Poverty Row Royalty

*The Films of Producer Sigmund Neufeld and
His Brother, Director Sam Newfield*

by
Thomas Reeder

Foreword by Ed Hulse

Afterword by Tim Neufeld

Split Reel LLC
Culpeper, Virginia
2024

Poverty Row Royalty:
The Films of Producer Sigmund Neufeld and
His Brother, Director Sam Newfield

© 2024 Thomas Reeder.

All Rights Reserved.

No portion of this publication may be reproduced, stored and/or copied electronically (except for academic use as a source), nor transmitted in any form or by any means without the prior written consent of the publisher and/or author.

All photographs from the author's collection unless otherwise noted.

Published in the United States by:

Split Reel LLC
P.O. Box 946
Culpeper, VA 22701
split-reel.com
info@split-reel.com

Cover design by Marlene Weisman

ISBN 978-1-964384-00-9 (Paperback)
ISBN 978-1-964384-01-6 (Hardcover)

Table of Contents

Dedication v

Foreword by Ed Hulse vii

Acknowledgements xi

Introduction xiii

Chapter 1: We Gotta Get Out of This Place 1

Chapter 2: There Comes a Time in Every Young Man's Life 9

Chapter 3: A Different Breed of Comedian 29

Chapter 4: What Poison Does to the Body (1932-1934) 43

Chapter 5: The Conning of Sigmund (1934-1935) 61

Chapter 6: The Real McCoy (1935-1937) 73

Chapter 7: Sam, Sans Sig (Part 1: 1932-1936) 85

Chapter 8: Sam, Sans Sig (Part 2: 1936-1940) 105

Chapter 9: Ben Judell Shoots for the Big Time (Sig, Sam, and PPC/PDC, 1939-1940) .. 161

Chapter 10: Like a Phoenix from the Ashes (Sig, Sam, and PRC, Part 1. 1939-1941) 177

Chapter 11: Growing Up in Hollywood – Part 1 203

Chapter 12: Buster Joins Fuzzy (Sig, Sam, and PRC, Part 2, 1941-1942) 209

Chapter 13: The War Takes a Bite (Sig, Sam, and PRC, Part 3, 1942-1943) 233

Chapter 14: Slaves of Formula (Sig, Sam, and PRC, Part 4, 1943-1944) 255

Chapter 15: The Entrance of Noir (Sig, Sam, and PRC, Part 5, 1944-1945) 275

Chapter 16: Growing Up in Hollywood – Part 2 291

Chapter 17: A Formula That Was Working (Sig, Sam, and PRC, Part 6, 1945-1947) 295

Chapter 18: Set Adrift (Sam, Sans Sig, 1946-1949) 325

Chapter 19: The Baby of the Industry (Film Classics, 1948-1949) 343

Chapter 20: When Hero Catches Crook, Time for Picture to End (Lippert, 1950-1953) . 353

Chapter 21: Too Many Fuzzys (AFRC, Regal Films, and Television, 1953-1958) ... 381

Chapter 22: The Twilight Years 401

Chapter 23: The Neufeld-Newfield Legacy 409

Afterword by Tim Neufeld 413

Filmography 415

Endnotes 459

Bibliography 489

Index 493

Producers Releasing Corporation/P.R.C. ad promoting the 1941-42 season's films, from **The 1942 Film Daily Year Book.**

Dedication:

For Tim, the keeper of the flame.

"Sig and Sam were a couple of wonderful guys."
Actor Glenn Strange

"Sig Neufeld has the knack of getting more picture for a dollar than any other producer in the business."

Uncredited Film Daily *reviewer*

"Sammy was very inventive and very, very kind; he was the nicest director I ever worked with."

Actor Sid Melton

"I remember one time when I was madly in love with a ballet dancer. I actually recorded a short ballet for her on one of their pictures. It was a western, you see, but they didn't care at all. One brother says to the other brother, 'Where's the music coming from? It's a cowboy picture, a period piece.' And the other brother says, 'Oh, maybe it's coming from the radio.' And the other brother accepted that. How charming they were."

Composer Paul Dunlap, on his experience with
Sig and Sam on one of their final films

Foreword
by Ed Hulse

In the first week of October 1941, principal photography on Sam Wood's *Kings Row* wrapped after nearly three months. The lavishly mounted Warner Bros. adaptation of Henry Bellamann's shocking best seller was already $300,000 over budget and 23 days over schedule. Several more days of retakes would be needed and it wasn't until early December that the final shot went before a camera. The film's "negative cost"—the total expenditure on production up to the point of having a finished negative from which release prints could be struck—came in at $1,081,698.

Director Wood, who already had a string of notable, big-budget, major-studio motion pictures to his credit, had enjoyed the services of Hollywood's top talents in every department, among them Oscar-nominated screenwriter Casey Robinson, Oscar-winning production designer William Cameron Menzies, Oscar-nominated cinematographer James Wong Howe, and Oscar-winning composer Erich Wolfgang Korngold. Producer David Lewis indulged Wood's every whim and defended him against studio chief Jack Warner's charge of profligate spending.

Kings Row, which starred Robert Cummings, Ann Sheridan, and Ronald Reagan, was a massive critical and commercial hit upon its April 1942 release, earning three Academy Award nominations (including Best Picture and Best Director) and grossing more than $5,000,000 worldwide. Sam Wood's next two pictures, *Pride of the Yankees* (1942) and *For Whom the Bell Tolls* (1943), also were big-budget productions utilizing the services of A-list actors and technicians. And they also enjoyed considerable success.

And yet, in none of these exceptional motion pictures—revered even to this day—did Sam Wood exhibit any discernible or identifiable directorial style. *Kings Row*'s striking visuals were devised to the nth detail by Menzies and Howe, who had collaborated numerous times previously, always to good effect. The production designer drew sketches for every single shot and had sets built to accommodate Howe's lighting schemes, knowing the veteran cameraman would painstakingly replicate the shadow effects indicated in Menzies' drawings. Sam Wood contributed not a single iota to the film's look, nor did he play any role in the story's development. Producer Lewis later admitted, "He knew nothing about the camera, nothing about script, and little about casting. . . . Before shooting he would [often] say to me, 'What's this scene about?' "

Sam Wood's director credit adorns many highly regarded films produced during Hollywood's Golden Age. His list of box-office successes is lengthy and includes pictures made at every major studio in town.

Why?

The answer is simple. Wood epitomized what used to be called a "traffic cop" director. He had no overriding creative vision, no particular skill. He simply knew how to marshal talented collaborators and let them operate at full capacity, unhampered by constraints on time and money. He made sure they wouldn't bump into each other. *Kings Row* could soar over budget by $300,000 and over schedule by nearly four weeks because studio moguls realized the likelihood they would wind up with a smash was so much greater because of gifted collaborators like Menzies, Howe, and Korngold. Then as now, it's not difficult to make a good picture in Hollywood when neither time nor money is any object and you're working with the best people the industry has to offer.

As principal photography on *Kings Row* was winding down during that first week of October 1941, another film was doing the same, albeit at a greatly accelerated pace. Director Sam Newfield was rushing to finish a cheap Western titled *Billy the Kid's Round-Up*, the second entry in a low-budget series starring former Olympic swimming champ and one-time Paramount contractee Larry "Buster" Crabbe as a greatly sanitized and considerably older simulacrum of the infamous New Mexico outlaw. Newfield's brother and producer, Sigmund Neufeld, had scheduled two weeks for the shooting of *Round-Up*. When edited—following a post-production interlude orders of magnitude shorter than that allotted to *Kings Row*—Newfield's opus would run 5,255 feet, yielding a running time of just over 58 minutes. Almost exactly half as long as *Kings Row*. It would be distributed by Producers Releasing Corporation (PRC), the perpetually undernourished runt of Hollywood's litter. But while Sam Wood's production had eaten up over one million dollars of Warner Bros.'s money, Sig Neufeld's ledger book recorded a negative cost of merely $13,188 for *Billy the Kid's Round-Up*.

Even by 1941 standards, producing a salable feature film for little more than thirteen grand was next to impossible. But Sig and Sam did it—not once, not twice, but dozens of times. They occupied a niche of the film market that the major Hollywood studios ignored. Their pictures never flashed across the huge screens of the downtown movie palaces; they mostly played the modestly appointed theaters in small towns and rural hamlets—the venues with three to five hundred seats. Every now and then PRC movies were booked into houses catering to the bedroom communities in and around larger cities, but almost always at Saturday matinees rather than evening double features.

Unlike the downtown theaters, which paid a percentage of the box-office receipts to major studios like Warner Bros., the smaller showplaces booked films from the likes of PRC, Monogram, and Republic for flat fees. Buster Crabbe's Billy the Kid epics, for example, rarely rented for more than $15 per engagement and frequently for as little as $10. At such rates, PRC needed more than a thousand bookings just to recoup a Western's negative cost, not to mention the added expense of prints, advertising, and distribution. Sig and Sam catered to a relatively small segment of the moviegoing population. They couldn't have made million-dollar films even if the money was available to them (and it wasn't), because they couldn't earn enough rental revenue to pay off the bankers.

Yet the brothers not only survived but thrived within the confines of their market niche. The profits were small but steady, and by cranking out product on an assembly-line basis—always within their minuscule budgets—Sig and Sam guaranteed not only their per-picture salaries but the continued viability of PRC as well.

Is the best Sam Newfield-directed Western as good as the worst Sam Wood-directed movie? If we're being honest, no, of course not. But Sam Wood had everything going for him. For *Kings Row* Menzies replicated an apple orchard on one of the sound stages in Warner's Burbank plant. The set was built for a single shot to be taken at a specific angle, from a specific distance, using a specific lens. When cinematographer Howe found he couldn't get the shot as designed without showing the overhead light banks, he spent the better part of a day having panels painted to resemble the sky, and then have grips hang them close enough to the camera to block out the lights. In the time it took to photograph that single shot, Sam Newfield and other directors like him could have done a couple dozen setups and knocked off several pages of script.

No director ever set out to make a lousy movie. No matter how small the budget, how tight the schedule, or how weak the script, every one of them showed up on the set wanting to do the best possible job and turn out a product that would entertain the grubby kids and working stiffs forking over their hard-earned dimes and quarters. But unlike Sam Wood, directors like Sam Newfield never had the opportunity to collaborate with a William Cameron Menzies or a James Wong Howe. They didn't have the luxury of spending a whole day to get a single shot. Instead they banged through the script as fast as possible, praying their lead actor wouldn't flub his lines and force them to waste time on retakes. They prayed it wouldn't rain on location the day they were scheduled to shoot horse chases, because the schedule might not allow them to return the next day.

I love classic movies as much as the next guy, but ever since beginning to research the world of "B" movies and Poverty Row studios I've had special respect for the guys like Sam Newfield—the filmmakers who labored against all odds to come up with pictures that, if nothing else, would entertain the audiences for which they were intended. And make enough money for their distributors to warrant continuation of a series like Sam's Billy the Kid Westerns.

Tom Reeder shares my affection for craftsmen—and they were craftsmen, not artisans—like the brothers Neufeld. Previously Tom has written about Ben Pivar, another hero to fans of low-budget second features. Now he's employed his considerable skills as a researcher to document the careers of Sig and Sam, in the process painting a vivid picture of a Hollywood most film historians continue to ignore. I thought I knew most of what there was to know about the brothers, but this book has added considerably to my knowledge of, and appreciation for, these unsung heroes. I've loved reading every word and I'm sure you will too.

Ed Hulse
Dover, New Jersey
March 20

This book is made possible through the generous support
of the following Kickstarter backers:

Bruce Simon, Jan L. Willis, Rodney Bowcock, Ronald Spayde, Karen Owen,
Ivan G. Shreve Jr., David Denton, Thomas Stillabower, Robert Lipton,
Jennifer Keenan, David Samuelson, Fred W. Johnson, Kevin Rollason, Bill Shute,
Rich Bush, Frank Thompson, Algie Lane, Robert Arkus and Jeni Rymer, Peter Cohn,
Edward Watz, R. Michael Pyle, Kevin Halstead, Elizabeth Maxim, Eric Cohen,
Jim Kerkhoff, Michael Gebert, Kenneth Cone, Sergey Kochergan, Joseph D. Moore,
Jim Cook, Keith Martin, Rick Pruitt, Kelly J. Kitchens, Jim Reid, Rowby, Jerry Beck,
Michael Aus, Linda Keenan, Peter Goldberg, John Nelson, Jared Stearns,
Mick O'Regan, Camille Scaysbrook, William Ferry, Kathy Fuller Seeley,
Michael Nella, Frank Flood, Steve Massa, Stephen M. Wolterstorff,
Jerome A. Dennis, Scott Galley, Dan Oliver, Russ Hughes, Ronald Larimore,
Mike Schott, Maurice Trace, Brent Walker, David Breakfield, Brett Prather,
William Barclay, Fotios Zemenides, Jeffrey Stundel, Paul Trinies, Timothy Neufeld,
Jean Newfield, Gilbert Sherman, Jose Ortiz-Marrero, Andrew Pearson,
Samantha Glasser, Peter Hillman, Beth Ann Gallagher, Will Sloan, Lisa Stein Haven,
Richard Novak, Michael Bannon, Suzanne Scherrer, Ryan Brennan, Kevin Deany,
Mark Bryan, Micheal D. Lang, Jakob Stegelmann, Ben Ohmart, Todd Terpening,
Tim Tucker, Michael J. Hayde, George Watt, Ben Model, Matthew Michael Barry,
Judith Redding, Rodney Haydon, Liz Lynch, Everett Haagsma, Steven Rowe,
Evan Stanley, Terry Adams, McKayla M, Elisa Townshend, Matt Stieg,
Heidi Liesman, Randy Skretvedt, ICSC.

Backers listed in chronological order of pledge.

Acknowledgements

This book would not exist without Tim Neufeld's considerable contributions, with strong support from his daughter Kathy. Tim got the ball rolling, contacting me out of the blue and piquing my interest in undertaking a biography of his grandfather, producer Sigmund Neufeld, and Sig's brother, director Sam Newfield. Not only was Tim able to regale me with numerous stories relayed to him by his grandfather, but he also provided many of the photos found in this book as well.

Tim put me in direct touch with Sig's son, the late Sigmund Neufeld Jr., who cheerfully sat through a half-dozen interviews, answering all questions in a frank and forthcoming fashion. That he never mastered the use of Zoom was not an impediment, as Tim contacted him through FaceTime, and the interviews proceeded uninterrupted in this jerry-rigged fashion. This led to contact with Sam's son Joel as well once I managed to track him down via Facebook, Tim and Joel reconnecting after several decades of losing touch. Both Sig Jr. and Joel were eager—and often amusing—participants in the retelling of their respective fathers' stories. The sons were observers and, on occasion, participants as well, both behind and in front of the cameras during the late 1930s into the 1950s. Sam's granddaughter, Laura Berk, graciously provided a number of stills from the photo albums of her mother, Sam's daughter Jackie.

Accompanied by his daughter Kathy, Tim spent several days digging through the United Artists/Eagle-Lion/PRC archives held at the University of Wisconsin-Madison's Wisconsin Center for Film and Theater Research. Tim further assisted by visits to (or contact with) the Tim McCoy archives at the University of Wyoming's American Heritage Center; the Margaret Herrick Library in Beverly Hills; and the Columbia Pictures archive at UCLA's Charles E. Young Research Library. I cannot overstate my appreciation of Tim's tireless efforts on this book's behalf, which included at trip over to Hungary in an attempt to track down further genealogical info on Sig and Sam's parents.

Other contributors include Ed Hulse, one of the leading authorities on low budget film, and the writer of this book's engaging and informative Foreword. Ed generously took time out of his demanding schedule to read through, and comment on, the manuscript, and provided identification of many of the actors pictured in the photos found herein; I wouldn't have had a clue otherwise. Western authority Boyd Magers, author of numerous books on the Western genre and the man behind internet's invaluable Western Clippings web page (westernclippings.com), also reviewed the manuscript and provided honest and frank comments about same.

Karl Thiede indulged me during my first cold call requesting budgetary information about many of the films Sig and/or Sam were involved in. He quickly warmed to my pestering and the project at hand, another four calls following over March and April of 2023.

Access to archival holdings, and permissions to use same was facilitated by Mary K. Huelsbeck, Assistant Director of the University of Wisconsin-Madison's Wisconsin Center for Film and Theater Research; Beth Harper of the University of Wisconsin-Madison's Memorial Library; and Mary Beth Brown, Toppan Rare Book Librarian of the University of Wyoming's American Heritage Center.

Other contributors in ways both large and small include Joel Newfield's wife Jean and son Greg; Julius Stern's grandson Gilbert Sherman, and Julius's daughter Marie Ariel; along with authors and film historians Mark Thomas McGee, Tom Weaver, Sam Gill, Richard Bann, and John Brooker. Ralph Celantano, Rob Arkus, Mark Heller, Geno Cuddy, and Doug Kennedy warrant mention, along with the New York State Archives. Unshredded Nostalgia, located in Barnegat, New Jersey, is always an excellent source of film stills, many of which can be found in this book. Sadly its owner, Jim Episale, passed on back in 2022; I'll miss our friendly chats each time I visited his store.

I'd like to thank the members of the Al Joy Fan Club for their moral support and relentless, good-natured ribbing. Members include Rob Stone, Steve Massa, Michael Hayde, Jim Kerkhoff, David Denton, Frank Thompson, Rob Farr, and Ben Model, the latter two having gone above and beyond the call of duty assisting Mr. Stone in a search through the LoC's massive collection of stills for potential candidates to help illustrate the text in this book.

A big thanks as well to this book's publisher, noted film historian and author Rob Stone and his Split Reel Books. Rob is the Library of Congress's Moving Image Curator at their facility in Culpeper, Virginia, and has recently embarked on the publishing of books on all aspects of film, along with curating collections of silent comedies on DVDs. Additional thanks to Split Reel's editor, film historian and author Michael Hayde, the most thorough, knowledgeable editor I've ever had the happy experience of working with. Michael served in this capacity on my earlier book, *Mr. Suicide: Henry "Pathe" Lehrman and the Birth of Silent Comedy*, as well, and the book was far better for his tireless contributions. I'd be remiss if I didn't mention graphic designer Marlene Weisman, of Marlene Weisman Design, for her outstanding work on this book's cover. Marlene's imaginative and eye-catching work has graced the covers of numerous other books on film, as well as the cases for DVD/Blu-ray releases with a decided silent film bent.

Last, but certainly not least, my wife Barbara, whose unflagging support has kept me going all these years; she keeps the ship afloat.

Thanks to one and all for helping to make this book that much better!

Introduction

In a way, it all kind of made sense. *Kismet*, some people would call it.

It started in 2017, when my decades-long research into the life and career of silent comedy pioneer Henry Lehrman was published as *Mr. Suicide: Henry "Pathé" Lehrman and the Birth of Silent Comedy*. Lehrman first came to prominence with the creation of his L- Ko Comedies in 1914, relinquishing it two years later for more prestigious and lucrative opportunities. L-Ko's new owners, brothers Julius and Abe Stern, nurtured the company to considerable profitability and success over the fourteen years that followed, rebranding and repositioning it along the way as Century Comedies and, later on, as Stern Brothers Comedies. I continued the story of the studio and its new owners in my follow-up book, *Time Is Money! The Century, Rainbow, and Stern Brothers Comedies of Julius and Abe Stern*, published in 2021. With that latter book's publication, I felt the story of this comedy company and its owners was finished.

That belief was soon to be quashed.

Fast forward to early June 2022, when I received an email from a sender whose name I didn't recognize. Its opening line grabbed my attention: "I am the grandson of Sigmund Neufeld, and I just finished reading Time is Money, in which there are many references to my grandfather." I recognized Sigmund Neufeld's name, of course, having just written about his lengthy stint with the Sterns, and was well aware that his brother, Sam Newfield, had worked for the Sterns as well. Additionally, my limited knowledge of the brothers extended beyond those early silents, my love of low budget films having "introduced" me to some of their sound output in years past, primarily that for Producers Releasing Corp. Sig had produced a significant number of that studio's films, most of which Sam had directed. Follow-up correspondences with that first email's author, Tim Neufeld, revealed that Sig's son, Sig Jr., and Sam's son, Joel, were both alive and well. To make a long story short, I was hooked. The legacy of that early studio and its various incarnations could be carried into the sound era and followed to its logical conclusion through the films of Sig and Sam. Putting my then-current project aside, I embarked on the whirlwind research of the brothers, and their involvement in the film industry from 1911 into the late 1950s. The result of that research is now in your hands.

There were several reasons I decided to undertake this research, aside from the obvious value of the availability of several surviving family members. First of all, I have always had a (qualified) love of the low budget B films of the 1930s, 1940s, and 1950s, the product of the independent producers whose operations resided primarily in Hollywood's "underbelly," disparagingly known as both Poverty Row and Gower Gulch. What always intrigued me about the makers of these films was their Sisyphean attempts to carve out a place within the industry under seemingly insurmountable odds. That they could produce arguably viewable films under the most spartan of budgets and unbelievably brief shooting schedules was a testament to their collective ingenuity, dogged determination, and, in many instances, creativity. Admittedly there were a lot of crummy films produced by the lone wolves behind them, but there was also a fair number of acceptable, modestly ambitious efforts produced and released to the public as well. The films of producer Sig Neufeld and his director brother, Sam Newfield, were almost always firmly placed in this latter group.

Sig landed a tentative foothold in the industry on the East Coast in 1911, talking his way into a job at Carl Laemmle's Independent Motion Picture Company (IMP). He relocated to join the Sterns at L-Ko on the West Coast in 1916, eventually advancing from editor to production manager in 1922. Sig was firmly entrenched and a significant contributor to the company by the late 1920s, by which time the Sterns had "reinvented" their company as Stern Brothers Comedies. In the meantime, Sig's brother Sam had relocated to the West Coast as well, and was brought on board in 1919, eventually working his way up to director of the company's popular comic strip-based series in 1926. By the time the Sterns called it quits in 1929, the brothers had both attained a solid education in the world of low budget filmmaking, adept not only in comedy construction, but in budgeting of both time and dollars as well. They were both well positioned to advance in the industry in the decade that followed, an initial run of comedy shorts quickly giving way to feature film production for a number of different independent filmmaking entities, Sig producing and Sam as director-for-hire. Their ambitions were modest, and they knew their market: the small neighborhood theatres and those in the more remote rural areas of the country, the theatres that survived on the lower-cost rentals of the independents to fill their single- or double-bills. Cost trumped all at these smaller, hand-to-mouth operations, and the brothers knew they could deliver product that would meet these exhibitors' needs.

It was with the company that came to be known as Producers Releasing Corporation (PRC) that Sig and Sam found their most productive and lucrative home, collectively responsible for more than one hundred films from 1939 into 1947. Stints with Film Classics in the late 1940s, followed by a string of films for Robert L. Lippert, Associated Film Releasing Corp. and Regal Films capped off their careers, Sam's last directorial efforts released in 1958, produced by his credit-shunning older brother.

It's the films for PRC that the brothers are most remembered for, if remembered at all. Sig's primary responsibility was for the company's Western genre output, contractually committed to churn out an unrelenting seasonal string of oaters. The Buster Crabbe-Al St. John "Billy the Kid" and "Billy Carson" series were the most prominent of these, released over the period 1941-46, Crabbe filling the shoes that Bob Steele had occupied during the previous season. Sam directed all of these, on tight schedules and parsimonious budgets that only deteriorated over time. As a result, the creativity behind these and PRC's other Westerns—the "Lone Rider," "Texas Marshal," and "Frontier Marshal" series among them—was, in a word, "compromised."

Take a look at the some of the films that the brothers made in addition to these Western series, however, and you'll find the occasional gem among the dross, benefitting from any combination of better scripts, bigger (by comparison) budgets, longer shooting schedules, and production niceties not afforded the Westerns. Among these are films that included the noirs *The Lady Confesses* and *Apology for Murder*, the "Michael Shayne" mysteries, the comedies *Hold That Woman!* and *The Kid Sister*, the horror entry *Dead Men Walk*, musicals such as *Harvest Melody* and *Swing Hostess*, and action-adventure films such as *Marked Men*. Not great films, by any stretch of the imagination, but standouts amongst their fiscally impoverished brethren.

Unfortunately for the brothers, it's the Westerns—with their cookie-cutter scripts and overly familiar plots—that they are most remembered for, to the exclusion of their one-off productions for PRC and the other studios they worked for, both pre- and post-PRC. Pulp fiction writer Frank Gruber wrote that there were seven basic Western plots, but looking at the brothers' output for PRC you'll only find a few of those seven employed. PRC's budgets didn't allow for the involvement of railroads, the participation of Indians, or any other plotline bordering on "epic," instead sticking to more modest (read "cheap") plots involving cattle rustling, stagecoach robbing, the swindling of ranchers and homesteaders, and the pitting of one rancher against another, plots that allowed for any number and combination of fistfights, gunfights, and horseback chases. Sig, it should be noted, claimed that there were ten basic plots rather than seven, but in the absence of his "list," one can only guess at just how finely he had to split hairs to arrive at that larger number.

To be clear, I am biased, because I enjoy this sort of film more than the average filmgoer, so this should be taken into consideration when reading what follows. Most important, my comments and thoughts about the brothers' films sprout from within the hermetic world of low budget, independently made films, considered solely amongst their threadbare peers and *never* against the output of the well-heeled majors. It would, of course, be sheer folly to compare any of the indie output to far better funded offerings like *Gone with the Wind* or *The Wizard of Oz*. Here it is "B" film world we are talking about, with nary an "A" film to be mentioned or even considered for comparison. Nevertheless, Sig's productions usually had every dollar up there on the screen, the results frequently belying their meagre budgets.

Sam's direction varied over the years, a direct byproduct of the various studios he was employed by, and the budget allotted to a given film. His initial features in the 1930s are notable for his occasional directorial flourishes and camera setups, but soon evolved into leaner, more streamlined, economically pared-down style, one that told each story in a succinct, no-nonsense fashion, effective and straight-forward. Always mindful of the budget and schedule he was operating under, Sam's direction was solidly workmanlike, utilizing an economy of setups with the occasional closeup for emphasis rather than show. Camera movement, a time-consuming and budget-eating "luxury," was kept to an understandable minimum, utilized primarily as either an opening shot to establish a location's setup, or to track in on one of the film's actors to emphasize the realization of some significant plot point; Sam used such movements judiciously. As B film producer William Pine explained in 1948, "We become ingenious because necessity, which is another word for budget in our dictionary, compels us to become ingenious."

Reviewers and historians tend to dismiss Sam's output based primarily on the sheer number of films he directed over his lengthy career; 270 by my count, but I'm certain there are other films for which he received no credit. This, to my way of thinking, was an incredible achievement, and one for which he should be admired; where's the *Guinness Book of World Records* when you need it? Unfortunately, the brothers' reputations have occasionally been demeaned over the years by critics such as Richard Corliss, who called Sam a "hack-of-hacks." It was, in my opinion, sheer laziness on Corliss's part, and on the part of any of the other condescending writers who denigrated Sam's directorial abilities, since he was a competent, hard-working, no-nonsense director who, as you will soon read in the pages that follow, frequently received good press in the various contemporary reviews. These critics' assertions are seemingly based solely on Sam's more necessarily hurried work for PRC, especially in the latter, cheaper films, than any of the numerous films that came before or after PRC. Or, just as likely, due to the expedient of parroting the words of uninformed others who came before rather than putting in any sort of personal effort. To avoid this trap, I've viewed more than 140 of the brothers' films over the past year, as preparation for this book, and for a more balanced assessment of their output.

And so, dear reader, and with an apologetic nod to Shakespeare, "I've come to praise the brothers, not to bury them."

Sam Newfield. *Courtesy of Laura Berk.*

Chapter 1:
We Gotta Get Out of This Place

In the latter half of the nineteenth century, life in Hungary depended on one's economic status. Most were engaged in the agricultural industry, and if you were a landowner in possession of a large- or medium-sized estate—then roughly one-half of Hungary's arable land—you were among the fortunate. Smaller landholders were able to make a living from their property as well, but if you were among those with only a few acres or, worse yet, one of the many landless workers, life could be miserable. This latter group suffered under inhumane working conditions, a situation exacerbated by overpopulation, which resulted in lower wages and less available work. Given that Hungary had little to offer in the way of industry, opportunities in nearby towns or cities were limited as well. The one seemingly viable option to these peasant laborers was to immigrate to the United States, where demand for cheap labor was booming. As a result, between 1870 and 1920 more than a million Hungarians—those so-called "huddled masses yearning to breathe free"—scraped together every penny they had, packed their meagre belongings, and obtained steerage to the United States. Life there, they figured, had to be better than their wretched life in Hungary; it couldn't be any worse.

Most of these immigrants arrived through the port of New York and gravitated to states with large concentrations of Hungarian immigrants. Pennsylvania, New Jersey, Ohio, and Illinois were among the chosen destinations, but New York provided the path of least resistance, and the Lower East Side a citified "home away from home." Those huddled masses soon found themselves huddled in one of the many tenement houses that dominated the area. One such couple was Simon and Josephine Neufeld, childless but with one on the way when they arrived in 1892.

156 Rivington Street, Lower East Side, Manhattan, circa 1915.

Manhattan's tenement buildings were low-rise affairs, an attractive option to the newcomers as their rents were comparatively modest—and for good reason. Squeezed onto twenty-five by hundred-foot lots, each floor would typically comprise six apartments of three-rooms each, squeezed into a 325-square-footprint. Six-story buildings were the maximum height allowed to be built; any higher would have required an elevator, an added expense that cost-conscious builders were sure to avoid. If you were the "lucky" renter of the sixth-floor apartment, you certainly would have gotten a lot of daily exercise trundling up and down those stairs. Simon and Josephine found an apartment at 156 Rivington Street, midway between Suffolk and Clinton Streets.

Born in Hungary in 1859,[1] Simon would go on to marry Josephine Neufeld, fifteen years his junior and possibly a cousin. Daughter Sadie was born soon after their arrival on August 14, 1892. Three more children would follow, all sons: Morris on February 17, 1894, Sigmund on May 3, 1896, and Samuel on December 6, 1899. Simon found work as a furrier, a job described as one who "Stitches together parts of pelts to produce completed garments such as coats, jackets, or hats, or parts of garments such as collars, or fur linings for coats; usually uses a zig-zag sewing machine."[2] Simon supplemented his meagre income by driving a horse-drawn beer wagon, making deliveries to the area's watering holes.[3] By 1900 the Neufeld family had relocated to another tenement apartment, this one at 230 East Second Street.[4]

Immigrating to the United States didn't work out so well for Simon, as he died at the comparatively young age of forty-two on March 4, 1901. Death was caused by some sort of lung disease, possibly tuberculosis, a condition likely caused or further aggravated by their cramped living conditions and the coal-burning, noxious fume-emitting stove used for cooking. The family's sole breadwinner now gone, Josephine had to take up the slack, finding work as the building's janitress. This was a thankless job, cleaning the latrines, scrubbing and cleaning the hallway, and whatever other tasks were given her. Free rent was her payment, so it meant they now had a permanent place to live, one in which they would reside for the next fifteen years. Josephine would earn a few dollars as well by taking in laundry for others.

Life at 230 East Second was far from pleasant. Sigmund described the living conditions at various times to both his son, Sig Jr., and grandson, Tim Neufeld. "To get water they had to go to a single tap of water that was behind the building outside, and bring it back to the apartment," explained his son. Tim elaborated: "There was a single tap for cold water and next to it [were] the two latrines. Nobody was conscious of public health in those days."[5] Nobody worried about weight gain back then, either:

The other story is that they could only afford for the family one piece of meat, and they would boil it on this coal stove every night for six nights and just have the soup for dinner, and on the seventh night, which must have been the Sabbath night, whatever meat was left they were allowed to eat the meat.[6]

The family continued to survive for several years on Josephine's salary alone. By 1905, all four children were still attending school,[7] and a studio-bound family portrait survives of the four children and their mother. It is visually deceptive, however, given that everyone appears to be living a solidly middle-class existence. That wasn't the case at all: everyone was garbed in outfits supplied by the photographer himself,[8] and any vestiges of semi-affluence were left behind in the studio's closets when they returned to their otherwise hand-to-mouth existence.

The Neufeld family, 1905. Left-to-right: Morris, Sigmund, Sadie, Josephine, and Sam.
Courtesy of Tim Neufeld.

By 1910 both Sadie, now seventeen, and Morris, age sixteen, were employed; Sigmund and Samuel were still both in school.[9] At some point Sigmund was apprenticed to a tailor, although this may have been a part-time position while he continued his schooling. Sig Jr. and Tim have conflicting recollections as to when Sigmund finally dropped out of school to go to work. Tim initially seemed to think it was second grade, but the 1910 Census has fourteen-year-old Sigmund still in school. "I thought he went a little bit further than that," said Sig Jr. "I thought he went to the ninth grade, or something like that. That's what I remember, I don't remember anything about the second grade. I mean he learned to read and write and do arithmetic and all that, and I don't think they learned that by the second grade." After a moment's pause, he added: "He read a lot of scripts!"[10]

Regardless of when Sigmund went to work for that tailor, it would lead to his first job in the film industry. This was a result of a planned encounter with Carl Laemmle, the president of the Independent Moving Picture Company—aka IMP—that would soon become part of the Universal Film Manufacturing Company, of which Laemmle would become president as well. Or, just as likely, Julius Stern, IMP's General Manager. Tim's recollection of the story, as told to him by his grandfather:

He was working in the tailor shop, he had to deliver suits, and he knew that the suits he was delivering were going to the head of the studio. He never told me a name, he just said the head of the studio, which I always assumed was Carl Laemmle. And he went to Laemmle's house which was somewhere in Upper Manhattan to deliver the suits. He knocked on the door…a [maid] opened the door, Laemmle was not there. It was cold, I think it was rainy, or it was terrible weather, and she said "I'll take the suits." He said "No, I want to personally deliver them to..." presumably Laemmle, but it's possible it was Julius Stern. And so he waited outside, and he waited outside for several hours until Laemmle returned. When Laemmle returned he gave him the suits, and he asked for a job in the studio. Laemmle said "Get in the car, ... we're going to go downtown [to IMP]." He was taken to the studio, and his first job was sweeping floors in the studio. And very quickly he ended up in the cutting room.... And he had the chutzpah to ask Laemmle for a job.[11]

Sig Jr.'s recollection of the events differs slightly:

The story you just told was a bit different than what I had heard; yours was more elaborate than mine...I always remember him saying that he delivered clothes to Laemmle [at the studio] once in a while, and when he delivered the clothes, he was fascinated by what they did there. He asked what they did and was told to take a look around the place: "It's where we make movies." Which he did, and then he talked to Laemmle and asked for a job. And [Laemmle] said, "Well, I'll tell you what. I come to work at 6:00 A.M. every morning and I go down such and such a street in New York, and if you're standing on the corner...I'll take you into the studio and we'll look into getting you a job," thinking that [Sigmund] wouldn't be there at 6:00 in the morning.... It was snowing, it was winter, and it was freezing out. But he was there, and Laemmle picked him up and took him to the studio, and that was the way it all started.[12]

The Independent Moving Pictures Company (IMP) logo.

IMP was formed in April 1909 by Carl Laemmle, with some financial backing from his brother-in-law, Julius Stern. The motivating force behind Laemmle's decision was simple enough, to provide a more dependable stream of product to his two-year-old film exchange, the Laemmle Film Service, and to the handful of theatres that he owned. In 1908, the Motion Picture Patents Company—aka The Trust—had been formed, a pooling of sixteen patents that related to the production and projection of motion pictures. The Trust soon had a stranglehold on the industry, with motion picture cameras, projectors, and film stock all falling under these patents. Production companies were now licensed by The Trust to use the affected equipment and film; distributors were licensed to handle films made solely by The Trust's licensee companies; and exhibitors to use projectors manufactured by Edison. Laemmle's Film Service had become the nation's largest film distributor, so Laemmle had a choice: acquiesce to The Trust's demands and its onerous licensing fees, or make his own films. The decision, it would appear, was an easy one for Laemmle. IMP's earliest films were made over in Consumers Park in Brooklyn behind the Consumers Park Brewing Company at 946-978 Franklin Avenue,[13] and on the open-air platform of the Harley-Merry Studio nearby at 947-951 Franklin Avenue. IMP's offices were located on the first floor of the building at 111 East 14th Street, and the factory on the floor above.[14] This was a modest setup to say the least. Jack Cohn, who along with his brother Harry would go on to create the studio that came to be known as Columbia Pictures in the 1920s, got his start at IMP:

In those days we developed and printed film in a small room where we were fortunate in making even a one-reeler. We would advertise the picture long before we started to make it. We would take a title and write a picture around that title, as we had to get the advertising into the trade papers before a picture was even started.[15]

By 1911, the year that Sigmund went to work for Laemmle, IMP had relocated a year earlier to more spacious offices at 102 West 101st Street in Manhattan[16] on the corner of Columbus Avenue. The growing company would churn out 120 films that same year.

Sigmund's janitorial duties were brief, the ambitious young man soon put to work as a cutter in the studio's editing room. Julius Stern (1886-1977), Laemmle's brother-in-law, had been managing Laemmle's theatres up until April 1911, when he was sent east to serve as IMP's business manager. Within a half year he was appointed general manager of the company,[17] and at some point took up residence at 417 Riverside Drive. That said, it is possible that the IMP executive that Sigmund had delivered clothing to—presumed to have been Laemmle—was instead none other than Julius Stern. Laemmle himself had relocated from Chicago to New York in November 1910,[18] so we'll never know for certain the individual's identity. Regardless, Sigmund now worked directly for Julius Stern, and would soon be promoted to a full-fledged editor.

Carl Laemmle (left) and Julius Stern, 1912.

1910 saw the formation of The Motion Picture Distributing and Sales Company, set up to distribute the product of most of the country's independent film producers. IMP was the principal unit of this concern, which would go on to be reorganized and renamed The Universal Film Manufacturing Company in 1912. Laemmle would serve as Universal's president,[19] the product of the independents now accounting for half of the market.[20]

Sigmund quickly became a proficient editor, working hand-in-hand with Jack Cohn, IMP's Jack-of-All-Trades who assisted with editing when he wasn't busy in the lab developing and printing film. If the edited footage was insufficient to fill a single reel, "we had to go out to find a little scenic to put into it to make it a full reel," said Cohn.[21] When projected, a single reel of film could take as little as ten minutes screen time, so a drama or comedy insufficient to fill a single reel was a rather simplistically plotted affair. Regardless of what filmgoers expected or wanted, Universal went all out in putting a "happy face" on its split reels. "A Saturday Success and Sensation, the IMP Split" declared the title of one such article in *The Implet*, Laemmle's short-lived house organ.

"The design of this release is to combine two short comedies on the one reel, or one comedy and an industrial," explained the article, going on to state that this "innovation" is "proven a striking success."[22] A full-page ad appeared several months later, ostensibly written by Laemmle himself, going on to tout that while the "Imp Splits" were "an expensive proposition for us to produce" and "costly from the very beginning," it declared that they are "a splendid thing" and that "you demanded them of us."[23] We'll take Laemmle's word for it.[24]

Jack Cohn mounting the running board for IMP's **Animated Weekly** newsreel car, 1915.

By 1912, IMP had established an additional temporary presence out in Los Angeles on two acres in a section oddly known as Brooklyn Heights (now known as Boyle Heights). "We are on the extreme edge of the bluff and can look down upon the city on one side and across the valley toward Pasadena on the other," wrote *The Implet*'s West Coast correspondent.

> This two acres is surrounded on three sides by a seven-foot fence.... Inside the fence is our studio and factory. We have a large open stage, Next to this is a barn, which we use for a storehouse. Then comes the beautiful seven-room bungalow, where the studio, office, projecting room, dressing rooms, wardrobe rooms, etc., are located. Then the factory building, where the developing, printing and cutting is done—also the assembling. You will observe that we have a complete plant."[25]

The IMP Film Company's California contingent, under the direction of Francis J. Grandin and comprising the small stock company of Margarita Fischer, Harry Pollard, Eddie Lyons, and E.J. Le Saint, departed for Los Angeles and this new studio on December 30, 1911.[26] And while the new setup was described as "Complete," the company would soon relocate to a new setup at 6100 Sunset Boulevard, at the corner of Gower Street.

By 1915 everyone in the Neufeld family was chipping in and pooling their earnings. Josephine continued as the building's janitress; twenty-two-year-old daughter Sadie held a position as a garment worker, operating some unspecified piece of machinery producing infant caps; Morris, age twenty-one, was a packer of coffee percolators; Sigmund, nineteen, was editing film for Universal; and fifteen-year-old Sam earned a few bucks as an errand boy.[27]

Within a year Morris, whom everyone called Maury, had left his previous job to become a chauffeur,[28] and Sadie had moved out of the apartment in June to marry a thirty-one-year-old fellow named Emmanuel "Mannie" Teitelbaum. Earlier in 1916 all of Universal's East Coast operations—Sigmund included—had been consolidated in their newly built half-million-dollar studio in the Leonia Heights section of Fort Lee, New Jersey. And now, in June 1916, Universal was shutting down production at the three-month-old studio, and shipping everyone out to its new West Coast facilities. "At present," said Julius Stern, "I am getting everything in shape preparatory to my leaving. All the companies are making strenuous efforts to have their pictures finished by the latter part of next week so that they will be able to leave for Universal City."[29] Sigmund was among those about to be uprooted. Julius went on to announce his supposed break from Universal: "I regret that I am leaving the Universal," said Stern. "But there comes a time in every young man's life when he wants to spread out and go into business for himself. I have that desire now, and it is this ambition which is causing me to leave this great organization."[30] One of Julius's plans was to go into partnership with his brother, Abe Stern (1888-1951), in Hollywood's L-Ko Komedy Kompany.

The L-Ko began operations two years earlier in 1914, organized by Henry Lehrman (1881-1946) and Julius's brother Abe; L-Ko released all its comedies through Universal. After two successful years of inventive comedies that rivaled those of Mack Sennett and his Keystone Comedies, Lehrman decided to move on to hoped-for bigger and better things, and soon found them over at Fox where he put together the more lavishly budgeted Sunshine Comedies. Lehrman had sold his shares in the company to Julius and Abe on July 8, 1916, and Julius's announcement signaled his intention to go into business for himself and focus on making comedies for his former employer. Here's where Sigmund received the second big break of his life. Tim Neufeld relayed the story:

> He went to work one day and his boss handed him tickets and said "Tomorrow you're going to Hollywood." [Sigmund] looked back at him…"Where's Hollywood? Where's Hollywood?" And he was told "Just get on the train and you'll be met at the station and be there tomorrow." The next day he had to go. And so he got on the train thinking he was going to Universal, because he's working at Universal. And when he gets to Union Station in Los Angeles, he's met by someone—I don't know who—and told "No, you're not going to Universal; you're going into Hollywood and you're going to work at…"—he always used the word "Century" or "Stern," he never used the word "L-Ko"— and he went over there and he had to get a room.[31]

Julius Stern (right) and his brother Abe, co-owners of the L-Ko Komedy Kompany, 1916.

A few words of explanation: The L-Ko Comedies would be rebranded as the Century Comedies by the end of the decade, with yet another makeover in 1926 as the Stern Brothers Comedies.

It seems unlikely that Sigmund was not aware of Hollywood, since Universal had had a presence there for several years, and was recently touting the grand opening of Universal City that had taken place a year earlier on March 15, 1915, some miles north of Hollywood in the San Fernando Valley. Universal's former—and far more modest—studio, was now L-Ko's studio, located in Hollywood on that southwest corner of Gower Street and Sunset Boulevard.

It is probable that Stern, well aware of Sigmund's capabilities in the editing room, was the "boss" who bought Sigmund's tickets to the West Coast. Sigmund found lodging in a boarding house at 6427 Sunset Boulevard, just a few blocks away from the L-Ko studios.[32] He was now employed by the Sterns and L-Ko, his five years with IMP and Universal having paved the way.

Chapter 2:
There Comes a Time in Every Young Man's Life

One can only imagine Sigmund's reaction when he first got a look at the ramshackle L-Ko studio complex, a series of shabby, retrofitted structures occupying a full city block that had all seen better days, and a world apart from that grand new studio back in Fort Lee. But it was a job, an interesting job at that, and one that provided a reliable weekly paycheck.

Julius immediately made his presence known and cleaned house. All of Lehrman's original stock company—Billie Ritchie, Henry Bergman, Gertrude Selby, Gene Rogers, Louise Orth, and Eva Nelson—were shown the door, leaving Alice Howell, Phil Dunham, Billy Armstrong, and a few others to carry on with the company's product, or at least for the short term. Sigmund was put to work cutting and assembling the films—all two reels in length by this time—made by L-Ko's current roster of directors, which included those with proven abilities—Jack Blystone, Noel Smith, Craig Hutchinson, and David Kirkland—along with some newbies—Jay "Kitty" Howe, Dick Smith, Vin Moore, and Frank "Fatty" Voss—culled from the acting ranks and shoved behind the cameras. "Now that Mr. Stern has been elected to the office of president and General Manager," wrote *Moving Picture World*, "he has swept aside all the old time methods of comedy productions, surrounded himself with the most capable comedy people in the business and is headed on the straight road to a huge success."[1] When it came to the business of making films, modesty in self-promotion was never one of Stern's weak points.

Filming at the ramshackle L-Ko studios at 6100 Sunset Boulevard, 1917.
Courtesy of Marc Wanamaker and Bison Archives.

After a somewhat rocky transitional period, L-Ko had regained its footing by the new year, once again providing a reliable stream of product for its one-per-week release schedule. Acting ranks were beefed up with the addition of heavyweight newcomer Merta Sterling, Bert Roach, Eva Novak, and others. Julius adopted the so-called "Star System" later in 1917, which added such notables as Hughie Mack, Gale Henry, Mack Swain, and Dave Morris to headline their own units.

The Sterns introduced a new brand as well toward the end of 1917, to showcase the talents of Alice Howell, one of their most popular and talented comedians. Century Comedies, as the new brand was ultimately named, would flourish, or at least up until Howell's departure two years later, requiring a lengthy reinvention of the brand and its focus. L-Ko soldiered on in concert with Century until 1919 when it was unceremoniously dumped, likely to clean the slate of any lingering hint of Lehrman's earlier participation and influence. The studio would henceforth be renamed the Century Studios as well, although industry insiders and those in the trades would stubbornly stick with referring to the studio by its former name. In L-Ko's stead was introduced the Rainbow brand of comedies, not at all different from its L-Ko predecessor, and ultimately short-lived; it was history after a single year. Concurrent with all this was the Sterns' dabbling in the chapter film arena, showcasing such serial stars as Frances Ford, Grace Cunard, and muscle-bound Elmo Lincoln. These were produced through the Sterns' Great Western brand and, it would appear, the Pacific Producing Company. The Sterns were also involved with the wildly popular *The Adventures of Tarzan* serial in 1921, produced by the newly formed Numa Pictures Corporation, on which Sigmund served as editor.

Sig Neufeld editing a film at the L-Ko studio, circa 1916. *Courtesy of Tim Neufeld.*

Sigmund's devotion to his mother and siblings remained undiminished despite his move to the West Coast. He would send a portion of every paycheck back to his mother, and she in turn would save—or attempt to save—every penny she could with the intention of one day relocating everyone to California to reunite the family.

Sigmund, as the story goes, was unaware of her plans, plans that were taking a bit longer than hoped for. Younger brother Sam was the problem, who by 1918 was holding down a job as a printer for the Carey Printing Company.[2] It seems that Sam had developed an interest gambling during his youth, shooting craps and the like with his friends, and becoming proficient as a pool hustler as well to supplement an otherwise meagre income. Gambling was an interest which quickly became a passion that plagued him—and those close to him—for the rest of his life. Frequently penniless as a result, he took to borrowing from his mother's savings. Despite this, Josephine was eventually able to save up enough money to move most everyone out to California in 1919.[3] The group included Sam, his sister Sadie, and her husband Mannie. Maury was part of the group as well, having just returned from a one-year stint with the army overseas. Their arrival by train came as a complete surprise to Sigmund, who had to scramble to find them a place to live. No one wanted to live at the beach back in those days, and the cheapest housing was in Venice Beach. There was a trolley—the Venice Short Line—which ran from downtown Los Angeles along what is now Venice Boulevard to the beach, so Sigmund rented a house there for the family, and they all settled in.

Sigmund quickly found work for his younger brother Sam, doing all manner of menial labor at the Century Studios, and for brother-in-law Mannie as a grip. "They never took breaks for lunch," recalled Sam's son Joel. "Sam's mother made sandwiches and she went to the set and sold sandwiches."[4] Maury—everyone called Morris "Maury"—was more of a problem, in that his year overseas had left him a changed man, or at least in the eyes of the family. Maury found initial employment as a chauffeur, but Sigmund soon got him a job at the studio as well, eventually working his way into a position as an electrician.

At some point Sigmund met the girl he would eventually marry, and remain happily so up until her death more than fifty years later. This fortuitous meeting took place during one of his daily trips to a nearby lab to deliver the day's work for processing, where he met a young lady named Ruth Auld. Ruth worked for the Chaplin Studios as a film cutter, and she too was delivering film for processing. A romance developed, even though Sigmund was Jewish and Ruth was a Protestant. Sigmund's adherence to Judaism was not at all strict, and during this time there was a dearth of Jewish females in Los Angeles, so nature and romance quickly sidelined any religious differences they may have had.

"To my dearest little friend Ruth. From Sig. L.Ko."
Sig Neufeld, looking dapper, circa 1916.
Courtesy of Tim Neufeld.

Ruth Emma Auld was born in the village of Dennison, located in Ohio's Tuscarawas County on October 24, 1897. One of nine children in a closely knit family, her older sister Alice had moved out to Los Angeles some time earlier for health reasons. Ruth wanted to follow—ostensibly for health reasons as well—and soon joined Alice on the West Coast. Ruth found employment at the Chaplin Studios, and was placed in the editing room as a film cutter. As such, the already edited workprint would be passed on to her, where she would cut the original negative to match the edited workprint. Then she would deliver the edited negative to the lab for the generation of release prints for shipment to distributors. It was paying work, but she had one major complaint about her boss; Sig Jr. explained:

> When she was working at Chaplin studio, she would go in when they had the daily rushes to screen each day, and she was part of that and would go in with the group. Chaplin would come in and bring all kinds of goodies and stuff to eat, and he wouldn't share with anybody. She thought he was so rude because he would bring all this food in and sit there and eat and watch the dailies and wouldn't offer any to anybody.[5]

Nitpicking, perhaps, but everyone has at least one complaint about their boss.

One of the reasons that the Sigmund and Ruth clicked as a couple was a similarly shared background: both had lost their fathers at an early age and were raised by their mother, although one can surmise that Ruth's mother had more difficulty in wrangling nine children to Josephine's four.

"Dearest little friend" Ruth Auld, Sig's love interest and future wife, circa 1917. *Courtesy of Tim Neufeld.*

Sigmund and Ruth would eventually marry in Los Angeles on March 9, 1920, the ceremony witnessed by a fellow named Robert F. Hill,[6] a director of shorts and more recently segments of the Stern Brothers' serials *The Great Radium Mystery* (1919) and *The Flaming Disc* (1920). Sigmund and Ruth moved into a new home located at 1354 Beachwood Drive—one block over from Gower and around the corner from the L-Ko/Century studios—while brothers Sam and Maury and their mother Josephine all moved into the house at 1312 Tamarind Avenue now owned and occupied by sister Sadie, her husband Mannie, and their two-and-a-half-year-old daughter Eugenia.[7]

Sigmund's technical abilities as an editor and his importance to the Sterns soon became apparent, when he came up with a seemingly obvious method of cutting down on studio waste and, as a result, putting more money into the Sterns' already bulging pockets. As told by Sig Jr.:

> They were walking down Hollywood Boulevard. My father said that he could make a two-reel comedy that they were doing into two complete separate shows. Stern told him "Well, if you can do that I'll give you anything that you want." "Well, I know I can do it because I figured it out already." They were walking by a jewelry store on Hollywood Boulevard. "Is there anything you can think of that you want?" They stopped and looked at the window. "Yeah, I'll take that ring right there." "Okay." And that's where he got the ring.[8]

Sigmund cherished that ring for the rest of his life, and after his death the ring eventually found its way to Sig Jr., who placed the ring's diamond into a new, larger setting, and wore it up until his death in 2022—a diamond that has remained on a Neufeld finger for over a century now.

Sigmund's importance to the Sterns was well known by 1921, as their head editor and, it would appear, title writer as well. One contemporary article wrote about Sigmund at some length, using the spelling of "Neufield" for his surname throughout:

> "Nothing ever looks funny to me!" This statement was made by Sig Neufield, film editor and cutter for Century Comedies, and known as one of the best judges of comedy in the business. Neufield doesn't express his enjoyment by smiles and laughs—mighty few people have ever seen him laugh at all, which is just the opposite of the popular conception of a funny man.
>
> Sig's job is to pay special attention to the gags, punches, and the theme of the comedy and he studies all the daily films with an eye to pick the best out of them. Like a kid with a set of blocks, he takes from five to ten reels of film and cuts them down to two; always retaining just the right thing and doing it with a face as dignified and as devoid of frivolity as that of a judge.
>
> After five years spent with Century his profession has become a sort of sixth sense with him. Almost unconsciously he can see a laugh and knows exactly where to insert it. While running off the rushes in the projection room Neufield has his ears all set for snorts, giggles and shouts. If he hears only half a laugh and he thinks he can get a whole one out of the situation in some other part of the picture he just naturally inserts the situation or stunt in some other part of the film. He does the titling last of all when he has reduced the comedy to screen footage.[9]

Sigmund had proven his worth to the Sterns. With eleven years practical experience, both in the editing room and by paying close attention to the production of their comedies, the Sterns promoted Sigmund to the important position of production manager in late 1922. Stern's editorial shoes were filled by Charles Wallach, an experienced vet with more than a decade in the industry, most recently as assistant to Jack Cohn on the *Universal Animated Weekly*.[10] Julius Stern's grandson, Gilbert Sherman, put Sigmund's promotion in this light: "Julius rewarded loyalty with loyalty, and I'm reasonably sure that's all there was to it. [Sigmund] wasn't family, but he was probably as close as it came without being family."[11]

Director Fred Fishback/Hibbard seventh from left with bow tie, boxer Jack Dempsey standing center with suit and tie, actress Louise Lorraine to the left of him, Brownie the Wonder Dog leaning on lion trainer Charles Gay. Far right: back row Bert Sternbach in black vest, Sig Neufeld with arms crossed in front of him, and director Charles Lamont to the right of Sig, March 1922. *Courtesy of Tim Neufeld.*

Lee Royal's contemporary *The Romance of Motion Picture Production* (1920) described a production manager as an "efficiency expert," and went on to say that:

> Figuratively he is the general in command of the various production units. It is his duty to see that there is no conflict between these companies. That is, he must start his companies at such times that while two or three of them are shooting interiors and using the stage space, the other two or three producing units can be taking exteriors. Again we find actors or actresses working in two companies at one time. The work must be planned so that the artist can work in the scenes of one production one day and play in the other production the following or a later day without any loss of time, or the "holding up" of either of the companies. An efficient production manager can save thousands of dollars every year for the larger organizations by preventing unnecessary delays and loss of time that would be inevitable were it not for the close cooperation between the various companies. This efficiency is the direct result of their being placed under the command of one head—the production manager.[12]

Needless to say, a position of extreme importance to the Sterns, and one they fully entrusted to Sigmund.

Concurrent with this was the promotion of a fellow named Bert Sternbach to casting director, replacing Zion Myers—now Harry Edwards's assistant—in that capacity.[13] Sternbach would come to be a huge part of Sigmund's future in film production, and a life-long friend as well.

Julius Stern indulges his pint-sized cash cow, Baby Peggy Montgomery, 1921. *Courtesy of Marc Wanamaker and Bison Archives.*

The studio's roster of comedians now comprised Baby Peggy, Brownie the Wonder Dog, Lee Moran (late of the popular Lyons and Moran comedy team), Buddy Messinger in a series of boys tales, and Queenie the Horse, along with supporting players Ena Gregory, Betty May, Max Asher, Blanche Payson, Joe Bonner, the "Human Beanpole" Jack Earle, Jack Cooper, and numerous others.[14] Part of Sigmund's new duties was the supervision of the studio's staff of gagmen,[15] his editing and fine-tuning of the company's comedies for the past six years evidently deemed sufficient training for such an important position. One of Sigmund's first undertakings was the preparation of Buddy Messinger's first film for Century, developed under the title *School Romance* but released as *Boyhood Days* (February 7, 1923).[16] *Film Daily* liked the results, deeming it an offering that "is amusing and should please the average audience."[17] In the months that followed Sigmund would work closely with director Herman Raymaker, co-writing the stories for films for both Century shorts and Baby Peggy's loan out to Universal for some Century Special features.

Sigmund's writing load was lightened somewhat with the hiring of cartoonist-humorist Vance DeBar Colvig—better known as "Pinto" to his millions of readers in the papers supplied by the United Feature Syndicate—to assist with the gag writing and script preparation.[18] In the months that followed, Sigmund and Pinto would collaborate with directors Jim Davis, Al Herman, former "Hall Room Boys" director Noel Smith, and others in the writing and fine tuning of scripts. Within a year Pinto would be promoted to head of the newly created Script Building Department. "His work," wrote *Exhibitors Trade Review*, "will bring all original and purchased material under his jurisdiction, and before a script is turned over to the director for production it will undergo rigid alterations and building-up." This was to be overseen by an advisory staff headed by Julius Stern, comprising Sigmund Neufeld, Bert Sternbach, and Stern's still-wet-behind-the-ears, sixteen-year-old nephew, Max Alexander,[19] whose bona fides in this capacity were, needless to say, questionable.

Sigmund's duties didn't end there. Whenever the Sterns crossed the country to meet with distributors and exhibitors—or would head to the East Coast for conferences with Universal officials, or made their annual summer pilgrimage to Europe for extended "working" vacations—Sigmund remained behind, entrusted with the oversight of the studio and ensuring that the day-to-day activities ran smoothly.[20] A more mundane, but nearly as important task assigned to Sigmund and Sternbach was the oversight of the studio's interior and exterior renovations, and the supervision of the sixty carpenters and twelve painters undertaking the improvements. The Sterns wisely headed to the East Coast while this was going on, once again entrusting Sigmund to handle it.[21]

Julius Stern leaving for (or arriving from?) Europe, 1920.
Courtesy of Marc Wanamaker and Bison Archives.

In the meantime, brother Sam was now taking uncredited bit parts in some of the Century Comedies. His earliest known appearance was in the Jay Howe-directed *Off His Trolley* (July 21, 1920) in support of star Billy Engle, and he's clearly visible at the wrong end of a club wielded by Baby Peggy Montgomery in one of her early comedies for Century. By 1923 Sam was co-writing scenarios as well with writer-director Al Herman, for films such as the Jack Earle vehicles *Oh Nursie!* (May 2, 1923), *Fare Enough* (June 6, 1923), and *Hold On* (July 4, 1923).

By 1925, Century was churning out fifty-four films for its upcoming 1925-26 season—a given season running from September 1 through the end of August the following year—at a reported budget of $500,000. The output of five units, the films featured the "stars" Wanda Wiley, Edna Marion, Eddie Gordon, and Al Alt, along with young Arthur Trimble in the upcoming "Buster Brown" series based on Richard F. Outcault's popular comic strip. "[Production Manager Neufeld] has already put the new schedule into effect," wrote the *Los Angeles Times*, "and the various comedy units will be kept active, with little intermission for several months to come." Julius Stern explained

Lobby card for Rainbow's **Off His Trolley** (1920). Sam Newfield (left) and Billy Engle at front of trolley, looking down at Clarence Hennecke on cowcatcher. *Courtesy of Jim Kerkhoff.*

Century Comedy cast and crew pose for the camera, April 5, 1920. Billy Engle seated, dead center, and Harry Keaton at the crank. Director Jay A. "Kitty" Howe far right, goggled Sam Newfield to the left of him. *Courtesy of Laura Berk.*

the apparent haste: "We are rushing production this year so that our exhibitors may preview our comedies before booking them. Heretofore it has been the custom of exhibitors to buy our comedies blindly. They would contract a series of pictures not knowing just what they were going to receive from a quality viewpoint."[22] Stern must have felt confident in Century's output by this time, or at least in bang-for-the-buck terms which appealed to so many smaller exhibitors.

While it was usually the lead comedians who suffered breaks and bruises during the filming of various stunts, it was Sigmund who fell victim during the shooting of a Wanda Wiley comedy tentatively titled *The Last Smile*, and all due to clumsiness. Perched high atop a camera stand and lost in thought, Sigmund backed up and fell off the edge, breaking his left arm in the twenty-foot fall.[23] Sigmund and Ruth now occupied a home at 915 Spaulding Avenue along with their first child—a son they named Stanley Neufeld—who was born two years earlier on May 1, 1923.[24] As such, Sigmund was now able to nurse his wound in the comfort of a new home, and without anyone else but Ruth and their young son around; their former Beachwood Avenue residence was now being rented to Josephine, Sam, and Maury for forty dollars a month,[25] having moved out of Sadie and Mannie's Tamarind Avenue home.

Sig Neufeld and wife Ruth with infant Stanley, circa 1923-24. *Courtesy of Tim Neufeld.*

1926 marked several firsts. Julius and Abe Stern had rebranded Century Comedies as Stern Brothers Comedies, a major step toward having their names known among the filmgoing public, just as Mack Sennett and Hal Roach had been doing for years with their respective companies. Another first was Sam's promotion to the directorial "big leagues." By April there were five units busy at work, two of them under the direction of seasoned veterans Gus Meins ("The Newlyweds and Their Baby" series) and Charles Lamont (the "Let George Do It" series). The other three units were headed by newcomers to the rank of director: former actor Scott Pembroke in charge of "The Excuse Maker" series, and former cameraman Francis Corby taking turns with Sam in directing episodes of the "What Happened to Jane?" series. Sam's first two credited offerings were titled *Which is Which?* (October 13, 1926) and *Please Excuse Me* (November 10, 1926), both "Excuse Makers" entries starring the series' regular, actor Charles King, followed by the Wanda Wiley vehicle *Jane's Engagement Party* (November 17, 1926).

Only a fraction of the hundreds of Century and Stern Brothers Comedies have withstood the ravages of time and man, and even fewer of those ones directed by Sam. Fortunately, *Please Excuse Me* is one of the lucky survivors, and it is quite good. In this one King loves the boss's daughter (Constance Darling), but his ongoing inability to arrive at work in a timely fashion continues to enrage the boss. On one such occasion King spins a wild story about encountering marauding Indians on his way and his valiant rescue of Darling, but her arrival soon puts the lie to his yarn. In an attempt to rid himself of this unreliable employee, his boss assigns him the thankless—and evidently dangerous—task of repossessing a ring from the brutish Mr. Sandow (Bud Jamison). After a violent encounter that leaves King the worse for wear, Darling saves the day with some quick thinking and the employment of her womanly charms.

The flashback as King weaves his wild Indian yarn is amusingly handled, and there are some great gags involving his Ford flivver interspersed throughout. Jamison, as always, makes a delightfully imposing heavy, and by now was one of the Sterns' most dependable actors. The story, while familiar, is competently executed by Sam, evidently a quick learner who had absorbed the techniques and approaches of the other house directors over the previous six years. All in all, a solid second effort for the novice director.

Century Studio entrance circa 1924. *Courtesy of Gil Sherman.*

The five abovementioned series now comprised the Stern Brothers' output for the 1926-27 season. The "Buster Brown" series, all directed by Meins, co-starred youngsters Arthur Trimble as "Buster," Doreen Turner as his sweetheart "Mary Jane," and Pete the Pup as "Tige." The "Let George Do It" series, based on the George McManus comic strip, featured rubber-limbed Sid Saylor, a former vaudevillian; most of these were helmed by Corby. "The Newlyweds and Their Baby" series, also directed by the seemingly inexhaustible Meins and based on another of McManus's strips, featured little Lawrence McKeen as the child-from-hell "Snookums," with Jed Dooley—another vaudevillian whose career in film ended almost as quickly as it began—and ingenue Ethlyne Clair co-starring as his harried parents—or at least for a short while. "The Excuse Maker" series, based on stories by William Anthony with Charles King in the lead, had Corby, Pembroke, and Sam all taking turns at direction. The "What Happened to Jane?" series lost its raison d'être after the departure of star Wanda Wiley for browner pastures elsewhere. Now limping through the remainder of the season's commitment with a dizzying array of starlets in the lead, the company's directors all took a shot at an entry or two, any thoughts of continuity left behind. As the company's production manager, Sigmund continued to oversee the productions of the active units.

The August 16, 1926, fire that destroyed the Century studios. The Sterns would relocate shortly thereafter to the former Francis Ford studios two blocks away.
Courtesy of Marc Wanamaker and Bison Archives.

The most significant occurrence of 1926, however, was the fire that destroyed the Century Studios at Gower and Sunset on August 15. This took place mid-afternoon during the studio's summer break while only the studio's watchman, David Frankel, was present. The studio was burnt to the ground, the loss estimated by Sigmund at between $400,000 and $500,000. Luckily, the negatives for all films produced to date were already on the East Coast for processing, so there would not be a significant impact on the upcoming release schedule. Sigmund sent an informative telegram the day after to the Sterns, then staying at Paris's Claridge Hotel:

Prop carpenter shop wardrobe all stages completely destroyed by fire. Fortunately cameras front offices vault & all records saved not even touched. Nobody knows how fire started watchman made rounds half hours before and everything was okay.

I left studio half hour before fire started. Generator okay. Wired Rubel Come here immediately. Behrendt man here will keep you posted please don't worry will do best I possibly can. Fire happened three o-clock Sunday afternoon = SIG =[26]

"Rubel" was Beno Rubel, Century's new secretary. Rubel rushed out from the East Coast to supervise, and within a month (and a questionable assist now eighteen-year-old Max Alexander, now the studio's technical manager)[27] they had acquired a replacement studio two blocks away from the ruins of their former base of operations. Built back in 1919 as the Francis Ford Studio, the new digs were located at 6040-6048 Sunset Boulevard, between the corners of Beachwood Drive and Gordon Street.[28] Production resumed by October 1926.[29]

The Disney Connection

There is a previously undocumented story that likely took place before the fire, a story that was relayed many times by Sigmund in his later years to his grandson Tim. One should keep in mind that memory can be a tricky thing, and that both the memories of Sigmund in his later years when telling those stories, and of Tim, recalling those same stories decades later, may not be entirely historically correct. That said, here is what Tim had to say regarding his grandfather's comments about an aborted deal, one that might otherwise have had a considerable impact on one of today's major studios:

My grandfather was quite definitive that he knew Walt Disney, and that while with the Stern Brothers they were going to acquire the Disney animation studio. And then there was a fire—I always assumed the fire was at Disney and not at the Stern Brothers; I didn't know about the Stern Brothers having a fire until I read your book[30]—and then the deal collapsed. I don't know whether there's any record of that, but he was always pretty clear, and all the stories that he's told me have all borne out by your research, and other research that I've done.[31]

Working under the premise that Tim's recollections are accurate, and that Sig's recollections were as well, here's what little I can speculate: Firstly, there were no fires at the various early Disney studios during the 1920s, so the fire referred to was undoubtedly the one that burnt down the Sterns' Gower and Sunset Century studio. That happened on August 15, 1926, so the referred to "deal" would have predated that.

Back in the mid-1920s, Walt Disney was not the famous animation powerhouse he would later become with the introduction of his "Mickey Mouse" cartoon character. In 1922-23 he had a short-lived series called "Laugh-O-Grams" based out of Kansas City, which were sufficiently amusing cartoons of contemporized fairy tales, but extremely crude by later standards. Financing was always a problem for Disney during these early days, and this early effort went bankrupt after a short run. Disney attempted to interest distributors—Universal included—in another series called "Lafflets," described as "animated cartoons and spicy jokes," but that series failed to garner any interest as well. Realizing that he needed to be where the action was, Disney left Kansas City behind and headed out to Hollywood in August 1923.

Operating out of two successive storefronts on Kingswell Avenue, Disney was attempting to interest distributors in yet another series, this one dreamed up back in Kansas City. The "Alice" series, as he called it, was something new and different, cleverly combining live and animated action in the same frame, the "live" action starring diminutive Virginia Davis. He successfully placed this with New York-based Margaret Winkler, the country's sole female distributor. Her contractual demands were for twelve "Alice" shorts to be delivered throughout 1924, and options for twelve additional shorts over each of the next two years. That, and she received full rights to all of them. Desperate for a foot into the industry, Disney agreed to her demands.

The series, beginning with the release of *Alice's Wonderland*, was an immediate success. Disney and Winkler's business relationship quickly headed south with her marriage to Charles Mintz, who, along with Margaret's brother George, quickly imposed their thoughts, wills, and demands on Disney, souring him in the process. It didn't help that the financial setup significantly favored the distributor, leaving Disney cash poor.

The newly negotiated contract for 1925 called for twenty-six films rather than twelve, and at terms that were even less favorable for Disney than the first year's terms. Here's where the Sterns come in, as explained by Neal Gabler in his exhaustive Disney biography, *Walt Disney: The Triumph of the American Imagination*. This took place early that year, a result of Disney's acknowledgement of an insufficient lack of knowledge of the intricacies of movie camera usage at that time:

> Walt admitted now that he had been a little too cocksure when he began the studio and that he had a lot to learn about making films, even hiring a cameraman from Century Studios, apparently at George Winkler's behest, because he conceded he did not know enough about running the camera himself.[32]

It's unknown who this cameraman was, but the important point is that negotiations were now opened between Disney and the Sterns.

Yet another contract was hashed out for 1926, but Disney's deepening financial crisis—stemming from the miniscule profits made on each short—was exacerbated by the move to larger space on Hyperion Avenue in February of that year. Disney was desperate for more favorable financial terms, and for a distributor he could work with. Making a huge leap of faith and attempting to connect some dots that should, perhaps, be left unconnected, it's not implausible that the Sterns, in their discussions with Disney over the use of their cameraman, may have proposed purchasing the studio under some mutually agreeable terms, and to go into effect with the termination of the 1926 contract. If that was indeed the case, however, the fire that decimated the Sterns' studio in August, and the immediate need to find new digs to resume production of their profitable comedies as quickly as possible, would understandably have derailed these talks.

From Neufeld to Newfield

But enough of speculation; let's get back to what we know. Sam was now directing under the Anglicized name Sam Newfield rather than as Sam Neufeld, although the Neufeld surname would reoccur with disconcerting regularity over the years to come.[33] Sam had begun directing shorts for the Sterns in early 1926 in anticipation of a 1926-27 season release. During the summer and fire-induced breaks of 1926, however, Sam did some moonlighting, heading over to competitor Jack White's studio where he directed a handful of Cameo Comedies for release through Educational. These included the single-reel shorts *Ask Dad* (February 27, 1927), *Auntie's Ante* (May 8, 1927), and *A Gym Dandy* (May 22, 1927). There was reportedly a Mermaid Comedy to be directed for White as well, co-starring Edna Marion and George Davis,[34] but whether this ever came about is unknown. It's possible that this was the film released as *Busy Lizzie* (January 23, 1927), purported to have been directed by a fellow named James Jones. Jones is credited as directing only four shorts in total, and all of them for White: *Midnight Follies* (October 21, 1926), *Busy Lizzie*, *Circus Capers* (May 15, 1927), and *Howling Hollywood* (April 21, 1929). Nothing else was ever heard from this James Jones, either before or after these four, so it's possible that "James Jones" was actually Sam, working under a pseudonym—something he would do with stunning regularity in the years to come—perhaps to avoid any additional fallout from the Sterns for a seeming lack of devotion. This is somewhat bolstered by the fact that Sam is clearly seen sitting in the director's chair in a posed crew still for the Poodles Hanneford short *Circus Daze* (August 1928; Weiss Brothers/Artclass), which starred Poodles Hanneford and was ostensibly directed by Charles Diltz; Hanneford was also the star of the Jones-directed *Circus Capers*. Sam directed at least one other short for the Weiss Brothers, *Nize People* (October 10, 1927), an entry in the "Izzie and Lizzie" series.

The cast and crew of the Weiss Brothers/Artclass comedy **Circus Daze** (1928) pose for the camera. Star Poodles Hanneford in drag, sitting center, Sam Newfield to the left of him, actress Betty Welsh to his right; Bert Sternbach standing far right. From his position of prominence, it would appear that Sam was the short's director, but others have attributed the film to Charles Diltz. *Courtesy of Tim Neufeld.*

Sam's output for the 1926-27 season consisted of ten two-reelers, but it was for the coming 1927-28 season that his worth as a director became apparent, his output increasing to fifteen films. As a result of the unprecedented demand for both the "Buster Brown" and "The Newlyweds and Their Baby" series, it was evident that film versions of popular comic strips were now the Sterns' biggest sellers. This led to the decision that the 1927-28 season's output would focus solely on adaptations of comic strips and jettison all other formats, retaining the above two series and the "Let George Do It" series, along with the addition of two newcomers: "Keeping Up with the Joneses" and "Mike and Ike (They Look Alike)." Based on the strip by Arthur "Pop" Momand, "Keeping Up with the Joneses" co-starred Harry Long, Stella Adams, and Addie McPhail as the upward-striving McGinis family. The other new series was the Rube Goldberg spinoff "Mike and Ike (They Look Alike)" which co-starred Charles King and Charles Dorety as the look-alikes, a concept difficult to swallow once you looked past their slicked-back hair and pencil-thin mustaches. The former of these two new series failed to click with audiences, petering out after a single season.

The Stern Brothers' "Mike and Ike (They Look Alike)" series director Sam Newfield and star Charles King.

The Sterns were now running a tighter ship, relying on their trio of reliable directors to handle the bulk of the season's output. Gus Meins was the best of the three, Corby oversaw an additional twenty-two shorts, while Sam brought in a respectable fifteen films. Twelve of Sam's efforts were entries in the "Let George Do It" series putting Sid Saylor through his paces. One such film was *High Flyin' George* (January 25, 1928), filmed under the working title *Up in the Air*. Saylor's co-star in this film was a former Ziegfeld Follies beauty, eighteen-year-old Jane Manners. "It was while she was playing in the Music Box Revue in Hollywood a few weeks ago that Production Manager Sigmund Neufeld saw her and signed her up," wrote *Universal Weekly*.[35] If Sigmund had high hopes for Manners, they didn't pan out; this was the only known film Manners would appear in for the Sterns.

Sigmund, now being touted as the studio's scenario editor as well as production manager, took a break from his hectic schedule after the 1927 holidays and headed back to New York for a vacation. It was his first time back in the city in twelve years,[36] and although the trip was promoted as a vacation, he was there to confer with Julius and Universal executives on new product. The result of these discussions was yet another increase in the studio's annual production budget, the amount now closing in at $1,000,000, a major increase in each upcoming film's budget.[37] Sam accompanied him on this trip, but direction beckoned, forcing him to return to Hollywood a week before his older brother.[38]

Upon his return to the West Coast, Sigmund spoke at length of his take on the public's attitude toward comedies, a change that demanded "comedies packed with thrills, and danger sequences." No longer was the public "satisfied with straight comedy and ordinary humorous situations," he claimed.

Sid Saylor and Jane Manners get hitched in director Sam Newfield's "Let George Do It" entry **High Flyin' George** (1928). *Courtesy of Robert James Kiss.*

The stunts which used to cause gasps of horror and breath-taking suspense in the old-time thrillers now are considered excruciatingly funny, when performed by a comedian. The situation may be just as nerve-racking or as dangerous as it ever was, but it now produces paroxysms of laughter where it used to curdle the blood.

I am not quite sure that I know the answer to this. Maybe the average man is becoming more bloodthirsty. Maybe he is just tired and fed-up with the old heart-grippers. Maybe he laughs at them in a superior, ridiculing sort of way. I have another theory for it, however. In applying these thrills to comedy, we are only superimposing the thrill and the comedy relief to it—giving the action and the reaction at the same time. This heightens the reaction and gives the audience a chance to laugh before the tension has let down. Therefore we get a more spontaneous and a bigger laugh than if the comedy relief be used as a follow-up of different material.

There is no question as to the danger our players now are subjected in order to inject the thrill element into comedies.[39]

Arguably nothing really new in the breakneck, thrill-seeking production of on-screen comedic daredevil sequences and the public reaction to same, but I'll cut Sigmund some slack here. Sigmund went on to describe a near miss that occurred during the filming of the "Let George Do It" comedy *Big Game George* (July 18, 1928), directed (somewhat recklessly, one might infer) by his brother Sam:

Sid Saylor, the star, was suspended high over the deck of a departing ocean liner by a derrick. The boat was supposed to go out from under him as he dangled in the air. It so happened that the after flag staff of the ship fouled some of the lines and began to drag Saylor's cable out of position. There was no stopping the huge boat, and it was only a question of a few seconds before the cable might snap, letting Saylor fall to the deck. He would have been killed or maimed for life in such an event. Luckily, the lines were cleared in the nick of time, just a second or two before the movement of the boat would have thrown its full power against the cable. It was a narrow escape and Saylor thought he was a goner. So did all of us. The funny thing is, that, although the cable sequence is shown as a thrill with dangerous aspects for its comedy value, only a small part of the actual danger and thrill of the situation appears on the screen in this instance.[40]

"Keeping Up with the Joneses" was jettisoned for the 1928-29 season, the remaining four series comprising the season's output. Meins, Corby, and Sam remained as the Sterns' powerhouse (and presumably overworked) trio of directors, each responsible for seventeen of the season's fifty-two film output; the fifty-second film was co-directed by Meins and Corby. Sigmund pushed the directors to get the upcoming season's films in the can as early as possible, the final season's output running the gamut of acceptable to poor. As a result of the push, the 1928-29 season's fare was finished and shipped by the beginning of 1929.

Three of Sam's efforts for this final season survive, and they are wildly uneven as entertainment (as was the bulk of the season's rushed output). The Sterns at some point decided that it was the comic strip titles that pulled in audiences, and that the acting talent employed was of secondary importance. This resulted in some lackluster leads as replacements for their more talented predecessors: Trimble remained as "Buster Brown," but gone was Doreen Turner, now replaced by Lois Hardwick—an okay replacement—but Pete the Pup was gone as well, now replaced by a talent-challenged mutt named Jerry, sporting the most absurd eyebrows in canine history. Also gone were King and Dorety from the "Mike and Ike" shorts, the charisma-less Joe Young and Ned La Salle the substandard—and wholly unamusing—replacements.

The first of Sam's final season films to survive was *Hold Your Horses* (January 16, 1929), easily the worst film of the trio. The first half takes place in a rooming house's dining room, the remainder of the film following the boys as they attempt to impress a pair of lovelies with their unfounded boasts about their prowess as horseback riders. One unamusing "gag" follows another at the Riding Academy as they get kicked through barn walls, accidentally ride a cow, end up at the wrong end of a mule's hoofs, and suffer a climactic ride through a campsite's tents and a group of picnickers; you get the idea. Young and La Salle simply walk through their paces, rarely eliciting a chuckle from the entertainment-starved viewer; one soon realizes just how accomplished and likable King and Dorety were in these same roles. If Sam had a gag writing team at his disposal, it must have been a very off day for them.

Buster's Spooks (June 26, 1929) and *Stop Barking* (August 21, 1929) fare better by comparison, the former of these two "Buster Brown" entries rather enjoyable. When they think they have accidentally drowned the chubby kid (Albert Schaefer) who has been annoying them, Buster (Trimble), Mary Jane (Hardwick), Oatmeal (Hannah Washington), and Tige (a woebegone Jerry) avoid a cop and take refuge in an unoccupied house. They think it's haunted, but it turns out that it is only the doing of the chubby kid who is trying to get even with them. There are lots of familiar (and by this time, tired) "spook house" gags employed, but the antics of Oatmeal and, surprisingly, Jerry as Tige, give the film a much-needed boost. Oatmeal's knee-knocking and the resultant falling of pants never fails to garner a laugh, but the biggest chuckles are courtesy of Jerry, demonstrating that in spite of his bizarre appearance, he was at times a borderline acceptable replacement for Pete. Mild laughs, admittedly, but a decided step up from a lot of the other later-era "Buster Brown" offerings, which had mostly grown stale and unimaginative of late; Trimble, after all, needed all the help he could get, and got it in this one.

Stop Barking was the next-to-last short ever released by the Sterns, and a sad, semi-swan song it is. Tige has a toothache, and the film follows Buster and Mary Jane's efforts to relieve him of his discomfort. That's pretty much it, and poor Tige—or should I say poor Jerry? —really takes a beating throughout this film. The poor mutt is visibly uncomfortable stuffed into the dental chair, and suffers multiple "imprisonments" as well squeezed into the bird cages. The ASPCA would have frowned on the proceedings, and I suspect that Jerry was relieved to have no further involvement in the "Buster Brown" series after this one. As for Sam's direction, it is workmanlike and unremarkable, but wholly acceptable.

Director Sam Newfield, center with gaudy socks, consults with brother Sig in white suit and tie, circa 1928-29. Bert Sternbach second from left in black suit, cinematographer and sometime director Francis Corby between Sam and Sig, young Max Alexander second from right, and cameraman Harry Forbes far right. *Courtesy of Marc Wanamaker and Bison Archives*

The Sterns were reported to be up in the air regarding the coming of sound and the prospect of retooling their studio to accommodate the new process. "At the studio recently [Julius] explained to employees that he knew nothing about talking pictures," wrote *Variety*, "but declared, 'We must drift with the tide. If it must be talkers it must be talkers. We will have to make them even though the expense will be more.'"[41] Rather than drifting with the tide, however, the Sterns decided to pack up and drift into retirement instead, the brothers doing so as comfortable millionaires. This decision was, in effect, made for them by a major rift with their brother-in-law and long-time advocate, Carl Laemmle. Laemmle, having some cash flow issues, asked Julius for a loan, and Julius—not unreasonably—asked for a repayment schedule. This sent Laemmle over the edge, sending a terse, single line telegram, and cutting all business ties with the brothers: "Decided make our own comedies,"[42] it read, and with that, the fifteen-year history of L-Ko, Century, and the Stern Brothers Comedies came to an abrupt end.

Laemmle made good on his threat, or at least for the short-term. Lawrence McKeen, the annoying (but evidently very professional) little brat who starred as Snookums in the Sterns' "The Newlyweds and Their Baby" series, was immediately hired by Universal to star as "Sunny Jim" in a series of ten sound shorts to be made at Universal City. Gus Meins, Sigmund Neufeld, and Sam Newfield were all hired as well, Meins and Sam initially to direct McKeen, and Sigmund to supervise.[43] Plans shifted, and Sam was soon reassigned to direct several of Arthur Lake's "Puppy Love" silent shorts, "ten sparkling comedies of youth on a rampage." Sid Saylor was another hire, to star in another series of ten comedies—silent as well—to be directed by Sam and Meins and supervised by Sigmund.[44] All in all, Sigmund was to supervise all fifty-two of the coming season's shorts.[45] Sam's output included such films as *Night Owls* (September 25, 1929) and *Doing His Stuff* (November 20, 1929) with Arthur Lake, *Outdoor Sports* (January 1, 1930) and *French Leave* (March 19, 1930) with Sid Saylor, and *She's a He* (June 4, 1930) and *Stop That Noise* (June 14, 1930) with "Sunny Jim" McKeen.

Once he was settled in at Universal City, and the long-term prospect of steady employment seemed at hand, Sigmund and Ruth decided to buy a new house. They found one they both liked at 340 North Sweetzer Avenue, closing on the newly built Spanish style house in December 1929. This was shortly after the stock market crash, so the previous, very short-term owners bailed out and, with $500 down, Sigmund assumed the mortgage. A little more than modest, but not opulent, it was a three bedroom, two bath dwelling in a nice, middle-class Jewish neighborhood. They had maids on-and-off, and tried live-ins, but Ruth didn't like that arrangement so, as Sig Jr. put it, "they had pain-in-the-ass maids coming in one or two days a week."

Fairfax Avenue was the main Jewish shopping street, and close to where they now lived. Ruth would make frequent trips to the Jewish butcher, bakery, and Canter's delicatessens to pick up the stuff that Sigmund loved, and that had been mostly absent from his childhood diet. Ruth, as Sig Jr. put it, "would go there shopping and get all that stuff that he liked. And I liked it too. I think my mother even liked it." Neither Sigmund nor Ruth practiced their respective former religions, agreeing early on that theirs would be a secular household. Still, they were, in a way, part of the Jewish community.

Knowing full well where his bread was buttered, Sigmund joined in with a raft of others in congratulating Laemmle on his twenty successful years in the industry, in half- and full-page ads placed throughout an issue of *Motion Picture News*. "Sig Neufeld Congratulates You Carl Laemmle" read the half-page blurb.[46] He may have had different feelings about Laemmle come mid-1930, however, when he was given notice that his services to Universal were no longer needed, an unceremonious end to a relationship, direct or indirect, that had lasted nearly two decades.

If you'd like to learn more about Henry Lehrman, Julius and Abe Stern, or the L-Ko, Rainbow, Century, and Stern Brothers Comedies, look no further than this author's *Mr. Suicide: Henry "Pathé" Lehrman and the Birth of Silent Comedy* (2017), and *Time is Money! The Century, Rainbow, and Stern Brother Comedies of Julius and Abe Stern* (2021), both published by BearManor Media.

Chapter 3:
A Different Breed of Comedian

After Sigmund's two decades working for Universal—be it directly or for one of its affiliated companies—he and his brother Sam were both shown the door. Sigmund's two decades counted for a lot within the industry, however, having learned the business from the ground up, and now with proven managerial talents to show for it. Sam's five years of direction would be in demand as well, although the industry's tunnel vision would think only in terms of comedy shorts; he'd never gotten anywhere near a feature-length film, nor a drama of any length.

The Stern Brothers had an industry-wide reputation for, shall we say, "thriftiness," and the brothers' years of cost- and corner-cutting experience working for them resulted in reputations as suitable hires for the many second-tier, budget- and schedule-conscious independent studios. The Sterns themselves were frequently the butt of mean-spirited jokes and apocryphal stories, but no one in the industry could deny their success. The year that followed the Sterns' retirement meant more of the same for Universal, providing the opportunity for both Sigmund and Sam to dip their toes into the sound film environment. Now that final relationship had come to an end, and none of the big studios like Fox, M-G-M, RKO, Warners, or Paramount showed any interest. There were dozens of smaller, independent studios around, however, many leading hand-to-mouth existences while they struggled to eke out a living from hastily filmed, low-budget quickies. These were the studios that would be interested in the talents that Sigmund and Sam had accrued to date, both having demonstrated their ability to work in a pressure cooker environment, to work quickly and efficiently, and to work within budgetary and time constraints. Many of these studios are now long forgotten—such as Continental, Sono Art-World Wide, Peerless, and Syndicate Pictures—while others managed to hang on for several years and acquire a certain level of success—such as Monogram and Tiffany. It was with this latter studio that Sigmund found a new home in May 1930.

The offer came from Phil Goldstone, Tiffany's head. In business since 1921, Tiffany was the baby of movie star Mae Murray, her director husband Robert Z. Leonard, and Maurice H. Hoffman, their films to be released through Metro-Goldwyn-Mayer. Murray and Leonard's divorce in 1925 brought an end to that relationship, however, but the studio soldiered on with its lower budget, lower production-value fare, populated by stars several notches shy of Murray's status and now released on the less rewarding state rights basis. As one of Hollywood's several independent studios, it was still the cream of the Poverty Row crop...or at least until the double whammy of the stock market crash of 1929 and the concurrent, costly switchover to talkies. As reality set in, Tiffany was forced to focus more on Westerns, a genre it had previously shunned.

Phil Goldstone (1893-1963) harkened from Omaha, Nebraska, where he had spent some time as a theatre owner and film distributor via his Sterling Film Exchange. The war resulted in a stint in the U.S. Navy from mid-1918 into 1919, where he oversaw the photographic department of the Navy Relief Society.[1] Goldstone relocated to Hollywood after his discharge, eventually going into production in 1920 with his Western Star Production Company. William Fairbanks was to star in a series of twelve oaters, to be released over the coming year on the state rights market.[2] That was the plan, at least, but it appears that only two of the twelve made it to the screen before the company folded. Undaunted by this initial failure, Goldstone regrouped with his Phil

Goldstone Productions, which cranked out a string of films from 1922 starring the likes of Richard Talmadge, Tully Marshall, and even lesser-known names. Goldstone was hired by Tiffany in late 1924 as the company's supervising director, producing his films at the Ince Studio.[3]

John M. Stahl (né Strelitzsky, 1886-1950) was named as Tiffany's vice president supervising production in 1927, the company now called Tiffany-Stahl Productions. Stahl had directed films since the early teens, moving into production as well by 1921. Prior affiliations with Louis B. Mayer, First National, and Metro-Goldwyn-Mayer led to overtures from M-G-M and Fox Films for his services, but Stahl decided to team up with Tiffany instead. Under Stahl's leadership, Tiffany-Stahl's production facilities were enhanced significantly with the acquisition of the Fine Arts Studios at 4500 Sunset Boulevard,[4] followed soon after with the additional space at 4516 Sunset. By 1930, however, Stahl had moved on to Universal, the studio reverting to its former name of Tiffany. Goldstone was now the studio's chief studio executive.

Producer Phil Goldstone.

Goldstone's offer to Sig—everyone called Sigmund "Sig" by this time—was to head a department to make "unusual short novelty productions." The initial three shorts were to be filmed in Technicolor, after which Sig would oversee several other, yet-to-be-announced series.[5] Nothing seems to have become of these fabled Technicolor shorts, but the first of the other new series was announced in July. Called "Classics in Slang," it was promoted as a series of six two-reelers to be based on stories by the late H.C. Witwer. Paul Hurst (1888-1953) was signed to star, having recently demonstrated his acting chops in three previous features for Tiffany, as the dimwitted sparring partner in *The Swellhead*, a bush league baseball player in *Hot Curves*, and the first mate *Paradise Island* (all 1930).[6] These were to be filmed as all-talkies.[7] Scott Darling, who had been churning out one scenario after another since the late teens, was hired to write the dialog for this series, as well as for a Charlie Murray-George Sydney feature *Caught Cheating* (1931).[8] Broadway comedienne Pert Kelton, the youngest of the Four Keltons and with only a single other film role to her credit—1929's *Sally* for First National—was signed to a three-year contract and added to the studio's roster of comedians as well.[9] Kelton would star opposite Hurst in several of the series' entries.

The second new series of two-reelers was announced that same month, this one to feature the so-called Tiffany Talking Chimps. This may have been Tiffany's attempt to jump onto the talking animal bandwagon that Jules White and Zion Myers had successfully introduced a year earlier with their "Dogville Comedies" for M-G-M featuring—you guessed it—dogs. "The chimpanzees are highly trained animals," wrote Dan Thomas, "Some of them, as a sardonic director [Neufeld] remarked, are practically as intelligent as lots of movie stars. In the films projected for them, these chimpanzees will sing, talk, play the piano and do all sorts of things that nobody would expect a chimpanzee to do." Sig oversaw the unit, and was ostensibly the series' director as well. Charlie Lewis and Madeline Beckwith were the simians' trainers, little doubt put through their paces wrangling the chimps in the films to come.[10]

Comedy shorts featuring anthropomorphized simians were nothing new, harkening back to 1916 with E & R Jungle Film's "Napoleon and Sally" series, Universal's "Mr. Joe Martin" series of 1919-21 and Century's derivative "Mrs. Joe Martin" shorts of 1919-20, William Campbell's (and others') "Snooky the Humanzee" shorts for Chester 1919-23, and "The Fox Monkeys" comedies of the mid-1920s. Tiffany's series would differ from these earlier efforts in two significant ways. First and foremost, these shorts would have sound, dialog, and music, while their predecessors were all silents. Also, the actors in the Tiffany series would all be of the hairy sort, nary a human being to be found in their casts; the earlier films all featured a mix of simians and humans, the latter group likely none too thrilled with being upstaged by their hirsute counterparts. One difficult-to-swallow claim was made at the time regarding trainer Lewis's wife, stating that she "was the first to introduce wild animals in a motion picture."[11] Sheer nonsense, one would presume.

Other shorts announced—or at least planned—for the 1930-31 season included twenty-six "The Voice of Hollywood" subjects, six "Musical Fantasies," six "Forbes Randolph Kentucky Jubilee Singers" musicals, six Technicolor "Color Symphonies" subjects, and six multi-color travel subjects named the "Rolling Stones Series." All of these were to be released as single-reelers, except for half of the six "Kentucky Jubilee Singers" entries, which were two-reelers.[12]

Tiffany, stretched to the limit at its current studio space by 1930, considered the acquisition of the Tec-Art Studios on Melrose. "There are two sound stages, one stage capable of handling any sized set and ample grounds suitable for street scenes or any outdoor location," wrote *Inside Facts of Stage and Screen*, adding "There are over a hundred offices and other conveniences for numerous producers.... Studio facilities at the Tiffany Studio are rather limited to permit the expansion necessary to take care of the other producers. Tec-Art would be a valuable acquisition to them at this time."[13] Those plans fell through, so they went ahead with plans to construct a 320 x 240 combination studio and office building on their existing lot, augmented by the acquisition of additional land.[14]

Sig's involvement with the Hurst shorts was primarily in a supervisory capacity, and only five of the proposed two-reelers were filmed. *One Punch O'Toole* was reported to have been the first of these to be filmed, but there were conflicting articles in the trades that make it impossible to accurately track down the correct sequence of production. Regardless, Sig is credited with directing *One Punch O'Toole*, with Frank Strayer—a journeyman director since the early 1920s—hired to direct the others. Hurst starred as "One Punch O'Toole," the none-too-bright and none-too-successful prizefighter whose fellow boarding house lodgers all place bets on. *Film Daily*'s reviewer was on the fence about the results: "Paul Hurst gets over a neat characterization, but he is far better than his material. This one is weak on story and gags."[15] That story and its gags were a co-effort of Sig and Scott Darling, so given the dearth of reviews for this particular short, we'll need to take this reviewer's word for their shortcoming. Pert Kelton co-starred with Hurst, with Bud Jamison and Eddie Boland rounding out the cast.

Hurst's other four shorts were *Ex-Bartender, De Woild's Champeen, The Missing Link,* and *The Tale of a Flea*, all Frank Strayer-Scott Darling efforts, and not necessarily released in that order. Hurst was sought for a role in another company's production after the completion of *The Tale of a Flea*,[16] and this would result in his severing of ties with Tiffany, although not necessarily of his choice. In early 1931 Hurst sued Tiffany for $16,000 he claimed due him, along with an additional $100,000 damages for breach of contract. He claimed that he was to be paid $1,000 per week for each of those six "Classics in Slangs" shorts, but that only two were ever made under that banner. "Also, he claims, Tiff loaned him to another studio at his Tiff salary, which hurt his rep, and finally dropped him."[17] Of the five he made, it's unclear which two of these were the "Classics in Slangs" entries, not that it's that important.

Paul Hurst in Tiffany's **De Woild's Champeen** (1930), Sig Neufeld producer, Frank Strayer director.

Sig's primary focus from 1930 into 1931 was on the planned series of twelve Tiffany Talking Chimps shorts. Harry Fraser (1889-1974), a writer-director of a half-decade's experience, was hired to write the stories and scripts. Jack Natteford was on board writing the clever dialog that the off-screen actors would lip-synch to the chimps' mouth movements, courtesy of some lip-smacking chewing gum. Along with the scripts and sets needed for the upcoming productions, costumes were needed for the stars as well. Goldstone assigned the thankless task to Fraser, who recounted the experience in his memoirs, *I Went That-a-Way: The Memoirs of a Western Film Director*.

> The scripts called for the chimps to be dressed up to fit their masculine or feminine roles. On this particular occasion, rather than let their costuming be handled by the studio wardrobe department, it was decided to have them outfitted at the May Company. Phil explained it this way: "It will make a great publicity story, Harry. You wrote these monkey epics, so you're elected to take the chimps shopping. I've ordered the limousine to drive you and the trainer and the two chimpanzees to the May Company." At that time there was only one May Company store, located at Eighth and Broadway in downtown Los Angeles.
>
> "How much am I supposed to spend?" I queried. Phil was not noted for his generosity, and the chimp pictures were being produced on a very tight budget.
>
> "Buy anything you want. I'll set it up with the store." So the very next day, in response to Phil Goldstone's orders, the big, black limousine pulled up in front of the store's Broadway entrance, and from it stepped the trainer, followed by Harry Fraser with Betty, the smaller of the two chimps, and Nellie, a big chimp gripped by hand, one on either side. The fun started the moment we stepped on the sidewalk. The customers and passers-by gasped at the sight of chimpanzees alighting from a big, black limousine. By the time we reached the stairs leading to the basement, we had a mob at our heels, as the word spread.
>
> We headed for the men's clothing department. The salesman paled as we approached.
>
> "I would like to see a suit to fit Betty, the little chimp," I said with a straight face, "and a larger size for Nellie. Oh yes, I will require derby hats and shoes to complete their wardrobes."
>
> The salesman looked at me in complete disbelief. "You're kidding."
>
> I shook my head. "No, I'm not." I explained that the costumes were needed for a comedy in production at the studio.
>
> "Well," he shrugged as he pulled a couple of suits off the rack, "my father-in-law is always telling me that I couldn't fit a monkey, and I guess for once he's right."
>
> By this time the chimps were getting annoyed by the crowd of people clustering around them. But we finally managed to squeeze Nellie and Betty into coats that fitted them, after a fashion. But the pants were a problem. The salesman reluctantly called the tailor, who, in turn, looked at me as if I were off my rocker when I asked him to shorten the trousers so the chimps could wear them. Derby hats were the next order of business. Nellie liked hers so well she refused to take it off. Fitting shoes to the oversize feet posed another problem. But the shoe salesman suddenly remembered he had had a special shoe made to order for a big seven-footer, who for some reason had never called for them. When he put them on Nellie, she fell in love with them, and screamed angry protests when we tried to take them off.
>
> By this time, the May Company basement was jammed with intrigued onlookers. The chimps, realizing that they were the center of attention, began to jump excitedly from one pile of clothing to another. In a short time, the place was a shambles. Finally, the trainer and I managed to get control of them and headed for the stairs, leaving the salesman jumping up and down in anger and frustration, as he helplessly viewed the disaster scene the chimps had left behind.

Back at the studio, Phil Goldstone practically had a heart attack when he discovered that the shoes Nellie was wearing with such pride had cost $25.00—a fabulous sum for a pair of footwear in those days. "Twenty-five shekels for shoes for a monkey—I won't pay it," he shouted."

To which I replied, "Tell you what, Phil, you inform Nellie that she can't keep her shoes and see what happens."[18]

Goldstone relented, but it would eventually lead to the formation of a special wardrobe department created solely for the chimps, under the direction of Mistress Caroline.[19]

Each film took longer than the usual comedy two-reeler to produce, and for obvious reasons: the stars weren't trained thespians, after all. The first four were in the can by late September,[20] and the initial two—*The Blimp Mystery* and *The Little Covered Wagon*—were previewed for reviewers that same month. "J.L.K." of *Exhibitors Daily Review and Motion Pictures Today* was ecstatic over the results, and dialogue writer Natteford's work in particular. "Whoever wrote the dialogue for this series immediately should be placed under a long-term contract, given a meal ticket, and carte blanc [sic] expense account," he wrote. "He, or she, supplied something that is 'gold in them thar hills.'" Regarding the series itself, he went on to say that "If Tiffany doesn't register on the dark side of the ledger, 100 per cent profit on this almost-human animal of the jungles, then this reviewer has spent 15 years in the movie game in vain."[21]

The first chimp comedy to be released was *The Blimp Mystery*, and it's a corker. The paper-thin plot involves the quest of detective Hemlock Domes and his assistant Watkins to track down and rescue Hemlock's girlfriend, kidnapped by a maniacally cackling bad guy; suffice it to say that she's rescued at the end. There's nothing particularly new that wasn't displayed back in those earlier "Napoleon and Sally," "Snooky the Humanzee," and "Mr." and "Mrs. Joe Martin" chimp-fests aside from the obvious novelty of sound, and here it's put to excellent use. The synching of voices to the simians' lip movements is smoothly executed, and the over-acted dubbed-in voices themselves quite amusing, from the girl's simpering, love-struck cooing to her later pleas for rescue, to the outraged chattering of the owner of a Chinese laundry when a disposed time-bomb disrupts his business.

It appears that Tiffany lavished some time and care and, perhaps, a few additional dollars to launch this new series, as the production values are excellent. Hemlock's small two-seater airplane is modestly impressive, tricked out with a smoke-spewing machine gun. Equally eye-catching and visually convincing is the TV-like, two-way audio-visual communication device the two lovers use to communicate, complete with seamlessly matted-in images of the two lovers at either end. (Hemlock tunes in unannounced a bit too early, catching his girl still dressing!) Director Neufeld has come up with some nice visual gags, such as Watkin's "black" eye, here a "white" eye to stand out on the chimp's dark skin; the kidnapper's cocktail shaking, which manages to splatter his poor abductee's face; and Hemlock's pursuit of the kidnapper's dirty footprints, across the floor, up one wall, across the ceiling, and back down the opposing wall. Jack Natteford's dialogue provides plenty of chuckles as well: Watkins, impressed by yet-another pithy observation by Hemlock, blurbs "Your deductions are marvelous, chief!" to which Hemlock blithely responds "Yeah, I'm good." A nice copy of *The Blimp Mystery* survives in the G. William Jones Film and Video Archive at SMU/Southern Methodist University.

Hemlock Domes's "modestly impressive" two-seater airplane, in director Sigmund Neufeld's **The Blimp Mystery.**

Barroom showdown in the Tiffany Chimps entry **The Little Covered Wagon** (1930), Sigmund Neufeld director.

The second film, *The Little Covered Wagon*, followed. "Should Be a Wow," wrote *Motion Picture News*' reviewer, deeming it "Something brand new in the line of comedies.... Phil Goldstone brings out this new series with trained chimpanzees, a gang of talented animals which should prove a big box-office bet.... [This] novelty subject should click in a big way."[22] The plot makes the leap from the covered wagon attacked by Indians to the surviving foundling growing up and cheating the crook out of foreclosing a mortgage. The reviewer had a sole complaint, albeit a minor one: "Goldstone made one mistake in not scaling some of the settings to the size of the chimps..."[23] Budgetary constraints, no doubt.

The Little Big House—a spoof on M-G-M's recently released prison drama *The Big House*—and *The Little Divorcee* were the other two among the initial four. "This is as clever a satire as we have seen anywhere on marriages that go wrong, letters left for the husband and the final reconciliation," wrote *Exhibitors Herald-World* in its review of *The Little Divorcee*. "All the credit must go to Charles Lewis who trains them and Sig Neufeld, the director. Both must have infinite patience, but the result is worth the effort."[24] *Motion Picture News* agreed: "These clever chimp subjects are little short of sensational, for the synchrony is nearly perfect, the chimps apparently talking the clever lines."[25]

It's life behind bars for the Tiffany Chimps, in **The Little Big House** (1930), Sigmund Neufeld director.

Sig directed approximately half of the initial series, with the remaining films assigned to other directors. *Nine Nights in a Bar Room* was a burlesque of the famous stage play *Ten Nights in a Bar Room*, and the story of a drunkard whose wife and baby are in need. "Sig Neufeld has directed a picture that will give lots of laughs to any audience."[26]

"'Sweet Patootie' calls for all the great histrionic powers of Mr. Chimp, and the subtle, alluring charm of his professional and matrimonial mate," wrote one reviewer, who was one of the few to see the film under that title."[27] *Sweet Patootie* presents somewhat of a problem in that there doesn't seem to be any contemporary evidence that it was released as such, its final release title unclear. Several different full-page ads appeared in the trades in 1930 listing the initial six films in the series as *The Blimp Mystery*, *The Little Covered Wagon*, *The Little Big House*, *The Little Divorcee*, *Chasing Around*, and *Sweet Patootie*. According to published release records, however, five of the above were among the initial six releases, but *Nine Nights in a Bar Room* was the sixth rather than *Sweet Patootie*, and *Patootie* is nowhere to be found among subsequent releases. Which suggests that it was probably renamed for release as *Nine Nights in a Bar Room*.

Sig Neufeld's opening title credit for **Apeing Hollywood** (1931).

"Chasing Around," wrote *Motion Picture* magazine, "starts off with a snappy family quarrel, in which the son—with an English accent that will panic you—attempts to act as peacemaker. Then father and son go for an airplane ride that is among the funniest bits ever filmed. The lines crack wisely, and the acting of the chimps is something to see."[28]

Apeing Hollywood is another survivor and readily viewable, and while it is sufficiently enjoyable, it pales in comparison to *The Blimp Mystery*, the series' first offering. The plot involves star-struck farm girl Fanny Applesass, who flees her abusive father and heads to Hollywood where she finds instant fame, a five-year contract, and a Rolls Royce to boot. Her farmhand lover follows, and after mistaking a scene being filmed as reality, beats up the male actor and is awarded a contract as well. There are nice touches throughout this frequently amusing spoof on all things Hollywood, such as

38 Poverty Row Royalty

Poster for the Tiffany talking Chimps' **Apeing Hollywood.**
Was it "*Apeing*" or "*Aping*"? Despite this poster's spelling
as "Aping", the released film spells it "Apeing" in its
opening credits.

farmhand's mistaking the Women's dressing room for the Men's, and the long, slow tracking shot starting with the back of the director's chair, labelled as such, to four additional chairs sequentially labeled "1st Assistant Director," "2nd Assistant Director," "3rd Assistant Director," and "4th Assistant Director." The German director's English, barely intelligible at first, eventually devolves into incomprehensible mutterings, and some of the earlier dialogue exchanges elicit some laughs as well. Fanny, being spanked by her father, wails "Oh, father, you are breaking my heart," and later recites a line from a script she is practicing: "Send me a sign from above," she implores, immediately followed by a hen laying an egg on her head and covering her with goo. Unfortunately, all that is good in the one viewable copy that survives in Ralph Celentano's collection is compromised and an unsatisfactory viewing experience, since the sound track is out of synch with the on-screen action by a second or two.

The Talking Chimp series previews were an immediate success, and deals were closed with Paramount to play in theatres throughout the Spanish speaking world, and with Fox for distribution in Australia, New Zealand, and Tasmania.[29] The future looked bright for the series.

A tender moment from **Cinnamon** (1931), the Tiffany Chimps' burlesque of the Richard Dix-Irene Dunne Western epic **Cimarron**. Sig Neufeld directed.

After a long layoff, production resumed in June 1931 on the remaining Chimp comedies. *Cinnamon*, a burlesque on the recently released Richard Dix-Irene Dunne Western epic *Cimarron*, was the first,[30] purported to have again been directed Sig. I say "purported" because it was well known that Sig didn't care for direction, much preferring the production end of the business. Sig's son shared his views as to why his father didn't direct more films than he did:

> My dad was not that outgoing…he was sort of intimidated by people and things, because he wasn't that well educated. I think that directing put him in a position that was uncomfortable for him, I really do, and I think that's why he preferred to produce, where he was just dealing with people but not being on the set and deal with the whole crew and all that sort of thing.[31]

Which brings us back to Sam. Sam was working over at the Tec-Art Studios filming a Sid Saylor short in June and July 1930,[32] but after that his credits have a gap until mid-1932. Sam's mini-bio in the 1937 *Film Daily* "Who's Who in Hollywood" claimed that Sam directed Chimp Comedies at Tiffany,[33] so it is likely that Sam joined Sig at Tiffany, co-directing—or perhaps solely directing—some of the shorts, and was content with an uncredited paycheck. After all, it was Sam who had six actual years of behind-the-megaphone direction of comedies for the Sterns, so who better to deal with this hairy horde?

Phil Goldstone's relationship with the studio during this time would appear to have been a rather shaky one. Rumors of his intention to resign were mis-reported as early as April 1930,[34] which was actually an intended leave of absence to deal with his ill mother; he was convinced to remain at his post.[35] Rumors resurfaced several months later regarding purported dissension within the studio, Goldstone's offer to buy the studio, and threats to quit. He denied it, "but with the understanding of closer relations and co-operation between east and west."[36] Things weren't going so well for Tiffany by 1931, the Depression having a major impact. The forced conversion to sound didn't help financial matters either. James P. Cunnigham, *Film Daily*'s Statistical Editor, explained in layman's terms:

> Motion pictures are photographed at the rate of 90 feet per minute, as compared with a former speed of 60 feet. The change was brought about when theaters increased the projection speed for a quicker turnover. Studios gradually raised the rate in order to maintain action at normal speed until 90 feet per minute was accepted as standard.[37]

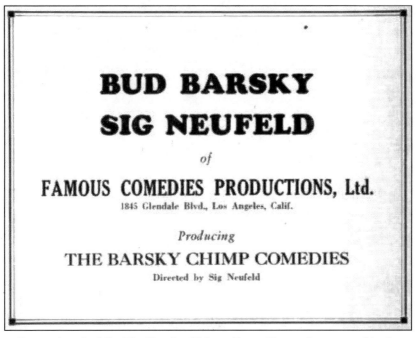

Promotional ad for The Barsky Chimp Comedies, as it appeared in the 1931 *Film Daily Year Book*. Nothing ever came of the proposed series.

An oversimplification and not entirely accurate—the frame-per-second increase was due to the switchover to sound, not the "quicker turnover" as stated—but the net result was a 50 % increase in footage used, and a corresponding increase in lab costs. This hurt the smaller, cost-conscious studios, an impact that was felt at Tiffany when Goldstone announced plans for the upcoming 1931-32 season: "No color or music will be included in the firm's new year features," he said, a statement that no doubt led to some concern among affiliated distributors and exhibitors.[38] By April 1931, Tiffany had merged with H.W. Hammon's Educational and World Wide. Numerous resignations of Tiffany staff resulted. "Disposition of Phil Goldstone, present Tiffany studio head, is still to be settled," wrote *Motion Picture Herald*. "He had attempted resignation on numerous occasions since Tiffany merger negotiations were started."[39] Goldstone's status was still a subject for conjecture as late as July, when *Motion Picture Daily* reported:

Is Phil Goldstone in or out? The veteran Tiffany studio head has been reported in and out probably more times than any other exec. Grant L. Cook in New York the other day stated that Goldstone definitely would stay with the company. Now, on the Coast, Goldstone says that's all wet and that he intends to quit on August 1.[40]

Goldstone followed through this time, and by year's end, when reports stated that he was now "closely identified with the financing of independent companies."[41] Goldstone remained in the industry throughout the 1930s serving as a producer—both credited and uncredited—on indie films that included Halperin Productions' *White Zombie* (1932), Larry Darmour Productions' *The Vampire Bat*, *The World Gone Mad*, and *The Sin of Nora Moran* (all 1933), and Criterion Pictures' *Damaged Goods* (1937).

Tiffany's merger and its attendant upheaval within the studio caused some major speed bumps with production, but the Chimp series limped on with entries that included *Africa Squawks* ("an interesting and very amusing travesty of the 'Trader Horn' theme," wrote *Film Daily*)[42] and *Skimpy*, a parody of Paramount's *Skippy*. *Gland Hotel*'s production was under way in September, yet another burlesque skewering M-G-M's hit *Grand Hotel*. It turned out to be Sig's last film for Tiffany, and the series' swan song. *Motion Picture Herald* reported the split and the reasons why, and if one reads between the lines, Tiffany's recent merger with Educational was likely the root cause:

> Tiffany-Educational will not release the Chimp two-reel comedies in future. "Gland Hotel," current release, is the last. Sig Neufeld, trainer and producer of the monkey shorts, now is looking for another producer to handle a new series of one-reelers which he contemplates for immediate production.
> Tiffany, it is understood, feels that the shorts have lost their novelty, and Neufeld is said to be in favor of other distribution.[43]

Gland Hotel, filmed last but the eleventh release in the series, was retitled *My Children* when released at the end of December 1931.

Film Daily reported that *Broadcasting* was "a travesty on Rudy Vallee. They show the gal in love with Rudy, and his rival, a German count.... Father Chimp doesn't like either one of the girl's sweeties, and expresses his dislike in typical monk style."[44] *Broadcasting*, the final entry in the twelve-film series released at the end of January 1932, was originally announced under the working title *Ex-King*.

A half-page ad was published soon after that appeared to confirm the next phase of Sig's career trajectory. It declared that Bud Barsky—an independent producer since 1924—and Sig Neufeld were partners in a new company—Famous Comedies Productions, Ltd.—located at the Hollywood Studios on Glendale Boulevard. The "famous comedies" were to be "The Barsky Chimp Comedies," a not-too-subtle offshoot of the Tiffany Chimps; Sig was to direct.[45] This was the rare mention in the trades of a company that seemingly existed solely on paper. Not to worry; Sig had yet another gig lined up almost immediately.

Sig's grandson Tim reminisced years later about his father—Sig's older son Stanley—and his life-long quest to track down one of the Tiffany Chimp shorts. "Dad always talked about the Chimp Comedies. He was searching during his life for a print of them and never could find them. He talked about it a lot...I guess he grew up and went on the set. Both my dad and Sig [Jr.] went to the set a lot with their dads, so my dad by then—he was born in '23—so he would have been seven or eight…it was a big deal, whatever it was. I think whatever it was that differentiated it was the fact that Sig [Sr.] was the director."[46]

It's too bad that Stanley didn't live long enough to be exposed to YouTube, and the heretofore rarities that continue to surface on that internet platform: both *The Blimp Mystery* and *Apeing Hollywood* can be viewed there.

Director Sig Neufeld's **Broadcasting** (1932), the final entry in the Tiffany Chimps twelve-film series.

Chapter 4:
What Poison Does to the Body (1932-1934)

The writing was on the wall. The deepening of the Depression had impacted theater attendance, which in turn led to the introduction of the controversial double bill by exhibitors desperate to lure their patrons back: two features for the price of one. One Los Angeles theatre owner claimed that "Ninety-five per cent of the exhibitors are forced to go double bill because they are afraid the competition is getting all the business," but wasn't happy about it, adding that "What poison does to the body, double billing does to the theatre" because it cuts their gross in half.[1]

As a result, there was a lessened need for shorts, and the resultant lowered rentals forcing the affected producers to cut their budgets. It was reported that Hal Roach planned to cut production budgets for its popular Laurel and Hardy series by more than 25 %, likely paring it down from $55,000 per two-reel short to a more modest $40,000. Other producers, it was claimed, were cutting their former average of approximately $35,000 by $10,000.[2] Which, of course, meant that it wasn't the best of times for those companies whose livelihood depended on the production and rentals of one- and two-reel shorts.

At thirty-five and approaching middle age, Sig wasn't a kid anymore. Family responsibilities had increased with the arrival of a second son, Sigmund Neufeld Jr., on May 12, 1931. Also, ever mindful of his younger brother's precarious status as a director of low budget, two-reel fare, he may have planned his future with the two of them in mind. To that end, Sig made two decisions: that he would no longer be an employee of others, his future security dependent on his bosses' day-to-day whims and the economic stability of their respective companies; and the world of shorts would no longer be his world. He wanted to enter the major leagues—perhaps *minor* leagues would be a more appropriate way of putting it—and become his own boss, return to production, focus on features rather than two-reelers, and leave any thoughts of direction behind. In later 1931, Sig teamed up with Morris Schlank, Joe Simmonds, and Joe Glucksman [as reported] to create a new independent production firm, with the lofty goal of eighteen features for the first year. The new company was named Tower Productions, Inc., and would release the films produced by Sig's Premier Attractions.

Fifty-two-year-old Morris Schlank (1879-1932) had been in the business since the late teens, a purveyor of independent low-budget fare sold on the state rights market. Initially producing a staggering number of comedies starring Hank Mann in 1919-20, by 1922 his focus had switched primarily to feature production. Typical of most indie producers, the bulk of his feature output were the more affordable Westerns starring Al Hoxie and others. Schlank took a break with the coming of sound but decided to jump back into the business with this new venture. Simmonds was a distributor of indie films, but his

A younger Morris Schlank, circa 1922, Sig Neufeld's partner in Tower Productions, Inc., which released the films produced by Sig's Premier Attractions.

focus would soon be diverted by another venture. The "Joe Glucksman" who appeared in early releases regarding this new venture, was likely a misreported Herman Gluckman, whose Capital Film Exchange had been distributing independent films for the past decade. Capital Film would distribute Tower's output in the New York territory, while Hollywood Films would handle New England, B.N. Judel Inc. in Illinois, and Gold Medal Films in Philadelphia.[3]

Simmonds touted his new company in the press and crowed about the advantages that indie producers had over their bigger competitors. "Independent producers occupy a happy position in the industry," he said, "insofar as they may make excellent productions on an economic basis at a maximum cost of 40 per cent less than the larger companies."[4]

Tower Productions' home office was back on the East Coast in New York City at 220 West 42nd Street, where Simmonds operated as the company's president.[5] Those eighteen proposed features soon were whittled down to eight—perhaps eighteen was a misprint—with each of the eight to be released at the rate of one every six weeks.[6] Sig's production company continued to work out of Tiffany Studios, where he befriended Hans Weeren, Tiffany's sound engineer and who, in a few years, would go to work for Sig. Max Alexander was there as well, having left Universal along with the Sterns and now served as Tiffany's purchasing agent.

Not one to dilly-dally, Sig went to work immediately on his first film for the new venture, *Discarded Lovers*. Edward Lowe was engaged to write a screenplay from Arthur Hoerl's story, Fred Newmeyer to direct, and William Hyer as cinematographer. The film was Tower's initial offering released on January 20, 1932. This was a decided change of pace for Sig, not only in that it was a feature, but a dramatic murder-mystery feature as well. The plot revolves around actress Irma Gladden, played by platinum blonde Natalie Moorhead, who is surrounded by those "discarded lovers" of the title: a persistent ex-first husband (Allen Dailey); a co-star second husband (Roy D'Arcy) who is driven to murderous rages over their impending divorce; the current film's screenwriter and her supposed fiancé (Jason Robards); the film's director (Robert Frazer); and—just maybe—her thieving chauffeur (Jack Trent). When she's murdered, seemingly most of the cast becomes a suspect, and that includes the director's wife (Sharon Lynn) as well. The film comes to a tidy, if not wholly convincing, conclusion via a screening of her latest film for all involved, which somehow manages to elicit a confession from the guilty party.

Discarded Lovers is a sufficiently diverting little mystery, chock full of all the stock characters one is used to in this sort of film, with a wise-cracking reporter (Russell Hopton), a blustery and thoroughly inept comic relief cop (Fred Kelsey, who else?), and his gruff captain (J. Farrell MacDonald). The acting is adequate but wildly uneven, talent-wise: Robards delivers an annoyingly mannered performance as the psychologically tortured screenwriter, and D'Arcy, as Irma Gladden's co-star and soon-to-be divorced second husband, overacts in such an amateurish fashion that one wishes he'd called it quits at the end of the silent era.

Director Fred Newmeyer—better known as a director of comedies—and cinematographer William Hyer work well together, delivering a visually satisfying film. The film's first extended shot is an eye-opener, an impressively long and fluid tracking shot that wends its way through a film studio being prepped for an upcoming scene, finally settling on the young lovers-to-be. Uncredited producer Sig puts every penny of the budget up there on the screen, with the interior set for Gladden's opulent mansion a lavish one, with in-studio sequences and numerous location sequences well-chosen money savers. *Film Daily*'s reviewer was impressed with the results: "Independent pictures of this calibre will make the larger companies sit up and take notice. Director Fred Newmeyer has turned out a sincere piece of work and the cast of seasoned players carries on in most convincing style."[7]

Lobby card for Tower Productions' premier entry **Discarded Lovers** (1932), star Natalie Moorehead at left. Fred Newmeyer directed. *Courtesy of Heritage Auctions.*

Arguably the most interesting thing about this film is its genre-upending twist of having its lead character and top-billed star bumped off at the film's midpoint, a gimmick to be revisited nearly thirty years later by Alfred Hitchcock for his stunning twist in *Psycho*. Moorhead had more than two dozen features to her credit in the mere three years since her first release in 1929 for studios that included Fox, First National, M-G-M, and Paramount, so her face was well known to moviegoers; her surprise demise so early in the film was likely as unexpected as that of Janet Leigh decades later. As the thirties rolled on, however, gigs with the top-tier studios became fewer and farther between, her career grinding to a halt by the end of the decade. Regardless of its shortcomings, *Discarded Lovers* was a respectable initial offering by Premier Attractions and Tower Productions.

Sig's next for Tower was *Shop Angel*, released in March, and he once again was omitted from the opening credits. Lowe wrote the screenplay and William Hyer returned as cinematographer, with E. Mason Hopper, a grizzled veteran who had been directing since 1911, brought in to put the actors through their paces. In this one, Marion Shilling plays a working girl in a big fashion establishment who, ambitious to become a foreign fashion buyer and expert, refuses to take heed to her fellow workers' warnings about her lecherous boss. "Here is one of the finest independent productions of the season," wrote *Film Daily*, "qualifying in all departments. Story, production, direction and acting would do credit to any big producing organization."⁸ *Hollywood Filmograph* was equally impressed with the results: "The direction of Mason Hopper showed his splendid experience and the photography of William Hyer was of the highest standard," going on to say that "this production for a Tiffany [sic] release shows careful treatment, fine direction and good acting and should be a good moneymaker for Morris Schlank and Tower Productions."⁹ Holmes Herbert, Anthony Bushell, and Walter Byron co-starred, and Hank Mann appears in a bit part as well, perhaps at Schlank's insistence for old times' sake.

Premier Attractions had by now relocated to leased space at Universal City, and Sig's next would be filmed at the Big U studios.¹⁰ Louis King was hired to direct Sig's third production, *Drifting Souls*, having a string of films—most of the sod-busting, cattle-roping, six-gun shooting sort—to his credit since 1921; it went into production on May 18.¹¹ The story involves a well-meaning small-town lawyer (Lois Wilson) who needs $5,000 to cover her father's costly operation, so she heads to the big city and offers herself in marriage to anyone who will pony up the money. There's a secondary plot wherein a young man thinks he's responsible for another's death in a hit-and-run, and she—now married to the fellow—goes to court to attempt to defend him. Not surprisingly, all ends well.

Film Daily was underwhelmed by the result, stating that "There is a little bit of everything thrown into this story, and the result is a very choppy continuity that fails to arouse any sympathy for any of the characters."¹² *Harrison's Reports* was just a tad kinder, calling it "A moderately entertaining program picture. The story is somewhat illogical, and the action is slow."¹³ You can't win them all.

Sig Neufeld's **Drifting Souls** (Tower Productions, 1932), Louis King director.

Exposure was the next in line being prepped by Schlank, but was sidelined by an unforeseen incident. Schlank, a semi-invalid for the past twenty years who had managed to function in the industry despite his physical handicaps, had travelled to Murietta Hot Spring in June for a rest, but instead ended up with perpetual rest.[14] Sig now succeeded Schlank as head of Premier Attractions, and took over where Schlank left off on *Exposure*'s preparation.[15] Despite the hiccup in the film's preparation, the film went before cameras in mid-July.[16]

Released a mere month later on August 20, 1932, the rival newspaper yarn *Exposure* was Sig's fourth for Tower. Hard-drinking, scandal-mongering reporter Andy Bryant (Walter Byron) goes to work for a failing newspaper primarily to exact revenge on the rival paper's owner (Tully Marshall) who had insulted him. Bryant turns the paper around and falls in love with its owner, Doris Corbin (Lila Lee), but when his proposal is rebuffed due to her concerns over a potential relapse with his drinking, he decides to pack up and head back to New York. Differences are all resolved in the end, Bryant has a change of heart and eschews the Yellow Journalism he was responsible for, the two papers merge, and Bryant marries the boss…and she has a baby.

Sig Neufeld's **Exposure** (Tower Productions, 1932), Norman Houston director. Here hard-drinking reporter Walter Byron threatens newspaper owner Tully Marshall.

This is a surprisingly good little film, with excellent production values on display once again and a cast of very competent actors. Byron is fine in the lead as the self-described "ink-slinger," as is Lee as his boss and primary love interest. As their cold-hearted rival, Marshall is at his most dislikable until his inevitable change of heart, and Nat Pendleton puts in a brief appearance early on as the so-called "Maniac Killer." Sig brought back two former Stern Brothers actors—Lee Moran and Spec O'Donnell—for roles as fellow newspaper employees. Norman Houston both wrote and directed the film, a curious choice given that as a respected screenwriter with nearly a decade of work behind him, this was only his third film as director, and as it turned out his last. Sig probably got him as a cost-saving package deal, but whatever the case Houston seems comparatively at home behind the megaphone, perhaps with a confidence-building assist from cinematographer Harry Forbes. Forbes' camera does a nice lengthy track and pan throughout the newsroom early on, and the only questionable choices in terms of visuals are the two extended fistfights, both executed in a continuous, unengaging long shot. As good as this film is, its status as a lower budget film only becomes evident in the stock footage employed, the police mobilization near the film's opening, and later with some equally familiar disaster clips of stock cars and airplanes crashing. Otherwise, the film has a pricier look than one might otherwise expect. Sig finally got his name in the credits, as "Associate Producer" to the late Morris Schlank's "Producer."

Meanwhile, two items of importance took place around this time. First of all, Simmonds and Gluckman teamed up with Phil Goldstone to serve as officers in his newly formed Majestic Pictures Corp., a "new national independent plan for producers and distributors." Majestic's plans for the 1932-33 season included sixteen features, four specials, and six Jack Hoxie Westerns.[17] Tower Productions and Simmonds' involvement with same was referred to as "a separate interest of his that will not in any way be tied to the new project."[18] If this announcement didn't concern Sig, Schlank's death two months later should have.

The second item of significance was brother Sam's marriage. His bride, Violet Evelyn Hollingsworth, was a younger woman he claimed to have met in a soda shop. Born in Sawyer, North Dakota on August 25, 1912, the newlyweds had moved into an apartment at 314 North Sierra Bonita Avenue.[19] Sig had hired directors with proven talents up to this time, but now looked upon Sam as a golden asset: he was loyal, dependable, a fast worker who stayed within budget, and came comparatively cheap. For his fifth production, *Red-Haired Alibi*, Sig would hire Christy Cabanne to direct, and Sam would serve as his assistant director while learning the ropes of feature direction.

A graduate of the US Naval Academy at Annapolis, Christy Cabanne (1888-1950) had a brief career in the Navy before entering film as an actor for D.W. Griffith at Biograph in 1910. Promoted to Griffith's assistant, Cabanne eventually moved into direction under Griffith's supervision in 1913. This association served him well, opening doors at studios—including Majestic, Mutual, Metro, Goldwyn, Columbia, and Robertson-Cole—for numerous projects of varying prestige throughout the silent era, directing the likes of the Gish sisters, Douglas Fairbanks, and Francis X. Bushman. With the coming of sound, however, Cabanne's career had taken somewhat of a dive, relegated to quickies for Tiffany, Columbia, Universal, Monogram, Majestic, and now Premier Attractions and Tower. What Cabanne had in experience, he now seemed to lack in industry clout. Still, he would be a good mentor for Sam.

With Morris Schlank's death, Sig may have thought he was finished with the Schlanks, but soon found himself saddled with Morris's son Mel. Sig assigned him as the fifth film's (uncredited) associate producer and hoped he'd stay out of his way.[20] Instead, Sam ultimately received the onscreen associate producer credit, perhaps a move on Sig's part hoping that Mel would take the hint and go away.

Red-Haired Alibi went before the cameras on September 6, 1932. As with *Exposure*, cinematography was handled by Harry Forbes, a former associate of Sig's back at Stern Brothers Comedies, and who would remain with Sig and Premier for the rest of its run.[21] *Red-Haired Alibi* starts out strong enough and engages for most of its length, but the last-minute surprise twist seems overly contrived and proves to be somewhat of a letdown. Good girl Merna Kennedy is hired by smooth-talking Theodore von Eltz to pose as his wife, but when she comes to realize that he's a ruthless gangster, she beats a hasty retreat from the Big Apple to nearby White Plains. There she reconnects with recently divorced Grant Withers, is hired as nurse to his four-year-old daughter (Shirley Temple), and ends up marrying him. When von Eltz, on the lam from the law and rival gangsters, shows up and attempts to extort $10,000 dollars from her, he instead ends up shot dead for his efforts, pistol-wielding Kennedy presumably the guilty party. Turns out she had a .33-calibre pistol, and he was killed by a .45, so goodbye jail, hello happy ending.

There's so much that's good about this film that I hate to quibble about its contrived denouement, but quibble I must. Regardless, the acting is convincing throughout, with Kennedy a very attractive presence in the lead as the personable but naïve heroine. Von Eltz's smooth, fast-talking gangster makes the leap from likeable to hissable without batting an eyelash, and Withers delivers a relaxed, breezy performance in the obligatory good-guy roll. Huntley Gordon, Pernell Pratt, and Fred Kelsey all play cops of varying ranks, with the latter seemingly locked into his usual dumb and belligerent cop character, but perhaps just a tad less stupid here. Christy Cabanne, a seasoned pro a few years past his career highpoint, was a good choice to helm the film, keeping the budget under control by utilizing a number of long takes, rendered less noticeable since Harry Forbes' roving camera makes up for the fewer editorial cuts. As for the sets, they are consistently impressive, and must have been built for some bigger-budgeted production and redressed for Sig's production. The nightclub set, a massive Art Deco affair, is complete with an attached dining room allowing the camera and cast to move from one room to the next. Both Travers' and Shelton's homes are visually lavish settings as well.

Sig Neufeld beams for the camera in this photo from 1933. *Courtesy of Tim Neufeld.*

Time would prove one of Sig's choices to be a savvy one, and that was the selection of little four-and-a-half-year-old Shirley Temple to star as Shelton's daughter. This was Temple's first ever feature film role, although appearances in several sound shorts for Universal and Educational preceded (and would follow) before she was snapped up by the Fox Film Corporation, where she would quickly rise to international stardom over the rest of the 1930s.

Daring Daughters, Sig's sixth Premier Attraction for Tower, and Cabanne's second with an assist from Sam, followed into release in February 1933. Fox writer Sam Mintz was hired to write the screenplay,[22] with Forbes back to lens the film. A drama bearing the working title *Wise Girl*[23] and released under the catchier title *Daring Daughters*, filming took place in November 1932[24] at the Tec-Art Studios on Melrose Avenue, then undergoing reorganization as Republic Studios.[25]

Poster for Sig Neufeld's **Daring Daughters** (Tower Productions, 1933). Sam Newfield assisted director Christy Cabanne.
Courtesy of Heritage Auctions.

"[Tec-Art] is one of the most thoroughly equipped studios in the industry," wrote *Inside Facts of Stage and Screen*,

> having all of the modern facilities including RCA filmtrack recording equipment and Harris disc recording device available. There are two sound stages, one stage capable of handling any sized set and ample grounds suitable for street scenes or any outdoor location. There are over a hundred offices and other conveniences for numerous producers.[26]

For the record, Tec-Art had one of the first sound stages in Hollywood, built in 1928 at Roy Disney's direction, with Patrick Powers's Cinephone sound equipment installed. The Disneys were making the switch from silent to sound cartoons, so the Disney Film Recording Corporation was set up at Tec-Art in rented space, as there was no usable space at the Disney studios over on Hyperion Avenue.

Daring Daughters is the story of sisters (Marian Marsh and Joan Marsh, *not* sisters in real life) who head to the big city, "one worldly wise, thinking evil of all men, taking what she can get and the devil take the hindmost," wrote *Film Daily*, "the other innocent and curious, who resents her sister's direction, strikes out and nearly fails."[27] According to *Hollywood Filmograph*, Cabanne told them "that of all the pictures that he has made this one came nearer to his ideals."[28] *Motion Picture Herald* provided its thoughts on the results: "The cast has a name or two which may strike a familiar note. In its quality of execution the picture belongs in the small town, small theatre class, but unfortunately in its theme and story development it is not of the best material for that category of trade, particularly that of the family."[29]

Meanwhile, there was growing dissent among the filmmaking technical ranks. Studio bosses were taking advantage of the Depression and the supposed impact it was having on the health of the industry. Wage cuts, they insisted, needed to be imposed to keep the studios open, and they were hefty: 50 % for all employees receiving more than $50 a week, and 25 % for those earning less. Realizing just how tenuous their collective position was in the industry, the Independent Motion Picture Producers Association (IMPPA), of which Sig was a member of the Board of Directors, got involved early on.

The IMPPA "has appointed a committee to work out details of a plan that will keep production going in spite of the present crisis," wrote *Hollywood Reporter*. Sig was part of this committee, along with IMPPA officers Nat Levine, Phil Goldstone, Larry Darmour, and Lester Scott. The article went on to say that:

> Sam Wolf, attorney for the organization, stated last night that the committee would first have a meeting with officials of the IATSE [International Alliance of Theatrical Stage Employees] and other studio labor locals to seek their advice, assistance and cooperation through the emergency period. The independent producers do not wish to aggravate the present unemployment crisis through a complete cessation of production, and they must look to their employees for cooperation until business returns and frozen assets can be released.
>
> The independents did not agree on any specific percentage of salary cuts for employees. The latter will be asked to lend assistance to their employers through a general resolution now being prepared by Attorney Wolf.[30]

Ninety-seven percent of non-union workers, including employees under contract—actors, directors, and writers—accepted the reduction. The unions, not surprisingly, voted unanimously to reject the wage cuts.[31] "Dark stages and silent cameras prevailed in all the major studios today," wrote Louella Parsons in her syndicated column. "The only companies working were the independents. They alone are not affected by union troubles." The independents paid union men less than the majors—15 to 20 % less—but an agreement provided that if a salary cut was agreed upon with the majors, they must take it from the independents as well.[32] The shutdown was looked upon as only a temporary event, and Sig was listed among other independents whose current production was unaffected.[33]

Employees finally agreed with the cuts for a two-month period, but in doing so the studios agreed to turn their books over to auditors representing the Academy of Motion Picture Arts and Sciences, who brokered the deal. Salaries would be returned to their original level upon an order by the Academy following a review of each individual studio's financial situation. All the affected studios agreed to this plan, with the result that within a month Columbia, RKO, M-G-M, United Artists, Paramount, and Hal Roach Studio all voluntarily resumed full pay. Only Warners balked,[34] but eventually came around. Peace was restored, but not for long: By July, approximately 665 sound technicians went on strike, and when the studios sought to replace them with nonunion men via ads placed in local newspapers, all hell broke loose. 2,765 other film workers from four unions followed, affecting production at Fox, M-G-M, Paramount, RKO, Roach, United Artists, Educational, Universal, Warners, and Bryan Foy Studios. The strike, however, did not impact some forty independent companies, both renting space or operating their own facilities.[35] Sig's Premier Attractions was among those "lucky" independents, and continued production unimpeded.

Sig now decided it was time to promote Sam to full director, transforming his Premier Attractions to more of a family affair. Former M-G-M writing staff employee George W. Sayre had banged out an original story that Sig purchased for his next production, titled *Reform Girl*, filmed at Metropolitan Studios on Las Palmas Avenue during January 1933.[36] An abundance of surplus studio space was currently available, with eleven lots bidding for rental business from independent producers not already locked into leases. The bidding studios included United Artists, Sennett, Fox for its Western Avenue lots, Warners for its Sunset lot, Republic, Pathé, Universal, Educational, International, Western Pictures, and Metropolitan.[37] Sig took advantage of this bidding war and relocated to Metropolitan, if only temporarily. Production was underway in February, interrupted only briefly on the twenty-seventh: "Their cigars smoked and candy eaten, employes [*sic*] at Metropolitan Studios were wishing Sam Neufeld would celebrate again today the birth of his first and only child, a girl," wrote *Los Angeles Evening Citizen News*. "Yesterday he exchanged cigars and candy for congratulations on the birth of a six pound, six ounce daughter, born Sunday to Mrs. Neufeld at the Cedars of Lebanon Hospital."[38] Sam, who was credited as Premier Attractions' "head director," had celebrated the birth of his and Violet's first child, Jacqueline, who arrived on February 26, 1933.

Sam Newfield's wife Violet and their first child, daughter Jacqueline "Jackie" Newfield, 1933. *Courtesy of Laura Berk.*

Reform Girl is the story of a dishonest politician who schemes to dishonor and discredit his opponent by paying former prisoner Noel Francis to impersonate his target's long-lost daughter, her assignment to secure some important papers. Skeets Gallagher plays the girl's pal who eventually gets her to see the error of her ways, getting shot in the process.

Noel Francis and Skeets Gallagher in Sig Neufeld's
Reform Girl (Tower, 1933), Sam Newfeld's first
feature as director. *Courtesy of Heritage Auctions.*

The New York State censorship board, a division of the Department of Education, rejected *Reform Girl* in March 1933, and again in August. Which is surprising in that it had already been passed by the National Board of Review in March and the Department of Public Safety of Massachusetts for Sunday showings without eliminations. Virginia and Ohio passed it as well without change, while Maryland and Pennsylvania had passed it with only minor changes. Unswayed by the decisions of its sister states, New York's censors summarized their vague complaints: "Many scenes are shown of the corrupt activities of the Boss; the intimidation of the officers of the law and the demoralization of the character of the girl." Which led to the rendering of their two decisions: "Immoral; tends to corrupt morals and incites to crime."[39] It's not clear just how they figured the film would corrupt morals, but whatever the case, reject it they did. The result was a whittling down of thirteen minutes of footage from 6,154 feet in length to 4,973 feet, forfeiting 20 % of its original length.[40] *Variety* was ambivalent about the heavily trimmed results: "Nothing unusual about this piece in manner, shape or form. A catalog yarn with a title that has only a hallucinatory relationship to the plot and creates every reason for the necessary existence of double features."[41] Sam's name was up there in the opening credits, but as "Sam Neufeld," his adopted "Newfield" surname temporarily shelved. He must have made a stink about it since he would be credited as "Newfield" in the following film's credits.

Dapper Sam sometime in the 1930s, all duded up. *Courtesy of Laura Berk.*

While the eighth and final film of the originally scheduled eight releases was in the works, Simmonds headed to Hollywood to confer on the 1933-34 season's eight film lineup.[42] Sig had purchased an original story titled "Night Coach," the story of an overnight Los Angeles to San Francisco bus trip, written by Gordon Morris, brother of popular actor Chester Morris. Neufeld retitled the story "Public Stenographer" and assigned Douglas Doty to write the screenplay. Leslie Simmonds, Joe Simmonds' son and now part of the team, was assigned to supervise. Sam would direct, the production tentatively scheduled to start at the end of March.[43] The "Public Stenographer" title promptly reverted to "Night Coach" when it was learned that producer Sam Katzman had production underway on a film of that same title starring Lola Lane, based on a story by Ellwood Ullman. Katzman's *Public Stenographer* went before George Meehan's cameras in May, going into release by Screencraft in November 1933.

Night Coach had a tentative start date of May 15,[44] eventually undergoing a title change to *The Important Witness*. Released in mid-July, Noel Madison starred as the public stenographer. *Film Daily*'s reviewer provided a succinct assessment of the general plot: "[The heroine] is witness to a gangster murder while taking dictation from the victim in his hotel room, so the killers kidnap her so she can't squeal. Then we see her the very next day sitting at her accustomed desk in the hotel lobby guarded by a gangster as part of the scheme to establish their alibi.... And so on through the commandeering of a trans-continental bus to capture the girl after she tries to escape." One might question why the gangster didn't simply kill her along with his intended victim as well, instead of the more elaborate, plot-extending activities that followed. Whatever, the reviewer summed it all up by calling it "another variation on the gangster story, and one that arouses little sympathy for any of the characters. The heroine is made to do some rather dumb things that result in interest being killed off early in the proceedings."[45] *Variety* was more charitable: "Gangster picture, but with the violence tempered with comedy and given an excellent production for indie product.... Probably can ride along where the general trend is against gang stuff, and not too heavy for the kids, who'll generally love it. Still an indie, but good for its kind."[46] Douglas Doty's adaptation of Morris's story, it would appear, left something to be desired; "it sags in the middle," added *Variety*, and *Film Daily* complained that "motivation is weak and a lot of important points are left to be cleared up." Sam's direction was rated as "Weak"[47] as well, but showed some imagination with the staging of much of the action on an all-night bus "of a kind not familiar in most parts of the country." Some bathroom comedy was added to break whatever tension the plot provided, Sam's experience with the Stern Brothers possibly the impetus to add such a scene.[48]

A disarming Donald Dillaway opposite Noel Francis, in Sig Neufeld's **The Important Witness** (Tower, 1933), Sam Newfield directing. *Courtesy of Heritage Auctions.*

The independents were in somewhat of a panic in mid- to later-1933, a result of proposed restrictions to production prompted by a new National Recovery Act code that appeared to propose an end to double bills. There had been talk of the NRA's plans to "increase employment in film and other industries to establish fair trade practices" as early as April, although just how "fair" those "trade practices" would be was a topic of considerable concern among many different segments of the industry "after a prolonged deadlock on a number of important proposals."

By June Congress had passed the NRA's measure, and President Roosevelt signed the act to make it a Federal Law. Three committees were formed—producers, distributors, and exhibitors—to study the various recommendations, each of which had its own personal agenda. "The principal problem of correlating occurred between the distributor and exhibitor committees," wrote *Film Daily*, "which drastically differed on a number of major clauses." A tentative code was completed by the committees by mid-August, but it had clauses in it that "represented the majority opinion, in many instances with the minority in hot disagreement." Six major issues of controversy were left unresolved for later determination.

Public hearings began in late August, and conferences later that month adjourned in September with "various factions deadlocked on all major controversial issues." More hearings and meetings followed but the deadlocks persisted, so by the end of September attorney Sol A. Rosenblatt, earlier assigned as Deputy Administrator in charge of the amusement field codes, decided to write the code himself, citing the failure of the various factions to come to any sort of mutually acceptable agreement. The presentation and examination of his first draft on October 4 led to the "open revolt" of the independents, "assailing the document as unfair." [49]

Twenty-nine independent coast producers jointly chimed in, stating that such restrictions would result in at least a 70 % cut in annual independent product. In a telegram wired to the Federation of the Motion Picture Industry, they stated that "Every member of the Independent Producers Asso. has been conscientiously adjusting methods of production to take care of the increased cost which will be necessitated by the NRA code, with great willingness to cooperate even though our budgets will be materially affected." They went on to point out the "vast amount of unemployment that the elimination of double bills will create" and added that "while independent producers do not have any great sum of money to expend on production, they nevertheless pay all laborers and technical workmen of all classes a sum equivalent and in most instances greater than that paid by major producing companies." Sig, his Premier Attractions, and Tower Productions were among the many signers of the telegram.[50]

On October 5, the following day, the independents walked out on the meetings. A revised draft followed on the 10th which was 90 % the same as the initial version, and still viewed with dissatisfaction by the independents. They were stuck with it, however, when the major company executives packed up and headed home two days later.

This may have impacted the 1933-34 season's original projection of eight films being pared down to a mere four films, along with Simmonds' new focus on Goldstone's Majestic and his ongoing intention to bring Tower to a close. Given the somewhat shaky position of the independents in the industry at this time, Sig and Premier had to concentrate on finishing those final films for Tower, and quickly. Sig relocated to International Studios over on Sunset Drive, and doubled down on his ninth, tentatively titled *Headin' for Heaven* and based on the stage play "Excess Baggage;" George Wallace Sayre handled the adaptation.

Regis Toomey entertains Gloria Shea in Sig Neufeld's **Big Time or Bust** (Tower, 1933), Sam Newfield director. *Courtesy of Heritage Auctions.*

Released near the end of 1933 under its new title, *Big Time or Bust* is a sort of poor man's *A Star is Born*. The film moves from carnival sideshow to Broadway as it follows the shaky marriage of daredevil high diver Regis Toomey whose assistant wife Gloria Shea becomes the overnight toast of Broadway, and the lascivious target of millionaire playboy Walter Byron. Humiliated that his wife is now the primary breadwinner, humiliation turns to bitterness as he comes to suspect—erroneously so— his wife's unfaithfulness. Driven to the brink of a planned suicide attempt during another high dive, he has a change of heart when his wife arrives at the last moment. The two are reunited and she quits the theater to, once again, become his dutiful "better half," but prospects for the future seem dubious at best. "For better or worse" she says, rather cheerlessly, to which hubby responds "Yeah: Better for me, worse for you." She should have stayed on Broadway.

Big Time or Bust is a rather predictable drama, saved primarily by the excellent performances of all involved. Toomey is fine as the cocksure thrill diver, his mood quickly devolving into a gloomy funk that renders his character a drag to watch; at one point he's so despondent that he becomes a borderline bum, as evidenced by his disheveled, soiled clothing and a heavily applied five o'clock shadow. Shea is adequate as his wife, provided the additional opportunity to perform three different numbers during the film's unspooling. Byron is as smooth and slimy as ever, and Edwin Maxwell—as Byron's counterpart and well-heeled producer of Shea's show—provides the proper amount of cynicism to the proceedings. "I never get involved with women" says he as he reprimands Byron for his skirt-chasing, his comment neutralized when his bathroom door slowly opens, revealing a robe-clad lovely inside, adjusting her stockings. In the small role of Toomey's small-time Jewish agent, Nat Carr provides the film its few sporadic moments of levity with his world-weary asides.

This was brother Sam's third go-round at feature direction, and he does a satisfyingly workmanlike job of it. Harry Forbes' camera work is competent but uninspired, mostly medium shots with a minimal number of cuts and a similarly minimal number of camera movements. Jimmie's high dives from hundred-foot towers into small pools of water below, dives no doubt filmed using a stunt double, are excitingly filmed, the dives themselves filmed from above the diver's head looking straight down at the pool far below as he descends. There are a few disconcerting bumps along the way, however, occurring as one scene leads to another. Early on—and seemingly out of the blue—Toomey asks Shea where his watch is, to which she responds that it's on her dressing table. They walk to the table and exit the frame as the shot fades, a rather curious, meaningless, and abrupt end to the scene. Later, another scene ends with Shea's happiness that Toomey has finally landed a job, but cuts to the following scene as she boasts about her new gig on Broadway, a gig she knows will not sit well with him. The transition is a jarring one. *Harrisons Reports* was overwhelmed by the results: "Mediocre program fare," sniffed the reviewer. "The story is trite, and the photography poor; and so is the sound at times."[51] Somewhat of an overreaction, in my humble opinion.[52]

There were a couple of pieces in the trades in November 1933 worth noting. *Motion Picture Daily* wrote that "Henry Ginsberg has signed Sig Neufeld, former production manager for Stern Brothers in the old silent days, as head of the Roach story department,"[53] and *Hollywood Filmograph* concurred, stating that "Sig Neufeld tops the writing staff at Hal Roach's studio."[54] If accurate, it was likely a move out of desperation on Sig's part due to uncertainty about the future, and an extremely short-lived position. *Hollywood Filmograph* had another article stating that Sig was starting production at the Talisman Studios—presumably Premier Attractions' *Beggars Holiday*—in that very same issue.[55]

Released in August 1934, *Film Daily*'s cutesy "Phil M. Daly" provided one of the few reviews-of-sorts, in another of that publication's annoyingly laid out "Along the Rialto" entries: "For its unusual sincerity...and a rare quality of humanness...we commend a little pix made by Tower Productions...'Beggars' Holiday'...in which Hardie Albright and Sally O'Neil score impressively in some touching and poignant love situations...the story material was there...and so was the Director, Sam Newfield...a lot of our major pix could use what this li'l pix has..."[56] Oddly enough, and at odds with all of Premier's previous efforts, there was virtually nothing in the trades about this particular film's production, nor reviews once it was released. One has the feeling that Simmonds was otherwise preoccupied with Mascot, his usual endless stream of press releases fed to *Film Daily* having come to an abrupt, if temporary, end; it would seem that *Film Daily* took pity on this hastily churned out quickie. Albright and O'Neil were supported by J. Farrell MacDonald, with direction again by Sam, and Harry Forbes lensing.

Sarah Padden out-stares Lucien Littlefield in **Marrying Widows** (Tower, 1934), Sig Neufeld producer, Sam Newfield director.

Marrying Widows was Premier's final production for Tower, going into production mid-February of the following year, with Sam and Harry Forbes brought back for this final collaboration. In the interim, Sig had packed up and moved production once more, this time to the Mack Sennett Studios in a deal brokered by Sennett rental department's Jed Buell.[57] Production commenced under the working title *Widows*, with a cast that featured Minna Gombell, Johnny Mack Brown, Lucien Littlefield, Bert Roach, Sarah Padden, and Judith Allen, borrowed from Paramount to round out the cast. Even Sam's old buddy Syd Saylor was brought back for a small role.

Completed in mid-March[58] and released in May, Judith Allen stars as the widow of a sewing machine magnate. Rival business owner Johnny Mack Brown woos her, solely to gain ownership of the inherited business. She didn't inherit it, however, but by the film's conclusion Brown has fallen in love with Allen anyway and marries her. The machinations of Minna Gombell—who knows that brother-in-law Lucien Littlefield had shielded Allen from her rightful inheritance—result in the business ending up in Allen's—and Brown's—hands.

"This film ought to provide a good deal of pleasure in neighborhood houses," wrote *Motion Picture Daily*. "Besides being endowed with a fine cast, the production has many moments of merriment. The story has been developed with a light hand and is told in a quick tempo."[59] *Film Daily* agreed, at least up to a point, stating that "this one is benefited by a pleasant cast, a nice production and some laughs," while adding that "its situations are hardly plausible" and once again rating Sam's direction as "Fair,"[60] not too divergent from that publication's ratings of "Weak" and "Okay" for several of Sam's previous efforts. All in all, another acceptable entry in Premier's output.

And that was it for Sig, moving on after only eleven of Tower's twelve releases. The slack was taken up by *The Big Bluff*, a Reginald Denny ego-fest—he wrote and directed it as well as starred—for his Angelus Productions, released later the previous year. Foreign rights to the twelve productions were acquired by Arthur Ziehm's General Foreign Sales Corp.,[61] and let us hope that he didn't lose any money on the deal.

Meanwhile, the controversy over double bills and the studios that provided the second features continued unabated, a thorn in the sides of exhibitors, the producers of shorts, and the owners of the major studios alike. Unemployment, which had been a mere 3.2 % of pre-depression 1929, had by 1933 increased to 25 % nonfarm workers. "Granted, the depression has caused the public to seek quantity at the cheapest price," wrote the manager of a theatre in Toronto,

> but the depression will not last forever, and, in addition, the old adage about fooling the public for some of the time, although perhaps dormant, still lives and is liable to pop up again in the very near future. When it does, the public will probably turn up its nose at poor product, irrespective of a three-hour performance for a quarter....[62]

E.W. Hammons, the president of Educational Pictures, commented on localized attempts to ban the double bill practice, conceding that while "It is true that double features have actually been prohibited as yet in a comparatively few locations.... Any further spread of the double bill habit would almost certainly have sounded the death knell of short subjects." Hammons, perhaps optimistically, added that "All branches of the business, including producer and exhibitor alike, stand to gain by the curtailment of the double feature practice."[63]

If the strongly felt opinions of the detractors of the sort of film that Sig was now producing concerned him, it shouldn't have, as the next fifteen years would clearly demonstrate. With his commitments to both Premier and Tower now behind him, Sig would stick with the lower budget fare that he was most comfortable with and move on to his next venture.

Chapter 5:
The Conning of Sigmund (1934-1935)

It didn't take long for Sig to land on his feet, and by April 1934 he was producing for Nat Levine's Mascot Pictures Corporation. A long-time producer of serials, Levine (1899-1989) now wanted to expand into feature production, announcing ten features and two exploitation specials for the upcoming 1934-35 season. To that end, production was to be split among four unit producers, each assigned to specific films they would oversee "from camera to cutting room." Sig was one of the four producers, whose unit was scheduled to produce four films. The other three producers included Martin G. Cohn, responsible for another four; Lou Sarecky to handle another two; and Louis Baum to handle those two "exploitation specials."[1] A total budget of $1,250,000 was announced for the season's output at an average of $105,000 per picture.[2] A staff of thirty writers would wrangle over the stories and screenplays.[3] Four titles were assigned to Sig's unit: *Along Came a Woman, Anything Once, The Man from Headquarters,* and *One Frightened Night,* the first of these already in production by late May.

Mascot Pictures Corporation's Nat Levine.

Nat Levine's assistant was a young fellow named Maurice Conn. Born in Concord, New Hampshire, Conn (1906-1973) was educated at Rhode Island State College and Brown University, with graduate work at USC. Conn had managed theaters in both Concord and Providence, Rhode Island before becoming Levine's assistant at Mascot, where he was involved in both production and distribution.[4] In July 1934, Conn resigned as Levine's right-hand man, promptly replaced by Jack Fier, formerly of National Screen and Consolidated Film.[5]

Conn's goal was to become an independent producer with his newly formed Ambassador Pictures, signing Kermit Maynard to star in a series of eight Westerns as an upright Northwest Mounted Policeman. The first of these, *Footprints,* was scheduled for an August 1 start under the direction of Otto Brower, who had churned out similar fare since the latter 1920s. The series was to be based on several of the stories by prolific—and popular—writer James Oliver Curwood,[6] or at least that's what the press releases claimed: the actual plots of the films rarely had anything to do with Curwood's originals. Rights to Curwood's stories had been acquired by William N. Selig some twenty years earlier, and he was now selling them off to producers shopping for controversy-free fare to avoid agitating the newly emboldened censors.[7] Herbert Aller joined the company as Conn's partner in late July,[8] and within a month Conn had lined up distribution through independent exchanges in a number of midwestern territories.[9]

Following in the footsteps of his older brother, popular Western star Ken Maynard, Kermit packed his bags and headed to Hollywood. Kermit was quite athletic and an excellent horseman, resulting in stunt work at Fox and other studios. Kermit's initial break came in 1927 when he starred as "Tex" Maynard in a series of Westerns for

Maurice Conn (left), Ambassador Pictures president, shakes hands with his father, veteran New England exhibitor Captain Jacob Conn.

producer Trem Carr and Rayart Pictures. An inauspicious start, for sure, since he was paid a paltry $250 for the experience—not per picture but for the entire series—as well as supply his own wardrobe and perform his own stunts.[10] Still, it was experience, if not necessarily a positive one. By 1930 he was with Mascot, appearing in a string of mostly uncredited roles until approached by Conn. At thirty-six years of age and willing to forgo a potential sixth-year win at the Pendleton Round-Up where he was already a five-time Pacific Coast trick-riding champion,[11] the prospect of a starring role in his own series was too hard to resist. Kermit made the leap.

Time would quickly prove Conn's choice to have been a savvy one: "This lad Kermit Maynard is as good as his famous brother, Ken," wrote one reviewer. "He is a handsome fellow who knows how to act as well as pull nifty stunts on his horse, and in rough-and-tumble fighting he is a bear."[12] Knowing "how to act" and being good at it really aren't the same, but given the level of competition in the other lower-budget Westerns proliferating at the time, I'll cut this reviewer—and Kermit—some slack. It didn't hurt that Kermit was a likeable, easy-going individual, a polar opposite from older brother Ken whose reputation within the industry was—in a word—toxic. "I don't think he felt second fiddle to his brother," recalled Beth Marion, who co-starred with Kermit in 1936's *Wild Horse Round-Up* (oddly billed as "Betty Lloyd"). "They didn't associate an awful lot. They were different personalities. I don't think Kermit smoked or drank. Brother Ken made up for it.... I had heard some wild tales about Ken Maynard, and was almost afraid. My goodness, I had no encounters with him."[13]

With a rugged Western star and eight Curwood stories to work from, things looked promising for Conn's new series. And then, like a shaky house of cards, Conn's setup fell apart: Aller was gone, and the scheduled Brower shoot in limbo.

In a panic and with little to show for his efforts to date, Conn regrouped and looked back to Mascot and the unit producers hard at work there, singling out Sig as the most viable—and likely to succeed—option. He approached Sig with the offer of a partnership, and to sweeten the deal offered to include Sig's wife Ruth as part of the package. Sig jumped at this attractive—and heretofore unprecedented—offer, and Ambassador was re-incorporated with Conn as president, Sig's wife Ruth as vice-president, and Sig as secretary-treasurer; the three of them served as the board of directors as well.[14]

Ambassador Pictures' golden boy, cowboy star Kermit Maynard, as he appeared in **Red Blood of Courage** (1935), Sig Neufeld and Maurice Conn producers, John English director.

It's not known whether Sig had finished his initial production for Mascot or started on any of the other three films, as he never received credit for any of that company's films. Regardless, by October he was hard at work supervising the first of the Maynard films for Ambassador, the one that Brower had been attached to, if only tentatively. Suggested by the Curwood story "Footprints," *The Fighting Trooper* was adapted for the screen by Forrest Sheldon. Direction was reassigned to Ray Taylor, who had been overseeing this sort of lower-budget fare since the mid-1920s.

Maynard plays the first of his stalwart Northwest Mounted Policemen, doggedly on the trail of the killer of co-worker Walter Miller, who had insisted on taking Maynard's place in the assignment that got him killed. LeRoy Mason, his sister Barbara Worth, and their gang top the list as suspects for both this, the robbing of stores, and the murders of trappers for their pelts. A reward is posted for Mason's arrest by "outraged" trading post owner Robert Frazer, which immediately pegs him as the likely culprit in the minds of Western-addicted filmgoers. Meanwhile, Maynard poses as an opportunistic crook, and infiltrates Mason's gang. Maynard eventually exposes Frazer as the real culprit, and after the usual donnybrook (with an assist from Mason), both Frazer and his henchman (Charles King) are arrested. There's the standard happy ending, where Mason and his sister Worth, now exonerated of guilt, open their own trading post. And, of course, Maynard and Worth end up as lovers.

As the series opener, *The Fighting Trooper* is a good first offering, not overly surprising since producers frequently lavished additional money and/or effort on a series' maiden effort to grab exhibitors' attention. This is a handsome looking film, location filming in the wilderness around Lake Arrowhead a decided plus, beautifully shot by cinematographer Edgar Lyons under director Taylor's guidance, and well worth the decision to pack up and film there. Undercranking—which serves to speed up the onscreen action—is employed during some of the fight sequences and the mounting of horses, but we can't really take him to task for that since he had good company elsewhere at this time in films of this sort.

Editor Ted Bellinger's handiwork falls short on occasion, this apparently his first time wielding the shears. In general it is acceptable and workmanlike, and even displays moments of creativity during several of the action scenes. Its awkwardness occurs during some of the dialog sequences, where sluggish cutting retains too much dead space between cuts, giving the appearance that the actors themselves hesitated before responding. This adds unwarranted emphasis to their performances which, truth be told, are occasionally lacking.

Kermit Maynard is perfectly adequate for these low-budget oaters. While he's not the best of actors when it comes to delivery, and his attempts to laugh on cue are forced, he shines in the action sequences. LeRoy Mason is smooth and likeable as primary suspect La Farge, and Charles Delaney, as Maynard's none-too-bright fellow Mountie, comes across as a "Syd Saylor" clone. Barbara Worth, while an attractive presence, remains far too bundled up for most of the footage. And four-legged Dauntless, portraying the canine role of Rowdy, comes across nicely given that he doesn't have any dialog. Nor, for that matter, does villain Charles King.

After all the action that has come before, the film attempts to end with a couple of hoped-for laughs. After both Frazer and King have been knocked senseless, Delaney bursts in and announces, "I've got everybody rounded up, but I don't know who's who." Which really doesn't make much sense but *sounds* kind of funny. The final scene is even more of a yawner, Maynard sneaking into the trading post, shrouding himself in an Indian blanket while grabbing some pelts, then approaching Worth as if to trade them. She finally recognizes him, and we're left trying to decide whether this was intended to be funny or charmingly cute; whichever, it was neither. Despite its occasional shortcomings, however, *The Fighting Trooper* was a solid opener for Sig and Conn's new series. *Motion Picture Daily* agreed: "Production as a whole should please all lovers of outdoor action pictures."[15]

In an interview conducted by John Brooker years after the fact, Conn would claim that these films each cost in the range of $9,000 to $12,000, his collaborations with Sig likely falling in this later range. Directors would be hired on a flat basis from $350 to $500, and the crew on the same basis. Actors and extras—excluding the star—would add another $1,200 or so to the budget, and any so-called "name" actors another $100 for a sole day's work. Cowboys came cheap, earning a flat $100 for the shoot's duration. Even the rented studio space was a flat deal. The flat fee basis, of course, worked in the producers' favor since it didn't matter how many hours or days a film took to complete. "Back in those days we would figure on having about two days of interiors and four days of exteriors," said Conn. "We'd shoot the entire picture in six days…sometimes even five days." The interiors were saved as protection against the weather.[16]

Kermit Maynard's pissed off in **Red Blood of Courage** (Ambassador, 1935), Sig Neufeld and Maurice Conn producers, John English director.

Half of Sig's Westerns for Ambassador were directed by his brother Sam, who we'll cover shortly. The other four were handled by John English, Forrest Sheldon, and the above-mentioned Ray Taylor. British-born John "Jack" English (1903-1966) was a novice when it came to direction, having previously served solely as an editor since the mid-1920s. Sig had a warm spot in his heart for editors, and with the deep-set conviction that editing was the best training ground for an aspiring director, Sig gave English his initial two opportunities to direct. The first of these was Ambassador's third release, *Red Blood of Courage*, filmed in March 1935 and released on April 20. Time would prove that Sig's intuition was spot on in this regard, as English would go on to become one of Republic's top two directors (along with William Witney) of serials and Westerns well into the 1940s.

Red Blood of Courage, while not nearly as good a film as *The Fighting Trooper*, stars Maynard as a Mountie, once again under cover in an oft-confusing tale of greed and the struggle of a gang to gain possession of some oil-rich land. Lead crook Peter Drago (Reginald Barlow) impersonates Mark Henry (also Barlow), the property's real (and now under wraps) owner, hoping to marry off Henry's oblivious niece, Ann Sheridan, to his henchman, Ben Hendricks. She and her proposed hubby will inherit the land and the crooks will be rich, or at least that's the half-baked plan until Maynard gums up the works.

This is a serviceable little Western, chock full of the requisite, and well-staged, fistfights, horseback chases, and gunplay. The acting is a notch better than usual, with teenager and aspiring young actress Ann Sheridan a standout—both acting-wise and in the looks department—borrowed from Paramount for this, her first real starring role after a year-long string of mostly uncredited appearances. Maynard's performance is his typical, but here he's allowed to demonstrate some of his impressive trick horseback riding: hanging upside down off the side of his horse Rocky, as if dead or unconscious, and later hanging off the tail-end of Rocky, out of sight, then somersaulting up and back into the saddle; impressive stuff! As for the outlaw gang, it's comprised of the usuals, Charles King—all of King's contemporaries referred to him as Charlie—given lines and more to do in this one, George Regas his usual menacing and leering self, and Hendricks doing a convincing drunk.

English's direction shows definite promise, one notable shot taking place as Sheridan recalls Maynard's suggestion that she too infiltrate the gang. The camera slowly tracks in to a closeup of her face as snippets of Maynard's words fade in and out, barely audible but enough to get the point across, a stylistic touch that works. English's direction picks up for the action scenes as well, one of the more spirited ones taking place in a cramped attic, as Maynard repeatedly vaults and swings out of his two opponents' reach, swooping in to deliver his well-timed and well-placed punches. "There is plenty of the usual Western-film hokum," wrote *Film Daily*, "but it is well done and should make a hit with the fans."[17]

English's other film for Ambassador was the company's seventh release, *His Fighting Blood*, wherein Maynard serves jail time for a crime his n'er-do-well brother (Paul Fix) committed, an inexplicably altruistic action that leaves the audience scratching their collective heads in bewilderment. Maynard joins the Mounties upon his release, only to find his irksome sibling having reneged on his earlier promise to go straight. Redemption occurs when the brother takes a bullet to save Maynard's life. "There is more drama and less fighting than in the regular Westerns," wrote *Film Daily*, "but there is enough action to keep things interesting throughout." English's direction was deemed "Satisfactory," while the camera work of Jack Greenhalgh—soon to play an important, years-long part in Sig and Sam's careers—was rated as "Good."

The other Ambassador directed by an outsider was *Wilderness Mail*, filmed in February and released a month later. *Wilderness Mail* was the final directorial effort from Forrest Sheldon, a prolific, decade long writer-director, Westerns his forte. Maynard tracks the murderer of his brother, a sergeant in the Mounties, with few clues to work with. Since he only has a brief sixty minutes to solve the crime, he does so, pinning it on villain Fred Kohler and, as a bonus, marrying Kohler's daughter, Doris Brook, by the fadeout. While *Film Daily* gushed that the film "Will rate with the best of thrill yarns,"[18] *Motion Picture Daily* was more measured with its assessment: "This 'action thriller' gets off to a good start and from the first reel or so promises to live up to its billing—well, almost—but in the end turns out to be rather weak-kneed and just another picture slightly lacking in entertainment values. Director Forest [sic] Sheldon seemed to be trying hard, but outside of Fred Kohler and Kermit Maynard the material with which he had to work seemed shy in histrionic ability."[19] Sig went uncredited with this one as well.

Kermit Maynard consoles his fallen comrade in **Wilderness Mail** (Ambassador, 1935), Sig Neufeld (uncredited) and Maurice Conn producers, Forrest Sheldon director.
Courtesy of Heritage Auctions.

That there was a sameness to each of these films was no accident, as they all adhered to a loosely defined formula that Conn and Sig worked under. As described by Conn in his interview with Brooker, "we'd concoct a story and put the greatest amount of stress on action on the basis that action would cover a multitude of sins in so far as story deficiencies were concerned." Conn went on to add that their formula was, in the simplest, most stripped down of terms, "a fight, a chase or a killing in each and every reel…"[20] Robert Emmett Tansey, the prolific producer-director-writer of Westerns of this quick-and-dirty sort, once summed up the unofficial "formula" as twenty minutes of riding, ten minutes of shooting, ten minutes of fighting, and twenty minutes of plot, some of the plot the "sacrificial lamb" if production were to run over schedule.[21]

Sam was bouncing around from one assignment to another elsewhere in the industry at this time—more on that in a later chapter—but Sig managed to reel him in to direct four of the eight Ambassadors. These were *Northern Frontier*, the company's second release; *Code of the Mounted*; *Trails of the Wild*; and the season's final entry, *Timber War*.

68   Poverty Row Royalty

Northern Frontier's plot features some eastern counterfeiters at work in the snowy wilds of Canada, the girl (Eleanor Hunt) forced to work as their expert engraver, and the two-fisted Mountie (Maynard, of course, and operating under cover, as usual) assigned to break up the gang and rescue the girl's father. "Here is red-blooded entertainment for young audiences. The film should satisfy to a 't' the most ardent of action fans," enthused *Motion Picture Daily*. "Its story, while by no means original, is told in a fast tempo with considerable suspense against a north country background that offers an opportunity for some fine outdoor shots captured by Edgar Lyons' camera. Hard riding, gun play, fisticuffs, these are to be found in generous proportions."[22] *Film Daily* rated Sam's direction as "Excellent,"[23] and Jack English did the editing for this as lead-up to his promotion to direction.

Code of the Mounted (initially announced bearing the wimpier title *Sandy of the Mounted*), which went into production on May 9,[24] was another of Sam's films for his brother, and this one is a revelation of sorts. Maynard stars as Mountie Jim Taylor, revisiting the oft-used plot of going undercover, this time to crack a ring of crooks murdering trappers for their pelts. Wheeler Oakman plays the gang's leader, who uses his trading post to acquire trappers' pelts at low-ball prices or, if they refuse, has the trappers murdered, acquiring the pelts cost-free. His partner, played by sultry Lillian Miles, is in it for the money alone, repeatedly rebuffing Oakman's lecherous advances. There are shootouts and fistfights galore, Mounties killed, and crooks shot or arrested before Miles saves Maynard's life as he's about to be killed by the last remaining crook. There's been a budding love interest growing between Maynard and Miles that must have left the kiddies squirming in their seats, hence her action.[25] Maynard, it turns out, is an old softie, so he lets her escape.

Mountie Kermit Maynard threatens helpless Roger Williams in director Sam Newfield's **Code of the Mounted** (Ambassador, 1935), Sigmund Neufeld and Maurice Conn producers. *Courtesy of Heritage Auctions.*

Maynard gets to show off his considerable trick-riding abilities during the opening scenes as he practices for an upcoming equestrian contest. Riding atop two side-by-side horses, with a foot planted on each, he coolly remains astride as they leap over a hurdle. His acting seems to have improved and become more natural since the series' opener, and the character he portrays is more serious. Whether this is a function of experience, or Sam's handling of him as an actor is anyone's guess. Syd Saylor is reunited with his former Stern Brothers director as Maynard's Mountie partner, and gives the breeziest, most likable, and convincingly relaxed performance of the film, punctuated by moments of throw-away comic relief. Charlie King is absent this time around, his place taken by an equally menacing Dick Curtis. Ben Hendricks makes an unbilled appearance of sorts, his villainous trapper named Benet—already executed when the film begins—pops up when a photo of Hendricks's character "Slager" from *Red Blood of Courage* illustrates a newspaper article about his hanging.

Sam's handling of this film demonstrates what a visually competent director he could be with just a little more time—and perhaps a few extra dollars—to crank out a film. A far cry from so many of his more rushed Westerns of the upcoming PRC years, this one boasts a nice intermingling of long, medium, and close-up shots and carefully chosen angles, avoiding the more expedient straight-on uninterrupted takes. The opener, where a group of Mounties grill captured gang member Raoul (Roger Williams), is a good example, Sam's direction, Edgar Lyons's camerawork, and English's editing working in harmonious concert.

There are two top-notch shootouts bookending the film, the first of these an ambush where two Mounties are killed. These are genuinely exciting in their execution—or at least comparatively so—enhanced by Jack English's rapid cutting. Hans Weeren's sound recording adds to the impact, the gunshots—and there are a whole lot of them—having auditory heft to them. *The Philadelphia Exhibitor* praised the series, writing that "Maurice Conn's Hermit [sic] Maynard series has held high reputation because of care in production, impressive scenic backgrounds," adding that Sam's "handling is above average of usual action dramas."[26]

Sig Neufeld's favorite and oft-used sound engineer, Hans Weeren.

Hans Weeren, late of Tiffany and by this time a renowned sound engineer, handled the recording for Ambassador's *Northern Frontier* and *His Fighting Blood* as well as for this film. A native of Amsterdam born in 1894, Weeren had been with Tiffany since 1930, earning a reputation within the industry for his technical capabilities and inventiveness. The research council of the Academy of Motion Picture Arts and Sciences, formed earlier that same year, took note. Its stated purpose was "to coordinate motion picture research and standardization efforts and to function as a central bureau for the exchange of technical and artistic information" and "consolidate the work of the film Academy's technical bureau, producers-technicians committee and art and technique committee." Weeren was chosen as Tiffany's representative to the group focusing on sound issues, such as the development of a quiet 35mm camera that would dispense with the cumbersome "blimps" used to muffle extraneous noise, advancements in "split recording" to allow two different sound tracks to be recorded on opposite sides of 35mm sound stock, and so forth.[27]

Weeren first made the news back in early 1930 when he was involved with nascent television transmission. On April 7, a 200-foot segment of director James Whale's soon-to-be-released *Journey's End* was to be transmitted from New York City to Weeren's set,[28] "probably at the Mayan Theater, where 'Journey's End' will open Thursday."[29] There doesn't appear to have been a reported follow-up about this experiment, so it's likely that it wasn't a success.

By the time Weeren was hired by Ambassador, he had assembled a sound truck for location recording, operating under the banner Cinema Sound, Inc. He was also still busy at work on what was described as "a television set which can be used to advantage in picture making."[30] While rather vague as to what its actual use would be in filmmaking, the inference is that perhaps this innovation might have somehow afforded remote monitoring of a scene being filmed, a variation of sorts predating director Jerry Lewis's novel approach of video playback thirty years hence. Regardless, Weeren would promptly become an integral part of both Sig's and Sam's films to come, ending with his premature death at age forty-nine in 1943

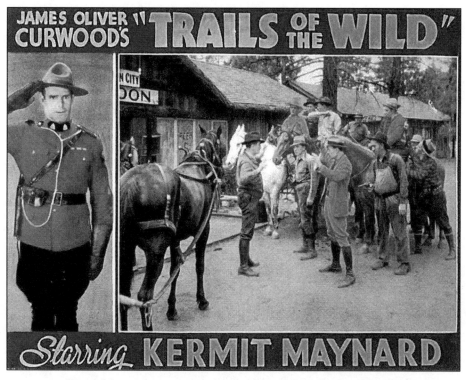

Kermit Maynard at attention, in this lobby card for **Trails of the Wild** (Ambassador, 1935), Sig Neufeld and Maurice Conn producers, Sam Newfield director. *Courtesy of Heritage Auctions.*

Trails of the Wild, Sam's third for Ambassador, was released in August. The story revolves around the kidnapping of mining engineer John Elliott by his partners, Robert Frazer and Wheeler Oakman. They hold him prisoner in an abandoned mine, hoping to force him to reveal the location of a new vein he has discovered. Meanwhile, Mountie Maynard is on the trail of Roger Williams, the killer of another Mountie, Monte Blue, and scripting shortcuts would have it a member of Frazer's gang as well. Working with fellow Mountie Fuzzy Knight and grizzled old prospector Frank Rice, Maynard manages to rescue Elliott, make a last-minute horse ride to obtain the cash needed to fulfill Elliott's contractual commitment to Frazer, arrest Frazer for kidnapping, and end up in the arms of Madison's grateful daughter Billie Seward.

There are so many villains in this one—Matthew Betz and Charles Delaney included—that the plot seems occasionally top-heavy with characters, but that's of little importance since Sam has punctuated the proceedings with several action-packed sequences, concluding with Maynard's dash atop Rocky over mountaintop and back to cash Elliott's check. As always, the location shooting gives the proceedings a visual boost, and Jack Greenhalgh's cinematography is a definite asset—*Film Daily* rated it "A-1". Greenhalgh has taken care to strive for a more natural look in several low-light interiors: the mine shafts illuminated solely by flashlight and a donnybrook in a darkened saloon both display just enough visual information to keep the viewer abreast of what's happening, while retaining a veneer of reality. Kids must have thought that secret stone door into the mine was cool, but to more discerning eyes it seems rather absurd. As the film's love interest, Billie Seward is a cute and competent—but sadly underused—addition. Reviews, as frequently happened, were at odds, *Film Daily* judging it to have been "Efficiently produced with a capable cast and nicely paced direction," adding that it "will fill its purpose in entertaining the followers of outdoor melodrama."[31] *Variety* was far less charitable, taking Sam to task for what were felt to be the film's shortcomings: "Weak picture because of failure to realize story possibilities and obviously for lesser duals. Director has failed to weave story together and there are numerous draggy episodes."[32] As for the exhibitors, some of them weren't impressed with Kermit's thespic abilities, dragging in brother Ken for comparison: "If Ken Maynard could have played the part that Kermit played, the picture would have gone over much better. Kermit don't hit so good with the audience."[33]

Sam's fourth and final directorial effort for his brother and the Ambassador series was *Timber War*, its production underway in October 1935 and rushed into release a mere month later. Studio publicists didn't hold back in their press release for the film:

> Riding the wheels of death Kermit Maynard and one of the most dangerous desperadoes of the West are locked in a struggle that means death to one or the other—or both. The train must drive through a trestle that has been put on fire—Maynard fights like he never has before. Will he come through safely[?].... "Timber War" is regarded as one of [James Oliver] Curwood's outstanding stories and has been produced for the screen with sweeping, life-like strokes. To admirers of two-fisted, red-blooded he-men and tales of the open spaces this film should carry great appeal.[34]

Regardless of other promotional releases that touted location filming way up in the Canadian Rockies, the film was in reality shot a mere eighty-five miles from

Hollywood, in and around Lake Arrowhead, California. "We shot up in the Redwoods," said Lucille Lund, Maynard's co-star in *Timber War*.

> It was a hard job—we had to stay at the Redwood Hotel with all the lumberjacks. The food was good, but it was very rustic. We had to get up every morning at 4 AM—there was no hairdresser, no makeup man. You did it all yourself. We went deep into the forest—there was no place for a bathroom! And, no other female! I remember one incident that happened off the picture. There was a dance—the lumberjacks and their girlfriends or wives were there. I came in after a long day's shooting; I overheard one woman say to another after she had looked me over from top to bottom, "I don't think she's so hot."[35]

Timber War would prove to be both Sig and Sam's swan song releases for Ambassador.

Exciting poster art for director Sam Newfield's Kermit Maynard starrer **Timber War** (Ambassador, 1935), Sig Neufeld and Maurice Conn producers. *Courtesy of Heritage Auctions.*

Chapter 6:
The Real McCoy (1935-1937)

By the time Conn's and Sig's eighth Maynard oater for Ambassador was released, however, Sig was long gone from the studio, deep into his next venture. It's unknown whether there was conflict between the two partners or if they merely disagreed on the future thrust for the studio, but whichever the case Sig had packed his bags by early 1935 even though he retained a loose affiliation with Ambassador and the production of the following season's eight films.

Sig's new independent concern, formed by Sig and Leslie Simmonds, once again bore the name Premier Pictures and would operate out of the Talisman Studios at 4516 Sunset. Nine action pictures were announced, the first with a tentative start on March 29, 1935.[1] The new company didn't exist for long under the Premier banner, however, a title conflict forcing a name change to Excelsior Pictures within a mere three weeks of their initial announcement.[2] All of the press releases touted this as being a co-venture of Sig and Leslie, but behind the scenes Leslie's father, Joe Simmonds, returned as the production company's president.

Sig and Ruth Neufeld pose with their sons Stanley (left) and infant Sigmund Jr., circa 1935. *Courtesy of Tim Neufeld.*

Sig needed a director for Excelsior's first production, so he turned to the guy he could trust, brother Sam. Announced as *Hell Breaks Loose* but ultimately released as *Crashin' Thru Danger*, the film co-starred Guinn Williams and Sally Blane.[3] Filmed and completed in April 1935, it was awarded a code number by the PCA sometime during November 26, 1935, and January 26, 1936.[4] For whatever reason, the finished film was not released theatrically until September 1938. Another story titled "Death on the Wing" was purchased for potential production, an original by Barry Barringer who had written several of the Maynard Ambassadors, but it doesn't appear to have gone anywhere.[5]

At the beginning of January 1935, a new production and distribution company named Puritan Pictures Corp. was formed by Louis Solomon and Dave Gross. With corporate offices located at 723 Seventh Avenue in New York, Solomon served as the company's president, and Gross its vice president and secretary.[6] By mid-March Solomon announced that a deal had been closed with popular Western star Tim McCoy, for a series of ten Westerns to be released on the state rights market come fall.[7]

Born in Saginaw, Michigan in 1891, McCoy had gotten the Western bug as a teen after seeing the Miller Brothers 101 Ranch Wild West Show, prompting a westward excursion. After serving a stint in the war, McCoy eventually landed in Hollywood, and by 1926 he was starring in films at M-G-M. With his departure from that studio in 1929, McCoy was featured in a couple of serials for Universal before heading over to Columbia in 1931, where he remained up until his hiring by Solomon. While Puritan may have seemed a step down from Columbia, McCoy explained the reason in his memoir, published a decade after his death:

> Columbia was not prepared to let me off to tour [with the Ringling Brothers-Barnum & Bailey Circus] in the summer and make films in the winter, though I explained that the promotion I would be getting across the country could hardly hurt at the box office.
>
> Thus, when my contract came up for renewal in 1935, I signed with Puritan Pictures, an outfit which fully appreciated the lure my tour with the circus would have. Puritan was not one of the more prestigious production companies and the quality of the films I made with them, which were sometimes completed after only three or four days' shooting, left much to be desired. Doubtless, it would have been better for my career had I stayed at Columbia. In fact, immediately after I signed the contract with Puritan, and as a couple of the outfit's executives and I toasted our hopes for future success in my apartment at Garden Court, the telephone rang and a man from Columbia offered to meet the needs imposed upon me by the circus. But I had given my word, and it was too late.[8]

McCoy's terms were the same as he had received at Columbia: $4,000 per picture for ten pictures, each film budgeted in the $10,000 to $12,000 range.[9]

Solomon engaged Nat Ross Productions to handle McCoy's first two films for Puritan, *The Outlaw Deputy* and *The Man from Guntown*. He then engaged Sig and Simmonds and their Excelsior Pictures to handle the remaining eight of McCoy's Western series, to resume in October after McCoy completed his most recent tour with the Ringling circus.[10]

Production commenced in October with the first of these, titled *Bulldog Courage*. Sig put together a team of sorts for his crew, several of whom would remain a constant through all eight productions. Brother Sam would handle the direction throughout, with Jack Greenhalgh manning the camera and Hans Weeren the sound for all entries as well. Editing was doled out to one of three individuals: S. Roy Luby, Jack English, and Holbrook Todd. Screenplays were mostly written by Joseph O'Donnell, with Jack Neville, Wyndham Gittens, or Arthur Durlam brought in as needed. Speed was of the essence, of course, with production of the eighth and final entry completed by end of March 1936.[11]

Bulldog Courage, released on December 30, 1935, follows Tim Braddock (McCoy) and his single-minded determination to avenge the death of his late father, also portrayed in flashback by McCoy. His father had been swindled out of his mine by banker Karl Hackett and his lawyers. He took to robbing the stages carrying the bank's gold shipments, but is shot by a pursuing posse, dying with his young son (Eddie Buzard) at his side. Now grown up, McCoy returns to town and finds that an old friend (John Cowell) is facing the same fate at Hackett's hands, so he spends the rest of the film evening the score. The film ends with a satisfying comeuppance for both Hackett and his partner in crime, mine owner Edmund Cobb, Hackett crushed in the mine explosion he had arranged, and Cobb at the wrong end of Braddock's gun.

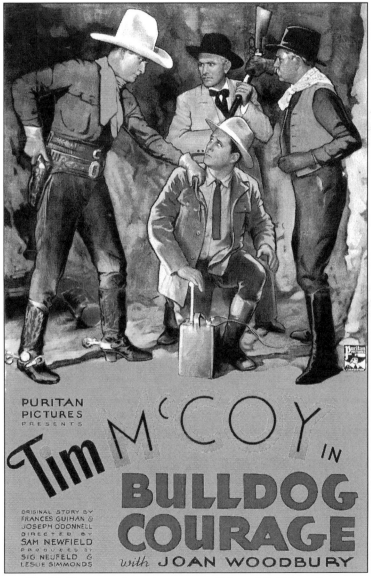

Tim McCoy puts a last-minute stop to Edmund Cobb's explosive intentions; Karl Hackett threatening with rifle. **Bulldog Courage** (Puritan,1935), Sig Neufeld and Leslie Simmonds producing, Sam Newfield directing. *Courtesy of Heritage Auctions.*

Sig and Sam must have been thrilled to have a star who could actually act, McCoy adequately conveying a range of emotions with only the rare moment of awkwardness. His physicality is evident, a solid five foot eleven, 170-pound immovable presence, convincingly intimidating those who need intimidating. Actor Paul Fix is on board as an explosives expert—a self-described "powder monkey"—who provides the film's comic relief, although I am sure that there were viewers who found him anything but comic with his rapid-fire, ethnically accented delivery. In one amusing scene, McCoy takes Fix's character's place, delivering the guy's own lines and garnering genuine laughs this time around. Joan Woodbury provides the film's love interest—or should I say *lack* of love interest—as Cowell's daughter, a childhood sweetheart of McCoy's who once promised to marry him and now, years later, seems present solely as a pain-in-the-ass contrarian. Once the action picks up, however, Woodbury pretty much disappears from the film. "Sam Newfield's direction plays the effort for all its thrill and action content," wrote *Motion Picture Daily*, "while Jack Greenhalgh's photography takes in the pictorial backgrounds and follows the action suitably."[12] As the series' opener, *Bulldog Courage* was a solid offering, arguably the best of Excelsior's eight, but inarguably having the coolest title.

Tim McCoy holds the bad guys at bay in **Roarin' Guns** (Puritan, 1935), Sig Neufeld and Leslie Simmonds producing, Sam Newfield directing.
Courtesy of Library of Congress.

Roarin' Guns (January 27, 1936) followed, this time with McCoy as the hired gun Tim Corwin. It's the age-old story of cattle barons vs. the helpless, little-guy ranchers. Wheeler Oakman and Karl Hacket are the barons of the piece, supposedly competing to acquire the various ranches in the area, but in actuality in cahoots, using all sorts of unscrupulous methods to threaten and drive the ranchers into selling. Rancher John Elliott calls in McCoy to help with the fight, but in time McCoy is framed for both the abduction of Elliott's niece (Rosalinda Price) and the murder of Elliott himself. McCoy clears his name, and in a climactic street-based ambush, shoots both Oakman and Hackett dead. As a clincher, McCoy proposes to Price, and the two will now raise Elliott's orphaned son (Tommy Bupp).

This one opens with a bang, with lots of stock footage of stampeding horses and a shootout outside a burning house, a not terribly convincing miniature. McCoy's anti-hero is a nice change of pace, and Bupp, as the kid who idolizes McCoy, has some cute moments and pulls them off nicely, but eventually wears out his welcome with an overabundance of saccharine cuteness. The film's requisite love interest is supplied by the cold-as-ice Rosalinda Price, one of the more curious looking actresses of the period, whose cheek-to-cheek lips give her the appearance of a human Pez dispenser. If you think you recognize her, it would be from this film only as it was her sole film role...unless, of course, she was one of those minor actresses who tried reinventing herself with one or more name changes. As usual, Oakman and Hackett both make eminently despicable villains. Jack Greenhalgh's nighttime photography once again warrants a favorable mention.

Border Caballero (March 1, 1936) is one of the best entries in the series, full of action and with a plot that engages. McCoy stars as undercover Federal agent Tim Ross—posing as slightly disreputable "Missouri"—and his efforts to break the bank robbing schemes of saloon owner Ted Adams, his boss John Merton, and J. Frank Glendon, the territorial bank examiner they collude with. The stolen money is being used to bankroll guns bought across the border in Mexico, so the villains of the piece, wanting snoopy "Missouri" out of the way, frame him for his old friend Ralph Byrd's murder. Merton has the hots for saloon worker Lois January, but angered over boyfriend Byrd's death and knowing that Merton was responsible, she provides her new friend Missouri with info that enables the staging of a phony monetary delivery to a bank, setting the trap for the gang. McCoy has the pleasure of shooting both Merton and Glendon dead in the street.

McCoy has a lot of fun in this one, allowed to expand his acting chops as he dresses and poses as the Mexican "José"—almost unrecognizably so—in a successful attempt to get into Adams's saloon. It's a broad performance worthy of Leo Carrillo, providing an immense boost to the viewer's enjoyment. Earle Hodgins appears as Doc Shaw, a travelling snake oil salesman, in a time-filling, throw-away subplot, that provides an enjoyable opening sequence where he's pitted against an ornery sheriff, broadly played by silent comedy veteran Robert McKenzie. Another silent comedy throwback has a brief appearance as well, James Aubrey playing a drunk satisfied with Doc's product; he doesn't once attempt to hide his British accent.

Sam's direction of this and the other series entries is commendable, at least within the budgetary and expectation limits of these state rights quickies. The productions are all handsomely mounted, and the acting uniformly excellent, an improvement over the more dramatically challenged performers of the Ambassadors that preceded them. Greenhalgh's cinematography is an undeniable asset, his nighttime shoots almost always visually convincing and moodily lit, especially with interiors. It would seem that Sam insisted on one or more nighttime sequences in most of these entries, given the visual boost and additional luster they add to the final product. Sam seems most at home when orchestrating the action sequences, the fistfights frequently brutal—for the era at least—and the gunfights fast, furious, and usually believably chaotic. As "José," McCoy's saloon-based slugfest with Merton features tight closeups of each participant as they take another sock to the jaw, the concluding shootout loud and violent. That McCoy always gets to shoot dead the bad guys of the piece at each film's conclusion is, well, as American as apple pie.

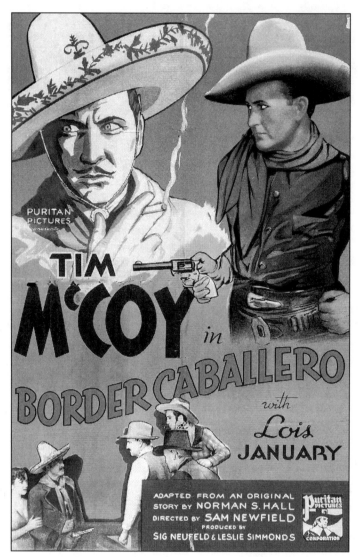

Tim McCoy in his guise as "Missouri" in **Border Caballero** (Puritan, 1936), Sig Neufeld and Leslie Simmonds producing, Sam Newfield directing. *Courtesy of Heritage Auctions.*

Lightnin' Bill Carson (April 15, 1936) came next, with McCoy now the no-nonsense, quick-draw sheriff of the title, hired by San Jacinto's banker Joseph W. Girard to clean up the town's corruption. Karl Hackett is on board once again, this time as "Stack" Stone, owner of the town's saloon who, along with "Breed" Hawkins (John Merton), runs a ruthless, murderous gang of stage robbers. The film changes course near the end—Hackett and Merton are merely arrested rather than shot dead as in earlier films—the story now shifting gears to follow "Silent" Tom Rand (Harry Worth), a former (and temporarily reformed) gunslinger. Worth goes after the sheriff and posse members responsible for the lynching of his innocent gambler brother, Rex Lease, gunning them down, one-by-one, in a sequence of quick cuts that only lasts for a couple of minutes. McCoy is last on Worth's list, but Worth has a change of heart and engineers the shootout that results in his own death. Lois January has a minor role, appearing briefly at both ends of the film, and inconsequently so, her Mexican accent at odds with her character's Irish surname "Costello."

This one's a curiosity, with the series' highest body count, courtesy of Harry Worth's vengeance-filled former gunslinger. It is also one of Sig and Sam's darkest offerings, highlighted by the slam-bang lynching of Rex Lease, the innocent and guilt-ridden gambler the viewer has grown to like; there's no last-minute rescue this time around. Later on, McCoy has his climactic shootout with Harry Worth, who has emptied his pistol before their showdown, an early cinematic twist on the "Death By Cop" syndrome.

Sam manages to add a few nice touches to the proceedings, one of which is Lease's lynching. A gunshot sends his mount running, followed by a shot of the ground beneath as his signature playing card, the Ace of Spades (aka the "Death Card"), drops into view, followed by his "last smoke." Cut to the sheriff, the hanged man's legs creating a moving shadow over his grimly set face. Then Lease's brother arrives, with a long point-of-view closeup as he slowly looks from one unseen member of the posse to the next, capped by his slowly delivered voiceover promise: "I'll remember every one of you, as long as I live." Simple in execution, but chilling in effect.

Visually the film is as handsome as those that preceded it, with one jarring exception: there are three successive closeup shots of a conversation between Dolores and Tom Rand, where in the first and last she's on the right looking left, and in the second she's on the left looking right. It's an Editing 101 no-no, the jump so noticeable that it's surprising that Jack English, the film's editor, allowed it to pass, but pass it did. Based on his future work, it would appear that he learned from his mistakes. Aside from that one technical error, the film is an oddity of sorts given its rather downbeat storyline, but all the more intriguing as a result.

Tim McCoy is Earle Hodgins's prisoner in **Aces and Eights** (Puritan, 1936), Sig Neufeld and Leslie Simmonds producing, Sam Newfield directing.

Aces and Eights (June 6, 1936), while perhaps a step down from its predecessors, still has enough moments of interest to warrant a viewing. McCoy plays notorious gambler "Gentleman" Tim Madigan, whose prodigious strength—he can tear a deck of cards into quarters with his bare hands—usually makes up for his lack of firearm. Pursued across state lines by the Marshal (Earle Hodgins) fixated on finding the killer of a card sharp, McCoy heads to the town of Roaring Gulch. He soon learns of Wheeler Oakman and his attempts to swindle the Hernandez family—father Joseph W. Girard, hopeless gambler and drunk son Rex Lease, and lovely daughter Luana Walters—out of their home and property. Oakman is aided and abetted by saloon owner J. Frank Glendon, and it takes the gambling talents of McCoy to win over the saloon, pay off the Hernandez debts, clear son Lease's conscience, and deliver guilty Oakman to the law. Add to that the promise of landing Walters.

Tim McCoy knocks one out of the park in **The Lion's Den** (Puritan, 1936), Sig Neufeld and Leslie Simmonds producing, Sam Newfield directing. *Courtesy of Heritage Auctions.*

The film's pleasures are simple ones: Jack Greenhalgh's photography and atmospheric lighting of the two saloons' interiors; and the film's lengthy prologue. The latter begins with several standard minutes' worth of silent film stock scenes of a wagon train besieged by marauding Indians. This is followed by a bit about Wild Bill Hickok (Karl Hackett) and his days in Deadwood, shot dead in the back while playing poker, a pair of aces and eights clenched in his hand—from then on known as the "Death Hand" and providing the film its catchy title. Hackett, according to one source, delivered the prologue's narration as well. Silent comedian Jimmy Aubrey makes a return appearance, this time as McCoy's sidekick and, for better or worse, for the film's duration.

The Lion's Den (July 6, 1936) followed, with trick shot artist McCoy and his dim-witted assistant Don Barclay hired by ranch owner Arthur Millett and his daughter Joan Woodbury. McCoy's assignment: help stave off greedy rancher J. Frank Glendon, who wants their land for its water rights, and will stop at nothing to get them. Glendon has hired notorious gunslinger John Merton to come to his ranch—and not for his health—but McCoy gets wind of this and shows up, convincingly posing as Merton. Glendon's gang is made up solely of wanted men, so McCoy works behind the scenes with Karl Hackett's sheriff (for once a good guy) to decimate Glendon's gang, one by one, either by arrest or death. When Glendon forecloses on Millett's outstanding loans and the ranch goes up for bid, McCoy uses the rewards he's collected to outbid Glendon and reacquire the ranch for Millett and Woodbury, Glendon and his surviving gang members arrested in the process.

The Lion's Den suffers from its lower budget look, with a lot of grainy stock footage of a big city's streets, trains, and cattle stampedes intercut at various times. As McCoy's partner, Barclay is on board presumably for comic relief, but his stupidity and habit of saying the wrong things at the wrong time quickly grows tiresome. The film's opening, which takes place in a fancy nightclub, features McCoy's character on stage demonstrating his prowess with both whip and pistol. Seemingly added as filler, it is far too long and should have been handled in a more economical fashion.

Reviews were mixed. *Film Daily* liked it, finishing its review by stating that the "original twists and surprises keep this one steaming all the way, and it will get over easily with the fans who want plenty of the thrill stuff."[13] *Motion Picture Daily* concurred: "The story contains a good degree of novelty, deviating from the routine.... The story moves lively on its clever way. There are twists and turns which make effective and pleasant entertainment."[14] *Variety* was a bit more downbeat in its assessment: "Very little action in the opus, sole thrills confined to a single gun fracas.... City slicker idea introduced at first promises something different, but it folds early. Later stanzas are worn, even though McCoy's label is there for the thrill addicts."[15] You win some, and you lose some.

The McCoy Westerns in this series did not adhere to any specific time period, jumping from era to era. *The Lion's Den* appears to take place in the later 1800s, given that one of the characters refers to a typewriter as a "newfangled" invention, while the camera focuses on a closeup of a very primitive model. *Ghost Patrol*, which followed, was a contemporary piece, with McCoy as G-Man Tim Caverly, assuming the identity of a rival gangster to gain access to a gang of robbers responsible for the downing of airplanes and subsequent deaths of all onboard. This is an oddball Western-Sci-Fi hybrid, the method used to down the planes the electric impulse generating invention of Lloyd Ingraham's professor, a prisoner of the gang. McCoy's cover is blown when word gets around that the gangster he's impersonating was arrested and in jail, but reinforcements have been called in and the gang's leaders, Walter Miller and Wheeler Oakman, are taken into custody after a ferocious gun battle.

One of the lesser entries in the series, *Ghost Patrol* (August 3, 1936) falls back on the old "assumed identity" gimmick that seems to resurface time and again in a lot of these films. The film itself suggests a hurried production, with Sam—either lazily or out of necessity—relying on longer, mid- to long-shot single takes, frequently eschewing cuts to closeups. There's also the use of rear projection, newly introduced to the series and blatantly obvious in early scenes where McCoy pilots a carriage, a curiosity given that so much of the film was shot on location. Even Greenhalgh's photography and Jack English's editing have a slap-dash look to them, stock footage of airplanes out of control intercut with static shots of pilot McCoy in the cockpit, an unconvincing "sky" backdrop behind him. As for the inventor's lab, it is equipped with paraphernalia that looks straight out of the earlier *Frankenstein* and *Bride of Frankenstein* films' labs (some contemporary sources say that it is the *same* equipment, courtesy of Kenneth Strickfaden). *Ghost Patrol* has its plusses, however, thanks to some good casting. McCoy's partner Jimmy Burtis is

Tim McCoy in Puritan's **Ghost Patrol** (1936), Sig Neufeld and Leslie Simmonds producing, Sam Newfield directing. *Courtesy of Heritage Auctions.*

for once played as a smart, resourceful sidekick rather than the usual comic relief idiots of some of the previous films. As the imprisoned professor's daughter, actress Claudia Dell is a delight, displaying considerable acting chops and a good sense of humor in a scene where she is demonstrating different hitch-hiking techniques; it doesn't hurt that she's easy on the eyes. Wheeler Oakman revisits his by-now familiar heavy, with Dick Curtis brought back as well for another henchman role.

The Traitor (August 29, 1936) wrapped up the series, with McCoy this time around as a Texas Ranger who—you guessed it—goes undercover to break a gang. His Captain, Karl Hackett, orchestrates it so that it appears that McCoy has been dismissed for cowardice, but the two alone know this secret. This allows McCoy to infiltrate the gang led by J. Frank Glendon, two of whose men—Pedro Rigas and Frank Melton—McCoy saves from a mob set on lynching them. Instead of taking them in, however, McCoy releases them with the intention of following them to Glendon. McCoy gains the gang's trust, but they are soon on to him, which now puts him in the crosshairs of both the gang and his former Ranger pals, who now think he's gone over to the dark side. After recuperating from being shot by fellow Ranger Jack Rockwell, McCoy eventually finds himself in a cabin along with Melton and Melton's sister, Frances Grant, besieged by Glendon's gang. The Rangers arrive in the nick of time, Regas is shot dead, and Glendon arrested. In the fracas, however, Melton is killed as well, as is Hackett, taking the secret of McCoy's "dismissal" with him. He had the foresight, however, to mail himself a letter exonerating McCoy, so all ends well.

This is an acceptable end to the series, with Greenhalgh's stunning exterior photography a standout. McCoy has the opportunity to deliver a measured speech to the assembled mob, explaining to them that to lynch the two captives would be doing them a favor, as the alternative—jail, trial, pleas, empty promises, and languishing in jail until the day of execution—would be a far more severe punishment. Some of the sets and settings were beginning to look familiar by this time, Mary's ranch house having already been used in at least two previous outings.

"In all my experience around pictures," supposedly wrote Sam, "I've never witnessed a more spectacular riding stunt than McCoy's breaking and taming an outlaw horse in the opening reel of the feature. It wasn't pretending, either, for the equine actor who fills the role of the horse Thunderbolt is a real bad actor in quite another sense of the word than it is applied theatrically." Sam—or more likely a press agent—continued:

> I was tickled to death when the scene was over and I knew Tim's neck and spine were still intact. When "The Traitor" was first opened at the Ideal Theatre, you ought to have seen how the audience reacted to that particular shot. Even the adult fans yelled in unbridled enthusiasm, and as for the youngsters they simply went crazy over it. I take my hat off to Tim McCoy as the greatest rider the screen knows today. It's no wonder the fans are clean ga-ga over him.[16]

There's little doubt that this is just a bunch of press agent puffery. Who really thought that Sam actually travelled to Corsicana, Texas to gauge the Ideal Theatre audience's reaction? That said, anything goes when trying to "sell" a film to a prospective audience.

Tim McCoy's in control in **The Traitor** (Puritan, 1936), Sig Neufeld and Leslie Simmonds producing, Sam Newfield directing. *Courtesy of Heritage Auctions.*

Which brings us back to the earlier mentioned *Crashin' Thru Danger*, filmed in April 1935 but given a very belated release in September 1938. Which is a surprise given that it was a comparatively good little film. A trio of fun-loving, skirt-chasing linemen—Ray Walker, Guinn Williams, and James Bush—are best buddies until they move in with cute Sally Blane, the daughter of their former boss Robert Homans, recently killed in a gas explosion. Jealousy soon creates a rift among them, coming to a head when Walker and Bush think (erroneously) that Williams and Blane are to marry. When Williams dies in a fall, Bush's jealousy—now redirected towards Walker—prompts him to ask to be reassigned to the lab. When a huge electric storm threatens the leader line to the General Hospital, Walker tries to deal with it solo, but Blane shames Bush into helping out and, in the process, saving Walker's life. Bush and Blane end up together, and Walker's now fine with it.

This one stands out among many of its low budget peers on several levels, the novel electrical grid setting a decided asset. The camaraderie among the trio of linemen is believable, with Walker the skirt-chasing jokester who takes a dark turn, Williams the gruff, no-nonsense co-worker who assumes Homans's position of authority, and Bush the serious, shy, and hopelessly love-sick moper of the group. Williams excels in his role, for once given a serious, sympathetic part which atypically credits him with a fair degree of intelligence. Blane is charming and convincing as the unintentional homewrecker, giving her younger sister Loretta Young a run for her money in the looks department. The film has its share of suspenseful sequences, including the gas leak and explosion that kills Homans, Williams's pole-top electrocution and fall to death, and the climactic attempts to fix the teetering pole during the raging rainstorm. There's a nightclub-based donnybrook that's nicely orchestrated, the fight brought about when a masher—Syd Saylor in a rare serious role—moves in on Blane. Sam's direction is quite good, handling his actors and action scenes with equal authority. Even the stock footage has been chosen with care, the exciting storm footage of particular note. The only blatant visual glitch came with Jack English's editing, where the cross-cutting between Homans and his Superintendent has both of them facing left as opposed to facing each other, a gaff that he'd revisit with McCoy's *Lightnin' Bill Carson*. English's fault, and not that of the director or cameraman, James Brown, Jr.? Even if so, the negative could have been flipped so that it cut properly.[17] Yeah, I know; nitpicking. *Film Daily*, one of the few trades to review the film, dished out the praise: "Here is a strong offering in the indie field, with a powerful melodrama of realistic action, in a new field for the movies to tackle," and finished off the review with a tip of the hat to Sam: "Director Newfield turned in an exciting and colorful production."[18]

With the earlier completion of *The Traitor* and his contract with Puritan, Tim McCoy moved over to Monogram to begin another series of Westerns. As we'll soon see, however, McCoy's connection with Sam was far from severed.

Guinn Williams and Ray Walker in the arm(s) of the law in Excelsior's
Crashin' Thru Danger (1938), Sig Neufeld and Leslie Simmonds
producing, Sam Newfield directing. *Courtesy of Heritage Auctions.*

Chapter 7:
Sam, Sans Sig (Part 1: 1932-1936)

The films that Sam directed at Tower, Ambassador, and Puritan for his brother were merely the tip of the proverbial iceberg. It didn't take long for Sam to gain a reputation among producers of low-budget fare as a director who would meet schedules, stick to budgets, work well with the actors and crew, and deliver an acceptable product. He never needed an agent, as word of mouth was all that was necessary to keep him in constant demand through the mid- to later-1930s. He directed no fewer than thirteen features in 1936, sixteen in 1937, sixteen in 1938, and eleven in 1939, and those are just the ones we know of. Sam adopted at least two *noms-de-plumes* for his many credits beginning in 1939—Peter Stewart and Sherman Scott—and may have used others that we are unaware of, such as the elusive "James Jones" mentioned as a possibility in an earlier chapter. Also, there was the occasional film that was released without any sort of directorial credit that Sam may have had a hand in. Regardless, and aside from the films he directed for his brother's various ventures in the early 1930s, Sam directed for a dizzying number of production companies during the 1930s. These included such companies as Progressive, Cavalcade, Supreme, Winchester, Booth Dominion, Colony, Spectrum. Lincoln, Stan Laurel Productions, Concord, Victory, Principal, Criterion, Fine Arts, Cinemart, and Arcadia, releasing on both the state rights market and through established distributors that included Republic, Monogram, Columbia, M-G-M, and Grand National.

As busy as he was, however, Sam would always finish each day's work in a timely fashion, allowing for the early dismissal of cast and crew. This was a result of both his efficiency and no-nonsense approach to direction, but also for a more personal reason—his passion for gambling—but more on this in a later chapter. The birth of his daughter in early 1933 didn't make him any more of a homebody, as his gambling continued unabated, and his socializing at nightclubs later that same year, as documented by the press. "Society rub shoulders with celebs of the amusement world at this spot" wrote *Hollywood Filmograph* about the New Montmartre Café, where Sam joined in with others of the film and sports worlds to celebrate.[1]

Universal's Shorts, and One Outlier

One company that Sam would return to sporadically in the early- to mid-1930s was Universal, the place where he got his start in the industry. This usually was to collaborate on the scripts for the company's two-reel shorts with James W. Horne or W.P. Hackney, on Horne-directed shorts that included *Oh! My Operation* (1932), *Picnic Perils*, and *Just We Two* (both 1934). The most significant of these was *You Can Be Had* (October 3, 1935), which Sam directed and was produced by Bert Sternbach, with whom he had worked many times before back on the Stern Brothers Comedies. This film was essentially an update of the former Tiffany Talking Chimps comedies, with the hairy leads once again acting out the various roles with human voices dubbed in. A takeoff on the popular Mae West films then in release, the film's lead "Fay East" gets caught up in a night club raid, the "man" she had her sights on turning out to be an undercover detective. *Motion Picture Daily*'s reviewer liked the results, calling it "fair entertainment" and giving "credit to the producers and Sam Newfield, the director, for the smooth performances of the 'players'."[2] *Motion Picture Herald* agreed: "The animals are admirably controlled, the dubbing adroitly done, and action is remarkably smooth considering the difficulties inherent in this type of production. The short rates high among its kind."³ The "City of Brotherly Love"'s *Philadelphia Herald* was one of the few dissenters, dispensing with brotherly love to question how "a company that can make such an inspired production like 'Magnificent Obsession' can release such a two reeler is a mystery. Poor." Reviewers aside, exhibitors found it to be a crowd pleaser—which was what really counted—as one Alabama-based theatre owner wrote in an ecstatic letter published in *Motion Picture Herald*'s "What the Picture Did for Me:" "One of the best comedies of its kind ever made…. If you want to get something that will cause a riot with the kids as well as please the adults play this two-reeler from Universal."⁴

Producers Bert Sternbach and Arthur Alexander's belated take on the Tiffany Chimps, **You Can Be Had** (Universal, 1935), Sam Newfield directing. *Courtesy of Heritage Auctions.*

Another two-reeler that Sam directed in 1934 was comedian Lloyd Hamilton's little seen swan song, *Wedding Belles*. Hamilton, whose career spanned a two-decade period, came to prominence in Kalem's "Ham and Bud" series with co-star Bud Duncan. Work followed in the late teens in some of Henry Lehrman's Sunshine Comedies for Fox and Henry Lehrman Comedies for First National, after which he starred in a successful run of comedies throughout the 1920s for release through Educational Film Exchange. Hamilton made a successful transition to sound, starring in a series for Mack Sennett and several more for Educational, but by this time alcoholism had taken a noticeable toll on his body and features. *Wedding Belles*, which was made for Cavalcade Film Corporation in early 1934,[5] survives, with Hamilton supported by Arthur Housman, Gertrude Astor, and Eddie Gribbon. Given that the sound was recorded by Hans Weeren, it was likely filmed at the Tiffany Studios. The plot is a slim one—or at least in the cut down version that survives—with Hamilton pursuing his bride-to-be aboard a ship, her father intending to marry her off to another. Hamilton rehashes some of his familiar gags from years gone by, most notably his oft-used fish-down-the-back-of-his-pants routine. The film's semi-climax involves an escalating, tit-for-tat seltzer battle. A mere shadow of his former self, Hamilton would be dead within less than a year at age forty-three.

Comedian Lloyd Hamilton's last starring role, here with Gertrude Astor, in Cavalcade's **Wedding Belles** (1934). *Courtesy of Ralph Celantano.*

Progressive Pictures Corporation

Sam directed the feature *Under Secret Orders* (January 1, 1934) in late 1933, a drama which follows a banker (Donald Dillaway) who is tasked to deliver some valuable bonds to an American client in Central America, and the gang of crooks out to gain hold of the bonds during the boat trip there. Filmed for Willis Kent's short-lived Progressive Pictures Corporation,[6] whose sole output during 1932-34 was a mere six features, *Under Secret Orders* was released on the state rights market. "Just another of those rambling semi-melodramas," wrote *Film Daily*, adding that "It is all very amateurish in plot and execution, and fails to impress." Sam wasn't let off the hook, his direction deemed "Weak."[7] *Variety*, in their usual snarky fashion, dismissing it as "One of those deliver-the-papers things."[8]

Supreme Pictures Corporation

Sam's 1935 was notable for two reasons, one personal and one professional. On the personal front, a son—Joel Clark Newfield—was born on May 1. On the professional front, 1935 marked the beginning of Sam's long and fruitful relationship with producer A.W. Hackel and his Supreme Pictures Corporation. Born in Krakow, Austria, Hackel (1882-1959) emigrated to the U.S. in 1889 and found employment in burlesque and on the Jewish stage. Tired of that life, Hackel got into the manufacturing of ladies' ready-to-wear clothing in New York, taking that business to the West Coast and expanding it there. His fortune evaporated in the 1929 crash, so he abandoned ladies' wear and went into film production in 1930.[9] Supreme was formed in 1934 to produce a series of Westerns featuring popular cowboy star Bob Steele, with Sam Katzman supervising and Robert Bradbury directing the bulk of them. Sam was brought in a year later to direct the first in a new series starring Johnny Mack Brown. Filming began on June 10, 1935, under the working title *Brand of the Coward*, the film released on the state rights market on August 1, 1935, as *Branded a Coward*.

Producer A.W. Hackel, circa 1938.

The film begins on a promising note: Twenty years after witnessing both his parents killed by a gang led by a fellow known only as The Cat, sharpshooter Johnny Mack Brown is left pathologically gun shy, cowering helplessly whenever there's serious gunplay. So far, so good, but then he undergoes an inexplicable conversion when witnessing a stage robbery, killing some of the gang members, driving off the rest, and safely returning its cargo of gold and future love interest Billie Seward. He's made the town's Marshal, with the result that he is now made the target of a gang—the one he did battle over at the stage robbery—led by a fellow calling himself The Cat. This all leads up to a violent fight between Brown and The Cat, with the film's twisteroo the revelation that The Cat is, in actuality, Brown's long lost brother Billy. Billy takes a bullet meant for his brother and dies.

This is a pretty good film, a semi-psychological drama notable primarily for its straying from the usual Western conventions. Kids of all ages must have been shocked by Brown's initial cowardice, but that didn't last long. As Brown's stuttering sidekick Oscar, Syd Saylor is on board for comic relief, but his stuttering quickly loses whatever questionable humor it initially provided. When Saylor's found dead, a victim of the gang, that too provides an unexpected jolt, and allows Brown to display a few moments of actual grief and tenderness. The last-minute revelation that The Cat—heretofore shown only in shadow (as if we'd even recognize him)—is Brown's brother, seems added solely for yet another unexpected surprise, but doesn't seem to make a whole lot of sense. Quibbles aside, there are several exciting action-filled set pieces, one set on the runaway stage which allows stuntman Yakima Canutt another opportunity to risk life and limb falling between the horses, the coach passing over him unharmed. The climactic fistfight between Brown and his brother is a genuine bruiser, the bulk of it filmed in one long take as just about every piece of furniture in the cabin is destroyed.

Reviews were mixed, although both Brown and Saylor were singled out for their "trim performing," the latter praised for his "bang-up job in the comedy assignment."[10] But it was the exhibitors, who had a good feel for what their patrons wanted, that really counted. One account reveals the reaction of Louis Korson, whose Masterpiece Film Attractions distributed the film throughout the Pennsylvania region and beyond:

> When a few months ago, he contracted to distribute A. W. Hackel's Johnny Mack Brown series, exchange owner Korson thought he was merely acquiring another western series. Month later when 'Branded a Coward' came into the exchange, he took a look at the picture, found, to his amazement, that while this was a western whopper, it was also a western melodrama, much on the same order as those which made George O'Brien famous.[11]

Frank McCarroll and Roger Williams, ready to open fire in producer A.W. Hackel's Johnny Mack Brown vehicle **Branded a Coward** (Supreme, 1935), Sam Newfield director.

Sam—or more likely Supreme's press agent—weighed in on the psychological aspects of the film in a long-winded, atypically thoughtful piece on the film:

> You might say there's quite an undertone of psychology running through the film. A hero who has to fight with himself to conquer fear, and makes good despite that handicap, is something of a new note in Westerns, where heroes are never known to make a bad break so far as courage goes. But that very thing gets Johnny Mack Brown a whole lot of sympathy, especially from the feminine patrons, and the men admire him too. The reason is that every one of us, at some time or another, has been up against fear in some form. And each one knows how he or she felt and acted, or would have liked to have acted, on such occasions. And that sense of fellow-feeling puts them right in touch with Johnny. That's the psychological slant—and judging by the box office reports, it has worked out nicely in the case of "Branded a Coward."[12]

Winchester Productions

In mid-1934, popular actor William "Bill" Boyd signed a four-picture contract to star in features for producer William Saal, and his newly formed Select Pictures. Formerly of Tiffany and KBS,[13] New York-based Saal's plans were to make films on both the East and West Coasts, with financing by Consolidated Film, of which Herbert J. Yates was president. Negotiations followed with Yates to consolidate exchanges throughout the country handling Consolidated financed films. Saal's Select and M.H. Hoffman's Liberty Pictures would be the first to take part, with other indie producers being financed by Consolidated to join in as their respective contracts with other exchanges expired.[14] Select's first effort, titled *Federal Agent*, went into production at the Talisman Studios on October 20, while another of its films—*Bad Penny*—went into production at the Biograph Studios in the Bronx.[15] *Racing Luck*, *Burning Gold*, and *Go-Get-'Em, Haines* were all to follow—all of them directed by Sam—and all of them initially advertised as Select Productions; *Federal Agent* was reviewed as such by *Photoplay* in March 1935.

And then George Hirliman got into the act. Hirliman, formerly the president of New York's Exhibitors Screen Service, Inc., had broadcast his "two cents worth" back in 1933 as to how depression-weary and -impoverished patrons could be lured back into theatres: "Reduced incomes everywhere demand that producers and theater owners cut down operating costs to a point where they can offer the public good entertainment at a price the public can afford to pay," he wrote. "Not until such economies are effected will the industry begin to recover."[16] Hirliman decided to put his money where his mouth was and headed to the coast in November 1933 to line up some talent for a series of lower budget films to be made in the east at the Biograph Studios. Yates and his Consolidated Film Industries were to back Hirliman's venture to the tune of $350,000.[17]

Republic Pictures Corporation was created in mid-1935 by Yates when he finally forced six independent companies, by now deep in debt to his Consolidated Lab, to "consolidate" under his leadership. These included the aforementioned Liberty Pictures, as well as Larry Darmour's Majestic, Trem Carr's and W.L. Johnston's Monogram, and Nat Levine's Mascot.[18] Republic worked out a deal to absorb and copyright the Select product as well—only *Federal Agent* had actually been released—and re-brand it under Hirliman's newly formed Winchester Productions. The four Boyd films would now be advertised and (re)released as such. Saal, presumably as part of the acquisition deal, was thrown a bone and made Republic's general sales manager.[19] Each of the four films was budgeted at $11,000, with domestic rentals ranging from a low of $34,536 (*Go-Get-'Em, Haines*) to a high of $47,147 (*Federal Agent*).

Racing Luck, the series' opener released first on October 31, 1935, was actually filmed after the series' final entry, *Go-Get-'Em, Haines*, going into production on March 17, 1935.[20] Boyd plays racehorse owner Dan Morgan, whose race-winning horse is disqualified when it's found that it was "hopped up," courtesy of the surreptitious maneuvering of rival Ernest Hilliard. He's soon reinstated and, with the assistance of impoverished stable owner Barbara Worth and her kid brother George Ernest, nurses lame horse Color Sergeant back to health. Color Sergeant loses another big race to Hilliard's horse Carnation, but is declared the winner when Carnation is proven not to be Carnation, but rather a ringer.

It's established early on that Hilliard is the bad guy: not only does he have Boyd's horse doped to have it disqualified, but he also demands that his lame horse be shot so he doesn't have to waste money on food for it. Later on, Hilliard has Color Sergeant's stable set on fire, but only manages to kill another horse in doing so. And if that wasn't enough, he's responsible for the death of stable worker Ben Hall, who had tried to stab Hilliard after having his hunchback rubbed for good luck, and for the umpteenth time. Screenwriters Jack O'Donnell and George Sayre weren't particularly subtle in driving home this point, even throwing in Hilliard's thoroughly unlikable companion, Esther Muir, just to annoy the males in the viewing audience.

William Boyd—not to be confused with William "Stage" Boyd—gives a relaxed performance, which isn't surprising since he had already starred in dozens of films since the late teens, and was on the verge of popularizing his "Hopalong Cassidy" character in films such as *Hopalong Cassidy* and *The Eagle's Brood*, both released shortly before *Racing Luck*. Barbara Worth, who plays Boyd's love interest in the film, was also a silent film veteran, here given far more to do than her counterparts in those numerous Westerns. *Racing Luck* would prove to be her last starring role, retiring from the business and eventually marrying producer Maurice Conn, Sig's former partner. As Worth's little brother, George Ernest is surprisingly good, less annoying than so many of his acting-challenged peers and giving a reasonably natural performance.

Sam must have felt right at home directing this yarn, set as it is at the race track and stables, the type of location he was intimately familiar with as a result of his obsessive gambling; *Film Daily*'s reviewer observed that the "plot carries a lot of inside dope on the tricks of the turf."[21] There's lots of location footage filmed at the tracks and stables intercut with the stock, and this enhances the film's visuals in a significant way. The scene where the stable has been torched is effectively handled, and rather emotional given the lives of the horses, pet dog, and kid brother Ernest involved. "Director Sam Newfield paces his direction toward an exciting climax," wrote *Motion Picture Herald*, and gave a well-deserved "thumbs up" to cinematographer Edgar Lyons.[22] Given a boost by better production values—presumably due to Winchester's association with Republic—the result has a slicker look than the norm. Sam managed to bring the film in only $290 over its $11,000 budget.

Bill Boyd and Barbara Worth in producer George Hirliman's **Racing Luck** (Winchester/Republic, 1935), Sam Newfield director.

Sandwiched in between *Racing Luck* and *Go-Get-'Em, Haines* were *Burning Gold* (December 16, 1935) and *Federal Agent* (April 10, 1936). Reviewers were underwhelmed and bemoaned the depths to which Boyd had temporarily fallen, adding that these films would probably do okay since he was now back in favor due to his Hopalong Cassidy offerings. *Film Daily* deemed *Burning Gold* a "Mildly satisfying action programmer of oil fields," adding that "Conventional elements of action melodrama are put to work again to make this one, resulting in only fair entertainment," and judging Sam's direction as merely "Adequate."[23] *Variety* was more succinct, calling it a "frail yarn" and calling the photography—no cameraman was acknowledged in the credits—and Sam's direction "ordinary."[24] *Motion Picture Herald* gave the series its most scathing review when writing of *Federal Agent*: "Republic would do well to eliminate the Winchester productions from its program as they do not compare favorably with the pictures made by the home studio." And while mentioning that this particular film was a "slight improvement over his previous films for this company," said that "Boyd's fans of the old days were disappointed in his latest appearance, and they are becoming fewer with each new picture."[25]

Letita Lane has Bill Boyd at a slight disadvantage in **Federal Agent** (Winchester/Republic, 1936), Sam Newfield director.

Go-Get-'Em, Haines (June 15, 1936), the first of the four to go into production in January 1935, ended up being the last to be released in June 1936, nearly a year-and-a-half later. The film was shot entirely on a round-trip voyage between Los Angeles and Panama, making the seven-day trip to on Panama Pacific's liner *Virginia*, returning after a few days' rest in Panama on the liner *California*. The company of twenty-eight—which included the stars Bill Boyd, Sheila Terry, and Eleanor Hunt—would use the liner's public rooms and exteriors during the early morning hours before most of the passengers had risen.[26] Nighttime scenes were shot on the return voyage between San Diego and Los Angeles, a dining room scene shot at midnight in the Gulf of California; half of the first-class passengers volunteered to take part in evening dress as extras to help fill the seats.[27] Sam's cinematographer was Edgar Lyons, who got his start in the early 1920s filming Westerns and dramas.

Boyd plays fast-talking reporter Steve Haines, assigned to get a story from Lee Shumway, a utilities magnate whose company's crash has ruined thousands of investors. Boyd follows Shumway, now attempting to escape by sea, disguised and with an assumed identity. Stuck on board, Boyd makes the best of it, flirting with fellow passenger Sheila Terry, daughter of fading stage actor Clarence Geldert. During a staged show hastily thrown together to entertain the ship's passengers, Shumway is shot dead, prompting Boyd to start his own investigation. He's later informed by his paper's editor, Ernest Hilliard, that the real utilities magnate has been found dead, and that the fellow murdered on board was actually magnate Shumway's twin brother. The twin brother's murder is finally resolved when Boyd tricks Lloyd Ingraham, the ship's captain, into a confession—his life savings were wiped out by Shumway's chicanery—moments before he expires from a healthy dose of his own poison.

Boyd looks like he's having fun in this serio-comic role, delivering a breezy performance and verbally sparring with pretty Sheila Terry. Jimmy Aubrey appears in this film's cut-rate version of an "Arthur Housman" drunk, a role well suited for him. Eleanor Hunt, who plays one of the film's many suspects, seems to be enjoying herself in her bits for the ship's performance of "Her Father's Revenge," delivering a syrupy little ditty titled "Oh Willie Come Back" (or something like that) and giving a hammy performance in the melodramatic play leading up to the twin's death. The show itself is somewhat of a time-killing, footage-filling diversion, but entertaining enough in its own right, and played for laughs.

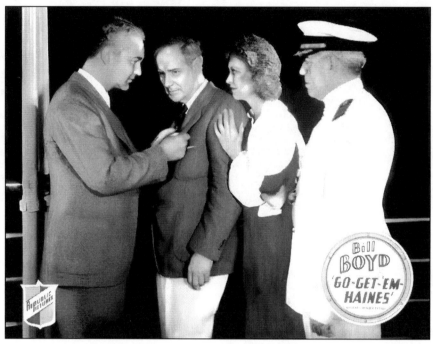

Hot-shot reporter Bill Boyd in **Go-Get-'Em, Haines** (Winchester/Republic, 1936), Sam Newfield director. *Courtesy of Heritage Auctions.*

The film's biggest asset is Sam's direction in concert with Lyons's cinematography. It's a handsome production, benefiting fully from—and making the most of—its on-board location filming. Interiors are nicely lit, and nighttime exteriors lit and shot at night—no day-for-night stuff here. George Sayre's screenplay, while adequate, is typical mystery film fare, even concluding with the obligatory gathering of the suspects in a stateroom while Haines delivers his suspicions, findings, and ferrets out the killer ("Its run-of-crop story will get by with average mystery fans," wrote *Film Daily*).[28] Terry, by the way, looks great in a bathing suit in a scene set by the pool; I wish I could say the same for Boyd and his noticeable girth. Hunt too, for that matter. Not to worry, though; Terry ends up in Boyd's arms in the film's final fadeout.

Producer Hirliman, I might add, fell head over heels for Hunt during the production and, I guess, she for him. Both divorced their respective spouses—her second—in Chihuahua in June 1935, the two marrying a few days later that same month. Cutting his losses with the Winchester offerings and Republic almost as soon as they were announced, Hirliman unveiled his new corporation, Regal Productions, Inc., in September, and his plans to produce eight features in color—it would be dubbed Hirlicolor—for "major company" (Grand National) distribution.[29]

Booth Dominion Productions

Sam's second journey beyond the U.S. borders took place less than a half year after his trip down to Panama, this time up to Canada where he was to direct two films for the newly formed Booth Dominion Productions, Ltd. This was the baby of J.R. (John Rudolphus) Booth, Jr., grandson of the staggeringly wealthy lumber magnate J.R. Booth, the "Grand Old Man of Canada." The elder Booth had passed away back in 1925, leaving an estate of $200,000,000 (some sources say $250,000,000, but a whole lot of money either way). Junior had inherited $12,000,000 outright, with even more to come in the years to follow.[30] By now a well-known sportsman and inventor, Booth was president of several Canadian enterprises as well as part owner of the Film Laboratories of Canada, Ltd., and Audio Picture Corporation. Booth, with his long-standing interest in the technical aspects of film, put together his production company with plans to make twelve features to comply with the British film quota law—the Cinematograph Films Act of 1927—which was created to stimulate the British film industry by requiring British cinemas to show 7.5 % of British Empire-made films, recently upped to 20 % in 1935.[31] Arthur Gottlieb and Jack Goetz, both of New York's Du-Art Film Lab, were partners in this new venture, Goetz as vice-president and Gottlieb as secretary and treasurer; Gottlieb served as the U.S. representative for the studio and its films as well.[32] Booth would make his headquarters at the Du-Art Lab.[33] Initial plans were to create a studio in Ottawa, Booth attempting to entice the members of the civic Board of Control with estimates of $65,000 in local expenditures generated by a first production as part of his pitch to lease the city's Horticultural Hall, which had been used a decade earlier in a similar capacity.[34] Other sites in Ottawa were considered as well, including the Coliseum at Lansdowne Park and use of the rink of the Minto Skating Club, but Booth soon settled—with regrets, he said—on Toronto and its now defunct Ravina Rink Building and pool, rebuilt for the company's purposes.[35]

Original predictions of twelve productions were soon halved, each to be an estimated six-reel, 5,300 to 6,000 feet in length. An arrangement with M-G-M gave that company distribution rights to the films in England and the Dominions—Canada, Australia, New Zealand, Ireland, South Africa, and New Zealand—and would pay Booth Dominion the entire negative cost upon delivery of each finished film,[36] while Booth Dominion Productions would retain the distribution rights for the U.S. and the rest of the world. Burt Kelly, formerly the "K" in KBS Productions, was brought on to handle the productions.[37] Hoping to get some Hollywood know-how behind their initial two productions, Sam was hired to direct, and some other experienced technicians were brought up to assist as well, cinematographer Sam Leavitt—billed as Sam Levitt—the most prominent of these. The first two productions would benefit from name recognition of their two leads, actor Charles Starrett for *Undercover Men*, and actress Toby Wing, borrowed from Paramount, for *The King's Plate*.

Sam arrived in Toronto in the first week of August, production on *The King's Plate* starting on August 12.[38] Sam's oft-used villain Wheeler Oakman was brought up for support and to essay a similar type role, along with Kenneth Duncan. Duncan, formerly with Paramount, had been reduced to appearing in industrial and non-theatrical shorts made by Associated Screen Studios, so he was probably thrilled to once again be part of a bigger production. Production for this race track-set story was to be completed in eight weeks,[39] with a budget of $50,000 and exteriors to be shot on location at the Woodbine track in Etobicoke, Ontario during the fall meet.[40]

96   Poverty Row Royalty

Down on his luck Kenneth Duncan (aka Ken Duncan, aka Kenne Duncan) is a hopeless gambler, up to his neck in debt and now fired from his newspaper job. He loses everything during yet another crap game, emerging with his sole winning, a race horse named Special Delivery. With the aid of his girl, Toby Wing, and her lunch stand-owning father Elliott Lorraine—both of them racing savvy—Duncan's horse proves to be lightning on four hoofs. Enter slimy Wheeler Oakman, who bribes jockeys to lose races so that his bets win big, Lorraine his reluctant go-between under the threat of having his dishonest past revealed. Special Delivery delivers, now entered in the famous "King's Plate" race at Woodbine, and the favorite to win. Oakman gets to Duncan via Lorraine, who agrees to throw the race for the sake of Wing and her father. Lorraine's last-minute change of heart allows Special Delivery to win, Oakman to be banned from race tracks forever, and the expected happy ending.

Star Toby Wing is prominent of this lobby card for **Thoroughbred** (Booth Dominion, 1936; aka **The King's Plate**). Sam Newfield directed in Canada for producers J.R. Booth and Burt Kelly.

This is a decent little film, retitled *Thoroughbred* for U.S. release since no one south of the Canadian border would have a clue what the King's Plate was or meant; it's Canada's oldest thoroughbred race since 1860, and the first race in the Canadian Triple Crown. Duncan tries hard in the lead as the smart alecky, devil-may-care former reporter, comfortable in the several gambling scenes rattling off the appropriate jargon with a knowing ease, but in general delivering an uneven performance, at times breezy, and at others awkward. Toby Wing, the poor man's Jean Harlow, is the real star of this film, giving a likably sassy performance as the wise cracking lunch wagon waitress who knows her way around race tracks and horses. Wheeler Oakman, in films from 1912 and the hardest working actor in Hollywood, excelled in this type of underhanded role, a good choice for his character. Young Romeo Gaskins, who plays Duncan's helper and pressed-into-service jockey, does his best in his sizable role, but his best wasn't quite best enough. Sam's direction was for the most part workmanlike, but displayed some creativity for the second horse race: Instead of relying on a mix of stock and newly shot racing footage, he instead cut back and forth between the race announcer in his booth and Wing and Lorraine in closeup on either side of a radio, listening to the race. Promotional materials touted Sam as "one of Hollywood's best-known directors," a bit of a stretch but a nice nod in his direction. *Philadelphia Exhibitor* gave it a lukewarm review, summing it up as "For nabes, twin bills."[41]

Undercover Men had much the same cast and crew, the second production starting immediately after the first's completion. While the stars Charles Starrett and Adrienne Dore were new to this film, Oakman and Duncan were back once again, as were the Canadian players Eric Clavering and Elliott Lorraine. Cinematographer Sam Leavitt, editor Alex Myers, and recording engineer Harry Bellock were back as well, with Sam once again assisted by John Chisholm. Sam was on familiar territory, revisiting a plot revolving around the Royal Canadian Mounted Police as he did back with Ambassador's Kermit Maynard films.

Branded a coward and fired when he fails to defend his bank against a notorious—and murderous—gang of robbers, Charles Starrett decides to join the Mounties and track down the gang lead by nominal boss Eric Clavering. When his good friend and fellow Mountie Philip Brandon is gunned down, Starrett is hopping mad, locates their hideout, takes gang member Wilbur Freeman prisoner, and forces him (with a red-hot poker!) to reveal a daring armored car robbery about to take place. Calling in reinforcements that include his boss, Wheeler Oakman's inspector and Austin Moran's sergeant, the robbery is foiled. Starrett somehow puts two and two together and comes up with the identity of the gang's big boss: It's Kenneth Duncan, the rich snob son of the bank's president, Farnham Barter, and the guy who's been sniffing around Starrett's girl, Adrienne Dore.

This is one of Sam's lesser works, and fault can be laid at the doorstep of its writer, Murison Dunn, a scribe for Canadian radio shows enlisted for this film, then promptly sent back to radio. Part of the script's weakness is that it frequently makes iron jawed Starrett look like a dolt. Sure, he's quick with his fists and somehow figures out things that others haven't, but as a Mountie he comes across as borderline incompetent. While in the midst of a conversation with friend Brandon, the latter is suddenly shot dead from afar before Starrett's eyes. Instead of jumping into action, however, he just sits there staring at Brandon's dead body, stumped by what has just happened, and looking about as ineffectual as imaginable—but perhaps the blame should be put on the director. At another point, Starrett—apparently ousted from the Mounties for another round of cowardice—goes to work at the hardware store of Elliott Lorraine, Dore's dad. Within five minutes of being hired and left alone to keep an eye on the place, what does he do? He wraps a package and heads out to deliver it, leaving the store unattended. The film's plusses—and there are a few of them—stem from Sam's direction, unimaginative for the most part but with the occasional visual flourish. Leavitt's camera does a nice, lengthy tracking shot through the hardware store following Starrett and his new boss from one end to the other; nothing particularly special but it stands out in the midst of mostly static shots. The visual high point, however, takes place when the heretofore unseen and unidentified boss of the gang visits the hideout and confronts Clavering. It's a long, tracking shot taken from the boss's point of view, approaching and entering the hideout, then faced directly by Clavering who holds a conversation with him, with only the occasional glimpse of the boss's hand as he grabs a drink, and wisps of smoke from his unseen cigarette. It doesn't hurt that the producers had the co-operation of the Royal Canadian Mounted Police, much of the action shot at their barracks and training grounds.

Cast and crew for producer J.R. Booth's **Undercover Men** (Booth Dominion, 1936). Back row: Director Sam Newfield and Adrienne Dore second and third from left, Kenne Duncan with black shirt and white tie, Wheeler Oakman far right. Front row: Charles Starrett second from left, Eric Clavering, Phil Brandon. *Courtesy of Mark Heller.*

As it turned out, there was another Canadian-based "Booth" production company—Booth Canadian Films, Ltd.—that had been active since 1929, and they were none too happy about the confusion created by J.R.'s new company. Things came to a head in early 1936, and Booth Dominion was forced to change its name to Dominion Motion Pictures, Ltd.[42] As for J.R. Booth, the two films that Sam directed for him would turn out to be the sole output for his production company. Booth's future was cut short five years later when he died of a heart attack at the comparatively young age of forty-seven, on his way back to Ottawa after attending the World Series games.[43]

Colony Pictures

Max and Arthur Alexander's Colony Pictures was another occasional stop along Sam's seemingly nomadic journey from one independent production company to the next, directing a mere three films for them over a four-year period. Max, as you'll recall, was Julius and Abe Stern's nephew, the son of their sister Frieda and a mere fifteen years old when he emigrated from Germany to join the Sterns in Hollywood. When the Sterns closed shop in early 1929, they had Phil Goldstone's National Film Recording Company install Biophone sound recording equipment at their 6040-6048 Sunset Boulevard studio on its largest stage, and rebranded it as the National Film Recording Studios.[44]

Max and his younger brother Arthur were put in charge of the new installation, the building's ownership now transferred to them. By June, producer Trem Carr was leasing space at the studio and filmed his first all-talking film, *Handcuffed*, at the facility.[45] By 1933 Carr had merged with Rayart Productions, the combined venture now known as Monogram Pictures, and by mid-1933 Monogram had relocated from 6048 Sunset to the Metropolitan Studios. The Alexanders were now able to offer additional space to outside independent companies, "and will give them every help and attention necessary to make their pictures at a more reasonable price than in the past."[46]

By 1934, the brothers had gone into production themselves via their newly created Beacon Productions, their first film a drama titled *I Can't Escape*, based on the Jerry Sackheim/Nathan Asch story "Decent;"[47] it was released on the state rights market. The studio was beefed up when the Cineglow Sound System created a theatre to be used for dubbing by independent producers.[48] The Western *Thunder Over Texas* followed on its heels, which *Hollywood Filmograph* praised, singling out cinematographer Harry Forbes's camerawork, and concluded with "Max Alexander has produced a come-on for more of this brand."[49] Half a dozen other films followed through 1935, but by 1936 Beacon had folded.

The Alexanders regrouped, and created what was called Normandy Pictures Corporation, signing cowboy star Rex Bell to a six-picture contract, with another six action melodramas in the pipeline as well for the upcoming 1936-37 season.[50] Normandy didn't last long, or at least under that name: the announced features were all produced and released as Colony Pictures. Colony operated out of 6044 Sunset, a smaller portion of their block-long complex bracketed by the corners of Beachwood Drive—number 6048—and Gordon Street—number 6040. Max and Arthur were Colony's chief executive and—curiously—assistant, respectively. Alfred Stern, son of Julius and Abe Stern's oldest brother Joseph, became Colony's general manager, and Charles Henkel the film editor.[51] Colony's first two films were released on the state rights basis, but the remaining four would be distributed by Grand National.

Sam was hired to direct Colony's initial offering, the Western *Stormy Trails*, adapted by former silent film comedian and current character actor Phil Dunham from the story "Stampede" by E.B. Mann. Corrupt land developer Stanton (actor unidentified) has been selling plots of land with the promise of water soon to come. The hitch is that the water is located on cattleman Rex Bell's land, which Stanton intends to gain possession of by causing Bell to default on a loan, thereby forcing a land auction. Stanton has henchman Karl Hackett do his dirty work, which leads to several deaths, Bell's brother Bob Terry among them, along with the stampeding of Bell's thousand head of cattle so that he can't sell them. Thinking that Hackett has killed Bell, Stanton forces the auction, but it is soon revealed that the money he's planning to buy it with was all stolen from the town's bank. Hackett turns on Stanton and kills him, but is overcome by Bell before he can escape and turned over to the sheriff and his posse.

This is an innocuous little film, boosted by wavy-haired Bell's earnest performance and Hackett's dependable menace as the film's sharpshooting killer. Sam makes the most of his meagre budget, sticking to the great outdoors whenever possible, returning to the spartan interiors only as need be; the poorly painted "exterior" views seen through open doors and windows a visual slap to the face whenever they come into view. Grainy stampede footage—and the stampedes in these B-Westerns are *always* grainy old stock footage—stand out like a sore thumb when intercut with Robert Cline's crisper, if unimaginative, camerawork. All in all, a modest, unassuming little Western. Bell's horse Sheik, by the way, looks like it has a severe case of freckles. Lois Wilde plays Bell's love interest, and as usual ends up in his arms, or as close to "in his arms" as these films usually get, not wishing to alienate the wee ones. Lloyd Ingraham pops in and out as her dad, with Earl Dwire delivering a solid, believable performance as Bell's lawyer. *Film Daily* liked it, saying that "this one packs its share of flying hoofs, barking guns, intrigue, danger and romance, with Rex Bell providing the heroics in generally exciting scenes."[52] *Variety* was a bit more downbeat in their review, singling out that grainy stampede stock footage: "What the producers had probably intended to make their big punch in the film, the stampede of a herd of cattle, turns out a sad botch."[53]

Rex Bell, held at gunpoint in **Stormy Trails** (Colony, 1936), Max and Arthur Alexander producers, Sam Newfield director.

It would be another three years before Sam would return to direct another Western for the Alexanders. In the meantime, Colony had signed a contract with popular Western star Hoot Gibson on August 14, 1936, to appear in six to eight pictures the following year. Gibson, who had been making Westerns since 1910 and now found himself taking a back seat to a much newer—and *younger*—crop of cowboy stars, backed out of this agreement for unknown reasons. The Alexanders, understandably annoyed, had a $32,000 breach of contract suit filed against him, anticipating a $4,000 loss of profit on the eight films that were not to be.[54]

Grand National, which had been distributing the Colony Westerns as well as some entries in "The Shadow" series starring Rod LaRocque and the "Flash Casey" series starring Eric Linden, was in desperate trouble by early 1938. Jimmy Cagney, GN's Great White Hope signed back in 1936 during one of his contractual disputes with

Warners, had by now secured a release from his contract. GN declared bankruptcy and filed a petition for reorganization under 77-B of the Bankruptcy Act. As part of this proposal, an optimistic twenty-six features were planned for the following twelve months. Federal Judge William P. James approved a contract that called for the distribution of Colony's *The Shadow Murder Case*,[55] which was in the can and ready to go, along with two Ken Maynard Westerns—*Whirlwind Horseman* and *Six-Shootin' Sheriff*—to be filmed over the next two months.[56] There was talk of a merger with E.W. Hammon's Educational Pictures to create a new company—New Grand National was one unimaginative name that was bandied about—but it fell through[57] and Edward L. Alperson, GN's head, was unsuccessful in obtaining new financing for the company. Alperson resigned in February 1939, the company going belly up soon after.

The Alexanders had bolted from Grand National during this period of turmoil after their few commitments were met. They terminated Colony and created Road Show Pictures, to feature musical star Gene Austin in a series of "outdoor romantic musicals" which would be toured through the South and Southwest. As an added enticement, Austin, along with his accompanists Candy and Coco, would make a personal appearance at each showing. *Songs and Saddles* was the first—and as it turned out, the last—of these.[58] With that behind them, Colony Pictures was resurrected, but with a change in its leadership: Herman and Alfred Stern were now president and secretary, respectively, with Max now listed as producer and Arthur as general manager.[59] Given this new hierarchy, it's likely the Sterns now had some money in the game.

The Alexanders approached Ken Maynard and got him to sign a six-picture contract, half of their twelve-picture program planned for the upcoming 1939-40 season. The remaining six would all be contemporary dramas, to be released on the state rights market.[60] Maynard only ended up making four of those Westerns for Colony, the first two directed by Sam, and the final two by Harry Fraser.

The first of these—*Flaming Lead*—started production on a four-day shoot on March 27, 1939, on location up in Newhall, California.[61] At the request of heavy-drinking Dave O'Brien, the cowardly, long-distance half-owner of a

Ken Maynard looking tough in producer Max and Arthur Alexander's **Flaming Lead** (Colony, 1939), Sam Newfield director.
Courtesy of Heritage Auctions.

ranch with Eleanor Stewart, out-of-work Ken Maynard impersonates O'Brien to help Stewart figure out who's been rustling their horses. Saloon owner Walter Long is conspiring with Army agent Tom London to steal the ranch's horses, to fulfill an Army contract, thereby grabbing the $150,000 that would otherwise go to Stewart. Working with ranch hand Ralph Peters, who gets killed for his efforts, Maynard finally figures that Stewart's foreman, Reed Howes, is in cahoots with London as well. The film culminates in a big slugfest with Maynard and O'Brien on one side, and Howes and London on the other, the former shot dead, and the latter turned over to the sheriff.

This is another routine Western, relying primarily on Maynard's fading charm to pull it off. Stewart is fine as the female member of the cast, giving a feisty performance as the so-called "female cyclone." O'Brien provides the film's comic relief—or should I say *forced* comic relief—as the film's spineless drunkard, a rather stereotypical film drunk at that. Howes makes a good heavy in his role as the duplicitous foreman, a highlight of sorts his rather spirited fistfight with Maynard. As for Maynard—who was a better actor than his younger brother—he was by the late 1930s a mere shadow of his former physical self, semi-bloated like a latter day, gone-to-seed Elvis. He's not as graceful as in earlier films, and the film's opener, where he performs some shooting and lassoing for a nightclub's patrons' entertainment, displays movements that look rather labored and clumsy. As for that slicked-back hair, the guy must have owned stock in Brylcreem.

The film itself is a visual hodge-podge, Art Reed's unimaginative cinematography frequently intercut with scads of stock footage, some of it seamlessly so, and at other times so dark and dupey that it's nearly impossible to make out what's going on. The producers didn't need to shell out any money for stunt men, either, since every fall from a horse is footage obviously cut in from some earlier film as well. As usual, Sam's direction rises to the occasion for the film's numerous shootouts, fistfights, and hoof-pounding horseback chases. The canned music over the opening credits, which continues over the first scene, is obtrusive, and launches into another dialog-muffling piece for the second scene. After that—mercifully—the lid was closed on the can. *Showmen's Trade Review* summed it up nicely: "So long as there's action and gunplay, it matters little to Western fans whether their favorite type of entertainment is good or bad."[62]

The Society of Motion Picture Film Editors (SMPFE) was formed in 1937 to protect its members from the unfair—and rampant—labor practices of the film studios, the majors, mini-majors, and independents alike. Of the latter, editors completed a push that by 1939 gave them virtually a closed shop in the indie field. The society's contract with the indies called for the following: a minimum of $100 weekly for the editors of features, and $75 for serials and shorts; along with $1.10 per hour for assistant cutters and 50 cents per hour for apprentices, with both guaranteed forty hours per week. Editors who accept pay that didn't adhere to these guidelines would face suspension from the society. The list of independents who signed with the SMPFE was lengthy, the Alexanders' Colony Pictures among them.[63]

Charles V. Henkel was a respected editor who had worked primarily for the indies from the late 1920s, and on Sam's first for Colony, *Stormy Trails*. Three years later, and after being suspended by the SMPFE, Henkel would file a $126,900 suit in Superior Court against the SMPFE, asserting that the suspension was illegal.

> Henkel's complaint alleges that his suspension is all part of a scheme on part of major producers to monopolize production and exhibition in California by forcing independents out of business. He asserts his suspension followed his refusal to testify to alleged fake criminal charges to be brought against Colony Pictures Corp., independent outfit.

Complaint states that Henkel was promised a steady editing job on a major lot if testimony was forthcoming, but if he refused, his membership would be taken away.

By-laws were violated, Henkel claims, when SMPFE suspended him on the asserted fake charge that he had accepted less than the minimum pay for editing a picture for Colony.[64]

The SMPFE must not have thought that Henkel had the cojones to make a stink, because they quickly agreed to reinstate him if he dropped the suit. Which he did.[65]

Sam followed up *Flaming Lead* with *Death Rides the Range*, a dull, credulity-stretching entry saved—as usual—by several satisfying action sequences, some strained humor courtesy of Maynard's "pals" Panhandle and Pancho, played by Ralph Peters—resurrected from the previous film's dead—and Julian Rivero, respectively. The film barely gets started when the story is brought to a grinding halt by the insertion of a time-padding, wholly inconsequential song—"Get Along Little Pal"—courtesy of Kenneth Rhodes as Slim, perched outside a trading post, and the film's intermittent canned score is just as lousy as before. There's less stock footage this time around, but there's one jarring insert—no doubt employed to save paying a stunt double—where white-shirted Maynard is about to be thrown from his horse, and the stock insert has a guy in a black shirt thrown and tumbling down a hill. The story itself has Maynard working to save the ranch of Fay McKenzie and her brother Julian Madison from the greedy hands of neighboring rancher Charlie King. King has promised to supply foreign agent Sven Hugo Borg and whatever unnamed country he hails from with helium, inconveniently located in a cave on the McKenzie property. The film ends with Maynard whupping King in yet-another slugfest, Borg arrested, and our hero revealed as an undercover FBI agent. That, and McKenzie agrees to marry him!

Maynard looks like he may have dropped a few pounds, that or saw the previous film's dailies and decided to suck in his stomach for this one. As the hero of the piece, he keeps having plot-advancing "hunches" that suggest a certain level of laziness on the part of screen writer Bill Lively. Charlie King revisits his stock villain role, but looks mighty convincing in his climactic fistfight with Maynard. John Elliott is an annoying delight as McKenzie's grouchy old uncle Hiram Crabtree, and for once we are actually happy to see our hero evict an old man with a game leg from his carriage and force him to walk. As the other villains of the piece, Borg, Michael Vallon, and William Castello pose as archeologists and probably wouldn't fool a first grader as such. Uncredited Richard Alexander is a convincing standout as Big Nick Harden, described as "one tough hombre" who terrorizes a saloon's inhabitants, gets in a fistfight with Maynard, and loses. Maynard's horse Tarzan—unlike in the previous film—gets to strut his stuff at several points, rescuing Maynard's hat and, amazingly enough, later unties the ropes that Maynard is tied up with (let's see Lassie do that!).

Fay McKenzie was the daughter of hard-working character actors Robert McKenzie and his wife Eva McKenzie, old-timers with hundreds of credits to their names since entering the business back in 1915. She spoke with interviewer Mike Fitzgerald about the film, and singled out Sam for some sincere praise:

That was a thriller—Ken Maynard and the director, Sam Newfield, were both so nice to me. Sometimes, if you work with big stars, like Ken Maynard, you could be overwhelmed, but Ken seemed to me to be a little long in the tooth at the time. (Laughs) Maybe I shouldn't say that. It's a wonderful thing to tell you, but amazingly, I have no ill will—I was very, very protected—and everybody knew my parents, so no one hit on me. They were told "She's the McKenzies' daughter—Watch it!" (Laughs) The director, Sam Newfield, was a friend of the family—he was good with comedy; an excellent director.[66]

Despite the fact that Sam had a lengthy working relationship with the Alexanders back with the Sterns through the better part of the 1920s, it's surprising that he wasn't hired to direct more of their films. They would be reunited several years later, however, when Sam would direct a trio of films for their newly named Alexander-Stern Productions.

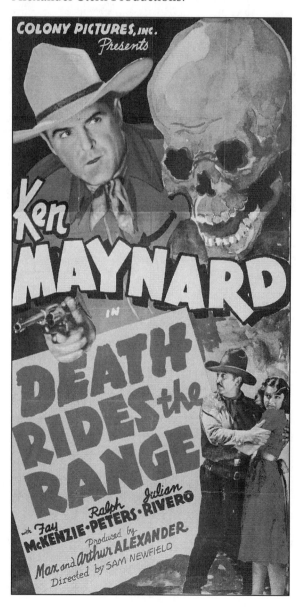

Ken Maynard in producer Max and Arthur Alexander's Death **Rides the Range** (Colony, 1940), Sam Newfield director. *Courtesy of Heritage Auctions.*

Chapter 8:
Sam, Sans Sig (Part 2: 1936-1940)

Sam bounced around between so many studios during the 1932-1940 period that an attempt to describe them in any sort of strict chronological order is impossible. The final years of the 1930s are significant in that Sig disappeared from the trades and active, credited production, leaving Sam to fully fend for himself. Which he did, and without a hitch, since his capabilities were by now well known throughout the independent production segment of the industry, and a next job always waiting for him.

Sig's absence remains somewhat of a mystery, or at least to his surviving descendants. Family lore places Sig at a bigger studio sometime during the 1937-1939 period, but for which one and for how long is unclear. Tim Neufeld seems to recall that Sig went with Columbia for a short while,[1] which wouldn't be a total surprise since Columbia was one of the so-called mini-majors—Universal was another—and they produced the bulk of their films on the cheap. Also, Sig had worked with Jack Cohn—one of Columbia's co-founders—way back at the start of his film career at IMP. *Variety* had a short piece in August 1936 stating that Sig had joined Columbia as an associate producer, but that's the sole mention found to date asserting as such.[2]

Sig Jr. thinks it was at M-G-M, a very short stint resulting from Sig's realization that he was totally out of his element at M-G-M, a whole different world than the Poverty Row studios where he felt at home. Sig Jr. elaborated on his recollection of this period:

> I know he had a relationship with the head of Columbia for a time.... He was trying to put some deals together; I know he didn't have anything going for a while.... He was trying to put together some deals and it took a while, but he finally did. He wasn't inactive, he just didn't have anything going.... M-G-M, if that was true—I think it probably was—they hired him over there to make their B movies, and after three days he didn't like it at all, and he quit. I think it's probably true.[3]

"He left because of the way they did business," added Tim.

Another hint as to what he was up to during this period was found in his possessions, passed on to his son. Contained therein were four tins of 16mm footage, two of which contained home movies, the third an amateur mini-film titled *The Curse*, made by Sig Jr. when he was a teenager. The fourth tin contains a short, single-reel professional film. Titled *Carnival Show*, this was a short produced by Milton Schwarzwald's Nu-Atlas Musicals for release through RKO on July 24, 1938. It's a compact musical revue set at a carnival, starring Clyde Hager as the carnival's barker, opera singer Jan Peerce as a frankfurter salesman, the dancers The Three DeLovelies, and a group of Black musicians called the Cotton Club Tramp Band. Schwarzwald produced these short, ten-minute musicals for several years, and while the film itself carries no credits, its copyright entry credits Schwarzwald as director. Given that there's no other obvious reason why Sig would have saved a copy of this particular film all those years, it would suggest that he had a part in its production and, possibly, some of the other Nu-Atlas productions as well. Pure speculation, of course, but a viable possibility. Whatever the case, Sig's whereabouts during this nearly three-year period warrants further research.

Sam was on his own during this period—on his own, but kept extremely busy. He began an on-again, off-again relationship with fledgling producer Jed Buell in early 1937. Buell (1897-1961), by this time involved in the industry in varying capacities for a number of years, reportedly got his start as a business manager and/or treasurer of several theatres back in his hometown of Denver, Colorado. Buell eventually headed out to California, where he managed Los Angeles's Westlake Theatre in the late 1920s, building it up to be Southern California's premiere preview house. From there he joined the Laemmle mini-chain until those theatres were sold to Fox, after which he switched gears and went into scenario writing, if only briefly and sporadically; Sono-Art's *Reno* (1930) was based on a Buell original. By 1930 he had landed himself a more secure position as chief of publicity at the Mack Sennett Studios,[4] or at least until Sennett closed shop, after which he became a free-lance publicist.

Producer Jed Buell (standing) signs a trio of little people to star in his upcoming **The Terror of Tiny Town** (Principal/Columbia, 1938). Little Billy Rhodes with pen, Johnny Winters center, and an actress identified solely as "Lady Little." Sam Newfield directed.

By mid-1934, Buell had made the decision to move into production with the formation of Rainbow Pictures. Rainbow was set up to make feature-length comedies, with the stars Andy Clyde and Harry Langdon touted as headliners. A first, tentatively titled *College Sweetheart*, was to star Clyde, with support from Grady Sutton and Mary Kornmann, followed by a second Clyde comedy, this time teamed with Langdon. Sounded promising, but nothing came of it.[5] By mid-1935, Buell was working as publicity manager for the startup Capital Pictures and its pie-in-the-sky plans to film eight "highway patrol action pictures," the first of which—*Double Spots*—was to be directed by Fred Newmeyer, but this fell apart as well.[6]

By 1936, Buell had hooked up with George H. Callaghan to organize a production company they named De Luxe Pictures, Inc. Two series of singing westerns were planned—although only one would come to fruition—to be filmed at the Talisman Studios.[7] Callaghan, as president would be in charge of distribution, while Buell, the company's secretary-treasurer, was in charge of production.[8] Former concert singer Fred Scott (1902-1991), who had appeared in occasional bit parts in films for Warners, Pathé, and RKO over the previous ten years, was signed to a six-picture contract to headline the new series; Spectrum Pictures would handle distribution on a state rights basis. Scott's abilities as a warbler were the draw here, commented upon several years earlier in *Motion Picture* magazine: "Then there is young Fred Scott, whose studies have been with one Signor Alberti of Hollywood. Scott has already sung several leading parts in talkies and now has been engaged to sing opposite Jeritza in the opera 'Salome' in Los Angeles."[9] Clearly the guy had musical chops, but could he cut it as a rugged western hero? Buell and Callaghan thought so.

Romance Rides the Range (September 28, 1936), which went into production in August with Harry Fraser helming, was the first in the Scott series, released in September 1936. *Motion Picture Herald* was rather blasé about the series opener: "In attempting to emphasize the singing voice of the star, Fred Scott, this western suffers from slow tempo" and went on to say "it misses fire somehow with the resultant lack of suspense and rapid-fire action commonly associated with productions of this type."[10] Boyd Magers, who has probably seen more low-budget Westerns of this type than anyone else on the face of the planet, was underwhelmed by the film and its obvious budgetary limitations: "Inept beginning as Grand Opera singer Fred Scott goes west. Several out of focus shots and sound so primitive you can hear the cameras whirring."[11] *Romance Rides the Range* was followed by *The Roaming Cowboy* (January 4, 1937) and *The Singing Buckaroo* (January 15, 1937), directed by Robert Hill and Tom Gibson, respectively. The "De Luxe Pictures" name disappeared after the initial release, with subsequent releases advertised solely as Spectrum Pictures releases.

Sam was hired in late February or early March 1937 to direct the remaining three Scott oaters in the series, the first of which was tentatively announced as *Song of the Prairie* before attaining its April release title *Melody of the Plains* (April 15, 1937). Former silent comedian Al St. John was by now Scott's sidekick, having replaced Cliff Nazarro who took part in two of the earlier outings in a similar capacity. *Moonlight on the Range* (October 6, 1937) and *The Fighting Deputy* (December 5, 1937) were to follow. Bert Sternbach and Hans Weeren were both now part of the crew as well, brought in as production manager and sound engineer, respectively.

Fred Scott, shooting instead of singing, in **Melody of the Plains** (Spectrum, 1937). Jed Buell producer, Sam Newfield director. *Courtesy of Heritage Auctions.*

"Here is a Western that can be played anywhere that entertainment of this type goes and be well received," wrote *Hollywood Reporter* about *Melody of the Plains*. "It has everything that it takes to please."[12] *Film Daily* concurred, stating that "Jed Buell's production is well-staged and contains all the necessary ingredients to make a successful western."[13] Even Boyd Magers deemed it "One of Fred's better ones."[14] *Moonlight on the Range* received typically nuanced reviews, always incorporating such qualifying phrases as "wholesome entertainment to the screen from a small budget"[15] and "sure fire for the juvenile trade."[16]

One would hope that *The Fighting Deputy* is not representative of the series as a whole, but I guess that's wishful hoping. Musical Westerns and their singing cowboys were very popular during this era, but nothing brings a film's pacing to a screeching halt than the periodic interruption to show off Scott's talents as a warbler. I lost count of the musical interludes, but there were at least four of them, and if you were to remove them and the comedic sequences involving Al St. John and his girl Marjorie Beebe, you'd be left with about ten minutes of plot.

Scott and St. John play deputies to the sheriff, who is Scott's dad, played by Frank LaRue. A gang of robbers led by Charlie King—as Scar Adams—return to town, King revealed as the brother of Scott's girl, played by Phoebe Logan. King wounds Scott's dad, so Scott is urged, and agrees, to become the temporary sheriff. That King is the film's unredeemable bad guy is driven home when he kills Scott's dad, dumping his corpse at the doorstep of where Scott and Logan's wedding is taking place. And if that wasn't proof enough, King goes on to shoot his own father (Lafe McKee), who saves Scott by shooting and killing his son before expiring.

Not much of a plot, and despite Scott's admittedly fine singing voice, the dubbing of his songs is poorly executed. As for his acting abilities, he's reasonably good in the role, but as with so many other newly minted cowboy stars there's lots of room for improvement. As far as I can tell, Phoebe Logan was a one-shot wonder, possessing a pleasant smile and here primarily for window dressing, her misguided loyalties aside. King, as usual, makes a believably menacing villain, clearly having found his niche in an endless string of Westerns after his brief, and wholly acceptable, turn as a comedian in silent comedy shorts for the Sterns. St. John and Beebe are here primarily for pace-interrupting comic relief, although he is allowed some more serious moments when alone with Scott. Frank LaRue, Lafe McKee, and King all add a level of professionalism to the cast.

Sam's direction helps to keep this disjointed hodge-podge from falling apart, his excitingly filmed action sequences involving horseback chases and gunfights engaging as usual, culminating with the knock-down, drag-out fistfight between King and Scott. Not surprisingly, the film has its share of the usual shoestring-budgeted film head-scratchers. King sneaks into a darkened room through a window and lights a wall-mounted lantern, the room coming to immediate blinding life as a bank of lights are turned on out of camera range. Later, Scott and St. John track down King and his gang when they spot the smoke from their campfire, so how does Scott alert the posse? By lighting a fire and sending a smoke signal which, of course, King immediately spots. Go figure.

The comedic sequences involving St. John and Beebe, while interrupting the film's pacing, are hit or miss affairs. St. John samples one pie after another from the restaurant where Beebe is employed so that she can paint the day's fare on the business's window, his efforts brought to a halt when he identifies one as cinnamon. Neither can spell it, so it becomes apple. Later, an accidental bump turns into a tit-for-tat rock-throwing melee, more at home in a Laurel and Hardy comedy and clumsily executed here. There's another humorless bit, courtesy of Eddie Holden, here playing a heavily accented Swede whose loud, gulping swallows give his fiancée pause. Silly, but I guess they needed some filler. All in all, a harmless but unimpressive conclusion to the first Fred Scott series.

Fred Scott sticks his nose in the cook's business in **The Fighting Deputy** (Spectrum, 1937). Jed Buell producer, Sam Newfield director.

As the Fred Scott series for Spectrum wound down, Buell got involved in another fast-paced project for a Santa Barbara financier named Sabin W. Carr. Carr had just formed Metropolitan Pictures, Inc.—or so it was reported—with the intention of making six singing Western features starring, and targeted for, African Americans. These were to be roadshowed at the nearly 800 so-called "race theatres" across the country. Sam was hired to direct, Bert Sternbach signed on as associate producer, and Hans Weeren handled the sound. The first production, *Harlem on the Prairie* (December 9, 1937), was to star Herbert Jeffries, with comedic support by F.E. Miller and Mantan Moreland as "Crawfish" and "Mistletoe," respectively; Maceo B. Sheffield in the role of "Wolf Cain," the obligatory heavy; along with Spencer Williams, Jr. and Connie Harris.[17] There seemed to be some confusion about the name of Carr's production company, as the "Metropolitan" name was replaced (or corrected) to Lincoln Pictures, Inc., and was changed to Associated Features, Inc.[18] shortly thereafter.[19] The screenplay was banged out by a fellow named Fred Myton, who would soon become Sig's go-to guy for quick-turnaround scripts.[20]

Born Umberto Alexander Ballentino in Detroit, Michigan, Herbert Jeffries (1913-2014) was a popular singer with Les Hite's orchestra when he was hired for this, his first screen appearance. Like so many kids his age, Jeffries grew up watching the endless stream of cowboy flicks at his neighborhood cinema, and learned to ride horses at his grandfather's dairy farm in Northern Michigan. The son of an Irish mother and mixed-race father ("He was Italian, French Canadian and…Ethiopian," claimed Jeffries[21]), dark makeup was applied to his face to hide his otherwise light skin from filmgoers. The budget for this film precluded the hiring of stunt men, so Jeffries gamely did his own stunts, and apparently safely so.

F.E. Miller was known on Broadway for his all-Black musical revue, *Shuffle Along*, which had a two-year run. Mantan Moreland, now a familiar face to most fans of films of the classic era, had earned his comedic chops in vaudeville but was relatively new to film at this time, with appearances in only two shorts and an uncredited bit in *The Green Pastures* before being hired. Connie Harris, who starred as the film's feminine lead, was a singer and dancer plucked from the Paradise Club in Yuma. Maceo Sheffield, a well-known theatrical producer of African American shows, was hired to supervise as well as act.[22] Lew Porter, the composer of the current hits "Frijoles" and "Vagabond Dreams Come True," was hired to direct the music, a combination of several of his numbers and some other tunes, to be sung by the quartet The Four Tones.[23]

The plot involves a medicine show performer Doc Clayborn (Spencer Williams) and his daughter Carolina (Connie Harris) who return to a town where, years earlier, he was part of a gang involved in a gold robbery. He had hidden the stolen gold, but now, recognized by his former gang members, is mortally wounded. Before he dies, however, he reveals the location of the hidden loot to young hero Jeff Kincaid (Herb Jeffries), with instructions to return it to its rightful owners.

Herb Jeffries (right) in **Harlem On the Prairie** (Lincoln Pictures, 1937). Jed Buell producer, Sam Newfield director.

Reviewers were pleased with the results. *Film Daily* led with "Negro musical Western has some fine singing and fast action," and praised Jeffries's "fine voice which he uses to advantage." The reviewer singled out Sam stating that "Newfield does a good job with the material offered and limited production facilities."[24] *Motion Picture Daily* had some perceptive comments about the film:

Its principal difference—an idea that sets it apart from all other westerns and makes of it a feature that has considerable exploitation value—is that it is played by an all-Negro cast. Thus it can be advertised as "something different." It may be anticipated that houses which cater exclusively to Negroes should find it a banner attraction. Yet on its entertainment merits alone, it might prove a novel attraction in other theatres. The audience which saw its preview in the Meralta Theatre, Culver City, and in which youngsters predominated, did as much cheering as such audiences usually do in the case of regulation westerns.[25]

According to *Film Daily*, *Harlem on the Prairie* was to follow its engagement at Harlem's Apollo theatre with a February 1938 run at the Rialto, the first "all-Negro motion picture to crash a first-run white theatre on Broadway."[26]

Harlem on the Prairie proved to be the sole collaboration of Buell, Carr, and their Associated Features, but the film's success prompted producer-director-writer Richard C. Kahn to engage Jeffries for three follow-up Western features, *Two-Gun Man from Harlem* (1938), *The Bronze Buckaroo*, and *Harlem Rides the Range* (both 1939), after which Jeffries returned to his first passion, singing.

There was an action taken in 1938 by the Screen Actors Guild that benefited seven independent producers. Known as the "Western Agreement," it allowed the affected companies to produce low-budget Westerns on a fifty-four-hour week. The producers maintained that unless they were allowed to employ a fifty-four-hour week they could not continue. If allowed, they had agreed to make at least four Westerns and two serials during each calendar year, and to make their financial records available for inspection to prove their inability to operate on the regular forty-eight-hour week. The affected indies would over time include Alexander-Stern Productions, Inc.; Cisco Kid Productions, Inc.; Great Western Productions, Inc.; Range Busters, Inc.; Harry Sherman Productions, Inc.; Stern Productions; and Sigmund Neufeld Productions, Inc. The "Western Agreement" remained in effect for seven years, but by 1945 it was decided that there was no longer any justification for the longer work week. Of the original seven indies affected by the agreement, only Sigmund Neufeld Productions and two others remained in business at the agreement's termination.[27]

Meanwhile, for the first time in ten years comedian Stan Laurel found himself without a partner. Laurel's 1935 contract with producer Hal Roach had expired, while his long-time partner Oliver Hardy had another two years left to go on his contract. Laurel had wanted production control and $100,000 for all upcoming features as part of any new contract, and Roach was loathe to agree to those demands.[28] Taking control of the situation in early 1937, Laurel announced vague plans to form his own production company to produce several feature-length comedies, to star other screen comics. The possibility of his starring in one of these was mentioned, along with the possibility of Oliver Hardy's involvement once his Roach contract expired.[29] This led, albeit briefly, to a four-picture deal inked with Roach, but that was promptly revised when Laurel formed the Stan Laurel Corporation. Under the new deal, Laurel's company would film two Laurel and Hardy features for Roach, another two for M-G-M, and the production of other features as well. Laurel signed Fred Scott to a five-year contract, to go into effect once Scott completed his contract with Spectrum. Buell was signed as well to produce the Scott series for Laurel, his commitment to Spectrum now finished,[30] and song writer Lew Porter signed to direct the music for the six films.[31] As for Associated Features, Sabin Carr, and those hoped-for six features, *Harlem on the Prairie* proved to be the first, and last, of them.

Sam Newfield was an obvious choice to direct, given his familiarity with both Scott and Buell, with Sternbach and Weeren making the transition as well to keep the core group together; Sam was hired in November 1937,[32] and Sternbach a month later.[33] Sam's first for Laurel was *The Rangers' Roundup*, quickly followed by *Knight of the Plains* and *Songs and Bullets*, all released in the first half of 1938. Buell threw together a new production company—Jed Buell Productions—to film the new Westerns for Stan Laurel Productions, these too released on the state rights market by Spectrum.

The Rangers' Roundup (February 15, 1938) is more of the Fred Scott same, pleasant enough viewing, with Scott's baritone on full display and enough humorous moments courtesy of St. John. As undercover Ranger Tex Duncan, Scott joins fast-talking Earle Hodgins's Miracle Medicine Show as both a singer (what else?) and sharpshooter, ostensibly to entertain the local yokels but in reality, looking to track down a gang of robbers, with a questionable assist from St. John. The gang, headed by boss Steve Ryan, includes Karl Hackett, hot-tempered Carl Mathews, Sydney Chatton—another Ranger who has managed to infiltrate the gang—and reluctant newbie Robert Owen, whose good-girl sister (Christine McIntyre) keeps trying to talk him into going straight. Suffice it to say that after a bunch of chases, gunfights, and two slugfests, Scott overpowers the gang, recuperates the money stolen from the Express Office, lets Owen get away, and ends up with McIntyre.

Fred Scott emotes in **The Rangers' Round-Up** (Stan Laurel Productions/Spectrum, 1938); Al St. John at left. Jed Buell producer, Sam Newfield director.

Lew Porter was responsible for the film's five songs, Scott singing both solo and in wholly acceptable duets with McIntyre. "[T]he musical numbers composed by Lew Porter," wrote *Motion Picture Herald*, "are not only high class but are worked in in such a manner that they bear a direct relationship to the theme and its action."[34] Sam even coerced Porter to take part in the film (and in others that followed), as the saloon's piano player accompanying Scott and McIntyre as they toss off "Jo-Jo from Mexico," and later as the unwilling subject in one of Scott's sharpshooting demos. That scene, wherein Scott is blamed for intentionally shooting another subject who was actually shot by another hiding in the wings, was almost a direct lift from the earlier Tim McCoy film *Border Caballero*, screenwriter George H. Plympton shamelessly borrowing from Joseph O'Donnell's former script.

The production has the same bare bones look as *The Fighting Deputy*, but given that one of St. John's supposedly funny sequences takes part concurrent with Scott's crooning, it frees up a couple of minutes for more plot, not that there's much plot to fill it. Sam's direction is rather flat with this film, the aforementioned song and St. John's silly antics taking place in a single, uninterrupted long shot. (In fairness, *Film Daily* said that "Sam Newfield's direction is competent.")[35] Weeren's sound recording and/or mixing leaves something to be desired, especially in some early outdoor scenes where shots with sound are jarringly intercut with soundless others. That said, Sam rises to the occasion for the film's obligatory horseback chase, gunfights, and two spirited fistfights, Scott slugging it out first with Mathews and later, at the film's conclusion, with Ryan. Sam once again employs his "signature" camera setups for these, closeup point-of-view shots of fists coming at the camera, cut to the recipient's head knocked back, that sort of thing.

Scott, who was by now known in the press as "The Silvery Voiced Baritone," hadn't improved measurably as an actor from his previous outing, but is likable enough and gives it the old college try in his action scenes. McIntyre, whose operatic soprano voice was cultivated at the Chicago Musical College, is fine in her duets with Scott and holds her own throughout the film. McIntyre had appeared in only a couple of films before this, but within a few years would be signed to a long-term contract at Columbia. From 1943 until her retirement in the mid-1950s, McIntyre would appear in countless short comedies for that studio, most memorably as a foil for The Three Stooges. The rest of *The Rangers' Roundup* cast is adequate, Hodgins revisiting his familiar, and always entertaining, snake oil salesman/huckster role. Hackett gets to squint a lot as the duplicitous henchman, and Ryan is menacing enough as the film's chief bad guy—not Charlie King, but good enough. The film's one false acting note comes from new-to-film, twenty-year-old, British-born Sydney Chatton, whose two one-on-one conversations with Scott are unbelievably bad, with all the authenticity of a sixth grader's first acting gig. It would be another five years before Chatton would take another stab at acting, and by that time he was notably better.

Knight of the Plains (May 7, 1938) was arguably the best of the three for Laurel, not that Fred Myton's screenplay was significantly better, but it had more precious time to develop since most of Scott's musical interludes were dispensed with. Lew Porter's "Paradise Valley" is heard at the film's opening and again at the conclusion, with only one other ditty inserted early on, and logically so. Gang head Richard Cramer sidelines his usual pastime of cattle rustling to get into the con man business, swindling gullible Frank LaRue into purchasing a "half interest" in a supposed Spanish Land Grant. Henchman John Merton poses as Pedro de Cordoba, the owner and seller of the deed. Scott and St. John arrive in Paradise Valley looking for the gang that rustled some of his cattle, falls for LaRue's daughter—played by lovely Marion Weldon—and takes the side of the homesteaders about to be evicted from the property. By the film's end he's beaten the stuffing out of Merton, forcing him to reveal the swindle to the sheriff and enabling the homesteaders to return to their homes.

Motion Picture Daily singled out Sam for praise: "Sam Newfield's direction, which concentrates on action, is sharp and consistent and takes full advantage of the materials provided in Fred Myton's screenplay."[36] Twenty-four-year-old Weldon, in the business since her mid-teens, had been signed by Fox in 1934, followed by a stint at Paramount where she was demoted to uncredited bit parts and loaned out to star in the occasional low budget oater such as this one. Within a year she gave up trying and retired from the business. Former stage actor Richard Cramer, whose gravelly voice and constant scowl usually found him in roles on the wrong side of the law, was the smarter half of this film's two primary villains. The dumber half was played by John Merton, who had started in the business back in the mid-1920s, initially acting under his birth name, Myrtland LaVarre. Merton found himself steadily employed from the mid-1930s on, a regular in B-films, most of them Westerns. When the genre finally petered out at the end of the 1940s, Merton made the logical transition to television, employed continuously up until his death in 1959 at the comparatively young age of fifty-eight. Emma Tansey, looking decades older than her then sixty-seven, plays one half of the poor old couple threatened with eviction, Western-regular Lafe McKee her husband. Actor James Sheridan, a perennial heavy in numerous other Westerns, was the son of Tansey, and appeared in this film under his birth name, Sherry Tansey.[37]

Al St. John was back once again as comedy relief, which came to him easily by this point in his life. Born in 1893, St. John was the nephew of comedian Roscoe Arbuckle, who provided the path for Al's entry into Mack Sennett's Keystone Comedies in 1913. St. John was a regular in his uncle's comedies, eventually going out on his own and headlining comedy shorts well into the 1930s when he transitioned into character acting, almost always in Westerns. He first adopted the character name of "Fuzzy" for these Fred Scott Westerns, soon to be billed as Al "Fuzzy" St. John, eventually shortened to simply Fuzzy St. John, and always the tripping and stumbling sidekick partnered with Bob Steele, George Houston, Buster Crabbe, Robert Livingston, and Lash LaRue. St. John's broad slapstick style of humor is not for everyone's taste, with recurring bits such as his tripping during a chase, his misfiring gun's stray bullet downing the bad guy. His antics always provided a break from a given film's action, however— whether welcomed or deemed an annoyance—and it surely made a hit with the younger folk in the audience.

Songs and Bullets (May 15, 1938), the third and final of Sam's directorial efforts for Buell and Laurel, while not as good as its predecessor, comes across far better than the series' first entry. Not that it's a better film, but the production is much slicker looking, the paper-thin plot serviceable, and the whole benefits from a sizable role for Charlie King as the stunningly ineffectual sheriff. King is in cahoots with "respected" citizen Karl Hackett, who oversees a rather large gang of robbers. Scott and St. John come to town to track down the fellow who shot and killed his uncle, the only clue the dumdum .45 bullets used. After an hour's worth of the usual songs, chases, and fistfights, Scott finds Hackett's revolver loaded with them, substitutes blanks, allows himself to be shot, then emerges alive and well and victorious. Between the seven interruptions for Scott's singing—and that damned "Prairie Moon" is sung not once, not twice, but *three* times—and the occasional pause for St. John's antics, there isn't much time left for plot, this one pieced together by George Plympton and Joseph O'Donnell working as a team. Lew Porter is once again pressed into service in a bit role as a piano player.

While some have attributed a perceived increase in the amount of humor in the three Stan Laurel productions as Laurel's contribution, that's arguable given that it seems to be on par with the pre-Laurel Westerns. There are a couple of humorous bits, the first when most of the town's menfolk show up to attend the first day of school taught by the new French school teacher. The second involves St. John, whose attempts to help Scott in an extended fistfight with a trio of robbers has the opposite effect. Laurel's one inescapable contribution, however, and one mercifully confined to this one film, was agreeing to have his then-girlfriend, French-born Alyce Ardell, play the feminine lead. Ardell's first stab at screen stardom was for producer Joe Rock, who starred her in a

Charles King has the drop on Fred Scott and Al St. John in **Songs and Bullets** (Stan Laurel Productions/Spectrum, 1938). Jed Buell producer, Sam Newfield director.

short-lived series of Blue Ribbon Comedies back in 1925-26. All silents, so her lack of English was not an impediment. Now a dozen years and perhaps as many pounds later, Ardell handles her part reasonably well, but she's saddled with a nearly impenetrable accent, and is not even remotely as attractive as the other two young actresses Scott was paired with. With all the male citizens of town going gaga over her arrival, one would suspect that she's the only female in a fifty-mile radius; her appeal is elusive. *Film Daily* was succinct in its comments about her: "Alice Ardell, a short and rather plump lady is the female interest."[38]

Former silent comedian Jimmy Aubrey, who pops up in small roles in countless Westerns, has non-speaking bits in all three of these Laurel productions, as a drunk in the first, and as gun-toting henchmen in the other two. Aubrey and Laurel's paths had crossed in the past when Aubrey had small roles in a couple of Roach's Laurel and Hardy Comedies, and it's been said—but unconfirmed—that Laurel directed, sans credit, Aubrey in several comedies for Joe Rock back in the mid-1920s. Was Aubrey's presence in these three Westerns another Laurel contribution, or simply a coincidence? Not that it makes any difference.

By April 1938, however, Buell had jumped the Stan Laurel Pictures ship, released from his contract to embark on a whole new venture. This was the production of a novelty titled *The Terror of Tiny Town*, starring "an all-midget cast," but more on that in a moment. Laurel stated that he intended to produce the remainder of the Scott series, with an assist by L.A. French,[39] a former production manager of the Laurel and Hardy unit back at Roach.[40]

Which sounded good, except for the fact that Stan Laurel Corporation and its Fred Scott series were effectively dead. Laurel, it was soon reported, was to star in a series of features for Mack Sennett, who had organized Mack Sennett Pictures Corporation to feature the comedian. The first in the series, tentatively titled *The Problem Child*, was to star Laurel as "the normal-sized son of a pair of midgets;" Buell was signed as associate producer for the film.[41] As with so many other projects bandied about in the trades, it never happened. As for Scott, his contract was with Buell, who turned around and sold it to producer C.C. Burr, who announced plans to film a six-feature series starring Scott at International Studios.[42] These would be the last six films Scott would make before leaving the business to concentrate on real estate.

Which brings us back to Buell and his little people. Back in April, Buell had closed a deal with the Singer Midgets for the troupe to star in his upcoming *The Terror of Tiny Town*, the script of which had been written by Fred Myton.[43] Sam was hired to direct, and Sternbach to associate produce.[44] One of Buell's first moves was to contract for forty "fast riding" Shetland ponies for his diminutive cowboys to ride.[45] The Singer group had been midway through a personal appearance tour in Honolulu when signed to the film, so the sixteen of them sailed into the port at San Pedro where Buell stood to greet them, accompanied by another eighteen homegrown little people signed from the mainland. Buell, it was reported, yelled out "Hyah, podners" in his best affected western fashion, only to be met by blank stares. One of them finally responded: "Sprechen sie Deutsch?"[46]

A popular group formed by Austrian Leo Singer and his wife Walberga a quarter century earlier, The Singer Midgets comprised European little people primarily of Bavarian stock. They performed throughout Europe until the outbreak of World War I, emigrating to the United States where they would continue in vaudeville for the remainder of the group's existence.[47] With thirty members at its peak, the group had by this time lost nearly half of its members.

Buell, who claimed to not be offended when called a "quickie" producer, offered up his version of his inspiration for making the film resulting from a talk with some associates: "And one of the props cracked that if I kept on trying to keep expenses down, I'd probably use midgets for actors. That struck me as a good idea—and that's what I'm doing. Only the expenses are going up, not down."[48]

Sam and Buell took their cast of thirty-seven north of Hollywood to film exteriors in Newhall and Placerita Canyon in California, after which they returned to town and filmed interiors on sets at International Studios. The film's leading man was played by twenty-nine-year-old Billy Curtis, "the Don Juan of the midget world" as one article put it.[49] Sixty-five-year-old[50] Billy Platt played one of the villains, and Charlie Becker, forty-four,[51] as the goateed cook. Twenty-one-year-old Yvonne Moray took the role of the heroine, accompanied each day by her full-sized mother, no doubt distrusting those European show people. Like something out of the M-G-M film *Freaks*, Curtis had married a six-foot-four nightclub bouncer named Lois de Fee in Miami the previous winter, and was now caught up in an impending divorce. Sam, given a typical eight-day schedule to make the film, didn't think that would be enough time. "His difficulty," he explained, "was keeping the midgets on their ponies long enough for shots. They always are falling off."[52]

Billy Curtis and Yvonne Moray take direction from Sam Newfield at the outdoor location of **The Terror of Tiny Town** (Principal/Columbia, 1938), Jed Buell producer, Sam Newfield director. *Courtesy of Laura Berk.*

Sol Lesser and his Principal Pictures came to the film's (and Buell's) rescue, investing another $50,000 into the production which allowed for an extra two weeks of shooting. As part of his investment, the cast was signed to contracts to appear in a series of "Class-A features burlesquing current film hits."[53] The first of these, scheduled for a late August start, was to be set at a lumber camp with a full-sized heavy (Charlie King, perhaps?) portraying mythical Paul Bunyon. Buell, it was reported, would head to Europe upon completion of *Tiny Town* to hire additional little people.[54]

There were several challenges unique to this production, as itemized—and perhaps embellished—in one article:

> It's a melodrama whose hero found it impossible to fire a man-sized six-shooter and so .22 blanks with reduced charges of powder had to be especially manufactured. It's a drama whose villain required intricate and technical sound apparatus because his piping voice properly belonged in the high soprano section of a boys' choir. It's an outdoor action picture whose fast-riding cowboys had to be taught to ride.[55]

Once the film was ready for release, Louis Hyman, distribution chief of Lesser's Principal Pictures, headed east in July to New York with a print in search of a distributor.[56] He found one with Columbia. "YOU NEED A REAL NOVELTY!" the ensuing full-page ads screamed, quick to note in fine print that "This picture is sold separately and not included in Columbia's regular 1938-39 product contracts." *The Terror of Tiny Town* was released on December 1, 1938.

I'm not going to disparage this film as so many others have—most notably the Medved brothers in their essentially worthless book *The Golden Turkey Awards*—because it's actually a pretty good little film. Once you get past its obviously exploitative nature, what you have is a rather standard Western, but one that benefits from Lesser's infusion of cash which (if press releases are to be believed) doubled its starting budget to the neighborhood of $100,000, a far greater sum than the majority of its lower-budget brethren. The film has a slick, professional look to it, Mack Stengler's crisp cinematography coupled with Sam's solid direction working in harmony to yield a Western heads and tails above so many of its genre competitors. Fred Myton avoided any pandering to the pint-sized cast, providing a straight-forward tale that could have been used unchanged with another, full-sized cast. All the elements are there: rivalry between ranches, a stagecoach holdup, a threatened lynching, a hissable villain, and even a climactic slugfest. Charles Becker, as the film's good-natured cook, provides the obligatory—and surprisingly enjoyable—comic relief. Even Lew Porter's songs—and there are a bunch of them here—are better than some of his contributions to other films, one of them—"Mister Jack and Missus Jill"—quite catchy and memorable.[57] Even the film's opening credits have a slicker look than the run-of-the-mill Poverty Row film credits, no doubt courtesy of the film's eventual distributor, Columbia Pictures.

The acting, not surprisingly, is all over the map, some of it raw and amateurish, and some of it quite good—but that's frequently the case with so many of the hastily produced, penny-pinched Westerns emerging from Hollywood's Poverty Row. Billy Curtis, as the film's hero Buck Lawson, is likable in the role, handling the dubbing of his song—"Down on the Sunset Trail"—seamlessly, and looks quite competent mounting and riding his white pony. As the film's heroine, Yvonne Moray is adequate, and sings well with her (presumably own) birdlike voice; her romantic scenes with Curtis are quite charming, even closing the film with a kiss. Billy Rhodes—who went by Little Billy and appears in the credits as such—chews up the scenery as the film's villain, Bat Haines, and clearly relishes the role that was handed him. As the spurned, vengeful dance hall girl Nita, actress Nita Krebs pulls off her role with a sultry, dare I say "sexiness," that befits her character, sort of a pint-sized Marlene Dietrich. As Moray's father, craggy-faced Billy Platt is another of the cast's more convincing actors. According to Sam's son Joel, not all the cast was made up of so-called midgets, beefed up somewhat by some smaller statured horse racing jockeys. They probably were pressed into service for some of the more spirited ponyback riding and, perhaps, the long shot where someone doubling for Curtis leaps from pony to runaway stagecoach. As for the ponyback chases, they look rather silly with those Shetland ponies prancing rather than galloping. And, as typical with films of this ilk, one of Curtis's rides starts and finishes on a black pony, but he's astride a white pony mid-ride.

The plot is standard Western stuff: Villain Billy Rhodes orchestrates a near-war between neighboring ranchers John T. Bambury and Billy Platt, each of whom thinks the other is rustling his cattle. Hero Billy Curtis (as Bambury's son) and heroine Yvonne

Moray (as Platt's daughter) are in love, and try to mend the rift, while Rhodes does his best to provide impediments at every turn, at one point framing Curtis for the murder of Moray's father. Rhodes's duplicity is finally revealed when he shoots the sheriff dead in front of others, and finally meets his comeuppance when blown to smithereens by a load of dynamite placed by his spurned dance hall girl Nita Krebs.

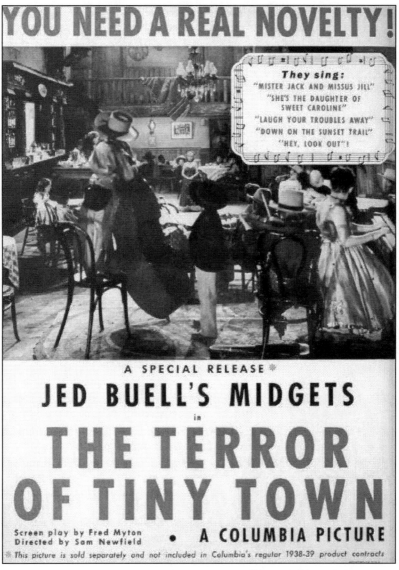

"You Need a Real Novelty!" Buell found his "White Knight" in Columbia, which distributed **The Terror of Tiny Town** independent of its 1938-39 product contracts.

Along with a number of other, mostly positive reviews, *Hollywood Spectator*'s reviewer provided a thoughtful analysis of the film:

Jed Buell had a good idea and has realized it handsomely. Midgets interest us because they are so exactly like us in all respects except that of size; but because there are so few of them among so many of us, and so few ordinary occupations available to them, they find the easiest way to make a living is to let us look at them, at so much a look, and that pleases both them and us. Jed's idea was to provide action with the look, so he rounded up a score of the little people, had a story written for them, and gives us, in The Terror of Tiny Town, one of the most interesting and pleasantly entertaining pictures I have seen in quite a spell of moons. Jed does not present his players as freaks, does not ask us to regard them as anything other than characters in a regular, true-to-type, as a line on the screen terms it – "Rollickin' Rootin'. Tootin'. Shootin' Drama of the Great Outdoors." Wisely Jed refrained from including anything never before seen in a Western. Therein lies the strength of this picture as entertainment.

We do not laugh at these nice little persons. We laugh with them as they strut importantly, and obviously with appreciation of the humor in it, through sets built to standard size and dressed with standard furniture. But the rootin', tootin', shootin' bad men, and the brave and honest guardians of the law, ride pint-size steeds when they dash madly hither and yon upon their respective missions. And strangely enough, as you watch them you become interested in the story as a story, view it as standard Western entertainment, wish the really handsome leading man well and fall quite in love with the beautiful heroine.... Little Billy—another Billy—makes a dastardly villain, a ruthless killer, and my hisses mingled with the others which bore testimony to the impressiveness of his villainy. All in all, The Terror of Tiny Town is good fun, a screen treat you should not miss.[58]

At least one Maine-based exhibitor was pleasantly surprised by how good the film was:

Business was so flat that I didn't care what happened so I booked this single, but did I get fooled? They liked it so well, some came back Saturday. It was a good story and was more carefully put together than the run of the mill westerns. The little fellows put all they had into it. It was something different and that is what we need in westerns.[59]

The film's production prompted a lot of interest prior to its release. Dr. Eugene Frenke and his United Players, Inc. jumped on the bandwagon and set plans in motion to feature a little person in the role of Half-Buck. Three films were planned—*Half-Buck Rides Again*, *Half-Buck Goes West*, and *Half-Buck Hits the Trail*—and it was reported that fifty midgets had been lined up and were heading to Chicago to star.[60] They were never filmed.

Billy Rhodes, as Little Billy, made plans with Leo Singer to open a "Tom Thumb eatery" somewhere in Hollywood, to be staffed solely with little people. "Little Billy's big idea," it was reported, "is to run everything in a dwarfish way, down to the tiniest detail." Along with the cooks and wait staff, a Little Theatre show was to provide entertainment as well. "The Vest Pocket," "The Atom," and "The Pinhole" were all names that were proposed for the place.[61] It was never built.

Buell's trip to Europe in search of little people never happened either, as a disgruntled Lesser decided not to exercise his option to finance any additional films of this sort, as paltry domestic rentals of $44,000 quickly put the kibosh on any plans for future films. Buell took his midgets and supposedly signed that long-term contract with Sennett to star in his newly formed company.[62] With the Sennett deal in the dumps,

Buell's future plans kept changing. Sam Decker of Majestic announced a deal in November to distribute six Westerns that Buell was supposed to produce,[63] presumably the new series of Fred Scott Westerns announced earlier for the 1938-39 market, but nothing came of that.[64] Buell was forced into an out-of-court settlement with John Leal, one of the uncredited stars of *The Terror of Tiny Town* who sued over the use of faulty makeup applied by makeup artist Louis Philippi that left a scar on his face.[65] The rest of his brief career was spent producing a series of race comedies, most of which starred Mantan Moreland, along with a short-lived stint as a producer at Producers Releasing Corp. Buell's career as a film producer came to an end with the release of *Mantan Messes Up* in 1946.

The Terror of Tiny Town almost resurfaced in late 1940, when Leon Fromkess, PRC's foreign manager, was offered the reissue rights (along with *Tarzan's Revenge*). "If we could get these pictures on equitable terms," wrote Lee Goldberg, president of Cincinnati-based independent exchange Big Feature Rights, to Fromkess, "I would like to handle them as I think that we can do business with them and not hurt ourselves in any way." It didn't happen; PRC's Executive Committee squashed the deal.[66]

One later aspect of Sam's involvement with this production really impressed his young son Joel, and that was the recognition he would receive while walking in Hollywood: "[The midgets] all knew him, and we would walk down Hollywood Boulevard and these midgets would come up and say 'Hi, Sam.' They all knew him." This street-based recognition extended to many of the African Americans who worked on *Harlem on the Prairie* and some of Sam's jungle-based adventures as well, who would great Sam with a similar warmth and friendliness.[67] To a little kid, out-of-the-blue greetings from this colorful assortment of strangers must have been an unusual, if somewhat confusing, experience.

Republic Pictures

Sam was incredibly busy during this period, with a total of forty-five films released over the three-year period 1936-1938. Eighteen of these were for Republic Pictures: a single film for producer Nat Levine in 1936, and the remaining seventeen films for producer A.W. Hackel over the following two years.

Sam's solo effort for Levine was an early entry in Republic's long-running "The Three Mesquiteers" series, based—initially, at least—on the popular Western stories by author William Colt MacDonald. In an obvious nod to Alexander Dumas's "Three Musketeers," these updated and transplanted stories were first brought to the screen by RKO in 1935 as *Law of the .45s* and *Powdersmoke Range*. Republic took up the reins in 1936, the series' opener simply titled *The Three Mesquiteers*, with the fictional trio of heroes—Stony Brooke, Tucson Smith, and Lullaby Joslin—played by actors Robert Livingston, Ray Corrigan, and Syd Saylor, respectively. Ray Taylor directed for producer Nat Levine, in charge of Republic's Westerns and serials since his former Mascot Pictures had merged with Republic the previous year. *Ghost Town Gold* followed, the second of the 1936-37 season's series eight entries, with Saylor replaced by Max Terhune as Joslin; Joseph Kane directed. Sam was hired to co-direct the series' third, *Roarin' Lead* (December 9, 1936), sharing the honors with Mack V. Wright. Wright, an assistant director of no particular note, had a prolific career nonetheless, spanning more than four decades; Westerns had predominated to this date.

The story centers on the Cattlemen's Protective Association and its corrupt general manager, played by Hooper Atchley. Scheming with his head ranger George Chesebro and head henchman Yakima Canutt, they orchestrate cattle rustlings with the hope of breaking the association via multiple payouts to the affected cattlemen. The association had been set up so that its proceeds would provide funding for the local orphanage, but Atchley wants the funding stopped, the orphanage shut down, and all those poor little orphans adopted. Here's where the Three Mesquiteers come in. They just happen to be the association's trustees, so they take over, fire Atchley and his gang of rangers—all nattily attired in matching outfits—and put a halt to the adoptions. Atchley doesn't take this lying down, but after a number of ambushes and fistfights, the Mesquiteers expose his corrupt scheme and he and his cohorts are hauled off to jail. Except for Canutt, that is, who was conveniently shot dead by Atchley in front of dozens of witnesses, thereby sealing Atchley's fate.

What saves this film is the likability of its three stars, and their breezy, humorous repartee. Livingston, who'd been in the business for years but finally hit his stride at Republic as a Western star, is the occasionally hot-tempered but good-looking member of the group, available to romance each film's ingénue; here he ends up with the orphanage's cute superintendent, played by newcomer Christine Maple. Corrigan, a former physical fitness trainer who appeared mostly uncredited in small roles until landing the starring role in Republic's serial *Undersea Kingdom*, appears as the trio's muscle-bound member. Corrigan displays a degree of patience, calming his hot-tempered compatriot on several occasions, but explodes into action when the need—or his mood—arises. Terhune, a former vaudevillian with a knack for ventriloquism, is the comic relief of the group, although the humor is played down and his usefulness to his two comrades made evident. There's one donnybrook where Terhune, spittoon caught on hand, dispatches one gang member after another with his new-found weapon. Some may grouse about the presence of Terhune's dummy Elmer and the ventriloquism he employs, but it's all harmless enough. What drags down the film is the presence of those annoying orphans, most prominent of which is played by feisty little Tommy Bupp. At one overly long point they put on a fund-raising show for the townspeople, and we are forced to sit through one act after another, which includes singers, tap dancers, a chorus line and, as a jaw-dropping capper, an Apache Dance performed by the brother and sister act Theodore and Kathy Frye—and these were reportedly students of Republic's talent school! As if watching forced tears and sobbing back at the orphanage wasn't enough.

As often happens in these mass-produced Westerns, whole storylines reappear in subsequent productions. One such example takes place early on when Atchley sends his henchman out to round up some "rustlers" to appease the townsfolk. The gang returns with the captured trio of Mesquiteers in tow, who are immediately identified as the association's trustees, their captors looking foolish as a result. This premise would be reused a couple of years later in *Songs and Bullets*, where Fred Scott and Al St. John are similarly pulled in as scapegoat rustlers, and set free when the town's prominent hotel owner identifies them as the singers he has hired. Oliver Drake and Jack Natteford were the writers of the former, while George Plympton and Joseph O'Donnell the writers of the latter, so who was responsible for this direct lift? Sam was the common thread between the two films, so my guess is that he suggested this particular bit for reuse, likely as a script-writing expedient.

The Three Mesquiteers pose between takes for **Roarin' Lead** (Republic, 1936), Nat Levine producer, Sam Newfield and Mack V. Wright directors. Left-to-right: Ray Corrigan, Max Terhune, and Bob Livingston.

Directing at Republic must have been a pleasant change of pace for Sam, with better production facilities and sets than the usual threadbare productions he'd been working under in the past. The film has a glossier look than his norm, and even music director Harry Grey's stock music is more thoughtfully applied, and for a pleasant change actually adds to the on-screen action. The film's stars are introduced as they approach on horseback, "Listen to the Mockingbird" accompanying them on the soundtrack, immediately bringing The Three Stooges and their theme song to mind; a whimsical, curious choice. *Film Daily* commented on the results, saying that "the picture is technically good. Sequences are smooth-flowing and nicely contrasted" and deemed Sam's direction as "Solid."[68] As always, the exhibitors had the last word: "What happened to Syd Saylor? He was good."[69] You can't please everyone.

As far as the series went, however, it was one-and-done for Sam, who moved on to other productions. The series' popularity guaranteed it a long life, however, lasting into 1943 with the leads replaced with a dizzying array of new actors that included Ralph Byrd, John Wayne, Raymond Hatton, Duncan Renaldo, Bob Steele, Rufe Davis, Tom Tyler, and Jimmy Dodd.

Sam was next reunited with both producer A.W. Hackel and actor Johnny Mack Brown, having worked with them two years earlier directing *Branded a Coward* for Hackel's Supreme Pictures. Alabama-born Brown (1904-1974) wasn't initially destined for Western stardom. Hired by M-G-M back in 1927, Brown was featured as the rugged, good-looking leading man in a string of contemporary films, playing opposite such leading ladies as Joan Crawford (*Our Dancing Daughters*), Greta Garbo (*A Woman of Affairs*), and Norma Shearer (*A Lady of Chance*; all 1928), and on loan-out opposite Madge Bellamy at Fox (*The Play Girl*; 1928) and Mary Pickford for United Artists (*Coquette*; 1929). Having seamlessly transitioned from silents to sound, there was the occasional Western thrown into the mix: Brown reappearing with Crawford in *Montana Moon*, and as the lead in King Vidor's big-budgeted *Billy the Kid*, both in 1930 for M-G-M. Released from his contract in 1931, Brown freelanced over the next few years for a slew of different companies that included First National, Paramount, and Fox, and as demand for his services lessened, Columbia, Mascot, Chesterfield, and Tower; Sig and Sam's *Marrying Widows* (1934), which was discussed in an earlier chapter, was for this latter company.

Brown's career trajectory took an abrupt turn in 1935, however, with his hiring by producer A.W. Hackel to star in a series of eight Westerns for release through Hackel's Supreme Pictures, *Branded a Coward*, the first in the series. The success of this first group of eight films prompted Hackel to sign Brown for an additional eight Westerns, now for release through Republic.[70] Sam was hired to direct six of these—*Bar-Z Bad Men*, *The Gambling Terror*, *Trail of Vengeance*, *Guns in the Dark*, *A Lawman is Born*, and *Boothill Brigade*—all released during the latter part of the 1936-37 season, and all budgeted at $13,000 apiece. Embraced by the public and comfortable with the genre, Brown would spend the better part of the next two decades as a Western hero in no fewer than 120 films.

The first of these, *Bar-Z Bad Men* (January 20, 1937), bore a familiar plot as penned by George Plympton, that of cattle ranchers manipulated to think that one is rustling the other's cattle. Character actor Tom London, who'd been featured in oaters for more than two decades, plays the town's "leading citizen" Sig Bostell, whose gang, headed by Dick Curtis, rustles the cattle from Frank LaRue's Bar-7 Ranch and rebrands it, changing the "7" to a "Z" and dumping the cattle at Jack Rockwell's Bar-Z Ranch. Enter Johnny Mack Brown as Rockwell's new partner, whose attempts to get to the bottom of things shifts into high gear when Rockwell is murdered. Lois January plays the feminine lead as LaRue's no-nonsense daughter.

Familiar stuff, but there are several elements that elevate this film above much of Sam's earlier Westerns. First is lead actor Brown himself, whose relaxed, more natural performance benefits not only from innate ability but from his schooling back at M-G-M as well; it doesn't hurt that he's physically convincing in the numerous fight scenes. Opposite him, Lois January, who had worked for both Sig and Sam opposite Tim McCoy in their earlier *Border Caballero* and *Lightnin' Bill Carson* for Excelsior, has far more to do in, and with, the film's plot than the usual dispensable female "leads." She takes part in shoot-outs and earns her keep by ensuring that daddy has a fully loaded pistol every time its predecessor runs out of ammo. And if her shooting isn't enough to satisfy the viewer, she initiates a romance with Brown mid-film that must have left the younger viewers groaning. Bert Longenecker's inspired cinematography is a definite asset as well, employing some visually interesting compositions and setups in the film's opening scene, where hell-raiser Brown (as Jim Waters, celebrating his upcoming partnership in the Bar-Z Ranch) and his fellow cowboys shoot up the town and make nuisances of themselves in the saloon. Longenecker, by this time in his sixties and the twilight of a lengthy career behind the camera, seems to have gotten a second wind as the end neared, filming no fewer than thirty films in the final three years of his career, 1937-39.

The cattle rustling gang features Dick Curtis as London's go-to, right-hand heavy, Westerns' premiere bad guy whose presence in most any film immediately signals to the viewer which side he's on. Ernie Adams takes part as well as the gang's weak link, a weaselly character who breaks down and reveals all after a few hard knocks from Brown, not that that's much of a surprise since these B Westerns frequently have gang members who give it all up after some minor skirmish. Silent comedian Milburn Morante has a prominent role as the town's inept deputy Sherlock ("That thick-headed deputy ain't got sense enough to pound sand in a rat hole") who, for once, rises to the occasion and assists rather than hinder Brown's investigation. Sam exceeded Hackel's $13,000 budget by only $123.

Dick Curtis (right) subdues Johnny Mack Brown while Ernie Adams disarms him, in **Bar-Z Bad Men** (Republic, 1937). A.W. Hackel producer, Sam Newfield director.

Johnny Mack Brown arrives in town to set up a gambling room in Sam's *The Gambling Terror* (February 15, 1937). The town is in the grip of terror by the "Protective Association," whose strong-arm tactics force donations' from the town's businesses and citizens. Dick Curtis is the head muscle, and if there is any doubt that he's a bad guy that's dispelled when he whips young Bobby Nelson, son of the newspaper editor, and later forces money from a simpering elderly couple played by Emma Tansey and Lloyd Ingraham. Charlie King's his boss, and the big boss who keeps his identity a secret turns out to be another of those supposedly respectable citizens, played by Earl Dwire. Brown gets involved, of course, in breaking up the gang and with the editor's cute daughter, Iris Meredith. And surprise: Brown's not a gambler after all, but an undercover lawman brought in to help by the town's sheriff, Ted Adams.

Engaging enough, and there's a nifty climactic fight between Brown and both King and Dwire aboard a runaway buckboard, Brown and kidnapped Nelson leaping to safety moments before it crashes. Meredith, in only her third credited role in a mini-career that would fizzle out five years later, goes from pacifist to organizing a secret band of vigilantes to kill off the gang members. Screenwriters George Plympton and Fred Myton rework some familiar plot devices to satisfactory effect, although *Variety*'s

Johnny Mack Brown feigns drunkenness while a distrustful Dick Curtis observes, in **The Gambling Terror** (Republic, 1937). A.W. Hackel producer, Sam Newfield director.

reviewer deemed it "formula authorship," adding both the sound recording and camera work among the film's "faults." It looked and sounded okay to me. Sam brought this one in $30 under budget!

Trail of Vengeance (March 29, 1937), his third in the series, began its seven-day shoot on Saturday, January 16, 1937. In this one Brown poses as a wanted murderer in order to investigate the killing of his brother. His bad rep preceding him, Brown finds that both sides in a range war want him for his talents. Who to side with: Iris Meredith and the other honest ranchers she bands with, or Warner Richmond, the film's featured bad guy? The choice is obvious, especially if Brown hopes to end up in the arms of someone by the film's end.

Variety commented on both lead and his rival:

Brown, a real husky, convincingly fits his western roles and looks the part of a guy who can handle himself in tight places. His principal opposition in this film is Warner Richmond...one of the more capable western heavies, and can incite plenty of audience opposition with the bronc fans by just doing a walkon.[71]

128 Poverty Row Royalty

Guns in the Dark (April 14, 1937) came next, covering some familiar turf but with a few twists. It's the old cattle ranchers teetering on range war over one's plans to dam a river and provide free water to neighboring ranchers, and the other who wants it stopped. Why? Because he's been rustling the other rancher's cattle and hiding them in a canyon that would end up being flooded. Johnny Mack Brown rides into town, gunless since he is convinced that he accidentally shot and killed his partner, Julian Madison. He has picked up a new partner along the way, stuttering Syd Saylor, who it should be said had one of the most infectious smiles ever seen on the screen. The film's twists: The rancher planning to build the dam is played by Claire Rochelle, for once a female given a meaty role, and showing a fair amount of spunk in her dealings with rival rancher Dick Curtis. Curtis is in league with a villainous Mexican played by squinty eyed Ted Adams. Curtis wants to eliminate Rochelle the old-fashioned way, while Adams plans to marry her and neutralize her in the process, resorting to kidnapping her. The other twist: Saylor, and *not* the film's lead, turns out to be the film's undercover agent—and he doesn't really stutter! Twists aside, the film grinds to an incongruous halt when Brown and Rochelle hold off a horde of gang members in a south-of-the-border cantina by

Johnny Mack Brown has the upper hand in **Guns in the Dark** (Republic, 1937). A.W. Hackel producer, Sam Newfield director.

throwing an endless stream of crockery and trays at them—even a well-aimed pie—and manage to knock them all out cold in the process. Not one of B Westerns' finest moments. Sam saved producer Hackel a few bucks by coming in $775 under budget, reinforcing his reputation for efficiency and thriftiness.

Iris Meredith provided the love interest once again in *A Lawman is Born* (June 21, 1937), which pits grocery clerk Brown—supposedly wanted for a murder or two down in Texas—against Warner Richmond and his head goon, Charlie King. When

King dispatches the town's sheriff, Earle Hodgins, the latter's wife pushes for Brown to replace him. He's elected, and goes after Richmond's gang, who have aggressively been driving the smaller ranchers away. Brown goes *mano a mano* in a showdown against gunman Dick Curtis and shoots him dead. Meredith is one of the ranchers' daughters, and she ends up being Brown's "reward" for his good deeds. Would it surprise you to learn that Brown was cleared of those earlier murder charges? I didn't think so.

Film Daily liked the results, stating that "Horse opera fans will like the picture. It has good tempo, is often exciting, and always well directed and photographed."[72] *Motion Picture Daily* seconded that last comment: "Bert T. Longenecker's camera work is easy on the eyes."[73]

Sam's sixth and final Johnny Mack Brown Western for Hackel and Republic was *Boothill Brigade* (August 2, 1937), a good little film that tones down the action in favor of story development. Brown and Rochelle are lovers, but that bond is broken when Brown learns that her father, Frank LaRue, has used some legal trickery to acquire all of the area's land, and intends to evict the settlers. Brown finds that Ed Cassidy, who holds the mortgage on LaRue's ranch and is the film's so-called "land hog," has used the threat of foreclosure to force LaRue to do his dirty work. Working with Rochelle, the two eventually convince her father that he should sign the deed over to the settlers rather than Cassidy, whose scheming, now exposed, is arrested. Horace Murphy keeps popping up as the film's comic relief, always yammering on about how his shotgun likes to "bark," but eventually proves to be a useful asset to Brown's investigation. Bobbie Nelson has a smaller role as the teen bound and determined to help Brown, whatever the cost.

Johnny Mack Brown and Claire Rochelle (center) in **Boothill Brigade** (Republic, 1937). A.W. Hackel producer, Sam Newfield director.

Boothill Brigade is atypical for the series given its more involved plot and comparative lack of action. There are a few fistfights and lots of horseback chases, and one delightful little sequence of tough talk between Brown and henchman Dick Curtis, but that's about it. No climactic fistfight or gun battle, just a simple little chase with Brown apprehending the fleeing Cassidy and turning him over for arrest. And if the viewer expected a showdown between Brown and Curtis, they were sorely disappointed, as Curtis simply disappears from the scene. Reviewers liked what they saw, and *Variety* singled out both Sam and cinematographer Bert Longenecker for their contributions, tossing in a nod to unnamed screenwriter George Plympton:

> Lenser Longenecker is rapidly distinguishing himself as one of the better muggers. Manages to get in plenty of good angle shots and unusual scenery in the hard riding sequences. Director Newfield, presumably the busiest director in the west if the recurrence of his tag on press books is an indication, does well with this, as with most of his other ones. But then he had something to work with, too...dialog throughout is way above the hackneyed.[74]

Hackel kept Sam busy, bouncing him back and forth between the Brown Westerns and those for popular Bob Steele. Sam directed three of the Steele Westerns released during the 1936-37 season, *Lightnin' Crandall*, *Gun Lords of Stirrup Basin*, and *Doomed at Sundown*, and all budgeted at $13,000 apiece as well. Many of the Steele Westerns that preceded these were directed by Robert N. Bradbury, but with his departure for Grand National and Monogram, Hackel hired Sam to take over the reins.

Born Robert Adrian Bradbury in Portland, Oregon, Steele (1907-1988) was the son of prolific director Robert N. Bradbury, who'd been helming Westerns since 1918 for Vitagraph and Select. In show business as part of the family's vaudeville act at age two, Steele and his twin brother Bill eventually starred in a series of comedy shorts directed by their father for Pathé from 1920-1922, beginning with *The Adventures of Bob and Bill*. Steele—still billed as Bob Bradbury Jr.—resumed his film career in 1925 once again for his father, in small supporting roles in films that included *With Daniel Boone Thru the Wilderness*, *With Davy Crockett at the Fall of the Alamo* (both 1926), and *With Sitting Bull at the Spirit Lake Massacre* (1927).

In 1927, Joseph P. Kennedy, president of F.B.O., announced the signing of Steele to a long-term contract; it didn't hurt that Steele's father was now the supervisor of Western units for that studio. Now bearing his new screen name, Steele would again be directed by his father, for his first starring role. "Now just 21 years of age," wrote *Exhibitors Herald*,

> and marking the fulfillment of a life long training, he is now on location at Red Rock Canyon, 60 miles from Mojave, Cal., on the desert to inaugurate filming on the exteriors of the first of his seven starring vehicles, "The Mojave Kid."
> When shooting begins, the newlymade star will have the opportunity to apply his experience in horsemanship, cowboy tricks, and acting for the first time in the role for which he has been intended since his birth. His father feels that he can do anything, and never needs a double on the screen.[75]

Steele's films proved to be popular with the filmgoing public. After his stint with F.B.O., Steele made a series for Syndicate in 1929, another for Tiffany in 1930 where he made a smooth transition to sound, followed by series for Sono Art-World Wide and Monogram. Steele began his lengthy association with producer A.W. Hackel in 1934, a thirty-two-film run lasting into 1938.

Lightnin' Crandall (March 24, 1937), the first of the Steele series that Sam was to direct, is another "range war" story, the looming conflict a result of ranch owner Frank LaRue's refusal to sell some adjacent property to neighboring rancher Charlie King. Nothing special there, but what makes this film a little bit different from the norm is Bob Steele's character, a former gunfighter—the fastest in Texas—who decides to go straight, hang up his guns, and settle down far away in Arizona as "a tenderfoot." He's sucked back in when "far away in Arizona" lands him in the midst of the rival ranchers. Initially wanting to remain neutral, falling for LaRue's cute daughter (Lois January) makes that a short-lived decision, and running afoul of King prompts him to strap his six-shooters back on.

Charlie King, of course, is another of the film's merits, not only with his endless stream of threats, but he's lecherous as well, drooling over January and promising to put an end to the war if she'll agree to marry him. One of the film's high points—perhaps its highest—is an early slugfest between Steele and King that takes place in a saloon. This is a real knock-down, drag-out affair that is stylishly filmed with many more camera setups and angles than usual, and convincingly violent with a broken furniture casualty rate far higher than the norm. Oddly enough, the film's sound mixer failed to lay in any sounds of the numerous punches connecting, which blunts some of the otherwise excellent scene's effectiveness.

Steele opened up about King in a later interview with Bobby J. Copeland, which provides a glimpse of the man behind the villain:

> He was so much fun in real life. In those days when we were all together so much, we became one happy family. If there was any larking around off-screen, you can be sure Charlie was in the middle of it. He was a big man—not too tall—but he weighed over 200 pounds. He was great to do fights with—so agile for a man his size.[76]

Lois January is back again as the female lead, and Sam gives her plenty of screen time. As in *Bar-Z Bad Men*, she is the aggressor in a rapidly budding romance with Steele, who locks lips with her mid-film, and has a repeat performance at the film's conclusion as they are married. Steele's performance is sincere, but his capabilities as an actor are somewhat limited. He comes across best during the film's more serious moments, but lighthearted Bob isn't always convincing, and displays a level of discomfort you'd think he would have gotten over by this point in his career. He really shines in his more physical moments, however, visually convincing in his fight scene with King. Ernie Adams has a nice little role as Steele's right-hand man, a far cry from his weaselly characters in other films. One of the film's gems is Earl Dwire, as the older gunslinger who taught Steele everything he knows, and whom Steele is forced to face off against in the film's climactic scene. It's Steele against both Dwire and King, Steele prevailing by killing King but only winging Dwire. That a wounded Dwire stands by in the background smiling as Steele and January are married fails to pass the reality test, but I doubt audiences cared.

One would think, after watching enough of these Westerns, that there was a perpetual war between rival ranchers taking place, and always instigated surreptitiously by respected citizens. In the *Gun Lords of Stirrup Basin* (May 10, 1937), it's the cattlemen led by Frank Ball vs. the homesteaders and Frank LaRue. Steele and Louise Stanley, son and daughter of Ball and LaRue, respectively, are in the thick of it, and the only voices of reason in the otherwise looming battle, orchestrated by local attorney Karl Hackett. When they marry against their fathers' wishes, neither side trusts them. When LaRue is shot in the back and dies shortly thereafter, all hell is about to break loose, but Steele rides to the rescue with proof that Hackett manipulated the conflict to gain control of the land, bringing the fight to an abrupt end and a reconciliation between the two sides. A fistfight between Steele and Hackett leads to the latter's death as he plunges over a cliff.

Bob Steele smiles for a change in a presumably posed shot from **Gun Lords of Stirrup Basin** (Republic, 1937). A.W. Hackel producer, Sam Newfield director.

A familiar plot, to be sure, but this film is so much better than many others that preceded it. For once there's no levity at any time, and Steele remains grimly determined throughout. Stanley, who got her start a year earlier in mostly uncredited parts, was one of the more talented and likeable feminine leads in B films of this sort, relegated primarily to Western parts after her appearance in this film. Her career came to a halt in 1940 when she married actor Jack Randall. Hackett, the scheming villain of this piece, is at his rabble-rousing worst in this film, a cheer no doubt going up in contemporary audiences when he plunged off that cliff. Ernie Adams has a smaller role as one of Ball's ranch hands, presented first as a staunch opponent of Steele's neutralism, but surprising the viewer when it turns out he's secretly on Steele's side. Broken nosed Lew Meehan is this film's scowling henchman, a suitable replacement for Charlie King when the latter was unavailable.

Sam, Sans Sig (Part 2: 1936-1940) 133

This is one of Sam's more visually stunning films, benefiting from Republic's technical crew and physical facilities. Working hand-in-hand with cinematographer Bert Longenecker, much of the outdoor photography and compositions are first-rate, a far cry from the more hurried oaters of the lesser Poverty Row studios. "The camera work by Bert Longenecker is a treat," wrote *Motion Picture Daily*,[77] while *Boxoffice* said that the film was "entertainingly directed by Sam Newfield."[78] The lead up to the confrontation and resulting shootout between the two sides towards the film's end is nicely orchestrated, Sam's direction, Longenecker's camerawork, and the film's editor[79]

Bob Steele holds dastardly Warner Richmond (far left) and Lew Meehan at gunpoint in **Doomed At Sundown** (Republic, 1937). A.W. Hackel producer, Sam Newfield director.

working together to create a scene of building suspense and dread. There's even a little girl who is playing with her doll as bullets ricochet around her to tug at the viewer's heartstrings. The screenplay, by co-writers George Plympton and Fred Myton, is a more mature piece than the norm. *Gun Lords of Stirrup Basin* is a surprisingly good little film, and among Sam's better efforts for producer Hackel and Republic.

Doomed at Sundown (June 27, 1937) was a step down, but not too far. This one's a grim tale of revenge as Steele goes after the murderer of his father, the town sheriff. Following a tip, he heads to the border and the notorious bandit hangout, Sprague's Cantina, where he manages to infiltrate a gang lorded over by rock-jawed Warner Richmond, Richmond's top two henchmen—Earl Dwire and Lew Meehan—aren't the most dedicated of employees, fully distrustful of their boss and scheming to get $12,000 of stolen bank checks away from him. When Steele's cover is blown by the film's love interest, Lorraine Hayes (aka Lorraine Randall), he still manages to orchestrate events so that the gang's two factions turn on each other. Richmond escapes with Steele in hot pursuit, and after two separate fistfights he is subdued. The law arrives just in time to prevent the pursuing gang from cancelling Steele's and Hayes's checks.

Sam's direction is as solid as usual, and Bert Longenecker's cinematography once again an asset on the exteriors. It falls short in one instance, however, when the two groups of gang members engage in a furious donnybrook. For whatever reason, be it Sam's or Longenecker's decision, the sequence is slightly undercranked, resulting in the on-screen action sped up slightly. It looks blatantly unrealistic, providing the film's one false visual note.

Lorraine Hayes, who gives a convincing performance, had a brief five-film career in 1937. Sans credit in one of them, she went by Lorraine Randall in two of the others. David Sharpe, who plays her brother, had a lengthy career that spanned more than fifty years, a lot of it spent doing stunt work as well. Sam brought both of these two latter films, *Gun Lords of Stirrup Basin* and *Doomed at Sundown*, in under budget.

Republic announced an ambitious output for the upcoming 1937-38 season, twenty-four Westerns out of a total of fifty-four productions. Gene Autry was to star in eight, the "Three Mesquiteers" series' entries another eight, and Bob Steele re-signed for the remaining eight.[80] These included *Arizona Gunfighter, Ridin' the Lone Trail, Colorado Kid, Paroled – To Die, Thunder in the Desert, The Feud Maker, Desert Patrol,* and *Durango Valley Raiders;* producer Hackel upped the budget on these by $500, to $13,500 per. Shooting on *Arizona Gunfighter* began in July 1937.[81]

Arizona Gunfighter (September 20, 1937) has Steele hooking up with Ted Adams, head of a do-good gang that takes care of the small ranchers. The gang eventually breaks up, and Steele goes straight, retiring to a ranch. The rest of the gang turns to outlawing, and under the leadership of Lew Meehan raises hell in the territory. Steele and Adams reunite and track down the gang and successfully do away with them in a furious gun battle. Steele ends up with adjacent rancher Jean Carmen, who just happens to be Adams's daughter.

Sam Newfield (left) gives direction to Ted Adams (center) and Lew Meehan in **Arizona Gunfighter** (Republic, 1937); A.W. Hackel producer. *Courtesy of Joel Newfield.*

Reviewers liked the film, but were surprisingly blunt in pointing out the inadequacies of Steele's acting. "One drawback is that the star of the piece, Bob Steele, is allowed to act," wrote *Variety*. "Of stature, build, mannerisms and even voice belonging to a cowboy, this agile western lad is shy of true thespian ability. He registers grief, anger and faithful loyalty in this picture with the same series of grimaces and misplacement of words."[82] *Motion Picture Daily* was more succinct: "The acting and characterizations are good although the leading man delivers his lines with a stiff-lipped monotone."[83] One wonders if Steele read his reviews?

Ridin' the Lone Trail (November 1, 1937) has Steele investigating the robberies of gold shipments from a mine co-owned by Frank Ball and Hal Price. Steele goes undercover and takes a job at Ball's ranch, and soon dreams of going undercover with Ball's daughter, Claire Rochelle. A trio of thugs—Charlie King, Julian Rivero, and Lew Meehan—are behind the robberies, masterminded by their mask-wearing boss. Rochelle's white horse, which only she can ride, has been spotted at the robberies, thereby adding to the confusion. The masked boss turns out to be Ball's ranch foreman, Ernie Adams. Steele wraps it all up as the gang robs another shipment, taking Rivero prisoner, shooting King and Meehan, and catching Adams as he attempts to escape on a railroad hand car.

"Blood and thunder, plenty of fisticuffs afoot are bountifully supplied in this western," wrote *Motion Picture Daily*. "Bob Steele is featured. He does not sing but uses his fists to exciting advantage and generally injects action in the scenes where he appears."[84]

Next for Sam was *Colorado Kid* (December 6, 1937). Steele, the foreman at a ranch he's just been fired from, is suspected of murder when his former boss, Horace Murphy, is found dead and $5,000 missing. Karl Hackett's the actual guilty party, and Ted Adams the sheriff he convinces of Steele's guilt. Arrested and sentenced to hang, Steele escapes with the aid of bartender Ernie Adams. Marion Weldon plays the daughter of Frank LaRue, whom Hackett is trying to force off his ranch. LaRue hides Steele, and Weldon tricks Adams into leading her to Hackett's hiding place, Steele follows her, and forces a confession out of Hackett.

Film Bulletin was unimpressed: "This is a routine western. Action is fairly fast, but the story presents nothing novel. It is, as a matter of fact, so patterned that even dyed in the wool western fans may find it a bit monotonous."[85] *Film Daily* said that "it falls short of the standard studio has set with recent westerns, as the story has been done too carelessly to carry much weight."[86] At least they didn't trash Steele's acting abilities in these reviews.

Paroled – To Die (January 10, 1938) was a decided step up from *Colorado Kid*. Banker Karl Hackett's gang robs his bank and plants evidence that points to Bob Steele, Hackett's rival for the hand of Kathleen Eliot. Steele is convicted and sent to the penitentiary, but not for long. Horace Murphy, a government agent posing as a dim-witted drifter, is on to Hackett and exonerates Steele. Now a free man, Steele goes after Hackett and brings him to justice. Eliot's father, the town's sheriff (Steve Clark), now approves of the romance between his daughter and Steele.

"This is a typical blood and thunder western with villains, double crossing, gun fights galore, fist fights, bank robberies, romance and a few other odds and ends put together in a fast moving pix that will please the western fans and the kids," wrote *Film Daily*, adding that "Bob Steele is his usual slam-bang self, and he mercilessly pursues the villains and swats them around in a thorough and convincing manner."[87] "Sam Newfield contributed lively direction," added *Motion Picture Daily*. "Miss Eliot rides better than most horse opera heroines. Her acting is convincing."[88] Which is somewhat of a shame since her career in film resulted in only three roles, this and two others for Monogram.

Bob Steele and Karl Hackett face off in **Paroled—To Die** (Republic, 1938). A.W. Hackel producer, Sam Newfield director.

Steele heads for the Circle R Ranch to try to find out who murdered his uncle, the ranch's owner, in *Thunder in the Desert* (February 21, 1938). With hobo Don Barclay in tow, Steele infiltrates Ed Brady's gang and finds that they plan to take over the ranch. They've managed to scare off everyone from the ranch except its foreman, Steve Clark, and his daughter, Louise Stanley. Steele's the rightful inheritor of the ranch, but switches identities with Barclay as part of his scheme to uncover the culprit. Charlie King, a neighboring rancher, is finally identified as the killer, and arrested.

Variety was impressed by comic Don Barclay, less so by Louise Stanley: "Barclay makes a good showing and is fairly sure of a permanent berth in the Steele pieces, having worked in a few before. His is the type relief Steele has needed for sometime. Girl is Louise Stanley, who has little to do and registers the same way." As for the film itself, it was deemed "the best of Bob Steele's breathless escape celluloidal sessions of the current program."[89]

Karl Hackett is the title's *The Feud Maker* (April 4, 1938), who pretends to work with both settlers and cattlemen as friction grows between them, while secretly stoking the fires with the goal of driving them all off and picking up the land for a song. Settler Frank Ball tries to keep the peace between the two groups, his daughter Marion Weldon along for the ride. Steele finally catches on to Hackett's scheme, biding his time until the two settle things in a showdown. Hackett is arrested, the settlers and cattlemen make peace, Steele is elected the town's sheriff, and he and Weldon end up together—big surprise there.

"Outside of being too generous with clips of Steele riding his horse pell-mell over the countryside, the film is compact and entertaining," wrote *Variety*.[90]

Film Daily was wincingly harsh in its review of *Desert Patrol* (June 6, 1938), wherein Steele is a ranger sent to investigate the murder of another ranger by Apache Joe (Ted Adams), a half-breed. "This western thriller gives every indication of having been shot from the proverbial cuff, or else turned out by a company that was away off the usual form. The story is very mediocre, and the acting likewise. In fact it is so poor that it is amateurish." And they didn't spare the film's love interest, Marion Weldon, adding that "The girl in the part recites her lines as though repeating them for a school reader."[91] Ouch!

Rex Lease (standing) in **Desert Patrol** (Republic, 1938). A.W. Hackel producer, Sam Newfield director.

Durango Valley Raiders (August 22, 1938) finds new-to-Durango Steele arrested by the town's sheriff, Forrest Taylor. He's accused of being the master criminal known only as "The Shadow," who's been looting and killing the locals. No one knows what The Shadow looks like, since he's another one of those B-Western villains with a penchant for hiding behind a mask. Louise Stanley, the daughter of the ranch owner (Karl Hackett) whom Steele had been working for, is kidnapped by The Shadow's right-hand thug, Ted Adams. Working with several others, Steele rescues Stanley and reveals The Shadow's identity: He's the sheriff! The taxpayers are saved the cost of jailing Taylor when Adams turns on him and kills him.

Exhibitors were mixed in their opinions and respective experiences. It did well in Oklahoma: "Played this picture old but did nice business. My patrons said they were tired of singing cowboys and were glad once more to see one who put up some fight and action."[92] Ohio, it would appear, was another story: "Just another western."[93] By the time *Durango Valley Raiders* was released, Sam was gone from Republic and with Buell finishing up *The Terror of Tiny Town*. In the meantime, releasing arrangements between

Republic and Supreme had not been renewed. This was likely due to the addition of the Roy Rogers series at Republic, joining their Gene Autry and Three Mesquiteers series. Hackel dropped Steele from his roster.[94]

Concord Pictures and Monogram

Sam had squeezed in a trio of films for Maurice Conn's Concord Pictures earlier in 1938 for Monogram. Conn formed Concord Productions specifically to make eight Westerns for Monogram release for the upcoming 1937-38 season. The Concord productions were to feature players supplied by Monogram, the upcoming season to include sixteen Westerns in all: four with Tim McCoy, four with Tom Keene, and eight with Jack Randall. This was separate and apart from Conn's Ambassador Pictures, which had plans for another sixteen films for the state rights market.[95]

Sam's output reunited him with Tim McCoy for both *Code of the Rangers* (March 9, 1938), the second in the season's series, and *Phantom Ranger* (May 27, 1938), while Sam's third for Concord, titled *Gunsmoke Trail* (May 8, 1938), starred singer Jack Randall.

Tim McCoy in **Phantom Ranger** (Concord/Monogram, 1938), Maurice Conn producer, Sam Newfield director. *Courtesy of Heritage Auctions.*

When a gang of bandits headed by Wheeler Oakman enters the territory patrolled by McCoy's troop in *Code of the Rangers*, McCoy soon finds that his duplicitous brother (Rex Lease) is tied up with them. The brother redeems himself by going straight and joining McCoy in his pursuit and apprehension of Oakman.

Film Daily seemed satisfied with the results, writing that "western fans will be satisfied with this new Monogram release as it has action, villainy and fine scenery in equal quantities," but dismissed Sam's direction as merely "Adequate" and cinematographer Jack Greenhalgh's lensing as "Fair."[96] *Variety* was less enthused, dismissing the film with "Tim McCoy's latest horse opera…gives him little more to do than be quick on the draw and handle his fists with equal dexterity. A minor mustanger…. For the kindergarten grade."[97] Exhibitors were much happier with the film and the audiences it drew, one in Indiana writing "No April fool joke, this picture. It's a whiz of a western, carefully produced, expertly acted by the old trooper, Tim McCoy. Monogram seems to possess the knack of knowing how to turn out good ones."[98] They agreed in Virginia: "Tim McCoy is fast becoming one of the leading western stars for me; each picture I play is getting more and more compliments. And this one is especially good."[99] So much for the reviewers.

Phantom Ranger places McCoy in the role of a secret agent sent from Washington to Arizona to track down a band of counterfeiters headed by Karl Hackett. The gang has kidnapped an engraver (John St. Polis) and forced him to make the counterfeits. McCoy hijacks a shipment of the phonies, is tracked down by the gang, and ends up joining them. St. Polis's daughter, played by Suzanne Kaaren, is on the trail as well, posing as a Mexican dancer. Both she and McCoy are forced to reveal their identities to each other before he saves both her and her father. The gang is arrested, and McCoy pursues Hackett who conveniently backs off a cliff and falls to his death.

This was Kaaren's second Western role—her first was with Johnny Mack Brown two years earlier—although she had been in films since 1933. Kaaren explained how she got the part to interviewer Mike Fitzgerald: "Tim personally selected me for the film. There were some 200 girls up for the part! Tim loved the way I rode horses. It was a nice association. I also got to sit on Tim's lap—just like I did Johnny Mack's."[100] Reviewers liked this one. "Tim McCoy gets a break with a good plot that moves along intelligently and gives him plenty of opportunity to show his riding skill and his shooting ability," wrote *Film Daily*. "The climax is plenty fast and exciting" and Sam's direction "good."[101] *Variety* concurred, but with some provisos: "There's action galore in this Tim McCoy western. A little too melodramatic and cluttered with implausibilities, the picture has several original twists and nice suspense. Should satisfy where McCoy is a fave. As with most oats operas, 'Phantom Ranger' is weakest when it becomes talky. Dialog is replete with mustang cliches."[102]

Singing cowboys were all the minor rage at this time, with Gene Autry at Republic, Fred Scott with Spectrum, and Dick Foran at Warners. Monogram figured they needed a crooner as well, and found him with actor Jack Randall, who had been relegated to supporting roles at M-G-M and RKO since 1933. Randall (1906-1945), the brother of popular "Three Mesquiteers" actor Robert Livingston, had appeared on Broadway prior to entering the film business, so he leapt at the opportunity to put his singing voice to use, and in starring roles. Monogram's studio chief Scott R. Dunlap was bullish on his new find. "Both Tim McCoy and Tom Keene rank high in the estimation of western fans," wrote *Film Bulletin*. "In addition, Dunlap has created a new singing cowboy star to rival the popular Gene Autry; he is Jack Randall, probably the most handsome of all outdoor yodelers. He may lure some feminine trade for the hitherto exclusively male horse opera."[103] *Riders of the Dawn* (July 14, 1937) was Randall's introduction to Western fans, and demonstrated that he was both a decent actor, could sing (albeit in a more operatic style), and possessed a deep voice that could measure on the Richter Scale. That said, he failed to click with audiences, and if the "feminine trade" was banging at the doors, it was more likely to get out of the theatres than in. After a mere five films, the suits at Monogram decided to jettison the singing and have Randall concentrate on his acting. This was where Sam came in, handling the directorial chores on *Gunsmoke Trail*. According to co-star (and future wife) Louise Stanley, Randall wasn't happy about the series' shift to straight action Westerns, but he didn't have any say in the matter. The film, which co-stars Al St. John, has John Merton posing as Stanley's uncle with the intention of gaining control of the estate left to her by her deceased father. Enter Randall, who immediately smells a rat, and eventually knocks some sense into Stanley.

Jack Randall in **Gunsmoke Trail** (Concord/Monogram, 1938), Maurice Conn producer, Sam Newfield director. *Courtesy of Heritage Auctions.*

Variety was happy about the new direction the series had taken, and Sam's handling of the film:

> Best Jack Randall western made to date, principally because it's strictly a western without the light opera touch of wagon-wheel harmony and solo badly bayed at the moon. Flick has action, covers all the well-known wrinkles in story and movement and is snappily done. It'll go a long way to bring Randall up among the mustangers now leading.... Screenplay, camera, sound and directorial departments commendable.[104]

The new tack the series had taken didn't help much, and by 1940 Monogram had shown both the series and Randall the door. To add insult to injury, the poor guy fell off his horse and died while making a film a few years later; he was only thirty-nine.

Fine Arts, Cinemart, and Arcadia, for Grand National

Sam also squeezed in another three films for release through Grand National during this time—all Westerns, not surprisingly—for three different production companies, and with three different stars. *Frontier Scout* (October 21, 1938) was the first, a Fine Arts Pictures production starring George Houston as Wild Bill Hickok. In 1865, Houston and his pal Al St. John head to Kansas after they are mustered out of the Union Army. They meet Dave O'Brien, head of a cattle commission house that's teetering on bankruptcy due to the rampant rustling of cattle. Houston is made the town's marshal, puts an end to the rustling, and falls for O'Brien's sister (Beth Marion) while doing so. "With its better story, splendid cast, and first-class production, it is a top-notch Western, one which can rank with the best in its class," wrote *Film Daily*. "Credit for this noteworthy western should go to Maurice Conn, who handled it as associate producer, Franklyn Warner, the executive producer, Frances Guihan, who wrote the story, and Sam Newfield, the director."[105] *Boxoffice* agreed, stating that as "a western action feature with a Civil War background it captures everything that could be desired and shows remarkably good production values for its budget classification."[106] Fine Arts had signed Houston to star in an eight-picture series of "outdoor action pictures,"[107] but given the film's splendid reviews it's surprising that *Frontier Scout* ended up being the sole film produced. Houston would find a new home in a few years over at Producers Releasing Corporation where he was hired as lead in "The Lone Rider" series. But more on that in an upcoming chapter.

Rugged George Houston has the upper hand in **Frontier Scout** (Fine Arts/Grand National, 1938), Sam Newfield director.

Trigger Pals (January 13, 1939) was the first entry in a six-film series made by Cinemart Productions starring band leader Arthur Jarrett (1907-1987), his first name reduced to a more rugged-sounding Art for the credits and promotional purposes. Former Grand National attorney Philip N. Krasne was put in charge of the newly incorporated production company to produce the Jarrett series, and a 300-acre tract dubbed Circle-K Ranch near Lake Sherwood would be the filming location for the oaters; it would be available for rent to other producers of Westerns as well. Sam was hired to direct a cast that included Lee Powell and the ubiquitous Al St. John, which went into production in November 1938.[108] Jarrett stars as the half-owner of a ranch, the other half owned by an eastern girl (Dorothy Faye) who wants to turn it into a dude ranch. Throw cattle rustler Ted Adams into the mix and you have a very familiar plot.

Trigger Pals (Cinemart/Grand National, 1939) pose for the camera, Philip N. Krasne producer, Sam Newfield director. Left-to-right: Art Jarrett ("apparently a better singer than a cowboy, but pleasant"), Al St. John, and Lee Powell.

The reaction to the film was mixed, which didn't bode well for Jarrett's future as a cowboy star. *The Exhibitor* was rather blasé, stating that Jarrett was "apparently a better singer than a cowboy, but pleasant."[109] Another insider, having viewed the rushes, was more taken by Jarrett's co-star:

Although Grand National signed Art Jarrett, the yodeler, to star in the western TRIGGER PALS, it looks very much as if a chap by the name of Lee Powell will turn out to be the real star. This handsome lad, who played THE LONE RANGER, will become G-N's western ace—unless the rushes betray us.[110]

Reviewers weren't overly impressed. *Boxoffice* dismissed it by stating that "An extremely thin story and weak comedy situations don't help this stock Western beyond stock values. It's not particularly in the film's favor that a tried and true formula is employed."[111] *Variety* sniffed that "There's little to redeem this production, even Art Jarrett failing to win his spurs either as an actor or singing cowboy."[112] Exhibitors, as always, had the last word: "Keep away from this. Impossible is the word. Even the kids walked out, and for two days I stayed out of the lobby."[113] It was one-and-done for Jarrett, who retreated to the more accepting world of music and stayed there until the 1950s when he started making some appearances on television.

Another six-picture musical Western series was launched in January 1939, starring Tex Fletcher (1910-1987), radio's "Lone Cowboy."[114] Producer Jack H. Skirball was the guy who hired Fletcher, an unusual choice for a singing cowboy star. Born Geremino Bisceglia to Italian immigrant parents, Fletcher had left home and traveled the country as a teen, learning the ways and skills of cowboys along the way. He landed at radio station WOR in Newark where, as *Variety* put it, "he used to kick rangeland musicales etherward into the wide open spaces around Manhattan."[115] A talent scout heard him, brought him to Skirball's attention, and Fletcher was signed.

Tex Fletcher does his damnedest to woo Joan Barclay in **Six-Gun Rhythm** (Arcadia, Grand National, 1939), the first—and only—entry in a proposed six-film series; Sam Newfield directed.

Fletcher could sing and ride, but it was in the looks department that he fell short. His first entry for the newly formed unit Arcadia Productions, tentatively titled *Rhythm Rides the Range*, was filmed under Sam's guidance and released as *Six-Gun Rhythm* (May 13, 1939).[116] Fletcher plays a college football hero who returns to the family ranch in Texas to find that his father is missing—as in murdered—the murderers still on the loose. As usual, they are cattle rustlers as well, led by silent leading man Reed Howes, but that kind of goes with the cinematic turf. Fletcher calls in his football pals and they help round up the culprits in a rather absurd semi-climax. What follows is perhaps the film's highlight, a fight between Fletcher and Howes amidst a raging sandstorm; something different for a change. Joan Barclay is in the cast to add some acting experience and sultry good looks to the otherwise uneven talent, with Ralph Peters adding some comic highlights whenever he attempts to dismount his horse. Some of Sam's directorial choices work against the film, Fletcher initially seen only from the back or at an oblique angle, his full face only revealed four minutes into the film. As for the outdoor sequences, most of them appear to have been filmed late in the day, the long shadows and dim lighting visually compromising many scenes. *Variety* pointed out that "Film has its selling troubles, except in those places listening to Fletcher for those six years he was committed to WOR."[117]

Grand National planned another musical Western series, this one to star ex-champion boxer Max Baer. Baer headed to Hollywood in mid-February to prepare for shooting, and Sam was set to direct, but those plans fizzled out.[118] By mid-1939, Grand National was in dire financial straits, and hadn't been able to supply its exchanges with films for the past several months. There was a brief flurry of excitement when they announced that the company had four features ready for release, *Six-Gun Rhythm* one of them.[119] The film suffered from spotty placements, so Fletcher rose to the occasion and made personal appearances nationwide to give the film a boost. Lucky for Fletcher that the Hazard Theatre in Hazard, Kentucky wasn't one of them, or at least on November 4. As the on-screen gunshots rang out, patrons failed to note the one additional gunshot that took place. When the lights came up, they were stunned to find a fellow patron shot to death, and by the theatre's jealous projectionist no less.[120] A film showing to remember.

After his brief experience with Grand National, Fletcher quit the business.

Victory Pictures

Meanwhile earlier in 1938, there was a lot of self-imposed belt-tightening at the majors due to the growing turmoil overseas. The foreign market, once the source of a third of Hollywood's income, had been halved due in no small part to the barring of some films in Japan, China, Germany, and Italy. The stateside market had shrunk as well, with a decline in many areas of 5 % to 30 %. This didn't sit well, so the majors went on a house-cleaning spree. The contract player ranks were thinned, and there was a decline in the renewal of featured players' contracts in those instances in which additional payment was guaranteed if options were renewed. M-G-M laid off 500 employees in one fell swoop, and RKO terminated a similar number; cuts at Paramount, Warners, and 20th Century-Fox, while not as severe, were ongoing as well. One of the first steps taken internally was the announcement that most of these studios would not make any more "B" grade films, "a statement that warmed the cockles of the anti-double-bill votaries," as it was reported by Wood Soanes in the *Oakland Tribune*. Well, not exactly; what they really meant was that they'd be more selective in the production of lesser fare, either spending a bit more to elevate a given script to programmer status, or junk it altogether. "These pictures have been useful to groom young players who show promise," the *Tribune* went on to report,

> and to provide employment for approaching has-beens who may still be useful in one way or another. But the young players are being routed out of the training schools maintained by the studios and the has-beens are being quickly dropped from the payrolls.[121]

The year 1938's projected production of an estimated 538 features was more than 30 % fewer than the 778 of 1937. This was music to the independents' ears, who were more than willing to take up the slack.

Within less than a half year the independent market was reported as "revitalized." Talisman Studios, which continued to rent space to the independents, installed an additional $10,000 worth of new sound equipment—new re-recorders, mixing panels, and a new sound room—to accommodate the expected increase in production.[122] As a result, the Independent Motion Picture Producers' Association (IMPPA) was revived after several years of dormancy caused by rising costs and the curtailment of indie production. The goal of the IMPPA was to gain concessions from the Screen Actors' Guild and other labor groups for lower labor costs than the scales set for the majors. Sig was reactivated as an officer of the group, along with Phil Goldstone, George Hirliman, and others.[123]

Meanwhile, the introduction of broadcasting had a huge impact on the entertainment industry, and by 1938 there were approximately forty million radios in households nationwide. Radio had become a favorite form of daily entertainment, cost-free after the initial expenditure to purchase the unit. This doesn't seem to have had much of an impact on the movie industry, however, one of the few businesses that did not suffer financially from the depression. By 1939, 65 % of the population was going to the movies at least once a week, and oftentimes more than once. Radio had become an entertainment adjunct, and not a replacement.

Sam, who was rarely out of work, benefitted from this increased production, entering into an agreement with producer Sam Katzman to direct eight Tim McCoy Westerns for Katzman's Victory Pictures. As initially announced, the titles for the upcoming productions would be *Lightning Carson Rides Again* (already in production by September 1938), *Texas Wildcats*, *Outlaw's Paradise*, *The Fighting Renegade*, *Singing Six Guns*, *Phantom Guns*, *Pecos Troublemakers*, and *Return of the Terror*.[124] Only the first four titles would be retained when the eight were finally released. All laboratory work for Victory would be handled by Nat Saland's Mercury Laboratories in New York.[125]

Producer Sam Katzman.

Sam Katzman (1901-1973) got his start during the silent era back in 1914 at Fox, initially doing a bit of everything from prop man to assisting producers. He later served as assistant director on a number of shorts and features, after which he functioned in the same capacity in the early 1930s for some of Bryan Foy's productions for Columbia. Katzman switched over to production manager, first for D.J. Mountan's Showmen's Pictures for Screencraft in 1933. In 1934, Katzman went to work for A.W. Hackel and his Supreme Pictures, serving as producer on a number of Bob Steele Westerns. (Katzman's wife Hortense later claimed that she had told him she would only marry a producer, prompting the change.) Cinematographer Richard Kline, who lensed a number of Katzman's later films, provided a rather humorous description of the outgoing producer to interviewer Tom Weaver: "Have you ever seen a picture of Sam Katzman? He looks just like you would think a Sam Katzman WOULD look like. He was the PERFECT Sam Katzman [laughs]!"[126]

Seeing how well Hackel was doing as an independent producer, Katzman decided to get into the game and formed his own Victory Pictures in May 1935.[127] Operating out of the Bryan Foy Studios in Culver City,[128] Katzman launched into a string of dramas (very) loosely based on stories by prolific writer Peter B. Kyne,[129] serials, and Westerns, the latter frequently starring Tom Tyler. In 1938, he signed Tim McCoy to star, and Sam to direct. It wouldn't be out of the old Foy Studios, however:

Clinching of an eight-picture deal with Tim McCoy, western star, will end a long period of idleness for Sam Katzman and his Victory Pictures. Katzman, whose Culver City studio was destroyed by fire last year, will shoot at Conn Studios, the first of the series to get into work before August 15. He will seek state-right releases.[130]

Katzman's studio had burnt to the ground back in January, an estimated $100,000 loss. Arson was suspected since his studio had nearly suffered a similar fate back in June 1937.[131]

McCoy needed the work. He had such a good time touring with the Ringling Brothers in the summers of 1935, 1936, and 1937, that he had decided to form his own show. His timing couldn't have been worse, as he explained in his autobiography.

It was 1938, a year many of us in show business later regarded as possibly the worst year of the Depression. The Hagenbeck-Wallace Circus closed down that year when, because of an inability to pay for it, their new canvas was confiscated by a sheriff in Riverside, California. Even Ringling Bros. and Barnum & Bailey, because of insoluble labor disputes, had been forced to cancel out dates and return to their winter quarters. So, with all the survival instincts of a lemming, I set about putting together America's last wild West show.[132]

The show was called Colonel Tim McCoy's Real Wild West and Rough Riders of the World, and it had its premiere on April 14, 1938, in Chicago's International Amphitheatre. It flopped, and closed twenty-one days later in Washington, D.C.

In Chicago a month ago Tim McCoy's Real Wild West and Rough Riders of the World were let loose with charging horses, yippiding cowboys, lassos thrown to rope in the general public. In Washington last week McCoy's broncos seemed all too sadly busted. First, F. Stewart Stranahan of Providence, R.I., with a $17,500 claim against the show, threw it into receivership. Then, padding at Stranahan's heels a delegation of McCoy's Sioux Redmen visited Commissioner of Indian Affairs John Collier, threatened a sitdown strike against Tim McCoy unless he: (1) came through with back pay, (2) furnished more than one clean shirt a week, (3) provided free war paint. Sent back to the show by Collier, the Sioux refused to perform. In a big frontier-drama act where white men were supposed to make Indians bite the dust, for two performances there was not a Sioux Indian to bite.

After that, there were no performances at all. Restrained by court order from moving on to Baltimore, the show folded for good in Washington, a martyr to McCoy's belief that the Buffalo Bill tradition still has life in it.[133]

The court appointed receiver divided what little money there was in the show's treasury among the roughly 500 now-jobless employees, which amounted to about $5 each. The show, it was reported, had $400,000 when it started out three weeks earlier.[134] "I lost about $300,000 on that deal," recalled McCoy years later.[135]

With that coffer-depleting fiasco behind him, McCoy needed to quickly recoup his losses, making a four-picture deal with Monogram—two of which Sam directed for Concord Productions—followed by this signing with Katzman.

Katzman—undoubtedly with some input from Sam—put together a production team that remained fairly consistent for the eight productions. Holbrook Todd served as editor on all eight, with Ed W. Rote functioning as production manager on all of them as well. Todd, who had first worked on Sig and Sam's *Border Caballero* for Puritan, would soon become an integral part of their production team, serving as editor on well over 100 films post-Victory. Rote, who was well into his sixties by this time, had gotten his credited start as production manager for Katzman back in 1935 with *Hot Off the Press*, and would continue in that capacity for Katzman up until he retired in 1944 after his work on the East Side Kids' *Bowery Champs*.

Hans Weeren (consistently misspelled "Weerin" in each film's credits) handled the sound recording on six of Katzman's Victory titles, Glen Glenn handling those chores on the other two. Weeren, who had first worked with the brothers back at Ambassador and for Sam on-and-off since then, would become a permanent fixture for them at Producers Releasing Corp. in the years to come, up until his untimely death in 1943. Settings for the Victory Westerns were cobbled together by Fred Preble on six films, Harry Reif handling settings on a seventh, and *The Fighting Renegade*—sans a credit for settings—is anyone's guess.

Charles Henry, an unknown both before and after, was Sam's assistant director for the first two films, after which Bert Sternbach was brought in for the remaining six films, beginning with *Code of the Cactus*. Sternbach would soon become Sig and Sam's most important collaborator and, as it turned out, lifelong friend.

Bert Sternbach

Born in Austria on March 12, 1887, fifteen-year-old Bert Nathan Sternbach emigrated to the U.S. in 1902, taking up residence in Newark, New Jersey. By 1918 Sternbach had relocated to Los Angeles, where he was hired by the Sterns to work at the L-Ko/Century Studios. Over the next eleven years, Sternbach's importance to the Sterns had grown, with promotions to studio casting director, purchasing agent, and location chief, along with the advisory staff of the Script Building department, and the co-writing of scenarios with Sig. In 1928, Sternbach was "placed in charge of comedy product,"[136] which one would assume was another way of saying he was made the studio's production manager. There was a brief break in Sternbach's tenure with the Sterns, resigning in 1925 to enter the theatrical costuming business,[137] and a few instances where he would serve as production manager on several late twenties Weiss Brothers/Artclass comedy shorts, but he returned to the Sterns and remained with them up until the studio's closing in 1929.

The cast and crew of the Weiss Brothers/Artclass comedy **Better Behave** (1928) pose for the camera. Star Poodles Hanneford in top hat, sitting center, production manager Bert Sternbach to the left of him, William McCall behind Sternbach with bowtie and mustache, Joe Young to the right of McCall in police uniform. *Courtesy of Tim Neufeld.*

Little mention was made of Sternbach over the following few years. Unmarried his whole life, Sternbach resided in a rental at 6004 Lexington Avenue in Los Angeles. In October 1933, Sternbach, Sam Newfield, and Arthur Alexander incorporated the Novelty Pictures Company.[138] The company's base of operations was located at the Alexander Studios, and it is unclear whether any films resulted from this venture, although 1935's *You Can Be Had*, which Sam directed with Sternbach and Alexander producing, is a likely suspect, and the only known collaboration of the trio at this time. By 1934, Sternbach had gone to work as a producer for Consolidated Pictures, Inc., whose output was distributed by Stage & Screen Productions, Inc. on a state rights basis. Sternbach oversaw two "Tarzan, the Police Dog" films—*Captured in Chinatown* (1934) and *Million Dollar Haul* (1935)—as well as the Robert Hill-directed Rex Lease starrer *Inside Information* (1934). Production of *The Drunkard* followed, for Weiss Productions.

Recently Bert Sternbach and Louis Weiss decided to film it [the 1844 melodramatic play, *The Drunkard; or, The Fallen Saved*] with fortitude and abandon. Loaded with gestures and the frightful acting of a century ago, it is about as uproarious a thing as has come along. Happily, the action of the yarn is broken by the observations of an audience of today, on which the camera swerves during the play's progress. One member of the audience, Milburn Moranty [sic], never says a word but his pantomime as he watches cursed drink get the better of the hero is as droll acting as the cinema offers.[139]

This may have been both Sam and Sternbach's "introduction" to Morante, who would be given numerous bit parts in so many of Sig and Sam's films that followed.

Sam, Sans Sig (Part 2: 1936-1940)   149

Sternbach rejoined Sig in 1935 when Excelsior Pictures was formed, and would remain with him for the next couple of years in the capacity of Excelsior's general manager and purchasing agent; don't look for his name in any of the credits. Sam and Sternbach's working relationship resumed uninterrupted from 1937 on while Sig was at parts unknown, with films for Jed Buell's Spectrum Pictures and Principal Productions 1937-38, and as assistant director on *Trigger Pals*, released a month earlier than *Code of the Cactus*. In the years that followed his stint serving as Sam's assistant on Katzman's McCoy series, Sternbach would remain a mostly permanent fixture on Sig and/or Sam's productions for the remainder of their collective careers.

Katzman had a closely knit stock company of sorts for these productions, the fact that they were knocked out one after another in rapid succession simplifying matters. Dependable character actors all, the recurring cast included some combination of Ted Adams, Forrest Taylor, Bob Terry, Slim Whitaker, Frank Wayne, Reed Howes, Karl Hackett, Frank LaRue, Alden Chase, and Dave O'Brien. Uncredited bits included silent comedians Milburn Morante, "Tiny" Lipson (usually as a café owner, waiter, or bartender), Jimmy Aubrey, and even Kermit Maynard as a back-of-the-pack henchman. Their professionalism and adequate, if not excellent, acting abilities were a definite asset to these otherwise threadbare productions.

Behind-the-scenes shot taken on the set of one of Sam Katzman's Tim McCoy entries for Victory Pictures. Sam Newfield at left, Tim McCoy sitting, Sam Katzman second from right. *Courtesy of Laura Berk.*

These films were made fast and cheaply, the environment in which Sam felt most at home. The McCoy Westerns had budgets approximating $8,000 per, $4,000 of which went directly into McCoy's pocket. McCoy remained a magnet to fans of Westerns, however, these films pulling in between $40,000 and $60,000 per picture.[140] McCoy would play the same character in all eight films, that of "Lightning" Bill Carson, introduced two years earlier in Sig and Sam's *Lightnin' Bill Carson* for Puritan. McCoy's quick-draw sheriff was updated to a Department of Justice agent for the series' initial entries. All of them were set in the current day, a move that further simplified production: no need to worry about background telephone poles or any other anachronistic item that might creep into a shot.

The story and screenplay for *Lightning Carson Rides Again* (October 10, 1938) and the film that followed were credited to "E.R. O'Dasi," which was a pseudonym used by screenwriter Isadore Bernstein.[141] Bernstein had been writing scenarios since the early 1910s under his real name, hiding behind the "O'Dasi" moniker for these two low-rent productions.

Bob Terry is sneaking up on Tim McCoy in **Lightning Carson Rides Again** (Victory, 1938), Sam Katzman Producer, Sam Newfield director.

When McCoy hears that his nephew, Bob Terry, is wanted for robbery and murder, he decides to investigate, heading to the small western town where this all went down. Disguised as gambler José Fernandez, McCoy infiltrates the local gang who had actually stolen the bank money and framed Terry, earns their confidence, and finagles it so that they trust him enough to take the $10,000 to Mexico to exchange it for "clean" money. Reed Howes, a gang member that "José" had fought with earlier, doesn't trust this newcomer, and eventually gets the evidence to break McCoy's cover. McCoy didn't earn the nickname "Lightning" for nothing, disarming Howes just as recruits arrive to arrest the remainder of the gang. Except for the big boss, that is, whose identity has been hidden up until now, when McCoy pursues and arrests him. It's the bank's cashier, played by Frank Wayne.

McCoy, evidently relishing the opportunity to revisit his Mexican characterization featured in the earlier *Border Caballero*, is the film's saving grace. Aside from that, what little there was budget-wise isn't up there on the screen. Sam's direction was hurried and perfunctory, editor Holbrook attempting to add—unsuccessfully, I might add—a tad of visual excitement by repeatedly cutting back and forth from the action to static medium shots of onlookers supposedly observing same. The rest of the actors give uneven performances, and poor Joan Barclay, here as Terry's sweetheart, is given pitifully little to do and is wasted. The plot device of the gang actually trusting this South-of-the-Border newcomer with their hard-stolen cash is ludicrous at best, and McCoy's makeup as José wouldn't fool a five-year-old. Sam manages to inject a few nice little bits of business, perhaps the best of these an offscreen showdown between McCoy and some hothead: the clock strikes ten, McCoy excuses himself and leaves the room, several shots ring out, and back he saunters to resume his card game.

Six Gun Trail (November 25, 1938), filmed at International Studios in early October,[142] is a better film, not that O'Dasi/Bernstein's script is any more plausible, but visually it is far superior. Sam rose to the occasion this time around, contributing a couple of rousing set pieces: the opening, violent robbery and shootout at the post office; and a later, extended shootout in a saloon, the first half with the lights on, the second in the dark. Cinematographer Marcel Le Picard—here billed as Marcel Picard—seems to have lavished more care on this production, perhaps a function of more time (doubtful), more money (doubtful), or pride (more likely). His camera work is fluid, his setups well chosen, and his lighting more natural or, in some instances, moody. It shines in the two set pieces just mentioned, and in an early scene where McCoy gives one of the robbery captors the third degree. Elsewhere it looks more hurried and unimaginative, but at least he took pains when able to deliver some nicer work.

The plot allows McCoy to delve into another silly disguise, this one of a fence of Chinese extraction, an impression that makes the previous film's "Mexican" Oscar-worthy by comparison. The story has McCoy heading south to a border town trailing the fellows who robbed the post office of a load of precious jewels. Posing as the Chinese fence, he once again worms his way into the gang, gains their confidence, and agrees to swap the jewels for a load of cash. Being the bad guys, they fully intend to grab the cash and keep the jewels, but with an assist from fellow Justice Department agent Magpie, played by Ben Corbett, McCoy overpowers the crooks and takes them and their unscrupulous leader (Alden Chase) prisoner. Like I said, it's the visuals that make this the better film.

Comedian Ben Corbett (1892-1961), who played a throw-away character named "Shorty" in the previous film, has a far meatier role here as "Magpie," McCoy's cohort, a competent cohort for a change, with only moments of levity allowed to creep in. Magpie would be a recurring character in the remaining six films as well; the cynic in me thinks he was chosen to make McCoy look younger by comparison. Nora Lane, whose character is out on probation thanks to McCoy, repays his former kindness with a warning that his life is in danger. Otherwise, she has little else to do but stand around, looking concerned and wringing her hands. There are two musical numbers in this film—some would say two too many—one a yodel-filled ditty crooned in the saloon by a singer named Hal Carey, and another sung (or should I say poorly lip-synched) by Lane. One exhibitor chimed in about the film in general and the singing in particular: "A good western picture with excellent photograph, a lot of action and a gal who can't sing. Why do the producers think it necessary to inject a coupla songs into a standard western?"[143] Beats me; maybe to pad an overly thin plot? Those songs, by the way, were penned by the composing duo Lew Porter and Johnny Lange, musicians who seemed to have had a lock on knocking out decent little songs for inclusion in Poverty Row quickies during the period 1936-1942, together or independently. Porter, once again, gets pressed into service as the saloon's piano player.

Tim McCoy and Nora Lane in one of those romantic moments that must have bored the wee ones to tears, in **Six-Gun Trail** (Victory, 1938), Sam Katzman producer, Sam Newfield director.

Katzman leased space at the Progressive Studios in December to film interiors for *Code of the Cactus* (February 25, 1939) and its follow-up, *Texas Wildcats*.[144] The plot of *Code of the Cactus* was beginning to feel familiar, but McCoy's winning personality saved the film, as usual, and the film's gimmick of using trucks rather than horseback for rustling, courtesy of screenwriter Edward Halperin, sets this one slightly apart from its predecessors. Halperin, you'll recall, was producer of the earlier horror films *White Zombie* (1932) and *Revolt of the Zombies* (1936), both directed by his brother Victor.

In this one Magpie is a rancher who calls on his old buddy McCoy when he's besieged by so-called truck rustlers, a gang led by Ted Adams who uses the "modern" conveyances to steal the local ranchers' cattle. Adams is stealing the cattle for his boss, Forrest Taylor, who uses the cut-rate cattle to underbid competitors to land a government contract. McCoy resorts to his Mexican masquerade, this time passing himself off as a hijacker named Don Miguel something-or-other. He infiltrates the gang, gains their confidence, then turns the tables on them. Adams is shot dead in a big shootout between the ranchers and gang members. McCoy pursues Taylor and shoots him dead as well. Dave O'Brien has a smaller role as a cattle detective working undercover at Magpie's ranch, wooing and ultimately winning over Magpie's daughter, played by Dorothy Short.

It's typical stuff, but handled well enough to appease the critics. "Here is a top-rating western, in the McCoy manner, that should prove a response-getter in western houses," wrote *The Exhibitor*.[145] *Motion Picture Herald* was a bit more reserved, stating that "[f]or entertainment and commercial purposes, 'Code of the Cactus' will offer a standard outdoor adventure story in which a few novelties have been incorporated.... The climax will not be different from the finale of 1,001 westerns, down to the chase and hand-to-hand fight." As for the man in charge, "Sam Newfield, who has handled as many western stories as any man in the business, is directing."[146] Faint praise, indeed.

Tea time in **Code of the Cactus** (Victory, 1939), Sam Katzman producer, Sam Newfield director. Left-to-right: Ben Corbett, Tim McCoy, Dorothy Short, Dave O'Brien.
Courtesy of the American Heritage Center, University of Wyoming.

Texas Wildcats (April 10, 1939) went into production on January 15, 1939.[147] Interiors were filmed at Progressive, heading to Chatsworth afterwards for location sequences.[148] One can question why McCoy dived head first into relying on masquerades to deflect blame from his Carson character—here he doubles as "The Phantom"—but dive he did. McCoy comes to town and poses as a gambler, aiming to find out who murdered his Ranger friend. Posing as The Phantom as well, he bedevils rich and ruthless Forrest Taylor, who along with his equally ruthless son Bob Terry intends to foreclose on the property held by Joan Barclay and her brother Dave O'Brien; seems like gold's been discovered there. Terry shoots and kidnaps O'Brien to prevent him from making that final mortgage payment, McCoy and undercover pal Corbett (as Magpie) get to the bottom of things and expose Taylor's gang. Taylor accidentally shoots and kills his son, mistaking him for McCoy.

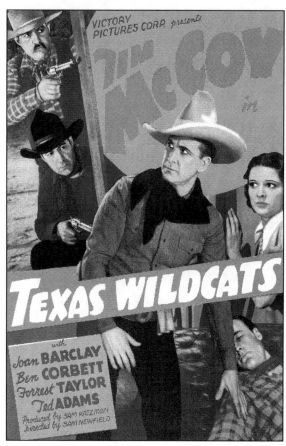

Tim McCoy at a slight disadvantage in **Texas Wildcats** (Victory, 1939), Sam Katzman producer, Sam Newfield director.

At least McCoy has left his Mexican and Chinese disguises behind for this one, less encumbered by a simple black mask when posing as The Phantom. The film is on par technically with its predecessors—no better, no worse—and Sam injects his usual energy in the film's fights and shootouts. He lazily resorts to the series opener's device of having McCoy engage another hothead—here Reed Howes—in an offscreen shootout. What stood out as a clever bit in *Lightning Carson Rides Again* comes across here as an uncreatively expedient shortcut, and to further compromise the scene's impact, Howes is later shown to have only an arm wound. McCoy is even stiffer, steely-eyed, and unemotional in this one, and that's okay. As Magpie—here given the surname of McGillicuddy and posing as a grizzled prospector—Corbett impresses once again, shifting easily and convincingly from menace to mirth. O'Brien's character makes a fortune-risking decision to go drinking with Terry, who is scheming to get his hands on that wad of bills, losing whatever audience sympathy existed, if any. As for his relationship with younger sister Joan Barclay, it feels just a little too "chummy." Barclay, initially enthralled by The Phantom, later (albeit unsuccessfully) blows his cover, but gets a pass since she's so darn cute.

The exciting and suspenseful *Outlaw's Paradise* is one of the best of the Katzman series, as long as you take it with a healthy dose of suspension of disbelief. McCoy, again as Dept. of Justice Carson, just happens to be a dead ringer for imprisoned gang leader Trigger Mallory, also played by McCoy. Trigger's old gang robs a post office of $30,000 in negotiable bonds, killing two in the process. Trigger is about to be released from prison, so Carson decides to impersonate him, worm his way back into the gang, catch them red handed rustling cattle, and arrest the bunch of them. Interim gang leader Ted Adams wants the gang to himself—and, for that matter, Trigger's sexy girlfriend Joan Barclay as well—so he resents "Trigger's" return. Adams catches on to the charade and is shot dead by McCoy, but things go from bad to worse when the real Trigger shows up and blows McCoy's cover. Fortunately, Magpie is on the job as well—undercover, as usual—and arrives in the nick of time. After a shootout and wild chase, the pursuing gang is subdued and arrested. As for Barclay, old softy McCoy lets her escape, his reasoning that she inadvertently "rescued" him. A stretch, but so be it.

Barclay, it was reported, had a close call with a Brahma bull that had escaped from the corral.

> Joan had just dismounted from her horse after a ride through the sagebrush for a scene while on location near Chatsworth. She had removed her coat and sat down to fix her makeup. Unknown to her, a Brahma bull had gotten loose from the lower corrals and charged up toward the company. Miss Barclay was right in the path of the animal, facing in the opposite direction. Recognizing the danger that threatened her, both Katzman and McCoy rushed in and headed off the super-heavy beast. They succeeded in roping the bull and returning it to the corral.[149]

Tim McCoy seems to have a thing for Joan Barclay, and who can blame him? From **Outlaw's Paradise** (Victory, 1939), Sam Katzman producer, Sam Newfield director.

The third in series to go into production the week of November 28, 1938,[150] *Outlaw's Paradise* was the fifth to be released on April 19, 1939. The film opens and closes with a bang, the initial robbery nicely orchestrated and satisfyingly violent, and the concluding showdown sufficiently exciting, with McCoy and Magpie using a trip-rope to tumble three pursuers from their horses, marred only by the insertion of a snippet of stock for the actual tumble itself. Bob Terry takes his by-now familiar surly gang member role, but for a change Dave O'Brien joins the other side of the law as a fellow gang member. Ted Adams is his usual sneering, scheming thug, but at least he's shot dead in this one rather than taken prisoner. McCoy appears to relish the opportunity to portray a swaggering, bellowing thug, and with this dual role dispenses with the stereotypical Mexican and Chinese masquerades. Barclay for a change plays the bad girl, hard-edged and cold, only allowed to show a fleeting moment of warmth at film's end. As for Corbett as Magpie, his recurring presence is one of the more satisfying aspects of this series, all the more so since he plays an effectual, active participant in the action, and not the broad comic relief of an Al St. John.

Reviewers, alas, were not as keen on the film, *Boxoffice* complaining that it "drags and drags until the last reel."[151] *Variety* was of a similar mindset: "This western will have to rest on the reputation of Tim McCoy for any business, even as a filler on double bills.... Plot has whiskers."[152] Yes, but they are *good* whiskers.

McCoy was well aware of—and seemingly okay with—the sameness of these plots as well as the liberties the screenwriters would take with historical accuracy, as he later explained to interviewer Anthony Thomas:

Westerns became stereotyped. They looked as though they had been cut out with cookie cutters. The truth about the real West was twisted to conform to the writer's preconceptions, and when historical figures were used there was so much fiction they could have been anybody. However, you always have to remember motion pictures are not made to serve as documents of history. Movies are entertainment, but even so, I've always maintained, you can give audiences authenticity *with* the entertainment.[153]

Straight Shooters (August 12, 1939), which went before cameras in late June, is barely worth mentioning since it is unquestionably the worst of the eight Katzman films. Not only is the production bare bones, but there is a whole, slightly re-edited six minute section midway lifted from *Six Gun Trail*, released the previous November, that covers Magpie conning a drink at the saloon's bar and the gunfights that followed therein. And as if that shameless padding and corner-cutting isn't bad enough, totally anachronistic dialog was left in to further muddy the waters. The plot has McCoy, now an agent for the F.B.I., tracking down the gang—led by reptilian Ted Adams, of course—responsible for the theft of a half million in bonds. One of the gang's elder members, who they unceremoniously dispatch in the opening sequence, had made off with the bonds, so the rest of the film has everyone trying to locate them; his niece Julie Sheldon shows up to provide the requisite love interest. Co-writers Basil Dickey and Joseph O'Connell should have been ashamed of themselves.

There's little commendable about this film, but I'll make a stab at it. First of all, Sheldon is an attractive presence, and an acceptable actress despite her mush-mouthed, Katherine Hepburn-ish delivery. That this is only the first of two credited film roles says something about her reception as an actress in Hollywood, but she's much better than some of the actresses McCoy was saddled with in this series. The only other positive thing is the stock music used in this and the other Katzman Westerns in this series, which is far more suitable and thoughtfully utilized than some of the lousy scores dumped into other comparable Poverty Row Westerns of the period. Faint praise, I realize, but the best I can do. *Variety* shared my reaction to this film: "Sam Newfield must have directed this one standing up and running, because balled lines, improper emphasis, and other inconsistencies didn't stop the headlong, one-take rush to get the pic done.... McCoy...can't go much further with this kind of actionless stuff if he's to survive."[154]

Unfortunately, the one takeaway that Sam may have gleaned from Katzman's penny-pinching bag of tricks was the reuse of footage and, in some instances, entire scenes from his earlier films in later films, a cost- and time-saving approach that would be revisited increasingly in the frenetic years ahead at PRC.

Ben Corbett, Julie Sheldon, and Tim McCoy seem to have things under control in **Straight Shooters** (Victory, 1939), Sam Katzman producer, Sam Newfield director.

McCoy reprises his Mexican masquerade for seemingly the umpteenth time in *The Fighting Renegade* (September 1, 1939), a necessity since "Lightning" Carson was believed to have murdered the head of an expedition six years earlier. As "El Puma," McCoy travels high and low with his gang hoping to track down Ted Adams, the real murderer. He runs into a new expedition headed by Forrest Taylor, determined to locate the Indian relics and gold that the earlier expedition was after. The murdered professor's daughter, played by newcomer Joyce Bryant, is along for the ride since she's the only one able to translate the Indian writing.

This one's a real snooze,[155] only marginally better than its predecessor. Sam directed this entire film on exterior locations with help from assistant director Bert Sternbach, thereby saving Katzman the added expenditure of renting studio space for interiors. Art Reed's cinematography is workmanlike, no more, no less. There are the occasional on-screen filmic blunders, most noticeable is Dave O'Brien's hat, knocked from his head when he's rendered unconscious on horseback, magically reappearing as he regains consciousness. Ted Adams plays his stock villain, which he's good at, less so when it comes to dismounting a horse or tentatively trotting down a hillside. Budd Buster, as a character called "Old Dobie," seems to spend half his screen time hiding in bushes spying on the others, in one cutaway after another. Forrest Taylor plays the short-lived professor heading the new expedition, the pince-nez he wears visually reinforcing his character's pompousness. Dave O'Brien doesn't fare much better as Joyce Bryant's fiancé, annoyingly condescending and even more pompous than Taylor, if such a thing is possible. Reed Howes gets to play a good guy for a change in a brief part as the sheriff. Curiously, Ben Corbett, as Magpie, delivers his lines in a more mannered, less natural fashion than in previous films, which leads one to suspect that Sam was determined to settle for single takes, regardless of how poorly any of his actors' delivery was. The film's acting standout is Joyce Bryant in one of her first released starring roles, hired by Katzman for *Trigger Fingers*, shot several months before but released after this film. Not only is she an extremely attractive presence, but her delivery and relaxed performance is far better than most of the starlets featured in this Katzman series. Bryant's career, such as it was, found her stuck primarily in low budget fare such as this and the random uncredited role, her stint in films effectively coming to an end in the early forties. The unremarkable script was by William Lively, who only had five other films to his credit before this, one of them Sam's Fred Scott-starrer *The Fighting Deputy*. Credit where credit is due, however: for once it didn't involve cattle rustling. *Variety* was quick to point this out, and the script's shortcomings as well. "Tim McCoy, disguised in a Mexican bandit...role, pretty familiar stuff by now, attempts to dress up Western bad man formula by cloaking the proceedings in a pseudo-scientific expedition. Idea had possibilities. Writer has mangled theme so badly, however, that final result is nothing more than the usual roundup of band of desperadoes and killers."[156] Screenwriter Lively's purview remained in films of this sort with the occasional serial thrown in, eventually turning to the television industry in the early fifties before retiring at decade's end.

It's unclear as to whether McCoy's use of disguises in most of the series' entries was his idea or Katzman's, but he was back at it in *Trigger Fingers*, the final McCoy/Katzman/Newfield offering to the public, released on November 1, 1939. Basil Dickey's screenplay didn't offer much that was new plot-wise, but there's enough in this film to like that helps it to stand out from the others. McCoy poses as a gypsy to investigate cattle rustling—what else?—but this time is joined by both Magpie (Corbett) and his secretary, Joyce Bryant, who don costumes as well. McCoy's accent is a mashup of intended Italian with unintentional overtones of his standard Mexican patois. Carleton Young appears as the head rustler, the ubiquitous Ted Adams his second in command.

Harley Wood has a starring role as well, billed above Bryant in the credits but with a much smaller part. A popular radio actress, Wood had entered films back in 1935, with random appearances under her own name and using the pseudonym Jill Martin for several of the Westerns she appeared in, this film included. She's not a particularly engaging actress, her two facial expressions switching between glum, turned-down mouth to blinding smile. Not surprisingly, this was her final film, deciding to concentrate on music composition with far more success. Bryant is the primary reason to like this film, an active participant in the proceedings from beginning to end (except during the fistfights), and a charming presence. The film's running joke is that both McCoy and Corbett refer to her by her nickname "Maggie," which she hates and frequently reminds them: "Margaret's the name." Sounds silly, but it garners a number of mood-lightening chuckles. Sam and Katzman are shameless in their cost-saving reuse not only of general stock footage, but from footage from at least three of their previous films together, *Code of the Cactus* and *Six Gun Trail* among them. One of the film's unintended charms is when one of the crew clears his throat offscreen, and they didn't bother to remove it—B-movie economics at its best.

Tim McCoy dons a gypsy disguise for a welcome change of pace in **Trigger Fingers** (Victory, 1939), Sam Katzman producer, Sam Newfield director.

Katzman's McCoy series, while not nearly as satisfying or technically proficient as Sig and Sam's earlier Excelsior productions for Puritan, still delivered the goods, albeit in a slightly compromised package. McCoy, of course, was the draw, and despite the wisdom of his resorting to donning costumes and characterizations to deflect attention from his character of Carson, remained the no-nonsense upholder of the law that the audience demanded.

With the completion of the McCoy series, Katzman had a decision to make. In January 1939 he had ambitiously announced a new season lineup of twenty Westerns.[157] Unfortunately, the indies' optimism about their future of only a few months earlier had soured, and prospects were dismal. "So far the many announced program have not even reached the scripting stage and there exists little likelihood that the first half of 1939 will see more than a handful of independent pictures completed," reported David James Hanna in *Film Bulletin*. "Veteran Sammy Katzman is proceeding very slowly and does not expect to complete his program of twenty pictures."[158] "Slowly," as in "Not at all;" Katzman finally decided to shut Victory down and head over to Monogram where he'd find a welcoming home for the foreseeable future until switching over to Columbia in 1947.

Hanna's primary explanation for the problems faced by the independents was the lack of distribution facilities, as few of the state rights exchanges were still available. As a result, some territories were not even available any longer, resulting in a loss of hundreds of potential playdates. His solution, and why it was a non-starter:

> One or two independent producers cannot work out a distribution set-up merely for themselves. Effective exchange representation requires the co-operation of every independent film man in Hollywood. What should be established immediately is a nation-wide system of exchanges to be fed by the combined product of all the indie producers. Yet every time the subject of a co-operative exchange system is brought up in indie circles, the idea is quickly abandoned because some of the short-sighted producers feel that there would be created a mutual feeling of antagonism should one man's film receive a better sales break than his associates.
> Frankly this belongs in the category of "little boy" stuff. This plan basically is the same as that under which United Artists has operated and prospered for many years. What minor injustices may be suffered by one producer or another are hardly sufficient reason for blocking consummation of a plan which would rescue all of the more substantial independent producers.

Hanna added that "Ben Judell, the former Chicago exchange man, has apparently withdrawn from the production end of the industry, having completed only three of the twenty-six features on his schedule."[159]

Judell would soon prove Hanna wrong.

Chapter 9:
Ben Judell Shoots for the Big Time (Sig, Sam, and PPC/PDC, 1939-1940)

For the first time in several years, Sig and Sam were to be reunited in what would become the most fruitful and lucrative collaborative period of their respective lives. This would be a result of the ambitions of Ben N. Judell, although their actual association with him would turn out to be short-lived.

Ben Judell (1891-1974) was not a newcomer to the business, with thirty-four years' previous involvement in the distribution and, more recently, the production of features. As early as 1912 Judell was handling the Mutual Film Corporation's films out of their Minneapolis office, having severed ties with the Western Film Exchange's Milwaukee office.[1] By 1915 he had been transferred to Mutual's Chicago office[2] as their western representative, and within three years had left Mutual to work for Universal's exchange back in Minneapolis. That didn't work out, so a mere three months later, Judell set up his own independent exchange—B.N. Judell, Inc.—in Minneapolis, with plans to open a branch office in Chicago[3] to distribute films on a state rights basis. Nearly twenty successful years passed before Judell took heed of the old adage that "the grass is always greener on the other side of the fence"—greener with dollars, that is—and decided to go into production. In late 1937, after two years spent on the Coast studying productions methods, Judell announced that he had "discovered what exhibs want—and they will get it!" With ambitious plans for forty-four features, Judell organized four new exchanges in Detroit, Kansas City, Los Angeles, and San Franciso, to be added to his existing string of established exchanges. Production was to begin on January 1, 1938, under the banner Progressive Pictures, a closed corporation.[4]

Within five months Judell's Progressive Pictures had wrapped on three "controversial and problem subjects" for release during the current season—*Delinquent Parents*, *Rebellious Daughters*, and *Slander House*—with another ten planned. Forty-two more features were announced for the upcoming 1938-39 season: thirty "exploitation features," six outdoor adventures, and six Westerns.[5] As it turned out, only those three completed features would be released before Judell closed the doors on Progressive; he had far bigger plans for the future.

A year would pass before Judell announced the formation of a new company—unnamed as of June 1939—to produce thirty-six features for the 1939-40 season with a budget of "about $1,000,000." Six of these were to be in the "A" classification, with distribution through a twenty-seven-franchise exchange setup, seven of which were Judell's own exchanges and the rest those owned and operated by others. Harry Rathner—more on him shortly—was the new company's New York-based sales manager and eastern representative, Jerry Olenick advertising and publicity manager operating out of Los Angeles, and Sig Neufeld—now back in the low budget game—in charge of production.[6] Within a week, production plans were upped to sixty with the addition of a series of twenty-four Westerns, and an expansion of the projected budget to cover the increase. The company, operating out of temporary quarters at 1033 North Cahuenga Avenue, now had a name as well: Producers Pictures Corp., with distribution to be handled by Producers Distributing Corp. Judell served as president and treasurer of both companies, the venture by now a family affair of sorts: son Harvey Judell was named as secretary of both, and Clara Judell, Ben's spouse, as vice president. Six associate producers were assigned to handle actual production under Sig's supervision.[7] By June the entire executive and production staff had been moved into a leased building at 1436 North Beachwood Avenue,[8] the former home of Bell Automatic Cinema Machines.

Tim McCoy was signed for a new series of eight Westerns, the first of which—*Texas Renegades*—was scheduled to go into production on July 24. Robert Tansey was scheduled to direct, but for reasons unknown production was delayed until December, with Sam now set to direct (nepotism, combined with the building of a new, Arizona-based studio, would be my guess). George Houston was announced to star in another series of eight under the title "Tales of Billy the Kid," the first entry tentatively titled *The Man from Oklahoma*. The Houston series never came to fruition, but he would be hired within a year for another series, and the "Billy the Kid" series resurrected with a new lead. Three other upcoming films were announced as well, to be shot at the Grand National Studios: the detective yarn *Wanted for Murder*; the melodrama *The Island of Fear*, based on a story by Jack London; and the big-budgeted, sensationally titled *Hitler—the Beast of Berlin*, which Judell described as "an expose of Nazi barbarism."[9] With those upcoming Westerns in mind, Judell had a new studio built in Granite Dells area of Prescott, Arizona. Bert Sternbach was brought on board as general manager of this new plant, the construction crew working overtime to achieve an October 1 production start. Both the McCoy and Houston films were to be produced there, as well as a feature tentatively titled *Brigham Young—Utah Miracle Man* for December release, and a third Western series of eight "Sagebrush Family" features to star thirteen-year-old junior cowboy champion Bobby Clark.[10] The new location was to have "an administration building and suitable living quarters for the production personnel, executives, players and technicians. These are being built under supervision of Peter Stewart [Sam Newfield] from plans by the company's art director, Fred Preble."[11]

The Island of Fear, more sensationally retitled as *Torture Ship* for its October 22 release, was loosely based the Jack London story "A Thousand Deaths." Adaptation was by screenwriter Milton Raison,[12] one in Sig's current stable of writers that at various times included Robert Emmett, Harvey Huntley, George Sayre, William Lively, Carter Wayne, and Sherman Lowe. The film's connection to the famous author, and the marketing hook that connection entailed, prompted Sig to put it into production first at Grand National Studios, bumping the previously announced *Wanted for Murder*.[13] Sig put together a cast that included a few names—not *big* names, mind you, but names nonetheless—that included headliner Lyle Talbot, Irving Pichel, and Jacqueline Wells, with Victor Halperin hired to direct, Halperin probably best known then (as now) as the man behind *White Zombie*. The plot promised the goods to ensure a turnout of horror and thriller fans, following the exploits of a doctor (Pichel) who is convinced that glandular problems are the root of all criminal behavior. Needing to experiment away from prying eyes, he charters a ship and turns it into an ocean-based operating room. His subjects, the eight killers he had helped to escape jail and took with him on his voyage, are soon on to him and none too appreciative of his "help." Talbot plays the hero—and crazy Pichel's nephew and human guinea pig—and helps the one female killer, Jacqueline Wells (Surprise! She's actually innocent!), to escape the mutinous rabble.

"As in the case of all new companies," wrote *Motion Picture Herald*, "it is to be expected that in this every effort will be made to insure that the picture's thematic, production and technical qualities will be of such a grade as to create a market for future releases."[14] Sig's choice for the opening salvo for Judell's company turned out to be a

The sensationally titled **Torture Ship** (PPC/PDC, 1939), loosely based on a story by Jack London; Sig Neufeld producer (uncredited), Victor Halperin director. *Courtesy of Heritage Auctions.*

good one, or at least as far as its cast was concerned; the actual plot and the film's technical aspects faring less well. "There can be no quarrel with the acting of the principals," wrote "Herb." in *Variety*, "it being of a rather superior grade than the story. Yarn has so many unreasonable and unexplainable points it will annoy even the most juvenile minded. Production is fair, not revealing the film's cheapie nature."[15] *The Exhibitor* was a tad more positive about the film: "Producer has, apparently, a register of good actorial material, the ability to come close to the bull's-eye in its field, and the stride is really hit, it should fill a void in the relatively inexpensive, yet entertaining, picture field."[16] *Film Daily* was similarly equivocal in its review, stating that "[w]hile failing to hold all the suspense and horror of the Jack London story from which it was adapted, this film has enough punch and drama to satisfy the nabe trade."[17] Not glowing reviews, for sure, but not too shabby either.[18]

Talbot, who just a decade earlier had been groomed as Warners' next great leading man, commented on his later career choices: "I was an actor who very seldom turned down anything, because I wanted to work. So consequently I worked in all kinds of pictures—good, bad, and indifferent."[19] *Torture Ship*, while acceptably entertaining, is sheer second-rate horror fare—*indifferent*, per Talbot—but aided in a big way by Greenhalgh's cinematography and effectively moody lighting. Spoiler alert: Pichel's experiments actually succeed, but go to the grave with him.

Inmate Robert Wilcox (second from left) has an oversized chip on his shoulder in the deceptively titled **Buried Alive** (PPC/PDC, 1939), Sig Neufeld producer (uncredited), Victor Halperin director.

Buried Alive (November 6, 1939) was directed by Halperin as well, from a screenplay by George Bricker. In spite of what the film's title may have suggested to prospective patrons, this one is a prison yarn, and a rather far-fetched but ultimately engaging one at that. Beverly Roberts plays the prison's nurse, who is catnip to several others of the prison's personnel, all of whom lust after her. These frustrated fellows include George Pembroke, as the prison's executioner; Ted Osborne as the prison's chaplain; and Alden Chase as the prison's doctor. Roberts will have none of this, falling instead for trustee Robert Wilcox, who manages to get himself condemned to death for a crime he didn't commit, his slide into despondency all stemming from an early altercation with sleazy reporter Wheeler Oakman. "With too many plots involving each other, this prison yarn gets all mixed up in itself and it falls short of being convincing drama," wrote *Film Daily*.[20] *The Exhibitor* gave a similarly lackluster review, stating that it "is similar to other prison pictures and should serve okay on the dual programs.... With a couple of feature names, the prison melodrama angles, 'Buried Alive' offers exploitation opportunities."[21] The film is somewhat better than these reviews suggest, at its best exploring the range of emotions leading up to an execution, and the grim staging of that event which follows. As for star Wilcox, we're supposed to sympathize with his plight, but his occasional knee-jerk reaction and accompanying short temper serve to dissipate whatever good will he's engendered up to that point. For both this film and *Torture Ship*, Judell was listed in the opening credits as producer, while Sig went uncredited. That basic inequity didn't last long.

Mercy Plane (December 4, 1939) was another early release, and by now Sig was finally credited as associate producer. The story involves a gang of crooks who steal airplanes and resell them. When the heat is on, they buy a bankrupt airplane factory and set it up as a new plant, and use it to rebuild the stolen planes before reselling them. The plot revolves around their theft of the spanking new hospital plane of the title, revolutionary in that it can "take off and land on a dime," a capability that must have been rough on the passengers. Throw in a romantic rivalry between air jockeys James Dunn and Frances Gifford, along with some unconvincing miniature work, and you have a typically unremarkable little film. Richard Harlan directed a cast led by Dunn and Gifford, with Harry Harvey added as Dunn's right-hand man. "Heroine Gifford is a pleasant adornment," wrote *The Exhibitor*, "while Dunn is his usual self."[22] William Lively was responsible for penning this yarn, which *The Exhibitor* deemed "a bit incredulous" while adding that "for the houses for which this is intended it will not matter."[23] Dunn and Gifford were husband and wife in real life, or at least for another two years.

The son of the American Ambassador to Peru, director Richard Harlan (1900-1968) was born in that country and raised in Havana. Actor Richard Barthelmess befriended Harlan when the latter was instrumental in securing a Cuban fortress for use in Barthelmess's *The Bright Shaw*. Barthelmess took him to New York and got him a job

Everyone seems in agreement in **Mercy Plane** (PPC/PDC, 1939), Ben Judell producer, Sig Neufeld associate producer, Richard Harlan director. Left-to-right: Matty Fain (bored), William Pawley, James Dunn, and Frances Gifford.

in the industry where he served in different capacities before becoming a full-fledged director, primarily of Spanish language films for Fox and Universal.[24] *Mercy Plane* proved to be one of the few English language films Harlan got to helm.

Sig—or perhaps it was Judell—had hired Halperin and Harlan to direct these earliest films, but Sig really wanted to bring his brother into the fold as Producers Pictures' director. Which he did, assigning him to direct *Wanted for Murder*, Sig's second production but the fourth to be released, retitled *The Invisible Killer* when it arrived in theatres on November 14, 1939. Curiously, Sam would adopt two faux personalities to "hide" behind for these productions for Judell, adopting "Sherman Scott" for this film as well as for *Hitler—Beast of Berlin*, and "Peter Stewart" for *The Sagebrush Family Trails West* and *Texas Renegades*. Sam would resort to using these two pseudonyms for years to come, interspersing them with his own name. Various reasons have been proposed for why Sam would adopt these secondary names for the credits, the one reason most often cited being the sheer number of films he was responsible for, and to make it appear that they weren't all the work of a single individual.[25] Another possibility for Sam's initial action would be for the directorial credit for *Hitler—Beast of Berlin*, his first released film for Judell. The trades had announced that Sam Newfield was to direct this film,[26] so it was no secret within the industry, but "Sherman Scott" appeared as the director for the film as released. Why the change? It is possible that the heated passions that were aroused by the making of this film within certain segments of the German-sympathizing populace may have led Sam (perhaps at his brother's protective suggestion) to adopt a false name to hide behind. Sam was, after all, Jewish, and a potential target of the more radical members of the German American Bund as a result. But more on this incendiary film in a moment.

Along with Sam's hiring to direct, Sig assembled a production team of proven talent that both he and his brother had worked with on different occasions over the years. Jack Greenhalgh, who had first worked with the brothers at Ambassador in 1935, would serve as cinematographer on all of Judell's seven releases. Holbrook Todd, who had worked with the brothers back at Excelsior/Puritan, was hired as editor, and Hans Weeren, first introduced to Sig back at Tiffany, hired as the unit's sound engineer. Bert Sternbach, who by this time had relocated to a rental at 5272 Hollywood Boulevard, was brought on as well to serve as the unit's production manager, his friendship with the brothers dating back to the early 1920s at Century. "He would go to the set more than my dad did," recalled Sig Jr., "he was around all the time, he'd supervise everything."[27] This team would remain in place with only occasional disruption for a number of years to come.

After his seemingly endless Western assignments, Sam was probably happy to be handed a contemporary piece by his brother. *The Invisible Killer*, while at face value is just another low budget murder mystery, is actually quite enjoyable viewing due to the undeniable chemistry of its two leads, perky Grace Bradley and Roland Drew. Bradley plays a crime reporter who is always one step ahead of police lieutenant Drew and his sardonic detective sergeant partner, played by William Newell. Bradley and Drew are lovers as well, her playful teasing leaving Drew frustrated, flustered…and smitten. Their back-and-forth arguing—interrupted for the occasional truce for romance—is delightful, and serves to boost the film a notch or two above the norm. The story involves a feud between rival mobsters (Alex Callam, Frank Coletti, and Sidney Grayler) involved in gambling, and the growing number of murders of those involved on both sides of the law. Each of the victims was shot, but autopsies reveal that they had all been poisoned beforehand. Leave it to the two leads to solve the murders, for once working in concert instead of independently.

Sam brought his usual on-screen energy to this film. An early highlight is the auto race between Bradley and Drew as both try to get to a crime scene first, excitingly filmed on the streets of Los Angeles. A later shootout between the cops and crooks at the latter's hideout, cleverly filmed in a single long shot through an open front door, is swift and violent. "Film is lively and has plenty of action to keep it moving," wrote *Film Daily*. "Nabe audiences will be satisfied...."[28] *The Exhibitor*'s reviewer concurred, and was taken with the film's leads, the dialog that screenwriter Joseph O'Donnell had given them, and Sam's direction: "Drew and Bradley bicker debonairly through the film, and she telephones her last story to the paper as they clinch. Bradley is cute, and the story is packed with action."[29] As far as B-level murder-mysteries go, this one is painless viewing, with Jack Greenhalgh's fluid camera work a definite plus. The opening credits have a roulette wheel spinning behind them that looks suspiciously like the same footage from the earlier Sam-directed *The Gambling Terror* for Republic.

Another one bites the dust in **The Invisible Killer** (PPC/PDC, 1939), Sig Neufeld producer, Sam Newfield (as Sherman Scott) director.

Sam headed out to Prescott, Arizona in late October for the filming of *The Sagebrush Family Trails West*. Accompanied by musical director Herbert May, Sam made an inspection of the studio and a western village under construction in anticipation of the November 13 start of filming.[30] Joseph O'Donnell was assigned as "western story editor" of the new studio's three units, acting as contact man from his office in Hollywood between Judell and Bert Sternbach, Prescott's general manager.[31]

Judell's new studio was a big deal in and around Prescott, and Judell went all out to cement relations with the locals. To that end he organized a studio inauguration ceremony for December 10 to mark the hoped-for completion of *The Sagebrush Family Trails West*. The fete was to be called "Bobby Clark Day," in "honor of the 13-year-old world's champion junior cowboy." Arizona state officials were invited, the most prominent of these the state Governor R. T. Jones, who would act as official host. A street parade would be followed by a rodeo and western barbecue at the studio.[32]

Filming of *The Sagebrush Family Trails West* wrapped a seven-day shoot on the night of December 15.[33] Young Bobby Clark, a champion trick roper, had starred in only two previous films to his credit—*Trigger Smith* and *Overland With Kit Carson*—both billed under his real name, Bobby *Clack*. Clark's co-stars for this and the remaining seven films would include Earle Hodgens, Joyce Bryant, and Nina Guilbert.[34]

Judell had high hopes for the "Sagebrush Family" series and its first entry, *The Sagebrush Family Trails West*, offering "theatres not currently booking so-called 'westerns' or outdoor pictures" free bookings:[35]

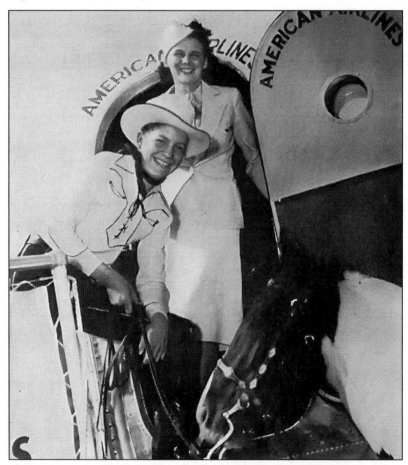

"Bobby Clark, Producers Pictures' 13-year-old world's champion junior cowboy, getting his horse, 'CHIEF', acquainted with an airplane..." Soon to be starred in **The Sagebrush Family Trails West** (PPC/PDC, 1940), the first in a planned eight-film "Sagebrush Family" series, the film tanked and killed any plans for follow-up entries.

We are so enthusiastic over the magnificent entertainment our "SAGEBRUSH FAMILY" will provide audiences everywhere, so "sold" on the consistent box-office value of these Great Eight screen jewels, that we are offering—absolutely free—without strings or reservations—to 100 selected U.S. theatres whose current booking policy does not include "outdoor" or "western" pictures. This is a bona-fide offer to acquaint exhibitors with this new series and will not be repeated. YOUR COMPETITOR, TOO, IS READING THIS AMAZING, UNPRECIDENTED OFFER—SO ACT QUICK...NOW!"[36]

Judell and Sig were so confident that the series would be enthusiastically embraced by the public that they had already mapped out titles for upcoming—but as yet unwritten or filmed—entries: *The Sagebrush Family Rides On*, *The Sagebrush Family Stakes a Claim*, *The Sagebrush Family on a Dude Ranch*, *The Sagebrush Family Across the Rio Grande*, *The Sagebrush Family at the Rodeo*, *The Sagebrush Family Meets the Outlaws*, and *The Sagebrush Family Fights Rustlers*.[37] The cast was set for the films as well, which included Bobby Clark, Earle Hodgens, Joyce Bryant, and Nina Guilbert; William Lively was to write the series' upcoming screenplays.[38]

The series' opener's plot was standard stuff. Earle Hodgins played the Sagebrush family's father, Guilbert the mother, with Clark and Bryant their two children. Hodgins has a traveling medicine show of which, true to typecasting form, he's the spieler. Their arrival in a town precedes a series of robberies, and Hodgins is accused. Clark teams up with a friendly deputy sheriff to track down the real culprit. Critics were unimpressed: "'Trails West' is nothing to brag about," groaned *The Exhibitor*. "Built largely—and ineffectively, as far as western entertainment is concerned—to show off the questionable prowess of 12-year-old Bobby Clark in rope manipulation, the picture is slow beyond the requirements of an introductory piece."[39] Another reviewer concurred, stating that "the picture as a whole fails to impress. The dialogue is outmoded, the direction stodgy and the photography poor, with the exception of some pleasing outdoor scenes. There are a few exciting moments, but not enough to lift the production to the action average."[40]

Judell and Sig's enthusiasm for the series' potential was misguided, to say the least, and after some later lip service suggesting that it might be continued with Bob Steele added to—or replacing—the cast,[41] there was no further mention; it died after the single entry.

The seventh of PPC's films was *Texas Renegades*, the first in an eight-film series that would reunite Sam with cowboy star Tim McCoy. The film's shoot was delayed for nearly a half year until its December 18 start at the Prescott studios. McCoy, not one to waste time with filming, had arrived the night before from his ranch near Thermopolis, Wyoming.[42] *Texas Renegades* was a definite step up from the McCoy films for Victory, with a much larger cast, a larger budget, more attractive location shooting, and little of the claustrophobic feel of those Katzman cheapies. While the plot's underpinnings are familiar—a respected member of the community of Rawhide is actually the leader of a band of notorious robbers—the film benefits from an interesting twist. Marshal "Silent" Tim Smith (McCoy), summoned to town to put an end to those robberies, is mistaken for a new, yet unseen gang member and poses as such, then as part of the gang's plotting assumes the role of the yet-unseen Marshal—himself! His ploy works for a while, but when the real expected gang member shows up and blows McCoy's cover, it all falls apart. This leads to a comparatively exciting climax, a large group of vigilantes after

McCoy whom they've been led to believe is the actual gang member, while the gang's leader (Lee Prather) has a herd of rustled steer driven through the town.

Thankfully, McCoy has dispensed with those silly costumes from the Victory series, sticking with his familiar all-black outfit and white neckerchief. And none of this shooting the bad guys in the wrist stuff, instead shooting a whole bunch of them dead at film's end. Prather is a good fit for "Bates," the gang's leader, and Harry Harvey provides slim comic relief as McCoy's sidekick "Noisy." Actress Nora Lane takes the part of the cattlewoman who summons McCoy to Rawhide, her performance unconvincing and leaving a lot to be desired—or at least in my opinion; her seventeen-year career and dozens of additional film roles would suggest that someone felt otherwise. As her foreman, Kenneth Duncan, who would start using his real first name—Kenne—by the mid-1940s, tries hard, but perhaps a bit too hard. Sam's direction is mostly utilitarian—lots of single setup scenes—but takes on some energy for the film's climactic shootout. And while the film is better than the Katzman series, it's still a low budget film, employing scads of stock footage for the closing sequence involving the stampeding cattle. That said, it's *good* footage.

Texas Renegades (PPC/PDC, 1940), Sig Neufeld producer, Sam Newfield (as Peter Stewart) director.

These lower budget features were intended to keep a flow of cash into the fledgling production-distribution company coffers, but Judell had bigger plans, plans that he hoped would give PPC some much-needed prestige and recognition, and perhaps a boost into a slightly higher league of filmmaking concerns. To that end he turned to a story titled "Goose Step," written by a fellow named Shepard Traube.

Shepard Traube (1907-1983) had produced and directed a handful of middling successes on Broadway by this time, shows that included *No More Frontier* (1931), *A Thousand Summers* (1932), *The Sophisticrats* (1933), *But Not for Love* (1934), and *Sailor, Beware!* (1935), none of which survived more than a two-month run. Turning to

Hollywood, Traube had a single screenplay to his credit for a low-budget crime drama titled *Prison Train* (1938). He decided to peddle a story he had written about the growing Nazi menace titled "Goose Step," and managed to interest Bennie Zeidman, an independent producer via his B.F. Zeidman Productions, Ltd. Operating out of the Talisman Studios, Zeidman engaged Traube to write and direct an adaptation of the treatment Traube had written from his story. In May 1939, Traube wrote to Joseph I. Breen, the no-nonsense and humorless head censor of the Motion Picture Producers and Distributors of America's Hays Office, asking for a review of his treatment. "Since the material is provocative and since I am very keen to go ahead with the writing of a screen play, which I am to direct, I should appreciate an early consultation with your office for advice and guidance," wrote Traube.[43] Breen responded that the treatment "meets the basic requirements of the Production Code" but went on to list a number of required changes.[44] For naught, as it turned out; Traube's association with Zeidman fell apart, so he hooked up with Judell and PPC. Judell didn't want a comparative novice handling the direction of what he hoped would be his premiere attraction, so he turned to associate producer Sig to choose a director, who in turn assigned his brother Sam to direct. Traube was thrown a bone and allowed to adapt his story for the screen. The film was placed on the fast track for production, scheduled for release on October 15, but rescheduled to a week earlier "because of the present war situation in Europe."[45]

Poster art for **Hitler—Beast of Berlin** (PPC/PDC, 1939), Sig Neufeld producer, Sam Newfield (as Sherman Scott) director. *Courtesy of Heritage Auctions.*

Judell went all out with advance promotion of his upcoming mini-blockbuster—now bearing the title *Hitler—Beast of Berlin*—and didn't stint on the hyperbole: "The Mad War Monster is Loose in Europe! Civilization trembles on the brink of disaster," screamed one ad in the trades. "It's a bonanza of timely dramatic, record-shattering screen entertainment."[46] The film's announced title immediately ignited a firestorm of controversy since President Roosevelt had made a plea for strict neutrality regarding the events in Europe, a plea that found receptive ears among many Americans. Judell walked a fine line regarding that neutrality: "The picture is not intended for propaganda," he said, "but will be the unvarnished, breathtaking expose of a demented fanatic's thirst for power—regardless of human rights, consequences or bloodshed. Secrets never before revealed will be depicted...and I promise you we will pull no punches."[47] Spoken like a true huckster!

"I can sympathize with both Mr. Judell's dislike of Hitlerism and his yen to cash in," wrote syndicated columnist Jimmie Fidler. "But someone should remind him—and I hope the United States Government will—that this is one time when Hollywood should tend to its proper knitting, the making of non-controversial entertainment. The United States, with sentiment already running high, will have a hard enough time keeping out of war without being forced to fight emotional excitation from Hollywood."[48] Judell was quick to try to calm the fires, reported *Boxoffice*, which wrote that he had "reiterated that the story, dealing with the underground anti-Nazi movement in Germany, is not war propaganda and is not intended to inspire hatred for any European political group."[49] One group that wasn't opposed to the film was the newly-formed HANL, the 250 member-strong Hollywood Anti-Nazi League.[50]

Oklahoma Senator John William Elmer Thomas withdrew a proposal he had made previously regarding a wartime censorship board for motion pictures, deciding that it wasn't necessary. Columnist Paul Harrison explained: "Against Hollywood," he wrote, "policies can be enforced by inaction. That is, instead of sending the marines to make the movies behave, the government can accomplish the same objective by NOT calling out the army or navy or air corps to help in the filming of pictures. The cooperation and good will of many of the departments in Washington are enormously important to the flicker industry." All well and good, but ineffectual in Judell's case. "[T]his is of little moment to Producer Ben Judell…so long as he doesn't need to borrow any battleships or squadrons of planes, he has nothing to fear from Washington."[51]

Traube's script, dated September 12, 1939, and still bearing the title "Goose Step," was submitted to Breen at the MPPDA, and a meeting was held between Breen, Sig, and Judell on the 19th. Breen summarized in a letter to PPC, stating that while that the story was acceptable under the Production Code provisions, "the advertising which has been broadcast in connection with this story, in which it is suggested that the title to be used is 'HITLER – BEAST OF BERLIN', together with the advanced advertising and publicity material, give us serious concern…." Breen called out Judell on his publicity's rhetoric, saying that his statements seem to not only "misrepresent your story, but suggest an inflammatory document, which, while it may not be a violation of the letter of the president's recent proclamation of neutrality, may be a violation of the spirit of that neutrality." Breen had suggested a title change and that advertising material be "kept within the spirit of your story," and Sig agreed to these "suggestions." Breen proceeded to itemize a number of mandatory changes to the script, closing with his customary "our final judgment will be based upon our review of the finished picture."[52]

The letter was never sent.

Shortly after the meeting, Judell's father Julius,[53] now in his mid-eighties, contacted Breen and wanted to know, in Breen's words, "What the hell all the trouble was about." Julius said that he had spoken with his son and Sig, but "did not agree at all with what they told him" and "got quite nasty over the telephone and gave [Breen] to understand that he would not change the title and would not amend the advertising…. He was a bit belligerent and gave me to understand that he didn't care whether we approved the picture or not."[54] Which left Breen and PPC at a stalemate. One suspects that elder Judell had a financial stake in PPC, and was fully behind the exploitative tack the production had taken.

Production commenced on September 20 at the Grand National Studios, the day after Sig and Judell's meeting with Breen,[55] with a budget of $100,000,[56] a huge sum by comparison to the modest budgets of PPC's other productions. While Sam had been initially announced in the trades as the director of *Hitler—Beast of Berlin*,[57] this credit was quickly reattributed to the fictitious Sherman Scott who, it was claimed, "has piloted several 'March of Time' reels in New York."[58] Jack Greenhalgh, as usual, handled the camera work. Sam's cast was far from powerhouse, starring Roland Drew, fresh off *The Invisible Killer*, Hungarian-born Steffi Duna, Greta Granstedt, Vernon Dent, and a young newcomer named Alan Ladd. Always looking to save a penny whenever possible, Sam pressed his two children—six-year-old Joel and eight-year-old Jacqueline (who everyone called Jackie)—into service as well. "Both me and Jackie were in that one," recalled Joel. "All I remember was we were in a park and it was 'Heil Hitler.' We were pretty small."[59]

Production was delayed, if only slightly, when the Los Angeles-based cell of Fritz Kuhn's German American Bund took umbrage at the film's proposed title and its anti-Hitler stance. A group of Bund members broke into the Grand National lot late one night, located Sig's sets, and destroyed them. Finding the wreckage the following morning, Sig and Sam marshalled the studio's workmen, and had everything reconstructed in short order.[60]

Sig and Judell received a copy of Breen's original letter of the 19th, made the required changes to the film (already shot and edited), and submitted the completed picture to the MPPDA. After review, Breen responded to Judell with only a minor trim required involving a prisoner "shown writhing and groaning while he is being beaten with a rubber hose." Otherwise, the film would be approved with three conditions: 1) the offending scene be trimmed; 2) a new, permanent title has been approved; and 3) assurance that all advertising, exploitation, and publicity be submitted to, and approved by, the Advertising Advisory Council of the Association.[61]

The MPPDA eventually approved the film for general release as *Goose Step*, reverting back to the story upon which it was based. Judell explained that without the Hays Office's title approval, the film would have been "barred from some of the larger producer-controlled theatre circuits."[62] In the meantime, the New York Censor Board had already approved the film with the alternate title *Beasts of Berlin*—a title that the MPPDA had already rejected—and a "slight revision" to the film itself, supposedly having addressed the board's original concerns that the film as submitted was "inhuman, sacrilegious and tended to incite crime."[63] It premiered at New York's Globe theatre on October 29, 1939. "The most noticeable reaction came whenever the 'Heil Hitler' salute was given," wrote one reviewer. "The reaction was general laughter. A scattering of hisses greeted the brief appearance of Hitler. Otherwise things were quiet."[64]

That didn't completely solve Judell's problems, as the film ended up being released under several different titles and with varying trims on a state-by-state basis. As Harry Rathner, PPC's Eastern rep put it, "Those who passed the picture, vetoed the title and others who did not object to the title rejected the picture."[65] Pennsylvania, New York, and Michigan all approved the film without trims, while Maryland, Ohio, Massachusetts, Chicago, Providence, and others demanded varying trims and deletions before approval.[66]

The film has a rather simplistic plot, designed primarily as anti-German propaganda. Unemployed civil engineer Hans Memling (Roland Drew) is a member of a clandestine anti-Nazi underground and has convinced his brother-in-law (Alan Ladd) to join as well. Drew's wife (Steffi Duna) is pregnant and wants to emigrate to the U.S., but patriotic (stubborn?) Drew resists, saying his job is there in Germany. The S.S. suspects Drew of anti-Nazi leanings and arrests him, placing him under "protective arrest" (after an energetic, two-on-one flogging). Storm Trooper Hans von Twardowski is sympathetic to, and a member of, Drew's secret group, but continues in his official position to gather information to be passed on to the group. He gets drunk with some fellow Storm Troopers, however, so drunk that he mumbles that he needs to inform Duna of Drew's arrest and inform the other members of the group as well, whom he goes on to name, one by one. His fellow troopers shoot him and arrest the others that he named. After a stint under protective arrest and placement in concentration camp-like detention center, most of them are released due to lack of evidence. Drew, who was to be released as well, is held back, having foolishly told off the camp's commanding officer. Seeing no future in Germany, Duna heads to Switzerland to have her baby. Drew's friends aid in his escape via a hay wagon while outside on a work detail. He joins Duna in Switzerland, where she convinces him that they should become the voice of a free Germany.

While not a great film, *Hitler—Beast of Berlin* certainly accomplished what it set out to do, and that was to arouse passions. After a brief opening sequence filled with stock footage of Nazis parading through the streets, greeted by the stiff-armed salute of the onlookers, the film moved forward with its simplistic storyline, pushing the occasional instigatory "button" along the way: the physical and psychological humiliation of a Jew, the brutal defrocking of a minister and the tromping on his fallen crucifix, that sort of thing. Sam's direction is straightforward, some scenes shot in single long takes as if viewing a stage play, while others employ numerous cuts and the occasional visual flourish. There are two scenes of torture, and while these both have been trimmed by the censors, they still manage to pack a punch. Sam's direction of these two scenes are the most stylistic sequences of the film, with atmospheric lighting and off-putting camera angles. Sig's increased budget—by comparison at least—is all up there on the screen, with solid-looking sets courtesy of art direct Fred Preble, who likely reveled at for once having a few extra dollars at his disposal. There are, of course, the usual B-movie rough edges and anachronisms. The most glaring of these is the continual appearance of swastikas reversed from the clockwise direction that the Nazis used, although whether this was an oversight or some sort of artistic slight on the part of the filmmakers is anyone's guess. The detention center's interior looks appropriately spartan and realistic, but the buildings' exteriors look a little too modern and architecturally slick. The film's score is, for want of a better word, inappropriately *cheerful* on occasion, and the cost-saving use of rear projection clumsily employed, as with the rooftops seen beyond the foreground refusing to remain in register. And, of course, the uneven—and frequently unconvincing—German accents.

Ben R. Crisler, the *New York Times*'s film reviewer, gave a balanced assessment of the film:

> We may not find it easy to view a picture like "Beasts of Berlin" objectively. To begin with, it is (in the unabashed words of the Pennsylvania Board of Censors, which unqualifiedly passed it) "100 per cent propaganda," and its very

frankness in this respect may alienate those who have a constitutional distaste for being sold even a reliable bill of goods under the guise of entertainment. On the other hand, persons who feel abnormally strongly on the subject of persecuted minorities may consider that it is a better picture than it is, while members of the Bund, presumably will feel positive that it is a much worse picture than it is.[67]

Variety reviewed the film on the basis of its box office appeal and artistry:

From a monetary standpoint, this picture should be a spectacular success. Its subject matter has an immediate draw, for one thing. And its treatment is precisely the sort calculated to inflame mob passions during a period of growing hysteria.... But if it's a boxoffice success, the picture is just as obviously an artistic failure, for its attacks on the Nazi regime merely scratch the surface, without ever even hinting at the fundamental evils of Hitlerism. Furthermore, its arguments are repetitious and, in any case, they've all been advanced more eloquently before.... So the film has nothing new or significant to say and it is framed in stupidly undramatic form.[68]

Motion Picture Review, which saw the film as *Goose Step*, provided the following age group ratings: "Adolescents, 12 to 16: Absolutely No" and "Children, 8 to 12: Frightful." They didn't bother with adults, aside from stating that 'such a picture should have no place upon the American screen."[69] I guess they didn't like it.

Director Sam Newfield pressed his children into service whenever children were needed in his films, as this still from **Hitler—Beast of Berlin** (PPC/PDC, 1939) demonstrates. Left-to-right in background: Jackie Newfield, Joel Newfield, and a third, unidentified child.
Courtesy of Joel Newfield.

Hitler—Beast of Berlin did little for Traube's film career. He would direct a few more films before returning to Broadway with what turned out to be the biggest success of his career, the drama *Angel Street*, which had a three-year run 1941-44, and an impressive 1,295 performances featuring co-stars Leo G. Carroll and Vincent Price. Traube would continue producing and directing on Broadway into the mid-1970s, his swan song a revival of *Angel Street* (1976).

Given the polarizing nature of the film, coupled with its general confinement to small rural theatres and neighborhood houses, *Hitler—Beast of Berlin* failed to be the big winner that Judell had hoped for and banked on. Production at the Prescott, Arizona studio was halted at the end of December[70] due to a lack of operating funds and growing debt, and by February Judell was forced to file for bankruptcy.

Judell's big dreams had come to a grinding halt after a mere seven films.

The franchise holders, who had embraced and were fully behind Judell's original plans, weren't about to let PPC/PDC go away. A gathering of these franchise holders was held in New York in late February to map out a course of action that would keep the business in operation. Judell was out by this time—"retired" was the word used—and former New York franchise holder and Eastern representative Harry Rathner was made president of the revamped company. Pathé, PPC/PDC's principal creditor, was to be active in the new operation, with the various franchise holders participating in the financing of production as well.[71]

Conferences were held with Robert S. Benjamin, attorney for Pathé Laboratories, to come up with PPC's production replacement, and Sig was the obvious choice. Sigmund Neufeld Productions, Inc. was formed[72] to function as PPC's successor, with actual production to resume on March 27 on a fifteen-picture schedule—seven westerns and "eight modest budget pix"—for the upcoming 1940-41 season.[73] PDC's successor, now named Producers Releasing Corp., filed for incorporation as a New York organization, with capital listed at 1,000 shares of no-par value stock. Incorporators were Robert S. Benjamin, Seymour Peyser, and Sidney Freidberg.[74] Rathner was named PRC's president, with franchise holders and stockholders Louis Ruttstein of Coast Picture Productions, and Boston exchange operator Harry Asher, made PRC's vice presidents; New York franchise operator Bert Kulick became secretary-treasurer.[75] Within a month George Gill would become PRC's third vice president.[76]

Producers Releasing Corp. would distribute the features produced by Sigmund Neufeld Productions, Inc., the latter's scheduled output upped from the initially announced fifteen films per year to two features per month.[77] With ambitious plans for his new production operation, Sig committed to an even greater output of thirty-six films—three per month—Harry Rathner "explaining that its exchange branches are prepared to absorb more than twice the number of pictures first planned." Eighteen of the thirty-six would be Westerns starring McCoy, Bob Steele, and a yet-to-be-announced singing cowboy.[78] Pathé committed to financing 66 ⅔ % of Sig's productions, each of which would be budgeted at roughly $25,000. Judell's remaining creditors were to be paid off from the receipts of PPC/PDC's original seven films; Pathé, a preferred creditor, would be first in line.[79]

Producers Releasing Corp. was now in operation, and Sig was to provide the product. Sam now had a permanent job.

Chapter 10:
Like a Phoenix from the Ashes (Sig, Sam, and PRC, Part 1, 1939-1941)

While *Hitler—Beast of Berlin* and its attendant cost had sunk the PPC/PDC ship, it lived on, exhibitions growing in demand as the European war raged unchecked, and with our eventual entry into the conflict after the attack on Pearl Harbor in December 1941. This had been actor Alan Ladd's first credited role after seven years in the business, but with his leap to fame in 1942 as star of Paramount's *This Gun for Hire* and *The Glass Key*, Producers Releasing Corp. was quick to re-release the film along with another, re-titled Ladd film—as *Gangs, Inc.*, formerly 1941's *Paper Bullets*—with Ladd now touted as the lead in both. *Beast of Berlin* was revived once again in 1948 under a new title—*Hell's Devils*—and with Ladd still billed as the lead, a shameless attempt to fool filmgoers into thinking it was a new movie. Sam's thoughts about Ladd's future in film were, at the time the film was made, unencouraging: "My dad thought he'll never make it," remembered Sam's son Joel. "Too short. Too small. He was used to the leading man being big."[1]

Benny Rubin sporting a coon skin hat in **Fighting Mad** (Criterion/Monogram, 1939), Philip N. Krasne producer, Sam Newfield director. *Courtesy of Heritage Auctions.*

Sam was always on the lookout for a next assignment, so during his down time between other productions and later, while Pathé and PPC/PDC's franchise holders were tied up in negotiations to restructure the bankrupt operation, Sam knocked off a few other films. One of these was *Fighting Mad* for Criterion Pictures, another north-of-the-border Mounted Police yarn which was one of those action-comedy hybrids that leaned a little too far in the latter direction. Warner Richmond and Ted Adams play a couple of bank robbers who head across the border into Canada to hook back up with their boss, played by Milburn Stone at his coldest. Along with them is hostage Sally

Blane—we are initially led to believe she's one of the gang—who ends up separated from the others, the stolen cash in her possession and now the object of the gang's search. Enter Mounties James Newill and Dave O'Brien, who seem conflicted over their duty to pursue the robbers and their collective lust over Blane. The film ends up with another of Sam's grand free-for-all fistfights, with the good guys overpowering the bad. Typical stuff—discredit where discredit is due goes to screenwriters George Rosener and John Rathmell—who took a standard Western plot and retooled it for the north country.

Newill plays "Sergeant Renfrew," author Laurie York Erskine's character who had first appeared in the pages of *American Boy* magazine back in the 1920s, then on CBS radio in 1936, and two films for Grand National, beginning with *Renfrew of the Royal Mounted* in 1937. The series moved over to Monogram with this film, and continued for another five. "Newell [sic] sings 'Trail's End,' 'Lady's in Distress,' and one other song," wrote *The Exhibitor*, "all of which are pleasant to hear."[2] I'm betting the kids in the audience thought otherwise. Comedian Benny Rubin provides the film's incessant comedy relief, and I use the word "comedy" loosely here since it's pretty much of the lame variety. Remove it from the film and you'd have about fifteen minutes left, and a sizable chunk of that wasted on Newill's singing. There isn't much to recommend this particular film, aside from the inclusion of a number of honest-to-God Indians for a whiff of verisimilitude, in throw-away bit parts; Iron Eyes Cody[3] and Chief Thundercloud were among them. *Fighting Mad* was released by Monogram on November 11, 1939.

"Teaser" poster art for the mildly exploitative **Secrets of a Model** (Continental, 1940), J.D. Kendis producer, Sam Newfield director.
Courtesy of Heritage Auctions.

A far more interesting assignment was Sam's direction of *Secrets of a Model*, an atypical (for him, at least) exploitation film with a title guaranteed to lure the most prurient of filmgoers into theaters, and not with wifey and the kids in tow. Produced by ultra-low budget producer J.D. Kendis, he of such uplifting fare as *Guilty Parents* (1934), *Gambling with Souls* (1936), and *Slaves in Bondage* (1937) and their attendant, borderline taboo topics of sex education and prostitution, *Secrets of a Model* focused on the age-old story of the naïve young girl corrupted by the big city. The film's crudely assembled trailer promised to reveal "The Shocking Story Behind the Glamour Girls on Magazine Covers!" and declared the film "A Fearless, Timely Drama That Dares to Tell the Truth!" This is followed first by a brief sequence of an artist and his briefly clad model, after which comes an extended scene of titillation: a rotter enters a bedroom on which a comely young lady is passed out on a bed. He removes his coat, then proceeds to undress her, first her shoes and then a cut to the floor where we see her shoes deposited, followed by stockings, belt, and skirt. Cut to the venetian blinds, nighttime dissolving to daylight. She awakens, presumably undressed under those covers, and looks to the bed

Like a Phoenix from the Ashes (Sig, Sam, and PRC, Part 1, 1939-1941) 179

next to her, which has been slept in as well. The trailer, unsubtle in its ham-fisted presentation, suggests more to come in the film itself, but if the heavy-breathing subset of the filmgoing public anticipated anything like the peek-a-boo nudity of Harry Revier's *Child Bride*, the perverse sexuality of Dwain Esper's *Maniac*, or anything even remotely in between, they were sorely disappointed.

The film's star—billed as Sharon Lee but in actuality actress Cheryl Walker, hiding behind a face- and reputation-saving pseudonym—is the film's saving grace. She can act, and is an attractive presence, but the story itself is lame. She and her roommate, played by Phyllis Barry, are carhops at a drive-in eatery hoping for better, fashion-modelling things to come. Milkman Julian Madison is in love with Lee but dumps her when she sees a pathway to success from wealthy, charming (but lecherous) Harold Daniels. Daniels gets her drunk with a promise of marriage, and the scene from the trailer follows, exactly as presented there. Humiliated and ashamed, Lee leaves town and attempts a few crummy jobs, growing more ill with each passing day. Back to health, she returns to her former roommate, reunites with her milkman, and the two get married. A final encounter between milkman Madison and rotter Daniels leads to a big fight, Daniels bludgeons Madison with a poker, the cops are called, a fleeing Daniels struck and killed by a passing car. Happy ending.

One can only guess where this is going to lead. Harold Daniels and Cheryl Walker (as Sharon Lee) in Sam Newfield's **Secrets of a Model** (Continental, 1940).

While it's never stated as such, one can read between the lines and attribute Lee's "illness" to the after effects of an illegal abortion. And while the film itself is a rather routine and unexceptional B-film, producer Kendis and director Sam toss in a couple of quickie scenes so as not to totally disappoint the ticket buyers hoping for more verboten footage: Lee and bad girl Grace Lenard stripping down to bra and panties in the drive-in's locker room; and artist Bobby Watson posing and ultimately dismissing one after another similarly clad model, four of 'em in total. Mild stuff, for sure, but "better" than nothing and the sort of mildly titillating stuff that had fallen by the wayside with the imposition of the Hays Code back in 1934. And while reviewers tended to dismiss the film ("Weak indie offering as program fare falls short in every department" wrote *Film Daily*[4]) at least one exhibitor in Iowa was happy with the film's B.O.:

> The Fourth of July has always been a flop for me until this year. "Secrets of a Model" run for "adults only" showed a nice profit. The advertising (heralds), window cards, photos and mats are very attractive and you do not promise your customers something that they will not see. During these times when the big pictures flop, anything with box office is welcome.[5]

Re-released in 1959 by Social Service Pictures of Hollywood as *Secrets of a Model School*, this would be the only film of its tawdry type to be directed by Sam, at least that we know of. *Secrets of a Model* was released on May 4, 1940, by Kendis's Continental Pictures on a state rights basis.

The other film that Sam directed during this period was for former employer A.W. Hackel and his Supreme Pictures. Hackel had been ill and out of commission from later 1938 into March 1939 with some unspecified, eight month-long ailment, forcing his retirement from his position as producer at Republic,[6] and keeping him out of active work.[7] His health regained, Hackel merged his Supreme Pictures in May 1940 with Million Dollar Productions, an Atlanta, Georgia-based company that specialized in what were then referred to as "race" films.[8] Hackel signed Ralph Cooper, the former star of *Dark Manhattan*,[9] *Gangsters on the Loose*, *The Duke is Tops*, and *Gang War*, to headline four films. "This can definitely be regarded as a step forward in racial advancement for a major film concern to sign a colored artist to star in a series of four pictures," wrote journalist Earl J. Morris. "Hackel, unlike other producers of Negro films, is a veteran in the business, and his first move was to recall Sam Newfield, prominently known Hollywood director, from one of the white film units of Supreme pictures, and assign him to direct Cooper."[10] In an effort to provide the films with just an extra touch of class, Sam was for once credited as "Samuel Newfield."

Production commenced on the first of what was announced as "4 Ralph Cooper All Colored Specials" for the upcoming 1940-41 season.[11] Titled *Am I Guilty?*, Cooper's co-stars were Sybyl Lewis, Lawrence Criner, Pigmeat Markham, and Marcella Moreland, the six-year-old daughter of popular film star Mantan Moreland. The plot involved doctor Cooper, forced to serve as physician to a group of gangsters, to the detriment of his clinic which had served his poorer neighbors. When the police finally round up the gangsters, Cooper gives himself up and throws his fate at the mercy of the jurors. He's sentenced to a year in prison.

The finished film premiered at New York's Apollo theatre on September 27, 1940, with a pre-showing stage "extravaganza" that, in the words of *Variety*, "put the show itself undeniably in second position with the audience." The so-called extravaganza was produced by Clarence Robinson; the performers included singer Roland Smith accompanied by Roy Eldredge's orchestra ("[Smith] is handicapped by the poor accompaniment provided by Roy Eldredge's crew, which manages later also to bollax up Billie Holidays' pipework."); a string quartet named Cats and the Fiddle; and comedic duos Johnny Vigal and John Mason, and Butterbeans and Susie—both duos Apollo regulars. Dancing team Tondeleyo and Lopez were "wild, frenzied and seductive" performing a South Seas dance session, Tondeleyo's attire described as "merely a tea-napkin size loin cloth, while the femme is dressed the same plus a net bra with pom-poms on it to add to the effect."[12] Customers got their money's worth.

"'Am I Guilty?' marks the debut of A.W. Hackel's Supreme Pictures Corp. into the all-Negro film field," wrote *Variety*:

> "Guilty," made in Hollywood, has a neatly-turned and adult story (despite its slightly trite vein), excellent acting and neat production values. It compares favorably in every respect with the B output of major lots. Current film brings an entirely new concept to the Negro picture field, which has heretofore limited itself to cheap comedy, much of it forced. Only difficulty it may run into is its effort to reach too far. In endeavoring to get away from the usual obvious Negro comedy style, it risks being too highbrow. It was well-received by the comparatively sophisticated audience of Harlem, but whether the more poorly-educated Negroes of the south, on which, after all, the picture must depend for a major portion of its income, would not rather see low comedy than a story of mental conflict is something else again.... Cooper is capable and sincere, showing considerably more talent—perhaps it's the direction of Sam Newfield—than previous efforts.[13]

Producer A.W. Hackel's first (and only) entry in the "all-Negro film field" starring Ralph Cooper, **Am I Guilty?** (Supreme, 1940), Sam Newfield (as Samuel Neufeld in the film's opening credits) director.

Unfortunately, Hackel's admirable ambitions with the planned Ralph Cooper series began and ended with this film. Hackel knocked out a couple of comedy shorts starring Pigmeat Markham before regrouping and signing a two-picture deal with Monogram to produce non-race films for the 1941-42 season.[14]

These few films marked the end of Sam's freelancing and the beginning of an eight-year commitment to the films of his brother and Producers Releasing Corp., churning out more than 100 features for PRC and its PPC predecessor from 1939 into 1947. PRC was unique in that its franchise holders would "dictate the policy and program of the production unit," and they liked Westerns. Lots of them.

Producers Releasing Corp.: 1939-1941 Seasons

Sig and Sam went to work almost immediately, their first feature for PRC in production by the beginning of May. Tentatively titled *Sons of the Finest*, the film was soon retitled *I Take This Oath*; former University of California football and track star Gordon Jones headlined. Tim McCoy, who had starred in *Texas Renegades* for PPC, was signed to a new six-film contract, his first—*Frontier Crusader*—set to roll immediately following *I Take This Oath*.[15] Bob Steele was signed as well, announced in April to take over the "Sagebrush" series with four new films, but the lukewarm response at the box office to *The Sagebrush Family Trails West* soon deep-sixed that project. By May, Steele was reassigned to a new six-film "Adventures of Billy the Kid" series, with Al St. John signed to co-star for comedy relief.[16]

Leon Fromkess, who was PRC's foreign manager, closed a deal with William J. Gell, managing director of London's Pathé Pictures, Ltd., to release twenty of PRC's upcoming films throughout the United Kingdom. British production was at a standstill due to the war with Germany, and in dire need of new product—that, and the price was likely right. These releases would begin with *Hold That Woman!*, which was to go into production immediately following McCoy's *Frontier Crusader*, the deal to remain in place for an extended period.[17]

PRC's premiere offering and the first of their so-called "specials," *I Take This Oath*, was released on May 20, 1940, and a viewing reveals that a bit more money and time was spent on its production. (Budgeted at $16,000, the negative cost ended up considerably more at $18,620.)[18] The acting is uniformly good, and it's evident that Greenhalgh gave more thought to the lighting of sets and camera placement. Sam's direction (as Sherman Scott) is a notch above his norm, with more cutting between shots within a given scene, and more attention given to his actors' performances. One would presume that after the relentless tedium of directing one Western after another, the opportunity to helm a drama of this sort was a refreshing change of pace; a scene where a main actor is killed in a bomb explosion is particularly well handled and convincing. Increased budget aside, it is after all still a lower budget film, most evident in the number of "exterior" shots where the actors do their thing in front of an obvious rear projection screen. The one exception is the sequence that takes place at the police academy's training grounds, filmed on location at some visually convincing facility.

Veteran cop Robert Homans's dogged investigation of the city's racketeering and quest to find the "big boss" behind it leads to his death by a bomb planted in his car. His son (Gordon Jones) vows revenge, but is convinced to do it legally by first attending the police academy and earning a badge. Learning takes a back seat to his own pursuit of those responsible for his father's death, however, putting that badge at risk and, ultimately, having it revoked. Meanwhile, Jones's girl (Joyce Compton) waits patiently for Jones to be finished with his obsessive pursuit, while Jones's best friend (Craig Reynolds) hopes to take Jones's place in Compton's eyes. After an hour's worth of investigation, Jones finally tracks down the big boss and political fixer, who just happens to be Reynolds's uncle (Sam Flint). During a climactic confrontation that involves both Reynolds and Flint, Compton, Jones, and Flint's gunman, both Reynolds and Flint end up shot dead.

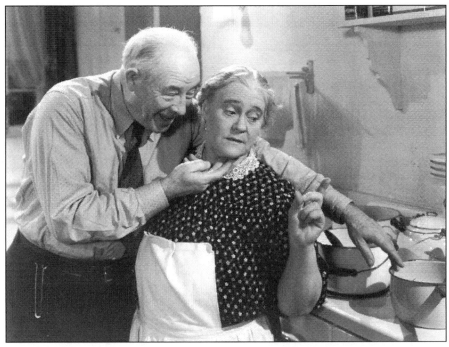

Doomed cop Robert Homans and his wife Mary Gordon in **I Take This Oath** (Producers Releasing Corp, 1940), Sig Neufeld producer, Sam Newfield (as Sherman Scott) director.

This familiar tale of revenge benefits primarily from the solid performances of all involved. Both Homans and Mary Gordon are fine as Steve's Irish parents, their comfortable and loving homelife presented at some length to render his death in the car explosion all the more shocking. As Steve's girl, Joyce Compton gives the film's most relaxed and convincing performance, her previous fifteen years in film an obvious benefit, although her rich southern accent seems somewhat at odds to all the Irish brogue around her. Craig Reynolds comes off well, he too benefiting from the large number of previous performances to his credit. In the lead, Gordon Jones gives a reasonably convincing performance, most of it with that perpetual frown etched in his forehead. His character suffers from the same personality shortcoming that so many lead characters display in films of this sort, and that is hot-headedness, immediately jumping to the conclusion that his girl is two-timing him when he spots her with another guy—laziness on the part of the writers, I'm guessing. *The Exhibitor*'s review summed it up rather well: "The acting, production, etc., are commendable, and although the nature of the yarn is not new, it should please in the duallers."[19] Another reviewer preferred to focus on feminine lead Compton and her ilk, stating that "Joyce Compton is pleasant to look at, but what trim young starlet isn't?"[20] Words of wisdom.

Son Gordon Jones consoles his mother Mary Gordon in **I Take This Oath** (PRC, 1940).

Skip tracer James Dunn skips after fiancé Frances Gifford in the PRC "special" **Hold That Woman!** (1940), Sig Neufeld producer, Sam Newfield (as Sherman Scott) director.

Another of PRC's first season "specials" was *Hold That Woman!* (June 28, 1940), an enjoyable little comedy featuring a return of James Dunn as a seemingly inept skip tracer who finally, and unintentionally, makes good. Frances Gifford returns as well, as Dunn's tolerant fiancée, their relaxed performances and playful banter once again a function of their real-life marriage. Sam's comfort level handling comedy is evident, easily switching over to the film's underlying crime story and its more hard-boiled stuff, particularly in a grim little sequence where the mobsters prepare to torture a jewel thief (George Douglas) by drilling his teeth. Dave O'Brien plays an overly confident fellow skip tracer who finally receives his comeuppance as reward for his conceit and smugness. The cast was rounded out by Rita La Roy as Douglas's partner in crime, Anna Lisa as the French actress whose stolen jewelry the plot revolves around, William Hall as her business manager, Paul Bryar as the ruthless notorious jewel thief who wants those jewels, and Guy Usher as Gifford's short-tempered police officer father who can't stand Dunn. *Film Daily*'s reviewer had particular praise for Sig's production efforts, this one budgeted at $17,928, and brought in at a thrifty $17,117: "Sig Neufeld has the knack of getting more picture for a dollar than any other producer in the business," he wrote. "He has made a good imitation of a major studio's medium budget film on very little."[21] For the record, Frances Gifford was one of the most gorgeous actresses at work during that era, and it's somewhat of a surprise given her screen presence and acting abilities that an earlier stint at RKO failed to boost her career, leading to a short absence from film and the eventual return to star in Sig's *Mercy Plane* and *Hold That Woman!* for PPC and PRC. Fortunately, better films were in her future.

Sig had assembled a tight group of technicians to handle his Sigmund Neufeld Productions, many of whom had worked on his films at various times in the past and had been brought on board for the production of *Hitler—Beast of Berlin*. Sam, of course, would be his only director, assisted by Mel De Lay, who had been serving in that capacity for other studios since 1930. Jack Greenhalgh remained as the company's cinematographer, along with Holbrook Todd as the company's editor. Hans Weeren continued as sound engineer, along with Bert Sternbach as production manager. Art direction was handled by Fred Preble, who had served in the same capacity for Sam and Katzman at Victory. The selection of music—mostly canned—was handled by Lew Porter, whose association with Sam dated back to Stan Laurel Productions and Buell's *Harlem on the Prairie*; Porter and David Chudnow[22] would, on occasion, pen original tunes for some of the films as well. Greenhalgh, Todd, and Sternbach would all be constants in Sig's productions for many years to come, along with Weeren.

Another "member" of Sig's group was a fellow named Roy Loggins. Born in Texas back in 1882, Loggins was a former chauffeur who had moved into the catering business, and Sig hired Loggins to provide meals for most of his location shoots for PRC. What set Loggins apart from most of the other studios' caterers was that he was an African American. "[M]y grandfather was very proud of the fact that they employed him," recalled Tim Neufeld, "because there was strict segregation in Hollywood in those days, and discrimination."[23] Loggins "paid it forward" in a sense, as described by the Denshō organization:

> When Japanese Americans returned to the West Coast as the WWII U.S. concentration camps began to close in 1945, many faced lingering racial animus. In Los Angeles, they found an unexpected friend in Roy Loggins, a Black business owner who ran a food catering company for Hollywood studios. While people of

Japanese heritage were being refused housing and job opportunities by white landlords and employers, Mr. Loggins went out of his way to share left-over food from catering events and even offered part-time work to members of the Senshin Buddhist Hostel, a refuge for former Japanese American incarcerees who had nowhere to call home. His acts of kindness were so seared into the memories of those whom he helped, that not only they, but their children, remember him with gratitude more than fifty years later.[24]

Loggins, sporting white chef's hat and apron, appears in several of the cast and crew group photos that survive from this era.

In early August 1940, PRC held its first national three-day convention in New York. Harry Rather presided over the affair, attended by franchise holders from twenty-eight key cities. Product and sales policies for the upcoming 1940-41 season, which now included four specials, sixteen features, and eighteen Westerns, were outlined by Rathner and Sig. Leon Fromkess and Pathé Laboratories president O. Henry Briggs attended the convention as well. Along with the previously announced McCoy "Frontier Marshal" series and Steele's "Adventures of Billy the Kid," a third series of musical Westerns—the "Lone Rider" series—was announced, with a yet-unnamed singer-actor to star; George Houston got the gig soon after. Sig outlined production plans and stressed the importance of the South American market, while Fromkess touted his success in landing the Great Britain market. With the convention's completion, Rathner headed out to conduct regional meetings nationwide[25] while Sig headed back to the Coast and work.

Attendees at the newly formed Producers Releasing Corp.'s first sales convention in 1940. Standing, left-to-right: Lou Lefton, Herbert Given, Bert Kulick, unidentified, Milton Lefton, Jack Adams Jr., Tom Flemion, Ben Agren, and Ike Katz. Sitting, left-to-right: Lee Goldberg, George Gill, Harry Asher, Sig Neufeld, Harry Rathner, Leon Fromkess, and Ann O'Donnell.

With those regional meetings behind him, Rathner announced his resignation as PRC's president in early September, effective at year's end. Pathé's stake in PRC appeared to take a firmer hold when O. Henry Briggs was elected Rathner's replacement, even though Briggs was reported to have resigned as head of Pathé. Briggs had been on Monogram's board of directors as well representing Pathé, which raised rumors of a Monogram-PRC merger, but his eventual resignation from that post brought those rumors to an end.²⁶ With this upcoming change in leadership, PRC was able to secure $150,000 additional financing from a group of New York Banks. PRC's producers at this time included Sig, Jed Buell, Ted H. Richmond, and E.B. Derr,²⁷ but all of PRC's films released during the 1939-40 season were produced by Sig and directed by Sam. Production was divided between the Talisman and Fine Arts studios.²⁸

George R. Batcheller, Jr. was appointed supervisor of production in early 1941 to coordinate the activities of PRC's other producers, who were to oversee twenty-two non-Western films that year. PRC's three Western units—Tim McCoy, Bob Steele, and George Houston's series—remained under Sig and his production company.²⁹ Cincinnati-born Batcheller (1911-1977) was the son of Chesterfield Pictures' president and founder, George R. Batcheller, Sr. Junior got his start at Chesterfield back in 1928 as head of the contract department, with later work for Invincible as general sales manager, and Republic in a production capacity. A short stint with Roland Reed Productions at Pathé Studios preceded his hiring by PRC in January 1941.

Tim McCoy yuks it up with Inna Gest as Lou Fulton and young Robert Winkler look on, in **Gun Code** (PRC, 1940), Sig Neufeld producer, Sam Newfield (as Peter Stewart) director.

Tim McCoy's "Frontier Marshal" series for Sig spanned the 1939-40 and 1940-41 seasons. The first of these, *Frontier Crusader*, released a month after *I Take This Oath* on June 17, 1940, was a particularly (and satisfyingly) bloodthirsty and action-filled entry, McCoy killing at least five gang members, and perhaps a few more during the climactic shootout at their hideout, the body count obscured by all the gun smoke. McCoy plays Marshal "Trigger" Tim Rand, summoned to the town of Monument City to help clean the place up, which of course he eventually manages to accomplish. There's the unseen "big boss"—we only see him in shadow until the film's end, a rather tired gimmick—who schemes to put the local mine out of business, assigning local hotel operator and respected citizen Karl Hackett and his flunkies—Ted Adams among them—to the job. The mine is blown up and the payroll shipment robbed, but to no avail. Reliable Frank LaRue played the beleaguered owner of the mine, with John Merton excelling as the knife-wielding thug-for-hire known as "Hippo Potts." Dorothy Short has a smaller role as a famous dancer brought to town to entertain, one of the more accomplished actresses to grace these films.

Sam outdid himself with the direction of this film, providing a number of nice little visual touches. At one point McCoy approaches a gunman known as "Mesa Kid" (Ken Duncan) and deftly kicks the guy's pistol out of his holster and snatches it in the air. Another gang member is dispatched offscreen by Merton's knife, his lifeless hand flopping into the frame still holding on to his unfired pistol. Later, McCoy engages Merton in a nicely staged fistfight, McCoy's final blow sending Merton to his death in a nearby well. The best sequence, however, involves McCoy's noontime showdown with Duncan and two of his cohorts inside the saloon. Outside, we hear a bunch of shots, followed by Duncan's exit from the front. He casually lights a cigarette and mounts his horse, then slowly topples over, dead. This ruse has been used in films numerous times over the years, known in the industry as "the long walk gimmick" and perhaps most memorably a year earlier in John Ford's *Stagecoach*, but is particularly effective in its staging and execution here. This was a decent opener for the McCoy series at PRC, and suggested good, if not better, things to come.

Gun Code's original script—as *Border Crossing*—didn't sit well with Breen and his censors, resulting in a four-page letter detailing all of the issues that needed addressing, eighteen of them in total. Breen's biggest beef was with a "boy of eight or ten years of age" named "Jerry." As written, the kid was to be abducted, "treated somewhat brutally," and involved in a shooting. While unacceptable as-is, Breen suggested two alternatives: change the character to a young man of seventeen or eighteen, or leave the kid in and remove any hint of danger to him.[30]

As released on July 29, 1940, *Gun Code* met no resistance from the various state censors—"Approved Without Elimination" was the phrase used—with only a few exceptions, Pennsylvania's objection worth noting: "Reel 3 – Reduce views of cattle mounting one another in herd of cattle moving to one flash of five feet."[31] (How did that get past Todd?) Breen's concerns about the kid, played in the film by young Robert Winkler, were dealt with, the gang members now treating him gently after they kidnap him, the kid escaping from them before any of the shooting starts.

The film's plot revolves around an extortion group known as "The Protectors," forcing payment from the business owners of Millers Flats to avoid ruin. McCoy's Marshal comes to town and poses as a blacksmith while he works to track down the gang and their leader—"The Big Fellow"—who, true to form, turns out to be one of the town's most respected citizens, this time a banker. Sam injects enough hard riding, fistfights, and gunplay to satisfy the filmgoing action addicts. Ted Adams is part of the cast once again, but this time on the right side of the law. *Gun Code* was brought in for a modest $11,392.

The remaining four series entries were more of the same. *Arizona Gang Busters* (September 16, 1940) tried something a bit different. "With its topical fifth column angle, this is good for exploitation and a little different from most westerns" wrote *The Exhibitor*.[32] Evidently that difference didn't sit well with some exhibitors and their patrons: "P.R.C. ruined a good western series with this one," complained a theater owner from Indiana. "The folks who like this type of picture don't want any sabotage or international situations in their horse operas."[33]

Like a Phoenix from the Ashes (Sig, Sam, and PRC, Part 1, 1939-1941) 189

Ted Adams (left) and his cohorts at Tim McCoy's mercy in **Riders of Black Mountain** (PRC, 1940), Sig Neufeld producer, Sam Newfield (as Peter Stewart) director.

Charles King (left) and his buddies have Tim McCoy under control, in **Outlaws of the Rio Grande** (PRC, 1941), Sig Neufeld producer, Sam Newfield (as Peter Stewart) director.
Courtesy of Heritage Auctions.

Riders of Black Mountain (November 11, 1940) fared less well, or at least according to one contemporary reviewer. "This is lacking in effectiveness," wrote *Motion Picture Daily*. "Flaws in sound and photography combined with generally poor staging are chiefly responsible. What appears to be the western's sole asset is the name of Tim McCoy...."[34]

Outlaws of the Rio Grande (March 7, 1941) features McCoy's marshal on the trail of a gang of counterfeiters, with an assist by his pal (Ken Duncan) and the Mexican secret service. "The action is fast throughout and should please Western fans who want something happening every foot of the film."[35] Charlie King is back again as one of the bad guys, prominent in what may have been the film's highlight, a knock down-drag out fight with McCoy. *Outlaws of the Rio Grande*'s negative cost was in line with the other series' entries, a typically thrifty $11,504.

The series' final entry, *Texas Marshal* (July 14, 1941), involves a phony League of Patriots, used as a front while its henchmen eliminate ranch owners to gain possession of their properties which sit atop a vein of valuable ore. Marshal McCoy to the rescue. All the McCoy films bore the "Peter Stewart" direction credit.

With the completion of his commitment to PRC, McCoy moved over to Monogram where he would team with Buck Jones and Raymond Hatton in a series of eight "Rough Rider" Westerns released 1941-42 before retiring from the business, or at least for the next thirteen years before he was lured back for the occasional role. "It was a lot of fun," reminisced McCoy decades later, "and darned remunerative. I liked the income and I liked the life. I certainly don't regret having gone into pictures."[36]

PRC's final first season "special" was *Marked Men* (August 28, 1940), a drama that mostly succeeds with its modest ambitions. A wrongly convicted and innocent convict (Warren Hull) escapes from prison, wanders the desert, adopts a stray dog, and ends up in a large town. Assuming a false identity, he soon falls in love and becomes a respected part of the community. The gang and its leader who had originally framed him arrive to rob a bank, and circumstances conspire to lead the townsfolk to think he's part of that gang. He escapes and hooks up with the gang, now stranded due to their broken-down car, and offers to lead them across the desert to Mexico. The gang's leader (Paul Bryar) decimates the gang along the way, but loses out in a confrontation with Hull, with a snarling assist from that adopted dog. A forced confession frees up Hull to marry his girl, played by Isabel Jewell.

A slightly more ambitious production on Sig's part, Sam took his crew to Tempe City, Arizona, a city just east of Phoenix and about 100 miles south of the Granite Dells studio, to film on location there and in the surrounding desert. This judicious decision provided the film a far richer and more realistic look than so many of the other studio- and Los Angeles-bound films of this era. "This afternoon many of our people enjoyed the experience of witnessing the filming of a motion picture," wrote the *Tempe News* about the July 23 filming.

> The Casa Loma hotel was used for the thriller, which embodied bad men with guns, racketeers and gangsters with high powered automobiles and Tommy guns, and all other paraphernalia and action that goes [with] that sort of picture. The producer is Sigmund Newfield [*sic*] Productions, Hollywood. The title of the

picture is 'Masked [*sic*] Men,' starring Warner [*sic*] Hull and Isabel Jewell and featuring the great dog 'Shadow.'³⁷

Sleepy old Tempe, it would seem, was excited about its fifteen minutes of fame, but accuracy was clearly *not* the writer's strong suit.

The desert sequences, both early on after Hull's escape and the later, grimmer trek of the exhausted gang members, are the film's visual highpoints. There's little subtlety to Bryar's gang leader, killing off four members of his gang, one-by-one, over noise and greediness toward their dwindling supply of water. Isabel Jewell, playing a good girl for a change, works well with Hull, although the premise that both she and her physician father (John Dilson) would invite this total stranger to become part of their household at their first meeting is a bit difficult to swallow. Al St. John has a small, and atypically straight, part as "Gimpy," the noisy gang member first to meet his maker after his ill-advised shooting at some howling wolves. The film's breakout star—and with only one prior film under his collar—was Grey Shadow, a German Shepherd whose first name's spelling vacillated between "Grey" to "Gray" from one film's credits to the next. The dog's episodes are nicely directed, and the early scenes where he fights off the wolves to protect Hull and is wounded in the process are rather touching. The film's lower budget ($20,087; Sam brought it in at $18,485) underpinning is obvious, of course, primarily in the screenplay's shortcuts and occasional implausibilities. There's the obligatory "police mobilization" montage filled with grainy chunks of footage seen dozens of times before, and there's actually a snippet of footage lifted from Sig's previous release, *Hold That Woman!* And if the film had an actual makeup artist on staff, he should have been fired; those desert-growth beards look terrible. Quibbles aside, it's a pretty

Lots of loot, but stuck in the desert in **Marked Men** (PRC, 1940), Sig Neufeld producer, Sam Newfield (as Sherman Scott) director. Left-to-right, standing: Al St. John and Art Miles. Sitting: Warren Hull, Paul Bryar, Ted Erwin, and Eddie Fetherston. *Courtesy of Tim Neufeld.*

good little film, benefiting considerably from the bulk of Greenhalgh's location-shot photography. In an unusual display of generosity, Universal, who owned the title "Marked Men," agreed to allow PRC the single use of it for this film while retaining to right to use it for one of its future films "whenever it so desires."[38]

The second Western series to premiere during the latter part of the 1939-40 season was Bob Steele's "The Adventures of Billy the Kid," opening on July 20 with *Billy the Kid Outlawed*. These were cut-rate entries budgeted at $11,000 per film, as evidenced by the opening montage of stock footage, lifted directly from one of Sig's earlier productions. That didn't matter to the kids and horse opera addicts in the audience, satisfied to watch Steele scowl his way through another fight-filled Western, lack of acting chops be damned. "Neighborhood houses the country over should welcome a new company with open arms such as Producers Releasing Corporation," wrote one excited exhibitor from West Virginia. "They put Bob Steele back in character. We almost had to tie the kids down while he was subduing the villain barehanded."[39] Louise Currie (billed as "Curry"), who co-starred in the film, gave this pocket assessment of Steele: "Bob Steele was sharp and busy; hustling, bustling. He was a real fighting cowboy, ready for a fight at a moment's notice."[40] Al St. John became part of the ongoing cast, providing his usual compliment of trips, falls, and dexterity with a pistol, occasionally rising to the occasion when need be. Carleton Young appeared in most of these as well as a character usually named "Jeff," whose connection to "Billy the Kid" would shift from film to film.

Billy the Kid Outlawed's story takes place in 1872 Lincoln County, New Mexico, or at least according to the trailer's opening crawl. A pair of law-abiding cattle ranchers are murdered at the order of the corrupt store owners (Ted Adams and Joe McGuinn) scheming to control the town. Steele comes to town accompanied by his sidekicks Fuzzy (Al St. John)[41] and Jeff (Carleton Young), and learns that his two friends were murdered by a gang led by John Merton. Adams gets elected as the town's sheriff and promptly declares Steele and sidekicks as outlaws. Through the machinations of Louise Currie, who Steele had earlier rescued, Steele is pardoned by the Governor. A climactic ambush by the gang members, mistaking Adams and McGuinn for Steele and his friends, results in their deaths. Steele, not trusting that he has actually been pardoned, rides off into the sunset to rest up for the next film, and a reputation that vacillates from film to film.

Next released on September 30, 1940, *Billy the Kid in Texas* has Steele still stuck on the wrong side of the law due to some recent trumped-up charges. He stumbles upon an express wagon robbery and manages to rob the robbers, intending to pass the money on to its rightful owners. Heading into town, it soon becomes evident that the men from the Lazy 8 ranch—Charlie King and John Merton among them—were the payroll robbers, and they aren't happy with Steele. After a bruising fight with King in the local saloon—the film's highlight—Steele, not recognized as Billy the Kid, is convinced to become the town's sheriff. A gunslinger (Carleton Young) is assigned to dispatch Steele, but upon the confrontation realizes Steele's his brother. He decides to go straight, and together they foil another robbery attempt by Merton and his gang. Now deemed heroes, Young is made sheriff, while Steele and St. John ride on to their next adventure. Included in the cast was Terry Walker as an express office employee, and Frank La Rue as her father.

Like a Phoenix from the Ashes (Sig, Sam, and PRC, Part 1, 1939-1941)   193

The filmic fights between Steele and Charlie King in this and other films were among the best staged in all of Sam's films. Steele biographer Mario DeMarco explained:

> I can only number one hero that could match [King's] skill with his dukes, and that was Bob Steele.... Steele, a one-time boxer...would first go over the fight scenes carefully with Charlie. The timing became perfect. When Bob would jab his left three or four times in quick succession, King's head would jerk back so realistic that the audience thought he was actually getting pulverized. Then Bob would finish him off with a left and a right cross that usually sent King sprawling across a table or two in a dead heap. Both were real experts in this particular scene. When Charlie took on a bit of weight in later years, it tended to make the thin, athletic Steele look twice as good.[42]

The Exhibitor liked the film: "A better than average Bob Steele western this has a good story and plenty of action, including fist and gun battles. Al St. John helps with his comedy relief which draws plenty of laughs."[43] *Variety*, on the other hand, didn't, deeming it "much duller than previous ones. Almost entirely quickie in acting and production.... Joseph O'Donnell's original looks like it was culled from several western screenplays of recent years. Peter Stewart's direction doesn't help much."[44] I lean more towards *The Exhibitor*'s assessment. One personal observation: The painting behind the opening credits, believe it or not, actually evokes—well, *sort of*—Vincent Van Gogh's "Starry Night."

Bob Steele and sidekick Al St, John hold Ted Adams (second from left) at gunpoint in **Billy the Kid's Gun Justice** (PRC, 1940), Sig Neufeld producer, Sam Newfield (as Peter Stewart) director.

Billy the Kid's Gun Justice (December 27, 1940) saw Steele protecting a group of ranchers from a bunch of real estate swindlers. After an hour's worth of the usual gun fights and fisticuffs, Steele out-swindles the swindlers, tricking them into paying many times a property's worth. Louise Currie made a return appearance as his co-star. The series' opener's budget of $11,000 was upped by $500 for this and the subsequent Steele entries, and was exceeded by a mere $377.

Billy the Kid's Range War (January 24, 1941) was more of the same, this one focusing on a gang chief scheming to stop the construction of a stage road in order to get a government contract for his steamboat line. A murder rap is pinned on Steele to get him out of the way. *Variety*, not a particular fan of these low budget oaters, called it "One of the less vigorous westerns. Meller is based on story material that impresses as too flimsy, though fist fights, a bit of gunplay and conventional horse-chase occasionally relieve tedious sequences."[45]

One exhibitor had both praise and complaint about this one, the complaint shedding some light on PRC's corner-cutting: "Good western. The print was terrible. That is a habit with P.R.C. This series draws well."[46]

Apropos of nothing, and it may be apocryphal, Bob Steele was credited as the inventor of the Steele Saddle, a modification of the old western saddle that was used extensively throughout the west at the time these films were produced. The royalties, it was claimed, helped to pad Steele's already hefty income.[47] The current makers of the saddle in 2023—Trail Saddles by Steele—claim otherwise.

Steele starred in two more "Billy the Kid" films: *Billy the Kid's Fighting Pals* (April 18, 1941)[48] and *Billy the Kid in Santa Fe* (July 11, 1941)[49] before leaving PRC and heading over to Republic. The initial four films in the Steele series were directed by "Peter Stewart," and the final two by "Sherman Scott." Despite Steele's departure, the popularity of the series was evident, and Sig wasn't about to let it die out; it would see new life come the 1941-42 season.

Al St. John's praying for a last-minute rescue in **Billy the Kid's Fighting Pals** (PRC, 1941), Sig Neufeld producer, Sam Newfield (as Sherman Scott) director.

PRC was having difficulty getting up to speed and delivering product, and it was evident to all that Sigmund Neufeld Productions alone would not be able to meet the fledgling company's needs. One exhibitor, while registering some complaints about *Marked Men*, was sympathetic of the studio's predicament: "Plot fairly good and acting not too bad. Photography only fair and sound not so good. However, Producers are trying hard to deliver so give them the break they justly deserve."[50] The other units that were created shortly after the company's reorganization would soon be augmenting the release schedule, but it wasn't until this second, 1940-41 season before any of them actually reached theater screens.

Sigmund Neufeld Productions' contract with PRC during this 1940-41 period stipulated that PRC "would advance certain sums to the PRODUCER upon the completion of each photoplay and upon the delivery thereof to DISTRIBUTOR" for each film, and that Pathé would "advance certain additional sums as therein specified upon the completion of each photoplay."[51] After each film went into release, there would be a fifty-fifty split of domestic and Canadian gross receipts after standard deductions for prints, advertising, local censorship, and so forth were taken off the top. Sig's company's split increased significantly for foreign receipts, at 90 % to PRC's 10 % for the United Kingdom, and 80 %-20 % for the rest of the world.[52]

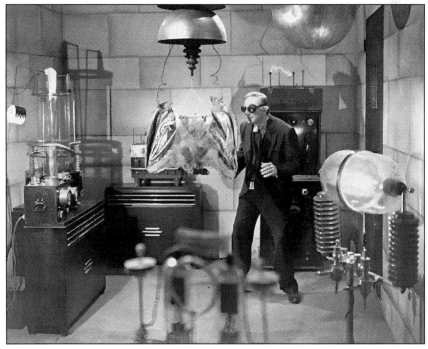

They don't get any battier than Bela Lugosi in **The Devil Bat** (PRC, 1940), Jack Gallagher credited producer, Jean Yarbrough director.

The earliest example of another producer's film to be released was with a genre new to PRC, *The Devil Bat* (December 13, 1940). Starring popular horror film star Bela Lugosi, Sig had been credited in the trades as the producer of this film, but when released the film's credits and advertising materials all credited Jack Gallagher as producer. Gallagher, the former president of Fanchon Royer Pictures and known primarily for his Spanish language films and later industrials via his Cinema Sales, Inc., was likely hired to assume Sig's production responsibilities when the latter's workload proved too unwieldy. Additionally, the film's director was Jean Yarbrough and not Sig's brother Sam, so it would appear that Sam was bogged down with Sig's other productions as well. It remained a Sigmund Neufeld Production, however.

The plot, based on screenwriter John T. Neville's adaptation of an original story by George Bricker, is a skimpy one. Cosmetics company scientist Bela Lugosi is in a snit over the wealth of the company's two owners (Guy Usher and Edmund Mortimer), wealth they made off his creation of a new cold cream. Utilizing his super-sized (via "glandular stimulation") killer bats, he proceeds to have the owners' three sons (John Ellis, Alan Baldwin, and Gene O'Donnell)—and one of the owners as well—murdered during the course of the film. The bats, you see, have been trained to sniff out and sever the jugular veins of anyone unfortunate enough to have agreed to test Lugosi's new experimental shaving lotion. The culprit is finally exposed by snoopy reporter Dave O'Brien and his inept photographer, Donald Kerr, Lugosi perishing under the snout of one of his flying beasts. Rather silly stuff, needless to say.

Jean Yarbrough's direction makes Sam's look flashy by comparison, the film returning to seemingly endless shots of Lugosi's attic window opening and bats emerging from within. David Chudnow's cobbled together musical score proves to be more grating than suspenseful, reused by scorer Leo Erdody five years later for *The Flying Serpent*, also scripted by Neville and a none-too-subtle reworking of this earlier film's plotline. The opening shot of the story's setting, "Heathville," was lifted directly from the previous year's *Marked Men*, a hilltop shot of Tempe City, Arizona. The film benefitted from its slightly increased budget—$20,000—if only in a minimalistic fashion.[53]

Actor Gene O'Donnell, whose role as one of the cosmetic manufacturer's sons meets an untimely demise, had few recollections about the production decades later. Aside from Lugosi keeping to himself, he recalled that the girl who played the maid—Yolande Mallott—was "a very cute girl," and that director "Jean Yarbrough went to AA meetings. He had problems."[54] Selective memory.

Producer Jed Buell contributed a trio of films to PRC schedule, all of them directed by William Beaudine: *Emergency Landing* (May 9, 1941), *Broadway Big Shot* (February 6, 1942), and the thoroughly delightful Harry Langdon starrer *Misbehaving Husbands* (December 20, 1940). *Boxoffice* was ecstatic over the latter film:

> To be considered in a class by itself was Jed Buell's initial productional effort for Producers Releasing Corp., "Misbehaving Husbands." Obviously Buell stretched every penny of a modest budget to the limit to turn out a compact little domestic comedy, well-equipped to do able service in the market for which it was geared.[55]

Director William Beaudine (1892-1970), a veteran of the industry from his start at Biograph back in 1909 who had peaked with his silent era features—Mary Pickford's *Little Annie Rooney* (1925) and *Sparrows* (1926) among them—had by now found himself exiled to the independents after he'd spent a few years directing over in England, and returned to find that Hollywood had "forgotten" him. Or at least the majors had; the independents leaped at the chance to hire a man of his vast experience and talent, and who was willing to work within their schedules and budgets. Beaudine directed an additional nine films of varying genres for PRC released through this and the following season, including such titles as the Ralph Byrd vehicles *Desperate Cargo* (July 4, 1941) and *Duke of the Navy* (January 23, 1942), Tom Neal in *The Miracle Kid* (November 14, 1941), and the Sydney Blackmer mystery *The Panther's Claw* (May 8, 1942). Producers John T. Neville, John T. Coyle, Martin Mooney, Ted Richmond, and Lester Cutler oversaw the production of one or more of Beaudine's other films, including *Mr. Celebrity* (October 10, 1941). Sig had some sort of connection to this latter film, although the specifics are unclear. Let it suffice to say that he continued to receive 12 % of the overages for this film for years to come,[56] so one can speculate that he held producer Martin Mooney's hand during the film's production.[57]

Producer Ted Richmond (1910-2013) had little experience prior to his films for PRC, a sole assistant producer credit on director Beaudine's *The Last Alarm* (1940) for Monogram. Richmond oversaw an additional four films for PRC before moving on to an extremely prolific career that lasted through the 1970s, having graduated to executive producer on films that included director Franklin J. Schaffner's *Papillon* (1973) and Ken Annakin's *The Fifth Musketeer* (1979). The other producers at work on films for the 1940-41 season were E.B. Derr—responsible for two films—along with John C. Bachman and the King Brothers—Maurice and Frank Kozinsky—for one film each. Direction of these films was in the hands of William Nigh, Phil Rosen, Albert H. Kelly—all seasoned vets whose careers stretched far back into the silent era—and German-born actor-director Max Nosseck, who fled that country back in 1933 due to increasing religious persecution.

George Houston catches the bad guy in the act in **The Lone Rider Rides On** (PRC, 1941), Sig Neufeld producer, Sam Newfield director.

The other producers and directors aside, Sig and Sam were still responsible for the bulk of the season's releases. Their "Lone Rider" series finally made its debut early in the 1940-41 season. Former "light opera baritone" George Houston had been hired as the series' star, his sole former experience with either of the brothers his starring role in 1938's *Frontier Scout* for Sam and Grand National. Houston (1896-1944) was a New Jersey-born son of a minister, his stint in the church's choir leading to musical training at New York's Institute of Musical Arts (now the Julliard School). Houston served during the First World War and eventually made his way onto Broadway in a series of short-lived shows from 1929 into 1935. This led to interest by Hollywood, his first starring role in producer Edward Small's *The Melody Lingers On* (1935). Nearly a dozen more films followed before Sig signed him to the series in early October 1940.

Houston's contract with Sigmund Neufeld Productions, Inc. called for six pictures within a year, with Houston to receive $1,000 per film. Two separate options were included, the first for an additional six films over a second year with Houston to receive $1,250 per film; and the second option for another six films during year three, with Houston to receive $1,500 per film. The contract stipulated that the years "shall be divided into 6 sixty day periods during each of which said sixty day periods the Producer must complete one picture with the Artist." Should Sig fail to meet those terms during any sixty-day period, Houston would receive his $1,000 regardless. A clause was included that stated that "said contract may and shall be transferred and assigned to Producers Releasing Corporation by said Sigmund Neufeld Productions."[58]

George Houston (center) and Al St. John seem to be in charge in this still from **The Lone Rider Crosses the Rio** (PRC, 1941), Sig Neufeld producer, Sam Newfield director.

Rathner had originally planned to assign a different producer to oversee the new series, but changed his mind and added the films to Sig's Western-heavy schedule,[59] an addition that wasn't expected and stretched Sig's production resources and technicians even thinner. Sam, for a change, dispensed with the Sherman Scott and Peter Stewart ruse for this series, although in hindsight he may have wished that he hadn't.

The series was rushed into production with inflated budgets of $12,000 for the series' first two films, and then into release, the initial two entries—*The Lone Rider Rides On* (January 10, 1941) and *The Lone Rider Crosses the Rio* (February 28, 1941)—

barely reviewed in the trades.⁶⁰ *Boxoffice* was unimpressed with the former, calling it "a strictly routine offering without particular distinction." The reviewer didn't hold back:

> Music [by John Lange and Lew Porter] saves it somewhat. It is played loud and long. George Houston is not up to regulation cowboy hero standards. He lacks a drawl and his acting talents need polish. Hillary Brooke, the feminine lead, sounds like a Park Avenue drawing roomer. Obviously a rush job, many of the sequences were filmed in overcast weather which could not wholly spoil the excellent scenic background.⁶¹

Not an auspicious series opener, and it exceeded its budget by more than a thousand dollars.

The series' third release, tentatively titled *The Lone Rider Gallops to Glory*, went into production in mid-April,⁶² and was retitled *The Lone Rider in Ghost Town* for its release on May 16, 1941. The film involves a daughter's search for her missing father, a mining engineer held hostage by some villains and their gang who want to force the location of a gold deposit from him. The "Lone Rider"—aka Tom Cameron (George Houston)—and his sidekick Fuzzy Jones (Al St. John, of course) ride into to town to do some prospecting on an abandoned property, now a so-called "Ghost Town." Cameron learns of her predicament and, after the obligatory gunfights, fistfights, and horseback dashes, proceeds to solve the mystery. Which, I might add, isn't much of a mystery. It's another of those musical Westerns, but we're fortunate that Houston only breaks out into song twice. The second of these, Johnny Lange and Lew Porter's "Old Cactus Joe," has, for better or worse, a verse sung by St. John. Lange and Porter's score for the film, by the way, overlays far too many scenes in an overly dramatic and inappropriate fashion.⁶³

Alaine Bandes comforts her father Edward Piel, Jr. while Al St. John looks on as George Houston holds them at gunpoint, in **The Lone Rider in Ghost Town** (PRC, 1941), Sig Neufeld producer, Sam Newfield director.

PRC entered into a promotional campaign with Sears, Roebuck and Company in an attempt to boost Houston's cred among the Western-going public, with the introduction of the "George Houston Boys' Cowboy Shirt." The stipulation: "that all printed matter, such as catalogs, counter placards and newspaper advertising, used in connection with said marketing, exploiting and selling of said boys' cowboy shirts, will bear the name of George Houston in a prominent position."[64] One wonders just how big of a seller these shirts were.

Watch enough of these low budget mysteries and you'll quickly become aware of the stunning similarity between plots, and the plot devices employed. This film's screenwriter, Joe O'Donnell, employed the expedient of reusing a sequence where Houston is required to make a breathless horseback ride over a mountaintop to another town to cash a check, the greenbacks needed to satisfy a pesky contractual stipulation. O'Donnell had used this same device six years earlier for Sig and Sam's *Trails of the Wild* for Ambassador. *The Lone Rider in Ghost Town*'s plot is mindlessly simplistic, not that its target audience would mind, and it's arguable whether St. John's admittedly juvenile antics actually save the film, but they sure don't hurt. Budd Buster assists St. John in the yuks department, earning some laughs as a grizzled prospector. As the film's lead, Houston has rugged good looks and considerable size—he's convincing in his fight scenes—and a good singing voice to boot, but the poor fellow falls short in the charisma department. That said, he soldiered on in this sort of role in the years to come up until his sudden death in 1944 from a heart attack.

Al St. John finds the secret entrance to the mine the hard way, in **The Lone Rider in Ghost Town** (PRC, 1941), Sig Neufeld producer, Sam Newfield director.

Feminine lead Alaine Bandes doesn't have a whole lot to do in this, her first credited role, but she can act and looks quite good up there on the screen. Within a year she would reinvent herself as Rebel Randall and continue in film for another decade, in both features and shorts, with and sans credit. Alden Chase and Frank Hagney play the film's "masterminds," with Charlie King on board once again for the expected thuggery and to take yet another beating, this time at Houston's fists. Which begs the question: Why in so many of these Westerns, when a free-for-all breaks out, does someone shoot out the lights? *Film Daily* was succinct in its summary: "Actionful but confusing story makes a weak entrance for new western star."[65]

The budgets for this series had by now been reduced to a contractually agreed upon $10,200 per, although this proved to be an impossible goal to stick to. *The Lone Rider in Ghost Town* ended up with a negative cost of $12,496, while the remaining three films never dipped much below that amount, and would hit a high of $13,614 for *The Lone Rider Ambushed*.

Houston demonstrates once again that size isn't everything in the follow-up *The Lone Rider in Frontier Fury* (August 8, 1941), delivering a performance even more stilted and lethargic than for the previous film. In this one, Houston is framed for the murder of a ranch owner (John Elliott), and sets out to find the real killer. The key is in the hands—*head*, actually—of a "touched" fellow named Loco Weed, played by Budd Buster. It turns out (no surprise) that Ted Adams and Karl Hackett want the dead man's property, and are scheming to get it from Hillary Brooke, who inherited the ranch.

George Houston launches into another unwelcome song while Maxine Leslie and Al St. John look on with bemused admiration in **The Lone Ride Ambushed** (PRC, 1941), Sig Neufeld producer, Sam Newfield director.

Fred Myton's screenplay is even more absurd than usual, with more plot-advancing coincidences than usual. Houston, wanted for murder and sought by half the vengeance seeking cowboys in the territory, merrily rides through the plains warbling "Ride 'Em, Cowboy, Ride 'Em" at full volume, and later belts out "Down By the Old Alamo" in the midst of the gang of cutthroats he's angling to convince that he too is a wanted murderer. Throw in a third song in that same setting—a duet with actress Virginia Card—and you start to wonder what makes this fellow tick. Perhaps the biggest groaner comes when Houston is found out and about to be murdered by the gang members. They are standing in a general store, and he just happens to notice a convenient canister of black powder on the shelf. He winks at Card and she dumps its contents on the floor while he convinces one of his captors to give him a cigarette. None of the group notices or suspects anything, allowing Houston and Card to escape in the explosion.

Sam manages to provide a few nice touches to help salvage the film. One extended sequence takes place during a raging nighttime thunder storm, which helps greatly to enhance the mood and heighten the suspense. The film's climax (aside from that silly black powder bit) has Houston, Brooke, Card, and Buster holed up and barricaded in a room surrounded by Adams and Hackett's men, a furious gunfight capped by some smoke bombs tossed in to drive them out. It doesn't sound like much, but for a PRC Western it's a comparatively ambitious sequence. In the feminine lead, Hillary Brooke is competent in this, her first credited starring role, although her character is far too quick to accept Houston's innocence. Al St. John is back as Fuzzy, and while his character furthers the plot and rides to the rescue, far too much time is spent tripping and falling over things. This isn't a very good film, and suggestive of why the series, and its star, failed to click with audiences.

The Lone Rider Ambushed (August 29, 1941) and *The Lone Rider Fights Back* (November 7, 1941) were both cut from the same cloth. Houston plays a dual role in the former, as both the title character and the bandit he is mistaken for. "This one rates below par for the sagebrush sagas," wrote *Film Daily*. "It is shy on action, has a poor script and generally has been handled in an inferior manner. Budget limitations are obvious."[66] *The Lone Rider Fights Back* has to do with the murder of a ranch owner and attempts by the villains of the piece to gain possession of the property from the victim's niece (Dorothy Short). Enter Houston and St. John to track down the murderer. "Fair direction and an inferior script [by Joe O'Donnell] place a great strain on the dramatic credibility of the yarn," wrote *Film Daily*. "Huston does okay but does not rate with the rest of the screen heroes. Al (Fuzzy) St. John furnished whatever comic relief there is."[67]

George Houston holds Charles King at gunpoint while Al St. John cowers in the corner, in **The Lone Rider Fights Back** (PRC, 1941), Sig Neufeld producer, Sam Newfield director.

As unpromising as this series' debut season turned out to be, PRC planned to stick with Houston for another six entries before the reins would be turned over to another.

It didn't quite turn out that way.

Chapter 11:
Growing Up in Hollywood – Part 1

By mid-1941, Sig's son Stanley was eighteen years old, and second son Sigmund Jr. ten years of age. Sam's children were younger, daughter Jacqueline and son Joel eight and six years of age, respectively.

There were, of course, both pluses and minuses to growing up in Hollywood as the children of fathers actively engaged in the production end of the industry. The pluses were all the cool things those connections afforded you. The downside was having fathers who were both workaholics, and rarely at home. "As a parent and father," reminisced Sig Jr.,

> he was so busy at the time that I felt as a kid I was somewhat neglected by him, he was so busy all the time. I didn't have a lot of communication with him, mostly with my mother. He would come home late—he'd be at the studio six-, seven-, eight o'clock at night, working all the time; very busy. He was a good man, but I just never felt super-close.... My father never had a breakdown or anything like that, but he did put in a lot of long hours, and was very wrapped up into the whole thing, very much so. That was the key to his life, was working.[1]

And these were the days back when a work week ran from Monday through Saturday. Sam's son Joel felt much the same way about his father:

I did not spend that much time with him. He was always working, or he was gone. As kids, we would go to bed like at six- or seven o'clock at night...they weren't home yet.... We didn't see them at night, we didn't see them in the morning because they left before we even got up. So they were gone.[2]

Sig Neufeld and his wife, Ruth. *Courtesy of Tim Neufeld.*

The lack of interaction with his father left him with some ambivalent feelings. "You have to understand, it's not that we were disappointed with our parents, we just felt like we never really had them.... He wasn't that great a family man, he wasn't a bad family man; he just didn't have time."[3]

Sig and Ruth and the kids still lived at 340 North Sweetzer Avenue, a home they would occupy throughout the 1940s. Hollywood was not nearly as built up (and run down) as it is today. "I actually remember some of the orange groves that were still there when I was a kid," said Sig Jr. "They were like a block east of Vine Street and Hollywood Boulevard, and they went up into the hills, and parts of those areas were still wheat fields."[4]

Sig Sr.'s mother Josephine had lived with her sons Sam and Maury for a while at their rented Tamarind Avenue home during the 1920s, and later at 1354 North Beachwood Avenue. She took ill in 1938, however, and moved over to Sig's North Sweetzer home. She was suffering from diabetes and lung cancer, and eventually succumbed on October 27, 1938, from a pulmonary embolism. While religion did not play a part in either Sig or Sam's life at this time, it did in Josephine's, and she was buried in a Jewish cemetery in East Los Angeles. On the day of her funeral, "They didn't invite me because they thought I was too young," recalled Sig Jr. "and would be too upset. I knew where they were going...they thought I didn't know, but I did."[5]

Sig and Sam's mother Josephine Neufeld, taken some time during the early 1930s.
Courtesy of Tim Neufeld.

As the older son, Stanley had gone to work as a teen and learned to drive. And he *really* liked to work, an addiction of sorts that would last his entire life:

> I like to work. I was brought up to work. When I first got my car, I got it and I worked at a drug store taking medicine and stuff to people in a car. Working, that's all I thought of, even when I went to school, high school. I didn't have to. But I somehow, I got it in my system that I had to work. And I'm going to get laid off every day of my life. You know? ... I don't know how to put it. I was in love with my work. And that's all I was in love with, was my work. And I wanted to keep working. And I kept working. And of course I say, well, I'll never get another job if I quit.[6]

Sig Neufeld and teenaged son Stanley in 1940. *Courtesy of Tim Neufeld.*

It wasn't all work for Stanley, however, and during his free time he'd head to his father's set:

> When I was in high school, I used to go to the set and I would be the guy running for the water to give to the actor, or doing little jobs like that, and I'd just like being around on the set, watching what they were doing, especially if they were doing a western. I got to ride the horses, and especially if the horses weren't working for a while, I used to be able to go to the stable and ride 'em.... I got pretty good at it.... I [also] got on a side saddle, and I was the only one that could ride on a side saddle, and I got a few odd jobs of doubling women riding side saddle, and so I was stuck to where I was going to stay in the film business.... I was about sixteen years old, and I went from there and it was fun because I knew all of the horses in the stable that just worked on films, and I used to be able to break 'em in, if a certain thing was going to happen, because I went

there...because to me it was all fun... [P]eople around me always thought I was working too hard on the horses.⁷

Sig Jr., on the other hand, didn't take to horses the way his older brother did. "I did a little bit [of horse riding], but I was never very good at it, I kept getting on the wrong side of the horse."⁸

Sig Jr. had fond memories of visiting his father's sets as well. "Every Saturday I would go and spend the day on the set at the studio, when they were shooting either on location or at the studio." The outdoor Westerns were "shot at a place called the Iverson Ranch. A guy owned this really large piece of land with all kinds of hills; it was perfect for making westerns.... That was used regularly; I spent a lot of time out there, that's where I watched them filming."⁹

The kids weren't spoiled, growing up in a comparatively frugal and conservative environment. "I think it was the background," speculated Sig Jr.,

coming from where they had very little, and had to appreciate what little they had, and I don't think [Sig Sr.] ever got over that. I mean we lived very nicely: the house was nice, but it wasn't in Beverly Hills. It wasn't a huge house, but it was a very nice house in a nice area, and he always drove a nice car, but he wouldn't get a new car every year; he'd drive the same car for four or five years. So he was conservative in that respect, and he respected the money that he was making.¹⁰

Religion was a non-issue in the Neufeld household, or at least according to Sig Jr.

My mother was protestant, and of course my dad was Jewish, and they agreed when they got married that religion was not going to be a major part of anything that they would follow so that it wouldn't interfere with their lives.... The family members—my dad's mother and all that—were a little disappointed that he hadn't married a Jewish person. They got along absolutely fine, they never had any problems or anything like that at all, so it worked very well. They said to me, whatever you want to do—if you want to go to church, go to church, if you want to go to the synagogue, go to the synagogue, and if you don't want to do anything or have any religious affiliation, do that. I remember they sat me down once when I was fourteen or fifteen years old [and said] anything you want to do is okay with us. So I just went along with what they were doing—and didn't do anything.¹¹

Oddly enough, Sam's son Joel remembers it somewhat differently: "[The Neufelds] were very Jewish, with the separate dishes and all. My dad [Sam] used to explain about the Jewish religion, 'cause Sig was very Orthodox. I thought they were very Jewish because the only thing I learned from my dad was how to order in a deli."¹²

Sig and Ruth were not big on entertaining. "My mother had friends, but I don't remember a lot of big parties or anything," recalled Sig Jr. "She would have an occasional dinner party for six or eight people but that was about it; they didn't do any big parties or big entertainment very often."¹³ But when they did, Sig's brother Sam and his wife Violet were rarely included. According to Joel, the two families "didn't have a close family relationship...it was all work...nothing was social."¹⁴ Sig Jr. elaborated on the rift: "My mother didn't like Sam, she didn't like him because of the way he was living and the gambling and all that, so she wouldn't have him over, she wouldn't go to his place, or anything like that. I don't remember there being any problem between the wives, but because of the relationship with him the families didn't mingle much."[15]

As infrequently as the boys got to see their Uncle Sam and Aunt Violet as guests at their home, they almost never got to see their father's other siblings, Aunt Sadie and her husband Mannie, and Uncle Maury. Over the years, Sig and Sam's sister Sadie had worked her way into real estate, finding a niche in her growing rental business. Sadie's rental receipts greatly increased her family's otherwise modest income from Mannie's job as a grip in the industry. "Sig and Sadie were the brains of the family," recalled Tim Neufeld, Sig's grandson, and Stanley's son, "and Sadie, of course as a woman, never got to work at Stern Brothers or Century or any of the films her husband did, but she took what money they had and bought real estate. She tried to maximize her real estate returns by being the landlord to inter-racial couples when in those days most people wouldn't rent to them, she would, and she could command more rent as a result of doing that."[16]

Brother Maury was another story. Sig had paved the way for Maury to become an electrician in the industry, and he was reasonably successful at it. In addition to working on Sig's various productions, he would freelance elsewhere. He was, however, incredibly shy. "[In] all the crew pictures I have yet to find one where he's in that picture," said Tim. "And even the family gathering for [an earlier] wedding, he's not in that picture." On the job, he'd stay in his place of comfort, up with his lights high above the set.[17]

The attendees at the wedding of Sadie Teitelbaum's daughter Selma (Sig and Sam's niece) to Sol Perlman, June 10, 1941. Selma and Sol center, Sadie to the left of Selma, father Mannie Teitlbaum standing extreme left. Sitting, Left-to-right: Sam Newfield, Sigmund Neufeld Jr., Jackie Newfield, and Joel Newfield. Ruth and Sig Neufeld standing third and second from right. *Courtesy of Tim Neufeld.*

Maury had served in Europe during the First World War. Sig Jr. thinks he enlisted to get away from the family, while Tim thinks he was drafted, but whatever the case, family lore has it that he was gassed during combat, and was never quite the same after that. "[That] may explain why he was reticent about being in the photos, and why he, as an electrician, he'd just stay up there with the lights, away from everybody else."[18] Tim's daughter Kathy speculates that it may have been "straight-up PTSD from being in the war, because we're not sure what he did."[19]

As time went on, Maury's options dwindled, and he ended up a parking lot attendant in Venice. "He lived down at the beach, because at the time living down at the beach was very inexpensive," recalled Sig Jr. "Doesn't sound like it would be because it's one of the most expensive places to live. But at the time it was very cheap. And, yes, he parked cars and did stuff like that to make money." He never married, but had a common law arrangement for a while.[20] When things got really tight, however, Sig would always step in. "Everybody got supported, when they needed it, by Sig. I think Maury, at the end of his life…was kind of a loner."[21]

But now that Sig was so incredibly busy producing one Western after another—with the occasional "special" added to his plate—his sons didn't get to see a whole lot of him. In Sig Jr.'s opinion

> He didn't seem like a driven person to me, he just seemed like a good worker, but I never felt that he was driven, that he had to go out and do all this stuff, to prove something. He enjoyed his work. He loved going to the studio, and always coming home late, which my mother was bawling him out for. If they were shooting at night, he wanted to stick around and make sure they got the work done before midnight. He loved what he was doing, and really enjoyed it.[22]

It wasn't going to get any better anytime soon.

Chapter 12:
Buster Joins Fuzzy (Sig, Sam, and PRC, Part 2, 1941-1942)

Towards the end of February 1941, PRC had acquired an advancement of $1,000,000 from Herbert J. Yates's Consolidated Film Industries towards the completion of the films for both the current and upcoming 1941-42 seasons. As part of this agreement, Consolidated's plants in Hollywood and Fort Lee, New Jersey would handle the negative developing, printing, titles, and insert business of PRC. Twenty-four features and another eighteen Westerns were planned for the upcoming season, which PRC was able to deliver. It was also announced that RCA would handle all of PRC's sound recording.[1] In June, Briggs and Yates agreed on some additional funding as well, prompted by the expanded production and increased budgets for the upcoming season. Consolidated agreed to lend $16,575 for the production of any melodrama, $9,350 for any Western in the Tim McCoy series, and $10,200 for any other Western. All but four of the current 1940-41 season's films were already in the can by the end of June, the remaining four in the midst of production.[2]

PRC chairman of the board Harry Asher speaks at the 1941 annual convention held in Chicago. Left-to-right at table: George Batcheller, Sig Neufeld, George Gill, Asher, president O. Henry Briggs, cowboy star Art Davis, and Bert Kulick. *Courtesy of Tim Neufeld.*

On March 22-24, PRC held its annual sales convention in Chicago where "the organization, production and sales policy [was] adjusted to conform to the greatly expanded operations of P.R.C." as well as celebrate the company's one-year anniversary. President Briggs hosted, accompanied by Leon Fromkess, now vice president in charge of domestic and foreign operations; George Batcheller, in charge of feature production; and Sig, in charge of Western production. PRC's current slate of producers made the scene as well: John T. Coyle, Jed Buell, Ted Richmond, and E.B. Derr.[3] "We have budgeted our pictures amply in order to get the type of product that has proved profitable to the exhibitor," said Briggs, who also announced tentative titles for a raft of "dramas, comedy-dramas, mystery melodramas and character comedies with music features," some of which actually made it to the screen. Sig detailed the upcoming season's eighteen Westerns—he had a contractual commitment to deliver a Western to PRC every three weeks[4]—and added that PRC would also make an outdoor action film set in an "Alaska locale."[5] According to *Showmen's Trade Review*, "Briggs pointed out that the market for P.R.C. product demands pictures with a maximum of action and a minimum of dialog...'and that's the kind of picture P.R.C. is pledged to produce and distribute.'" William Gell, managing director of Pathé Ltd., distributor of PRC's product in London, came up with a slogan that was embraced by the convention's attendees: "Persistency—Reliability—Consistency".[6] Catchy, huh?

A round-table conference between PRC big-wigs and western exchange men at the 1941 convention in Chicago. Back center, left-to-right: Sig Neufeld speaking, George Gill, and O. Henry Briggs with head tilted and listening to a private comment. *Courtesy of Tim Neufeld.*

Sigmund Neufeld Productions' agreement with PRC during the 1941-42 season modified their split on the gross receipts. The fifty-fifty split of domestic and Canadian receipts remained, along with the 80 %-20 % split for the rest of the world, but Sig's share of the United Kingdom receipts dropped to 75 %.[7] Sig's production contract with PRC now had some more specific stipulations included, among them the requirement that each of the season's films must be at least 6,000 feet in length, that stock shots were not to exceed 500 feet in length, and that all stock shots had to be approved by PRC. "With respect to the stock shots inserted in the photoplay," the contract went on to clarify, "the negative thereof must be of such quality as to permit first class, clear, positive prints to be made therefrom." (It would appear that PRC was rather lax in following through with its demands regarding the stock shots, since a quick review of Sig's various Westerns reveals some rather shoddy stock inserts.) Additionally, the three principal cast members, director, cameraman, and editor of each film needed to be approved by PRC at least fifteen days in advance of actual production—pretty much a non-issue given that Sig reused the same crew and casts for his Western series—along with the title, budget, and anticipated schedule.[8]

With Sig's return to the coast, one of his first orders of business was to line up a replacement for Bob Steele, who would soon finish his commitment to the "Billy the Kid" series after his sixth entry wrapped in June. The series had proven popular with exhibitors and their patrons, due in no small part to Steele's presence. St. John would continue on as the new lead's sidekick, bouncing back and forth between this series and his similar sidekick character to lead George Houston in the "Lone Rider" series. Sig needed an actor who could readily fill Steele's boots, and found him in mid-May when he hired popular star Buster Crabbe.[9] Sig also acquired nine outdoor stories by author Johnston McCulley to be used as the basis of screenplays for his three Western series. The titles of the nine stories were "One Way Trail," "Romance of Roaring Valley," "High and Mighty," "Frontier Frameup," "Cowboy Afoot," "Cowboys Never Walk," "Caliente Kid," "Whelp of the Fox," and "Saga of Smoky Farm."[10] (Good luck trying to connect any of these stories to the completed films.) Now all he had to do hiring-wise was find a suitable replacement for Tim McCoy as well, who had finished his commitment to the "Texas Marshal" series. At one point Tom Tyler and Lee Powell were announced as McCoy's co-starring replacements, but that teaming never came to pass; Tyler was given a release from his contract with PRC[11] and the series was discontinued.[12]

Larry "Buster" Crabbe (1908-1983) would prove an excellent choice. Born in California and raised in Hawaii, Crabbe's swimming ability became evident in college, leading to two Olympic medals for freestyle events, a bronze in 1928 and a gold in 1932. Hollywood took notice of the ruggedly handsome six-foot one-inch, 195-pound Crabbe, his first appearance of note the starring role in producer Sol Lesser's *Tarzan the Fearless* (1933). "I go to college for four years, I even take part of a law course," recalled Crabbe eight years later. "Then when I have a chance to be in movies, they put a loin cloth on me and have me going around muttering: 'Uh-Uh.' I've been trying to live that down since."

This led to starring roles more to Crabbe's liking that included *The Sweetheart of Sigma Chi* (1933) opposite Mary Carlisle, before leading to his breakout role as the star of Universal's 1936 serial *Flash Gordon*. The popularity of this initial serial led to three more outer space, multi-part sagas for Universal, *Flash Gordon's Trip to Mars* (1938), *Buck Rogers* (1939) and *Flash Gordon Conquers the Universe* (1940). Popular with both children and adults alike, Sig decided that Crabbe would be an ideal replacement for Steele; it didn't hurt that Crabbe had a deferment from the armed forces as well. Crabbe was to star in "Water Follies of 1941," a road show version of Billy Rose's famous Aquacade at the Minneapolis Aquatennial, having appeared in Rose's Aquacade at the New York's World's Fair the previous year. The show would tour for a month, then disband for the remainder of the summer, allowing for an August start in Sig's "Billy the Kid" series with exterior shooting at the Placeritas Ranch,[13] by now commonly known as the Monogram Ranch since Monogram had signed a long-term lease on the property in 1937. "I do like appearing in westerns," said Crabbe, looking to the future. "As a western star you don't have to remain perpetually young. You can last a long time in such pictures."[14] Al St. John would continue providing a questionable level of humor to the series as Crabbe's sidekick "Fuzzy Jones," and Carleton Young would take turns with Dave O'Brien and Bud McTaggart playing the character of "Jeff."

Sig increased the budget for the series opener and Buster Crabbe's introduction in the lead, *Billy the Kid Wanted*, released on October 24, 1941. "Where last season's 'Kid' westerns, with Bob Steele, were 'quickie' horse operas and suitable only for the kids," wrote *Film Bulletin*, "this should satisfy wherever cowboy action films are popular."[15] Sig increased the amount of time allotted for Sam to shoot the film's episodes, reportedly at fourteen to sixteen days,[16] or at least initially. Sam directed all the season's six as "Sherman Scott."

Glenn Strange (later *Gunsmoke*'s bartender) plays the owner of the Paradise Land and Development Company, who bleeds dry the homesteaders he's suckered into buying property through exorbitant water rates and prices at the local store. Charlie King plays a rival gang leader aiming to take over Strange's lucrative business. Fuzzy (St. John) learns of this from one affected family, informs Billy (Crabbe) and friend Jeff (Dave O'Brien for this installment), and the trio sets out to make things right. After an extended ruse where Crabbe and O'Brien convince the rival factions of their hatred for, and determination to do away with, each other, they are found out. Just when things look bad for Billy and Jeff, now prisoners and being forced to fight the other to his death, Fuzzy arrives with a posse of homesteaders. Strange and King are arrested, and the trio of heroes ride off into the sunset. Atypically for any film having Charlie King as a heavy, he isn't once involved in a fistfight with anyone. For that matter, neither is anyone else except for Crabbe and O'Brien, who perpetuate their ruse by engaging in two extended slugfests with each other, Sam pulling out the stops for these two sequences. They must have both had some bruising by each workday's end.

Lest anyone paying to see this film think that *this* film's Billy the Kid is a bad guy, Fuzzy reminds us early on that Billy hasn't broken any laws, but the sheriffs still think otherwise and continue their relentless pursuit. Fred Myton's script is typically simplistic, the gullibility of the two rivals and their willingness to let Billy and Jeff become their respective gang's de facto strategists, rather difficult to swallow. O'Brien's devil-may-care attitude while tied to a chair by King and threatened with unstated torture is equally unbelievable, but I suppose this was intended to put the audience's wee ones' minds at ease. Crabbe is fine as the series' new Billy, and O'Brien at his comparative best as this film's Jeff. As for St. John, this particular episode provides his character some depth, or at least early on. His character is initially serious and sympathetic as he yearns for an end to their ongoing flight from the law, his desire for a stress-free life prompting his interest in abandoning his two pals and moving on to a place of his own. Not to worry: his spontaneous habit of injecting bits of business into any given film soon returns with the usual pratfalls and slapstick physicality pushing any hint of seriousness aside. For example, there's a scene where O'Brien breaks St. John and Crabbe out of jail. Crabbe later commented on St. John's improvisation, and willingness to take risks:

> Listen, he could take some great falls. One time we broke our way out of jail in a picture by sawing through the roof. We were about eighteen feet off the ground. We got up on top and I told the director I'd make the jump if Fuzzy'd jump. I thought Fuzzy would say, hell no, bring in the double. But he said, yea, I'll jump – he'd changed his shoes to sneakers beforehand and there I was with cowboy boots on. So I had to jump. The ground was harder than hell. Down comes Fuzzy and darned if he doesn't fall again after he got up. *Then* we jumped onto our horses. He was always doing some damned thing like that.[17]

For the record, the kid playing the homesteading family's young son was Joel Newfield, Sam's six-year-old son. "I was always in them when I went," recalled Joel when asked about his visits to his father's sets. "He would put me in them, in the movie;

these were all the Buster Crabbe movies."[18] Unfortunately for Joel, half of the reviews for the film credited him as "Joe Newfield," and at least one as "Billy Newfield."

Howard Masters protects wife Choti Sherwood and young son Joel Newfield from strangers Buster Crabbe, Dave O'Brien, and Al St. John in **Billy the Kid Wanted** (PRC, 1941); Sig Neufeld producer, Sam Newfield (as Sherman Scott) director. *Courtesy of Joel Newfield.*

"Chief ingredient of this one is action, supplied by frequent fisticuffs, gunplay, and a lot of frothy riding," wrote *Film Daily*'s reviewer. "Stands in market for prairie pix will find the footage good fan fare, with the heroics of Crabbe and O'Brien augmented by the comedy supplied by Al 'Fuzzy' St. John.... Direction: Firm. photography: Solid."[19] As the debut of Buster Crabbe in the lead, *Billy the Kid Wanted* was a very acceptable second-season series opener.

Screenwriter Fred Myton (1885-1955) got his start writing scenarios for Universal back in 1916, then switched to semi-freelancing in 1919, bouncing between independent producers, mini-majors, and major studios such as Pathé, First National, FBO, Paramount, and Columbia over the next fifteen years. A several-year dry spell followed in the mid-1930s, after which he found less profitable but far more prolific work for the independents such as A.W. Hackel and Jed Buell. Myton wrote eleven of the films that Sam directed before Sig hired him on a "flat deal" basis to write the screenplays for his Sigmund Neufeld Productions—nearly two dozen of them—with later work for Sig at Film Classics and Lippert. In 1946, Myton would defend his work—and that of the producers he worked for—in a letter to *The Screen Writer* magazine. This was in response to an earlier article titled "Your Minimum Basic Flat Deal" in which screenwriter Patricia Harper wrote:

> The most prevalent gripe among lower bracket writers seems to be against the so-called flat deal.

> In fact, our Thousand Dollar Minimum Basic Flat Deal is held in such opprobrium that the average writer will accept such a contract only under the stress of economic pressure, and then, with the defensive attitude that he therefore is at the producer's mercy, believing that the contract is so executed as to throw the balance of advantage in favor of the producer.
>
> I have yet to hear of any writer (myself included) who would admit that he or she would accept a minimum flat deal in preference to a weekly salary deal.[20]

This is the deal under which Myton had been writing his screenplays for Sig and others, knocking them off at $1,000 apiece. He fired off a letter in response to Harper's article and its assertions:

> I have been a screen writer since 1916, which, as I count it up, is thirty years. Up until the time of the [Screen Writers] Guild [1933], I rarely bothered with a contract. The Producer would say: "Nuts" or "Okey," and that's all there was to it. In my thirty years experience, I never received a dirty deal from any Producer, except once.... He was a big shot but he is now dead and there were political complications in the matter and I would not like to mention his name.
>
> Throughout the years, I have worked at most studios on salary, and not a bad salary at times, and, of late, I have been working with Sig Neufeld on flat deals and I, by far, prefer the flat deal. I work as I please. I don't have anyone breathing down the back of my neck while I'm working or drop around to count the number of pages I have written during the day. When I finish the job, it's done and I'm paid off. Of course, there's one thing to take into consideration, I'd rather enjoy life than make a lot of money.
>
> And I have a funny idea about not wanting to get paid for something I don't deliver. If I don't turn in a satisfactory job, and it can't be fixed up, I don't want to be paid for it.[21]

Prolific screenwriter Fred Myton, 1927.

Calculated for inflation, Myton had earned what would now be approximately $83,000 and $92,000 for the years 1945 and 1946, respectively. Not a huge annual salary, but not too shabby, either; as he said, he'd rather have time to enjoy life than make a lot of money, so his arrangement with Sig met both parties' needs. Harper, it should (and will) be mentioned, penned a handful of screenplays for Sig as well in the early 1940s, several years before this article was printed and likely fodder for her anti-flat deal stance.

Billy the Kid's Round-Up, brought in for a modest $13,188, followed on December 12, 1941, wherein saloon owner Vic Landreau (Glenn Strange) schemes to replace the town's sheriff with a more malleable, semi-corrupt puppet, Charlie King. The current sheriff calls in Billy, accompanied by Fuzzy and Jeff (Carleton

Young for this film), but gets shot dead before their arrival. The town paper, now in the hands of Joan Barclay, persists in printing stories placing both Strange and King in bad light, so she's next in Strange's sights. After several back-and-forth kidnappings and the usual gunplay, the film is capped off with a by-now-traditional slugfest, this one between Crabbe and Strange. St. John ends up elected sheriff, but flees at the first hint of trouble.

Any increases in the series' entries' budgets aren't readily apparent aside from the increased number of cowboy extras milling about in the various scenes' periphery, but perhaps Crabbe's salary was a bit heftier than that of Steele's. Newcomer Glenn Strange (1899-1973) makes for an imposing, six-foot five-inch heavy, turning from charm to threat at the blink of an eye. Strange became part of Sig's roster of bad guys for the next few years, even elevated to horror film star for Sig and Sam's *The Mad Monster* in 1942. A former country singer, Strange started making appearances in uncredited bit parts in 1930, racking up an impressive number of film roles before finally seeing his name up there on the screen in 1935, almost exclusively in Westerns from that year on, and a lot of them still sans credit. As the years rolled on, Strange would move over to television where he was most often found behind the saloon's bar in the long-running series *Gunsmoke*, a place he could call home up until his death in 1973. Years after his association with the brothers, Strange told interviewer Boyd Magers that "Sig and Sam were a couple of wonderful guys."[22]

Carleton Young plays Jeff as a more impatient, hot-headed character than O'Brien, ready to "string up" or "shoot dead" the bad guys, but always restrained at the last minute by cooler-headed Billy. The addition of this character was a logical one, a sidekick who could help Billy with his various plans and add a second set of fists in the numerous fights, since Fuzzy was of little use in the latter. Fuzzy begins this film once again yearning for a "calm and peaceable life," but quickly sets aside such notions once the action starts. Joan Barclay, as always, is a welcome, talented addition as the film's newspaper woman, a far meatier role than the seeming female "afterthoughts" of so many other of PRC's Westerns.

Billy the Kid Trapped (February 20, 1942), with its screenplay by Joe O'Donnell, brought something new to the series. In this one Billy, Fuzzy, and Jeff (the perpetually smiling Bud McTaggart for this sole entry), in jail for reasons unknown to them, are being blamed for the crimes committed by a trio of crooks masquerading as our heroes. The crooks want to continue having the blame placed on these unwitting dupes, so they break them out of jail. And so it goes until Crabbe catches on and the real culprits are exposed. "This western does not bother with frills," wrote *Motion Picture Herald*, an observation that could be made of most any of the series' entries.[23] Glenn Strange is back as the crooks' mastermind, while Ted Adams makes a return visit to the right side of the law as a sheriff.

The plot of *Billy the Kid's Smoking Guns* (May 29, 1942) involves the corrupt doctor (Milton Kibbee) who inflates the prices at his co-operative store so that his rancher patrons will eventually run up debts they cannot pay, paving the way for him to seize their property in anticipation of a cavalry post planned for the land. Murdering them, however, is an expedient when he's in a rush. Billy, Fuzzy, and Jeff to the rescue, putting Kibbee and his fellow thugs, John Merton and Ted Adams, behind bars. "[T]his tale is as incredible as most," sighed *Motion Picture Herald*.[24]

Al St. John, Buster Crabbe, and Carleton Young mean business in **Billy the Kid's Round-Up** (PRC, 1941), Sig Neufeld producer, Sam Newfield (as Sherman Scott) director.

Lawman Ted Adams isn't quite sure he should believe Al St. John's explanation in **Billy the Kid's Smoking Guns** (PRC, 1942). Left-to-right: Adams, St. John, Curley Dresden, Dave O'Brien, Buster Crabbe, and Joel Newfield. Sig Neufeld producer, Sam Newfield (as Sherman Scott) director. *Courtesy of Joel Newfield.*

Sam put his son Joel in this one as well, which caused no end of jealousy on the part of Sig's ten-year-old son, Sig Jr. "I really got pissed off about it," recalled Sig Jr. "Why didn't they put me in anything, and my dad was the producer. Sam kept putting his kids in…I was really angry. 'When do I get a part?' 'We'll get you something someday,' but they never did."[25] Sam's nepotism extended to his daughter Jackie as well, who had a small role in 1944's *Nabonga* as well as that miniscule bit in *Hitler—Beast of Berlin*.

Dave O'Brien (1912-1969) was back as Jeff for this and the season's final two entries, sometimes billed as "Tex O'Brien." O'Brien ran away from home in his mid-teens, hired by the Harley Sadler Stock Company where he would sing, dance, tell jokes, and play the ukulele.[26] Stage work followed before he worked his way into the film industry back in 1929, with uncredited gigs as stunt man, extra, and bit player in numerous films into the mid-1930s. O'Brien found his happy place on Poverty Row, with starring and supporting roles in a seemingly endless string of low budget films, 1936's *Reefer Madness* likely the most well-known of these. O'Brien ended up in nine films directed by Sam before his first jobs for Sig, resulting in another nine films through 1942. O'Brien continued in Westerns until 1945, when he moved over to M-G-M to multi-task in Pete Smith Comedy novelty shorts. Starring in most of these, he would also alternate between any combination of writing, narrating, and directing for more than ten years. O'Brien ended up as a successful comedy writer for television (as David Barclay) with a fifteen-year stint at *The Red Skelton Hour* that lasted until his death from a heart attack.

Between the scenes shot taken during one of Buster Crabbe's early "Billy the Kid" shoots. Left-to-right: Crabbe, producer Sig Neufeld's son Sig Jr. and wife Ruth Neufeld, Al St, John, his daughter Mary Jane (unconfirmed), and Dave O'Brien. *Courtesy of Tim Neufeld.*

The bad guys don't get any more unscrupulous than they do in *Law and Order* (August 21, 1942). Charlie King attempts to orchestrate the marriage of one of his cohorts to a wealthy blind woman (Sarah Padden) to gain access to her fortune. Billy and his boys get wind of this so Billy poses as her nephew, whom he resembles, to get to the bottom of things. Wanda McKay plays a niece who arrives to attend the wedding, and once the crooks are dealt with, she remains behind to care for Padden. "Western fans should get a bang out of this exciting and actionful piece of entertainment," wrote *Film Daily*. "Sherman Scott's direction carries a wallop."[27] There's one unintentionally amusing shot where Crabbe is in a rush to mount his horse, but the horse moves at the last moment, resulting in a rather clumsy fumble as Crabbe misses the stirrup and is forced to regroup. There was, evidently, no retake.

Crabbe plays a dual role in *Sheriff of Sage Valley* (October 2, 1942), as Billy who takes the job of sheriff of Sage Valley, and as chief villain Kansas Ed. Kansas Ed takes Billy prisoner and poses as the sheriff, leading to no end of confusion and suspicion. It turns out that Kansas Ed and Billy are brothers, but during a climactic struggle between the two, Jeff intervenes and kills Kansas Ed as he's about to kill Billy. Crabbe looks like he relished having the opportunity to play a villain for a change, with Charlie King, Kermit Maynard, and John Merton along for the usual thuggery. Actress Maxine Leslie has a plum role as Kansas Ed's gambling hall entertainer girl, and St. John of course is back as Fuzzy. *Variety* called it "an indie-made western that ranks with the best in the field although palpably having cost less than most."[28] *Sheriff of Sage Valley* was filmed for a slightly higher $14,381.

PRC seemed to be off to a good start, reportedly showing a profit for its first year in business—although the actual amount of that "profit" was not disclosed.[29] By the end of August, eight production units were lined up to make product for PRC, and by November sales for the 1941-42 program were 100 % ahead of the previous season's 4,000 accounts served. Arthur Greenblatt, PRC's sales manager, attributed the increase in sales and new accounts to "the record established by the company last season of having delivered all the pictures promised on schedule, and that continuation of this schedule of delivery had brought about greater confidence on the part of exhibitors, both circuit and unaffiliated, as to the stability and reliability of the company."[30] Greenblatt was fairly new to PRC, a former executive with Monogram whose earliest employ had been as sales manager for the Gaumont British company, followed by a stint with the Alliance Film Corporation.[31]

The hiring of Buster Crabbe—a *big* name for tiny PRC—and the revitalized "Billy the Kid" series were in part responsible for that uptick in sales and accounts. The downside was that all those extra dollars allocated to the series had to come from somewhere, and the budgeting for the ongoing "Lone Rider" and the new iteration of McCoy's "Texas Marshall" series were likely impacted. The former McCoy films, which had come to be known as the "Texas Marshal" series, were replaced by a new group bearing the "Frontier Marshal" banner. The films were to feature a trio of leads in another of those musical Westerns: Art Davis, Bill Boyd, and Lee Powell. Sam would direct all six as "Peter Stewart."

Lee Powell (1908-1944) had a handful of earlier roles to his credit as well, most of them bit parts, and two of them for Sam, *Trigger Pals* and the more recent *The Lone Rider Rides On*. He also had worked as a trick rider for the Barnett Brothers Circus, those proven abilities a decided asset for the roles ahead of him. His career was cut short went he went into the Marines, his life cut short as well in 1944 when he was reported killed in combat;[32] the reality was that his death resulted from a lethal batch of home brew tossed together by one of his fellow Marines—or at least according to author James Wise.

Art Davis (1913-1987) had a number of films under his belt by this time, most of them in uncredited bits and several where he was credited as Audry Davis. He (or someone else) wisely changed his rather unmasculine first name to "Art," and he appeared as such in a bit part for Sam back in that Tex Fletcher film *Six-Gun Rhythm*. With the "Frontier Marshal" series, he was finally promoted to semi-lead, a move that must have seemed like the big time to him. Davis was starring on a western radio show out of Tulsa, Oklahoma when signed by PRC.[33]

Bill Boyd (1910-1977) was not *that* "Hopalong Cassidy" Bill Boyd, although I'm sure that Sig and Sam had no qualms over potential filmgoers mistaking him for his more famous namesake. This fellow was known as Bill "Cowboy Rambler" Boyd[34] after his popular Cowboy Rambler Band, a regional favorite that had played over the airwaves for several years on radio station WRR, emanating out of Dallas, Texas.[35] Sig no doubt hoped that his popularity would be a draw in the Southwest among his base of fans. Boyd had by this time more than fifty published songs and 200 recordings to show for his twelve years in the business.[36] If he couldn't act, at least he could sing. Sig's contract with Boyd stipulated "not less than six (6) nor more than eight (8)" films during a one-

Cast and crew pose on location during the production of **Texas Manhunt** (PRC, 1942), Sig Neufeld producer, Sam Newfield (as Peter Stewart) director. Stars Lee Powell, Art Davis (left and second from left), and Bill Boyd (right) in rear on horseback. Sig Neufeld sitting front row, legs crossed, Bert Sternbach standing to the left of Sig, Sam Newfield sitting far right, looking at cameraman Jack Greenhalgh in all white, leaning. *Courtesy of Tim Neufeld.*

year period, beginning on or about September 15, 1941. Boyd would be given at least one week's notice before production of each film was to commence, and would receive $500 for each film in which he appeared. Options were included for a similar number of films in each subsequent year, with Boyd to receive $1,000 per film the second year, $1,750 the third year, $2,500 the fourth year, and $3,500 the fifth year. The contract added the proviso that "the PRODUCER [has] the right to use a double in place of the ARTIST to simulate his voice or personage if the PRODUCER so desires."[37] Perhaps Sig was hedging his bets on Boyd's untested acting abilities.

Powell, Davis, and Boyd would all play marshals, their characters bearing their real names with the sole exception of the series opener where Powell plays "Lee Clark." If Sig thought that one singing cowboy was a draw, then *two* singing cowboys would really reel them in, he was sadly mistaken. Ultimately, the series proved to be a dud. The opener, *Texas Manhunt* (January 2, 1942), which came in with a negative cost of $13,562—more than half of which went towards Sam's and the cast's salaries—involved a Nazi spy (Arno Frey) recruiting some "upstanding" Americans—Karl Hackett and Frank Hagney among them—to assist in his plans to disrupt the Allied food supply. The results garnered a withering review from *The Exhibitor*. "Unimpressive opener for a new western series," was the lead, going on to say that star "Boyd may be able to sing in western fashion, but he shows nothing else."[38] Lee Powell stars in this one as the Federal Marshal, while Boyd and Davis play a pair of radio personalities who like to interrupt a film's flow with their warbling.

Art Davis, Bill "Cowboy Rambler" Boyd, and Lee Powell (all kneeling) attend to Karl Hackett in **Texas Manhunt** (PRC, 1942), Sig Neufeld producer, Sam Newfield (as Peter Stewart) director.

Raiders of the West (February 13, 1942) has Boyd and Davis taking a break from their singing to pose as horse traders to infiltrate a counterfeiting ring, headed by Charlie King. Powell's marshal poses as a counterfeiter in order to worm his way into the gang as well. Powell and King duke it out in what turned out to be an unintentionally realistic fashion. "Charlie was having one of those fights with Lee Powell down in a basement," reminisced Bill Boyd regarding Powell's apparent lack of screen fighting ability. "Lee accidentally hit Charlie so hard that it sprained Lee's wrist. Charlie was knocked back, and hit his head on the edge of a chair. It took twelve stitches to close up the wound on Charlie's head. The scene was left in, and if you look closely you can see it."[39] Cowboy star Eddie Dean elaborated, based on his experiences filming fight scenes with Powell: "He was awfully rough to fight with because he didn't know how to pull a punch. He'd hit you! The other actors tipped me off. They said, 'Don't let him hit you; he's big! Don't let him hit you because he doesn't know how to fight without hitting somebody. He doesn't know how to angle it.'"[40]

Rolling Down the Great Divide (April 24, 1942), presumably representative of the series, involves another war-related story. Powell's marshal investigates the rustling of cattle intended for use by the U.S. Army by a bunch of horse thieves, the gimmick here the use of short-wave radio to keep on top of the horses' whereabouts. Marshals Boyd and Davis assist by going undercover and posing as singers in need of a job—talk about typecasting. Glenn Strange makes yet another appearance as the brains behind the rustlers, with Ted Adams one of his lackies. Wanda McKay appears as a waitress who works in Strange's saloon, and while she doesn't have a lot to do, she's a lot easier on the eyes than Boyd and Davis. Loads of stock footage grace this one whenever scenes of those rustled horses are needed.

Lee Powell, Bill Boyd, and Art Davis "cleverly" alert their hoped-for rescuers to their whereabouts via some broadcast warbling in **Rolling Down the Great Divide** (PRC, 1942), Sig Neufeld producer, Sam Newfield (as Peter Stewart) director.

222 Poverty Row Royalty

This one's pretty bad, and the primary reason that the series failed to click with audiences is rather apparent: Boyd and Davis can't act. Sure, their duets are pleasant enough, but when they are actually required to emote, they are both stiff and awkward and lacking any sort of charisma. Even their fight scenes are painful to watch, thrown punches obvious in their lack of connection, although one would assume that their fellow actors preferred these less-accident prone staged fisticuffs to those with Powell. Powell, on the other hand, could act, at least by comparison.

Prairie Pals (September 4, 1942), has a credulity-stretching plot revolving around a kidnapped scientist's discovery that converts Vanadium ore into synthetic gold. A huge vein runs under the local ranchers' land, and once again Stanford Jolley—aided by incompetent henchmen Charlie King, John Merton, and Kermit Maynard—schemes to drive those ranchers off their land. Pudgy warblers Boyd and Davis infiltrate the gang and feed raid-thwarting info back to Powell. Routine stuff, but this one is notable primarily for having Al St. John in an atypical straight role as the owner of the land atop the area's largest vein. "Just another oatie opera," dismissed *The Exhibitor*'s critic.[41] This one came in with a negative cost of $14,575.

Lee Powell strongarms Stanford Jolley in **Prairie Pals** (PRC, 1942), Sig Neufeld producer, Sam Newfield (as Peter Stewart) director.

The remaining series entries were *Tumbleweed Trail* (July 10, 1942) and *Along the Sundown Trail* (October 19, 1942) before Sig and PRC pulled the plug and sent Boyd, Davis, and Powell packing. *Along the Sundown Trail* would prove to be Powell's last film before joining the Marines, a sergeant at the time of his death in 1944. For that matter, it was the last feature film for all three of its stars—which tells you something.

Despite the series middling popularity, Sam continued to direct the "Lone Rider" series using his own name in the credits. George Houston was back in the lead for the second go-round, although by all reports he wasn't overly thrilled about it—so much so that he bolted from the series after the fifth entry and quit the business altogether. Fortunately for the followers of this particular set of films, Al St. John—one of the hardest working actors in the business, bouncing back and forth between this and the Crabbe series—was back once again as—who else?—Fuzzy. Sig, or perhaps the powers at PRC, seemed to think that their three Western series all needed a trio of leads this season, so Houston and St. John were joined by Dennis Moore, his character in these films known as "Smoky Moore." Moore (1908-1964) had been a regular presence in low budget Westerns and serials since 1932, under his birth name of Denny Meadows for the initial four years before reinventing himself with his new moniker. Hundreds of films followed after his stint in this series, ending up like so many of his fellow B-movie brethren in television. Moore retired from the industry in 1961, reportedly moving to Big Bear, California where he operated a gift shop up until his death in 1964.

George Houston "entertains" the barroom regulars with yet another unrequested song while Al St. John listens with stunned amazement, in **The Lone Rider in Cheyenne** (PRC, 1942), Sig Neufeld producer, Sam Newfield director.

Reviewers tended to ignore the series during its second season run, but those who took the time generally labelled the films as routine while tossing a bone to Houston's singing and St. John's comic relief. In most instances, only a brief synopsis of each film was published, a stunning example of editorial laziness. The season's entries were *The Lone Rider and the Bandit* (January 16, 1942),[42] *The Lone Rider in Cheyenne* (March 20, 1942), *Texas Justice* (June 12, 1942), *Border Roundup* (September 18, 1942), and *Outlaws of Boulder Pass* (October 28, 1942)[43] before Houston turned his back on the industry and was replaced by Bob Livingston. *Overland Stagecoach* (December 11, 1942) was intended as the following 1942-43 season's initial entry, but moved up when Houston called it quits. PRC, aware of Houston's unhappiness with the role (or, perhaps, fed up with his moaning about it) had hired Livingston as Houston's intended next-season replacement, Livingston late of Republic's "Three Mesquiteers" series. What differentiates this entry from its predecessors (aside from its new lead) is St. John's narration for a portion of the film. *Overland Stagecoach* came in with a negative cost of $15,790.

Sig took pride in the treatment of animals for his Western productions. "It is Neufeld's contention that devotees of western films are natural lovers of the wide-open spaces, and of the fine horsemanship and horseflesh that are featured in this type of production," wrote one reporter. "Accordingly, while others were experimenting with the Running W and other devices which caused the unsuspecting animals to crash to the ground before the cameras, often sacrificing their lives for the sake of a few cheap thrills, Neufeld has steadfastly maintained that no movie goer wants to see a horse hurt or even feel that one could have been hurt while making the film."[44] Of course if Sig excluded scenes of this sort from his films for budgetary reasons, it became a non-issue: there was always footage available from earlier films by others that could be reused, and the opening, stock-heavy montage in *The Lone Rider and the Bandit* bears mute witness to this "benign" approach. Sam was in synch with Sig on the humane treatment of the horses in his films, or at least tried to be. "With several hundred western pictures to his credit," wrote one reporter from studio-supplied info, "Director Sam Newfield holds a perfect record with no cowboy mount ever having been seriously injured although the riders have suffered plenty of bruising falls and cracked ribs."[45]

Cast and crew pose for this group photo, taken on location during the production of **Texas Justice** (PRC, 1942), Sig Neufeld producer, Sam Newfield director. Mannie Teitelbaum, Bert Sternbach, and Jack Greenhalgh to the immediate right of the camera; Sam's wife Violet center holding another's hand; sound engineer Hans Weeren fourth from right leaning against wagon; Stanley Neufeld holding clapperboard to right of Al St. John.
Courtesy of Tim Neufeld.

Aside from this mind-numbing, seemingly endless stream of quickie Westerns, Sig and Sam were able to undertake two of PRC's specials as well, the first the horror film *The Mad Monster*, followed by the jungle-based *Jungle Siren*. PRC had existed almost solely on a steady diet up to this time of Westerns, comedies, mysteries, and dramas, and had only once dipped its toes in the horror film genre with 1940s *The Devil Bat*. A revitalized horror film craze was in full swing now, the spark that lit it Universal's successful reissue of its classics *Dracula* and *Frankenstein* back in August 1938. This had led to the big-budget, A-status *Son of Frankenstein* with its $500,000 budget[46] in 1939, which in turn revitalized the genre and led to Universal's revisiting some of the studio's popular hits of the past, *The Invisible Man Returns* and *The Invisible Woman* in 1940, along with *The Mummy's Hand* that same year. 1941 saw Universal's introduction of a brand-new creature in the form of *The Wolf Man*, the success of which may have prompted Sig to come up with a similarly hairy PRC-bred creature. The result was *The Mad Monster*, released five months after its supposed inspiration on May 15, 1942.

Cast and crew pose on the indoor set for **The Mad Monster** (PRC, 1942), Sig Neufeld producer, Sam Newfield director. First row sitting center with legs crossed, Sig Neufeld (left) and Sam Newfield; second row Bert Sternbach far left; Hans Weeren, Johnny Downs, Jack Greenhalgh, and Glenn Strange third through sixth from left; Mannie Teitelbaum behind tree; Stanley Neufeld holding clapperboard. *Courtesy of Tim Neufeld.*

Sig turned once again to Fred Myton to churn out an acceptable screenplay—acceptable to PRC's needs, at least—which went before Jack Greenhalgh's cameras in March 1942. British actor George Zucco starred, with Anne Nagel as his daughter and Glenn Strange in the role of the unfortunate subject of Zucco's crazed experiments. Johnny Downs, inexplicably top-billed, appeared as the film's typically annoying reporter. As far as horror films go, this one is merely passable, but you have to give Sig and Sam credit for trying. The basic premise is a woefully familiar one, that of the "misunderstood" (read *crazy*) scientist out to prove the naysayers wrong. Here it's

Zucco's Dr. Lorenzo Cameron, discredited by his fellow faculty members for his theories about mixing the blood of animals with that of humans or some such nonsense—actually *not* nonsense since he gets the near-last laugh. Experimenting on his dim-witted handyman Petro (an overly padded Glenn Strange), Zucco uses a "catalytic agent" along with a wolf's blood to temporarily turn Strange into a wolf man. His stated goal: to create an army of wolf men to face off against the Axis powers! An admirable goal, it would seem, but first he'll use his current army of one to dispatch the four former faculty members who each had the temerity to question his genius. His daughter, played by Anne Nagel, hangs around to alternately defend him and his genius to nagging at him to be nicer to her reporter boyfriend Johnny Downs, who has inserted himself in Zucco's remote swamp-based mansion uninvited, and seems to think he has the right to play detective. Zucco's plans regarding the elimination of those faculty members only extends to two of them before Strange, no doubt annoyed with Zucco for those constant whippings he endures, turns on him. In a climactic Act of God, lightning strikes a table of chemicals during this confrontation, burning the mansion down around them.

Mad scientist George Zucco and one of his canine blood contributors in **The Mad Monster** (PRC, 1942). *Courtesy of Tim Neufeld.*

It is apparent that a few extra dollars were spent on this one—$21,211, to be exact—although those spent for David Chudnow's score should have been used elsewhere: it's just plain weird, out of place, and not at all atmospheric. The sets range from impressive—the soundstage-based "swamps" are dead-on for this type of film—to cheesy—Cameron's lab's amateurishly painted stone block walls. Strange's makeup as the wolf man isn't half bad aside from the prominent dime store teeth and Marty Stuart-like hairpiece, and the on-screen transformations from man-to-wolf visually comparable to those over at Universal. The film doesn't beat around the bush, however, and starts off with a bang, Zucco overseeing Strange's first transformation within a minute or two of the opening. We get a full dose of Zucco's madness shortly after, as he lectures and harangues his former detractors—or at least his ghostly visions of them—regarding his genius and their collective small-mindedness. His ambitions, or at least as presented in this film, are small (befitting a small film), the hinted-at army of wolf men sidetracked for the planned one-on-one killing of those faculty members. But before we even get to that, and perhaps the film's one comparative stunner, is Strange's killing of a child, which is handled off-screen and suggested solely by the child's ball slowly rolling from her doorway. If this was Sam's nod to Fritz Lang's far more stylish murder of Elsie in his classic *M*, it was only a nod, and not a deftly handled nod at that.

Glenn Strange's hapless Petro is about to taunt the censors by dispatching with a young girl—off-screen, of course—in **The Mad Monster** (PRC, 1942). *Courtesy of Laura Berk.*

Second-billed George Zucco (1886-1960) gives an over-the-top performance, but that's likely what viewers expected from this type of film: emphatic madness. Now looked upon as the film's "star," Zucco was a native of Manchester, England, with a considerable career in vaudeville and the British stage before entering the film industry. Zucco relocated to the United States in the mid-1930s, hired for character roles in numerous high-profile films that included *After the Thin Man* (1936), *Marie Antoinette* (1938), and *The Adventures of Sherlock Holmes* (1939). Universal's sequel *The Mummy's Hand* (1940) was a turning point of sorts in Zucco's career (although perhaps in a direction he may have preferred not turning), where he became increasingly associated with this type of film into the 1940s. With Sig's *The Mad Monster* under his belt, Universal's *The Mummy's Tomb* (1942), *The Mummy's Ghost* (1944), and *The Mad Ghoul* (1943), would follow, along with PRC's *Dead Men Walk*, *The Black Raven* (both 1943), and *Fog Island* (1945). Many others followed for these and other studios, and while he may be best remembered today for parts in these low budget quickies, Zucco continued to take small roles in a wide variety of films and genres as well up until his retirement in the early 1950s.

Ann Nagel gives a decent performance, but despite her character's prominence it's a throw-away role, alternating between concern and slack-jawed wonderment. After a long string of uncredited bit parts from the early 1930s at Fox and Paramount, a mid-1930s contract with Warners brought her some recognition in competently executed B's and the occasional A, such as Ray Enright's more prestigious *China Clipper* (1936). After Warners and, for that matter, the suicide of her husband, Nagel was all over the place in an endless succession of low budget films at Monogram, Republic, Universal, and now, at PRC.

Johnny Downs plays the typical scoop-hunting snoop, his entitled pushiness actually leading one to side with Zucco in his dislike for the fellow. Then there's Glenn Strange as Petro, tapping into his inner "Lennie" in an embarrassingly silly performance as the dim-witted victim of Zucco's experiments. As the wolf man, however, he's far better, his imposing bulk giving Lon Chaney Jr. a run for his money. That said, he was better off sticking to the old west. Unfortunately for PRC, they lost their British market for this one, since all "horror" films were banned from exhibition over there for the duration of the war.[47] "England clamped down," wrote *Variety*, "because of effects, actual or expected, on bomb-tinged nerves of wartorn populace required to walk home from their nightly cinema along blacked-out roads." Oddly enough, this ban was a one-eighty on the earlier British vs. American tolerance level for films of a horrific nature. As *Variety* went on to explain, "England's pre-war stuff in many instances was even too tough for U.S. theatregoers and on many occasion distribs here found it necessary to trim."[48] All in all, *The Mad Monster* gets a B for effort and a C for execution. It's kind of fun, though.

By the early 1940s, burlesque shows were at the peak of their popularity, with the exception of New York City, where Mayor La Guardia had banned them several years earlier.[49] One such performer of note was Ann Corio (1909-1999), who had left home at age fifteen and eventually became a striptease artist on the Mutual burlesque circuit in 1925. Later work for Minsky's Burlesque in New York was cut short by La Guardia's edict, prompting Corio to head west to California. Someone at PRC had the bright idea of capitalizing on her popularity and fame by putting her in a film, and one which could show off her impressively robust figure to best advantage. The result was 1941's *Swamp Woman*, one of PRC's "specials" directed by Elmer Clifton and produced by Merrick-Alexander Productions, a co-teaming of the aforementioned Max Alexander and fellow producer George Merrick. Corio was reportedly paid $1,000 for her six-day shoot plus a per centage of the profits. The film proved to be wildly successful, no doubt luring a healthy number of the male populace hoping for a peak at a little more flesh than usual, and on an exceedingly attractive woman. Corio's eventual take? According to *Variety*, "Stripeuse [Corio], from salary and per centage on 'Swamp Woman,' will net better than $25,000, according to present indications." If accurate, which is somewhat difficult to fathom: that's more than a half-million in 2023 dollars![50]

Despite the crummy reviews doled out for *Swamp Woman*, the box office take spoke volumes to PRC, so they quickly planned a follow-up picture, going all-out—for PRC, at least—with an increased budget, and a whopping seven-day shooting schedule as opposed to the previous film's six. The production was turned over to Sig to produce, teaming Corio with the studio's most bankable male star, Buster Crabbe.[51] The other "ambitious" film on Sig and Sam's roster for the 1941-42 season, the marginally exploitative *Jungle Siren* began its seven-day shoot on June 17, 1942. At a regional meeting held in Chicago in July 1942, it was decided that two films each season would receive extra exploitation and increased advertising. The current year's product to receive that extra attention was *Jungle Siren* and *The Yanks Are Coming*.[52]

Released on August 14, PRC's promotional materials hinted at what filmgoers might expect—or *hope*—to see, or at least as far as Ms. Corio was concerned:

> To say that Miss Corio is alluring in her new-style sarong is to put it mildly. She calls it a "nurong," and claims that it is half the weight of the usual sarong worn by other under-dressed screen stars in these outdoor romances.... You will enjoy the antics of a trained chimpanzee, which is the constant companion of the jungle girl, Kuhlaya, as Ann is called. In one scene as she swims in a pool, the mischievous simian steals her scanty sarong, and she is forced to chase it through the jungle.[53]

As Corio once put it, "A woman's greatest asset is a man's imagination."

Bert Sternbach (standing) and star Ann Corio are riveted by the antics of Greco the chimp, while Sam seems more riveted by Corio, during the production of **Jungle Siren** (PRC, 1942), Sig Neufeld producer, Sam Newfield director. *Courtesy of Tim Neufeld.*

The result, brought in with a negative cost of $25,762, is a rather silly jungle-based yarn by screenwriters George W. Sayre and Milton Raison which involves Nazis as well as rival groups of natives. Engineers Capt. Gary Hart (Buster Crabbe) and his wise-cracking assistant (Paul Bryar) are hired by the Free French to plot out an airfield for the Allies in deepest Africa. They trek to the village of Carraby where they encounter sexy Corio as Kuhlaya, the daughter of murdered missionaries who was brought up by Milton Kibbee's protective—but heavy-drinking—doctor. Nazis Arno Frey and his wisp of a wife Anna (Evelyn Wahl) are there as well, feigning friendship while scheming to incite a native uprising against the French to pave the way for the Germans to arrive. Jess Lee Brooks plays the native chief who is in cahoots with the Nazis, but is hated by Corio. Both Corio and Wahl fall for Crabbe, and hard, jealousy soon running rampant. A number of natives are dispatched during the proceedings before Brooks sets up Crabbe, Bryar, and Kibbee for torture and death. Lukas shoots his wife while she attempts to set Crabbe free; Corio skewers Frey with her trusty bow; and Crabbe shoots Brooks. The airfield somehow ends up ready for the arrival of Allied planes, and Crabbe tells them to bring a chaplain along so that he and Corio can tie the knot.

Buster Crabbe and Ann Corio goof around for the cameraman during the production of **Jungle Siren** (PRC, 1942). Crabbe seems to have everything in hand. *Courtesy of Tim Neufeld.*

Corio isn't much of an actress, but she's just so damn likeable in the role that she makes the film trashily enjoyable. The film's other saving grace is the endless string of wise cracks delivered by Bryar, some of them groaners ("Well, if it isn't William Tell in a sarong") while others are embarrassingly funny. Initially encountering Corio, Crabbe says "Wait, it might be a trick" to which Bryar responds "Yeah, a cute trick." Later, while admiring his unimpressive biceps, Bryar mutters "Another ten days of this and I'll have a physique like Buster Crabbe." Admittedly not the funniest of lines, but you take your little pleasures where you can find them. While Corio is obviously placed in this film as considerable eye candy for the male moviegoers, a bone is thrown to the females in the audience as well by having Crabbe go shirtless for several scenes. As the film's requisite wartime cinematic Nazi, Arno Frey is your standard two-dimensional duplicitous Hun. As his wife, Evelyn Wahl is an attractive presence who can act, but looks in desperate need of a good meal. Surprisingly, her career in film only placed her in two other films. As the scheming and ruthless native chief, Jess Lee Brooks is far too good and distinguished an actor for this sort of nonsense.

Quality aside, the film exceeded PRC's expectations. Within two months the film had been booked by more than 600 "major circuit theaters" and had established a new record for PRC bookings in "Class 'A'" theaters. *Jungle Siren*'s success prompted the immediate production of yet another film with a come-on title, this one titled *Secrets of a Co-Ed*, released a mere two months later. "[I]ndications are that the contracts may surpass in number those of 'Jungle Siren'" wrote *Film Daily*.[54] Monogram lured Corio away from PRC, however, and starred her in a trio of films over the next two years, *Sarong Girl*, *The Sultan's Daughter* (both 1943), and *Call of the Jungle* (1944), after which Corio called it quits—from films, that is.

Given its comparatively longer shooting schedule and higher budget, Sig had made several concessions to get *Jungle Siren*'s production underway. The most significant of these was agreeing to reduce his usual 35 % share of profits to 30 % for this one film. "I don't have to go into detail about how fair Sig has been on this matter, and he realizes that the additional monies that he has put in will enhance the value of his profit sharing participation," wrote Fromkess to O. Henry Briggs at the time.[55] Sig's contract reflected this lower amount, but an internal mixup reduced it by another 5 %, as reflected in the first profit check he received eight months later in March 1943. Sig sent off several letters in an attempt to receive the additional 5 % due him, but ultimately had to turn to Fromkess for help. "Evidently when the contract was prepared I failed to correct the copy that was sent to New York," wrote Fromkess, "and let it stand as printed, namely 25%, though my office copy and Sig's copy both show 30%."[56] The issue was ultimately resolved.

PRC's Los Angeles exchange, hoping to introduce its films to new accounts, came up with a seven-picture deal that included seven of the year's biggest "hits." *Jungle Siren* was one of the seven, accompanied by *Prisoner of Japan*, *They Raid By Night*, *A Yank in Libya*, *Bombs Over Burma*, *Inside the Law*, and *Prison Girl*.[57] Another deal PRC tried out was its "Package Plan" which called for the selling of two similarly themed films under a single "catchy" title. *Jungle Siren* was paired with *Swamp Woman* under the package title "Sarong Review," while *Bombs Over Burma* and *Prisoner of Japan* were packaged as "Slap the Jap"![58]

Film Bulletin's pocket assessment of the film was in line with those of most of the other reviewers: "To say that this jungle melodrama is an improvement over the former burlesque star's first film, 'Swamp Woman,' is faint praise. In this case, Sam Newfield has directed the wildly-improbable story with a faintly tongue-in-cheek style which takes away some of its curse."[59] Well said.

PRC needed to keep its franchise holders happy and meet its commitment to them, which required the output of a number of different producers to supplement Sig's Westerns and occasional "special." In a few instances these were producers who directed their own films as well, such as Bernard B. Ray and Arthur Dreifuss, who between them served double duty on four films for the 1941-42 season. Other producers generating one or two films each for the current season included the previously mentioned Ted Richmond and John T. Coyle, Martin Mooney, the team of Lou Brock and Jack Schwarz, Leo McCarthy, Walter Mycroft, Dixon R. Harwin, Lester Cutler, and Seymour Nebenzal. The directors employed by these producers included the season's workhorse William Beaudine with seven films,[60] along with names both familiar and obscure, both seasoned and green, such as Harry Fraser, Elmer Clifton, the tag team of

George M. Merrick—a rookie at direction—and writer-director Oliver Drake, Victor Halperin, Fred Newmeyer, Albert Herman, Harold Huth, Hamilton MacFadden, Joseph H. Lewis, Spencer Gordon Bennett, and Arthur Ripley. Unquestionably the most prolific producers contributing films for PRC release—and second only to Sig—were the Alexander brothers, Max and Arthur, who together or independently were responsible for thirty-six films released during the period 1941-46.

Max Alexander teamed with George Merrick under the aegis of M & A Productions—the "M & A" being Max and Arthur Alexander's first initials—to produce four films for the current 1941-42 season. These included the Elmer Clifton-directed, Corio-curve displaying *Swamp Woman*, along with director Al Herman's *A Yank in Libya* (1942). Max would also team with Alfred Stern, Julius and Abe Stern's nephew and son of their oldest sibling Joseph. Together they would produce thirteen films for the 1941-42 through 1945-46 seasons, initially as M & A Productions for the first season, and as Alexander-Stern Productions for subsequent seasons. These included *Secrets of a Co-Ed* (1942; Joseph H. Lewis director), a bunch of Westerns starring Dave "Tex" O'Brien, the Erich von Stroheim starrer *The Mask of Dijon* (1946; Lew Landers director), and *Secrets of a Sorority Girl* (1946; Frank Wisbar).

Max's brother Arthur Alexander produced another nineteen films for PRC on his own, released from 1943-46; all were Alexander-Stern Productions as well. Almost all of these were Westerns starring either Dave "Tex" O'Brien or, later on, O'Brien co-starring with Tex Ritter. The sole exceptions were a trio of Westerns co-starring Bob Steele and Syd Saylor, and the mysteries *Waterfront* (1944; Steve Sekely) and *Arson Squad* (1944; Lew Landers). Alfred Stern oversaw another four Alexander-Stern productions for PRC as well during the 1943-44 season.

Jungle Siren's extras pose for the camera. Ray Loggins, the fellow with the white apron (center), was the caterer that Sig would hire to feed cast and crew for most of his productions for PRC. *Courtesy Tim Neufeld.*

Chapter 13:
The War Takes a Bite (Sig, Sam, and PRC, Part 3, 1942-1943)

America's entrance into the war at the end of 1941 had an immediate impact on the film studios and their operations. Multiple restrictions were placed on all current and future productions, coupled with numerous eyes reviewing and—ideally—approving every planned step along the way. "Studio lawyers are working harder than they ever had to work before to earn their retainers keeping the bosses in the clear on matters of protocol, diplomatic regulations, obtaining censorship clearances, etc." wrote *Variety*. Those "numerous eyes" included not only the Army, the Navy, the Marines, and the Air Corps, but diplomatic and other representatives of the United Nations as well. Toss in the inconvenient censorship overseen by Byron Price in Washington, Colonel Watterson Rothacker in Hollywood, as well as Nelson Poynter and Warren H. Pierce of Elmer Davis's Office of War Information, and the studios had a whole lot of people and entities with their own personal agendas to placate and please.

One major imposition was a $5,000 limit on set-building, which led to the construction of multi-purpose sets that could be reused from film-to-film with only minor redressing. Location shooting was impacted as well due to regional restrictions and the availability of fuel. The Salton Sea and surrounding Imperial Valley desert became make-do locations for films that otherwise would have been filmed at now-restricted Catalina Island and the sands of Yuma, Arizona, respectively. "In one way it's costing them," continued *Variety*, "but in another way the exigencies of war will prove a godsend in the long run, for the studios for the first time in their profligate, spendthrift career are learning the meaning of frugality. In years to come many a common dividend will be paid to stockholders eked out of the habit of saving enforced by wartime necessity."[1]

Sig Neufeld poses with visitors to the outdoor location of one of his Westerns, circa 1942. Kneeling center: Bert Sternbach and Jack Greenhalgh. Directly behind them: Sig Neufeld and Leon Fromkess (ugly sweater), with O. Henry Briggs centered behind them. A dapper looking Al St. John far right. *Courtesy of Tim Neufeld.*

Raw footage restrictions were impacting the studios as well. By late summer producers had committed to a voluntary plan to reduce raw film stock usage by amounts ranging from 10 % to 24 % of 1941's usage. The majors' pledges ranged from 24 % for M-G-M, 22.5 % for Paramount and 20th Century-Fox, 20 % for Warners, 17.5 % for Columbia, Universal and RKO, and 12.5 % for Republic. PRC, United Artists, and Monogram, already stingy with the footage used on a regular basis, would only commit to a 10 % reduction.[2]

Not that all of the frugality-induced restrictions impacted Sig. Working as he had throughout his career on paper-thin budgets, any steps he could take to save an otherwise wasted dollar was common operating procedure for his productions. What impacted Sig's productions for years to come was the slow upward creep of the cost of things. Money was always tight with the independents, and cash-flow was an overriding concern in the plans and decisions made by PRC and Sigmund Neufeld Productions. Agreements reached over the past two years had a major impact on Sig's little company and the budgets allotted to its various films. Sig had already agreed in early 1940 to a 10 % wage boost for members of the Society of Motion Picture Film Editors, in his particular case impacting the pay of his go-to editor, Holbrook Todd. Sound Technicians Local 695 had also reached an agreement with Sig, impacting Hans Weeren's salary.[3] While the moneys allotted to any given production may not have changed, what that money could buy certainly had. With each passing year, Sig was forced to cut more and more corners, in terms of length of shooting schedules, the bodies needed for any given film, the sets and locations used, and the amount of footage shot. More stock footage would find its way into his films as the years went by, both from outside sources and from reuse of footage and scenes lifted from his earlier productions. Sig's son commented on the fluid nature of making some of these films, the seat-of-the-pants decisions made to streamline production and save a few dollars:

> They would go over the script and talk story a little bit, talk about how certain scenes should be handled and done. Whether they could afford to have 20 extras or 40 extras in a scene, things like that.... If things were too complicated and the director felt it was going to take a long time to shoot something, they'd rewrite it to simplify it. If they had a scene where they should have eighty or a hundred extras, they'd have a big meeting and end up with thirty-five or forty, to save money. If they couldn't do it themselves [simplify a scene], they'd get the writers on the phone and try to do it on the lunch break or something like that.[4]

Another potential cost savings was implemented by a trio of the independents. The cost of renting items needed for any given production had risen nearly 300 %, so members of the IMPPA named a committee in October to plan a joint property stockpile for use by the various association members. Sig was made chairman along with Arthur Alexander—both of PRC—as well as Martin Mooney and Sidney Williams of Monogram. Materials would be collected for use in dressing sets, all of which would be added to Sam Katzman's collection.[5]

The industry went all out in its support of the war, creating a "Victory Caravan" of Hollywood stars and personnel to blanket the nation's cities in a campaign for the sale of War Savings Bonds. More than 300 studio and allied industry employees took part as bond salesmen, with Sam and Bert Sternbach joining in to help out. The immediate goal of the campaign was to secure the pledge of as many industry employees as possible to commit 10 % or more of their salaries to the War Savings program. According to one report, "the response has been enthusiastic."[6]

At the beginning of 1942, Pathé gained near-complete control of PRC, acquiring 68 % of PRC's stock for $750,000. "Part of that will be used to pay current indebtedness and part for new working capital," wrote *Variety* in January 1941. "Deal by PRC with Pathé supersedes the optional three-year arrangement with Consolidated Film Laboratories (headed by Herbert J. Yates, prez of Republic), by which latter was to finance PRC with $675.000." Pathé's acquisition did not affect PRC's current leadership, Briggs retaining his position as president and Fromkess as vice president in charge of production. George Batcheller remained in charge of PRC's feature production, as did Sig with his Western productions.[7] A new building was being constructed for Sig's exclusive use, but in the meantime, he operated out of leased space at the Chadwick studios. By the end of February, Pathé had acquired the remaining 32 % of PRC's stock and was now in complete control of the studio.[8] There was talk of replacing the Producers Releasing Corporation name with that of Pathé, or at least according to George Bonwick, Pathé's vice-president and treasurer, and PRC's treasurer. "Just when this will happen I can not say at this time but we have been thinking about it," he said.[9] Needless to say, the change never took place.

Cast, crew, and attendees of the May 1942 PRC convention pose during a break in the filming of **Tumbleweed Trail** (PRC, 1942), Sig Neufeld producer, Sam Newfield (as Peter Stewart) director. Sig is in the center of the trio sitting in the foreground.
Courtesy of Tim Neufeld.

A national convention of PRC franchise holders took place at the Hollywood Roosevelt Hotel over May 4-7th, 1942, where Fromkess, Batcheller, and Sig had been scheduled to coordinate and outline production activities for the upcoming 1942-43 season.[10] It didn't turn out that way when Batcheller, formerly in charge of feature production for less than a year, announced his resignation in April. Fromkess became Batcheller's replacement and put in charge of all PRC production, permanently relocating to the West Coast in shared office space with Sig at his temporary setup at the Chadwick Studio at 1440 N. Gower.[11] The convention convened with Briggs opening and Greenblatt presiding. Fromkess outlined general production plans, and Sig discussed his program, one of his planned non-Western films tentatively titled *Berlin Revolts*;[12] it doesn't appear to have been made. New films were shown to the attendees, followed by a "ranch party" at the Iverson Ranch in Chatsworth (where Sam was currently filming *Tumbleweed Trail*), followed by an evening banquet back at PRC's studios. Fromkess announced that "We are going to get dollar-for-dollar in production values, and we are going to pass that value on to the exhibitor," adding that every feature would have an outstanding "name" player.[13] His definition of "name" likely differed from others, but that was of little concern. As for those shared quarters at 1440 N. Gower, they proved to be a little too tight, so PRC's Hollywood headquarters were moved over to the Talisman Studios on Sunset Boulevard on September 15. Expansion plans dictated the need for more space, so use of the Gower St. studio continued.[14] The Talisman space would be vacated within a year after a long-term lease was signed with the Fine Arts Studio at 7324 Santa Monica Boulevard, possession taking place in May 1943; PRC would share space in the new digs with Pine-Thomas Productions, whose output was released by Paramount.[15] Bob Baker, a puppeteer who worked on several of Edgar Ulmer's films at PRC, described the studio—and the vibe there—to interviewer Peter Bogdanovich:

> It was a nice studio. It was clean and it was well kept. Yet, you felt—you felt a kind of [strangeness] there because as you looked around, most of the people in the way of actors and actresses were on the rebound…or just beginning. It wasn't like going into Paramount, MGM, or Fox, or even Universal.[16]

Lunch time at the Iverson Ranch for attendees of the May 1942 PRC Convention. Sig Neufeld sitting third from right on foreground bench. Leon Fromkess, Jack Greenhalgh, and O. Henry Briggs standing center far back. *Courtesy of Tim Neufeld.*

Leon Fromkess (1901-1977) hadn't intended to become a film company executive, it just turned out that way. Born in New York City, the five-foot-six Fromkess attended De Witt Clinton High School and Columbia University. Upon graduating, Fromkess became a member in the New York Curb Exchange, which was renamed the American Stock Exchange in 1953. It was through financing that he became interested in the motion picture business, beginning in 1929 when he handled Wall Street financing for Columbia Pictures. In 1937 he handled Wall Street financing for Monogram, and in 1938 became treasurer of Monogram; he resigned a year later. In 1940 Fromkess took part in the formation of PRC, elected executive vice-president a year later in 1941. And now, with Batcheller's resignation, he was in complete charge of production.[17]

In July, titles were announced for the upcoming 1942-43 season's forty-two productions of twenty-four features and eighteen Westerns. The features would be divided into three classes: "Victory Specials" (aka "V-Specials"), "Pacemakers," and "Spitfires."[18]

Buster Crabbe's popular "Billy the Kid" series continued for another six films during the 1942-43 season with Al St. John's "Fuzzy" at his side. One change from the previous season was the elimination of the third sidekick "Jeff;" otherwise they were much more of the same. The other change that had taken hold was with the leading "Billy the Kid in..." dropped from each film's title, a change that had begun to take place with the previous season's entries, and a change that applied to the "Lone Rider" series as well. The season's "Billy the Kid" entries included *The Mysterious Rider* (November 20, 1942), *The Kid Rides Again* (January 27, 1943), *Fugitive of the Plains* (March 12, 1943), *Western Cyclone* (May 14, 1943), *The Renegade* (July 1, 1943), and *Cattle Stampede* (August 16, 1943). The budgets increased midway through this series, *The Mysterious Rider* budgeted at $13,000 and *The Kid Rides Again* increased to $13,500; they were brought in with negative costs of $13,619 and $14,005, respectively. *Cattle Stampede*, the season's final entry, had a negative cost of $15,465.

Kermit Maynard has Al St. John pinned while Buster Crabbe holds John Merton and the others at gunpoint, in **The Mysterious Rider** (PRC, 1942), Sig Neufeld producer, Sam Newfield (as Sherman Scott) director.

Filmed on a twelve-day shoot with a negative cost of $13,779, *Fugitive of the Plains* offered a twist and novelty of sorts, with actress Maxine Leslie portraying the female leader of a gang. *The Exhibitor* summed up the general plotline of these films in a mere two sentences about *Fugitive of the Plains*: "As usual, Billy, the Kid, Buster Crabbe, is being blamed for all sorts of crimes he didn't commit. Faced with the alternative of either giving himself up as guilty or unmasking those posing as him, he chooses the latter course..."[19]

Gang leader Maxine Leslie holds Buster Crabbe at gunpoint in **Fugitive of the Plains** (PRC, 1943), Sig Neufeld producer, Sam Newfield director.

Charged with coming up with six acceptable screenplays per year and making decent, patron-friendly films from them was a difficult task at best, so it's not surprising that the results would fluctuate from film to film. For the most part reviews remained favorable, and dealt with each film with the audience for which it was intended firmly in mind. There was the occasional clunker, however, as one frustrated exhibitor was quick to note in his comments about *Fugitive of the Plains*:

> I regret very much that a good western star such as Buster Crabbe has to be put on the spot, by performing in such poorly produced westerns. If he continues he will surely go stale. It is about time that some of these companies woke up to the fact that the best stars in pictures can be ruined if not properly directed and produced. These westerns are a joke.[20]

Another exhibitor had a similar reaction to the film, while conceding that his patrons seemed to like it:

Personally thought it terrible, but it seemed to please the Western fans. Recording on these films is not very good, in my opinion.[21]

On the other hand, *Variety* gave an enthusiastic thumbs up to *Western Cyclone*, and with Al St. John's performance in particular:

This is one of the best of the 'Billy the Kid' series starring Buster Crabbe, not only because it has plenty of action and lively dialog but also as a result of the laugh value. Al St. John...has been provided with plenty of good comedy situations and, apparently with Crabbe's blessings, is given wide opportunity to show his stuff. That is to Crabbe's credit or the credit of director Sam Newfield, who appreciates his value.[22]

Al St. John rides along as Buster Crabbe and Lois Ranson share a buckboard in **The Renegade** (PRC, 1943). Sig Neufeld producer, Sam Newfield director.
Courtesy of Tim Neufeld.

It's likely that Sam's background in slapstick comedy with the Stern Brothers prompted him to give St. John free rein with his on-screen antics, and Crabbe was quick to note St. John's contributions to the films: "The things I did with Fuzzy—you know, he saved so many westerns for us. He was always good for two, three or four good belly-laughs—you never knew what he was going to do."[23] While acknowledging and appreciating St. John's considerable contributions to the popularity of the series, Crabbe was rather blasé about his own career, and didn't hide it from a contemporary interviewer. When asked if he preferred movie work above all else, he responded "No, I'd rather run a gas station. That's always been my ambition, for since I was a kid I liked to monkey around with machines and in garages. I've also always wanted to own an apple ranch. I have the ranch now, and I'm angling for a gas station."[24]

Kermit Maynard, who had a small role in this film as well, once relayed an interesting tidbit of info to St. John's wife Flobelle, that she in turn passed on to historian Sam Gill. Maynard said that Al "was no slouch as a horseman.... Few people know that Al used to have to hold his horse back, because Crabbe was the leading man, and that little Pinto Al had would take up and go!"[25]

All of the Western series' entries were usually rife with money-saving stock footage, and the Crabbe series—although its first few films managed to avoid stock—soon succumbed as well. Sig rarely, if ever, visited the location shoots, but made his presence known. "[Sig] never came on location. But [he] called in. [He] had lots of stock footage that [he] expected us to match our shooting with," recalled Crabbe.[26]

> We were scheduled to do a "big" cattle drive this day and arrived on location to find 20 head of tired cows. Sam told Bert to call Sig, got Sig on the phone and shouted "How the hell do you expect me to shoot a drive with 20 lousy cows?" [Sig's] answer "Mill 'em around."[27]

Crabbe's quibbles aside about the series and his pie-in-the-sky occupational preferences, it was money in the bank, and he had no real illusions about his place in the industry. "I don't think I'll ever be a big star. I had a chance to be one when I first went into pictures, but the producers fumbled it by 'typing' me. As soon as I learn the movies can get along without me—and I'm sure they can—I'll get out. There's always my apple ranch to go to. You know—apples, apple cider, and so forth."[28] He'd stick with the "Billy the Kid" series for another three years. And to that end both he and Al St. John committed themselves to the series by signing long-term contracts with Sig.[29]

Any complaints about the sound recording in PRC's films may have been another fallout resulting from the wartime restrictions placed on the studios. Restrictions on the building of sets resulted in a considerable increase in outdoor shooting, requiring a comparable increase in the use of sound trucks and portable sound equipment. According to one report, the majors and mini-majors had a total of eighty-eight sound recording outfits, owned outright or under lease. The independent producers used unlicensed equipment, however, and there were only three unlicensed outfits used to any great extent in 1942. Glen Glenn had a lone truck that was used almost exclusively by Monogram for its Westerns and occasional feature; Arthur Alexander had a single sound truck as well for use on his cowboy series; while Sig had a single outfit—Weeren's truck, no doubt—used for his annual commitment of Westerns for PRC. To add to their woes was the fact that nearly everything used to make a sound truck was in demand by the military as well, hindering any needed repairs or replacements. Patchwork fixes may have negatively affected sound recording on occasion.[30]

The "Lone Rider" series now featured Robert Livingston in the lead, a most welcome replacement for George Houston. Livingston's contract was for the standard six films, but only five were released during the season; the sixth, initial release had plugged the hole in the previous season's schedule resulting from former star Houston's premature departure. The new season's films were *Wild Horse Rustlers* (February 12, 1943), *Death Rides the Plains* (May 7, 1943), *Wolves of the Range* (June 21, 1943), *Law of the Saddle* (August 28, 1943, and the only one to be directed by Melville De Lay, usually Sam's assistant director on these films), and *Raiders of Red Gap* (September 30, 1943). *Law of the Saddle*, it's worth noting, was the first Western to be filmed at Corriganville on its western streets, built by Ray "Crash" Corrigan on the 1,740-acre spread he had purchased back in 1937 for $11,354.[31] It would be the first of many to make use of Corrigan's spread, De Lay bringing it in at $15,154.

Bob Livingston and Al St. John are about to get a "Get Out of Jail Free" card in **Wild Horse Rustlers** (PRC, 1943), Sig Neufeld producer, Sam Newfield director.

Livingston was a whole different animal than Houston, and brought about a notable change. Western aficionado Boyd Magers explained, regarding the previous season's *Overland Stagecoach* and Livingston's debut in the lead: "When George Houston returned to New York, Livingston took over the Lone Rider series from Houston with this film, causing the series to undergo a complete metamorphosis. Houston sang, Livingston didn't. Houston did not wear a mask, Livingston did, as he'd done in some Three Mesquiteers films—making a loose 'Lone Ranger.'"[32] One can only imagine just how happy the young ones attending these films were about the change, those former sappy musical interludes now replaced with a few more minutes of action!

After a stint with the Pasadena Playhouse, Robert "Bob" Livingston (1904-1988) segued into the film industry with bit parts for Universal and Fox. Signed by M-G-M in 1934, Livingston appeared in a number of films in parts both large and small before being dropped in 1936. Work for the indies followed, Livingston seemingly content with his reduced status within the industry. His most notable roles were as Stony Brook in Republic's long-running "Three Mesquiteers" series (1936-41), as well as the starring role in *The Lone Ranger Rides Again* (1939) serial.

Wolves of the Range has nothing to do with wolves, but then the titles of these Westerns rarely had any connection to the film itself. There's a drought in Little Rock, and the ranchers are in a panic over the looming loss of their cattle. The town's banker, played by Ed Cassidy, extends loans to help them ride out the drought, but the "respectable" Cattlemen's Association head, I. Stanford Jolley, has the banker killed. It seems that there's an "Eastern Syndicate" that wants to take over the valley for an irrigation project, and is orchestrating the drought. Enter the "Lone Rider" (Livingston) and Fuzzy Q. Jones (St. John), who eventually save a run on the bank and bring the bad guys to justice.

There's nothing new in this one aside from the gimmick of having Livingston suffer from amnesia and unable to recall what he did with the money to save the bank from that run. St. John plays it straight for a short while, but soon descends into his usual zaniness, capped perhaps by a visit to a fortune teller, purchasing a medallion that will supposedly save him from death, then saved from a thug's bullet when it imbeds itself in that same medallion. And why Livingston's character dons that Lone Ranger-like mask for a single early scene is beyond me since *everyone* knows he's the famous Lone Rider. And for that matter, why does he bear this name given that he's never alone, always with Fuzzy at his side?

Frances Gladwin doesn't seem to take Bob Livingston seriously in the lobby card for **Wolves of the Range** (PRC, 1943), Sig Neufeld producer, Sam Newfield director.

Director and part-time actor Robert Hill, who had served as Sig's best man at his wedding to Ruth years earlier, has a bit part as a judge in this film, and would pop up occasionally in small roles in other films as well, such as *Fuzzy Settles Down*, another entry in the ongoing Crabbe-St. John series. Frances Gladwin, who appears in this film as the banker's distraught daughter, was an ingénue borrowed by Sig from 20th Century-Fox,[33] and would appear in an additional five films for Sig while on loan; her role as a jaded cigarette girl in Sam's *Harvest Melody* was so insignificant, however, that it must have proved to be a major disappointment for the fledgling actress. *The Exhibitor* was happy with the direction the revitalized series was taking, stating that "This, like others in the series, shows improvement,"[34] while *Variety* gave a nod to the pairing of the two leads, stating that "Livingston and St. John, as usual, make a smooth-working team."[35] The film, perhaps, benefitted from the extra dollars spent on it, coming in at $16,547.

Bob Livingston's about to take one on the chin in **Law of the Saddle** (PRC, 1943), Sig Neufeld producer, Melville De Lay director. *Courtesy of Heritage Auctions.*

Raiders of Red Gap, which was filmed for $14,387 and released at the beginning of the 1943-44 season on September 30, was the final entry in this series, freeing up some of Sig's time to focus on additional non-Western themes in the years to come. Livingston continued in Westerns and other low budget films up until his retirement from the industry in 1958, but was lured back fifteen years later by producer Sam Sherman to star in the career-capping epics *The Naughty Stewardesses* (1973), *Girls for Rent* (1974), and *Blazing Stewardesses* (1975).

The production of eighteen Westerns each year occupied a lot of both Sig and Sam's time, but there was downtime as well, especially for director Sam and the films' other technicians. Sig and Sam would jointly make two "specials" for the season, the horror film *Dead Men Walk* and the mystery *The Black Raven*, but while Sig became increasingly more involved in the day-to-day business of running PRC, Sam was put to work elsewhere. One such film was for producer Peter R. Van Duinen and his comedy *My Son, the Hero* (April 5, 1943), for which Sam changed hats and provided some additional dialog. The film's director (and co-writer, with Doris Mallot) was Edgar Ulmer, who had hooked up with PRC a year earlier to direct the drama *Tomorrow We Live*, starring fading former silent screen idol Ricardo Cortez.

Edgar G. Ulmer (1904-1972), whose directorial career had peaked briefly with Universal's sensational Karloff-Lugosi co-starrer *The Black Cat* (1934), had screwed himself professionally when he exercised the poor judgment of screwing Max Alexander's wife whose husband, it just so happened, was Carl Laemmle's nephew; the breakup of Max's marriage prompted an unhappy Laemmle to have Ulmer blackballed throughout the industry. After a few lean years directing Yiddish films in the wilds of New Jersey and any other quickie project tossed his way, Ulmer finally hooked up with PRC, the studio no doubt giddy over landing an experienced and creative talent they could hire for cheap. Finally put under contract to the studio in later 1943,[36] Ulmer would go on to direct a string of comparatively successful films between 1942 and 1948, most famous of which was the John Carradine vehicle *Bluebeard* (1944) and the early noir *Detour* (1945). Ulmer's contributions to PRC extended beyond the writing and direction of his films, at least according to his several self-serving interviews.

Cinematographer Jack Greenhalgh was loaned to Van Duinen as well to lens *My Son, the Hero*, but his involvement was short-lived. With the U.S. now at war with the Axis powers, Greenhalgh had applied for a commission with the Army Air Corps and its photographic unit. His application came through on December 11, 1942, shortly after filming had begun. Greenhalgh was told to report for duty first thing the following morning, so he scrambled to find a suitable replacement to complete the filming of Ulmer's film. He found him in the person of Robert Cline, a forty-seven-year-old cinematographer with behind-the-camera experience since the mid-1920s. Cline was well known to both Sig and Sam, Sig having worked with him as early as 1930 on some of those Tiffany Chimp Comedies, and Sam on films for Colony, Spectrum, Supreme, and Republic. Cline would shoot more than twenty films for Sig at PRC before Greenhalgh was given a medical discharge from the Air Force in late 1944, after serving a stint in charge of the 5th Combat Team shooting battle-action films.[37] Two days after his discharge, reported *American Cinematographer*, "Sig Neufeld called him back to work. [Greenhalgh] hopes all the other boys will receive such considerate treatment when they come home."[38]

New York-born Jack Greenhalgh (1904-1971) stumbled into his life-long career purely by accident. As a seventeen-year-old, he had accompanied his father in 1923 to a location shoot at what was then called Las Turas Lake. The film, part of a series produced by Harry Joe Brown that Al Rogell was directing, had Ross Fisher as cameraman. Fisher's assistant failed to show, so Fisher pressed Greenhalgh into service, the one-day fill-in becoming a fulltime job. Greenhalgh was young and gung-ho, so he occasionally agreed to fill in for the stunt man as well. One such stunt required him to descend from the top of Los Angeles's ten-story Flatiron Building by rope, and carrying the heroine no less; the film's usual stunt man had had last-minute cold feet regarding the assignment.

As second cameraman, Greenhalgh had moved on to the Fred Thompson Company, followed by a stint with Pathé assisting cameraman Norbert Brodine, and Greenhalgh's first experience with sound. Work for both First National and Fox followed,[39] eventually hooking up with Sig and Sam in 1935 at Ambassador. Work for the brothers would follow at Sig's Excelsior Pictures for Puritan, and for Sam at Colony and Grand National before Sig hired him to film *Hitler—Beast of Berlin* and become a permanent fixture with Sigmund Neufeld Productions. Greenhalgh's contributions to the sort of low budget films Sig and Sam were turning out were invaluable. *American Cinematographer* explained:

> Most of these pictures were made on modest budgets which means, of course, that the cameraman was limited in the amount of time he could spend in setting up for, and composing each shot, a condition that calls for a cameraman with the utmost skill and a perfect understanding of his craft if the picture is to finish on time and not suffer photographically.[40]

The article was written about fellow A.S.C. cameraman Vincent J. Farrar, but the sentiments expressed apply equally to Greenhalgh's efforts for Sig.

Sam's other film for PRC was the "higher-budgeted special" *Queen of Broadway* (March 8, 1943), co-starring Buster Crabbe and Rochelle Hudson. Bert Sternbach made the leap from production manager to producer for this film, teaming with Sam for their newly formed S&N ("Sternbach & Newfield") Productions; Sig served as executive producer for this one. Filming of its six-day shoot began on October 8, 1942, working from a script written by George Sayre and Milton Raison. Sternbach received $1,034 for producing the film, which came in with a negative cost of $22,000.

Hudson stars as a famous—and very successful—forecaster of sports outcomes. While she herself never places bets, her followers all do and have done well with her predictions. She has a combative relationship with boyfriend Crabbe, the owner of a professional football team. He wants to marry, but she doesn't. Enter little Donald Mayo as a six-year-old whose mother has just died. The kid doesn't know of her death, but Hudson does, and is coerced into taking him in until he can be placed in an orphanage. She falls for the kid and decides to adopt him, but her petition for adoption is denied based on the biased testimony of a pair of old investigative biddies. Crabbe comes to the rescue, adopting the kid and then marrying Hudson. Hudson thinks that the nuptials were solely to facilitate the adoption, so she sends an embittered Crabbe packing. Leave it to the kid to bring the two sparring adults back together.

The cast and crew of **Queen of Broadway** (PRC, 1943) take a break to pose for the camera. Mannie Teitelbaum kneeling lower left, Sam Newfield sitting center with script in hands; Rochelle Hudson sitting at desk, Buster Crabbe behind her; Bert Sternbach dead center in black suit, Jack Greenhalgh behind with hand on Bert's shoulder; Stanley Neufeld standing far back center, Hans Weeren with hand on Stanley's shoulder. *Courtesy of Tim Neufeld.*

This is a pleasant enough film with a decided Damon Runyon-esque vibe, Hudson always surrounded by a rough assemblage of fast-talking bookies, fading sports figures, and other shady types. Her right-hand man Rosy (Paul Bryar) is an English-mangling, malaprop-spouting ex-prizefighter, and gets the bulk of the film's most humorous lines and asides. Sternbach's production has a "richer" look than the preponderance of PRC's output, and Sam's direction is straight-forward and adequate for the story being told. One can readily imagine that Sam felt "at home" with this story, centered as it is around all manner of sports betting. Sayre and Raison's script is better than the average for PRC, full of snappy dialog and biting comebacks. Hudson, who is gorgeous in this film, makes a convincing foil for Crabbe, who must have been happy to don a suit and tie for a rare occasion. Little Donald Mayo, only six when he made his debut in this film, gives as credible a performance as a six-year-old could be expected to give. Unfortunately, PRC's shot at more mainline adult fare with this one falls short after the engaging first half, tipping a bit too far in the direction of maudlin once the whole adoption wrangling takes over. That said, it's a far more enjoyable film than so much of PRC's other output, and a very acceptable effort. "A neatly done picture," wrote *Film Daily*. "One that embodies all the essences of good entertainment—comedy, drama, smooth movement and heart-felt emotion, whipped into film fare that will find approval among audiences and exhibitors." The review went on to say that it was "ably produced by Bert Sternbach" and commented on "the well-knit direction of Sam Newfield."[41]

The War Takes a Bite (Sig, Sam, and PRC, Part 3, 1942-1943) 247

Buster Crabbe, Rochelle Hudson, and their "rough assemblage of fast-talking bookies, fading sports figures, and other shady types" look on as little Donald Mayo lands a right in **Queen of Broadway** (PRC, 1943), Sig Neufeld producer, Sam Newfield director.
Courtesy of the Library of Congress.

Sig's oldest son Stanley was now nineteen years of age. Because of his years watching his father at work, he decided to go into the production end of the business. Since his father was rarely on the set when Stanley was, it was Bert Sternbach who Stanley looked up to and learned from. Stanley's enthusiasm earned him a spot assisting Sternbach on *Queen of Broadway*,[42] but with its completion he headed to San Francisco to join the Merchant Marines as a marine engineer.[43] "I could have gone into the Navy," said Stanley later in life. "I wanted to go in as an engineer and [after] three months at school in San Francisco…I was supposed to go out for three months on a ship." He was gone for eighteen months rather than three, and the ship was a mess when it returned to the States, "but it was exciting because I was a young guy and I was looking for action…."[44]

Surprisingly, Sam, who was extremely patriotic, wanted to enlist in the Army. According to his son Joel, however, he was rejected because of what he did for a living. Directing movies "kept him out of the Army. He wanted to join, and they wouldn't let him because he was making these movies. They needed the movies."[45] Sam's physical condition may have played a part in the Army's decision as well. Both Sig and Sam would contribute to the war effort, however, by producing a series of training films.

Stanley, by 1944 an Ensign, was given a leave of absence to marry Marie Scott and go on a honeymoon in June of that year.[46] The marriage took place in San Francisco, which might have presented an issue for the Neufelds and Newfields, who were based nearly 400 miles south in Los Angeles; gas was rationed and flight availability reduced due to the ongoing war. Not to worry: "[Sig] went through the studio and got a limousine with a chauffeur. Bert [Sternbach] hired a limousine, and of course limousines had unlimited access for gasoline because that's their business. So we drove up to the wedding in a chauffeur-driven limousine that he hired for the trip," recalled Sig Jr., who was quick to add that "I always sat up front with the driver."[47]

Sam's other film independent of Sig was for producer Jack Schwarz. Back in April, PRC had closed a radio "package" deal with the National Concert and Artists Corporation for the acquisition of the title, story, and cast of a recent radio show, "Danger, Women at Work." Recently broadcast on the West Coast, PRC's purchase included the show's "name" cast: Patsy Kelly, Arline Judge, Mabel Todd, Cobina Wright, Sr., and Allan Byron. Original plans were for it to be produced the following month by Peter Van Duinen, with direction by Edgar Ulmer.[48] Within a month, however, production reins had been turned over to Schwarz and direction to Sam. Gertrude Walker was brought in to adapt her original script with Ulmer, but it was Martin Mooney who was credited with the final screenplay as filmed. Arline Judge had to back out when she was called east to do a stage play, Una Merkel named as her replacement.[49] Merkel too ended up being replaced. The film took slightly longer to shoot than usual—seven days rather than six—and exceeded its rather generous $32,841 budget by nearly 14 %, coming in at $37,389.

Warren Hymer and Patsy Kelly try to get a marriage license in **Danger! Women At Work** (PRC, 1943), Jack Schwarz producer, Sam Newfield director.

Danger! Women At Work, as released on August 23, 1943, co-starred Patsy Kelly, Mary Brian, and Isabel Jewell as a trio of war-time women who decide to get into the hauling business when Kelly inherits a ten-ton truck. There's a load waiting for them in

Las Vegas, but the need to fill their empty truck for the ride there from California is filled with the offer of a bunch of gambling furniture and paraphernalia. The trip is eventful, the girls quickly acquiring a colorful load of hitchhikers: a socialite with amnesia (Cobina Wright Sr.), a fortune teller (Betty Compson), and the millionaire's daughter (Wanda McKay) fleeing daddy's grasp to meet her beau out in Boulder, Colorado. They end up with a multitude of pursuers that include the finance company planning to repo the truck, some crooks hoping to steal their load, detectives hired by the millionaire to return his daughter for the $5,000 reward he has offered, a bunch of gamblers who lost out to Kelly in a game of dice, and the girls' boyfriends hoping to rescue them; lots of traffic cops along the way as well. After the girls are arrested on a bogus charge brought by the gamblers, all ends well, of course, the film closing with a three-way wedding ceremony.

A screwball comedy of sorts, there are enough laughs to hold the interest, Kelly not surprisingly the source of most of them. These are mild laughs at best, the film as a whole providing an hour's worth of only moderate entertainment. The film starts off with an interesting premise, but there are so many characters introduced and at such a frantic pace that the viewer soon gives up trying to keep track of who-is-who and why, and just goes along for the ride. It was another nice change of pace for Sam, however, and painless viewing.

It should come as no surprise that reviewers were mixed in their reactions to the film. "Reasons for laughter are frequent and spontaneous in 'Danger! Women at Work'," wrote *Motion Picture Herald* in its positive review. "[I]t is fresh, fast and filled with capable performers."[50] *Harrisons Reports* was more qualified in its review: "In spite of the fact that the story is far-fetched, this program comedy has enough laughs, fast action, and amusing situations to satisfy undiscriminating audiences in smalltown and neighborhood theatres. Discriminating patrons may find it a bit too inane."[51] Fair enough. *Photoplay* gave it a thumbs down—literally, stating "Don't thumb a ride on this one"—adding that "Wanda McKay and Betty Compson whirl around the story that isn't worth the whirl, believe us."[52] Cute. And, of course, there was always a disgruntled exhibitor to write in with his two-bits' worth of complaint, this one based in North Carolina: "Another flop from PRC. As was to be expected, we had several walkouts, but maybe the heat had something to do with that."[53] My money is on the heat.

Sig had two suspense-filled films lined up as well, the second and third films for George Zucco in his three-film contract. The first—*Dead Men Walk*—was an unapologetic horror film, while the second—*The Black Raven*—was a murder mystery with mildly comedic overtones. Sam collaborated with his brother, serving as director for these two films, with Jack Greenhalgh handling the camerawork on the former, which had begun shooting back in September 1942. Greenhalgh had joined the Air Force by the time *The Black Raven* went before cameras on February 9, 1943, however, so Robert Cline took over for him.

Variety commented on the current popularity of horror and mystery films, providing a reason for Sig's sudden interest in these two genres. "The chillers are cleaning up in most spots around the country, even getting first-run and downtown bookings in unprecedented manner, and, because of their usually low budgets, are, as a class, reaping comparatively greater profit than other picture types." Music, no doubt, to Sig's ears. *Variety* continued:

Chalk it up to the war. Studio and film-row execs point out that World War I gave a needle to gangster themes, and that although horrifics and whodunits were always around, World War II, with its greater and swifter destruction, is encouraging more of their production to satisfy public taste whetted by star [sic] realities.... Whodunits, on the average, run budgetwise somewhere around the western brackets. But some distribs get three times, and more, in gross rentals from the former.[54]

Sig and PRC weren't about to let the hottest current cycle get past them, a cycle as *Variety* put it "given impetus by the one item around which cycles always revolve: new momentum to the tingling of dimes, quarters and halves on boxoffice."[55]

George Zucco is introduced to niece Mary Carlisle's fiancé Nedrick Young in **Dead Men Walk** (PRC, 1943), Sig Neufeld producer, Sam Newfield director.

"Sig Neufeld, who makes 'em for PRC release, says that when you make a horror picture, you've got to make it so the skin will crawl off the customer's bones," wrote Ed Riaden, *Showmen's Trade Review*'s West Coast Editor, of *Dead Men Walk*. "His next one, a vampire story, starts in a fireplace with a small fire, and ends in a big fire that takes all the players with it. Sort of like Hamlet, where the King dies, the Queen dies, Laertes dies, Ophelia dies, and Ham dies."[56]

Almost. The film opens with a closeup of a book, "History of Vampires," which is then tossed into the fireplace. A face appears superimposed over the flames, launching into a lugubrious speech about the occult, the undead, and what have you. It's reminiscent of the face-in-the-crystal-ball opening of those Universal "Inner Sanctum" mysteries, but solely coincidental; *Dead Men Walk* was released on February

10, 1943, a full ten months before Sanctum's initial entry, *Calling Dr. Death*. With that atypical opening behind us, we're on to the funeral for the late Dr. Elwyn Clayton (Zucco), a little-loved occult-worshipping member of the community. In the audience is Elwyn's twin brother, kindly Dr. Lloyd Clayton (also Zucco), Lloyd's niece and ward (Mary Carlisle) and her fiancé (Nedrick Young). Elwyn doesn't stay planted very long, returning as a vampire, assisted by fanatical and none-too-bright Dwight Frye. As it turns out, Elwyn and Lloyd had a life-long hatred of each other, the former killed when he attacked Lloyd and was pushed off a cliff during the scuffle. Elwyn confronts his brother with a promise: because Lloyd took Elwyn's "mortal life," Elwyn would now take the life of the one dearest to Lloyd—Carlisle, of course—and *very* slowly, with the eventuality that Carlisle would join Elwyn among the undead. The rest of the film involves Lloyd and Young's quest to track down Elwyn's daytime napping place, that is after Young has been convinced that Lloyd himself is not responsible for Carlisle's slow descent into anemia and looming death. The film concludes with a fiery climax, Lloyd giving his life to ensure that Elwyn is consumed by the flames. Frye, pinned beneath a fallen pedestal, goes along for the ride.

Lobby card for **Dead Men Walk** (PRC, 1943) highlights George Zucco struggling with himself. *Courtesy of Heritage Auctions.*

This is an effective little chiller, benefiting from what would seem like an enhanced budget. Not so: it finished its six-day shoot on September 17, 1943, with a negative cost of a modest $21,995. Sam's direction ($750), while not flashy, is assured, with Greenhalgh's cinematography more fluid than usual and enhanced by moody, atmospheric lighting throughout. The sets are more convincing than the norm, particularly the stage-bound "outdoor" sets which are for the most part visually convincing; one only need compare this film's cemetery to the zero-budget cemetery of Ed Wood's *Plan Nine from Outer Space* to see the difference a larger budget can make. The performances are quite good as well. Zucco dominates in his dual role, calm and soft-spoken as Lloyd, and maniacally threatening as Elwyn; all the shots where he appears as both brothers are executed in a technically proficient fashion as well. Mary Carlisle, a twenty-year veteran of the business, gives a decent performance but really has little to do except lie around looking listless and sighing deeply. Carlisle recalled working at PRC in an interview with Don Leifert:

> How was PRC different from the major studios? There was little time for lighting and rehearsing. Everything was different. On an A picture, a designer designs the wardrobe. At PRC, we'd go to wardrobe and pick out something that had already been worn two or three times on other pictures.[57]

As Carlisle's lover, newcomer Nedrick Young—the previous year's *Bombs Over Burma* was his sole role to date—gives it the old college try, but he's one of those bland, draft-deferred fellows likely chosen more out of need than for talent. That said, his acting here is sufficient, if a bit overwrought, but would improve with experience in a career that would last through the 1950s, a comeback of sorts in 1966's *Seconds*. Dwight Frye, by now thoroughly stereotyped as the dim-witted lacky of horror films gone by, returns here sporting a shifting hunchback and giving the performance his usual, over-the-top gusto while appearing rather haggard doing so. Frye would die later that same year at the comparatively young age of forty-four. And then there's Fern Emmett as Kate, the mother of a murdered child, who serves as sort of a Greek Chorus of one, popping in at random moments to "educate" those in the scene with her on the workings of vampires. The most notable of these is that the only way to kill a vampire is by fire, a significant change from Universal's standard death-by-stake-through-the-heart. The viewer is never quite certain whether to take her performance seriously or with a touch of tongue-in-cheek, but her off-screen murder midway dispenses with that issue.

Reviews, for a rare change, were almost unanimously positive—or at least not overly negative. *The Exhibitor* called it "One of the best vampire pictures since 'Dracula'"[58] *Harrisons Reports* called it a "horror melodrama [that] should appeal to the followers of pictures of this type" while adding the caveat that it was "Too horrifying for children."[59] *Showmen's Trade Review* deemed it "Just what the horror fans like for entertainment,"[60] and *Motion Picture Daily* concurred: "Here is an above average horror picture that should please all the mystery fans."[61] *Variety*'s "Rose." appears to be among the dissenters, opening with "PRC's excursion into black magic…fails to ring the bell as a horror story" before proceeding to trash most aspects of the film, including Sam's direction, which she said failed "to inject proper punch and excitement in development of yarn."[62] I think the wrong reviewer was assigned to review this film, given that it's a far better film than she would lead the reader to believe. That, and she was a notable outlier.

The *Black Raven* isn't nearly as successful, being one of those storm-tossed, suspect-heavy mysteries with red herrings galore and not an iota of chance for the viewer to deduce the guilty party based on the clues—or lack thereof—provided. That said, it's still a fun little film if one is content to sit back and enjoy the combative interactions between all involved. George Zucco plays the proprietor of the remote hostelry near the Canadian border named The Black Raven. It is a name Zucco's also known by among the lawbreaking sort, who occasionally use his less-than-legal assist while avoiding pursuit to cross that nearby border. On one rain swept night where a nearby bridge has been washed out, Zucco soon finds his inn inhabited by an eclectic bunch of misfits and travelers: his former partner (I. Stanford Jolley) who has escaped prison and intends to kill Zucco; gangster Noel Madison, who wants Zucco to get him across the border; Byron Foulger with his satchel full of embezzled cash; Wanda McKay and Robert Livingston (billed as Robert Randall for this film), eloping lovers trying to escape her domineering father; and as B-film coincidence would have it, Robert Middlemass, her father and "dirty politician" who hates her beau. Middlemass gets wind of Foulger's ill-gotten gains and commandeers them, but when he's found dead from a blow to the head and the money gone missing, the mystery begins. All of the film's characters are obsessed with something: Jolley with killing Zucco; Madison with locating the missing money; the pig-headed sheriff (Charles Middleton) with finding the killer; Livingston with proving his innocence to the sheriff; and Foulger with getting the hell out of this increasingly threatening madhouse. It will come as no surprise that the guilty party is finally found out, but after three more of the film's characters are dispatched—four dead out of nine: that's a rather hefty body count!

Pretty much the entire cast of **The Black Raven** (PRC, 1943) is featured in this poster for the film. Sig Neufeld producer, Sam Newfield director.
Courtesy of Heritage Auctions.

Filmed on a quick six-day shoot with a negative cost of $21,996, the film benefits from good production values and decent performances, but Fred Myton's screenplay is heavy with the usual (and by this time rather stale) "mystery" conventions. Sam's direction emphasizes a few of the more obvious cliches with his choices: the face that reappears at the rain-swept window, shadows of unseen individuals creeping across nearby walls, that sort of thing. Glenn Strange has a role as the inn's all-around gofer, included for questionable comic relief that is anything but comic and of little relief; just how many times can a guy humorously fall down a flight of steps? *Film Bulletin* commented on same, stating that "Glenn Strange's cowering servant is practically a burlesque portrayal. It's so bad that it will draw laughs from the audience."[63]

Variety pointed out another reason for the studios' current embrace of the mystery film, saying that "with limited sets required—frequently not much more than a mystery house along the roadside, a dark night and an eerie storm...[t]his lends itself readily to [Office of Price Administration's] $5,000 set ceiling. Tension on the actual or threatening shortage of talent is also relieved a bit by the comparatively limited cast required, with mobs hardly ever needed; ditto for top talent."[64] *Variety* wasn't referring specifically to *The Black Raven*, but they might as well have been.

Reviewers took note: *Motion Picture Daily* called *The Black Raven* "a lot of picture for the money spent" and said that the trio of Myton, Sig, and Sam turned in "a balanced job."[65] *Motion Picture Herald* gave it a similar nod while keeping its PRC-origins firmly in mind, stating that "For the time it takes and the money it cost, this hour of melodrama conducted in surroundings of suspense...measures up to par for product in kind.... [I]t tells its tale and maintains its spell with effectiveness."[66] PRC's suits must have been happy with these two films, and the comparatively positive acceptance they received.

The Black Raven's production cost summary provides a detailed glimpse at the sort of salaries the film's participants could expect to receive during this period of time, and for a producer of Sig's admittedly parsimonious sort. Sig paid himself $1,200 for producing the film, and his brother Sam $1,000 for directing; Sam's assistant, Mel De Lay, received $175 for helping out. The film's tight little cast received a total of $4,105, which included $135 for the bit players. Screenwriter Fred Myton received $600 for his cliché-heavy script—$1,000 per film was a few years off—while Bert Sternbach received $221 to make sure that every penny spent needed to be. Hans Weeren received $1,209 for his efforts, assistants, and equipment, while replacement cinematographer Robert Cline was paid $340, along with an additional $277 for his two assistants. Editor Holbrook Todd earned $363 for his creative snipping, and composer David Chudnow a mere $100 for his five compositions, itemized as "Shadows," "Despair," "Nightmare," "Main Title," and "End Title," a pretty good deal for Sig since canned music wouldn't have cost him a whole lot less.[67]

There were two other projects that Sig was to produce during this period, but don't appear to have come to fruition. Fromkess purchased an original story from Martin Mooney titled "Convict Battalion," described as being based on "the so-called suicide squad at San Quentin prison which offered its services in fighting the Japanese."[68] Sam and Bert were both involved with this project initially, but rights were eventually turned over to PRC and original costs of Mooney's story "absorbed by PRC in the final settlement of the cost of the production of the motion picture THE CONTENDER."[69]

The other film was tentatively titled *Ex-Racketeer* about a racketeer who "goes all-out for war."[70] Neither appears to have been produced, or at least not by Sig, and not with these titles. Based on the skimpy description of *Ex-Racketeer*, it's possible that they were both one and the same. Not that it really mattered, since both Sig and Sam were spread rather thin as it was.

Fromkess, it should be noted, took a liking to producer-writer Mooney and appointed him to his personal assistant and PRC's story editor in early 1943.[71]

Chapter 14:
Slaves of Formula (Sig, Sam, and PRC, Part 4, 1943-1944)

PRC's annual meeting of franchise holders was held in Kansas City, Missouri in mid-June 1943. It was, once again, opened by O.H. Briggs, who gave his usual self-congratulatory progress report, and chaired by Arthur Greenblatt, who detailed the upcoming season's program, sales policies, and distribution plans. Fromkess and Sig, who by now worked well together and had a healthy respect for each other's capabilities, attended from the West Coast to bring the franchisees up to date on actual production. "This young organization continues its fast pace, accelerated by substantially increased budgets from Pathé on various productions in prospect. Leon Fromkess has proven himself a first class production executive" wrote *Film Bulletin*. "It is evident that PRC is making a bid for 'A' playing time and will soon have a product capable of traveling in big league company."[1]

Forty features were planned for the 1943-44 season, with an increase in budget more than double any previous year's. Of the planned forty, sixteen would be Westerns: eight of Sig's "Billy the Kid" series,[2] and another eight of Alexander-Stern's "Texas Rangers" series co-starring Dave O'Brien—now billed as "Tex" O'Brien—and Jim Newill. The other twenty-four features were to be divided into four major groups, explained Greenblatt, an increase over the previous season's three: "Producers Specials," "Victory Specials" (aka "V-Specials"), "Pacemakers," and "Spitfires."[3] Greenblatt failed to explain what differentiated the films from one group to another, not that it was of particular importance. For some perspective, Sig and Sam's *Dead Men Walk* and *The Black Raven* of the previous season turned out to be in the "Pacemakers" class, along with Sam's *Queen of Broadway*.[4]

Also discussed was Fromkess' "decision" to take the first step in what was viewed as an attempt to acquire the status of a major company. Fromkess had decided that PRC should start making its own films, with PRC Productions, a subsidiary of PRC, formed for that purpose. Five units would become the production apparatus within the new company, with the parent company financing all production. All five had been operating independently and releasing through PRC up to this time, but would now be functioning entities within the company itself. The named companies were headed by Sig Neufeld (Sigmund Neufeld Productions); Bert Sternbach and Sam Newfield (as S&N); Jack Schwarz; Max Alexander and Alfred Stern (as Alexander-Stern); and Arthur Ripley and Rudolph Monter (as Ripley-Monter). Active production was to commence in June 1943 filming at PRC's new studio space at Fine Arts Studios.[5]

Not so fast, said Briggs. While Fromkess was fully behind this decision to grow PRC into something more closely resembling a "respectable" motion picture studio, both Briggs and the others at the company's financial end were far less enthusiastic about the move, feeling it would entail too much risk.[6] It would be another month or so before Fromkess could calm their collective jitters, and by mid-September filming had started on PRC's first in-house production, the Fromkess-produced *Jive Junction*, directed by Edgar G. Ulmer.[7] PRC Productions, Inc.'s executive setup included Briggs as president, Fromkess as vice president, Karl Herzog as secretary and treasurer, and Arthur Johnson as assistant secretary and treasurer; Sig was among others on the board of directors.[8]

PRC Productions was to be housed at the Fine Arts Studio—formerly the now-defunct Grand National Studio—which PRC now owned. With a bid in September of $305,000 in cash plus $33,000 for back taxes, PRC had outbid Columbia's offer of $300,000 plus $33,000 for the back taxes. PRC took possession on October 1, 1943.[9] Extensive improvements were made to the studio, which included equipment such as electrical fixtures, generators, sets, and flats, all recently acquired from the I.E. Chadwick studio, along with newly purchased equipment.[10]

The signing of contracts in September 1943 gave PRC possession of the Fine Arts Studio for $305,000 in cash plus $33,000 for back taxes. Left-to-right standing: Sig Neufeld, assistant secretary-treasurer Arthur Johnson, and secretary-treasurer Karl Herzog. Sitting: Leon Fromkess, vice president, and O. Henry Briggs, president. *Courtesy of Tim Neufeld.*

The unfortunate death of Sig's sound engineer Hans Weeren at the beginning of August did not come as a total surprise. Weeren had been a patient at Cedars of Lebanon hospital for the past two months, so it must have become evident at some point that his end was nearing. Still, at only forty-nine years of age, a better outcome had been hoped for. Weeren was interred at Forest Lawn Cemetery on August 7,[11] his last released effort the "Billy the Kid" entry *Blazing Frontier*, released less than a month after Weeren's death. In the years that followed, Sig would fill the position with a number of different sound engineers, including Ben Winkler, Lyle Willey, and Corson Jowett, but it was with Glen Glenn that he felt most comfortable, utilizing his services on fifteen films over the years 1944 to 1952. Sam too had earlier experience with Glenn, having worked with him on two of Sam Katzman's Victory Westerns.

Sig's production contract for the 1943-44 season, while essentially the same as the previous season's contract, tacked on some additional, potentially intrusive stipulations. Sig was barred from issuing any sort of advance publicity material or releases without first receiving PRC's approval, and PRC now reserved the right to have one or more of its reps on the set for the filming of any of the film's scenes, for post-production sound recording, as well as in the editing room breathing down the necks of the editor and cutter. PRC also reserved the right to retake and reedit individual scenes for any given film, and to audit the books and records related to a given film for up to twelve months after each film's delivery to PRC. The 1940-41 season's two-page production contract had by now ballooned to a wordy thirty-three page contract.[12] Additionally, Sig's agreement with PRC for the Westerns during this period covered the negative costs, payable by PRC upon delivery of the completed film, limited to the increased $13,500 per film for the "Lone Rider" series, and now $16,000 per for the Buster Crabbe series. After each film went into release, the fifty-fifty split of domestic and Canadian profits remained, along with the 75 %-25 % split for the United Kingdom. Sig's take on the rest of the world dropped however to a 65 %-35 % split. Domestic television, 16mm, and trailer receipts had by now been added to the contracts with a fifty-fifty split for these as well.[13]

Westerns continued to provide strong revenues for PRC. In April 1943 it was announced that grosses on the Western series were up 47 % from the same period a year earlier.[14] Sig's "Billy the Kid" series was the primary earner in this group due to the popularity and warm camaraderie of its leads, Buster Crabbe and Al St. John. There were seven entries released during the season—*Blazing Frontier*, with a negative cost of $17,219 (September 1, 1943), *Devil Riders* (November 5, 1943), *The Drifter* (December 20, 1943), *Frontier Outlaws* (March 4, 1944) *Thundering Gun Slingers* (March 25, 1944), *Valley of Vengeance* (May 5, 1944), and *Fuzzy Settles Down* (July 25, 1944)—all of which were directed by Sam and credited as such. Sam dispensed with his Sherman Scott and Peter Stewart aliases beginning with this season, or at least as far as the Westerns were concerned. The Sherman Scott moniker would only be used in later years for PRC's *The Flying Serpent* (1946) as well as two more films for Eagle-Lion, the entity that absorbed PRC in 1947. Both aliases, however, would be trotted out on a sporadic basis for some of Sam's later assignments for Paramount, Film Classics, and Lippert.

The season's first, *Blazing Frontier*, is significant for one series-altering reason: it was the last time that Crabbe would portray the notorious outlaw of yore William Bonney, more commonly known as Billy the Kid. All the preceding entries in this series took pains to drive home the (historically incorrect) point that Crabbe's Bonney was only a fall guy for the crimes of others, pursued by the law as a path of least resistance. That the screen Billy would occasionally bend—or break—the law to achieve a greater good was conveniently overlooked, as in this particular film where he orchestrates both the robbery of a stage coach and the rustling of cattle to infiltrate and get the goods on the villains of the piece. By this film, however, Crabbe's character had been so sufficiently whitewashed otherwise that a change to jettison all that "wanted by the law" baggage seemed in order. That change would come with the next film.

Blazing Frontier, which *Motion Picture Daily* deemed "sub-par,"[15] involves the scheme of colluding railroad agent and chief detective—I. Stanford Jolley and Frank Hagney, respectively—to pit ranchers against the railroad in order to gain possession of their land. The beleaguered rancher's lawyer (Milton Kibbee) contacts his old friend Billy to help gain evidence to expose the swindlers' scheme. To that end (and as usual), Billy and his sidekick Fuzzy infiltrate the swindlers' gang, get the goods, and bring the two villains to justice.

Buster Crabbe (far right) bends the law just a bit when he orchestrates a "robbery" of a stage coach in order to get the goods on a gang of outlaws, in **Blazing Frontier** (PRC, 1943), Crabbe's last appearance as Billy the Kid before becoming Billy Carson. Sig Neufeld producer, Sam Newfield director. *Courtesy of Tim Neufeld.*

Blazing Frontier's screenplay was written by a young woman named Patricia Harper. Born in Indiana in 1908, Harper had headed to Los Angeles for work at a newspaper. She sold a story to M-G-M that was never filmed, but her interest in the industry was now piqued. Having had dance lessons in her youth, she managed to wrangle jobs as a chorus girl in musicals for Warners and Goldwyn, which petered out when interest in musicals waned. Killing time in a movie theater featuring a Western double bill, Harper sat through what she called "the worst pictures she's ever seen." Putting her writing talents to work coupled with some intensive research, Harper launched into the writing of Western scripts, twenty of which had been filmed by various studios by late 1943. Sig would produce five of them between 1942 and 1943.[16] Given that the majority of these were for Sig and other indie producers, her aforementioned 1946 article in *The Screen Writer* decrying the flat fee seemed like a case of biting the hand that fed her. Her career as a screenwriter, not surprisingly, didn't last for much longer after the posting of that article.

Motion Picture Daily's dismissal aside, the film is another typical entry in the long-running series. The enjoyment level of these films varies from film to film, needless to say, but most of them provide enjoyable viewing if taken at face value: simplistically lightweight entertainment designed to provide an hour's worth of action and comedy for the lower half of a twin bill. It doesn't hurt that both Crabbe and St. John are undeniable pros whose ongoing teaming provides the viewer a comforting familiarity. Wisely on the filmmakers' part—and with Crabbe's generous acquiescence—St. John's roles grew from one film to the next, largely left to his own devices to provide considerable (if sometimes questionable) humor to an otherwise straightforward Western. The film's final scene includes one of St. John's throwaway actions, his singlehanded rolling of a cigarette, one of his Uncle Roscoe "Fatty" Arbuckle's signature moves that was likely passed on to his nephew. As for the "blown lines" observation that critics readily lob towards PRC's output, they are rare in Sam's film, but one is actually mis-delivered by Frank Hagney in this film. That said, Hagney was a seasoned pro with hundreds of roles to his credit since the late teens, and made such a quick recovery that most viewers wouldn't even notice it and, if they did, would accept it as intended realism in an otherwise unrealistic film.

Al St. John, Milton Kibbee, Buster Crabbe, and Marjorie Manners in **Blazing Frontier** (PRC, 1943).

The second of the season's entries was *Devil Riders*, and this one was significant for three reasons: Crabbe now portrayed squeaky-clean Billy Carson, his former Billy the Kid character now consigned to the dustbins of film vaults. Gone was Billy's familiar black shirt, replaced with a "good guy" one of a lighter color, and Crabbe now had second-billed Falcon as his trusty steed. The plot has cohorts Charlie King and John Merton attempting to thwart a stage road being built through land they want for their own. As part of their plan, they scheme to pit stage line owner Frank La Rue and local Pony Express operator Billy Carson (Crabbe), both bidding for the same mail contract, against each other. Fuzzy (St. John), the town's blacksmith, is Billy's partner as well, while Patti McCarty appears as La Rue's daughter.

This is an action-packed film—action-packed and little else. Seemingly one horseback chase, stage pursuit, shootout, and fistfight after another, there's little else going on in this film. The one major exception is a considerable chunk of unnecessary padding midway through the film, for a barn dance featuring Fuzzy's acrobatic dance steps (one of which sends his partner through a window) and two musical numbers. And just when you think the action has all petered out, a mad stagecoach dash to deliver some desperately needed serum is thrown into the mix. Screenwriter Joe O'Donnell must have been hard up for inspiration this time around, although he received $500 for his lackluster efforts.

Motion Picture Herald's reviewer was spot on with his observations about the film and its major structural flaw:

> As everyone knows, producers of Western pictures have long been slaves of formula. The basic ingredients of the formula have always been two way conflicts, virtue in opposition to evil and virtue in opposition to virtue, the latter combination always arising out of a misunderstanding only to be patched up in the denouement. This latest of the Buster Crabbe series defies the formula.
> There is no misunderstanding between Buster Crabbe and Patti McCarthy who is on hand to supply the romance, and there is no substitute for the secondary theme. This omission produces an unhappy necessity of repetitious action. It is almost entirely a picture of pursuit.[17]

Devil Riders is one of the lesser offerings in an otherwise entertaining series, with a negative cost that exceeded its predecessor, *Blazing Frontier*, by more than $4,000, coming in at $21,650.

The rest of the season's entries demonstrated that the "revitalized" series still had some gas in its engine. Of *Frontier Outlaws*, *The Exhibitor* wrote that "Director Samuel Newfield wisely lets the story worry about itself, concentrating on getting plenty of action and several laughs. This has the ingredients demanded by its patrons…"[18] *Motion Picture Daily* stated that "Sig Neufeld's production makes it a topnotch example of this studio's offerings in the category."[19] *Showmen's Trade Review* added that the "Well-paced direction by Sam Newfield keeps the picture moving, with some extra good outdoor shots adding to the scenic value."[20] *Motion Picture Herald* chimed in with "Sam Newfield, director, has a achieved for producer Sigmund Neufeld a robust, action-filled film that should satisfy Western fans."[21]

Al St. John's increase in screen time was noted by *Film Daily* in its review of *The Drifter*. "Comedy is purveyed by Al 'Fuzzy' St. John who is before the camera so much that 'The Drifter' is more properly a comedy western rather than a western spiked with comedy," an observation that could be made of an increasing number of other entries as well.[22] *The Drifter* has the distinction of being the first in the series where PRC proclaimed Crabbe as "King of the Wild West" in its opening credits.

Thundering Gun Slingers, while not garnering the same level of reviews, climaxes with a genuinely brutal slugfest between Crabbe and Charlie King, the film's chief villain. Crabbe, who plays a far grimmer, revengeful Billy Carson in this film, commented years later on King's apparent strength and physicality, saying that "Charlie was a big man, but he was agile as a cat. He moved like a gazelle. He fought a lot of the movie cowboys and always lost, but I doubt any of them could have whipped him in a real fight. I know I wouldn't have wanted to take him on. He was not only agile; he was very fast for a big man, and as strong as an ox."[23] Evidently, only in the movies can a guy Bob Steele's size whup Charlie King. Oddly enough, Crabbe is back in his black shirt in this one, which leads one to believe that it was filmed earlier as a "Billy the Kid" entry but rebranded later as a "Billy Carson," not that it's of any real importance.

Showmen's Trade Review rated *Valley of Vengeance* "One of the better Buster Crabbe pictures"[24] while *Motion Picture Daily* deemed it "A Western that lives up to the standard set by the capable team of Sigmund Neufeld, producer, and Sam Newfield, director."[25] *Film Daily* singled out St. John's performance, noting that "The comic virtually takes the play away from Buster Crabbe, the star of the show, his antics being good for plenty of laughs."[26] The Hays Office's only quibble about the film as submitted to them resulted in this proviso: "This certificate is issued upon your assurance that you will trim some of the killing from all prints released."[27]

Director Sam Newfield and Al St. John on the set of **The Drifter** (PRC, 1943), Sig Neufeld producer, Sam Newfield director. *Courtesy of Joel Newfield.*

Al St. John's popularity was readily apparent when the title for the season's final entry—*Fuzzy Settles Down*—was chosen. *Independent Film Journal* declared it "One of the best western programmers to come from PRC," adding that "this opus has a good story that builds up a nice combination of fast action and clever corn. Because the dialog [from screenwriter Louise Rousseau] is a bit more natural, the action and comedy appears believable."[28] "Buster Crabbe has considerably less to do," observed *Motion Picture Herald*'s reviewer of St. John's thrust to the forefront in this one, "and spends most of the picture just biding his time."[29]

The initial, pre-approved budget for the season's Crabbe Westerns had been set at $16,000 per film, but was renegotiated to $17,000 per for the final three entries.[30]

While Sigmund Neufeld Productions continued to be PRC's most dependable and prolific supplier of films, a number of other producers provided product as well. Some were one- and two-film pickups, a group that included producers Warwick Ward, James Sloan, Walter C. Mycroft (alone or with Jack Buchanan), John Argyle, William Rowland, and Arthur Ripley, all with one film each; Seymour Nebenzal, Donald C. McKean and Al Herman (Herman directing as well), and Peter Van Duinen, with two films each. Dixon Harwin and Lester Cutler delivered four and five films, respectively. PRC's most productive producer during this period (aside from Alexander-Stern, mentioned in an earlier chapter) was Jack Schwarz. Schwarz (1896-1987), a former Indiana and Kentucky theatre owner, moved into independent production for PRC in 1942, with ten additional films to his credit through the 1943-44 season in addition to the Sam-directed *Danger! Women at Work* and *Tiger Fangs*. Fromkess had dipped his toes into the production waters as well during this period, overseeing Edgar Ulmer's *My Son, the Hero* and *Jive Junction* (December 16, 1943), along with director Joseph H. Lewis's *Minstrel Man* (August 1, 1944). Fromkess would become more deeply involved with production during the 1944-45 and 1945-46 seasons, overseeing another dozen films during that period. The most prolific directors during the 1942-43 and 1943-44 seasons, aside from Ulmer and his five efforts, were Elmer Clifton with six, Al Herman and William Nigh with five each, Oliver Drake with four, and Arthur Dreifuss, Alexis Thurn-Taxis, Wallace Fox, Harry Fraser, and Steve Sekely with another three each. Pikers all, compared to Sam's thirty-two directorial efforts released during this same two-season period.

Sig received a boost of sorts within the industry in October, a boost that must have felt like a validation of his long years as a producer. A month earlier, I.E. Chadwick, president of the Independent Motion Picture Producers' Association (of which Sig was a member in long standing), approached the Academy of Motion Picture Arts and Sciences, citing "the commonality of all producers in participating in war, charity and other non-profit-making activities." While producer membership to date consisted almost solely of those working for the majors, the association had no rule against the inclusion of independents. As a result of Chadwick's request, AMPAS extended the invitation to join to fifteen independent producers, all of whom were admitted to membership on October 5. The fifteen producers included Sig, Leon Fromkess, Sam Katzman, Max Alexander, Peter R. Van Duinen, Arthur Ripley, A.W. Hackel, Edward Finney, I.E. Chadwick, Jack Schwarz, Trem Carr, George Weeks, Scott R. Dunlap, Max King, and Lindsley Parsons. A sixteenth, W. Ray Johnson, was admitted as well.[31]

Now that Sam's contractual responsibilities were limited to the one Western series, his time was freed up to take on some assignments for PRC's other producers. For the 1943-44 season, these included *Tiger Fangs* (September 10, 1943) for producer Jack Schwarz and star Frank Buck, *Harvest Melody* (November 22, 1943) for producer Walter Colmes, and the Buster Crabbe vehicle *The Contender* (May 10, 1944) for Bert Sternbach—whom Sam would frequently refer to as "Mr. Money"—as another of their S&N Productions.[32]

Tiger Fangs starred famous American wild animal hunter and collector Frank Buck, a fifty-nine-year-old celebrity more than a few years past his prime. Perhaps most famous for his published account of his expeditions, *Bring 'Em Back Alive*, Buck had just recently quit the wild animal business and sold his remaining stocks of critters that reportedly included 1,000 monkeys, eleven elephants, a dozen pythons, some tigers, and other four- and two-legged creatures. Buck had recently received word from Singapore, where he had made his headquarters for more than thirty years in what was described as "a handsome and comfortable house, decorated with tiger skins, equipped with electric refrigeration, and suitable for a king." He wasn't happy about what he heard. "Who do you think's living there now?" said Buck to reporter Frederick C. Othman. "It's breaking my heart, a dirty little Jap admiral is living in my house." They didn't mince with words during the war.[33]

Buck interrupted a lecture tour he was giving in the east to make the film,[34] which went before Ira Morgan's cameras on June 21, 1943, and required an atypical eight days to shoot. Within a few days he had managed to wrench his back, and spent the rest of the shoot hobbling around on crutches when not filming a scene. Sam, described as wearing a yellow necktie and a double-breasted coat, looked somewhat out of place in the faux jungle setting, while Buck was described as looking somewhat embarrassed acting with the tamed animals. It would be the last film Buck would star in, aside from a minor role along with Clyde Beatty in director Charles Barton's comedy *Africa Screams* in support of Abbott and Costello six years later.

A past-his-prime Frank Buck is the lackluster star of **Tiger Fangs** (PRC, 1943). Jack Schwarz producer, Sam Newfield director. *Courtesy of Heritage Auctions.*

Tiger Fangs has one of those "timely" war themed plots, and as soon as you see Arno Frey's name in the opening credits' cast list, you know who the bad Nazi is going to be. Buck, playing himself, joins his buddy Duncan Renaldo in a journey to Penang at the bequest of old friend J. Farrell MacDonald. The native workers of MacDonald's rubber plantation are being mauled by wild tigers, tigers the superstitious bunch think are possessed by "Chindock," the evil spirit of men turned into the beasts. Buck meets up with the area's (and modest budget's) assortment of characters: June Duprez, MacDonald's granddaughter and assistant to the plantation's doctor, Arno Frey, a toxicologist and specialist in rare tropical diseases. The nearby Asiatic Animal Export Company's head is the obsequious Dan Seymour, who Buck takes an immediate dislike to: "He smells like a Hun." It turns out that Seymour is an agent of the Reich, having his Japanese lackey Pedro Regas deliver darts loaded with a toxin developed by Frey to drive tigers wild, then unleashing them in the jungle to have their way with the natives. The goal: disrupt the flow of much-needed rubber to the Allies. Buck, of course, figures this all out, and within the film's brief running time. He avoids a blow art delivered by Regas which accidentally kills Frey, and Regas in turn is stabbed by Alex Havier, MacDonald's faithful assistant. Seymour gets squashed by a marauding herd of wild elephants.

This is kiddie stuff, for sure, and it would appear that Buck's anger over that Japanese admiral commandeering his old home in Singapore impacted some of the dialog in Arthur St. Claire's screenplay. When Buck comments on the natives' belief in Chindock, he says "they're positive the Japs, or 'monkey people' as they call them, have possessed the souls of the tigers." While contemporary wartime viewers probably didn't bat an eyelash at lines like that, they jump out at today's viewer. The film's biggest problem, aside from its rather juvenile plot, is the acting. Buck doesn't make a very convincing action figure, overweight and somewhat haggard looking; he tries, but his delivery is uneven and at times outright awkward. June Duprez is a mystery to me given her many starring roles and evident experience on stage. Her belabored, breathy manner of speech is off-putting, delivered ponderously as if on the verge of slumber, coming across at times like an overly winded Katherine Hepburn. Duncan Renaldo doesn't seem overly enthusiastic about his role, and gives a lackluster performance, although *Film Bulletin* thought otherwise, stating that "Duncan Renaldo is the best of several capable players in the cast."[35] Seasoned pro J. Farrell MacDonald, on the other hand, always delivers a relaxed, believable performance, and both Seymour and Frey are allowed free rein to ham it up as the film's two villains. Reviews were mixed, *Film Daily* calling it a "well-handed jungle melodrama with topical theme,"[36] while *Harrisons Reports* dismissed it as "Mediocre program fare."[37] To each his own. The film ended up with a negative cost of $44,472, exclusive of promotion and distribution.

Harvest Melody, in my opinion, fares better. At face value, credited producer Walter Colmes appeared to have had more time, money, and talent on hand for Sam to work with, and the result is a pleasant, admittedly lightweight musical with enough comedy interspersed with the frequent breaks for those musical numbers to maintain the viewers' attention. And make no doubt about it, *Harvest Melody* is first and foremost a musical—okay, it's a propaganda piece as well—cram packed with a dozen interludes provided by Eddie LeBaron and His Orchestra (the "Rajah of Rhumba"), The Radio Rogues, and The Vigilantes, along with the occasional solo and a couple of duets featuring co-stars Rosemary Lane and Johnny Downs. On the random occasions when the actors get to do some acting, big band music frequently serves in the background, resulting in one of the more palatable music scores to be found in a PRC feature.

The paper-thin plot involves the machinations of a down-on-his-luck press agent Sheldon Leonard to reinvigorate the career of his leading client, actress Gilda Parker (Rosemary Lane), equally down on her luck after her contract with Zenith Pictures is not renewed. Leonard gets the idea from his wise-cracking assistant Claire Rochelle:

create a "Back-to-the-Farm" movement to help out at understaffed farms, the nation's "breadbasket" needing support during these lean wartime years. Lane is joined by other "celebrities" that include actress Charlotte Winters and Billy Nelson, a former boxer aspiring to become an actor. At Leonard's urging, Lane manages to break the heart of farm boy Johnny Downs's sweetheart, Marjorie Manners when an affair and marriage proposal is orchestrated between Lane and gullible Downs. After several awkwardly inserted patriotic speeches, those numerous musical interludes, and an overlong and not particularly amusing segment of celebrity impersonations, all ends well. Lane eschews stardom to continue supporting the farm movement, Downs and Manners are reunited, Nelson returns to the ring and emerges as champ, and Lane has a huge film contract awaiting her once the war is over.

Producer Walter Colmes (1916-1988) may have seemed an odd choice to oversee this film, given that it was his first effort in that capacity. At twenty-seven, Colmes had had a surprisingly full and diversified career up to this time. After a stint teaching dramatics and public relations in Boston, Colmes went on to produce musicals and dramatic plays along with radio programs for several national networks. He authored the play "Here's to Happiness" as well, which had a short Broadway run but found a second life on the road. Colmes relocated to Hollywood in 1940 with the motion picture industry his goal. There he established his own publicity agency, served as an actors' agent, and later worked as a Hollywood columnist, most recently in support of Hedda Hopper.[38] PRC must have been sufficiently impressed with his background to offer him his first job as a film producer, the result a decent little time-killing diversion.

Producer Walter Colmes and star Rosemary Lane consult the script with Sam during production of **Harvest Melody** (PRC, 1943), Walter Colmes producer, Sam Newfield director. *Courtesy of Laura Berk.*

The top-notch cast—for PRC at least—helps to carry this film over. Rosemary Lane, having left the industry after her contract with Warners failed to yield any career-making roles, returned to the screen for a short while in films for lesser studios such as Republic, Universal, Columbia, and PRC. Her singing, not surprisingly, is fine given her earlier background as a vocalist for bandleader Fred Waring and His Pennsylvanians, and Downs manages to hold his own in their two duets. The Radio Rogues—Eddie Bartell, Sydney Chatton, and Jimmy Hollywood—are somewhat of a curiosity, here primarily to serve more as a very low wattage comedy team than as a singing group.[39] Sheldon Leonard is a welcome addition to any cast, with smaller roles by the likes of Syd Saylor, Luis Alberni, Marin Sais, and Billy Nelson (who comes across as a sort of poor man's Lionel Stander) all providing solid performances.

Reviews were almost unanimously favorable, praising both the film and its director in terms of the market for which it was intended: "Timely musical with back to the farm setting should satisfy easily. Walter Colmes makes a promising debut as a producer with this timely musical comedy.... Sam Newfield did an excellent job at directing," wrote *Film Daily*.[40] *Motion Picture Daily* declared the film "maintains a steady pace throughout under direction of Sam Newfield,"[41] while *Motion Picture Herald* rated it "a solid entry in its musical class."[42] *Showmen's Trade Review* was most effusive in its piece on the film: "[T]his is a class show and should please all members of the family. The music has an extra attraction for the high school agers. Easily qualified to head the bill in all nabes and subsequents. Will round out a very good bill where it supports an important feature."[43] Oddly enough, exhibitors were less than enthusiastic about the film's performance at their respective theaters. While some wrote in to *Motion Picture Herald*'s "What the Picture Did for Me" with (semi-)positive reactions such as "A very pleasing little show"[44] and "This was slightly above average as a small musical. It has good music and laughs, which are all a feature needs these days,"[45] other exhibitors were outright hostile to the film's performance. "This is the type of picture I like to see down the street at my competitor's house," wrote one sarcastic exhibitor in Michigan,[46] while another complained, "This did not register with my patrons. I had more walkouts on it than I care to repeat."[47] Perhaps the topper came from an irate exhibitor in Minnesota: "I would entitle it Melody of Disaster. One of the biggest mistakes I ever made was to allow this film running time. If you've got it you are due for a fine letdown. It wouldn't even hold up its end of a double bill. Had numerous walkouts and frankly if I paid to see it I would squawk too."[48] Evidently there's no accounting for taste.

Given that producer Walter Colmes was immediately signed to a six-film production deal with Republic after completing this film, it would suggest that his work was viewed favorably within the industry. Having come in with a negative cost of $61,230, *Harvest Melody* ended up with respectable domestic rentals of $134,675, and another $18,347 in foreign receipts thrown in on top.

Colmes had entered into the original agreement with PRC on June 25, 1943, to produce the film on a $45,000 budget, with Joseph Berne proposed as director, Ralph Spence as screenwriter, and songs by Harry Akst and Al Jolson; the tentative cast included Johnny Downs, Wendy Barrie, Vera Vague, George Givot, Cliff Edwards, Maxie Rosenbloom, Harry Barris, and Marjorie Manners (only Downs and Manners would make it into the final cast). Colmes stuck with Ralph Spence to write the screenplay from an original story by Ande Lamb and Martin Mooney, and supplemented Harry Akst with Benny Davis and Leo Shuken for the film's music and lyrics; so much for Al Jolson.

Fromkess had high hopes for the film and Colmes's handling of same:

> If this production comes through with the cast that is listed, it should really make an "A" picture for us. The way Colmes is working this out most of the cast, the Director, writer, and song writers, etc. are performing for a profit sharing participation, and while the budget is for $45,000.00, in reality if all the salaries were paid, the cost would be $100,000.00, so it is quite possible if the picture comes off that we could sell it as one of our SPECIALS in the $75,000.00 bracket.[49]

Fromkess's optimism resulted in the increase of the film's budget to $60,000, with Colmes to receive $2,750 for producing.[50] Fromkess's faith in Colmes's untested abilities turned out to be, in a word, *misguided*.

The reality is that Colmes's involvement in the film's production was somewhat limited. It didn't take long before Colmes realized he was in over his head when it came to actually producing a film, so on August 2, 1943, Walter Colmes Productions entered into a contractual agreement with Sigmund Neufeld Productions, Colmes assigning all rights to the property in return for 50 % of the producer's fee, along with 50 % of the gross profits. Sig in turn entered into a contract to produce the film for PRC on this same day, with the budget remaining at $60,000 and the promised delivery date of October 1, 1943, retained. From this moment on the film became a Sigmund Neufeld Production in all respects except for screen and publicity credit, the film remaining in name only as a "Walter Colmes Production."

Sig dispensed with Colmes's original plans for profit sharing, turned the script over to Allan Gale (who received sole screen credit), and put most of his usual team to work on the film. Salaries were higher on this particular production: Sam received $2,600 for directing; Sig and Colmes split the $2,750 producer's fee; $2,500 covered everyone involved in the story and screenplay; cinematographer James Brown and his two assistants received $1,012 in total; Holbrook Todd and his two cutters another $641; and the cast a total of $17,223, which included a $9,489 entry for "Welfare Workers," suggesting that Sig put a number of unemployed individuals to work as extras and bit players. David Chudnow was brought on board once again as musical supervisor and to compose some additional background music as well, Chudnow and the songwriters accounting for another $5,791 of the film's budget. The film's negative cost came in slightly over budget at $61,230.[51]

Colmes's comparative inexperience as a producer resulted in some financial issues as well, likely a result of those initial profit-sharing plans being terminated. As a result, Colmes was forced to sign over his share of the profits to his Los Angeles-based lawyer, Herbert T. Silverberg.[52] Four years later Silverberg unsuccessfully attempted to sell his interest in the picture to PRC's successor, Eagle-Lion Films.[53] *Harvest Melody* was sufficiently successful, however, with worldwide rentals more than double its initial cost, so Colmes's track record as a newbie producer looked promising, or at least to those unaware of Sig's behind-the-scenes involvement; Republic Pictures took note. Colmes's next film, *Trocadero*, co-starred Lane and Downs and was filmed at the Fine Arts Studio as well,[54] but after the completion of this and five others for Republic (and several others as associate producer), Colmes would oversee his last film in that capacity in 1949. As for Lane, a final Western for Columbia followed *Trocadero* and would serve as Lane's swan song, after which she bid the industry a less than fond farewell.

Sam and Sternbach's *The Contender* provided a decided change of pace for star Buster Crabbe, for once placing him in a straight drama with a story arc that allowed him to display a wide array of emotions. Crabbe's truck driver Gary Farrel needs money to keep his young son (Donald Mayo) in military school, so he trains for a big company prize fight to win the $500 pot. From there he rises through the fighting ranks, his head swelling with each subsequent win and the growing fame that he accrues. When gold digging blonde Julie Gibson gets her claws in him and plays him for a sucker, he loses sight of what is really important to him, becoming an obnoxious boor, ignoring his training, and alienating everyone close to him: his best friend (Glenn Strange), his sports reporter girl Arline Judge, his trainer Milton Kibbee, and his manager Roland Drew. It's a downhill slide from that point on, losing one fight after another. A group confrontation by Mayo, Judge, Strange, and Drew brings him to his senses, and in the happy ending he quits boxing, is reunited with his son, and faces marriage to Judge.

Former professional boxer Jack Roper dwarfs Buster Crabbe in this scene from **The Contender** (PRC, 1944), Bert Sternbach producer, Sam Newfield director.

This is for the most part a good-looking film, budgeted at $37,500 and brought in a few dollars under, and despite the overly familiar storyline succeeds as acceptable entertainment. The fact that Crabbe quits the game rather than making a triumphant comeback is a nice twist from the norm, although the rather abrupt ending is a bit too pat and hard to swallow. The smoke-filled boxing ring arena set is visually convincing, and the fight sequences therein nicely orchestrated by Sam, with sound technical advice from former boxer Art Lasky. The screenplay's trio of writers—George Sayre, Jay Doten, and Raymond Schrock—have provided some bitterly snappy comebacks, and the bit of presenting an oversized hat to Crabbe—so that his swelled head can grow into it—a good one. The cast is uniformly good as well, particularly Glenn Strange in a quietly understated role as Crabbe's buddy. Crabbe's obvious physicality is an asset to this particular role, and he makes the time-constrained transformation from nice guy to unlikable bastard convincing; he even gets to slap his son to the ground! Arline Judge is solid as his sports reporter love interest, and you know right away that Julie Gibson's character is a gold digger since she's the only one consistently showing cleavage. As Crabbe's son, young Donald Mayo is surprisingly effective, with only the occasional inexperienced misstep. The film's lower budget roots are not nearly as evident as usual, apparent only in the several exercise, training, fight, and newspaper headline montages. There are the random inserts of fight scene stock footage that stick out due to their lack of clarity and mismatched speed ("clips from actual fights awkwardly inserted into the continuity" complained *Variety*) which is unfortunate since the ring-based footage shot for the film looks so good.

While far from a great film, *The Contender* isn't a bad one, either, but suffers from its overused storyline. *Motion Picture Daily* liked it more than most reviewers, with kind words for the film's producer-director team: "Strung on a straight story line held taut by tight direction, this melodrama of the prizefight field delivers a plentitude of entertainment in its 63 minutes.... Bert Sternbach produced, getting utmost values from his budget, and Sam Newfield directed tellingly."[55] Other reviews were less charitable.

Roland Drew, Arline Judge, Milton Kibbee, and Glenn Strange confront failing boxer Buster Crabbe in **The Contender** (PRC, 1944).

The film almost didn't get made. Fromkess had fired off a letter to PRC's new general sales manager Leo J. McCarthy in mid-December 1943, stating that "In making up the Release Schedule, will you please eliminate the picture THE CONTENDER as we have to cancel out this production." Fromkess was miffed that his intention of having the film made on a budget of $27,500 had been shot down by Sternbach and Sam, who insisted that it couldn't be made for less than $36,000. "So therefore," continued Fromkess, that's out and we are cancelling the picture. I will have some other picture replace it in about a month or two, therefore, please advise the Exchanges. Frankly, I am just as well satisfied as we would be having Buster Crabbe in too many pictures in too short a time."[56]

So much for digging in his heels: By late January 1944, Fromkess had not only returned *The Contender* to the production schedule, but had upped the budget to $37,500.[57] Whether it was the intervention of Sig, the exchanges and their thwarted expectations, Crabbe's increasing popularity, or some other factor, the reasons for Fromkess's reversal are unknown. Whatever the case, the film got made, and with a negative cost of $36,075, increasing to $37,803 when sound royalties were factored in. With *The Contender*'s completion, S&N Productions was dissolved, with all future receipts for this film and *Queen of Broadway* to be sent to Sternbach and Sam directly.[58]

Aside from Sam's efforts for several of PRC's other producers, his primary function was to serve as brother Sig's on-call director. Sig, however, was increasingly tied up with the day-to-day affairs of PRC and his assistance to Fromkess, so aside from the Crabbe Westerns his personal productions were few and far between. There were two such efforts for the 1943–44 season, the jungle-based "thriller" *Nabonga* (January 25, 1944) and another stab at horror, *The Monster Maker* (April 15, 1944).

Nabonga, which went before cameras from October 27 to November 4, 1943, had numerous tentative titles along the way to the screen, including *Jungle Fury*, *Drums of the Jungle*, *Jungle Terror*, *The Girl and the Gorilla*, and the more descriptive *Nabonga Gorilla*. It really wouldn't have mattered too much which title it had ended up with since the finished film was an exceedingly juvenile affair, clearly aimed at the nose-picking set. Ray Gorman (Buster Crabbe) heads to deepest Africa to recover the jewels stolen years earlier, and to clear the name of his late father, who committed suicide after being wrongly accused of helping the thief, Herbert Rawlinson. Crabbe learns of a feared "White Witch" and the "house" that had fallen out of the sky, and quickly deduces that's where he needs to go. Accompanied by native Prince Modupe, whose life he saves twice before Modupe ends up killed by a gorilla, Crabbe finally tracks down Rawlinson's daughter, played by Julie London. A child at the time of the plane crash that stranded them in the jungle, she's now an attractive young woman. London had befriended "Samson," the gorilla (Ray Corrigan) she had comforted back when she was a child, the beast now serving as her protector. Crabbe is unaware that he has been followed by scheming Barton MacLane and Fifi D'Orsay who want the stolen jewels for themselves. After numerous confrontations that end up with Crabbe badly beaten and MacLane about to make off with the jewels, Samson kills both D'Orsay and MacLane, expiring shortly thereafter from MacLane's gunshots. London, now all alone, agrees to return to America with Crabbe so that he can return the jewels to their rightful owners.

"It is an implausible and confusing story and Crabbe's heroics brought many unintended laughs from the usually indulgent audience at the New York theatre, the Times Square house that specializes in Westerns and scare pictures," wrote *Motion Picture Herald*.[59] *Harrisons Reports* wasn't impressed, either, calling it "A pretty dull jungle melodrama of program grade.... The story is up to the intelligence of ten-year-old children; adults will consider it too ridiculous to take it seriously." Most of the reviews noted the extensive use of jungle-based stock footage intercut with the staged scenes. The back-and-forth shift in image quality is readily—and distractingly—apparent, and there is such an extensive use of it that its acquisition must have put a sizable dent in Sig's $42,500 budget.

PRC's press releases for *Nabonga* were shameless with exaggeration regarding the wild animals featured in the film, stating that "working with animals is always difficult, but working with two huge gorillas, including the huge Nabonga who has the title role, is something else," as if Ray Corrigan's gorilla suit would fool viewers. It went on to add that "Buster Crabbe, star of the picture, had to wrestle with an alligator for one scene in the picture…. The alligator was rather sluggish in the cold morning when the river shots were taken, but nevertheless he managed to give a fairly good account of himself and Crabbe had to call upon all his strength to subdue the thrashing reptile."[60] Right. Given that his ill-suited stunt double is blatantly obvious during his fight scenes with MacLane, would Sig and Sam actually put Crabbe in a river with a live alligator? And if that release didn't stretch credulity far enough:

> One of the most impressive scenes in PRC's 'Nabonga'…is a fight between two gorillas, which one of them is supposed to be killed. The shooting of the sequence of the Sigmund Neufeld Production, was fraught with danger for director Sam Newfield and Crabbe and actors Barton MacLane, Fifi D'Orsay, Julie London and other set workers, should one of the trained beasts have become really angry, the trainers could not have held them in check.

This particular piece went on to add that "The scene had to be a "one take" shot because of the huge strength of the animals."[61] One take, likely, but not for that reason.

Bert Sternbach (second from left) and Nabonga (Ray Corrigan) flank young Jackie Newfield while a slim Sam Newfield (second from right) looks on with some trepidation. From the set of **Nabonga** (PRC, 1944), Sig Neufeld producer, Sam Newfield director.
Courtesy of Tim Neufeld.

Nabonga was seventeen-year-old Julie London's first acting role, and she delivers an adequate performance. "London shows promise for the future," wrote *The Exhibitor*,[62] seconded by *Motion Picture Daily* which wrote that "Miss London, in her film debut, is pleasing."[63] Talent aside, London gives Ann Corio a run for her money in the form-fitting sarong department. (And just where does a girl, living alone in the jungle with her gorilla, acquire a patterned sarong?) D'Orsay, a French-Canadian who had been pigeon-holed in French roles since her debut in *They Had to See Paris* (1929), was now forty and a bit past her prime. She had signed a three-picture deal with PRC,[64] with *Nabonga* her first; Albert Herman's *Delinquent Daughters* and Jack Schwarz's *Dixie Jamboree* would follow later in 1944. Barton MacLane always makes a convincing heavy, and does so here as well. Sam saved a few dollars by casting his young daughter Jackie as London's character as a child, and she delivers a surprisingly nice performance for a novice.

Sig and Sam went way over the film's $30,000 budget, ending up with a negative cost of $40,355. As a result, Sig offered to sell the film outright to PRC for $42,500 and relinquish all future rights to profits, which Fromkess immediately agreed to.[65] Sig may have come to regret that decision, since the film, aside from its silliness, ended up being a hit. Sig announced a sequel titled *White Gorilla*, to be directed by Sam as well and with Buster Crabbe planned as its star.[66] Presumably this ended up released a year later on November 2, 1945, as *White Pongo*, with Richard Fraser in the role originally intended for Crabbe. Just to confuse issues, there was a *White Gorilla* released three months earlier, written and directed by Harry Fraser, produced by Louis Weiss, starring Ray Corrigan, and with a lot of "white gorilla" footage incorporated from a silent film.

Sig and Sam decided to have another go at the horror genre with the effective little chiller *The Monster Maker*—working title *The Devil's Apprentice*—which went into seven days of production on February 7, 1944, with a budget of $37,500, and into release on April 15th. Originally planned as a Jack Schwarz Production, Schwarz had conveyed the rights to Sig back in October 1943. Sig managed to secure the services of a semi-name star as lead, the established character actor J. Carroll Naish, who had achieved an extra iota of fame with his Academy Award nomination the previous year for his supporting role in Columbia's *Sahara*. Working from a screenplay co-written by Pierre Gendron and Fromkess-assistant Martin Mooney, the result, while far from subtle, offered a new and marginally unpleasant twist. Naish plays crazed (of course) Dr. Igor Markoff, who becomes obsessed with pretty Wanda McKay, the spitting image of his dead wife, and daughter of famed pianist Ralph Morgan. Naish makes overtures towards McKay, and when they fail gets pushy about it. Morgan pays Naish a visit to tell him off and gets conked for his efforts. While Morgan is unconscious, Naish injects him with a new serum he has been working on—X-53—which affects Morgan's pituitary glands and introduces the glandular disorder acromegaly, and on the fast track. Soon Morgan's extremities begin to deform, resulting in an inability to play the piano and, for that matter, to be seen in public. Finding out from his reluctant assistant Tala Birell that his new batch—X-54—can reverse the effects of X-53, Naish delivers his ultimatum to Morgan: tell McKay to marry him and be returned to normal, or remain afflicted. Morgan breaks loose of his bonds, they struggle, and Naish is shot dead. Birell delivers the antidote, telling onlookers McKay and her beau Terry Frost that Morgan will be back to normal in no time. And—*Voila!*—there he is giving another piano recital in the very next film-concluding scene.

Naish is adequately unhinged and menacing as Markoff, and it is revealed at one point that he isn't a doctor at all, having killed the real Markoff. And as if that wasn't dastardly enough, he also infected his late, cheating wife Lenore with acromegaly so that no man would ever be attracted to her again, prompting her suicide. Morgan is fine as the tortured pianist, giving the film's best performance and sympathetic in his unpleasant role. His slapdash acromegaly make-up was handled by Maurice Seiderman, who was anything but prolific, his few credits scattered across a number of low budget efforts as well as three marginally more prestigious gigs for Orson Welles: *Citizen Kane* (1941), *Jane Eyre* (1944), and *Touch of Evil* (1958).

A misshapen Ralph Morgan in **The Monster Maker** (PRC, 1944), Sig Neufeld producer, Sam Newfield director. *Courtesy of Heritage Auctions.*

Wanda McKay gives another of her solid performances, and for once gets to wear some expensive looking finery. European actress Tala Birell is convincing as Markoff's assistant, who inexplicably sticks with him because she's in love with him—or at least up to a point; what is suggested, but never made sufficiently clear, is whether Markoff has a hypnotic hold over her. Terry Frost is there for the obligatory younger male lead and to keep each scene filled with cigarette smoke, and Glenn Strange gets to play yet another imposing, muscle bound assistant. For whatever reason, there's also a caged gorilla (Ray Corrigan again) who gets to annoy the lab's dog Ace (Ace, the Wonder Dog!) and escape his cage once to scare Birell, only to be ushered back by Ace; perhaps Sig had worked out a two-for-one deal with Corrigan.

The film looks somewhat slicker than the norm, with effective lighting and camera placement that appears to have been given some time and thought. The sets run from lavish—Lawrence's mansion's interior—to insubstantial—the mansion's exterior entrance. The film's music score—for a rare occasion written for the film rather than pulled from stock—was the work of first-time credited film composer Albert Glasser (1916-1988), then a twenty-eight-year-old who had learned his craft at Warners under Max Steiner and Erich Wolfgang Korngold. He was a fast worker, his talents consigned almost solely to an endless string of B-grade efforts, his body of work over the next three decades resulting in scores for well over a hundred films, including *I Shot Jesse James* (1949), *Invasion U.S.A.* (1952) Ulmer's *Murder is My Beat* (1955), and *High School Confidential!* (1958). Glasser, who was paid a paltry $250 for his score, told B-film aficionado Tom Weaver "I composed, orchestrated, copied, conducted, worked with the music cutter. What the hell? If I didn't want it, they had ten guys waiting. I wanted credit."[67]

Film Daily approved, stating that "Horror fans will find this one right down their cinematic alley" and added that "Sam Newfield turned in a good job directing, and Sigmund Neufeld supplied satisfactory production values."[68]

Escaped gorilla (Ray Corrigan) terrorizes Tala Birell in a superfluous sequence in **The Monster Maker** (PRC, 1944). *Courtesy of Heritage Auctions.*

Chapter 15:
The Entrance of Noir (Sig, Sam, and PRC, Part 5, 1944-1945)

PRC had undergone a shift in leadership at the end of January 1944 when O. Henry Briggs resigned, necessitating a settlement of his contract that was to run through the end of the year.[1] His exit was precipitated "as a result of unreconcilable differences over management policy," reported *Film Daily*.[2] He packed his bags and headed to his Cape Cod estate, leaving the position of presidency vacant, and while there was no immediate successor in line, Fromkess ended up being elected to the long-vacant position in July.[3]

While still in his position as vice-president in charge of production, however, Fromkess had announced back in February that budgets for several of PRC's biggest features for the 1944-45 season would run as high as $300,000, while Western budgets would remain at a stingy (as reported) $17,000 each. As planned, there would be twenty-four features and sixteen Westerns, and producers independent of PRC would contribute about half of the upcoming season's product.[4] Contracts were signed with Sigmund Neufeld Productions for the 1944-45 season to make eight more of the Crabbe-St. John Westerns, along with six features; *Swing Hostess* was to be the first of the latter group.[5] Sig's contract with PRC for the six features stipulated that four of them would have budgets of $45,000, and the other two budgets of $60,000.[6]

Sig Neufeld (sitting center, arms folded) and Leon Fromkess (sitting second from right) pose with distributors and exhibitors circa 1944. *Courtesy of Tim Neufeld.*

Plans had been firmed up somewhat by the time of PRC's fifth annual sales convention held at New York's Essex House in late June. Fromkess presided, while general sales manager Leo J. McCarthy droned on with the specifics. Product for the upcoming season would now be divided into two military themed groups (how's that for supporting the troops?): the "Army" group and the "Navy" group. The Army group had three subdivisions producing films, four "Generals," eight "Colonels," and eight "Majors." The Navy group would consist of four "Admirals," eight "Commanders," and eight "Captains." Titles of most of the films planned for each group were provided.[7] The estimated budget given at this time for the upcoming season's films was $7,385,000.[8]

PRC wanted Sig to continue with the reworked "Billy Carson" series, and why wouldn't they? Crabbe recalled that Sig budgeted the "Billy" Westerns to ensure that they made back their production costs on domestic release, and that the real profits would roll in from foreign release in South America, Italy, and Japan.[9] Sig and Sam could knock out these Westerns in an assembly line fashion by this time, given that their technical crew had, with random exception, remained unchanged since the series began. Along with Sig and Sam and co-stars Crabbe and St. John, production manager Bert Sternbach, editor Holbrook Todd, and cinematographer Jack Greenhalgh and his wartime-dictated replacement Robert Cline served as the nucleus, working from screenplays thrown together by a small, rotating group of writers that included Fred Myton, Joseph O'Donnell, George W. Sayre, and Patricia Harper, supplemented by the occasional wild card. Working together from film-to-film was unusual for the time, but akin to today's production crews for any given television series, working as a unit for six-to-ten months at a time. Sig had a team and enough work that he could keep the team together, or at least during the PRC era. The season's seven released "Billy Carson" entries—*Rustlers' Hideout* (September 2, 1944; filmed for $20,122), *Wild Horse Phantom* (October 28, 1944), *Oath of Vengeance* (December 9, 1944), *His Brother's Ghost* (February 3, 1945), *Shadows of Death* (April 19, 1945), *Gangster's Den* (June 14, 1945), and *Stagecoach Outlaws* (August 17, 1945)—however, were beginning to show their age, with previous plotlines revisited and tweaked with annoying regularity.

Sig Neufeld relaxes at the location of one of his Western productions. *Courtesy of Tim Neufeld.*

Sig's contract with PRC for the 1944-45 season's Crabbe Westerns called for eight films of at least six reels each, with budgets of $20,000 per. Options increased the budgets to $22,500 per for a second year, $25,000 for a third year, and $26,500 for a fourth year. Sig's share of profits remained at 50 % for the U.S. and Canada, but dropped to 70 % for the United Kingdom and 60 % for the rest of the world.[10]

One thing became apparent during the season was the growing popularity of Al St. John's character of Fuzzy Q. Jones. So much so that Sig allowed the writers to beef up St. John's role in some of the films at the expense of Crabbe's. Fortunately for all involved, Crabbe didn't seem to mind—or care; he still received a hefty paycheck either way. The final three films were examples of St. John's increased presence, and how the films benefitted and were reenergized from this altered direction. Regarding *Shadows of Death*, *Motion Picture Daily* wrote that

> Sam Newfield and Sigmund Neufeld present another Western winner. Old slapstick routines are dragged out and dressed up for Al 'Fuzzy' St. John, who does a slick job in his role, which for the first time, allows him to carry the picture practically alone. There is no attempt this time to push Fuzzy in the background in favor of Buster Crabbe, and the results are highly pleasing.[11]

Gangster's Den elicited similar observations, *Motion Picture Daily* stating that "Buster Crabbe, standard hero of the Sigmund Neufeld-Sam Newfield Westerns, takes a back seat in this one while Al (Fuzzy) St. John assumes the task of seeing it through. The veteran comic runs the gamut of routine slapstick, adroitly transplanting Sennett-era gags to the saddle of a horse."[12] One exhibitor, tired of the series itself, reserved a positive comment for St. John: "This is the same as all of Crabbe's. Again Fuzzy saves me from walkouts with his comedy."[13] *Stagecoach Outlaws* received a similar thumbs up: "Al St. John, in charge of comedy, has more and better to do than commonly,"[14] wrote *Motion Picture Herald*. By the time the series' final entry—*Outlaws of the Plains* (September 22, 1946)—was released, St. John's character was the main focus of the film, Crabbe not appearing to utter a single line until the twenty-minute mark, after more than a third of the film had unspooled. Crabbe was by now making $2,500 per film, while St. John earned $758 for *Gangster's Den*.

Reviewers would on occasion include a word or two of praise for Sam's handling of these films. *Motion Picture Herald* acknowledged his contributions to *Shadows of Death*, writing, "The usual blend of exciting action and comic interludes, tempered by Sam Newfield's seasoned direction, gives the film greater entertainment value than the usual production from the Western mill."[15] *Showmen's Trade Review* singled him out for his direction of *Stagecoach Outlaws*, stating that "Direction by Sam Newfield, an old hand with western sagas, keeps the action in the outdoor tenor that fans have a right to expect."[16] That said, there was the occasional review that wasn't nearly so positive, but in most cases they at least acknowledged that his films would entertain those for whom they were really intended, and that he always delivered the goods as far as non-stop action was concerned.

The season's screenplays, with contributions from writers Joe O'Connell, Fred Myton, George Milton, and George Plympton, frequently yielded less-than-enthusiastic reviews due to their growing familiarity. Of *Rustlers' Hideout*, *Motion Picture Daily* wrote "It's a routine story in which the local bankers…scheme to swindle an honest rancher…out of his property by hiring thugs to steal his cattle" while saving some words of praise for Sam's direction: "Under the direction of Sam Newfield, the film maintains a steady pace, the emphasis on the action."[17] Crabbe relayed an amusing anecdote about one of the series' entries in a 1973 letter to Tim Neufeld:

> One day toward 6:00 P.M. when the 10 horses in our posse would go on overtime ($2.50 per horse), Bert whispered to Sam, Sam whispered to me and I said to Fuzzy and the cowboys – "Do what I say in this next scene." We rode fast to the bottom of quite a hill – I raised my arm to halt the guys then said as seriously as I could, without laughing – "Dismount men, It'll be faster on foot." We

dismounted and started up the hill – such was the life of the independent productions.[18]

Cast and crew pose on the set of **Wild Horse Phantom** (PRC, 1944), Sig Neufeld producer, Sam Newfield director. Standing, second from left, middle row: Bert Sternbach, Sam Newfield, Al St. John, unknown woman, Jack Greenhalgh, and Buster Crabbe. Mannie Teitelbaum slouching far left. *Courtesy of Tim Neufeld.*

Wild Horse Phantom was deemed "a routine western, with familiar story and typical performances,"[19] while *Oath of Vengeance* was dismissed with "Possessing a standard plot, this effort is just another western. Action lags in spots, and the production is routine."[20] *His Brother's Ghost*, notable primarily in its total absence of females in its cast, received similar words of dismissal: "This effort follows the well-worn path of the series."[21]

As for the series' sets, ever-cranky *Variety* topped off its lukewarm review of *Stagecoach Outlaws* with a shot at the apparent seediness creeping into the on-screen surroundings, stating that "Sets seem to be wearing out. Maybe PRC ought to get some new ones now that the war is over."[22]

Crabbe didn't hide one of his reasons for sticking with the series, and that was the obvious one: money.

Actors' salaries seem high to the average person, but when you consider that the actor doesn't work a full year, he has to maintain a high living standard, a good part of his salary goes to the income tax man, and the star's career is a comparatively short one, there is no reason to be envious of the movie star's salary. Many once famous players have died in debt or near poverty. I made $12.50 a week in my first job. I started in movies at $100 a week. It seemed like a bonanza, but I soon learned it wasn't for I needed so much more to maintain the high standard of living required from a Hollywood actor.[23]

Crabbe had a comparatively high standard of living, and intended to keep it.

Sam's son Joel was one of the lucky few to be present at one of the location settings when an unplanned, but very exciting incident took place:

We were on location, and evidently there were two companies shooting. I thought it was Corrigan[ville], but it might have been somewhere else. But there was an island...and they were doing a jungle picture and my dad was doing a Western. They had [Johnny] Weissmuller; my dad had [Buster] Crabbe, and both of them being the Olympic swimming champion, you saw this kind of developing. I was pretty young, but I could figure out what was going on. And they started betting on who was better. The thing was to swim out to the island, and back again, and they'd win the pot. And both crews on both sets got involved in betting, and I looked at the two and I thought for sure that Crabbe would win, because he looked fit—he was in good shape—and Weissmuller wasn't—he was kind of flabby. And they went off and, boy, Weissmuller just killed him.[24]

Joel never learned who his father bet on.

Buster Crabbe and Al St. John at odds with Charles King, second from right; Kermit Maynard behind him, in **Oath of Vengeance** (PRC, 1944), Sig Neufeld producer, Sam Newfield director. *Courtesy of Heritage Auctions.*

Reviewer and exhibitor reactions aside, the day-to-day operations seem to have been comparatively pleasant, reasonably conflict-free affairs. According to Sig Jr., his father "got along great with his cast and crew," adding that "everybody worked together constantly; what I'd call a well-oiled machine."[25] Sam's son Joel described his father's temperament on the set, saying that

> He was very easy-going, he never yelled or screamed, got upset with anybody. No matter if the light fell down and almost hit somebody, he wouldn't get upset. It just wasn't in him.... If an actor wanted to try something, fine; he let them. It wasn't like 'No, you can't do that.' Sometimes the actors wanted to embellish their part, and he let them.[26]

A hairy Glenn Strange "terrorizes" (left-to-right) Bert Sternbach, Sam Newfield, Jack Greenhalgh, and two others in this gag shot taken on the set of **The Mad Monster** (PRC, 1942). *Courtesy of Tim Neufeld.*

"I would see [Sam] sitting around talking to the actors before takes and going over things, giving them ideas," recalled Sig Jr. "I think he was pretty good with that, actually."[27]

Sig Jr. described the day-to-day functions of his father, Sam, and Bert Sternbach:

My father was kind of the boss, the producer. He oversaw the things, he worked very much with the writer of the scripts, that was the big thing he did in prepping the scripts, and making sure they could be filmed for the amount of money they were going to spend.... He was very much involved with the casting...and the business aspects of it. Sam was strictly the director. I don't think he paid any attention to producing or anything that went into that. He'd just go to the set and direct; that was his thing. The quicker he'd finish the day's work the quicker he could get out to the racetrack. Bert [Sternbach] was the production manager, and production managers are really kind of involved in running the company, and making sure everything gets done on time, making sure the equipment was all available...and breaking down the scripts and figuring out how many days they're going to need to film the show, and doing all that stuff.... He does so in coordination to some degree with the director, and of course with the producer. But the production manager is really the guy who figures out "Yes, we can do the script for the money and on time," or "No, we can't; it's too over written, we'll go over schedule and over budget; you got to cut it down" or something like that.... It's kind of a producer in training.[28]

Sam's love of gambling was one of the things that brought him closer to the crew, in that they could count on him to conclude most days' work on time. "[Gambling] had an impact on his social life," recalled Sig Jr. "His career was fine, and he always went and did his job as he needed to, but he couldn't wait to get his day's work—that's why he was so fast—he couldn't wait to get the day's work done so he could get to the race track...and catch at least the last race; that I remember vividly."[29] It also provided some barrier-breaking, one-on-one between him and the crew on the way to location shoots. "They frequently had poker games on the bus—instead of him going out in a car, which of course the director generally does—he'd go out on the crew bus in order to get a crap game going on the bus while they were driving to the location."[30]

When Sig Jr. was asked how his father's personality compared with Sam's, he responded:

The differences are easier: My dad was shyer, and Sam was more outgoing. So it worked very well that my dad became the producer and Sam became the director, because you need to be outgoing to be a director, and the producer didn't need to be so outgoing. But he was kind of a shy man. I think he felt a little bit intimidated because he didn't have a great education and all that, but he was dealing with a lot of people who were very well educated. I think that put a little stress on him. That didn't bother Sam at all, he was very outgoing. They both ended up in the right jobs.[31]

Sig Jr. liked that about Sam, liked that he was more "Hollywood" than his father. "My mother's opinion, [Sam] was a spendthrift. But I liked him, I liked the idea. I mean he took the mold of somebody in the motion picture business better than my dad did."[32]

While Sig and Sam would collaborate on the actual production of each film as far as script and logistical considerations were concerned, that collaboration ended at the door to the editing room. Sig, with his lengthy background in editing back at Universal, couldn't keep away from it, while Sam was happy to leave it to Sig.

[Sig] was very much involved with the editing, having come from that background. He would go and spend time in the editing room, going over the [film] with Holbrook, making changes, adjustments, and so forth. He spent a lot of time with him.... Most directors do it, but I don't recall Sam ever doing it. He may have, but I don't think he cared that much about it. My dad would march into it, but [Sam] just left it there.

Gag shot taken on the set of 1942's **Billy the Kid's Smoking Guns**. Left-to-right: Milton Kibbee, Buster Crabbe, Bert Sternbach, Jack Greenhalgh, Sam Newfield, unknown.
Courtesy of Tim Neufeld.

With only the "Billy Carson" as their ongoing commitment to PRC, the brothers were able to undertake two other films as a team, the musical *Swing Hostess* (September 8, 1944) and the comedy *The Kid Sister* (February 6, 1945). Sam would also direct two other films on loan out, *I Accuse My Parents* (November 4, 1944) and *The Lady Confesses* (May 16, 1945), both for Alexander-Stern Productions. There was a trade ad stating that, in addition to *Swing Hostess* and *The Kid Sister*, Sig would also produce "Four Other Features."[33] *Motion Picture Herald* stated that *His Adopted Daughter*, the aforementioned *White Gorilla* (aka *White Pongo*), and four Westerns were in Sig's future,[34] and a later trade ad added *Thirty for Tonight* and *Flying Serpent* into the mix.[35] It's not clear whether *His Adopted Daughter* and *Thirty for Tonight* ever got made and, if so, by whom and under what title.

Back in April 1943, Sig purchased an original story by Louise Rousseau titled "Records for Romance" with the intention of adapting it as a musical comedy.[36] He hired Rousseau and Gail Davenport to write the screenplay, and within a month it was one of twenty-five scripts being readied for production, the biggest backlog of properties in PRC's history.[37] It would be another year before the film was put into pre-production, one that according to reports would "carry one of PRC's biggest budgets." Singer Martha Tilton was hired to star.[38]

Twenty-eight-year-old Texas-born Martha Tilton (1915-2006) was then best known as the popular former lead vocalist on bandleader Benny Goodman's radio show and on his recording "And the Angels Sing," and a later recording artist for Capitol

Records. Known as "Liltin' Martha Tilton," she had made sporadic appearances in features and shorts since 1937, sometimes as a bit player, sometimes as herself, and at other times solely on the film's music track, but for most filmgoers she was known only by her voice. Sig's contract enabled her to showcase her talents and demonstrate that she could act, and make her face known to the film-going public as well.

Singer Martha Tilton looks like she's about to tip over on this lobby card for **Swing Hostess** (PRC, 1944), Sig Neufeld producer, Sam Newfield director. *Courtesy of Heritage Auctions.*

Swing Hostess, as the film came to be known, was released on September 8, 1944, to surprisingly consistent, albeit lukewarm reviews. Most of these spotlighted her pleasant singing and added that she could act as well, while dismissing the story she found herself in as unexceptional. "This is a routine musical," wrote *The Exhibitor*. "Tilton makes a nice impression, and some of the tunes are engaging. Otherwise, this lacks any particular distinction."[39] *Harrisons Reports* offered a similar assessment, stating that "Martha Tilton has a pleasing voice, and some of the songs she sings are catchy tunes. The story is rather lightweight, but it is no worse than the stories used in the majority of program musicals turned out by the larger companies."[40] "The best thing about 'Swing Hostess'," wrote *Motion Picture Herald*, "is its star, Martha Tilton, best known as a singer with Benny Goodman's band and familiar to followers of swing," adding that it had a "hackneyed story."[41] *Photoplay* was right in line: "Martha Tilton, for so long heard on the radio, makes her debut as an actress-singer and proves the adage, seeing is believing, for we believe now Miss Tilton may win her way to a niche of her own in movies…. The story you can skip over lightly…."[42]

They are, of course, correct. An attractive, petite blonde, Tilton has a great voice and holds her own as the film's lead character. Tilton plays aspiring singer Judy Allen, but when her audition record gets mixed up with unpleasant fellow border Betty Brodel's record, it's the latter who lands a contract with lascivious agent Harry Holman, and a primo premiere spot on The Tropic's opening night as lead singer with bandleader Charles Collins's orchestra. In the meantime, Collins and Tilton make cute, Tilton not realizing who Collins is during their initial meetings. Her hard-boiled, wise-cracking buddy, Iris Adrian, and Collins's buddy, Cliff Nazarro, likewise fall for each other. Come opening night, Brodel delivers a disastrous performance. Tilton's fellow boarders, a misfit assemblage of whacky vaudevillians, have learned the truth, however, interceding to whisk Brodel off-stage and interject Tilton as her replacement. She delivers her powerhouse performance, and seals it with a kiss from Collins.

Cliff Nazarro and Charles Collins put in their juke box request in **Swing Hostess** (PRC, 1944). *Courtesy of Heritage Auctions.*

This is lightweight, for sure, but enjoyable nonetheless. Some of the comedy in this wannabe screwball comedy falls curiously flat, and Tilton's fellow rooming house boarders seem more like a by-the-number collection of likeable misfits—Emmett Lynn's scatterbrained Blodgett and Philip Van Zandt's Merlini the Magician among them—still there are enough chuckles here to make for painless viewing. Iris Adrian is all enjoyable tough-talk and bluster, while Nazarro earns the most laughs from his unintelligible double-talk. Porcasi's exasperated nightclub owner is a hoot, and Holman's blonde-obsessed booking agent equally so. Perhaps the film's funniest moment occurs when Blodgett, consistently blocked at the last moment from arriving at the common bathroom on time, finally realizes that every other boarder has just left the building. Rushing up to the bathroom, he grabs the knob—which comes off in his hand. Trust me, it's far funnier than it sounds. On the more serious side, underrated and underused actor Charles Collins delivers a perfectly adequate performance as Tilton's amused bandleader lover-to-be, as does Earle Bruce, a good-looking one-shot wonder who is likeable as Joe Sweeney, the recording employee responsible for coaxing Judy to lay down those initial tracks.

Martha Tilton's oddball fellow rooming house occupants are featured in this lobby card for **Swing Hostess** (PRC, 1944), humorless magician Philip Van Zandt center.
Courtesy of Heritage Auctions.

Aside from Tilton's six numbers, one of the film's pluses is that it has a richer, more lived-in look than the typical PRC output. Sets are solid and convincing, and Sam, who brought the film in at $70,485[43] and received $1,500 for his efforts, makes the most of his (slightly) longer shooting schedule to include more varied camera setups and movement. The screenwriters have tossed in a few throwaway references to the war—audiences had grown weary of them by this time—and there is an interesting look at how the jukebox industry operated circa 1944 for today's otherwise oblivious viewer. It's a perfectly acceptable little film, but as *Photoplay* put it at the closing of its review, "We wouldn't want to see it twice, you understand." Understood.

The Kid Sister went before cameras on October 16, 1944, the finished film going into general release the following February. Screenwriter Fred Myton finally delivered with this one, and Sam stepped up his game with the direction; the result a thoroughly delightful romantic comedy. Twenty-year-old actress Judy Clark, hired based on her performance in PRC's *Minstrel Man*, is a delight in the lead, delivering her rat-a-tat snappy dialog in a voice vaguely reminiscent of Mae West's. As younger sister Joan Hollingsworth, she is forced by her domineering mother (Ruth Robinson) to take a back seat to her older sister, Constance Worth, whom mother thinks should be the first to marry. Ma has set up Worth with wealthy neighbor Roger Pryor, but Clark falls head-over-heels for him, leading to all sorts of hairbrained confusion stemming from Clark's initial posing as a maid to be near him. Throw a ruthless burglar (Frank Jenks) and Clark's childhood friend Richard Byron into the proceedings, and it is one merry mixup after another. By the film's end, Clark manages to capture the burglar, and Pryor's heart as well.

Clark is utterly charming in the lead, and directly responsible for much of the film's success, occasionally breaking the fourth wall to directly address the viewer with her familial complaints. Roger Pryor, while not the most dashing of leading men, handles the light comedy in a confident fashion. Constance Worth is the stereotypically imperious, condescending older sister, while Ruth Robinson hovers over the film as the mother who pig-headedly adheres to "the science of child rearing" gleaned from "Little Ladies and Gentlemen: Child Guidance By Love and Reason" by Matilda Boggs. Smaller roles are nicely handled by Minerva Urecal as Pryor's head housekeeper, and Tom Dugan as an exasperated cop. Sig, evidently pleased with Albert Glasser's score for *The Monster Maker*, brought him back to compose the perky score for this film—pleased, and likely happy to find a competent composer willing to work for a pittance.[44]

Judy Clark, in disguise as a maid, has the neighbors fooled as part of her scheme to be near Roger Pryor in **The Kid Sister** (PRC, 1945), Sig Neufeld producer, Sam Newfield director.

Reviewers were mixed. *Variety*, usually quick to pan PRC's output, called it "an example of a good light comedy done well on a very light budget."[45] *Showmen's Trade Review* called it a "neat little picture" and a "zany comedy" while acknowledging Sam's handling of the film, stating that "Direction by Sam Newfield has the picture moving fast, with plenty of excitement for the spectator."[46] *Film Daily* agreed, saying that "Under the supervision of Sigmund Neufeld and the lively direction of Sam Newfield, the production moves along pleasantly and smoothly."[47] *Motion Picture Herald* gave Myton's screenplay a nod, stating that "There is a quality of freshness about the screenplay…which provides Miss Clark with snappy repartee."[48] *Motion Picture Daily* and *Harrisons Reports* were more reserved in their reviews, calling it "An unpretentious little film of modest proportions"[49] and "Just a minor program comedy."[50] *The Kid Sister* came in with a $45,044 negative cost.

I Accuse My Parents is one of those well-intentioned social commentaries that tries hard and accomplishes its goals, albeit with a healthy dose of suspension of disbelief. Based on a story by Arthur Caesar and adapted for the screen by Harry Fraser and Marjorie Dudley, one needs to subscribe to the idea that the actions of parents are directly and wholly responsible for any negative outcome for their children, no matter the degree of that outcome. Some writers have viewed this film as a forerunner of sorts to Nicholas Ray's *Rebel Without a Cause* (1955), although I'm sure I'm an outlier when I say that I was never overly sympathetic to James Dean's woe-is-me whiner in that one. Regardless, Sam's direction for producer Max Alexander was singled out by *Motion Picture Daily* for mention: "Sam Newfield's direction brings out both emotional and dramatic values."[51] Sam once again received $1,500 for his efforts.

James Wilson (Robert Lowell) inhabits a self-fabricated fantasy world where he lives in the perfect household with the perfect parents—or at least that's the way he presents it to others. In reality, his parents (John Miljan and Vivienne Osborne) spend their waking hours drinking, smoking, gambling, partying and incessantly arguing, the only "love" they show Lowell the repeated doling out of cash with the hope that he'll go away and make his own fun. Lowell gets a job in a shoe store, but his real problems begin when he falls head-over-heels for lovely young Mary Beth Hughes, a singer at the "Paradise" nightclub. "Businessman" (read "crook") George Meeker looks upon Hughes as his girl, and she's too afraid to tell him otherwise. As Hughes's and Lowell's relationship deepens, Meeker woos an oblivious Lowell into a life of crime by having him make pickups and deliveries of packages, the contents of which remain a mystery to the naïve youth. Assigned to drive a pair of hoods to another "pickup," a nightwatchman is shot dead during the ensuing theft, and now the cops are after Lowell, who rented the car used in the heist. He blows town and ends up with the sympathetic owner of a greasy spoon, the first person who has actually taken an active interest in the boy's welfare. Lowell decides to turn in both himself and Meeker, so he calls the cops and confronts Meeker, who is shot dead in a struggle for his pistol. On trial for both robbery and Meeker's death, Lowell tells the judge the above sad story, and for his effort is acquitted of the killing and given a five-year suspended sentence for the robberies, with two years' probation under his parents' custody.

As Jimmy, Robert Lowell gives an impassioned performance, although his not-so-gradual transition from squeaky-clean high school student to heavy-spending, nightclub-hopping lover seems a bit of a stretch, compounded by his blatant naivety regarding the errands he's been running for such exorbitant pay. This was Lowell's first film role, however, and his performance is both sympathetic and sensitive. As his conflicted girl, Mary Beth Hughes was a perfect choice: she can act, sing—three numbers in total—and looks good doing so. John Miljan, Vivienne Osborne, and George Meeker round out a consistently good cast. The film tends to be a bit preachy about its subject, culminating with the judge delivering a closing speech on the "neglect of children," accompanied by the strains of "There's No Place Like Home" on the soundtrack. And while Jimmy's parents look sufficiently contrite after being accused by their son and with the judge's following tongue lashing, one wonders just how pleasant Jimmy's next two years in the custody of his parents will actually turn out to be.

Robert Lowell (right), on trial for murder, faces his hard-partying and neglectful parents, Vivienne Osborne and John Miljan, in this lobby card for **I Accuse My Parents** (PRC, 1944), Alexander Stern producer, Sam Newfield director. *Courtesy of Heritage Auctions.*

Sam's other directorial effort for Alexander-Stern Productions and producer Alfred Stern was the mystery *The Lady Confesses*, a surprisingly satisfactory and taut little murder mystery that succeeds in generating some real suspense towards its conclusion. Mary Beth Hughes was back as the lead, this time as a brunette.

Mary Beth Hughes and Hugh Beaumont's plans to marry are cut short when his wife (Barbara Slater), missing for seven years and thought dead, puts in an appearance at Hughes's home. When she's found strangled to death later that same evening, the list of suspects starts to grow: Hughes, of course, due to the evening's earlier visit from Slater; Beaumont, due to the upsetting of his marriage plans; Edmund MacDonald, manager of the 7-11 nightclub and a secret lover of Slater's since her reappearance weeks earlier; and Claudia Drake, in love with MacDonald and now feeling like the spurned lover. Homicide cop Emmett Vogan doggedly pursues the case, quickly eliminating Hughes who has turned amateur detective and keeps feeding him clues. As for Beaumont, his "perfect alibi" is deemed "too perfect." That Beaumont, with his "perfect alibi," turns out to be the psychopathic murderer comes as no real surprise given the way these films tend to work with intentional misdirection and red herrings galore. His reveal midway through the film helps to add to the suspense, as he adds Drake to his list of victims and makes several attempts on Hughes as well, the last of which is cut short when the cops barge in and shoot him to death.

Hughes is fine in the lead, playing the snoop and fending off lascivious bartender Dewey Robinson's clumsy moves. She's both help and hinderance, however, passing on found info to both Vogan and Beaumont, leading the latter to go after and strangle Drake to death. Beaumont excels in the lead, at first stumbling about as a very convincing drunk, later in his soft-spoken, romantic moments with Hughes, and finally as he topples over the edge into full-psycho mode and attempts to strangle Hughes while they are together on a seaside stroll. MacDonald makes for a good red herring, blatantly refuting Beaumont's alibi, slinking in and out of the nightclub at various times, and just coming across as a rather shady and slimy character in general. As for Vogan, he's your typically persistent detective, and handles the part well. Sam adapts well to the direction of this noirish murder mystery, staging scenes for maximum effect and cutting back and forth in tight closeups during some of the interrogations; Jack Greenhalgh's camerawork and Holbrook Todd's editing both add considerably to the film's overall look and feel. Given its modest ambitions and filmed for $54,500, *The Lady Confesses* is a delightful surprise.

Critics, for once, took notice, and were almost unanimous with their positive reviews, making this Sam's best received film for PRC to date. "This murder mystery...holds interest to the end and is a worthy PRC release," wrote *Film Daily*. "It has been given good direction by Sam Newfield and praiseworthy production guidance by Alfred Stern. The acting is splendid...."[52] *Box Office Digest*, while not quite as effusive with its praise, stated that "'The Lady Confesses' through workmanlike scripting in the mystery formula, crisp direction, and personable trouping, rounds up a satisfactory item on the PRC list.... Sam Newfield's direction extracts all possibilities of the script, and the cast is an excellent selection of troupers."[53] *Variety* agreed: "'The Lady Confesses,' starring Mary Beth Hughes, is likeable mystery melodrama with more twists and turns than a scenic railway, projecting good cast performances and sparked direction by Sam Newfield."[54] Critics took note of Beaumont's convincing turn as the fiancé gone psychopath. "Because of the well-built suspense and the absorbing story, this picture turns out to be one of the better program offerings," wrote *Showmen's Trade Review*. "Its cast is well chosen, with Mary Beth Hughes' performance, under Sam Newfield's able direction, achieving conviction and sincerity. Hugh Beaumont does very well as the psychopathic killer..."[55] *Motion Picture Herald* chimed in that "Hugh Beaumont's portrayal of the killer is of a kind to make his identity familiar to the public later on."[56]

Given the positive critical reaction to *The Lady Confesses* and the acknowledgment that Hugh Beaumont was a star to watch, the film would have a greater impact on the upcoming 1945-46 season's offerings than one might have imagined a mere month before its release. Sig and Sam both took note.

Hugh Beaumont, Mary Beth Hughes, and homicide cop Emmett Vogan in **The Lady Confesses** (PRC, 1945), Alfred Stern producer, Sam Newfield director.

Chapter 16:
Growing Up in Hollywood – Part 2

By the end of the 1944-45 season, Sam's daughter Jackie was twelve years old and son Joel ten. Violet's mother lived with the family, and given that both Sam and Violet worked—she was an uncredited script "girl" on a number of Sam's films during this period—Joel and Jackie's grandmother assumed many of the childrearing responsibilities.

[My mother] came out from the Midwest with my grandmother. First you have to remember my mother and father never raised Jackie and I. My mother's mother raised us. She ran the house, and did the cooking, took care of us, and made sure we went to school; stuff like that, because my mother and father would get up early in the morning, be leaving the house by six and wouldn't get back until eight. We hardly ever saw them.[1]

It didn't help that the family moved around a lot, living in rented dwellings on North Beachwood Drive, North Myers St., South Mansfield Ave., and Maryland Drive over the ten-year period 1935-45. "We had a lot of houses," recalled Joel, "and we moved around and finally settled in Beverly Hills, up in the Canyon area [at 1518 North Beverly Drive]. That was through our high school ages, and then we moved out."[2] There was also a weekend beach house in Malibu that Sam would use on weekends during his more affluent, Beverly Drive years.

Sam at the beach with his kids Jackie (left) and Joel (right), circa 1938. *Courtesy of Laura Berk.*

As with most grownups, Joel's childhood and teenage memories veer to the highpoints, the more mundane, day-to-day experiences somewhat of a hazy blur. Future actor Doug McClure was a fellow high school student, and the two of them were best friends, hanging out in the same group. Buster Crabbe had become a good friend of Sam's by this time, would visit the house on occasion, a big thrill to any kid in Joel's age group. Sig Jr. has fond memories of Crabbe as well: "I knew Buster [Crabbe] quite well. He was a good guy, an outgoing guy. In fact, he taught me how to swim. I learned from the best because he was the world champ in 1931."[3] Sid Melton was also a good friend of Sam's in later years, the two of them bonding during the filming of ten features for Lippert, which will be covered in an upcoming chapter.

One of the things that stuck with Joel was his father's sense of humor. "I remember when I was young and we were going up an elevator and it was kind of crowded, quite a few people, and he started doing a soft shoe dance. And you have to see this guy is kind of short and very heavy—probably 300 pounds and a short guy—doing a soft shoe dance."[4] Sam's sense of humor extended itself to the set as well: "He loved humor on the set. He would disrupt a scene for a joke, to be amusing, to have a laugh," said Joel. He cited an example, which took place during the filming of one of Sam's jungle epics. The natives were instructed to talk among themselves during one of the scenes, and didn't know what to say, or how to say it. Not wanting to waste any time, Sam came up with a solution that likely amused him: he gave them some lines in Yiddish.[5]

Sam's sense of humor would occasionally take an odd turn, such as the running gag they would play on onetime neighbor Edward G. Robinson. "[Robinson] lived at the end of the street," recalled Joel. "We had a dog, a Collie. If you let him loose, he would run away, and he always ran to Edward G. Robinson's house. And so if people were over [we'd] ask 'Do you want to meet Edward G. Robinson?' and we'd just let the dog out, and he'd bring him back."[6] One would imagine that Robinson was not nearly amused by this as the Newfields were. Other stars lived nearby at different times as well, and Joel and Jackie would play with the neighborhood kids. According to Joel, Andy Devine lived next door, and Bing Crosby two doors down.

Joel's memories of his father were mixed, and some of them were colored by Sam's love of gambling.

Stanley Neufeld wields a clapperboard during the production of **The Mad Monster** (PRC, 1942).

As far as the relationship between my dad and I was, I think, pretty strange. Because he was not your normal father. He tried, I mean he took me to a baseball game here and there, but he was all work. And his only fun was gambling. He was nice to us, and he would buy us stuff, but we never really vacationed together or anything like that.... He got most of his ideas from detective magazines. We would go down to Piggly Wiggly in Beverly Hills—he loved ice cream—and he would take his kids and we would go down. We'd get to buy comic books, and he would buy the racing form and the detective stories. From the detective stories he got the plots.[7]

As previously mentioned, Sig's son Stanley's fascination with the industry finally paid off when he was nineteen, serving as the assistant to the production manager on 1942's *Queen of Broadway*, although he served in more menial capacities for some time before this (he appears prominently in a cast and crew photo from 1942's *The Mad Monster*, which was in production in early spring of that year). One of Sam and Bert Sternbach's S&N Productions, *Queen of Broadway*, was produced by Sternbach, but it is reasonably safe to assume that he served as his own, uncredited production manager as well. According to Tim Neufeld, his father Stanley looked up to Bert because his goal was to go into production. Brother Sig, on the other hand, looked up to Sam because his goal was to become a director.[8] Both of them had excellent "teachers" at their fingertips.

Merchant Marine Stanley Neufeld poses with his wife Marie (far right) and (left-to-right) dad Sig Neufeld, Marie's mom Alice Scott, and Stanley's mom Ruth.
Courtesy of Tim Neufeld.

Now twenty-two years of age, Stanley arrived home during the last quarter of 1945 after three years' service in the merchant marines. "[The] last ship I was on came back into San Francisco, and I got off there and said goodbye... I wanted to return to the movies," recalled Stanley. "I really missed it." Stanley and his wife Marie moved in with Stanley's parents for a while before buying a house on Otsego Street in the Valley, eventually ending up by the end of the decade in Sherman Oaks at 4919 Mammoth Avenue.

> I came back in the end of 1945, and I went right to work in the film business. Now I don't know if people understand the film business, but if you're going to go anywhere in it, you gotta give your life to it, and I'm not kidding. At least that's what I did, to make a name for myself, and consequently I was working all the time, day, night, weekends, it didn't matter. I had no other life but making movies, television shows, and so on.... I wanted to be there...but the war came along and I came back, and I went back with my father, and I worked on several films as a Second Assistant [Director] on them, and I was learning more and more and real happy, and then I decided that I wanted to work at a big studio, and I got into the big studio with the help of my dad.

Stanley served as second assistant director of the Buster Crabbe films *Prairie Rustlers* and *Lightning Raiders* before graduating to assistant director to Sam, replacing Sam's long-time assistant Mel De Lay. The "big studio" that Stanley referred to—bigger than PRC, at least—was Columbia. "And I was learning what was happening there, and the first thing they told me, 'Don't sit down or you'll get fired.'"[9]

By 1945, Sig had made Stanley vice-president of Sigmund Neufeld Productions as well, with Sam continuing as secretary and Sig's wife Ruth as treasurer; all four were on the board of directors as well. Production offices were now located at the PRC studios on Santa Monica Boulevard.

Years later, Stanley ruminated about what his war experience had taught him.

> I didn't want to go through anything real, like [the war]. But I learned a lot there because I had to stand up for my position, and I had to know everything that I hadn't worked with. I had one guy that helped me a little bit, and I said, "Well, you know something… you've got to learn what you're doing before you get any respect," and that's… I think it helped me later on in life…. it made me want to be respected. I don't care what they called me or what they said about me, but I want to have a little respect.[10]

Cast and crew pose on the set of **Gangster's Den** (PRC, 945), Sig Neufeld producer, Sam Newfield director. Charles King, third from left, leaning; Jack Greenhalgh two to the right of King, Sam Newfield sitting below him; Buster Crabbe and Al St. John, standing dead center, Stanley Neufeld sitting below Crabbe, his wife Marie to the left of him and Bert Sternbach to the right. *Courtesy of Tim Neufeld.*

Chapter 17:
A Formula That Was Working (Sig, Sam, and PRC, Part 6, 1945-1947)

Fromkess announced plans for the upcoming 1945-46 season at a luncheon held at New York's Hotel Warwick in July 1945. There were to be fifty films—five more than the current season—eight of which would be in color, a first for the studio. Thirty-four features and sixteen Westerns would comprise the fifty, and two of the color films—Jack Schwarz's *The Enchanted Forest* and Robert Emmett's *Song of Old Wyoming*—were already in the can.[1] In addition to the films produced by Fromkess and his associate producers, Martin Mooney, Harry Sauber, and Leon McCarthy, the rest of the films would be handled by the producers and production units of Sig Neufeld, Alexander-Stern, Jack Schwarz, Clarence Greene and Russell Rouse, Sam Sax, Robert Emmett (Tansey), Georgio Curti, Henry Brash and Associated Producers. Neufeld, Schwarz, and Alexander-Stern were all independent producers distributing their product through PRC, while the others were contract producers for the company.[2] The announced fifty features would be produced at a cost of $8,000,000.

Sig's contract for the upcoming 1945-46 season's six non-Western features stipulated a $52,500 budget for each, with the caveat that "If the picture is to be made in color, then the price is to be agreed upon." Three of these were to be "Michael Shayne" mysteries—more on that in a moment—and the other three subjects yet to be chosen. As before, the contract gave PRC's pre-approval for use of Sam as director for any of these films, but went on to say that "if Producer desires to employ other directors, then such other directors shall be subject to the approval of PRC." Sig's profit-sharing for these remained at 50 % for the U.S. and Canada, and 60 % for the rest of the world, but was reduced to 60 % for the United Kingdom.[3]

Sig Neufeld and his wife Ruth bracket son Stanley and his wife Marie outside Sig's bungalow at PRC. *Courtesy of Tim Neufeld.*

Expansion plans were in the works as well, predicated on the availability of construction materials over the following six months. A new four-story administration building was planned to house executives, writers, the publicity department, makeup, commissary, and all other departments then scattered throughout the lot in a number of bungalows.[4] Sig had finally moved into his new, private digs at PRC's Santa Monica Boulevard studios by this time, one of those soon-to-be-eliminated bungalows. "Sigmund Neufeld Productions" read the sign that Sig had hung over its front door. "There were different bungalows for different production companies," recalled Sig Jr.,

> but dad, being the main money, had the biggest bungalow, outside of the main building, which is where you came in and out of. It was simple: you walked in, you had a place where the secretary would be sitting, and then you had an office on each side of the building; one was for dad and the production company, and the other was for Sternbach and that group. So it was basically like two offices with a secretary sitting in the middle.[5]

Once the administration building was completed, however, the bungalows would all be eliminated—Sig's included—making space for two new sound stages.[6]

Despite Fromkess's plans for PRC's future, there was growing internal conflict within the company between Fromkess and the members of the Young family. Unfortunately for Fromkess, PRC's financial backing stemmed from the Robert R. Young interests. Young, chairman of the board of Pathé Industries and heavily invested in the railroad industry, wielded considerable influence over PRC and its operations. Brothers Kenneth M. Young and John S. Young were co-owners of Pathé Film Laboratories, but Kenneth had a say in the day-to-day matters at PRC as well, having become chairman of the board of directors of PRC back in 1942. Things came to a head in August, and Fromkess submitted his resignation on the 27th, effective immediately, citing the standard "differences of opinion regarding the future operations of the company." Red Kann, writer of *Motion Picture Daily*'s "Insider's Outlook" column, explained:

> Leon Fromkess' break with PRC was not unexpected. He had considered withdrawing on several earlier occasions because of inability to reconcile the future with that of the Young interests which control the company. Fromkess had been stepping up negative costs on an increasing number of pictures. His theory—and correct—was termination of the war would place a greater demand on quality, not quantity. The Youngs did not agree. Fromkess refused to give ground. That's why he stepped out.[7]

Sounds reasonable, but somewhat at odds with Kenneth Young's comments to trade reporters a year earlier, having stated that the Young interests would make PRC a top company if they had to spend "$25 million to do so." Regardless, Fromkess was now out, joined by Ben Schwalb, executive producer, Harry Sauber, producer, and Don McElwaine, director of advertising and publicity.[8] Production matters previously handled by Fromkess were turned over to Reeves Espy, now the new vice-president in charge of production. Kenneth Young succeeded Fromkess as president, and to keep things in the family, Raymond E. Young—the studio's business manager for the past six months—was appointed general studio manager.[9] *Film Bulletin* commented on the upheaval at the studio following Fromkess's resignation:

Following this came word that the entire foreign department, headed by Robert Socas, had resigned…. The move put production virtually at a standstill with no one certain of what course might be taken…. [It] is hoped that whatever the cause for such a blanket walk-out has been removed. The studio started out with high promises about product and distribution but the difficulties seemed to have mounted much faster than did the product. The quality of production has been under par, even for independent product and undoubtedly the rift was caused in part by sales staff protests about selling inferior material. However, the company, which is a subsidiary of Pathé Industries, Inc., will undoubtedly right its problems since there is money for the purpose.[10]

Kenneth didn't remain as president for long, however. Within three months Harry H. Thomas was elected president and Lloyd Lind vice-president. By January 1946, PRC's revised plans were "to make one or two biggies a year itself and to handle the product of loners using studio facilities," reported *Variety*. "On the lot at present are Sig Neufeld, Jack Schwartz [*sic*], S-N Productions and Alexander Stern."[11] By February, production at the studio was pretty much at a standstill, a situation attributed to the extensive renovations taking place. By April, however, when only *Queen of Burlesque* was filming at the studio, it was reported that "None of the nebulous expansion plans hinted at some months ago seem to be assuming reality at this point, although the studio heads maintain there is progress afoot."[12]

The core team of Sigmund Neufeld Productions, circa 1945. Left-to-right: Bert Sternbach, production manager; Sam Newfield, director; Sig Neufeld, producer; and Jack Greenhalgh, cinematographer. *Courtesy of Tim Neufeld.*

During this period of flux—and aside from Buster Crabbe's "Billy Carson" series—Sig and Sam had already completed two of their three other features that would be released during the upcoming season, with the third currently in production. The murder mystery *Apology for Murder* had been filmed back in March under the working title *Highway to Hell*, and would go into release on September 27, 1945. *White Pongo* had been shot in April under the tentative title *Congo Pongo*, and would go into release on November 2, 1945. *The Flying Serpent*, one final stab at the horror genre, began shooting in mid-August, and would go into release the following year on February 20, 1946. By November, however, PRC's production unit was at a complete standstill. There was a new series yet to be started by Sigmund Neufeld Productions—a decided change of pace for the brothers—which will be discussed later in this chapter.

Derivation aside and taken at face value, *Apology for Murder* is a slickly stylish film noir that delivers the goods. Sig's core team of Sam, Fred Myton, Jack Greenhalgh, Holbrook Todd, and Bert Sternbach deliver their best work to date for this film, aided by an atypically—for PRC at least—good score by Leo Erdody. It's a handsome film, stylishly lit and filmed by Greenhalgh, with solid acting from leads Hugh Beaumont and Ann Savage, backed by a capable cast that included Russell Hicks, Charles Brown, Pierre Watkin, and Sarah Padden. Sam's direction matches the mood of the film perfectly, the climactic three-way shootout viscerally satisfying in its violent execution. That said, the film is a blatantly shameless reworking of Billy Wilder's classic *Double Indemnity* (1944), released by Paramount less than a year earlier to much success. According to Edgar Ulmer, *Apology for Murder* was originally titled *Single Indemnity*, but the threat of a suit by Paramount over the similarity of the title to their Barbara Stanwyck-Fred MacMurray thriller prompted the title change. "At the beginning of the season," claimed Ulmer,

> Fromkess would sit down with me and Neufeld and we would invent forty-eight titles. We didn't have stories yet—they had to be written to fit the cockeyed titles.... I knew nothing was impossible. When *Double Indemnity* came out and was a huge success, I wrote a picture for Neufeld which we called *Single Indemnity*. We were able to write that junk in about two weeks.[13]

Fred Myton is credited with both the original story and screenplay,[14] so if Ulmer actually had anything to do at any point with the "writing" of *Apology for Murder*, it has been lost to time. Forget about its roots, however, and the film stands solidly on its own as an engaging little thriller.

Reviews were mixed, several of them commenting on the film's similarity to *Double Indemnity*. *Motion Picture Herald* called it "a melodrama in the style of Paramount's 'Double Indemnity,' which this picture closely resembles in plot, characterization and technique."[15] *Motion Picture Daily* praised the film, and in words echoing the *Herald*'s review, stated that "Producer Sigmund Neufeld and director Sam Newfield, well known for their excellent Western pictures, have ventured into the field of melodrama, and come up with a tightly-knit, suspenseful feature which bears a close resemblance in story, characterization and technique to Paramount's successful 'Double Indemnity.'"[16] *Variety* was more balanced in its review, but commented on the "neat direction by Sam Newfield."[17] Sam received $1,500 for his efforts, and Sig another $2,250 for producing.[18]

Paramount was quick to note the released film's similarities to *Double Indemnity* as well, and the possibility—a remote possibility, admittedly—that this minor upstart might have some sort of impact on any future second run releases of their film. Paramount's lawyers contacted PRC and demanded that the film be withdrawn from release until after a two-year period from *Double Indemnity*'s April 24, 1944, release had elapsed. Not wishing to go head-to-head with a firm of Paramount's size and clout, PRC quickly rolled over and acquiesced to Paramount's demands. After contacting its distribution exchanges and demanding that all prints must be returned to Pathe's Bound Brook, New Jersey facilities "at the earliest possible moment," PRC went on to emphasize that "It is extremely important that this picture is taken out of circulation with all possible haste." PRC then dashed of a letter to Paramount:

> We agree that until April 30th, 1946, we will not distribute "Apology for Murder" in the United States, except in first run and subsequent run situations in the cities discussed with you in which we had theretofore exhibited this film. We also agree that until April 30, 1946, no further exhibitions will be taken in Louellen, Kentucky and San Diego, California.
>
> We have issued firm instructions to our independent foreign distributors to withhold distribution of this picture in their territory until March 31st, 1947.
>
> In sending you this letter, we do not admit the commission of any infringement of any rights which you have asserted. We have entered into this amicable arrangement in order to continue to maintain a friendly association between our companies and their associates.[19]

Conflict resolved.

Hugh Beaumont and Ann Savage, his two-timing partner in crime in **Apology for Murder** (PRC, 1945).

Apology for Murder's dark plot follows *Daily Tribune* reporter Kenny Blake (Hugh Beaumont), who falls hopelessly in love with Ann Savage, the wife of wealthy, and much older, Russell Hicks. Savage, who is evidently quite good at seduction, uses her feminine wiles to convince Beaumont that her husband plans to dump her without a cent, and that they should murder him via a faked "accident" before he can do so. Beaumont bludgeons Hicks and the two push his car off a cliff, but police lieutenant George Sherwood quickly susses out that it was a murder, not an accident. Kirkland's business associate Pierre Watkin is judged guilty of the crime on purely circumstantial evidence, and sentenced to be executed. Beaumont is plagued with guilt over this turn of events, but when he finds that Savage has played him for a sap and dumped him for slimy lawyer Norman Willis, he loses it. Confronting the two, Savage shoots and wounds Beaumont, who in turn shoots both Willis and Savage dead. Mortally wounded, Beaumont manages to make it back to the newspaper and type out a story for the lead, "'Murderer Confesses' by Kenny Blake." City editor Charles D. Brown, who has been conducting his own investigation into the murder, accepts Beaumont's "confession" before the reporter drops dead at his feet.

Apology for Murder's lower budget[20] underpinnings are barely in evidence, only noticeable in the occasional "exterior" filmed in front of a hazy rear projection, the plunge of deceased Kirkland's auto occurring off-screen and only heard but not seen, and in the breathless jumps from one scene to the next to pack a lot of story into the film's brief sixty-six[21] minute running time. Beaumont gives a convincing performance as we witness his rapid descent from a personable but hard-drinking and flirtatious reporter to a reluctantly scheming murderer, and eventual cold-blooded killer of his earlier love interest. Twenty-four-year-old Ann Savage was an excellent choice as the conniving wife, a blatant tease and sexy in a superficial sort of way; "good looking gams" comments a paper's photographer regarding the legs she has taken pains to show off. Twisting Blake to her perverted will, she fluctuates between needy and cold-hearted in a performance suggestive of her more famous one to follow in Edgar Ulmer's now-"classic" *Detour*, the second in Savage's two-picture contract for PRC, which went into production four months later. If you get to watch this film, put aside any fond memories you may have of Beaumont's "Ward Cleaver;" the characters are worlds apart.

"Good looking gams" comments a newspaper's photographer regarding the legs she has taken pains to show off, from **Apology for Murder** (PRC, 1945). Hugh Beaumont seems to be checking them out as well.

Leo Wald Erdody (1888-1949), the film's prolific composer, was born in Chicago to Hungarian parents. Erdody is most likely remembered today—if at all—for his collaborations with director and good friend Edgar G. Ulmer at PRC. After a musical education and training in Berlin, Erdody returned to the states and established a reputation of sorts as a writer of songs such as "Only a Song," "My Dream Rose," "A Garden By the Sea," and "Senorita Chula," his "A Little Song" (among others) peddled by New York music publisher C. Schirmer, Inc. for sale to accompany showings of Metro's *A Man and His Soul*.[22] In the years that followed, Erdody organized the New York-based dance band Erdody and His Famous Orchestra, and by the mid-1930s was appointed musical director of World Broadcasting System, a transcription service offering pre-recorded music to more than 150 radio stations nationwide via series recorded by Leo Erdody and the World Symphony Orchestra.[23] Hollywood eventually beckoned, Erdody becoming active in the independent film industry from 1941 up until his death in 1949 at age sixty of arteriosclerosis.[24] Erdody served as composer and/or musical director for Sig and Sam from 1942, on films that included *Overland Stagecoach*, *Queen of Broadway*, *Dead Men Walk*, *Apology for Murder*, *White Pongo*, *The Flying Serpent*, *Larceny in Her Heart*, *Gas House Kids*, *Money Madness*, and 1948's *Miraculous Journey*, his final effort before his death. Erdody, it should be noted, was responsible for PRC's sole Academy Award nomination when both he and Ferde Grofe were thus honored in 1944 for their musical score for Ulmer's film *Minstrel Man*.

"A Beast with Human Instincts!" all of which seem to be directed to young ladies in distress. Lobby card for **White Pongo** (PRC, 1945), Sig Neufeld producer, Sam Newfield director. *Courtesy of Heritage Auctions.*

I won't say that *White Pongo* is terrible since it boasts a whole lot of unintended laughs, but it is pretty bad. The paper-thin story focuses on an expedition to Africa to track down the "White Pongo," a white gorilla believed to be the missing link between man and monkey, possessing human-like intelligence. After interminable stretches of canoe trips down rivers, treks through the jungle, and oodles of stock wildlife footage intercut willy-nilly, a mutiny by head guide (and gold-hungry) Al Eben—you know he's a bad guy since it's 1945 and he's a German—and a laughable climactic fight between Pongo and a brunette gorilla, Pongo is captured and caged for a trip back to London. Despite all that stock footage,[25] the film still cost a surprising $67,811 to produce, well over its $60,000 budget.

The cast—chock full of bad British accents—includes Gordon Richards as Royal Society of Explorers expedition head Sir Harry Bragdon. Maris Wrixon co-stars as his vacuous daughter, seemingly along solely to incite jealousy and fistfights among the two smitten by her, taciturn guard Richard Fraser, and Richards's hot-headed personal secretary, Michael Dyne. Dyne, who in a fit of pique hooks up with Eben, gets shot in the back for what turned out to be an unfortunate decision. An uncredited Ray Corrigan dons a gorilla suit once again—this one an expressionless shaggy white one—as White Pongo, spending most of the film hopping about in the perimeter, grunting and beating his chest and displaying not one iota of that "human intelligence" he was earlier credited with. He does appear to have some "human lust,' however, carrying an unconscious Wrixon back to his lair instead of killing her, as he has done to every other human with the bad timing to cross his path. The standout performance is given by sexagenarian actor Egon Brecher as the aged survivor of a much earlier expedition who now lives among the natives. The expedition's head porter, played by African American actor Joel Fluellen, is named "Mumbo Jumbo," which pretty much tells you all you need to know about this film. That is, of course, unless you are a ten-year-old, in which case you may like it.

"The picture was shot in Santa Ana," recalled Wrixon. "I was under contract to Warner Brothers at the time. We worked night for day and summer for winter. We shot White Pongo in a week. We never even saw a makeup person. I also remember that Rod Cameron was in the ape costume."[26] Wrixon went on to add that "The picture is etched in my memory because President Roosevelt died when we were shooting. All others closed down. We were the only studio that continued shooting."[27]

At least *The Flying Serpent* offers something different in the way of horror films, providing an all-new creature with some historical context. Original story and screenwriter John T. Neville, who loosely reworked the plot of his earlier *The Devil Bat*, wove a tale around the ancient Aztec god Quetzalcoatl, a feathered serpent who, according to the *Encyclopedia Britannica*, with "his companion Xolotl, a dog-headed god, he was said to have descended to the underground hell of Mictlan to gather the bones of the ancient dead. Those bones he anointed with his own blood, giving birth to the men who inhabit the present universe."[28] Now *that* would have made for an interesting movie!

For this film, Quetzalcoatl was given the ability to fly, although it's questionable whether the Aztec's version had that ability as well, or simply used its feathers for show. According to the film's simplistic plotline, Dr. Andrew Forbes (George Zucco), discoverer of the hidden treasure of Montezuma in a cave near Azteca, New Mexico, has caged the treasure's guardian, Quetzalcoatl, for safe keeping. Having discovered that Quetzy will kill to retrieve one of its feathers—a lesson learned the hard way by Zucco's now-deceased wife—Zucco now utilizes Quetzy as an instrument of death against anyone with the poor judgment of approaching the cave. Three earlier-dispatched victims are soon joined by Henry Hall's sheriff, investigating those deaths, and Wheaton Chambers's ornithologist, drawn to the cave by an article written by James Metcalfe.

Famed pipe-smoking mystery writer Ralph Lewis is sent to the area to investigate and deliver daily radio reports on his findings, before exposing Zucco and his mad scheme. Crime doesn't pay, of course, and Zucco becomes Quetzy's final victim (why doesn't he just drop the damned feather? He should know better by now) before Quetzy is shot dead. Hope Kramer plays Zucco's step daughter and the film's requisite love interest, with Terry Frost along as a treasure hunter who is one of Quetzy's lucky survivors.

Filmed over an eight-day schedule beginning August 17, 1945, this is a rather routine horror film despite the comparative novelty of the flying serpent.[29] Quetzalcoatl itself is a rather nicely articulated puppet—courtesy of Ray Mercer & Company—that looks reasonably convincing while in flight despite the visibility of the guiding wires and its rather silly design, wings merrily flapping. Several of its attacks are handled nicely by Sam, the serpent flying directly at the camera from a distance, a cut just before it arrives and connects with its intended victim (and collides with the camera). Sam used his "Sherman Scott" alias in the credits for this film, and while one might assume that he did so to distance this sort of film from his more adult features, that would not explain why he allowed his real name to be used on such dreck as *White Pongo*. Sig spent a few extra dollars of the film's $48,887 cost on an artist to paint three separate matte paintings of various Aztec temples and ruins in the distance, with cars arriving and departing in the foreground. Sam—or perhaps editor Holbrook Todd in an effort to pad and stretch the running time—reuses these mattes far too many times, two of them five times each and the third two times. That said, they are rather impressive for a PRC effort, and provide the film with a modicum of class. Zucco, as usual, plays his typical over-the-top deranged archeologist, even getting to spew the lines "It's mine! It's all mine!" as he drools over the hidden treasure in his step daughter's presence, it slowly dawning on her that she's his next intended victim. The rest of the cast tries to work with what they were given, but Hope Kramer is saddled with the familiar role of good-girl relation to an older bad-guy. As the mystery writer turned sleuth, Lewis is okay. *The Flying Serpent* gets by on novelty and that trio of matte paintings, but that's slim recommendation.

PRC's concept of the Aztec god Quetzalcoatl, aka **The Flying Serpent** (PRC, 1946), Sig Neufeld producer, Sam Newfield director.

For this, Sig paid himself $2,250, Sam another $2,000 for direction, Neville $1,450 for his rather sophomoric script, Zucco $2,000 to ham it up on screen, Greenhalgh $603 for his camera work, Leo Erdody $1,428 for his score, Ray Mercer $2,518 for his not-so-special effects, and Roy Loggins $142 to feed cast and crew while on location at the Iverson Ranch (another $325).[30]

Al St. John, Buster Crabbe, and sheriff Budd Buster prevent a stabbing in **Lightning Raiders** (PRC, 1946), Sig Neufeld producer, Sam Newfield director.

Buster Crabbe was still under contract to Sigmund Neufeld Productions, but his contributions were now reduced solely to the "Billy Carson" Westerns. There were a final ten entries in the series, the final film's release spilling into the first month of the 1946-47 season. The films were *Border Badmen* (October 10, 1945; filmed for $21,094), *Fighting Bill Carson* (October 31, 1945; filmed for $20,090), *Prairie Rustlers* (November 7, 1945; the sole film in production in mid-September at the height of the fallout from Fromkess's resignation, filmed at the Corrigan Ranch for $23,304), *Lightning Raiders* (January 7, 1946; filmed for $23,349), *Gentlemen with Guns* (March 27, 1946; filmed for $22,671), *Ghost of Hidden Valley* (June 3, 1946), *Prairie Badmen* (July 17, 1946), *Terrors on Horseback* (August 14, 1946), *Overland Riders* (August 21, 1946), and the series' final release, *Outlaws of the Plains* (September 22, 1946). St. John was prominently featured in these final entries, his newly arrived mail order bride-to-be a source of considerable jealousy in *Gentlemen with Guns*, and the murder of his niece affording St. John one of his rare onscreen opportunities to display genuine emotion in *Terrors on Horseback*. These films were thrown together and filmed at such a hectic pace that *Film Bulletin* complained about them in their ongoing "Studio Size-Ups" column where they attempted to give updates on each studio's forthcoming films:

Only one feature in work this week and that a Buster Crabbe film titled at the moment "No. 8." These Crabbe features are made so fast and with so little preparation that even an accurate chart like FILM BULLETIN'S Production and Release Record misses one, now and then. Titles change quickly, since they all start without them. Story facts are not available until the picture is finished. Sometimes we wonder if even the PRC people know the current title of a Crabbe film at any given hour during the day. They are "quickies" in the truest sense.[31]

Budd Buster, Al St. John, George Chesebro, Frank Ellis, Buster Crabbe, and Steve Darrell in a posed shot not to be found in **Gentlemen With Guns** (PRC, 1946), Sig Neufeld producer, Sam Newfield director. *Courtesy of Tim Neufeld.*

Crabbe had grown weary of the films, of their reduced budgets and the shortened shooting time resulting from those cuts,[32] which led to the end of his association with Sig.

First we did them in fourteen, sixteen days. When the unions got stronger—more money for the grips, more money for the cameramen, whatever—in order to counteract that, we were shooting in twelve, ten, then eight days. My last western of the series was done starting on Monday and then Thursday night we wrapped the damned thing up. That's when I marched into [Sig's] office and said, that's it, no more westerns for me. That's when they got Lash Larue to come in."[33]

The screenplay for *Outlaws of the Plains* included a throwaway dig at the unions. When communication between fortune teller Fuzzy Q. Jones and bogus Indian spirit guide "Standing Pine" is abruptly cut short by the latter, Fuzzy mumbles "I wonder if he belongs to a union?"

With Crabbe's departure from the series, Al "Lash" LaRue was signed to a seven-year (as reported) contract by PRC. It was rumored that Sig was to produce this new series of Westerns as well,[34] but it was just that—a rumor.

The production records for *Ghost of Hidden Valley* provide an idea of what Sig and Sam had to work with. According to the records,[35] the film was budgeted at $22,500 and shot over a six-day period, coming in slightly over budget at $25,578. Crabbe's cut was $3,000, while popular sidekick Al St. John received $1,000. Sig received $1,200 as producer, while Sam received $1,250 for directing. Screenwriter Ellen Coyle received the standard flat rate of $1,000 during this period. The remainder—$18,128—went towards the supporting cast— Jean Carlin ($125), John Meredith ($227), Charles King ($175), Jimmy Aubrey ($155!), John L. Cason ($150), Zon Murray ($118), and others— as well as the technical crew—cinematographer Jack Greenhalgh ($1,038, which includes his assistants), editor Holbrook Todd ($581), production manager Bert Sternbach ($645), and many others (including Stanley Neufeld as second assistant director; $368). Sam fared well when you compare these costs to those of Westerns made at another studio, for example the Rod Cameron Westerns for Universal. While the budgets for Universal's Westerns made some months earlier—*Boss of Boom Town*, *Trigger Trail*, *Riders of the Santa Fe*, and *Beyond the Pecos*—ranged between a low of $54,625 and a high of $55,300, the director fees were all less than Sam was receiving—$1,000 for Ray Taylor and Lew Collins, and $1,050 for Wallace Fox and Lambert Hillyer. When considered as a portion of the total budget, however—roughly 5½ %—not only does it demonstrate how well Sam was making out salary wise, but how little was left over for everything else involved in the making of the film. Actor Jimmy Lydon, the lead in Edgar Ulmer's *Strange Illusion* (1945), made this analogous observation about the budgets at PRC: "You didn't fit the shoe to the foot. You fit the foot to the shoe. You made the budget first, and then you made the picture fit into the budget."[36]

Frank Ellis and Steve Darrell have Al St. John in an uncomfortable spot in this gag shot taken during the production of **Gentlemen With Guns** (PRC, 1946). *Courtesy of Tim Neufeld.*

One of St. John's lighter moments in **Terrors on Horseback** (PRC, 1946), Sig Neufeld producer, Sam Newfield director. *Courtesy of Heritage Auctions.*

Some of those "stronger" union issues that Crabbe alluded to were detailed at a Congressional hearing conducted by Rep. Carroll D. Kearns, chairman of a House of Representatives subcommittee investigating union practices. "Unless we get protection from Congress, we are finished" testified I.E. Chadwick, president of the Independent Motion Picture Producers' Association, regarding the impact that union "featherbedding" and other impositions were having on the IMPPA's twenty-nine small studio members. Chadwick claimed that fifteen members had already been put out of business and that fifty films had been lost to production, a "lessening of production with consequent increase in unemployment." The committee's Counsel Irving G. McCann asked Chadwick if there were union members sitting around at the IMPPA's various studios "drawing pay and doing nothing?" After answering in the affirmative, Chadwick went on to say that "Members of our association have considerable featherbedding...practically every union group tells you how many men you must employ." Chadwick cited an example, saying that up until September 1946 the small producer of Western pictures was required to use eight members of the Musicians' Union at $30 each. Bad enough, but now that same producer was required to employ a twenty-one-man group of union musicians on an annual basis of $6,900 each, and permitted to use them for a maximum 520 hours.[37] Assuming that these same—or similar—requirements were imposed on Sigmund Neufeld Productions, it's little wonder that much of each film's budget was being frittered away on non-essential employees.

Crabbe was pragmatic about his career in film, and what the future might hold for him. "Movies are strictly a business with me. I know that the life of the average movie star is ten years. That's why I would like to be a character actor—they last much longer.

And I would rather be the villain than the hero. I can be much nastier than nice. I would rather have the audiences hiss at me."[38] Little did he realize that he and Sam would work together in short order—if only briefly—and once again a decade later in the arena of television production.

Al St. John and Buster Crabbe in yet another fight, while Kermit Maynard looks on in **Prairie Badmen** (PRC, 1946), Sig Neufeld producer, Sam Newfield director.

If Crabbe thought he was finished with the "Billy" series, however, he was wrong. PRC decided to take some of the best of the earlier "Billy the Kid" Westerns, cut them down to forty-minute lengths, tweak and retitle them—the recuts budgeted at a surprisingly high $4,000 per film[39]—and reissue them in 1947 to plug some holes in the release schedule. Among these, *The Mysterious Rider* became *Panhandle Trail*, *Fugitive of the Plains* became *Raiders of Red Rock*, *Western Cyclone* became *Frontier Fighters*, and *The Renegade* became *Code of the Plains*.[40] These reissues proved to be a thorn in Sig's side since the cost of retooling them had a negative impact on future revenues derived from each. Sig dashed a letter off to Eagle-Lion Films, Inc. on December 18, 1948, "requesting a complete detailed explanation and accounting of the charges for negative reconstruction," but didn't hear back from them. On January 3, 1949, Sig's lawyer, Emil K. Ellis, sent a more strongly worded letter to Pathe Industries, Inc. regarding this issue, and cc'd Eagle-Lion Films, Inc.[41] An eventual response briefly citing "Negative Cutting Charges," "Negative Cost," and "Adjustment of Producer's Costs and Overhead"[42] proved to be "very unsatisfactory," and Ellis responded in no uncertain terms that if they were "unable or unwilling to furnish [him] the information requested...then [he would] insist upon the right to examination and inspection under the terms of the contract."[43] That got their attention, and a detailed, seven-page inter-office memo was quickly cobbled together minutely itemizing the charges for each of the films, the contents of which were forwarded to Ellis, who in turn forwarded them to Sig.[44] The sender, Eagle-Lion treasurer A. E. Bollengier, provided an overview as well:

> Our accounting department informs us that the original pictures were seven or eight reels in length and each was cut to a short of three or four reels. The music work involved obtaining all of the original music tracks and cutting such tracks in such a manner as to produce music bridges over those parts of the picture that were removed. Obviously, the same work was required to be done in connection with the sound. Furthermore, I am informed that this re-cutting necessitated a complete re-recording session. Other charges were made for fades and dissolves, and for new titles for the various pictures.[45]

The "seven or eight" reel original lengths was somewhat of a stretch, but whatever the case, Sig's reaction to the charges and Bollengier's explanation of same is unknown. It's a safe bet, though, that he wasn't overly happy about them.

Perhaps sensing the changing mood of the filmgoing nation, Sig decided to make the leap into more hard-boiled, noirish fare. His brother's *The Lady Confesses* and their joint production *Apology for Murder* were tentative steps in that direction. To that end, Sig purchased an initial three original "Michael Shayne" detective stories from author Brett Halliday for production, "protecting" his interests with an option for an additional three stories per year for the next few years if the series proved successful.[46] Author Brett Halliday—one of several pen names for Davis Dresser (1904-1977)—had spent a dozen years pounding out short stories for the pulps before he finally landed his first Michael Shayne mystery with a publisher in 1939. Nearly seventy Shayne mysteries were published between then and 1976, many of the latter ones bearing Halliday's name but written by ghost writers.

Twentieth Century-Fox had produced seven "Michael Shayne" films starring Lloyd Nolan that were released back in 1941 and 1942, but the character had been missing from the screen for the past three years. Now that Sig had the rights, Buster Crabbe was announced early on to star—perhaps erroneously so—but that never came about. Hugh Beaumont's performances in *The Lady Confesses* and *Apology for Murder* had demonstrated that he could handle the tough guy stuff, and the critical reaction to his acting surely didn't hurt, so Sig signed Beaumont to star. "Lloyd Nolan couldn't be more pleased about Hugh Beaumont getting the title role in the Michael Shayne detective series," wrote columnist Sheila Graham. "As you know, Lloyd was the original Shayne and became very tired of the role."[47]

The first three films in the series were *Murder is My Business*, *Larceny in Her Heart*, and *Blonde for a Day*. According to Beaumont, work at PRC for him was twelve-hour days. "I had to be Michael Shayne from 7 a.m. when I entered the P.R.C. makeup department, until 7 p.m. when I left the lot." As tiring as that must have been, that was merely the tip of Beaumont's workload iceberg, for in addition to being an actor Beaumont was also the yet-to-be-ordained minister of Los Angeles's Vincent Methodist Church. The filming of *Murder is My Business*, the first in the series, "was really rugged," said Beaumont. "There were the usual quota of weddings and funerals, and there were the regular Sunday sermons to prepare. And I had to keep up with my studies at the U.S.C. graduate school of religion." Add to that the boys' club that he organized for the kids in his neighborhood, and Beaumont was a very busy man. "I think I'm fortunate to be doing the two things I love best—spiritual guidance and acting. How long I'll be able to continue doing both is another question. If it becomes a matter of one or the other, I'm afraid P.R.C. will have to look for a new Michael Shayne."[48] Given Beaumont's last comment, I suspect that Sig may have been "afraid" as well.

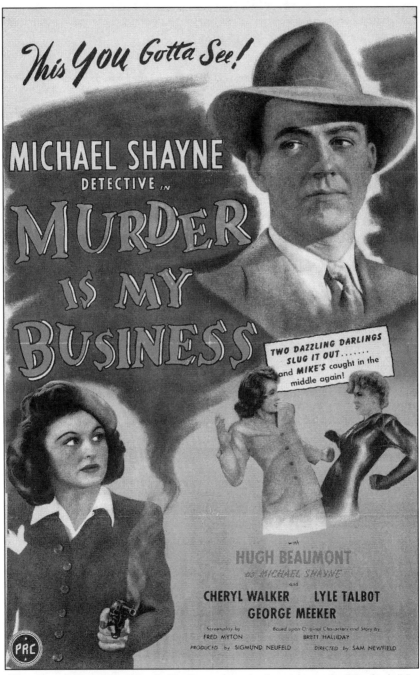

"Two Dazzling Darlings Slug It Out," or at least in the poster art for **Murder is My Business** (PRC, 1946), the first in the five film "Michael Shayne" series; a gun wielding Cheryl Walker and tough guy Hugh Beaumont get some space as well. Sig Neufeld producer, Sam Newfield director. *Courtesy of Heritage Auctions.*

Murder is My Business was filmed over an eight-day shoot from December 14th to the 22nd, 1945, going into release four months later on April 10, 1946. Unfortunately, the results are somewhat of a disappointment. All the elements that should have made this a better film are there, but the whole fails to gel into anything more than a mildly diverting mystery. Halliday's main characters are all present: Beaumont as the sarcastic sleuth Michael Shayne, who is always three or four steps ahead of everyone else; Cheryl Walker as his likable—and foolishly industrious—secretary and girlfriend Phyllis Hamilton (although why her name was changed to "Phyllis" from the later books' "Lucy" is a mystery); Ralph Dunn as blustery cop Pete Rafferty, who hates Shayne and hopes to have his P.I. license revoked; and Richard Keene as Shayne's newspaper reporter friend Tim Rourke, always willing to lend a hand. Fred Myton's screenplay is full of the usual cynical banter, red herrings, and plot twists—perhaps too many of them—but squeezed into the film's brief running time is annoyingly confusing at times. Greenhalgh's cinematography is spot on, with nicely chosen angles and evocatively moody lighting. The supporting cast all deliver solid performances as well: Lyle Talbot as a quick-with-his-fists ex-con and nightclub owner; Carol Andrews as the nightclub's flirtatious hostess; George Meeker as a sleazy, womanizing playboy; Virginia Christine as the wife of another ex-con (played by Parker Garvie) whose death she blames on Shayne; and Pierre Watkin, Helene Heigh, Julia McMillan, and David Reed, as the father, stepmother, daughter, and son, respectively, at the center of the murder being investigated. Walker, you'll recall, appeared six years earlier in the Sam-directed exploitation film *Secrets of a Model*, wisely hiding her real identity by adopting the pseudonym "Sharon Lee." Beaumont was paid $2,500 for his services, Walker $750, and Talbot $500. Sam, who brought the film in at $52,776, was paid $2,000 for his services, while Sig pocketed $2,625 for producing.[49]

The plot is far too involved to recount here, but let it suffice that the stepmother is murdered, and suspicion at one time or another falls on just about everyone listed above, including Shayne himself. Shayne, of course, solves the crime within the allotted hour, and in such a well presented and inarguable fashion that his nemesis, cop Rafferty, accepts it as presented and arrests the guilty culprit. Fred Myton wrote the script, and as usual Joseph I. Breen deemed the initial version unacceptable because of its "exceedingly low and criminal tone" and pointed out "that the police are shown as 'little more than heavies'."[50]

Beaumont was a good choice for Shayne—here a habitual eater of peanuts—delivering a relaxed performance, alternating between breezy one-liners and more threatening demands, and not above roughing up someone if the situation calls for it. He's believably tough, which is to say he has his physical limitations as well: finding himself at the wrong end of Talbot's fist three different times, he's knocked cold two of them, his own punch bouncing harmlessly off Talbot's jaw. Sig's older son Stanley served as Sam's assistant director on this and the films that followed, by now having replaced Mel De Lay in that capacity.

"Being the first of the series, it is not a very auspicious start" wrote *Harrisons Reports*,[51] and *Film Bulletin* agreed, deeming it a "tepid start for new mystery series."[52] Sadly, they were both correct.

Larceny in Her Heart, the second entry, went into production from March 1-9, 1946, under the working title *Crime in the Night*. As far as entertainment value is concerned, this was less successful than the first, although I suspect that others would disagree. Beaumont, Walker, and Dunn were all back portraying their former characters, but Paul Bryar took over from Richard Keene as reporter Tim Rourke, here given a far meatier role and benefiting from Bryar's engaging personality. Raymond L. Schrock wrote the screenplay from another Halliday original, a break from the Fred Myton screenplays written for the other films in the series. The mystery here involves greedy stepfather Gordon Richards, who schemes with corrupt sanitarium owner Douglas Fowley to keep his stepdaughter (Marie Hannon) drugged and under lock and key. Richards hires Shayne to find his "missing" daughter, but unfortunate circumstances lead to another young lady's death (also Hannon), her body dumped in the river and later "identified" as Richards's stepdaughter so that he can gain control of the estate left to her. Shayne catches on to the plot and has himself committed to the sanitarium under a false name to confirm his suspicions and effect Richards's and Fowley's arrest.

Director Sam Newfield (in doorway, holding script) and star Hugh Beaumont to his right on the exterior set of the Club Magnolia during the filming of **Larceny in Her Heart** (PRC, 1946), Sig Neufeld producer, Sam Newfield director. *Courtesy of Tim Neufeld.*

The problem with this film (if you want to call it that) is the inclusion of a lot of unnecessary lighthearted moments and unwelcome humor, totally at odds with the former film's darker approach. Poor Beaumont is required to play the fool early on, awkwardly stumbling about and nervously stammering away in a ridiculously futile (and unbelievable) attempt to keep his girl Phyllis Hamilton (Walker) from discovering the prostrate, unconscious body of Marie Hannon, spread out on a sofa in an adjoining room. Whether this change in tone was solely Schrock's contribution, or at the behest of Sig and Sam is unknown, but it severely diminishes the film's impact. *Larceny in Her Heart*—a title that has absolutely nothing to do with the plot—was released on July 10, 1946.

A Formula That Was Working (Sig, Sam, and PRC, Part 6, 1945-1947)

During the early- to mid-1940s, occasional actor Jack Roper worked for Sig and Sam at PRC, and possibly as part of their crew. Roper (1904-1966) was a former professional boxer, with 116 bouts to his credit spanning the years 1924-1940, with sixty-three wins, forty-three losses, and ten draws. Roper would regale his fellow cast and crew members recounting what was perhaps the most famous bout of his career, when he went up against reigning champion Joe Louis back in April 1939. At that time, Roper "was on one of the best runs of his well-travelled career" wrote sports writer Aaron Sutcliffe, "but lacked consistency as a fighter, having endured 39 professional losses before his bout with Louis."[53] Joel was present as Roper recounted the experience:

> He had a great story about boxing Joe Lewis. Joe Lewis was fighting a "Bum of the Month Club," and he would go all the way around the United States fighting one person a month, and usually the state champion. The state champion didn't want to fight him, so this guy stepped in…. He said that he went out and Joe Lewis had no defense whatsoever, and his gloves were down by his knees, and he hit Joe as hard as he could, and he didn't even blink. That was it; he was looking for a place to lay down.[54]

Roper only lasted two minutes and twenty seconds. Another five fights would follow over the next eighteen months—two wins and three losses—before Roper hung up his gloves and made the film industry his vocation of choice. Joel recalled Roper as being a member of the crew, which he may have been, but he was definitely an occasional actor at PRC as well. Look hard enough and you can spot Roper in bit parts in some of Sam's films, such as *Rolling Down the Great Divide* and *The Contender*. Roper appears in this second Michael Shayne entry as well, playing the small part of a bouncer.

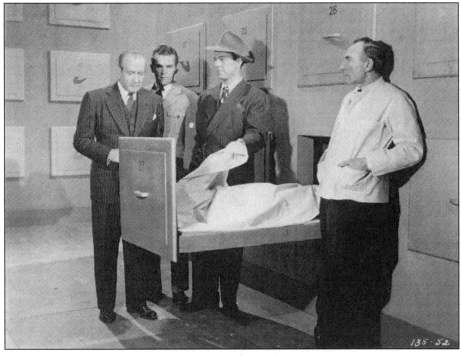

Gordon Richards "identifies" the unseen stiff as his daughter, Hugh Beaumont handling the sheet-lifting honors in **Larceny in Her Heart** (PRC, 1946).

Followers of the Shayne series were fortunate that Sig decided to assign the scripts of the following entries to Fred Myton once again, who wisely dispensed with much of the humor and lighter aspects of Schrock's screenplay for a more serious, straight-forward mystery.⁵⁵ Admittedly there are times when some humor creeps into the third film, *Blonde for a Day*, specifically with the back-and-forth between Shayne and his slightly dim arch nemesis, police detective Pete Rafferty, and a closing gag that is totally unnecessary and, in a word, humorless. Poor Myton had to settle for seeing his last name spelled "Miton" in the opening credits, a slap in the face of sorts since he'd been writing screenplays for thirty years by this time.

"Kathryn Adams, as Beaumont's faithful girl Friday, redeems a colorless performance in the final sequence by delivering one of the most professional right crosses ever uncorked by a cinema heroine." Hugh Beaumont is impressed. From **Blonde for a Day** (PRC, 1946) ; Sig Neufeld producer, Sam Newfield director.

Blonde for a Day's eight-day shoot began on May 1, 1946, with an approved budget of $57,130 and bearing the tentative title *Blondes on the Loose*;⁵⁶ it went into release four months later on August 29, 1946. Reviewers had mixed reactions to the film, *Harrison's Reports* calling it "an improvement over the other two pictures"⁵⁷ while *Motion Picture Herald* dismissed it by sniping that "Producer Sigmund Neufeld and Director Sam Newfield are more at home in the western field."⁵⁸ Beaumont returned as the famed detective, and Paul Bryar was back again as reporter Tim Rourke, given a far meatier role that dominates the film's first ten minutes. For whatever reason, casting changes were made for the other two recurring roles, Kathryn Adams replacing Cheryl Walker as Shayne's "girl Friday" Phyllis Hamilton, and Cy Kendall replacing Ralph Dunn as detective Rafferty. Neither of these two replacements are nearly as satisfying in their respective roles as the actors they replaced, but both Walker and Dunn would return for the eventual fourth in the series, *Three on a Ticket*, released in 1947. Adams, who consistently seems uncertain in her delivery, has one standout moment in the film, nicely described by *Motion Picture Daily*: "Kathryn Adams, as Beaumont's faithful girl Friday, redeems a colorless performance in the final sequence by delivering one of the most professional right crosses ever uncorked by a cinema heroine."[59] Agreed; it may be the highlight of the film! One wonders whether the fact that Adams was Beaumont's wife in real life had anything to do with her landing this role.

In this film, Bryar goes after the local gambling syndicate in an ongoing series of no-holds-barred articles, naming names and making accusations. After he's beaten up as a warning to lay off, he summons Shayne to come back to Los Angeles to help him track down a mysterious blonde who had killed three unlucky winners at the local casinos. Before Shayne arrives, however, Bryar is shot and hospitalized, near death. As usual with these mysteries, suspects are numerous: Mauritz Hugo, manager of several local gambling establishments and one of Bryar's targets; newspaper editor Frank Ferguson, who has fired Bryar due to the latter's refusal to stop writing those incendiary articles; Sonia Sorel, Ferguson's wife who "carries a torch" for a disinterested Bryar; Richard Fraser, who attempts to blackmail Ferguson with the pistol he has in his possession; and Marjorie Hoshelle, the neighbor of a murdered woman who has a very dark secret revealed later in the film. You'll go blue in the face attempting to figure out who the guilty culprit is, but naturally Shayne works it all out in the end.

Cinematographer Jack Greenhalgh (checkered shirt) sets up another shot for **Blonde for a Day** (PRC, 1946), while star Hugh Beaumont patiently waits in the doorway.
Courtesy of Tim Neufeld.

In the meantime, Robert R. Young had been busy overseas on matters that would ultimately affect PRC. Young, reported as "chairman of the board of the Chesapeake and Ohio Railroad and of the Allegheny Corp., who also holds the controlling interest in Pathé and PRC Pictures," entered into an agreement near the end of 1945 with England's J. Arthur Rank, to create a new worldwide distribution organization to distribute twenty "A" productions—ten British and ten American. The new company was to be known as Eagle-Lion Films, with the Young interests having distribution rights in the U.S., Central and South America, while Rank would handle distribution elsewhere. "Although controlled by the Young interests," reported *Film Bulletin*, "PRC will not participate in the operations of the new company, which will have its own distribution force."[60] That statement was clarified a few days later when *Showmen's Trade Review* reported that "the physical distribution of the Eagle-Lion products would be handled by the 22 wholly owned and operated PRC branch offices. In the remaining exchange centers where PRC operates under franchise, the physical distribution will be handled by other arrangements."[61]

A half year later, after *Blonde for a Day* had wrapped and shortly before *Larceny in Her Heart* was released, PRC was undergoing considerable change:

> The PRC lot is changing complexion, with the departure of the older producers and the gradual emergence of the new Pathé Eagle-Lion setup. Already ensconced on the PRC premises are Bryan Foy, new Eagle-Lion studio chief; Sam Israel, publicity head; Aubrey Schenck, Foy's executive aide; James Vaughn, production manager; David Stephenson, story department head; Ben Stoloff and Harold Gottlieb, producers; and others.[62]

Edgar Ulmer had obtained a release from his seven-year contract with PRC, having served only four of the seven years. "The old PRC lot," wrote *Showmen's Trade Review*, "which was used on a rental basis, is being repaired for exclusive use of Eagle-Lion.... Eagle-Lion will make more moderate budget films at first to fulfill needs of its distributors for product as quickly as feasible."[63] Sig and Sam, however, were still at work on yet another Buster Crabbe Western, then titled *Dangerous Men* but retitled *Prairie Badmen* for eventual release.

With all the changes taking place, dissatisfaction with the new regime, and uncertainty about the future, the old ranks were thinning. "Virtually all of the former PRC department heads are severing connections with the company" reported *Showmen's Trade Review*.[64] Rumors circulated throughout the industry. One of them concerned an impending merger between PRC and Eagle-Lion, but PRC's home office shot that one down. There were other rumors that Sig was planning to bolt from PRC, but vice-president Lind "flatly denied reports that Sig Neufeld had or was pulling out of the company to organize a new producing-distributing organization."[65] The future of PRC, however, quickly became evident. "It doesn't require any special gift for deciphering handwriting on the wall to observe that PRC is in the process of being eliminated as a film company," wrote *Showmen's Trade Review* in late June.

> Headman Robert Young has hitched his movie wagon to the Eagle-Lion banner and the only reason for PRC's continued existence obviously is the company's commitments to exhibitors. For the time being, it seems that PRC will continue to release through its former 36 exchanges, now bearing the Eagle-Lion name. In addition to avoiding any possible law suits for non-fulfillment of contracts, the ill-fated company is determined to maintain the best product possible under the circumstances. Harry Thomas, Young's top executive for PRC, is to be commended for this resolution in the face of such tough odds.[66]

Film Bulletin had similar thoughts:

It may be somewhat premature to sound the death knell for this little organization, but it has become obvious that either Producers' Releasing Corporation will soon cease to exist as a production outfit, unless its remnants should buy out from the status of stepchild to Pathé Industries-Eagle-Lion set-up and affiliate with some other organization. Even if this were done, it would probably spell finish to PRC as a name.[67]

Gentlemen with Guns, released on March 27, 1946, was the first film to be copyrighted by Pathé Industries, Inc. rather than the former copyrights by P.R.C. Pictures, Inc. *Murder is My Business* and all subsequent releases were now copyrighted as such.

Stripper Evelyn Ankers gives show owner Craig Reynolds an earful over the unexpected promotion of rival performer Jacqueline Dalya in **Queen of Burlesque** (PRC, 1946), Arthur Alexander and Alfred Stern producers, Sam Newfield director.

Sam was loaned to Alexander-Stern Productions once again to direct the Evelyn Ankers vehicle *Queen of Burlesque*. First announced in the trades at the end of 1944 as an upcoming project, preproduction plans were underway in March 1945 with Elmer Clifton assigned to write the screenplay.[68] By May, however, Clifton was history and Paul Gerard Smith was named to write it;[69] he too fell by the wayside. A strike by disgruntled union workers had been under way since March, which was delaying the start of numerous films at the various studios, PRC among them. *Queen of Burlesque* and Sig's *The Flying Serpent* were among PRC's affected films, production starts now tentatively set for June.[70] Production delays on *Queen of Burlesque* continued into the latter part of the year, ultimately impacted by the regime changes taking place. "Alexander Stern Productions will carry out their commitments for PRC," reported *Showmen's Trade Review* in November, "in spite of changes in policy at the studio."[71] It would be late March 1946 before actual shooting began under Sam's direction, working from a script ultimately turned out by David Lang. Cinematographer Vincent J. Farrar, recently returned from military service, was lensing the film. All of a sudden it was on the fast track: "PRC is rushing production of 'Queen of Burlesque' for an early release," reported *Variety*, "to take advantage of the controversy about the proposed revival of burlesque in New York."[72] It was the only film in production at the studio in April, working under a comparatively comfortable budget of $100,372. *Queen of Burlesque* was finally released on July 24, 1946, more than eighteen months since it was initially announced back at the end of 1944.

Burlesque show performer Jacqueline Dalya uses blackmail to coerce show owner Craig Reynolds into making her the star, replacing former star Evelyn Ankers, whose work had proven most satisfactory to date. Rose La Rose, another performer angling for the star role, is angered by the unexpected promotion as well. When Dalya is murdered, both Ankers and La Rose are suspected, along with most everyone else connected with the show. La Rose and fellow dancer Marian Martin join Dalya in the morgue before the guilty party is exposed by reporter Carleton Young, who happens to be in love with Ankers.

Reviews were generally favorable, with comments such as "a fast-paced murder story" and a "very good, suspenseful murder-mystery well above the average in its class." Sam's direction, however, almost always warranted mention: "Top credit goes to Sam Newfield for the way he handled the direction," wrote *Showmen's Trade Review*.[73] Other favorable mentions included "Sam Newfield, who directed, got every ounce of talent out of the cast,"[74] "Sam Newfield blends his elements in a workmanlike package,"[75] and "the direction of Sam Newfield make[s] this a film which should hold the interest of murder-mystery fans."[76]

Rose La Rose, "a burleycue specialist on and off the PRC screen," was one of the more exploitable members of the cast. Born Rosina Da Pello in Brooklyn in 1919, Rose complained about the restrictions imposed on her when appearing before the camera. "When I feel like bumping, I bump," she stated, "but in the movies they tell me: 'Rose, keep your hips still. No bumps, please.'" Rose continued with her complaints to the receptive reporter:

> They even put me behind a screen so [my] fans couldn't see all that was going on. They also put clothes on me—a harem routine. It was dreadful. But, I didn't keep my hips still. The censor said "You can move your hips only in an Oriental dance." So I changed the title of my "Sex dance" to an "Oriental" dance. The censors then said that everything was all right. But they had to stop the camera several times when my impulses got the best of me.[77]

Rose had only one other film credit to her resume, playing a stripper in the low budget exploitation film *The Wages of Sin*, released back in 1938.

Sig and Sam completed the eighth and final entry in the Buster Crabbe series—*Outlaws of the Plains*—by the end of June a few dollars under its $25,500 budget, and said goodbye to their long-time star.[78] With that series and all other productions behind him, Sig had settled his obligations to PRC. He arranged to take over the Morey and Sutherland Studios in August—soon to be known solely as the Sutherland Studio—where he would launch three final productions for PRC release, *Gas House Kids*, *Lady Chaser*,[79] and the fourth Michael Shayne entry, *Three on a Ticket*.

In the meantime, Max Alexander and his brother Arthur weren't content with their earnings from their new productions for PRC and others. Looking to squeeze every last penny out of their many shoestring productions, the Alexanders had turned to the fledgling television industry back in 1940, testing the waters by renting a handful of their earlier Westerns to NBC, and following up with some of the more recent Ken Maynard Westerns from 1938.[80] The Alexanders continued to produce films throughout the 1940s, then made a half-hearted stab at some syndicated television production. Come 1952, and still working out of their Sunset Boulevard location, Max and Arthur were doing quite nicely by selling older feature films to television stations, owning the rights to one hundred twenty-five films which included many of their own indie features as well as forty other British productions.[81]

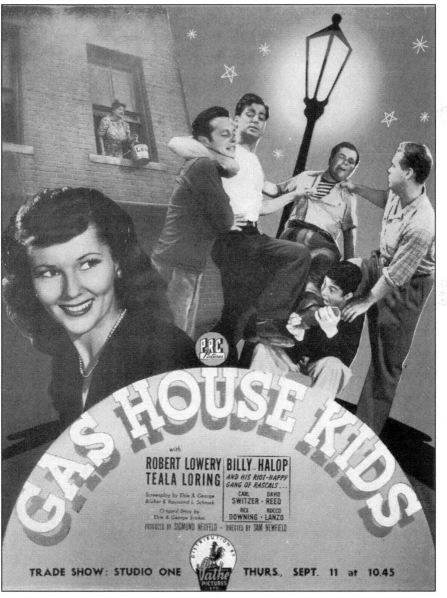

Poster art for **Gas House Kids** (PRC, 1946) gives off a definite "East Side Kids" "Bowery Boys" vibe; Sig Neufeld producer, Sam Newfield director.

Sig and Sam's final commitments to PRC/Eagle-Lion's 1946-47 season were all filmed at the Sutherland Studio in August and October 1946. *Gas House Kids* was the first of these, with interim titles of *East Side, West Side* and *Eastside Robinhoods* before settling on *East Side Rascals* with an intended July 29 start.[82] Production was delayed until the first week in August, and there was a problem with that proposed title, necessitating a change to the final *Gas House Kids*.[83] The "problem" with the title probably stemmed from the recent restoration of Sam Katzman's previous "East Side Kids" comedies by producer Jan Grippo—teamed with actors Leo Gorcey and Huntz Hall—as "The Bowery Boys." It wouldn't come as a surprise if Grippo sought to avoid any confusion among filmgoers that *East Side Rascals* was yet another "East Side Kids" film. Billy Halop had been part of an earlier incarnation of the group known as "The Dead End Kids and Little Tough Guys," and was an original cast member along with Gorcey and Hall in Stanley Kingsley's 1935-37 play *Dead End* and the Samuel Goldwyn film of same from 1937. Halop was named to star in *East Side Rascals*' cast, which could potentially add to the confusion. Regardless, anyone going to see *Gas House Kids* expecting a film along the lines of any of those earlier series would have been very disappointed.

When Robert Lowery returns from the war, everyone is stunned to see that he has lost the use of his legs and is a cripple. His fiancé, Teala Loring, sticks with him, and their long-held dream of owning a chicken farm in New Jersey resurfaces since they think that is something a fellow in his compromised condition could handle. The neighbor kids—Billy Halop, Colleen's brother David Reed, Carl Switzer, Rex Downing, and Rocco Lanzo—struggle to come up with a plan to get enough money to put a down payment on a farm that the couple has fallen in love with. Halop finds a satchel of money that Paul Bryar, a wanted bank robber, had taken from a rent collector he had killed. Not realizing the money's source, Halop and the gang use it to place a down payment on the farm. The cops think that Halop killed and robbed the rent collector, but Bryar gets to him first. Everything is eventually straightened out and Halop collects the $10,000 reward for Bryar's capture, using some of it to pay back the stolen money and the rest to cover the farm's down payment.

The film provides acceptable, more adult entertainment, and the benefits of its $85,259 budget are immediately apparent with the film's first scene, which takes place on the expansive and densely populated Lower East Side slum set, surrounded by numerous businesses and tenements. Sam had Greenhalgh open the film with a lengthy, high level tracking shot that wends its way down the street and through the crowds, ending up at the window of the Loring family's tenement; it's an impressive shot, and even more so for a PRC film. Sam's direction of a later amateur boxing match is deftly handled as well, with fighter Halop opposite real-life Middleweight Boxing champ Noble "Kid" Chissell as K.O. Burke. The screenplay, by Elsie and George Bricker and Raymond Schrock, stretches credulity to the breaking point, but that really comes as no surprise. Oddly enough, this film still bore the PRC copyright notice, at odds with the films that immediately preceded and followed it into release. Two more "Gas House Kids" films were to follow in 1947 before the series was terminated, *Gas House Kids Go West* and *Gas House Kids Go to Hollywood*. Reviews, it should be noted, were mostly favorable. Filmed over nine days, *Gas House Kids*' negative cost came in under budget at $83,874—Sam saved Sig $1,385—with domestic rentals a comparatively healthy $164,143; Sam went home with $3,000 in his pocket, his largest payday to date.[84]

Lady Chaser was the second to be filmed at the Sutherland Studios, going before cameras on August 16 under the tentative title *Lady Killer*.[85] Fred Myton returned to write the script, based on an original story by G.T. Fleming-Roberts, a prolific writer for the pulps with only one other story previously adapted for the screen. Watch the first few minutes of the film and you'll quickly see that you are in for another of Myton's convoluted mysteries. Here's the setup:

Inez Marie Polk (Ann Savage) gives an aspirin to a total stranger, Dorian Westmore (Inez Cooper), who has complained of a headache. Cooper dumps it in her purse, but later when her wealthy uncle complains of a headache, she passes the aspirin on to him. It turns out to be poison, and her uncle keels over dead. To complicate matters, Cooper is engaged to Robert Lowery, a fellow her uncle disliked so intensely that he had threatened to disinherit her. That's enough to convince the police and jury that Cooper poisoned him, so off she goes to the big house. All that, and in just the first few minutes of film!

Lowery spends the rest of the film trying to track down the aspirin's origin and clear Cooper's name. The mystery becomes less so about midway through the film when we learn that attorney Frank Ferguson had originally given the poisoned aspirin to Savage, who had been blackmailing him over a murder he had committed. To top it off, and in one of those hard-to-swallow B-movie coincidences, Ferguson was Cooper's attorney as well and, needless to say, not a very good one since she was found guilty. After several extended fistfights that would ruin a mere mortal, Lowery solves the mystery and turns Ferguson over to sympathetic police inspector Ralph Dunn.

Robert Lowery is about to strong-arm Marie Martino in **Lady Chaser** (PRC, 1946), Sig Neufeld producer, Sam Newfield director.

The film, which is sufficiently enjoyable on its own modest terms, benefits from some nice location photography and a uniformly fine cast. Ann Savage was a perfect choice for the brassy, screechy blackmailer, and William Haade fine as her dim, horse race-addicted boyfriend. Ralph Dunn appears as yet another cop, but this time he plays it straight and not for subtle laughs. Frank Ferguson, who was so good as the city editor in *Blonde for a Day*, is equally good here as the seemingly sympathetic attorney harboring a very dark secret. Charles Williams earns some chuckles as the very high-strung apartment manager. Lowery is good enough in a role that requires more action than chatter, a far cry from his wholly believable role as the crippled war veteran in *Gas House Kids*. Inez Cooper, who spends most of the film on a prison cot, was in the process of resurrecting her film career after a several year hiatus spent traveling from one Army post to the next, entertaining the troops. *Lady Chaser* was her fourth role since V-J Day.[86] For whatever reason, Sam exceeded his $70,648 budget by nearly $6,000, coming in with a negative cost of $76,558; he took home another $3,000 for his efforts.

Sig acquired additional Brett Halliday stories for production. The first of these, and his fourth in the Shayne series for PRC, was tentatively titled *The Corpse Came Calling* when filming started in late October 1946. It would eventually go into release the following year on March 3, 1947, as *Three on a Ticket*. Screenwriter Fred Myton concocted another Byzantine plot, this one involving embezzled cash and the stolen plans for a new secret weapon. When former, ethically challenged private investigator Brooks Benedict arrives at Shayne's (Hugh Beaumont) doorstep and dies of a gunshot wound, Shayne finds a portion of a baggage claim slip in his hand. It isn't long before a lot of people want that slip back, including blonde seductress Louise Currie; her sleazy escaped con husband Douglas Fowley; government agent Gavin Gordon in tandem with inspector Ralph Dunn; and assorted thugs. Gordon claims that the baggage slip is the clue to the stolen weapon plans, so both Shayne's secretary/girlfriend Cheryl Walker and reporter friend Paul Bryar try to convince Shayne to turn over the slip, and are disappointed with him when he doesn't. Shayne ultimately exposes the various thugs as former cohorts in the embezzlement of their firm's cash, and "agent" Gordon as one of them.

This is perhaps the best of the Shayne series to date, with loads of violence and gunplay to liven up the proceedings. Beaumont gets worked over several times, and in one nicely handled sequence gets beaten off-screen, collapsing into view several times onto a filthy mattress. Sam's direction is solid with one very disappointing, visually jarring scene where Beaumont and Currie meet up in a restaurant. Seated at a table, the left-right rule is broken several times, with Beaumont and Currie flipping back and forth from one side of the screen to the other. Aside from that one misstep, the film is a handsome one otherwise, with more lavish sets and lots of well-chosen location photography. Sam brought his old friend Charlie King back for a juicy bit part as a drunk, but poor Brooks Benedict is on the screen for barely fifteen seconds, and you never once get to see his face.

Three on a Ticket had a far higher negative cost than the earlier Shayne mysteries, coming in at $92,500; *Larceny in Her Heart* and *Blonde for a Day* had been filmed for $58,400 and $54,820, respectively. This was the last in the Michael Shayne series that Sig and Sam were involved with, although there was one final entry, *Too Many Winners*, directed by William Beaudine for producer John Sutherland and released two months later. The opening credit proclaimed that it was a presentation of "The New PRC".

As late as September both PRC president Harry Thomas and Pathé board chairman Robert Young were maintaining the line that PRC was to continue in parallel to Eagle-Lion. Thomas stated that the 1945-46 season had been the "most successful" year in the company's history, and that the new 1946-47 season would be a period of even greater expansion. Young, in a letter to Thomas, commended the company's performance over the past year and the individuals responsible for its success, stating that all "who have so magnificently contributed to the upward climb…will inevitably lead the company to the top…. I am talking officially when I say that there is absolutely no foundation whatsoever to any stories which you may have heard regarding our company, except that we are going to grow even more than we have grown during this past year."[87]

Director Sam Newfield got his actors' positions reversed when moving from two-shot to closeups, and editor Holbrook Todd left them as-is, in **Three On a Ticket** (PRC, 1946), Sig Neufeld producer, Sam Newfield director.

A mere two months later in November, however, Thomas announced that "all affiliations with producers of low-budget films would be severed at the termination of current existing contracts." Sig, the "leading producer in that field," was finished with PRC.[88] Sig's son believes that his father's "termination" was by mutual agreement:

> It was evidently by choice. I remember them having conversations that [Sig] didn't like, what they were proposing and what they were going to do with the company. I think he basically just walked away from it.... What I heard was that they wanted to upgrade everything, instead of producing good B movies they wanted to start making some A movies, and he felt they wouldn't be successful, and didn't want to be involved. That was the basis of the disagreement.... They had a formula that was working, and why mess with it.[89]

There was another conflict between Sig and the studio that likely added to Sig's decision to sever relations. Six months earlier back in May 1946, Sig sent a letter to PRC reminding them of their production contract dated May 23, 1944, wherein provisions were made to offset the eventual results of various unions then negotiating for wage increases of ten percent. When eventually agreed upon, these increases could, in whole or in part, come due retroactively. To that end, PRC added to each film's budget a reserve for the payment of same, if and when wage increases were granted and made effective. The unused monies in the reserve not required for the payment of retroactive wage increases would be paid to Sigmund Neufeld Productions "as a payment upon the negative cost of the picture."

Sig stated that he had paid out approximately $1,800 during the two-year period as a result of the outcome of those union increases, and wanted to be reimbursed.[90] This dragged on for more than a year, and by February 1947, PRC was still withholding reimbursement. "We will now proceed to check his figures and send you the computations," stated an internal PRC document written by Arthur B. Johnson. "In the meantime, please withhold any overages which may have accumulated to Mr. Neufeld's credit," eighteen films the focus of these overages. "As you know," added Johnson, "relations with Sig are a bit strained..."[91] A check made out to Neufeld Productions was finally cut in mid-May, but put on hold a day later before it was mailed.[92] The reason? "[Sig] has been rather disturbed about holding up his check and we didn't want to have it released until he had signed the contract on the last picture which he made for us wherein his participation in the profits of the picture had been eliminated." Sig, no doubt thoroughly fed up with the stonewalling, signed the contract, so "there is no reason why any check that he has coming for overages should not be released to him."[93]

Whatever the reality, Sig, who had produced nearly a hundred films for PRC, had moved on. There was speculation that Sig would move over to Screen Guild to produce. Screen Guild and Golden Gate Productions had a distribution advantage over most independent producers, composed of a network of 1,800 theater owners in the U.S. and Canada ready to exhibit its product. Headed by San Francisco- and Los Angeles-based theater owner Joe Blumenfeld, former PRC producer Jack Schwarz had already hooked up with Screen Guild. It was anticipated that both Alexander-Stern Productions and Sigmund Neufeld Productions would affiliate as well.[94] Sig confounded the pundits, however, and made other plans.

As for "The New PRC," by the end of 1947 it had been totally absorbed by Eagle-Lion, and there would be no further films bearing the PRC logo.

Chapter 18:
Set Adrift (Sam, Sans Sig, 1946-1949)

With the leadership changes taking place at PRC back in the latter part of 1945, and a growing uncertainty over what the company's future held for all involved, Sam's previously non-stop directing schedule began to cool somewhat. Needing to supplement his dwindling income, Sam had looked outside for some additional work, and found it with Ted Toddy and his Toddy Pictures. Newfield reportedly directed four unnamed features in rapid succession for Toddy back in Hollywood—three of them starring African American actor Dewey "Pigmeat" Markham—then headed East to direct a feature with an "all-colored cast" of sixty headed by Markham at New Jersey's Hudson Heights-based Ideal Studios.[1] With its completion, Sam went to work on a second for Toddy, both films shot in November 1945.[2]

Russian-born Ted Toddy (neé Meyer Tartakoff; 1900-1983) had fifteen years' experience working for both Universal and Columbia before breaking out on his own, first to form the Atlanta-based Dixie Film Exchange in 1938, followed by Dixie National Pictures in 1940. He started Consolidated Film Exchange to distribute the films of Dixie National and Million Dollar Productions,[3] the latter company purchased in 1940. Toddy consolidated his companies under the name Toddy Pictures Company in 1941,[4] and by late 1945 provided a somewhat misleading list of Sam's fellow directors at Toddy as Jed Buell, Harry Popkin, Harry Fraser, A.A. Brooks, William Nolte, William X. Crowley, and William Beaudine, working under producers Buell, Popkin, Al Westen, and Clifford Sanforth. David F. Friedman, the self-proclaimed "Mighty Monarch of Exploitation" and the man behind such 1960s drive-in cinematic fare as *Blood Feast* (1963) and *Two Thousand Maniacs!* (1964), described Toddy as a "dapper, balding, mid-sized, middle-aged, energetic, extroverted, fast-talking fellow," the "chairman of the board, president, secretary-treasurer, head of production, general manager, salesman, booker, and sometimes shipping clerk" at Toddy Pictures.[5]

By early 1946, Toddy was touting expanded production, announcing that in addition to the ten features he'd already announced, he was contemplating an additional six musical Westerns and a serial—with all-Black casts—along with a weekly "Negro News Review." Sam had by this time already directed a trio of features for Toddy, *House-Rent Party* (March 10, 1946), *Fight That Ghost* (April 10, 1946)—both starring Markham—and *Mantan Messes Up* (February 10, 1946) starring Mantan Moreland.[6] Markham was reported to have signed a four-picture contract with Toddy,[7] but aside from the Sam-directed short *Pigmeat Markham's Laugh Hepcats* (aka *Pigmeat's Laugh Hepcats*), a combined re-release of Toddy's earlier featurettes *Mr. Smith Goes Ghost* and *One Big Mistake*, there are no other known films that Markham made for Toddy.

Toddy once described the kinds of films his target audience wanted as ones that feature "light comedy, outdoor adventures, musical comedies with an abundance of singing, dancing, and comedy-romances."[8] Here's Friedman's critical assessment of Toddy's self-produced films:

> The characters and plots of Toddy's films were outrageous stereotypes, completely confirming the crude, cruel conceptions of blacks by the most bigoted racists. The male players were either lazy, shiftless, or small-time crooks, carrying outsized straight razors, gorging on watermelon and fried chicken, running from the police, frightened by "ghosts," shuffling, scratching, and muttering inane

lines in almost unintelligible dialect. The female players were either Aunt Jemima types or "red hot mammas."[9]

An exaggeration, perhaps, but since so few of Toddy's films are readily available for assessment, I'll let Friedman's recollections stand as presented. That said, based on the scant reviews published at that time, Friedman's comments seem to be somewhat of an exaggeration.

John "Rastus" Murray (top left) and Pigmeat Markham are "A Pair of Flat-Foot Floogies" in **House-Rent Party** (Toddy, 1946), Sam Newfield director.
Courtesy of Heritage Auctions.

House-Rent Party has Markham as a barber who teams up with his pal Shorty (John "Rastus" Murray) to try to track down and capture jewel thief Slippery Slim (Rudolph Toombs) for the $1,000 reward. *Fight That Ghost* reteams Markham with Murray as proprietors of a Bootery and Tailor shop whose mounting problems prompt thoughts of suicide. Those thoughts are put aside when the reading of a will names them both as beneficiaries of $2,500 each if they spend a night in the deceased's bedroom; "the comic duo literally run through walls trying to escape the imaginary spooks pursuing them," wrote historian Mel Watkins.[10] *Mantan Messes Up* follows star Mantan Moreland as he wanders into a new television station, and is left in charge when the boss heads off to lunch. Taking advantage of the situation, Moreland lets everyone think he's the office manager and conducts his own personal interview of an auditioning dancer (Doryce Bradley). Aside from these three features and the one known short, it's likely that Sam was involved with some others. Given Toddy's stinginess with credits, however, the full extent of Sam's contributions remains cloudy.

Mantan Moreland can barely keep his eyes in his head when he spots a lovely in **Mantan Messes Up** (Lucky Star/Toddy, 1946), Sam Newfield director.

With PRC's absorption by Eagle-Lion on the fast track and Sig's decision to terminate his relationship with the new regime, Sam was on the lookout for new engagements to fill the void until Sig needed him back. He found some quick work for Pine-Thomas Productions, directing two adventure films for release through Paramount, both of which he squeezed in before heading back to the Sutherland Studios to direct Sig's final PRC release *Three on a Ticket*. Producers William H. Pine and William C. Thomas had just signed a new two-year contract to produce for Paramount, their fourth in a relationship that had begun back in 1941 and yielded thirty-five films to date.[11] Affectionately known within the industry as "The Dollar Bills" for their lower budget productions, Sam was just the sort of director they needed: fast and dependable. For reasons that one can only speculate on this many years after the fact, Sam chose to use his "Peter Stewart" and "Sherman Scott" aliases on all the films he directed through the end of the decade, and that includes the two directed for his brother as well. He would revert back to using his own name for the series of films made for Lippert—the first released at the beginning of 1950—and for all subsequent films that followed.

Jungle Flight, the first of the two films, was a fairly routine, South-of-the-border mining camp melodrama co-starring Robert Lowery, Ann Savage, and Barton MacLane. Going before cameras on June 20th and lasting into early July 1946, the film involves fliers Lowery and Robert Kent (here billed as Douglas Blackley, his birth name), flying machinery and ore back and forth over a mountain range to MacLane's mining camp. Kent is killed when his overloaded plane crashes, leaving Lowery to find solace—and eventual lust—in the arms of Ann Savage, whom he takes back to camp to serve as the much-needed cook. All goes to hell when her ex-con ex-husband Douglas Fowley shows up and is eventually revealed as a freshly minted murderer. I'll let you guess who eventually prevails by the film's end, but suffice it to say there's the mandatory happy ending.

This is a reasonably engaging action-adventure film, well-acted with some decent aerial footage to liven things up. Savage displays a softer side in this film, less abrasive than usual and far more appealing. Fowley oozes menace as her unrepentant ex-husband, and MacLane is tough but ultimately a softy as the camp's gruff owner. Lowery is Lowery, good enough in the hard-drinking, bad singing, two-fisted role, a serviceable actor who never seemed to claw his way out of the lower budget arena. Curt Bois provides the film's moments of humor, as the English-mangling Latin who aspires to be a pilot. The film's lower-budget roots are in evidence, particularly with the two airplane crashes, one shown as an after-the-fact ball of flame, and the other simply mentioned in passing. Sam's direction and Jack Greenhalgh's camera work—yes, he was on this film as well—raise the film's cachet up a notch or two. Curiously, the fuddy duddies at the National Legion of Decency gave the film a "Class B/objectionable in part" rating on the basis that the film's plot "reflects the acceptability of divorce"[12]

Reviews were mixed but generally favorable. *Film Bulletin* rated it a "lukewarm action dualler" and "a routine entry in the Pine-Thomas series,"[13] and *Harrisons Reports* deemed it "weak in story values but with sufficient melodramatic action to make it an acceptable supporting feature in secondary theatres."[14] *Motion Picture Daily* was more favorable, saying that "The Pine-Thomas talent for telling a straight adventure story in a manner to get the most out of it is on display here in characteristic effectiveness, extracting a maximum of entertainment,"[15] while *Variety* praised its "good cast" and said the "offering holds the interest effectively."[16] They were all right in their way.

Robert Lowery's unhappy with his food, while Barton MacLane looks on with astonishment in **Jungle Flight** (Pine-Thomas/Paramount, 1947), William H. Pine and William C. Thomas producers, Sam Newfield director.

Jungle Flight may have been offered to Sam to direct so that Pine and Thomas could determine if he was the man to helm their follow-up film—*Adventure Island*—among the most expensive of their productions to date and the first to be filmed in the Cinecolor process. Loosely based on the Robert Louis Stevenson short novel *The Ebb-Tide*, the film was a remake of Paramount's 1937 *Ebb Tide*, which co-starred Oskar Homolka, Ray Milland, and Frances Farmer. Going before cameras in September and running into early October 1946, this new version co-starred comparative newcomers Rory Calhoun and Rhonda Fleming, both borrowed from David O. Selznick for the leading roles. This was only Fleming's third credited role after her debut performance in Hitchcock's *Spellbound* two years earlier, and Calhoun's third credited role as well, and only the second billed as Rory Calhoun.

Sam led a troupe of 147 cast and crew members to Catalina Island, the "largest in history of the Pine-Thomas unit."[17] Most filming took place at Catalina and aboard the rented schooner *Seaward*, the group later relocating to Sunland, California where interior sets were constructed. The film was cut and ready for release by the end of November 1946, but would sit on the shelf for some time before actually making it onto the nation's screens.

Both Pine and Thomas had begun their industry careers as press agents, so they decided to give their big new film—their first in color—a fitting publicity and exploitation campaign. Five key cities were chosen, and each received a different campaign, the one that proved to be the most effective and productive would be used when the film went into general release.[18] As evidence of the faith the powers at Paramount had in the new film, the advertising-publicity budget for *Adventure Island* was reportedly four times the amount ever previously allotted for a Pine-Thomas film.[19]

Rhonda Fleming, front and center, on this poster for **Adventure Island** (Pine-Thomas/Paramount, 1947), William H. Pine and William C. Thomas producers, Sam Newfield director. *Courtesy of Heritage Auctions.*

Sneak previews proved to be revelatory, for "every time Calhoun appeared in closeup, the bobbysoxers drowned out the dialogue with screams and shrieks." Pine and Thomas took note, and had three additional closeups of Calhoun shot for insertion into the film, closeups they called "screaming footage."[20] To further plug the film and its two stars, radio transcriptions were made of five-minute interviews with both, released to stations as another element of the promotional campaign.[21] Yet another gimmick was a contest to find the theatre manager who came up with the best exploitation campaign, the prize dangled before them their choice of an all-expense-paid vacation to either Cuba or Hawaii.[22]

Bill Pine was interviewed about the making of this first Pine-Thomas Production in color:

> I was pretty nervous when we decided to go ahead with "Adventure Island" in Cinecolor. It was quite an undertaking for us. Color costs a lot of money and in our setup we had to be very conscious, if not self-conscious, about money. We had to be more than half safe. The outcome there was that we shot only 26,000 feet to get 6,300 in the release prints. One out of four on the screen is cutting it very fine. A lot of people in Hollywood said they were impressed.... We have to plan, and plan damned carefully.... We become ingenious because necessity, which is another word for budget in our dictionary, compels us to become ingenious. Indiscretions in the use of color would have murdered us.[23]

Cinecolor was one of the early two-color processes developed in 1932 by William Thomas Crespinel and Alan M. Gundelfinger as an alternative to the Technicolor Corporation. Its advantages proved unavoidably attractive to the independent producers: the Cinecolor process cost only 25 % more than black-and-white photography, retrofitted black-and-white film cameras could be used, and rushes in color were available within twenty-four hours of shooting. Used primarily for short films and the very random feature during the process's first dozen years, it wasn't until 1945 when it was embraced by several denizens of Poverty Row, PRC, Monogram, and Screen Guild Productions chief among them. The Cinecolor process was not entirely accurate with its reproduction of the spectrum of colors, able to produce vibrant reds, oranges, blues, browns, and flesh tones, while other colors such as greens and purples tended to be muted.[24] View a faded print of *Adventure Island* or *State Department: File 649* and you'll have a rough idea of what the process's results looked like.

The film's plot is somewhat disjointed, the first half of the film set aboard a schooner given to disgraced sea captain Paul Kelly, whose drunkenness had resulted in the loss of both his former ship and papers, and left him stranded. Now given a major break, he takes old friend John Abbott and new acquaintance Rory Calhoun with him to assist with the ship's delivery of wine to Sydney, Australia. Kelly soon decides it would be more profitable to redirect the ship to Peru, sell the contents, and pocket the cash. That plan falls apart when they discover that the wine bottles all contain water, the result of the former, now-deceased captain's plan to cheat the insurance company. Just to complicate matters and add some sexiness to the film, the captain's daughter, Rhonda Fleming, is on board as well. Then the film shifts gears. They spot a remote island and head there in the hope of finding some much-needed food to restock their depleted supplies. There they find it governed by a murderous madman, Alan Napier, who rules the natives—who are convinced he's a god—with an iron fist. He's willing to trade food for Fleming, which is unacceptable, so the new arrivals all plan their escape. With limited success, I should add, since everyone ends up dead with the exception of Calhoun and Fleming, who make it back to the ship and sail off with a load of pearls.

The film's Cinecolor was the selling point of this otherwise implausible and admittedly rather silly adventure yarn, but there's enough action throughout to hold the interest, and Rhonda Fleming is attired in such a way as to please the male viewers. A raging fire in the ship's hold is a standout sequence, well-orchestrated and visually convincing. Napier's nastiness is driven home when he punishes one disobedient native by his usual method of discipline: tossing him into a pit filled with poisonous snakes. The climactic confrontation is rather fun, too, with Abbott attempting to neutralize Napier with a champagne bottle filled with sulfuric acid, but expiring from same when shot by his intended victim. Napier gets a taste of his own medicine when he's shot and stumbles backwards into that same pit of vipers. The film's biggest asset, perhaps, are the members of its cast, all giving solid performances that help to elevate screenwriter Maxwell Shane's story a notch above what it might otherwise have been with a less competent selection. As for the Cinecolor, it's somewhat difficult to judge today given the prints available, and referring to contemporary reports doesn't help much. *Motion Picture Herald* wrote that Cinecolor "adds luster and exploitability,"[25] while one exhibitor wrote in to complain that the "color isn't too good—in fact we have had lots better Cinecolor than this."[26]

Rhonda Fleming, in only her third credited film role, is pawed by lecherous (and wide-eyed) John Abbott in **Adventure Island** (Pine-Thomas/Paramount, 1947).

Due to a record backlog of produced films, both *Jungle Flight* and *Adventure Island* would sit on the shelf for a year before going into release[27] on August 22, 1947, and October 10, 1947, respectively, with Sam credited as director Peter Stewart in both.

Sometime during the first quarter of 1947, Sam was contacted by producer Sam Katzman, for whom he had directed those eight Tim McCoy Westerns back in 1938-39 for Katzman's Victory Pictures. Katzman's Victory was by now a distant memory, replaced by his longer-lived Banner Pictures, which had produced an endless stream of films for Monogram from 1940, the last of these—*Vacation Days*—released on January 25, 1947. Katzman had entered into a parallel relationship with Columbia Pictures back in 1945, producing both features and serials under his Sam Katzman Productions banner—aka Esskay Productions—the first of the latter the thirteen-chapter *Brenda Starr, Reporter* (1946), based on the popular comic strip by Dale Messick. Other serials followed, based on both original subjects and other popular comic strips; *Hop Harrigan America's Ace of the Airways* (1946), based on the "Hop Harrigan" strip by Jon Blummer, was one of them. Now that his lengthy stint producing for Monogram had come to an end, Katzman was doubling down on his films and serials for Columbia. Katzman had acquired the rights to Jon Blummer's "Captain Silver's Log of the Sea Hound" comic, and hired Sam to direct the fifteen-chapter serial from a script by George Plympton, Lewis Clay, and Arthur Hoerl. Buster Crabbe had been hired to star, which may have been instrumental in Sam's hiring given their comfortable and efficient working relationship of the past half decade. After looking over the schooners in San Pedro's harbor for two suitable vessels to be used for the film, production was ready to get underway.[28] This was to be Sam's first shot at directing a lengthy serial, an attractive proposition given the longer shoot and enhanced pay it would provide. It didn't turn out that way.

Buster Crabbe, star of the serial **The Sea Hound** (Esskay/Columbia, 1947), Sam Katzman producer, Mack V. Wright and Walter B. Eason directors. Sam Newfield only got to direct the first five days of production before being sidelined by a major accident.

The Sea Hound, as the serial was titled, began production on May 12, 1947. On the fifth day of production, May 16, shooting was taking place aboard the 105-foot two-masted schooner *Seaward* near Santa Catalina Island.[29] Sam, his attention focused on directing Crabbe, tripped and fell down the engine-room hatch, sustaining a fractured skull, internal injuries, and brain concussion. After some emergency treatment by studio first aid man William Tierney, the forty-eight-year-old director was first taken to Catalina Hospital, and then flown by seaplane to Long Beach and Cedars of Lebanon Hospital where emergency surgery was performed. Five days after the accident, Sam was reported to be "out of danger," but it would be another four months before he was able to return to work. In the meantime, Katzman immediately promoted assistant directors Walter B. Eason and Mack Wright to co-director status, and completed the film. Sam's name didn't make it into the film's credits.[30]

Sam had recovered sufficiently by September to accept a job directing *The Counterfeiters* for Edward Small's Reliance Pictures. Maurice Conn, whose heyday as an independent producer petered out in the late 1930s, was now in the midst of a three-film mini-revival. Based on his original story with adaptation for the screen by Fred Myton and Barbara Worth, *The Counterfeiters* would be the second of Conn's three late-1940s films, this one for distribution by Twentieth Century-Fox. Filmed at the Nassour Studios under the working title *Triple Cross*, Sam—as Peter Stewart—directed co-stars John Sutton, Doris Merrick, and a supporting cast that included Hugh Beaumont, Lon Chaney, Jr., and Herbert Rawlinson.

This crime drama has Scotland Yard Inspector John Sutton teaming up with U.S. Treasury Department agents Don Harvey and Robert Kent (again billed as Douglas Blackley) to put an end to a counterfeiting ring headed by cautious Pierre Watkins and his chief operator Hugh Beaumont, the latter saddled with dim-witted "muscle" Lon Chaney Jr. Beaumont's girl is played by Doris Merrick, whose father, Herbert Rawlinson, was the original engraver of the plates used to print the bogus bills flooding Europe. Sutton infiltrates the gang, and soon finds himself involved in multitudinous crosses, double-crosses, and triple-crosses, everyone wanting the valuable plates for themselves.

This would have been a better film if Chaney's roommate, played by George O'Hanlon, had not been added as unnecessary and unwelcome comic relief, which continuously distracts from the otherwise taut and engaging story unfolding on the screen. Most likely screenwriter Myton's unfortunate contribution, it reduces what could have been a hard-boiled thriller to something more closely approximating soft-boiled. Otherwise, the cast is fine, with Beaumont a standout as the smooth-talking but violence-prone hood who schemes to replace his 20 % cut with the more attractive 80 % that possession of the plates will yield. Brit John Sutton gives a relaxed performance as the gang infiltrator and recipient of a brutal beating by Beaumont. Merrick is a curiosity in that the way she plays her role it's a surprise that *anyone* trusts her, but I suppose we're to believe that her feminine wiles trump all. Chaney, for better or worse, is once again required to revisit his brain-addled "Lennie" persona. O'Hanlon, as alluded to above, is simply annoying. Reviewers liked the film, and made a point of complimenting O'Hanlon's performance—go figure. *The Counterfeiters* was released in May 1948.

Lon Chaney Jr. is being restrained from doing some major damage to John Sutton in **The Counterfeiters** (Reliance/Twentieth Century Fox, 1948), Maurice Conn producer, Sam Newfield (as Peter Stewart) director. Foreground, left-to-right: Robert Kent, Don Harvey, Chaney, and Sutton.

Pride had nothing to do with earning a living, and Sam probably didn't care too much where his next paying job came from, so he accepted an offer to direct two films for producer John Sutherland—he of Sutherland Studios—for release through Eagle-Lion. Directing as Sherman Scott, Sam helmed *Lady at Midnight*, filmed in March 1948, and *The Strange Mrs. Crane*, filmed three months later in June.

John Sutherland (1910-2001) was a former actor in stock 1929-30, followed by a stint with the U.S. Park Service, and studies at U.C.L.A. that led to a short-lived teaching job there. On to Hollywood, where he wrote and directed for Disney 1938-40, produced for M-G-M in 1941, then into the military and the U.S. Signal Corps 1941-43. He then went into business for himself, forming John Sutherland Productions where he produced a series of Technicolor cartoons for United Artists, as well as establishing a studio for production of both theatrical and commercial films. His first feature was the Michael Shayne mystery *Too Many Winners* for PRC, and had now landed this two-film contract for Eagle-Lion. Sutherland continued his work in the 16mm commercial field while fulfilling this contract.[31] While Sig had no known connection to Sutherland at this time, the fact that his son Stanley assisted Sam with the direction, and that both Jack Greenhalgh and Bert Sternbach were involved with these two films suggests otherwise.

Back to *Lady at Midnight*. Radio broadcaster Richard Denning and his wife Frances Rafferty are in a mild panic when they learn that someone is contesting the adoption of their seven-year-old daughter Lora Lee Michel, claiming that Rafferty was underage when it took place. Her birth certificate was lost years earlier, and they now discover that her baptismal certificate has gone missing as well. Needing some other form of proof, they involve their attorney Harlan Warde and private investigator Ralph Dunn to track down the birth mother, Claudia Drake, to testify that Rafferty was of age at the time. Matters are complicated when a wealthy neighbor—who turns out to have been the birth mother—is murdered, and thugs warn Denning not to get involved. After Denning is accosted on the street and beaten to a pulp, he undergoes a miraculous, time-compressed recovery and finally solves the mystery of the who and why behind the effort to take his daughter away.

Lady at Midnight is a serviceable, if slowly paced, murder mystery with a plot by writer Richard Sale that's a wee bit better than a lot of its lower budget competition. Denning is solid in the lead, although he smiles far too much for someone in such dire straits. Rafferty is perfectly charming as his wife, displaying a low-key believability. Dunn, as always, is a welcome presence as the P.I., and garners some honestly earned laughs as he continues to place horse race bets based on his *hunch du jour*, and regales young Michel with exaggerated stories of daring do. Former child actor Jackie—now Jack—Searle has a small role as a weaselly neighbor, but any cuteness he may have had in his youth was well behind him by this time. Sid Melton has an uncredited role as a two-bit hood, his presence here notable only in that he would soon reappear in many of Sam's upcoming films for Lippert in just a few years. As the young daughter at the story's center, Lora Lee Michel shows future possibilities as an actress, but her precociousness here defies belief. Reviewers were lukewarm in their reactions to the film, and one of them took pains to comment on the "ordinary directing by Sherman Scott."

Private investigator Ralph Dunn regales young Lora Lee Michel with tall tales of his past exploits, in **Lady at Midnight** (John Sutherland Productions/Eagle-Lion, 1948), John Sutherland producer, Sam Newfield (as Sherman Scott) director.

The Strange Mrs. Crane was adapted by screenwriter Al Martin from an episode of the long running "The Whistler" radio show. Beautiful young Marjorie Lord finds her charmed life as wife to older gubernatorial candidate Pierre Watkin threatened when Robert Shayne, her con artist partner from a former life and identity, resurfaces and blackmails her. Her new position threatened, she stabs and kills him. Ruth Brady, a co-worker and naïve lover of Shayne's, is arrested for the crime, and as B-film coincidence would have it, Lord is selected as a member of the jury hearing her case. Selected as the jury's foreman, Lord successfully pushes for conviction, and fills out the note to be passed on to the court clerk. At the last moment, though, she reaches into her pocket for the note and accidentally passes along a letter proving her guilt!

This is a good little courtroom drama despite its abundant implausibilities and coincidences. Lord and Brady "coincidentally" pass each other in the hall outside Shayne's apartment, not just once but several different times, and would Lord actually be chosen to sit on the jury given her close relationship with defense lawyer James Seay, who also just happens to be her husband's campaign manager? And why the hell doesn't a smart former con artist destroy that incriminating letter as soon as she got her hands on it? Regardless, the film is engaging, the viewer actually rooting for Lord to get away with it, or at least up to a point. This is one of Sam's better-directed films, with a number of nicely arranged compositions, solid camerawork from Greenhalgh, and seamless editing by Martin Cohn. Sam always seemed to be able to find a bit part or two for old friends and co-workers, in this instance for Charlie King, used here as one of the members of the jury (and expectant father!), and Spec O'Donnell, who had worked for the Sterns for a year or two twenty years earlier, as a telegram delivery "boy." *The Strange Mrs. Crane* was released on January 1, 1949.

Marjorie Lord plays the murderer we actually root for, or at least up to a point, in **The Strange Mrs. Crane** (John Sutherland Productions/Eagle-Lion, 1948), John Sutherland producer, Sam Newfield (as Sherman Scott) director. Left-to-right: Chester Clute, James Seay, and Marjorie Lord.

Sam was to direct one additional final film for Eagle-Lion Classics, the next iteration of Eagle-Lion, but more on that evolution in a few pages. Released on April 20, 1951, with the rather silly title *Skipalong Rosenbloom*, the film co-starred two former boxers from the 1930s, heavyweight champion Max Baer and light middleweight champion "Slapsie" Maxie Rosenbloom. Dean Reisner and Eddie Forman's screenplay had a rather novel approach for the era, presented as a television broadcast of a Western feature with frequent interruptions for commercial breaks, poking fun at both the Western genre and television broadcasting circa 1950. The film's independent producer, Wally Kline, said that the film's goal was to send owners of television sets away from the theatre "sharply aware of the contrast between theatre entertainment and the stuff TV's been feeding them."[32]

The story takes place in Buttonhole Bend, terrorized by outlaw Baer and his gang who have killed every sheriff unfortunate enough to accept the job. Saloon owner Hillary Brook is the brains of Baer's gang, but when they attempt to take over Raymond Hatton's property, Hatton sends for his nephew, Rosenbloom, for questionable help. This film was not available for viewing, so I'll defer to contemporary reviews for comment, *Motion Picture Daily* writing that

> The burlesque depends heavily upon slapstick, malapropisms and old puns for its comedy. It is boisterous, rough-and-ready fun with all the merits and faults of this type of humor. Those who like the nonsequitur joke, the obvious play on words and double-talk will probably enjoy "Skipalong Rosenbloom," a lampoon of television Westerns which ribs TV, video addicts, sponsors and, of course, the Western itself.[33]

Fuzzy Knight (center) is about to bring an unexpected end to the one-sided fight between Max Baer (left) and Maxie Rosenbloom, in **Skipalong Rosenbloom** (Wally Kline Enterprises/Eagle Lion Classics, 1951), Wally Kline producer, Sam Newfield director.

Harrisons Reports reviewed in kind, saying that

> There is nothing subtle about the comedy, which is played in the broadest slapstick style. Many of the gags and situations are so forced that they fall flat, but there are others that are genuinely funny and should provoke hearty laughter. The picture, which lampoons practically every western-feature cliché, is presented as a television-sponsored film, with a bubbling television announcer breaking into the action at intervals to plug the sponsor's products with fantastic claims. These claims provide the film with some of its choicest gags.[34]

There's a five minute fifty-five second excerpt on YouTube that provides a hint of what the film was all about, and depending on your tolerance for broad slapstick and questionable puns, you may or may not care for it. Personally, I thought it was rather funny in its own sophomoric way.

Sam, it would seem, was a perfect choice to direct, given his solid roots in silent slapstick comedy and his lengthy involvement with filmed Westerns. Kline, as it turned out, ran out of money on the film which eventually cost a reported $100,000 to produce. A syndicate of eight New York distribution executives—all officials of Eagle-Lion Classics—bailed Kline out by purchasing the negative at a profit to Kline.[35]

There was one more known solo effort for Sam towards the end of the 1940s, this one a more sensational effort exploiting the dangers of marijuana. Filmed at the Hal Roach Studios with the working title *The Devil's Weed* in later May 1949 as one of producer Richard Kay's Franklin Productions, the film starred aspiring actress Lila Leeds in an effort to cash in on the recent notoriety stemming from her August 1948 marijuana arrest with actor Robert Mitchum.[36] After serving sixty days in jail and placed on five years' probation, Leeds soon found that her previously none-too-healthy film career was now dead. Hoping to revive it in any way possible, Leeds accepted the offer to star in this blatantly exploitative exposé that, as the finished film's opening crawl explained, was "the story of 'tea' – or 'tomatoes' – the kind millions thru ignorance, have been induced to smoke…. If its presentation saves but one young girl or boy from becoming a 'dope fiend' – then its story has been well told." Leeds was paid $2,500 and 5 % of the gross, the latter of which never materialized.[37]

Initially released as *Wild Weed*, Leeds stars as a dancer introduced by her friend Mary Ellen Popel and pusher Alan Baxter into the clandestine world of marijuana, and begins her downhill descent from there. Straight arrow brother David Holt, whom she is working hard to put through school, discovers what she's gotten into, and commits suicide! Fired from her job due to her increasing lethargy—not to mention the adoption of a *really bad* attitude—Leeds soon finds herself and friends busted. Narcotics cop Lyle Talbot and his two agents, Robert Kent (yet again billed as Douglas Blackley) and Don Harvey, fail to get her to see the error of her ways, but two months in stir drives her to the brink of madness. Eventually recovered, she does a 180 and agrees to work with the cops to bring down the drug gang and its leader, Michael Whalen. The film ends with one of Sam's typically bruising fistfights, after which the miscreants are cuffed and hauled off.

The story, of course, is sensationalized, over-the-top nonsense, but production wise it is a genuine surprise, given that it's one of Sam's most stylishly directed films to date, benefitting from solid production values, excellent camera work and lighting, lots

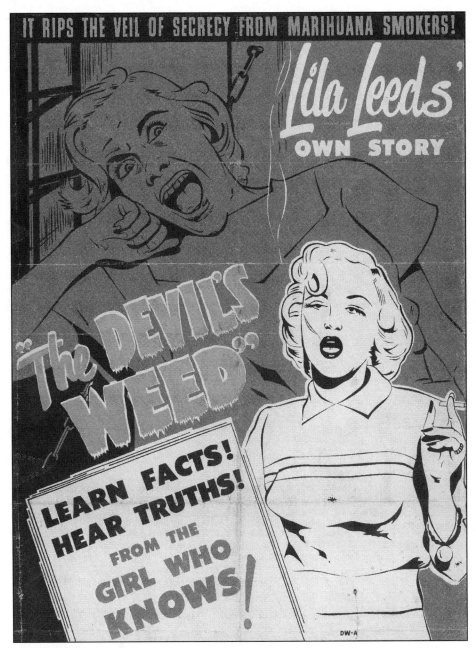

"Learn Facts! Hear Truths! From the Girl Who Knows!" Poster art for **Wild Weed**, here retitled and further sensationalized as **The Devil's Weed**. *Courtesy of Heritage Auctions.*

of tight closeups, and a theremin-heavy score courtesy of composer Raoul Kraushaar and Dr. Samuel J. Hoffman that tips the film's mood in an other-worldly direction; art direction by Eugene Lourie and editing by Richard Currier doesn't hurt, either. The acting is almost uniformly good, with Baxter a standout as the weed-pushing, conscienceless hood. Leeds does okay in the lead and tries hard in what ultimately proved a vain attempt to resurrect her career, but her lack of experience trips her up on occasion. There's one attention grabbing sequence set in the prison as Leeds slowly loses her mind, when she peers into a mirror and watches as her visage ages before her eyes, finally morphing into her dead brother. Given the film's somewhat tawdry reputation, it is actually a pretty good film that belies its lower budget, exploitative roots.

The film premiered on July 15 at Chicago's Rialto theatre, where Leeds put in a personal appearance "lecturing on dangers of marijuana" as part of a contractual forty-week tour at $1,000—or at least according to Leeds's memoirs.[38] *Variety* deemed the film's first week's take "Tame" at $12,000, dwarfed by RKO's *The Judge Steps Out* at $35,000 and United Artists' *Champion* at $32,000.[39] Sam Cummins, general manager of Eureka Productions, distributed *Wild Weed* on a roadshow basis,[40] but according to David F. Friedman, the film "played a couple of dates to disastrous results." The film was picked up by producer Kroger Babb "for almost nothing,"[41] Babb and his Hygienic Productions the ones behind the notorious exploitation film *Mom and Dad*.

Lila Leeds consults with Jack Greenhalgh (left) and Stanley Neufeld between setups on **Wild Weed** (Hallmark, 1949), Richard Kay producer, Sam Newfield (as Sherman Scott) director. *Courtesy of Tim Neufeld.*

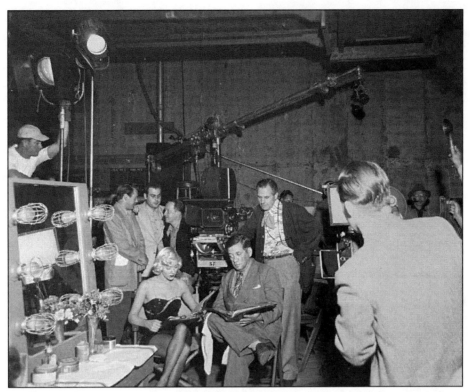

Lila Leeds continues to consult, this time with director Sam Newfield as Jack Greenhalgh quietly observes. **Wild Weed** (Hallmark, 1949). *Courtesy of Tim Neufeld.*

Babb had recently given his unfortunately named production company a new name, Hallmark Productions, and decided to give the film a fresh start. He produced new promotional materials that emphasized sex over drugs, with taglines such as "This Kansas Blond made 'Just One Mistake'" and "A Teen-Age Thunderbolt!" Coupled with a new title, *She Shoulda Said "No"!*, Babb hoped his new approach would lure in the overcoat crowd with different, lower expectations. The film, not surprisingly, faced a bumpy reception as far as the censors and morality police were concerned. The National Legion of Decency slammed it with a "Condemned" rating,[42] and Ohio's censor board banned the film outright; even an appeal to the state's Supreme Court—only the second in its history—failed to overturn the ban.[43] Overseas, the British Board of Film Censors refused to give it a certificate of approval.[44] Friedman was merciless—and likely exaggerating—with his recollections of Leeds, but they are so *colorful* that I reprint them here:

> [Mitchum] did about six months at the county farm; the judge let her go because she was a good-lookin' blonde. We had Lila out on the road telling about the evils of dope, but unfortunately she was blowing the operators and blowing the stagehands and messing around with the ushers, and we were getting closed up on morals charges because of her...[45]

As I said, most likely exaggerated. Unfortunately for Leeds, there was only one more film role in her future, and a tiny, uncredited one at that, in Warner's low budget *The House Across the Street*.

Chapter 19:
The Baby of the Industry (Film Classics, 1948-1949)

In the meantime, Sig was taking it easy, freed up as he was from the day-to-day, year-to-year grind of life back at PRC. His son Stanley and wife Marie had a son, Timothy Lee Neufeld, on April 23, 1947, so Sig and his friend Bert Sternbach would frequently stop by to visit Sig's first grandchild. This brief respite from filmmaking came to an end with an offer by Film Classics to produce a film tentatively titled *The Easy Way*, based on an original story and screenplay by Al Martin. Film Classics, Inc. was formed back in 1943 as a national distributing company of important older films produced by others. Along with the initial acquisition of thirty-six Gaumont-British films previously released by Twentieth Century-Fox, other films were acquired as well. "Among the stars featured in the films," reported *Independent Exhibitors Film Bulletin*,

> are Madeleine Carroll, Walter Huston, Herbert Marshall, Robert Young, Margaret Lockwood, Constance Bennett, George Arliss, Richard Dix, Claude Rains, John Loder, Wallace Ford, Richard Arlen, Boris Karloff, Constance Cummings, Conrad Veidt and Roland Young. The directors…include: Alfred Hitchcock, Carol Reed, Robert Stevenson, Victor Saville, Raoul Walsh and Michael Balcon.[1]

More recently, Film Classics had acquired fifty Universal Realart features, to be released at the rate of ten a year. While acknowledging that the company was "the baby of the industry," it was aiming for "major company status." "We want theatremen to know they can rely on Film Classics in any contingency," stated assistant general sales manager Jules K. Chapman at its first regional sales meeting in September 1947, "and only by giving them every cooperation can we [give] them this assurance."[2] A month later, Cinecolor Corporation entered the distribution field by acquiring 100 % of the stock of Film Classics and International Film Classics. In conjunction with this, Cinecolor formed the Cinecolor Finance Corporation to provide financing of lab charges and release prints for productions utilizing the Cinecolor process, relieving producers and distributors of the immediate need of putting up those elusive dollars. Film Classics would distribute both Cinecolor and black-and-white productions from independent producers and continue the rerelease of older productions, while trending toward new productions in Cinecolor.[3]

Showmen's Trade Review reported that "Sig Neufeld came out of retirement to produce 'Money Madness' for Film Classics," but he was never really retired, just taking a well-deserved break. That break was over now, however, and shooting began on January 15, 1948, at the Sutherland Studio.[4] Sam, of course, was the director (as Peter Stewart) of this Sigmund Neufeld Production, released for screening on April 15, 1948. A week before the film's release, *Film Daily* wrote that "The Hollywood grapevine hints Film Classics has a 'sleeper' in 'Money Madness'."[5]

Hugh Beaumont starred once again, and gives a convincingly unnerving performance as the film's cold blooded, manipulative psycho. He arrives in Los Angeles, deposits $200,000 in a safety deposit box, and takes a job as a cabby. He insinuates himself into the life of diner waitress Frances Rafferty, who lives with her bitter old aunt, Cecil Weston. After a whirlwind romance, Beaumont rushes Rafferty into a marriage, then sets about slowly poisoning the aunt. With her death, he forces Rafferty to go along with his scheme, claiming that she found the $200,000 in her aunt's trunk. Rafferty is cowled into agreeing to all this since Beaumont has implicated her in her aunt's death—she unknowingly delivered the poisoned drinks—and tells her that, as his wife, she can't testify against him. Rafferty's lawyer, Harlan Warde, begins to smell a rat, and things really fall apart when Danny Morton shows up, given that half of that stolen $200,000 "belongs" to him. The film ends with Morton shot dead by Beaumont, then Beaumont shot dead by some cops who were lured to the house by its booming radio. Rafferty is sentenced to ten years imprisonment as Beaumont's supposed accomplice.

Hugh Beaumont as the cold blooded, manipulative psycho in **Money Madness** (Sigmund Neufeld Productions/Film Classics, 1948), Sig Neufeld producer, Sam Newfield (as Peter Stewart) director.

This is a taut little thriller, and one of Sig and Sam's better films. Rafferty is excellent as Beaumont's dupe, as is Cecil Weston as her chronically complaining aunt. As Rafferty's lawyer, Warde comes off as stunningly unprofessional, pushy and annoying in his continuing romantic pursuit of Rafferty. That said, I seemed to have thought more highly of *Money Madness* than a lot of the contemporary reviewers. So much for *Film Daily*'s belief in the "Hollywood grapevine."

Karl Herzog, Cinecolor Corp.'s executive vice-president and Film Classics' vice-president and treasurer, was sufficiently impressed with *Money Madness* and Sig's capabilities that the two of them created a new production company, Sigmund Neufeld Pictures, Inc. Herzog, you'll recall, knew Sig from back at PRC where he had served as secretary-treasurer of PRC Productions in 1943. Incorporated in late March or early April 1948, incorporation papers were filed in Sacramento;[6] Sig was the new production company's president, Herzog its secretary-treasurer, and film attorney Monte Livingston the vice-president.[7]

Producer Sig Neufeld poses with son Stanley's wife Marie (black top) and her friend at the outdoor location of **Miraculous Journey** (Sigmund Neufeld Pictures/Film Classics, 1948), Sig Neufeld producer, Sam Newfield (as Peter Stewart) director. *Courtesy of Tim Neufeld.*

Sig already had a couple of projects in the works at this time. He had acquired the screen rights to Douglas Carter's novel "Fatima," a story with a carnival background that doesn't appear to have made it to the screen.[8] The other property, then working under the tentative titles *Jungle Night* and, soon after, *Jungle Blindness*,[9] finally landed the title *Miraculous Journey* by the time it became the first film of Sig and Herzog's new production company. Sam directed the film, which went into production late in March 1948 and was released in September. Sig used his usual technical crew of Greenhalgh, Todd, son Stanley, and Sternbach, and hired composer Leo Erdody once again to write the score, bringing back Lew Porter to write the lyrics for the film's one unmemorable song. Greenhalgh and Sam's earlier experience with Cinecolor for the Pine-Thomas production *Adventure Island* provided familiarity with the process.

Jack Greenhalgh checks the lighting for an upcoming shot with co-stars Rory Calhoun and Audrey Long in **Miraculous Journey** (Sigmund Neufeld Pictures/Film Classics, 1948).
Courtesy of Tim Neufeld.

As a first effort, it wasn't very impressive. The story was simplistic: A plane full of passengers crash lands in the middle of an African jungle, and they struggle to survive until the pilot cobbles together a dugout canoe, floats back to civilization, and returns in a helicopter to rescue everyone. Fred Myton's embarrassingly cliched screenplay is peopled by the usual stereotypes: Rory Calhoun (again borrowed from Selznick) as the tough, resourceful pilot; Audrey Long as the blind good girl; Virginia Grey as the wealthy, entitled, and murderously jealous woman; June Storey as the brassy girl from the East Side who at first tries to fool everyone by faking a French accent; Thurston Hall as the condescending financial wizard who fixates on the jungle's diamonds; Jim Bannon as the ruthless crook perpetually at odds with Calhoun; Carole Donne as the helpful stewardess; and George Cleveland as the jungle-based hermit who offers up pearls of wisdom throughout, managing to effect a change for the better in most of the stranded individuals. The hermit has a dog (Flame), a crow (Jimmy), a chimp (Charlie), and a pair of big-eyed owls hanging around to up the film's "cute" quotient. The dog figures prominently at two different points, alerting the others when the blind girl is sinking in quicksand, and later saving the day by shoving the crook, who has forced the hermit to accompany him, into the swamp as hors d'oeuvres for the crocodiles. And that crocodile: when it first opens its mouth it looks more like a sock puppet than a threat. Calhoun being Calhoun, all the female survivors lust after him, but he only has eyes for the one whose eyes don't work, fodder for seething jealousy among the other women. Sam fits in two fistfights amidst all the tough guy posturing between Calhoun and hissable Bannon, one of them outside the plane's wreckage—pretty good—and the other inside—not so good. The film manages another pugilistic highlight in a juicy catfight between Storey and Grey, the two of them slapping the hell out of each other. I suppose there's some sort of uplifting "moral" or "message" buried herein courtesy of the hermit's many inspiring homilies, that result in a mini-epidemic of hard-to-swallow forgiveness. Maybe one can begrudgingly accept the hermit forgiving Storey for helping Bannon kidnap him, but when Long forgives a jealous Grey for leading her into the quicksand where she almost perishes, up to her non-functioning eyeballs in the stuff before the obligatory last-minute rescue, that's choke-worthy! Toss in an appearance by the gorilla (Ray Corrigan) who dispatches an unfortunate Donne offscreen, and you end up with a rather silly film. Full disclosure here: Almost all of the contemporary reviewers liked the film, or at least gave it a pass, lauding it for its "exploitability" and its improvement over some of Film Classics' previous efforts. Greenhalgh's Cinecolor cinematography always warranted positive mention, which may have helped boost their reviews to a slightly higher level; what I viewed was a dupey, black-and-white copy, not that I had a choice.

Rory Calhoun's about to plant one on Audrey Long in **Miraculous Journey** (Sigmund Neufeld Pictures/Film Classics, 1948).

Sandwiched in between *Miraculous Adventure* and Sig's next credited film for Film Classics was the prehistoric monster thriller *Unknown Island*, released in November 1948. This one is an oddity in that Sig's name is prominently displayed under the film's pre-release promotional photos as "SIGMUND NEUFELD Presents," while lobby cards, posters, and the like released along with the film bore the caption "Produced By ALBERT JAY COHEN." These earlier photos are the sole association I've found between Sig and this film, his name and credit absent from the trades and online resources as well. I suspect that this was an unfortunate error on Film Classics' part, akin to syndicated columnist Louella O. Parsons's erroneous—and promptly retracted— claim that Sig had produced *Rocketship X-M* two years later.[10] This remains a topic for future research, to confirm that it was indeed an error rather than a legitimate, uncredited role that Sig played on this film.

Three rather unconvincing Tyrannosaurus Rex clomp about in this promotional still. Sig Neufeld was associated with **Unknown Island** (Albert Jay Cohen Productions/Film Classics, 1948) only in these early promotional materials, but had little or nothing to do with the actual film. Albert Jay Cohen producer, Jack Bernhard director.

Stanley Neufeld (left) and Sam Newfield consult with a State Department official in Washington D.C. to get some facts straight. **State Department: File 649** (Sigmund Neufeld Pictures/Film Classics, 1949). *Courtesy of Tim Neufeld.*

Sigmund Neufeld Pictures relocated to the Nassour Studios as the company's new headquarters[11] for its next production for Film Classics, *State Department: File 649*, then going by the flipped title *File 649: State Department*. The Cinecolor production reportedly budgeted at a generous $750,000, filming was to commence on September 15.[12] Sig wanted to get the technical details right, and for once had the bucks to do so. To that end, John E. Peurifoy, assistant secretary of state, was invited to attend a buffet dinner held in Beverly Hills and hosted by Cinecolor and Film Classics. Conferences followed with Peurifoy, Sig, and Joseph Bernhard, president of both Cinecolor and Film Classics, to discuss the production.[13]

William Lundigan and Virginia Bruce star as freshly minted employees of the U.S. Foreign Service, assigned to the northern-China post at Ming-Goo after several Americans have been killed back in Peiping. Trouble arises when exiled Mongolian warlord Richard Loo and his rebels arrive and make all of the Americans and their Chinese employees prisoners at the consulate, and begin a reign of terror among the local villagers. Loo's goal is to use coercion or force to get the government in Nanking to appoint him the area's governor. He is ruthless, of course, the point driven home when he has the arms cut off the consulate's ham operator, Victor Sen Yung. If that wasn't evidence enough, Loo is unfazed later on when his caravan drives over a little kid, leaving him to die. When the Americans back in Peiping realize that Loo has taken prisoners, they prepare to send planes. Loo and his cohorts take Lundigan with them as they flee the area, but Lundigan has made advance plans to dispatch Loo. He has placed dynamite under the warlord's personal trailer, to be activated when the radio inside is turned on. After delivering a fiery patriotic—and borderline jingoistic—speech to Loo, Lundigan is shot, but in a final altruistic move activates the radio, blowing Loo and his aides into the clouds above China.

Fuzzy snapshot of director Sam Newfeld (second from left wearing suspenders) on location at the White House to get some establishing shots for **State Department: File 649** (Sigmund Neufeld Pictures/Film Classics, 1949), Sig Neufeld producer, Sam Newfeld director.
Courtesy of Tim Neufeld.

State Department: File 649 is a film of its time, and while it was well received when released in February 1949, it hasn't aged all that well. It is certainly a good-looking film, that reported $750,000 budget all up there on screen. Exterior locations and interior sets have been convincingly provided by art director Edward Jewell and set decorator Elias Reif. Jack Greenhalgh's attractive cinematography makes good use of the Cinecolor process, with some location photography in Washington, DC to add to the verisimilitude.

The film boasts a much larger cast than usually present in films of the lower budget class, with Asian actors predominating. There's only one unfortunate exception, that of actor Robert Stephenson, who plays a Mongolian spy and looks about as Asian as Popeye the Sailor, perhaps less so. Lundigan and Bruce, low-wattage leads at best, deliver strong performances, as do most of the other lesser-knowns populating the cast, such as Frank Ferguson as a Peiping-based consul, and Milton Kibbee as a grizzled old trader. Milton Raison's screenplay results in a reasonably taut thriller, although most of the action (with the exception of that exploding trailer) takes place offscreen. The film's weak points include an intrusive voice-over narration that, while intended to give the film a documentary-like feel in its earliest scenes, instead comes off more like a 1950's classroom instructional video. The film's score, composed by Lucien Cailliet, has been laid in with a heavy hand, overwhelming several otherwise quietly romantic scenes between Lundigan and Bruce. As for that highly touted $750,000 budget, it appears that it was somewhat of an exaggeration: the film, it was later revealed, had a final negative cost of $257,000, with domestic film rentals an unspectacular $230,076. Not what one would call an impressive showing.

Cast and crew pose on one of the "exterior" sets for **State Department: File 649** (Sigmund Neufeld Pictures/Film Classics, 1949). Sig Neufeld and Karl Hertzog sitting at left, Sam Newfield whispering to Virginia Bruce while co-star William Lundigan ignores them, sitting at right. *Courtesy of Tim Neufeld.*

Motion Picture Daily praised Film Classics for delivering "an honest-to-goodness thriller,"[14] and *Variety* made note of Jack Greenhalgh's "beautifully photographed Cinecolor."[15] *Showmen's Trade Review* called it the "most pretentious production yet made by Film Classics," going on to say that "it will entertain audiences generally because of its lively action, its scenic background, the excellence of most of the acting, and its bang-up ending."[16] New York Democratic Representative Arthur Klein got his two cents in, placing a statement into the *Congressional Record* praising the contributions of Film Classics president Bernhard and sales vice-president B.G. Kranze. It read in part that the film "tells in an interesting manner how the unsung heroes of the State Department's Consular Service perform their varied functions, sometimes in the face of great danger."[17] None of this helped with ticket sales.

State Department: File 649 co-stars William Lundigan and Virginia Bruce.

Sig's relationship with Film Classics didn't last beyond this film. By mid-1950, Film Classics had merged with Sig's *bête noire* Eagle-Lion to create Eagle-Lion Classics.[18] There were signs of trouble soon after, however, *Film Bulletin* reporting that "the company is in dire need of more quality products is obvious, and until such time as it is available the company will continue to cut its operating expenses wherever possible." The article went on to add that Eagle-Lion Classic's 25-27 % distributing fees were to be upped to 30 %, and might go even higher.[19] Within a year of Eagle-Lion Classics' inception, United Artists' new regime purchased all films about to be released or already in release by ELC, which was in the process of going out of business.[20]

With the production of *State Department: File 649* now behind him, it would be another year before Sig would return to active production. Sig's battles with Pathe Industries and Eagle-Lion Films were annoyingly ongoing, and in April 1949 he dashed off another letter:

> I do not have to point out to you that reports and remittances for my participation in all of my pictures from 1940 to 1946 are far behind. According to my Distribution Agreement entered into during 1940, 1941, and 1942 the terms call for reports every thirty days. Subsequent Distribution Agreements call for reports every thirty days for the first fifteen months and every ninety days thereafter. The last reports and remittances received were in November 1948 covering my participation to June of 1948. You are therefore nine months behind in remittances and reports.
>
> I am aware of the trying conditions of the industry, but in order to protect my interests, your prompt reply will be greatly appreciated.[21]

Eagle-Lion Films finally got their act together with more prompt reporting. By September 1949 they forwarded a detailed listing of all Sigmund Neufeld Productions covering the 1940-41 season through the 1945-46 season, and remitted a check in the amount of $6,280.08.[22]

Aside from Sig's correspondences with Eagle-Lion, he continued to pursue other production options throughout the year, eventually landing a lucrative gig for both he and his brother later that year. Sam had managed to find some work directing the aforementioned *Wild Weed* in May 1949, but aside from that one job there was little else to do in the meantime.

Chapter 20:
When Hero Catch Crook, Time for Picture to End (Lippert, 1950-1953)

Back in mid-1945, theater owners Robert L. Lippert and John J. Jones decided to get into the production and distribution end of the business. They formed two companies: Action Pictures, to produce the films, and Screen Guild Productions to distribute them. Jones was president of Screen Guild, with Lippert vice-president, general manager, and in charge of sales. Lippert was president of Action Pictures as well, and would oversee all films produced in house. Action Pictures' first released effort was the Western *Wildfire, the Story of a Horse*, followed by *Northwest Trail* and *God's Country*. By early 1946 Action Pictures had been renamed Golden Gate Pictures, with Joseph Blumenfeld—of San Francisco's Blumenfeld Theatres—installed as president.[1] By 1947, Golden Gate was history as well, Screen Guild having taken over all in-house production. Over the next few years, Screen Guild's output would comprise a mix of in-house product and independently produced films picked up for distribution.

By 1949, Jones was no longer involved, and Lippert had assumed Screen Guild's presidency. By June Lippert's stranglehold on the company was completed when Screen Guild Productions was merged into Lippert Productions, with offices and production moved over to the Nassour Studios.[2] The surprise success of writer-director Sam Fuller's *I Shot Jesse James*, released in early 1949, had been the impetus to create Lippert Productions. According to Lippert biographer Mark Thomas McGee, "Using Fuller's film as leverage, Lippert persuaded the 28 franchise holders to merge Screen Guild with Robert L. Lippert Productions, an action that put Lippert in charge of the distributing-producing combination. His first order of business was to liquidate Screen Guild's assets for a 5 % overhead charge, after which he bought out the franchise holders and set up his own string of exchanges."[3] Lippert now held the reins.

In conjunction with this, Lippert incorporated the Motion Picture Financial Corp. in New York, its primary purpose to finance Lippert Productions, and possibly other producers' films as well.[4] Lippert was a wealthy man by now, a youthful obsession with film evolving into career that first involved theatre ownership having expanded to production and distribution.

But now decreasing revenues were becoming a concern. Impacted primarily by the rapid spread of televised programming and the resultant decrease in theatre attendance, Lippert laid the blame at the feet of the exhibitors, saying "I can make these statements because I can prove them." Lippert had first-hand experience with exhibition, owning sixty-one theaters in forty towns in California and Oregon. "Most circuit heads do not look at the product, or much of it, before they buy it, and they put no showmanship into the selling of it to their patrons. They leave the operation in charge of hired subordinates." Setting himself as an example of what the exhibitors *should* be doing, he claimed that he saw every film produced, and operated his theatres with no opening dates so that every film could run as long as there was a demand, and yanking it as soon as there wasn't. Advertising, he added, was customized to the likes and dislikes of a given community.[5] Lippert would go on to accuse industry leaders of ignoring the threat presented by the burgeoning broadcasting media, stating that "in Los Angeles, where there are more television sets, per-centage-wise, than in any other U.S. city, neighborhood theatre business is off forty per cent and first-run business is the worst in the country."[6] More had to be done to counter the growing influence and popularity of at-home (and free) viewing. Lippert liked to complain.

The name change went into effect on September 12, 1949, at which time Lippert laid out ambitious plans for the 1949-50 season's thirty-three films. Included among these would be three "high budget films," another four "intermediate 'A's," six of producer Ron Ormond's "Black Rider" Westerns, and twelve program features.[7] As initially announced, plans were for two films to be released per month, effective October.[8] Within a week, however, those two-films-per had been upped to three films per month.[9] As part of this enhanced schedule, Lippert had lined up Sig to produce films for the "program" feature category.

Between the two of them, Sig and Sam were responsible for fourteen films released from early 1950 into later 1953. Eight of these were team efforts, Sig producing and Sam directing. Another five were directed by Sam for other producers, and there was a final film produced by Sig that was directed by Reginald LeBorg. There was another, fifteenth film as well, a hybrid of sorts cobbled together from three separate Sam-directed episodes of the popular television show *Ramar of the Jungle*, but that will be discussed in the next chapter. Sam's involvement with the *Ramar* show precluded his involvement with Sig's final film, hence LeBorg as a fallback choice.

Stalwart Ralph Byrd, on the job for the U.S. Government's Radar Secret Service, ready for action by the department's silly looking vehicle, in **Radar Secret Service** (Lippert, 1950), Barney Sarecky producer, Sam Newfield director.

The first for Lippert was an action film titled *Radar Secret Service*, filmed at the Sutherland Studios in October and November 1949 under the working title *Radar Patrol*. Sam directed for producer Barney Sarecky from a screenplay by Beryl Sachs, the film released to theatres on January 28, 1950. None of his usual crew was present for this one, required instead to use Lippert's crew of cinematographer Ernest Miller, editor Carl Pierson, and sound engineer Earl Snyder. This exceedingly farfetched tale involves the

U.S. Government Radar Secret Service's pursuit of the crooks behind a stolen shipment of atomic material. Agents John Howard and Ralph Byrd tail the crooks in their tricked-out sedan, a huge radar device prominent atop their vehicle, following the guidance of those back at headquarters under the leadership of Pierre Watkin. As if having the RSS on their tail isn't enough cause for concern, gang leader Tristram Coffin is at odds with underling Tom Neal, both of whom lust after sexy cohort Adele Jergens; fellow crooks Sid Melton (questionable comic relief), Robert Kent, Riley Hill, and Kenne Duncan mill about on the periphery. Myrna Dell, as the bad-waitress-gone-good, rounds out the cast, all managing to deliver their lines with straight faces. The RSS finally gets its act together and uses a helicopter to track down the crooks and stolen material, the crooks either shot dead or arrested.

You'd have to be an eight-year-old or one hell of a rube to fall for film's basic premise, that using radar can bring in images of moving vehicles on a telescreen, and shot as if from a moving vehicle in front of it! Yeah, I know, the film's opening narration extolling the wonders of radar and possible future uses for scientific investigation set the flimsy scene, but talk about suspension of disbelief. The result is about as exciting as watching laundry dry, with interminable scenes of cars, trucks, and helicopters in motion using up what feels like half the film's length. A snippet of stock footage of a car crash that uses a vehicle that doesn't look anything like the one used in the newly shot footage only adds to the visual absurdity of the film. All-in-all, the film has the appearance of a 1940s action serial cut down to programmer length, and if that's the audience this was intended for, I guess filled some need or other. Sam appears to have been directing by the numbers for this one.

Sig and Sam were reunited for a second film for Lippert, this one the nifty *Western Pacific Agent*. Filmed over six days with the cooperation of Western Pacific Railroad, shooting began mid-December 1949.[10] Some framing scenes were shot aboard the railroad's streamliner "California Zephyr," much of it in the Vista-Domes as the train made its way through the Feather River Canyon. Passengers, who were supposedly surprised to see the heavy sound equipment moved onto the train, were provided some extra, mildly intrusive, "entertainment."[11]

Frank Wicken (Mickey Knox), a restless "bad penny" who only drifts back to his home town of Chester when he's hungry or broke, shows up once again and puts the squeeze on his father. Rebuffed, he gets wind of a huge payroll shipment that just arrived aboard one of the Western Pacific's trains, on its way for delivery by Robert Lowery. Knox heads over to the station agent and tries to force him to open the drawbridge to waylay Lowery, and ends up killing the agent when he refuses. Lowery arrives and, unable to get across the open bridge, heads inside to see the agent and he too is murdered. Knox makes off with the $50,000 payroll, only to later find that the bills' serial numbers are all known, and the money unspendable. Railroad special agent Kent Taylor is assigned to investigate, and over time gathers enough clues and fingerprints to identify Knox as the thief and murderer. In a climactic scene, Knox is surrounded by the law and attempts to escape by climbing the drawbridge's superstructure, but is shot dead.

This is an engaging action-thriller that benefits greatly from a lot of scenic location settings, the train and the action set on and around the drawbridge in particular. Kent Taylor is fine as the investigating agent. Robert Lowery has one of the smaller roles

Bad penny Mickey Knox threatens his father Morris Carnovsky with physical violence in the hard-hitting **Western Pacific Agent** (Lippert, 1950), Sig Neufeld producer, Sam Newfield director.

of his career as the paymaster who is murdered early on. Sheila Ryan is Lowery's grieving sister, and budding love interest for Taylor, Morris Carnovsky plays the murderous drifter's father, and Sid Melton—for better or worse—appears as a somewhat dimwitted local who "aids" Taylor with his investigation. The film's standout is Mickey Knox, who delivers a powerhouse performance as the remorseless, toothpick-chewing killer. And if three senseless murders aren't enough to establish his ruthlessness, he even gets to knock his father out cold, and then later shoot the defenseless fellow dead. Reviewers were nearly unanimous in their praise for Knox and the film in general, *Motion Picture Daily*'s reviewer particularly effusive:

> Standout performance in this direct-line murder story...is contributed by Mickey Knox, a grim, dynamic young man reminiscent of the early James Cagney. Kent Taylor and Sheila Ryan are the names for billing, and they acquit themselves ably, but the totally unsympathetic and entirely unextenuated killer, portrayed by Knox, is the character that dominates and carries the picture. It is, within its dimensions, one of the best of its kind in many months.[12]

When Knox was asked in 1997 by interviewer Patrick McGilligan what his favorite parts were, Knox was quick to respond that "I had the lead in a very low-budget picture called *Western Pacific Agent*, and all of the reviews were put on a poster with a drawing of me climbing up a bridge. The reviews compared me to Cagney and Garfield. I played a nogoodnik. It was directed by a guy named Sam Newfield. You can't find it anywhere today. That was fun, because I had the lead."[13] You couldn't find it back in 1997, but a print is available for viewing today on YouTube. *Western Pacific Agent* more than makes up for the "bad taste" left by *Radar Secret Service*. After this and few other film roles both before and after, Knox's career tanked in 1951 when he came under the scrutiny of HUAC and found himself unemployable.

Sig's base of operations was at the Nassour Studios, having relocated there back in 1948 for *State Department: File 649*. Edward Nassour had purchased a studio at 5746 Sunset Boulevard back in May 1945, initially naming it Consolidated Studios before changing it to the more ego-satisfying Nassour Studios;[14] the six-stage complex now covered nearly two square blocks near the NBC and CBS Broadcasting Stations. Sam's next film was made at Nassour, although it was for producer Barney Sarecky once again rather than for his brother. Produced in collaboration with the traffic division of the Los Angeles Police Department and based on factual material gleaned from their files, *Motor Patrol* "boasted" a comparatively nondescript cast that included Don Castle, Jane Nigh, Bill Henry, Gwen O'Connor, and others of similarly little renown. And, of course, Sid Melton as well, who shows up in every one of the first ten films that Sig and/or Sam made for Lippert. The filming of Maurice Tombragel and Orville Hampton's screenplay took place from February 1950 into March, going into release on June 29, 1950.

Vengeful cop Don Castle (left), on a quest to track down the killers of his future brother-in-law, grills Sid Melton in **Motor Patrol** (Lippert, 1950), Barney Sarecky producer, Sam Newfield director.

The slim plot involves an auto-theft ring indirectly responsible for the death of a young motor cycle patrolman, and the pursuit and infiltration of the ring by the fellow's future brother-in-law to bring them to justice. Bill Henry played the dead cop, Don Castle the vengeful cop, and Gwen O'Connor the dead cop's sister. Jane Nigh plays the film's "bad girl," and Charles Victor the ring's head. "At a preview showing of 'Patrol' in

Hollywood, the other day" wrote *Film Bulletin*, "the press generally rated it as one of Lippert's best, to date."[15] Which, at face value, sounded promising, and seems to have been confirmed by reviews. *Motion Picture Daily* said that it was "A new and stimulating insight into the activities and responsibilities of the 'motorcycle cop'" and concluded by calling it "a brisk, competent and incidentally informative accounting."[16] *Harrisons Reports* observed that "the picture has been given the care usually accorded to much bigger productions" and singled out Sam's contributions, saying that the "direction is so good that one feels as if seeing a real-life occurrence."[17] *Variety* praised the leads, saying that "Castle pleases as the hero, and Jane Nigh makes a comely villainess."[18] *The Exhibitor*'s review offered an aside that could be made about any of these films, referring to "some misplaced comedy," no doubt from the lips of Sid Melton.[19] It would appear that the film provided a welcome antidote to Sarecky's more childish *Radar Secret Service*.

Orville H. Hampton (1917-1997), the screenplay's co-author, was a former journalism major, radio news editor and announcer, and survivor of a five-year tour of duty with the Army overseas during WWII. Heading out to Hollywood and turning to screenwriting, Hampton spent several unsuccessful years trying to sell his scripts before finally landing a three-year contract with Lippert. *Rocketship X-M* was the first of these to be produced, concurrent with his rewriting of Sam's *Motor Patrol*. Hampton had served as dialogue director on Lippert's *Western Pacific Agent*, and would serve in a similar capacity on *Motor Patrol* and three of Sig's future films—*Lost Continent*, *Leave It to the Marines*, and *Sky High*—as well as writing the screenplay for a number of them.[20]

Sig and Sam were back together for the drama *Hi-Jacked*, filmed in April into May 1950 at the Nassour Studios. "One more threat to the American pocketbook is described in some detail in Lippert's 'Hi-Jacked'" began *Motion Picture Daily*'s review of

Framed parolee truck driver Jim Davis (center in jeans) is bound and determined to clear his name in **Hi-Jacked** (Lippert, 1950), Sig Neufeld producer, Sam Newfield director.

the film,[21] which follows parolee truck driver Jim Davis, whose attempts to lead a reformed life fall apart when his truck is hi-jacked a second time. Blamed for presumed involvement and fired from his job, his attempts to track down the responsible parties are thwarted when the criminals plant incriminating evidence, forcing his investigation under cover. Marsha Jones plays his faithful wife, with Ralph Sanford the trucking company's dispatcher who is in cahoots with the crooks. Reviews were mixed, *Motion Picture Daily* calling it "a fair production"[22] and *Variety* "an okeh crime yarn."[23]

The film's musical score was composed by newcomer Paul Dunlap (1919-2010), whose first film was Lippert's *The Baron of Arizona* (1950), followed soon after by this assignment. "Lippert would usually hand me $5,000—it seemed like a great deal then—and I would pay all the musicians, the copyists, pay all the taxes, everything, and what was left was mine," recalled Dunlap in an interview with Frederick Rappaport.

So I had to be very clever, very exigent. In fact, I've done plenty of scores where I helped time the music, wrote and orchestrated it, and sometimes did a little of the copying, conducted it, went back in the dubbing room and helped lay it in, and ended up, say, with $1,000.[24]

While *Hi-Jacked* was filming, Sig and Sam's favorite cinematographer Jack Greenhalgh was in Gallup, New Mexico, filming director Irving Allen's Western *Slaughter Trail*. While covering a scene of fifty charging Indians on horseback, Greenhalgh was trampled by one mounted Indian, suffering ten broken ribs, a broken collarbone, and had a lung punctured by a bone fragment. Greenhalgh was hospitalized for four weeks,[25] but had recuperated sufficiently to lens Sig's next film, *Three Desperate Men*.

In later summer 1950, Sig took his first tentative steps into the world of video broadcasting, joining with some others to create Mutual Television Productions. *Variety* explained:

New television film production unit, capitalized at $1,000,000, has been formed by a group of Hollywood indie producers, including Sig Neufeld, Rudolph Monter, Edward M. Gray, William Cane and Victor Mindlin. Most of the coin for the outfit, named Mutual TV Productions, is said to have come from backers in N.Y. and San Francisco.[26]

The initial goal was to turn out four series, the first of which was *These Are Our Children*, based on stories supplied by a California adoption agency named Children's Home Society. Within a few months those plans were jettisoned in favor of a series deemed more saleable, one based on the actual case files of Los Angeles County Sheriff Eugene Biscailuz. Viewed as television's answer to the successful *Dragnet* radio series, which was based on Los Angeles Police Department files, the thirteen half-hour video films were to begin in early December, with background scenes to be shot in the Hall of Justice. G. Pat Collins was to star, with direction by George Green, scripting by Doris Schroeder, and production supervision by Sig.[27] It doesn't appear that the filming of this series ever took place, but whatever the case, Sig severed his relations with Mutual TV shortly thereafter. By the mid-1950s, Mutual was fending off suits filed by the heirs of Monter in excess of $37,000, as well as by SAG over non-payment of residuals, both over the thirty-nine episodes of the syndicated series *Cowboy G-Men*.[28]

In the meantime, Sig had sold his North Sweetzer home and moved with his wife Ruth and son Sig Jr. into another, smaller home at 12837 Hortense Street in the San Fernando Valley.

In October, Lippert entered into an equal partnership with actor Gary Cooper to make a series of moderately budgeted films. They created Mayflower Productions as the production entity, and while Cooper would be active behind the scenes, he would not appear in any of the films, nor would he receive any on-screen credit. Two Westerns were initially planned, with more to follow if the films' reception was sufficient.[29] According to Lippert biographer Mark Thomas McGee, screenwriter Carl Foreman was one of the shareholders in the new deal, but it all blew up when the HUAC hearings accused Foreman of being a communist. Pressure was placed on Cooper, who reluctantly backed out of the deal while continuing to support Foreman. According to McGee, the film then being planned was *Three Desperate Men*.[30]

Producer Robert L. Lippert and actor Gary Cooper "clinch a deal for the formation of Mayflower Productions in which they will be partners." (*The Exhibitor,* November 1, 1950, p.30)

Three Desperate Men, whose original title was *The Dalton's Last Raid*,[31] had been announced back in August with a planned starting date in Utah of September 22.[32] Filming was delayed until October 10 and wrapped on October 23, with Jack Greenhalgh and Bert Sternbach back on the crew. By the time the Mayflower Production was released on January 12, 1951, it had been retitled *Three Outlaws* before finally settling on *Three Desperate Men*; Cooper's attorney forced the title change since some of the real Daltons were still alive, the "Daltons" becoming the "Dentons."

Ross Latimer, Jim Davis, and Preston Foster (the desperate men, left-to-right) make a big mistake by listening to the advice of career criminal William Haade (far right) in **Three Desperate Men** (Mayflower/Lippert, 1951), Sig Neufeld producer, Sam Newfield director.

Jim Davis attempts to help wounded brother Ross Latimer while Preston Foster breathes his last in **Three Desperate Men** (Mayflower/Lippert, 1951).

Young Joel Newfield face-to-face with Virginia Gray. "My big scene was I had to drive a buck wagon up to the door of Virginia Gray, knock on the door, and take her for a ride somewhere. That was my scene.... That was my bowing out of acting." After the scene was shot, Joel returned to his high school, but left his makeup on to impress his classmates. From **Three Desperate Men** (Mayflower/Lippert, 1951). *Courtesy of Joel Newfield.*

When Fort Grant deputies Tom and Fred Denton (Preston Foster and Jim Davis) learn that their hot-headed brother (Ross Latimer)[33] has been wrongly convicted of murder in California, they set out to exonerate him with iron clad evidence. When they arrive, sheriff Rory Mallinson attempts to divert them from their brother's hanging, then about to take place. Learning of this, they head to the hanging to free Latimer, and during the scramble Davis shoots and kills one of the guards. A vengeful posse now on their trail, the brothers flee, and day by day they are accused of more crimes they didn't commit, the reward for their capture or deaths climbing incrementally. They hook up with career criminal William Haade, and decide that since they are being blamed for all these crimes they may as well start robbing banks and express offices to survive. Foster learns that his fiancé (Virginia Grey) has died during their absence, so as the reward climbs to $40,000, they plan one big double score back at their home town, but the law is waiting for them, and all go down in a hail of bullets.

There isn't much plot—but a whole lot of riding—in this routine Western. Foster's presence was the film's draw, but Sid Melton, sporting the phoniest looking sideburns imaginable, took part once again in another humorless scene as a cocky station master. Sam's direction is unremarkable, but he does contribute a few memorable moments such as the near hanging, the assembled townsfolk patiently awaiting the culmination of the event while munching away on their respective lunches. Virginia Grey doesn't have much of a part, and is dispensed with unceremoniously with a few words from Foster's aged mother (Margaret Seddon) who simply states that she is dead. An opening crawl attempts to provide a historical perspective to the proceedings, but the film only limps along from there until the climactic gun battle, which livens things up a bit before all the protagonists are dead. Sam pressed his fifteen-year-old son Joel into service once again as George Denton, presumably another, younger brother.[34] Georgie arrives in a buckboard to pick up Grey as she embarks on a doctor-ordered trip to New Mexico for her health; a trip, needless to say, with very limited success.

Later in 1950, Lippert and some "unnamed investors" formed Spartan Productions as a permanent production unit to make films for release through Lippert. Sig and Sam were attached to the first two films made by Spartan, *Fingerprints Don't Lie* and *Mask of the Dragon*.[35] The two films were made back-to-back, *Fingerprints Don't Lie* going before cameras in December and *Mask of the Dragon* following shortly thereafter, both having most of the same cast members, as well as the same screenwriter (Orville Hampton) and technical crew. *Fingerprints Don't Lie*'s rather lethargic plot follows police fingerprint expert Richard Travis, who has doubts about the evidence he has provided that will surely convict artist Richard Emory of the murder of the city's new mayor. Aided by Emory's fiancé, played by Sheila Ryan, Travis sets out to disprove himself, and through a lot of scientific gobbledygook eventually uncovers a tangled web of deceit that involves police commissioner Michael Whalen, illegal gambling czar George Eldredge, and Eldredge's edgy girlfriend Dee Tatum. Sid Melton, of course, is back as an inept newspaper photographer, and Tom Neal actually jumps the fence to the side of law and order to portray a prosecuting attorney. Lippert's behind-the-scenes mistress Margia Dean appears as one of Emory's models, trading places with Syra Marty and ending up in a clinch with Travis.

This overly talkie drama misses the mark, with each new scientific discovery— Palm prints! A strand of hair! Forged fingerprints!—simply adding to the tedium. The cast is fine, although the running "joke" about Melton's flashbulbs never functioning properly wastes far too much time. The sets are uneven and visual evidence of the film's threadbare budget, Travis's lab looking more like an oversized kitchen, and the "grand" hallway outside the courtroom walled with hastily assembled flats whose seams are clearly evident. The absolute worst aspect of this film is the music score provided by Dudley Chambers, with an uncredited assist from Bert Shefter. It is, in my opinion, awful, performed primarily on an organ and sounding like an unwelcome cross between a soap opera and horror film. A mournful, second-rate church chorus joins in at one point, but thankfully departs shortly thereafter. Perhaps Chambers was aiming for something different, perhaps 1951's cut-rate answer to Anton Karas's zither score for *The Third Man*, but if he was, he blew it. *Fingerprints* was released on February 23, 1951.

Annoying newspaper photographer Sid Melton can't decide whether he should interrupt the smooching between Richard Emory and Sheila Ryan (left), and Margia Dean and Richard Travis (right). **Fingerprints Don't Lie** (Spartan/Lippert, 1951), Sig Neufeld producer, Sam Newfield director.

Mask of the Dragon has Richard Travis as a detective on the trail of the killer of his partner, Richard Emory, just returned from a stint in the military over in Korea. Emory had been paid to bring a jade dragon with him to the U.S., for delivery to Jack Reitzen, the Chinese owner of a Los Angeles based curio shop. Emory knew something was fishy, so he instead mailed the dragon to Travis's girl, police lab technician Sheila Ryan. Hoods Karl Davis and Sid Melton murder Emory, only to find that he doesn't have the dragon with him. After a lengthy investigation that involves police lieutenant Lyle Talbot, Army major Michael Whalen, and Emory's girl Dee Tatum, Travis uncovers the plot: the jade dragon was filled with $100,000 worth of contraband uranium, to be used in a sabotage plot cooked up by Reitzen and Whalen.

This one's a lot more fun than its predecessor, with enough action to keep viewers interested, including a lengthy scene where Travis is tortured for information, and Tatum's broadcast performance cut short when she's stabbed through the curtain behind her. Melton's introduction as one of the murderous hoods suggests a welcome change of pace for him, but when he shows up later dressed in Chinese garb and reverts to his comedic persona, any hopes for a straight role are dashed. Reitzen, as curio shop owner Professor Kim Ho, is another of those blatantly obvious Caucasians in Chinese garb so unfortunately prevalent in film for so much of its history. Former professional wrestler Karl "Killer" Davis appears as muscle in both this and the previous film, a threatening presence who can actually act. Charles Iwamoto has a nice part as another of the group's thugs, and ends up at the wrong end of a pitchfork after a climactic fight with Travis. Sam includes a few amusing bits, one of them having Travis absently mindedly playing with a knife while Ryan prepares a bandage for the cut she knows is about to come. Another scene takes place at a TV station, the program being broadcast interrupted by a tongue-in-cheek sponsor break. Sam had just directed *Skipalong Rosenbloom* at the KTTV television studios, and likely took his inspiration from that film's bogus commercials. This film's television studio sequence, while ending with the surprise murder of singer Tatum, otherwise provides some of the usual, film-lengthening padding by including a musical performance by country singers Curt Barrett and the Trailsmen. Alas, Sig retained Dudley Chambers to compose the score for this film as well, another of his organ earsores that, come to think of it, may have been "composed" on the fly rather than ever committed to paper.

Detective Richard Travis ponders the death of his good friend while lab technician and main squeeze Sheila Ryan looks bored in **Mask of the Dragon** (Spartan/Lippert, 1951), Sig Neufeld producer, Sam Newfield director.

One interesting note: the jade dragon was originally supposed to contain a shipment of opium, but the Production Code enforcers put the kibosh on that, necessitating the change to uranium. The film concludes with a not-so-amusing bit where Travis, having just exited the room, makes a brief return to face the camera in closeup and says "Confucious say 'When hero catch crook, time for picture to end.'" Truer words were never spoken.

Lippert had a surprise success with the release of Kurt Neumann's *Rocketship X-M* in mid-1950, hastily put together to ride on the coattails of George Pal's heavily promoted *Destination Moon*; it beat its inspiration into theaters by two months. Lippert quickly registered two additional titles for upcoming, higher-budget production, Jules Verne's *Twenty Thousand Leagues Under the Sea* and the yet-to-be-written *Lost Continent*.[36] The Verne tale ended up with Disney, but *Lost Continent* was turned over to Sig to produce.

Richard Landau was assigned to write *Lost Continent*'s script, but as coincidence would have it Landau's writing was interrupted when an expedition of the Navy and the University of California announced the supposed discovery of a "lost continent" in the Pacific between Hawaii and Wake Island.[37] Not one to miss a promotional opportunity, Lippert wanted the film's start pushed up from June to February 27.[38] Preproduction wasn't ready for the four month leap, however, so filming was delayed until April, getting underway on the 16th at the Goldwyn Studios, where two connecting stages were used to build the film's massive mountain set. F. Paul Sylos handled the production design, and Augie Lohman was in charge of special effects. Greenhalgh was back to handle the filming—the 212th film of his lengthy career—with Ernie Smith operating the camera and Bennie Coleman assisting. Greenhalgh explained their objective:

> Our aim was to create a feeling of vastness within the limited confines of the sound stage. Also, we had to give the "lost continent" sequence a mood of ominous fantasy, while still preserving a strong enough link with reality to convince the audience that these were situations that could and did actually happen to characters in the script.[39]

Jack Greenhalgh, A.S.C., on the set of **Lost Continent** (Tom Productions/Lippert, 1951), Sig Neufeld producer, Sam Newfield director. Assisting Jack are Ernie Smith, camera operator; Bennie Coleman, assistant (background); and Georgie Breslau, gaffer (right).

Sets included a conventional jungle, a "lost continent" jungle chock full of unusual plants and rock formations,[40] and a fifty-foot rockbound peak. The peak set was lovingly described by *American Cinematographer*:

> The mountain itself was a masterpiece of construction. Fashioned of materials strong enough to simulate actual rock and support the weight of seven actors clambering upward, it was mounted on rollers so that it could be wheeled around to provide a variety of set-ups and camera angles. It is a tribute to Greenhalgh's lighting skill that the 50-foot segment of man-made rock could be used as a background for a climb supposedly covering several thousand feet of mountainside. In most cases a shifting of the lights plus a fresh camera angle made a previously photographed segment of terrain appear completely different. Clouds photographed on transparencies were projected on a huge screen behind the rock, creating a realistically luminous sky effect.

Greenhalgh's camera was mounted on a boom so that it could rise along with the actors as they climbed upward, and hydraulic light stands were employed so that the lights could be raised along with the camera, or lowered slowly to achieve a setting sun effect. Clouds were created by blowing dried ice vapor into a scene.[41] Filming took far longer than the average Lippert production, nine days by one report, eleven by another, and fifteen by yet another. Regardless, it was more than Lippert's five-day average.

Screenwriter Orville Hampton was initially brought on board as dialogue director, but soon found that his creative talents were in desperate need. He explained the situation to interviewer Paul Woodbine:

> I had nothing to do with [*Lost Continent*] until the production date came. I was called into the production meeting by Sigmund Neufeld on a Friday—before shooting, on the following Monday, at [Goldwyn] Studios. All the sets were built and everything. This was a big production for Sig. Well, we were appalled.

Woodbine asked what happened:

> The script happened. Nobody had read it up until now. Sig was horrified and so was Sam Newfield, Sig's brother, who was going to direct it. I couldn't believe it myself. The script had pages filled with huge, long lectures. No way in hell this script could be filmed, I told Sig that I'd go on the set and find out what had to be shot. Then, I'd look for the scene in the script and paraphrase the dialog...scribble it out in long hand, then give it to the actors.[42]

Perhaps the hastened production schedule and the interruption of screenwriter Richard Landau's writing led to a less-than-optimal script, but that's just speculation. Whatever the case, it sounds as though the screenplay needed some work.

A loose reworking of Arthur Conan Doyle's *The Lost World*, the slim plot follows the six-man search party out to locate an experimental rocket that inexplicably crashed. Flying above the approximate location, the plane's engine shuts down and they make a crash landing. Finding a mostly deserted village, one of its two remaining inhabitants pinpoints the plateau atop the nearby "sacred mountain" as the crash site.

The team ignores warnings that it is hazardous to one's health to go there, making the arduous climb to the top, losing one of their members along the way. Arriving at the top—the black-and-white film takes on a green tint from here—they find a land that's a "throwback to prehistoric times" and teaming with dinosaurs. After days of aimless wandering, they finally locate the crashed rocket and recover its 1950-version of a data recorder, lose another member to a triceratops attack, and scurry back to the bottom as the whole island is reduced to rubble by an ill-timed earthquake.

Hugh Beaumont takes direction from Sam Newfield on the set of **Lost Continent** (Tom Productions/Lippert, 1951). *Courtesy of Tim Neufeld.*

This is a surprisingly good science fiction-adventure hybrid, with an exploitable Cesar Romero in the lead as the macho playboy pilot in charge of flying the team to its eventual destination. The other team members would have been familiar to B-film devotees of the era: Chick Chandler as Romero's cynical co-pilot, Sid Melton as the group's sergeant-level flunkee, Hugh Beaumont as the Geiger counter wielding scientist responsible for relaying so much of the film's scientific gibberish to the audience, Whit Bissell as another, unphysically fit scientist, and John Hoyt as the team's third scientist, initially distrusted by Romero since he's a Russian. The cast's two female additions, Hillary Brooke and Acquanetta, are both wasted in blink-and-you'll-miss-them roles, although the latter remains easy on the pre-blinked eyes while in the final throes of a career in freefall.

Lippert's, Sig's, and Sam's ambitions are admittedly undercut by the film's budget, but they get a whole lot of points for trying. Paul Dunlop's score is excellent, and Greenhalgh's cinematography the most fluid of his career. The film's strong point is that incredible mountain set, realistically rendered and utilized during the arguably overlong ascent to the plateau. The suspense builds nicely as they navigate the crevices, outcroppings, and sheer cliffs, the latter providing the film's most nerve-wracking scene where they need to climb a rope to get to the next level. Bissell is an early casualty from a well-staged fall to his death, filmed from above as he drops screaming, disappearing through a cloud into the depths below. Melton, whose toned-down presence in this film is welcome change, is the adventure's other casualty, gored to death by a charging triceratops.

The core group of explorers in **Lost Continent** (Tom Productions/Lippert, 1951). Left-to-right: Cesar Romero, John Hoyt, Hugh Beaumont, Sid Melton, and Chick Chandler; Whit Bissell "bought the farm" in an earlier scene. *Courtesy of Tim Neufeld.*

Which brings us to the film's special effects, which are for the most part handled adequately. An early encounter with a first "dinosaur" is a poorly executed shot of a lizard that evokes unfortunate memories of all those silly-looking, unconvincing lizards used in Hal Roach's *One Million B.C.*, a pathetic substitute for anything that actually *looks* like a dinosaur. Viewer concerns are quickly pacified in the five dinosaur-encounter scenes that follow, all of them utilizing a far more satisfying stop motion animation technique a la Willis O'Brien and Ray Harryhausen. I'll be the first to admit that the models used—a brontosaurus, a pair of triceratopses, and a pterodactyl—aren't nearly as slick as those employed by O'Brien and Harryhausen, and the actual animation of these not nearly as smooth and convincing, but kudos to the producers for opting for a technique that more closely approximates the real thing rather than taking the easy way out and filming a bunch of photographically enlarged lizards. The best of the five scenes is the first, where a brontosaurus spots and goes after Beaumont, who climbs to the top of a palm tree in an unsuccessful attempt to escape the beast. A blatant redo of an extremely similar scene in O'Brien's *King Kong*, it still manages to generate a fair amount of excitement. In later years, actor Whit Bissell attempted to distance himself from the film and its dinosaurs: "I didn't know it was going to be that bad. That picture had terrible special effects!"[43] Not top-of-the-line for sure, but not terrible.

Acquanetta emotes while Cesar Romero's ready for action in front of a backdrop in this posed shot for **Lost Continent** (Tom Productions/Lippert, 1951). *Courtesy of Tim Neufeld.*

Paul Dunlap, who was brought back to compose *Lost Continent*'s score, was usually given a couple of weeks to do so. One of the reasons he liked working for Lippert was that he was given cart blanche and left alone,

> since [Lippert] didn't know what the hell you were doing. He gave you the money, usually half up front and half later, and you did what you wanted to. Like on *Lost Continent*, which many regard as an excellent score.... My goodness, all that

goddamn rock climbing. All those stupid rubber animals. And when I composed the score the dinosaurs hadn't even been superimposed yet.... In any event, that was a big budget picture for Lippert. I had a huge orchestra, the largest on any of my Lippert pictures—four trombones, four trumpets, six French horns, violas, cellos and basses. They wanted a bigger sound—the picture needed all the help it could get. It must have been an interesting score, though. I remember for instance in London, Elmer Bernstein coming out of CTS, that cavernous basketball court of a studio, and he actually stopped to tell me how marvelous he felt the score was. I had no idea he'd ever heard it, much less having endured the movie.[44]

When *Lost Continent* was released on August 17, 1951, Lippert offered, for rent, a promotional theatre front for exhibitors to ballyhoo the film's showing at their theatre. "We don't know just how it is built up but it at least is an exploitation front that the average exhibitor could not afford and does not have the personnel to create," wrote *Film Bulletin*, which went on to write that the exhibitor who informed the publication of Lippert's offering claimed that it was responsible for doubling his average business.[45]

Interviewed by historian Tom Weaver, some of Sid Melton's comments revealed the depth of his admiration and respect for Sam:

My favorite director then, and will be one of my favorites forever, was Sam Newfield, who did *Lost Continent* and many other great pictures. His *Lost Continent* is an epic that was waaay ahead of its time. He could do anything. Sammy Newfield, he was one of the most wonderful directors. He used to let me re-write my own scenes in the various pictures, which I did.... Newfield knew what he was doin'. I think that guy has gone down on record as being the fastest B picture director, and he was (I think) superb at what he did. Sammy Newfield was an ace behind the camera, knew what he wanted. He was one of the most wonderful directors and one of the most underrated.... I thought so much of Newfield, he was that easygoing and that tremendously gifted. He was the sweetest guy in the world, and I was so sorry when he [died].[46]

Sig and Sam's next two films were churned out quickly, *Sky High* going before cameras on May 14, 1951, and *Leave It to the Marines* a mere seven days later, on May 21. Both comedies had military themes, screenplays by Orville Hampton, the same crew, and many of the same cast members. Sid Melton was elevated to lead in both films, with newcomer Mara Lynn his co-star.

Sky High is likely representative of the two films since they both have so much in common. At various times during its production referred to as *Off We Go* and *Up and At 'Em*, the film provides Melton the opportunity to unleash his particular brand of comedy unhindered, rather than have it awkwardly wedged into a drama. His dimwitted but well-meaning characters are admittedly an acquired taste, and not a taste shared by everyone. In *Sky High*, he is so incredibly stupid that it is difficult to sympathize with him. The premise is that he's a lowly private and tail gunner in the Air Force, and Mara Lynn, his girlfriend of three years, thinks he should set higher goals for himself and become a pilot. She finally browbeats him into taking the appropriate tests, all of which he fails, miserably. Douglas Evans, a high-ranking former buddy, notices Melton's resemblance to a spy (also Melton) who has plants inside the air base, so with fake mustache applied Melton struts around the camp impersonating the spy, who is elsewhere in jail. Melton's to report back to his superiors once he's approached with the keyword, "Hello, handsome." Sexy plant Margia Dean says those magic words to him, but he's so stupid he thinks she's flirting with him. His ruse falls apart when Dean and her two cohorts, Paul Bryar and Marc Krah, are reunited with the real boss spy, who has escaped from jail. Needless to say, Melton manages to turn the tables on his captors, imprisoning them in the top secret, radio-controlled test plane whose secrets they were after. Melton, the idiot, is now a hero.

The inanity aside, the film manages to elicit the random chuckle. The paper-thin plot is padded with all sorts of extraneous scenes, such as Melton's grilling during his pilot tests, and Lynn's surprisingly enjoyable (and seemingly off-the-cuff) jitterbug to swing music throughout her diner, shot by Sam in just two uninterrupted and lengthy takes. Lynn's acting ability is not of the highest calibre, but she's just so darn likeable and uninhibited in this role that she provides the film with what little energy and interest it has. Sam Flint plays the overly amorous colonel who lusts after Lynn, she performing a rather sexy—and censor bating—weight-loss routine for him that demonstrates just how athletic and limber she was. As for the film's questionable humor, there's a running gag involving Melton and a combative juke box, and an overly familiar bit involving his extended struggle with fly paper. Another scene has Melton and Lynn attempting to level a dining table by placing books under its legs, eventually raising it to such a height that they can't even see their plates while eating. One of the funnier bits is a scene where Melton is treated by psychiatrist Fritz Feld, the latter slowly becoming the patient and revealing his obsession with food, often viewing other people and pets as prospective meals. You get the idea, and the lower level of humor.

Mara Lynn and Sid Melton have successfully leveled their dining table in **Sky High** (Tom Productions/Lippert, 1951), Sig Neufeld producer, Sam Newfield (as Samuel Newfield) director.

Released before *Sky High* on September 28, 1951, *Leave It to the Marines* is another low-humor comedy wherein Melton, accompanied by his girl Mara Lynn, goes to city hall to obtain a marriage license, but idiot that he is inadvertently signs up with the Marines instead. Shipped off to boot camp, Lynn decides to follow and joins the Marines as well, catching the roving eye of sergeant Gregg Martell, who has acquired an intense dislike of Melton in the interim. The film's conclusion has everyone thinking that Melton is dead after the shed he was in is blown up, but he emerges, safe and sound, with twelve puppies (don't ask). He's awarded a medal for heroism, only to find that his girl is being shipped overseas. *Harrisons Reports* opened its review with "Indifferent. A noble attempt was made at comedy, but without much success."[47]

Sid Melton's in the dog house once again as his girl Mara Lynn lectures him, in **Leave It to the Marines** (Tom Productions/Lippert, 1951), Sig Neufeld producer, Sam Newfield (as Samuel Newfield) director.

The Western *Outlaw Women* was next for Sam, for independent producers Joy N. Houck, president of Joy Theatres, and his partners J. Frances White and Ron Ormond. This would be the premiere film for their newly formed, South Carolina-based Howco Productions,[48] boasting a higher budget and filmed in Cinecolor. Ormond, a producer who had a lot of experience directing low budget Westerns as well, was to co-direct; Sam directing the film's actresses, and Ormond handling the actors.[49] Filmed in late November and December 1951 at the Los Angeles-based KTTV studios, Houck closed a deal two months later in February for Lippert to distribute the film.[50] Concurrent with Lippert's move to higher-budget and higher-quality product, he was also making the switch from flat rate to per-centage deals with exhibitors. The feature length *Outlaw Women* was to be among the first films released under these new terms,[51] reaching theatre screens on June 2, 1952.

The Western town of Las Mujeres is different than most: It is run entirely by women under the stern control of Paradise Saloon owner Iron Mae McLeod (Marie Windsor), emotionless and tough, but fair. While Las Mujeres is thriving, the town of Silver Creek is dying, and a number of its citizens end up in Las Mujeres: Allan Nixon's doctor; saloon owner Richard Rober, Windsor's former lover and, we are led to believe, the cause of her current bitterness; and aging gunslinger Peyote Bill (Jackie Coogan). When it is learned that Silver Creek's bank's assets—a huge chunk of which are Windsor's earnings—are to be shipped elsewhere, outlaw Richard Avonde teams up with Leonard Penn, just out of prison where he did time because of Rober and Windsor. Rober has the law on his side, working with Lyle Talbot's judge to bring elections to Las Mujeres, and since women can't vote or hold office, it looks like Windsor's days of power are soon to come to an end. Windsor learns of the plans to rob the bank's assets, so she has her gang of women "rob" the stagecoach before Avonde and Penn can get to it, and take the loot back to the saloon for safe keeping. Avonde, Penn, and their gang arrive in town to steal the money from Windsor, and in the ensuing gun battle both Avonde and Penn are killed, along with one of the saloon girls.

Shot in attractive Cinecolor, *Outlaw Women* is a handsomely mounted production that benefits from a unique premise. Interest is maintained throughout by the various twists and turns and shifting allegiances, but the unfortunate copout "happy" ending somewhat neuters all that has gone before.

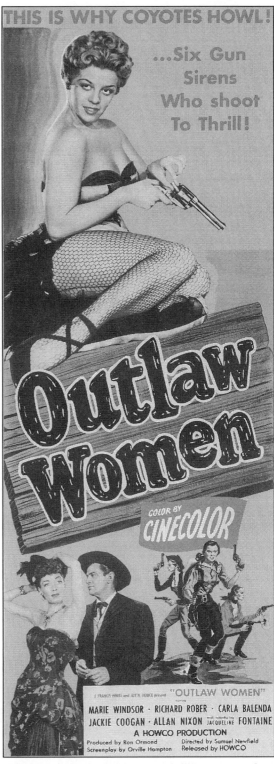

"Six Gun Sirens Who Shoot to Thrill!" Poster art for **Outlaw Women** (Howco/Lippert, 1952), Ron Ormond producer, Sam Newfield and Ron Ormond directors. *Courtesy of Heritage Auctions.*

Windsor gives and maintains a delightfully cold performance up until that unexpected and unfortunate ending, and Rober is fine as her business foil, who ultimately softens his stance and ends up marrying her. Nixon is okay but rather bland as the doctor kidnapped and forced to Las Mujeres to work. Carla Balenda is cute as his kidnapper, who does so only because she has fallen for him, and Jacqueline Fontaine plays the saloon's star performer, Balenda's older sister, who also has her eyes on the doctor. Maria Hart is a standout as the Paradise's stern-faced, tough as nails, cigar smoking enforcer, her brief five-film career spent primarily in Westerns. Former child star Jackie Coogan is almost unrecognizable as the mustached gunslinger, providing the film with some lighter moments, his appearance evoking memories of a younger, slimmer Charlie King. Rober never had a chance to see the released film, killed in an auto accident in Santa Monica a mere week before the film's release.[52]

In late summer 1951, Lippert entered a twelve-picture partnership with James Carreras's England-based Exclusive Films. Motion picture distributor Exclusive Films Limited was incorporated back in 1935 by Spanish immigrant Enrique Carreras and muti-faceted vaudevillian Will Hammer,[53] initially reissuing films by British Lion and the Korda brothers' London Films, while Hammer moved into production with the short-lived WH Films. Settling in with his Hammer Productions, his first production under this latter banner was the Bela Lugosi vehicle *The Mystery of the Mary Celeste* (1935). By the time that Lippert partnered with Exclusive Films, Enrique's son James Carreras, and Will Hammer's son Anthony Hinds were both firmly entrenched in the family business. Hammer Film Productions concentrated on what were known as "quota quickies," shorter, low-budget films, designed as bottom-half-of-the-bill filler and a workaround to the nation's Cinematograph Films Act of 1927, briefly described back in chapter 7. The Act, you'll recall, stipulated that a per-centage of all films shown had to be of British origin as a buffer against the overwhelming influx of American product, hence the creation of the quota quickies to right that imbalance. James Carreras' son Michael explained to the authors of the excellent *The Hammer Story: The Authorised History of Hammer Films*, Marcus Hearn and Alan Barnes:

Because of the quota law, a British second feature had to play with the American main feature. That meant the American studios had to give away a portion of the box office receipts to the second feature. The studios astutely decided to make these second features themselves, to retain the receipts. But to satisfy the quota law, the films had to actually be made by a British associate.

Carreras went on to explain that Twentieth Century-Fox released their films in Britain on the same circuit as Exclusive and Hammer. Spyros Skouras, Fox's head and a close friend of Lippert, worked out a quiet deal with Lippert to partner with Exclusive to co-produce these lower-budget films.[54] As part of the agreement, Lippert would provide and pay for any combination of one or two American actors to star, a director, and/or screenwriter. The proviso was that the American contingent could not exceed the newly formed Eady Levy's requirements that, to qualify as a British production, 85 % of the production had to be shot in the United Kingdom, with only three non-British salaries as part of the production's costs. Exclusive's distribution rights included England, Scotland, Wales, Northern Ireland, the Channel Islands, Malta, and Gibraltar; Lippert got the rest of the world.[55] The inclusion of an American actor helped with marquee value stateside, or at least that was the hope.

Lease arrangements were made with two studios for their use, eight films planned for production at London's Riverside studios, and the other four at the Mancunian studios in Manchester. The first film of this arrangement starred American actor Zachary Scott in the thriller *Dead On Course*.[56] As part of this deal, Lippert would pay two American stars for five weeks' production time, with any spillover to be paid by Carreras. Carreras had produced his films on six-day work weeks and expected to continue to do so, but a wage dispute in November between the Association of Cine and Allied Technicians and the Producers' Association over the former group's insistence on five-day work weeks, threatened the fulfilment of his commitment to Lippert. This resulted in the abandonment of a film planned for a January 8, 1952 start to co-star Cesar Romero and Arlene Dahl.[57] The issue appears to have been resolved by April when *Scotland Yard Inspector* was under way bearing its British release title *Lady in the Fog*; Romero now co-starred with Lois Maxwell.[58] Lippert and Carreras had agreed on having Sam direct, and Britain's *Kinematograph Weekly* was quick to report that "Experiment by Exclusive in bringing over American director Sam Newfield to direct Cesar Romero in 'Lady in the Fog,' at Riverside, has made an encouraging start."[59]

In London, American magazine writer Romero teams up with Bernadette O'Farrell to look into the suspicious hit-and-run death of her brother. While Scotland Yard remains skeptical that it was anything but an accident, reluctant and occasionally ineffectual amateur sleuth Romero eventually manages to uncover the thirteen-year-old death of the inventor of a super-charged carburetor by his former partners, film producer Geoffrey Keen, nightclub proprietor Lois Maxwell, and sanitarium-confined fellow inventor Lloyd Lamble, now all wealthy having reaped the rewards of their victim's invention. They use their thug, Reed De Rouen, to kill loose cannon Lamble, but Romero finally corners the other two, Keen falling to his death from a scaffold, and Maxwell dying in a fiery car crash while attempting to flee.

Cesar Romero takes direction from Sam Newfield on location for **Scotland Yard Inspector** (**Lady in the Fog** in Britain; Exclusive/Lippert, 1952), Anthony Hinds producer, Sam Newfield director.

Not surprisingly, the British cast all deliver fine performances, O'Farrell perhaps the standout as the grieving sister who slowly succumbs to Romero's charms. While a murder-mystery at face value, Sam and screenwriter Orville Hampton lace the film with liberal moments of humor, most prominent of these the running joke regarding the continuous delays of Romero's plane flight back to the U.S., and the growing frustration of ticketing agent Frank Birch in his attempts to appease Romero. Other intended comedic bits aren't quite as successful, such as Romero's repeated accidental smashing of Scotland Yard inspector Campbell Singer's cigar, and his pub-based concoction of one of his signature drinks, the "Dusseldorf Detonator," as former RAF friend and current publican Wensley Pithey looks on. As Romero adds the final drop of some unidentified liquor, there's an explosion followed by a superimposed image of an atomic bomb cloud above it; not subtle, but kind of funny. Sam seems to have worked in smooth concert with the studio's British technicians, cinematographer Walter Harvey's contributions a visual plus to the proceedings.

Kinematograph Weekly described the Brits' initial apprehension about having an unknown American director on board:

Doubts as to how the British technicians might adapt themselves to American methods were dispelled on the first day when, with 25 camera set-ups, no fewer than 9.05 minutes of good quality screen time was put in the can. Sam has already cabled his Hollywood company praising his British colleagues and saying he would like to stay over here and direct another picture with the same crew.[60]

One would assume that it didn't take Sam those Carreras-approved five weeks to shoot this film.

Sam's request to stay over was honored with his follow-up assignment, *The Gambler and the Lady*, a small but serviceable crime thriller. In *The Gambler and the Lady*, Dane Clark stars as an American crook in England, his wealth stemming from his high-end nightclub as well as the illegal gambling dens he runs. His one goal in life is to be accepted into society, dressing accordingly, and taking lessons in etiquette. He falls for society woman Naomi Chance, infuriating his former girl and the nightclub's brassy star performer, Kathleen Byron. Chance's family convinces him to buy 10,000 shares in a new gold mine, so against advice he sells everything to do so. When the "gold mine" turns out to be a huge swindle, he is rendered penniless. He goes on a bender, but when the mobsters (Enzo Coticchia and Eric Pohlmann) who bought his gambling businesses think he's ratted on them, they come gunning for him. After a big shootout in which the gangsters are killed, Clark emerges with an arm wound, only to be run down by his jealousy-crazed former girlfriend. Not what you'd call a happy ending.

Filmed in May and June 1952 under the working title *In the Money*, Sam ostensibly shared directing credits with Patrick Jenkins, his dialog director on *Scotland Yard Inspector* and assistant director on a handful of other British films leading up to this; one can assume that Sam did the heavy lifting. *The Gambler and the Lady*, despite its rather lackluster title, is a reasonably diverting crime drama peppered with enough suspense and action to keep one from nodding off. Walter Harvey's camera work is a definite asset, with some moody nighttime, fog-bound exteriors opening and closing the film, and a climactic shootout in a darkened room that evokes memories of some of those similarly dimly lit shootouts in Sam's earlier Westerns. Clark's character is cursed with a short temper—even shorter when he has a snootful—which results in a couple of nice action scenes, one of which is the huge donnybrook that engulfs an entire pub's clientele. The British cast is the usual mix of dependable pros, with memorable performances by George Pastell as Clark's vengeful former cashier, Meredith Edwards as his heavy-drinking and sensibly cautious bookkeeper, and Anthony Forwood as Chance's snobbish brother. A solid, if minor, British crime film.

Lippert, one of the last of the independent producers churning out low-budget fare, soon came to realize that the market for his modestly budgeted product was evaporating. "[W]hat the industry needs more than any other single thing is 'bigger pictures'," wrote *The Independent Film Journal*. "Lippert pointed out that theatremen can

Dane Clark (center) has gotten on the wrong side of gangsters Eric Pohlmann and Enzo Coticchia (to the right of Clark) in **Gambler and the Lady** (Exclusive/Lippert, 1952).
Courtesy of Library of Congress.

no longer afford to play in-between product; a movie-going habit no longer exists in the minds of the paying public, he said. People today, he added, can 'smell out the good ones'." With that in mind, Lippert said that it might benefit his company to turn out six-to-eight films using the same budget he'd otherwise produce twenty-four films with.[61] His first stab at a "bigger" picture was the Biblical epic—and I use the word "epic" loosely here—*Sins of Jezebel*. Bible-thumping films of this sort were experiencing a stunning period of popularity, sparked by Cecil B. DeMille's lavish *Samson and Delilah* in 1949, with M-G-M's Mervyn LeRoy-directed *Quo Vadis* and Henry King's *David and Bathsheba* for Twentieth Century-Fox following in 1951. In Hollywood, "bigger is better" seems to be the mindset producers operate under, so Fox rushed Henry Koster's *The Robe* into production, notable as the first feature filmed using the new widescreen process CinemaScope. Lippert decided to get in on the game and make his own Biblical mini-epic, hiring Sig to produce the film and his other go-to screenwriter, Richard Landau, to knock out an acceptable—and filmable on a slightly larger budget—script. Sam was off directing a television series at this time, so Sig hired journeyman director Reginald LeBorg to direct. They needed someone sufficiently sexy to portray the supposedly "very beautiful" Jezebel—"the most wicked woman who ever lived!"—settling for the forty-three-year-old Paulette Goddard, still good for some sort of marquee value but just a tad long in the tooth by this time.

Filmed in the KTTV television studios, cinematographer Gilbert Warrenton shot it in Ansco color using a 2-1 aspect ratio widescreen process, a switch from the standard 1-1.85 ratio.[62] "The largest cooperative trade press, newspaper and TV campaign in Lippert Pictures' history was announced" to promote the film, wrote *Motion Picture Herald*,[63] and Lippert engaged Hollywood's National Screen Service Corp. to create fifty- and twenty-second television trailers to promote the film in various TV markets nationwide.[64] An outsize three-color pressbook was prepared as well, Lippert's first to eschew his standard black-and-white.

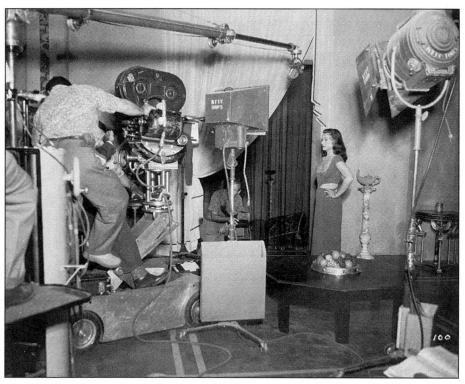

Paulette Goddard takes position for the camera at the KTTV Studios set for the Bible thumping **Sins of Jezebel** (Jezebel Productions/Lippert, 1953). *Courtesy of Tim Neufeld.*

The plot in brief: Princess Jezebel of Phoenicia (Goddard) marries weak Israeli King Ahab (Eduard Franz), and against the dire warnings of prophet Elijah (John Hoyt) and minister of state Naboth (Ludwig Donath), convinces him to build a temple to her god, Baal. Elijah prophesizes that the Israeli's god Jehovah will punish them with a drought, and sure enough it happens. The citizens are understandably angered by this turn of events, so Jezebel sends her priests to Mount Carmel to pray to Baal for rain and make her the hero of the piece. Elijah shows up and gets into the act, and it is his prayers to Jehovah that do the trick. The onlookers go after the priests, and when Jezebel learns of this, convinces weakling Ahab to have Elijah and his followers arrested. Elijah escapes, so Jezebel has Naboth stoned to death. The film ends with an oddly rushed sequence briefly covering Ahab's death in a war with the Syrians, followed by the people turning on Jezebel, who is slain by an arrow, tossed over the wall to the throngs below, and—just to make sure—run over by a handy chariot.

The film is terrible. Reginald LeBorg, the film's self-important director who always felt like he was slumming by taking the assignments offered him, didn't rise to the occasion for this one. He wrapped one uninspired take after another, letting the actors walk through their roles, evidently with only a modicum of guidance. The minimalistic sets are anything but epic, and screenwriter Landau's dialog laughable ("What's become of that girl I once knew?"). The ceremony accompanying the unveiling of Baal's new temple includes singers praising Baal who sound more like a barbershop quartet, and the scantily clad dancers look like a bunch of Las Vegas showgirls. The crowd scenes are anything but crowded, and Goddard looks like she's struggling to keep from bursting out laughing in some of the earlier scenes.[65] George Nadar, as Jehu, Captain of the King's Chariot's, is seduced by Jezebel as soon as Ahab leaves the room, and spends most of the film lost in thought or, when Jezebel's around, breathing heavily. John Shelton, who plays Loram, Jezebel's lead escort and counselor, has the most leaden delivery imaginable. Eduard Franz has the thankless role of the milquetoast King, alternating between lusting for his queen-to-be and moping about once they are married. Perhaps the film's unintentionally funniest scene takes place on the night of their wedding. As they approach the bedroom and the moment when lust-filled Ahab will finally get to consummate their marriage, he takes two steps into the room, falls to the floor, and passes out, drunk. Nice planning, Ahab. But then there's Joe Besser as Yonkel, added to the film as comic relief and, for once, the film's bright spot. His character hates his name, complaining whenever someone utters it, and kvetches about Baal, whispering to his horse "I don't like this Baal!" He manages to brighten up an otherwise dreary film with his asides, and that's about the best I can say for this misguided, cheesy Biblical epic. The *San Francisco Examiner*'s film critic summarized it nicely: "There must be more to this film than meets the eye—my eyes at least—because I didn't get a thing out of it except absolute boredom…. For this I would stand in line—to get out!"[66]

With the completion of *Sins of Jezebel*, Sig's involvement with Lippert would come to an end, Sam's having ended a year earlier with the direction of those two British-made films for Exclusive and Hammer.

Chapter 21:
Too Many Fuzzys (AFRC, Regal Films, and Television, 1953-1958)

By the early 1950s, Sam's homelife had fallen apart. Fed up with Sam's obsessive gambling, his wife Violet filed for divorce and got custody of the kids, Jackie and Joel. She fell back on her old job as script "girl" and went to work on one of the Western television series then in production, as well as serving as script supervisor for some features at Columbia. "She had a sister who was also a script girl, Emilie Ehrlich," recalled Joel. "They were doing script work for quite a while. My mother would break away and do something else when nothing was going on."[1] Violet, who was very outgoing, remarried in 1953 to a fellow named Robert McComas, a lawyer for Lockheed. The newlyweds moved into a house at 5124 Encino Avenue. "As soon as [Jackie] was old enough," recalled brother Joel, "she got out and left. Like she told me: 'I'm going to UCLA to find a husband.' It was just a matter of getting out. We were tired of being raised by our grandmother."[2] Twenty-year-old Jackie married David Gornel, a former neighbor, in August 1953.

Sam Newfield peacefully coexisting with former wife Violet at their daughter Jackie's wedding. *Courtesy of Laura Berk.*

Sam moved out of their home on North Beverly Drive and headed to Hollywood, where he resided most of the time in one of downtown Hollywood's hotels. "I'd see him occasionally, no more than normal," recalled Joel. "If he was working, I'd never see him."[3] Directorial opportunities were now thinning, although he found work during 1953-54 directing for television rather than motion pictures, helming fourteen episodes of the syndicated television series *Ramar of the Jungle*, featuring actor Jon Hall; Sam's nephew Stanley Neufeld served as his assistant director on some of these episodes. Former PRC president Leon Fromkess executive produced the series, which may have been instrumental in Sam's hiring. Three of Sam's episodes were reedited into a feature by the show's editor, Dwight Caldwell, and released in April 1955 by Lippert as *Thunder Over Sangoland*, the title of the first used episode that had aired in October 1953.

Star Jon Hall consults with director Sam Newfield as assistant director Stanley Neufeld observes, on the set of the television series **Ramar of the Jungle** (Arrow Productions, 1953-55), Rudolph C. Flothow and Leon Fromkess producers, Sam Newfield director (14 episodes). *Courtesy of Tim Neufeld.*

Sam's other engagement with a new television series reunited him with Buster Crabbe in later 1954 into 1955. Crabbe's popularity had reignited as result of the sale of his older Westerns for television broadcast, leading to an offer in 1951 to host a local half-hour kids' show in New York City called *The Buster Crabbe Show*. Crabbe would screen cut-down versions of his older Westerns and "Flash Gordon" serials for half of the show, and interact with the assembled kids—"Buster's Buddies"—during whatever time remained after the airing of commercials. The offer of a nationally broadcast television series on NBC was accepted, resulting in sixty-five episodes of the half-hour show *Captain Gallant of the Foreign Legion*; Crabbe starred along with his ten-year-old son Cullen. Asked who he'd like for a sidekick in the series, Crabbe immediately thought of his good friend and long-time sidekick Al "Fuzzy" St. John. So he requested Fuzzy. His hopes were dashed when he found that they had hired Fuzzy Knight instead, thinking that *he* was the "Fuzzy" that Crabbe had asked for.[4]

Variety provided some background on the first season's production:

Producers have gone to a great deal of trouble on this one, filming the series in North Africa with the cooperation of the French Foreign Legion. Use of Legion troops, North African natives, ancient French forts, Moroccan street scenes and expanses of Sahara Desert give the program a certain exotic appeal and authenticity.... Buster Crabbe makes a manly Captain Gallant, and his son, Cullen, an appealing waif whom the captain adopts. Fuzzy Knight is the heavily-humorous aide.[5]

Sam shared first season direction with American workhorse Jean Yarbrough, Tunisian Marcel Crevenne, and Parisian Pierre Schwab, all working from scripts written by William N. Robson, Gene Levitt, and Jack Andrews. The show ran for two seasons, but Sam cut short his affiliation with the series after the first when brother Sig had a renewed need for his assistance.

Buster Crabbe and son Cullen from an episode of **Captain Gallant of the Foreign Legion** (1955).

In the meantime, Sig and Ruth had grown to dislike the house they had bought on Hortense Street a few years earlier. Grandson Tim explained that San Fernando Valley "is extremely hot compared to the other side of the Santa Monica Mountains where Hollywood is," and described the house as

> kind of a ranch house in the Valley without air conditioning, and I can only imagine how miserable the summers were. They didn't stay on Hortense for very long, and they then rented back in Hollywood, and it was on—I think it was called Rossmore—and they rented in a very nice old Hollywood building that was in a collection of old classic Hollywood buildings—apartment houses—Mae West

lived a couple of doors down the street. They went back to their Hollywood roots. It's a little bit south from Sunset, but Rossmore is not that far from Vine Street or Gower Street and any of the old haunts....[6]

With *Sins of Jezebel* and his arrangement with Lippert now well in the past, Sig continued to look for a new deal for his Sigmund Neufeld Productions. He finally found one with former Lippert associate E.J. Baumgarten, by now Lippert Pictures' president. In late summer 1955, Baumgarten announced the formation of a new producing-distributing concern, Associated Film Releasing Corp. (AFRC), of which he was president as well. Baumgarten outlined plans for eight-to-ten "outdoor action pictures" to be released every six weeks, beginning in October.[7] Baumgarten arranged his own financing, and announced that the initial batch of films would be in the "$100,000 or under class."[8] The films were aimed at the second feature slot of small-town markets. "Or under" was the budgetary norm for the first two releases, but due to the "good acceptance" of those early films, Baumgarten upped future budgets to the reported $100,000.[9]

The first of AFRC's releases was *Two-Gun Lady*, co-starring Peggie Castle and William Tallman. This was followed by *Last of the Desperados*, the first of Sig's four films for Baumgarten, already in production under the working title *The Story of Pat Garrett* when Baumgarten broke the news of his new concern. Sig would follow *Last of the Desperados* with *The Wild Dakotas*, *The Three Outlaws*, and *Frontier Gambler*. It would appear that promotion of these films was not as robust or attentive as many of AFRC's competitors since prerelease materials in the trades and reviews of each film are fewer than the norm.

Former sheriff James Craig (left) and his deputy Jim Davis pose with director Sam Newfield on the set of **Last of the Desperados** (Associated Film Releasing Corp., 1955), Sig Neufeld producer, Sam Newfield director. *Courtesy of Laura Berk.*

Sig, as usual, brought Sam back to direct, along with his good friend Bert Sternbach as production manager. Holbrook Todd was able to serve as editor on two of the films, but Jack Greenhalgh was elsewhere on other assignments, so either Eddie Linden, William Bradford, or Kenneth Peach took over the lensing duties. Frequent screenwriting collaborator Orville Hampton penned three of the four scripts, and prolific musician Paul Dunlap, who had composed the scores for Sig's earlier *Hi-Jacked* and *Lost Continent*, was retained to write the scores for the four films as well. Dunlap relayed an amusing story about Sig and Sam that occurred during the production of one of these four final Westerns:

> I remember one time when I was madly in love with a ballet dancer. I actually recorded a short ballet for her on one of their pictures. It was a western, you see, but they didn't care at all. One brother says to the other brother, 'Where's the music coming from? It's a cowboy picture, a period piece.' And the other brother says, 'Oh, maybe it's coming from the radio.' And the other brother accepted that. How charming they were.[10]

Jim Davis takes part in some gunplay in **Last of the Desperados** (Associated Film Releasing Corp., 1955).

Last of the Desperados was the second film of Baumgarten's new concern, produced by Sigmund Neufeld Productions and released on December 1, 1955. After Pat Garrett (James Craig) kills outlaw Billy the Kid, most of the townspeople turn on him, believing the killing to have been cold-blooded murder. This prompts Craig to quit his job as sheriff and relocate under a false identity, where he falls in love with one of Billy's former wives, saloon operator Sarita (Margia Dean). Craig's former deputy (Jim

Davis) finally tracks him down and returns his sheriff's badge to him. Four of Billy's former gang members—Barton MacLane and Bob Steele among them—eventually track down Craig as well, who manages to kill them all in the gunfight that follows. He's saved from a bullet by the badge that Davis had returned to him. *Variety* called it a "good programmer" while saving most of its praise for Sam, finishing with "Sam Newfield's direction is good, highlighting the action values without sacrificing plot."[11]

The Wild Dakotas came next, released sometime in February 1956. Brutal, nononsense wagonmaster Jim Davis leads his weary group of settlers west into the wild Dakotas where they hope to settle in Powder Valley. The Arapaho Indians view the land as theirs, so Davis, who knows that the army is following, hopes to goad the Indians into attacking so that they will be massacred by the army. Frontiersman Bill Williams, a friend of the Indians, attempts to bring the two sides together to arrive at some sort of understanding. When that doesn't pan out, Davis has Williams whipped, but he later escapes and convinces the Indians to delay their attack. He returns to the wagon train, kills Davis during a fight, and takes the corpse back to the Indians as proof of the belligerent wagonmaster's demise, thereby preventing the attack. Colleen Gray figures into the plot as a sympathetic gambling girl who attracts Davis's unwanted attention.

Director Sam Newfield and his former wife Violet (both holding copies of the script) at an outdoor location, likely for the film **The Wild Dakotas** (Associated Film Releasing Corp., 1955), Sig Neufeld producer, Sam Newfield director. *Courtesy of Laura Berk.*

"INDIAN SAVAGERY...SWORN TO MASSACRE ON THE TERROR TRAIL TO POWDER RIVER VALLEY!" screamed the not-so-subtle posters, dominated by the fearsome visage of one of those Arapaho "savages." *Motion Picture Exhibitor* seemed to like the results: "Produced by some old hands in the action film field,

Neufeld and Newfield, and enacted by a cast also well versed in outdoor and western films this is an average entry of its type. There is plenty of action and the Indians always add excitement to this sort of thing."[12] One note of interest regarding this film is that despite all the Westerns Sig and/or Sam had made over the past two decades, the budgets had always precluded the option of incorporating Indians into the plots. *The Wild Dakotas* is notable for having a budget sufficient to do so.

The Three Outlaws followed, another fictionalized retelling of the notorious Wild Bunch story, penned by Orville Hampton. Filming was scheduled to roll in Mexico City on November 21, 1955, but was put on hold when there were no Mexican crews available. By mid-December, available Mexican crews were still a month away, so with a supposed spring release date looming, money flowing out the door, and little to show for it, Sig was forced to regroup and head back to the U.S. for location filming there, finally underway by mid-February.[13] Cinematographer Kenneth Peach filmed using the more cost-effective SuperScope 235 process, which produced a 2.35-1 aspect ratio image on standard 35mm film. The spring release date fell by the wayside, the film finally arriving on theatre screens in August.

Outlaws Butch Cassidy (Neville Brand), the Sundance Kid (Alan Hale), and Bill Carver (Robert Christopher), having grown weary of their trade, decide to retire. They head south into Mexico with the $57,000 stolen during their most recent train robbery, buy a ranch, and deposit the remainder in a local bank. Weaselly El Raton (Jose

Sam Newfield poses with some of the cast and crew of **The Three Outlaws** (Associated Film Releasing Corp., 1956), Sig Neufeld producer, Sam Newfield director. Left-to-right: Sam Newfield, Alan Hale Jr., Neville Brand, two unidentified actors, and Stanley Neufeld. *Courtesy of Tim Neufeld.*

Gonzalez Gonzalez, and, no, that is not a typo) is witness to the deposit, so he takes the news to bandito Rudolfo Hoyas who, once convinced of its veracity, has his gang blow up the bank and make off with the money. Railroad owner Stanley Andrews sends both his security head and top agent (Jonathan Hale and Bruce Bennett, respectively) to track down the thieves, and after a lot of plot has been expended, the three outlaws—and Hoyas—have all been shot dead.

Newcomer Jeanne Carmen has a small role as Hoyas's greedy girl, while Lillian Molieri has a slightly meatier role as the daughter of government police colonel Henry Escalante. Carmen relayed an amusing story to interviewer Ted Okuda about landing this part, her film debut:

> [It's] funny how I got that part. When I interviewed for the role, this guy handed me a script and said "Can you do a Spanish dialect?" I said, "Sure I can." I was lying, of course. So I read for him, and when I got through, he said, "I said *Spanish*, not *Jewish*!"

Sam Newfield clowns around with actress Jeanne Carmen and former wife Violet on the set of **The Three Outlaws** (Associated Film Releasing Corp., 1956). It would appear that Sam and Violet's divorce was an amicable one. *Courtesy of Laura Berk.*

Carmen had some very strong opinions about some of her co-stars, Neville Brand in particular. "Brand was a cranky sonofabitch. I can't remember him speaking off camera; if he did, it was probably something unpleasant. But," she added, "he was perfect for the part of an outlaw." Bruce Bennett was deemed "a nice guy, but too old at that point to be playing a leading man." As for Alan Hale, she felt that he "was better suited for comedies; it was so ludicrous to see him as the romantic figure."[14]

Motion Picture Daily had some kind words for the brothers and their most recent joint effort, stating that "Sam Newfield directed and Sigmund Neufeld produced, with the attraction reflecting their experienced handling all the way down the line."[15] The film was structured with an opening sequence that suggests the outlaws' fate, followed by the meat of the story as flashback. The review added: "That unlawful hombres will be ultimately apprehended and, in turn, killed is a foregone conclusion from the opening sequence."[16] *Motion Picture Exhibitor* commented in a similar fashion, stating that "A novel story twist is to be found in part of the plot framework, but aside from that the balance of the film is average."[17] Sam's direction appears to have been affected by the late-to-start rushed schedule, as some of the scenes are shot as single uninterrupted takes, usually as a medium two-shot. A time-saving expedient, for sure, but not typical of Sam.

Frontier Gambler, the last of Sig's films for AFRC, was arguably the weakest of the four. It is notable that Sig hired Sam's ex-wife, now remarried and going by Violet McComas, as script supervisor for this film (as well as the two films that preceded it), suggesting that the divorce was amicable, or at least something approximating amicable. Paul Dunlap, the film's composer, seems to have dashed off this particular score, which doesn't add much to the film. Dunlap wrote the music for one of the film's songs as well, "Your Heart Belongs to Her," with lyrics written by co-star Margia Dean.

Sam Newfield (to right of camera holding cigarette) and crew on a Western set, likely for **Frontier Gambler** (Associated Film Releasing Corp., 1956), Sig Neufeld producer, Sam Newfield director. *Courtesy of Laura Berk.*

The film starts off strong enough, with a series of nighttime shots following the footsteps of an unseen man approaching a home, the woman inside whose face is hidden by shadow, her shooting death, and the conflagration that follows when her home is engulfed in fire from an overturned lamp. Deputy John Bromfield is summoned to investigate her death, the woman thought to be Colleen Gray, whose successful gambling den business has provided her the funds to buy up half the town, making a large number of enemies while doing so. The film's gimmick is that Gray is alive and well; it was another woman who was in her house, her face burnt beyond recognition. The film's "surprise" really isn't much of one, since the purposefully obscured face of the victim in that opening scene immediately prompts the question "why?", and the obvious reason why.

Colleen Gray defends herself in **Frontier Gambler** (Associated Film Releasing Corp., 1956).

Motion Picture Exhibitor's review adequately summed up the film's shortcomings. "There is so much talk here and so little action," wrote the reviewer, "that were it not for the costumes and a few horses, this wouldn't be classified as a western in the accepted sense of the word. What starts out as a mystery with possibilities soon sinks to a routine level."[18] *Frontier Gambler* was released in September 1956.

Baumgarten's attention to Associated Film Releasing Corp. had been sidelined by a new venture a few months earlier, but more on that shortly.

In the meantime, Sig had reunited with former PRC president Leon Fromkess to form another production company that would prove to be a real family affair, involving not only his brother Sam, but his sons Stanley and Sig Jr. as well. Only this time the company's focus would be television production rather than that of feature film.

Fromkess, who had been functioning as production chief for Samuel Goldwyn Productions since his departure from PRC, resigned from that position on April 15, 1951.[19] Having made the decision to move from film production to the fledging television industry, Fromkess was hired for a short-lived executive position at Music Corporation of America (MCA) to produce television films for their Revue Productions. It wasn't long before Fromkess decided to start his own company, partnering with Harry S. Rothschild to form Arrow Productions Inc. Arrow's first series was *Ramar of the Jungle*, for which he hired Sam to film a number of the first season's episodes.[20] In 1953, Milton Gordon and Edward Small, president and vice-president, respectively, of New York-based Television Programs of America (TPA), bought into Arrow as partners, and as part of the deal Fromkess was made executive producer for TPA.[21] Popular TPA television series *Lassie* (1954-74) and *Fury* (1955-60), among others, were soon to follow.

In July 1956, Television Programs of America entered into a co-production agreement with the Canadian Broadcasting Company (CBC), to jump-start Canada's telefilm industry with a new television series. Announced as *Last of the Mohicans*, the thirty-nine-episode show was to be produced over a six-month period, on an estimated $1,500,000 budget. TPA would supply the series' two stars, John Hart and Lon Chaney Jr., as well as the director, Sam Newfield. The rest of the cast would be Canadian, as well as the technical crew, with the exception of a few key creative spots that would eventually be turned over to Canadians once they were up to speed. About 40 % of the footage was to be shot on location "in former French and Indian war country," with interiors filmed at the studios of Audio Pictures, Ltd., located in Toronto at 310 Lake Shore Road. Production was to commence on July 23, 1956, with newly formed Normandie Productions Ltd., a subsidiary of TPA, working in concert with CBC-TV.[22] Fromkess, who was well aware of Sig's abilities and efficiency as a producer from back at PRC, hired Sig to serve as Normandie Pictures' general manager, ostensibly serving under president Vincent Melzac but in actuality assuming control of the production. Bert Sternbach was brought along as production manager, Sam was hired as Normandie's director, and Sig's sons Stanley and Sig Jr. were brought along as well to gain further experience. TPA, CBC, and Normandie would jointly co-finance the series. Once completed, CBC would telecast the series, and TPA would distribute elsewhere under an agreement set by the three co-producing parties.

The deal was announced by Arthur Gottlieb, Audio Pictures' president, who knew Sam from back in 1935 when Sam went to Canada to make two films for Gottlieb's Booth Dominion Productions. Problems arose almost immediately when the limitations of Gottlieb's studio became apparent, requiring an increase in the outdoor shooting. According to *Variety*:

> Principal factor in deciding to shoot 70 to 75% of "Mohicans" outdoors was that Audio Pictures studio here, where interiors are filmed, is so small it can only handle two sets. There's no room to fly either one, so one has to be struck when the other's in use. Studio also has no light grid, which means lights have to be hung from the set itself and rehung, reset and refocused for every take.[23]

A replica of an Indian Village replica was built on Gottlieb's Pine Ridge Farms thirty miles east of Toronto in Pickering.[24] Gottlieb's farm needed a little work, however, requiring a road to be bulldozed into the wooded area, and a small bridge to be built to accommodate the vehicles bringing in the various equipment needed for filming. Sig Jr., who was there on location, recalled that Gottlieb had "built a little sound stage and had some space on his back property; he lived out on a big ranch. He would film commercials and things like that. The territory around it was perfect for the landscape and the backgrounds required, and they built the fort set, and they shot all of the shows right around there."[25] Snow and ice were written into the scripts to account for inclement weather.

Each episode took approximately one week to film, and more than 1,300 Canadians found some sort of employment by the time the series was completed. The touted $1,500,000 budget, as so often happened in press releases, was overstated, in reality slightly more than $1,000,000. German cinematographer Eugen Schüfftan, it should be noted, was behind the camera for a large number of the series' episodes.

John Hart (as Hawkeye) and co-star Lon Chaney Jr. (as Chingachgook) in Hawkeye and the **Last of the Mohicans** (Normandie/TPA-CBC, 1957), Leon Fromkess and Sig Neufeld producers, Sam Newfield director.

Set in the 1700s, the series was loosely based on James Fenimore Cooper's classic about the Mohican chief Chingachgook, and his woodsman friend Hawkeye. Chingachgook was played by Chaney, and Hawkeye by John Hart, both of whom were paid "about 800 bucks a week."[26] Chaney, who was notorious for his heavy drinking, made no exception for this series. "I remember that very well," recalled Sig Jr. "When they hired him to do the show, he said he'd love to do the show, but they should try to plan all of his work—particularly scenes where he had dialog—to be done in the morning because he starts drinking around noon. He said, 'I'm not going to change that, so if you want me that's the way it is.' And they took him and that's exactly the way he worked."[27]

Replacement "stuntman" Stanley Neufeld (pictured) rode side saddle in drag as none of the stuntmen in Canada knew how to do so. Stanley was an expert rider as he used to ride for free at the Fat Jones Stables in North Hollywood because his father used their horses so often.
Courtesy of Tim Neufeld.

John Hart was provided an apartment below Chaney's in a large apartment building overlooking Lake Ontario. Chaney's tipple of choice was Jim Beam, and he had a bottle with him each day of filming. "You could tell what time of day it was by the bottle," claimed Hart in an interview by Tom Weaver, but he was quick to add that "Chaney was never late, never didn't know his lines. He got a little 'juicy' by about three in the afternoon, but he was a professional actor and knew his part and did a good job. He was never out of control."[28] Sam's son Joel recalled that Chaney "was not what you might expect...he wanted to go fishing. He had a motorhome, and he was like a country guy and just wanted to go out and go fishing. And he didn't take any of it too seriously."[29]

The Canadian actors hired were not always as camera-ready as expected, causing the occasional delay. "Although the Hollywood actors are accomplished horseback riders after years of appearing in westerns," wrote a local paper, "many Canadian actors have been found to have little skill in the saddle. Stand-ins take over for the tricky riding shots."[30] Stanley Neufeld was one such "stand-in," according to his son Tim. "Because Sig produced westerns, my dad [Stanley] had unlimited access to free horses [during the PRC years]. [The horses] used to be in North Hollywood in the valley right over the hill from where they lived—maybe a twenty-minute drive. He became an expert horseman...and when they filmed 'Last of the Mohicans' he was a stunt double for a woman on a horse. We have some photos of that, him wearing a blue dress and a blonde wig."[31]

The actors were expected to perform their own stunts, although Chaney had a tendency to go overboard with the physicality, as he once did a decade earlier when he almost killed older character actor Oscar O'Shea while filming a tussle in one of Universal's "Mummy" sequels, *The Mummy's Ghost* (1944). Hart commented on this:

> We'd have all these Indian battles, and the producers would get these poor kids out of Toronto who wanted to get in the movies. They'd come out there, *not* dressed for the cold or anything, and they'd have to fight Chaney and me. Chaney would be about three sheets to the wind, and he'd grab these kids up and *slam* 'em into a tree…! And one day the "Indians" quit fighting, they wouldn't fight anymore![32]

Sam directed the bulk of the episodes. Sig's son Stanley, who had a decade's experience functioning as Sam's assistant director at PRC, Film Classics, and Lippert, now served as the series' production manager for most of the episodes. He also acted as Sam's assistant director on several other episodes, and finally got to direct, megging a few of the episodes as well.

Stanley's younger brother Sig Jr. was also part of the production team, but the film industry as a lifetime goal evolved more gradually than his older brother's lifelong obsession. "When I was nineteen," recalled Sig Jr.,

> I had to take a year off from school when I was a kid because I was so sick with asthma and hay fever. I had it terrible when I was young, and my mother kept me out of school for an entire year because of it, so I was always a year behind. So I didn't graduate high school until I was nineteen because of that, and when I got out of there, I remember my family said "Whatever you want to do is okay with us. If you want to go to college"—nobody in the family had gone to college—"so if you want to go to college, we'll pay for that. If you don't want to go to college we'll help you get a job." I loved to visit the set, and I decided that's what I wanted to do, what [Sam] was doing. He didn't really take me under his wing, although I do remember a few times talking to him very briefly about how he made certain decisions, so he was a little bit helpful. But I didn't talk to him a lot about it, I just observed."[33]

Deciding you want to be a director, and actually *becoming* a director, are two different things, however. His father offered him some solid advice, explaining that the best place to learn to be a director was in

> the editing room…because you can learn the most about film in the editing room. You learn what you need to film, what you need to shoot, the different camera angles, and how to move people, and how to move the camera, and all that stuff, because you are dealing with it on a daily basis. You are the director's biggest critic in the cutting room.[34]

So Sig put his son to work in the editing department.

> They put me to work as an apprentice, a learning thing which you had to do for like two years, and then you could move up to first assistant. When I started editing, I worked with Holbrook [N. Todd], before he retired…. Holbrook was a

good editor, and that's where I learned, started to learn about editing, because that's what I did for a long time before I directed.... I was with Holbrook Todd for two years.³⁵

Sig Jr. was now part of the *Mohicans* production as well. Sig Jr. and his cousin Joel drove to Toronto, Sig taking all his books and other personal belongings with him because he was planning to stay. They almost didn't make it, as Joel explained:

We drove across country, and when we got to Niagara Falls, they wouldn't let us in.... They asked [Sig Jr.] 'What are you doing in Canada?' and he said 'We're working.' Well, you had to have a work permit, and they checked and couldn't find one. And so he called the studio...and of course they were really mad at him, and they gave Junior a lot of trouble because he wasn't supposed to say that. Then we went down to Hamilton, down south, to cross over there. Of course the first question that came up: 'What are you doing in Canada?' and he said 'Oh, we're just vacationing.' And they open up the trunk, and he had books and lamps and stuff, and stuff you don't take on vacation. But they let us in.³⁶

Sig Jr. wore several hats during the production, serving as film editor, as sound effects editor, and music editor. "I actually have a recollection of being in the studio in Toronto when they were doing [the sound editing], and there was no live orchestra, they were just matching music to the film,"³⁷ recalled nephew Tim. "They sent me canned music," added Sig Jr., "and I put it together as best as I could with what I had, but I finally complained that I didn't have enough music, and they finally agreed to send me more..."³⁸

Sam's son Joel got involved as well, taking a break from college to join the crew as some sort of assistant. "It was like a summer break for me."³⁹ They called him an assistant director, but he says that he was no more than a glorified gofer.

The Last of the Mohicans' premiere episode was broadcast in Canada by CBC on December 6, 1956. Stateside broadcast followed a month later, premiering in Los Angeles on January 24, 1957. Episode one, *Hawkeye's Homecoming*, the sole episode directed by Sidney Salkow before Sam took over, takes place in 1757 along the Iroquois Trail in upstate New York. Hawkeye's brother Tommy (Don Garner), who has joined the British Army, is assigned to deliver a dispatch to Fort William Henry requesting additional troops to quell an Indian uprising. He doesn't get very far, betrayed and shot by Ogana (Michael Ansara), the Indian guide accompanying him. Ogana has the Brits bamboozled, leading then to believe that Tommy was a spy for the Huron Indians, but Hawkeye and Chingachgook don't fall for it and set out to clear Tommy's name. The truth comes out when Ogana and his fellow Indians attack the fort, a leering Ogana making off with an officer's daughter Marian (Lili Fontaine). All ends well when Hawkeye kills Ogana in a reasonably exciting knife fight.

Location filming certainly helped with the visuals, a trio of shots in the premier episode enhanced with scope-enhancing matte shots. The sets are solidly constructed, although some of the stage-bound exterior sets have an artificial look to them. The cast all handle their roles adequately, and for a nice change of pace the Indian attack is peopled by a whole slew of "Indians," and sufficiently savage in its execution. Ansara's duplicitous Indian spy adds an element of threat to the proceedings, and you can tell by his drooling leer as he snatches Marian away from the fort that she's in for one of those "fates worse than death." In most of the film's longer shots it actually looks like he shaved his head for the role, but his bald head appliance becomes painfully apparent during close shots during the climactic knife fight.

Variety's critic was not overly impressed, calling it the "Latest bid for moppet attention" in a rather lackluster review, although some of his comments were on target.

It's located in Northeastern U.S. and Canada in pre-Revolutionary time and as such is different in that it has the redskins skulking through a forest rather than riding down off a mesa. The difference is one of the prime assets of the series, judging by the initialer, since the story line clings to a rather outdated strict black-and-white treatment of heroes and villains that may not register too strongly with today's sophisticated sprouts.

The reviewer, "Kap.," went on to add that "some of his Indian braves appear to be more than a trifle too pudgy to instill much fear into viewers."[40]

The Last of the Mohicans was a success, one of the season's top twenty shows. Both Hart and Chaney assumed that it would be renewed for a second season, and made plans accordingly. Hart, needless to say, was dismayed—okay, *bitter*—when he learned that it was not going to be renewed. "Well, the dumb shits never made another *one!*," he told Weaver. "They got in a big hassle, the producer and the sponsors and the networks, and it all went in the toilet. That's life in Hollywood, it just happens like that."[41]

Stanley Neufeld (standing) oversees a setup with star Minerva Urecal (sitting center) for **The Adventures of Tugboat Annie** (Normandie/TPA-CBC, 1957). *Courtesy of Tim Neufeld.*

With *Mohicans* finished, Normandie embarked on a second, thirty-nine-episode half-hour television series, *The Adventures of Tugboat Annie*. Leon Fromkess served as executive producer once again with Sig as producer. Based on author Norman Reilly Raine's stories that had appeared in *Saturday Evening Post* magazine, Minerva Urecal took the part of Annie, with Walter Sande as rival tugboat operator Captain Bullwinkle.[42] Filming commenced in July 1957 with another reported budget of $1,000,000.[43] Sig reported that thirty of the thirty-nine episodes were in the can by December 20, the beginning of the production's Christmas break, and was set to resume filming on January 6, 1958.[44] Both Stanley and Sig Jr. were part of the production crew on the series as well, but with its completion, Stanley would return to Los Angeles to serve as assistant director on Lee Marvin's *M Squad*, while Sig Jr. would remain in Canada to edit the *Hudson's Bay* television series.

Back in June 1956, Associated Film Releasing Corp.'s president E.J. Baumgarten announced the formation of another company named Regal Films, Inc., to produce films for release through Twentieth Century-Fox.[45] Fox contracted Regal to produce ten low budget, black-and-white CinemaScope quickies, dubbed RegalScope for these colorless releases. Baumgarten was president of the company, but Lippert was behind it all and running the show, reportedly hiding his name from all publicity and each film's credits due to his ongoing clash with the Screen Actors Guild over royalties, or lack thereof. Lippert's behind-the-scenes involvement wasn't a secret for very long. "As we get the story," wrote *Motion Picture Exhibitor* in November, "Spyros Skouras, of 20th Century-Fox, authorized the advance of the production dollars to Bob Lippert and his associates in Regal. They, in turn, have worked hard to make every buck they spend 'look like five on the screen.' And the resultant CinemaScope, black and white, action pictures will be in *addition to* the regular 20th Century-Fox lineup." *Stagecoach to Fury* was announced as Regal's first release, *Motion Picture Exhibitor* declaring that while it "may never play the Music Hall or Grauman's Chinese, it is certainly useable by 90 per cent of the theatres of the nation."[46] "Lippert," reported *Variety*, "will act in an advisory capacity for the company."[47] Regal Films set up offices in Lippert's new Culver City-based office complex.[48]

Sig took a break to accept an executive production assignment for two Regal productions bearing the working titles *A Boy and His Dog* and *The Flaming Frontier*. He hired Sam to direct these two films and gave him credit as producer as well, but Sig would keep his involvement under wraps, refusing screen credit. Filming would take place in Canada at the studios of Canadian Film Industries, which would also provide technical and lab facilities, the two films qualifying for the United Kingdom quota.[49] *A Boy and His Dog* and *The Flaming Frontier* would be released a year later as *Wolf Dog* in July 1958, and *Flaming Frontier* a month later in August.

Wolf Dog co-starred American actors Jim Davis and Allison Hayes in support of twelve-year-old Tony Brown, a Canadian newsboy from Bolton, Ontario who had his start in a small role in *The Last of the Mohicans*. The film's real star was Prince, a seven-year-old German Shepherd and a great-great-great-grandson of Rin Tin Tin, or at least if press releases were to be believed. Sam was reported to have tested "hundreds" of German Shepherds before discovering Prince at the Royal Canadian Mounted Police training school in Bolton, where the dog had served since his release from army duty in 1954.[50] A simple but engaging story of good-vs.-evil, *Wolf Dog* follows parolee—and former decorated war hero—Jim Davis's attempt to settle down with his wife Allison Hayes and young son Tony Brown on a ranch deeded to him by his sympathetic former Marine colonel. Greedy neighbor rancher Austin Willis is determined to drive Davis off his land, first allowing his vicious dog to kill Tony's dog, and later stampeding Davis's small herd of cattle, whose sale was intended to pay off some bank debts. Bad goes to worse when former convicts and current bank robbers Don Garrard and Juan Root show up and take over the house, threatening to kill everyone if they resist. The film ends with all the loose ends tied up: Tony's new dog—half wolf—kills Willis's dog, Davis beats the daylights out of Willis who has come to kill Tony's dog, the law arrives and both Garrard and Root are shot dead, and Willis reimburses Davis for the lost cattle. Admittedly, too good to be true, but a happy ending, nonetheless.

Twelve-year-old Tony Brown and his four-legged co-star Prince on this lobby card for **Wolf Dog** (Regal Films/Twentieth Century Fox, 1958), Sig Neufeld producer (uncredited), Sam Newfield director.

Young Tony Brown was a good find, a natural, if slightly over-enthusiastic, actor throughout. Prince, while not in the same class as his supposed distant ancestor, is adequate in the title role. Davis and Hayes are fine as his parents, with support from an uneven assemblage of Canadian actors. Hayes, for what it's worth, was one of the 1950s' most voluptuous actresses, her physical attributes shown off to good advantage a mere two months earlier in Allied Artists' *Attack of the 50 Foot Woman*, which probably didn't hurt this film's box office at all. Sam's direction is somewhat dictated by the super-wide RegalScope process, British cinematographer Frederick Ford shooting most scenes in mid- to long-shot with the goal of filling the image. Ford, who was filming for the first time on this side of the pond, wrote a lengthy, enthusiastic, detail-filled letter describing his experiences on *Wolf Dog*:

I am delighted at being here to photograph the first black and white CinemaScope feature being produced in this country by a Canadian company. I never thought I should have an opportunity of shooting a modern cowboy story.

I have a complete crew: Operator Jackson Samuels (Canadian), 1st Assistant Manny Alpert (American), 2nd Assistant Don McMillon (Canadian), 3rd Assistant Ted Winters (Canadian), Clappers Loader Denny Murphy (Canadian) and two Grips (Canadian).

Just returned from our first week's shooting on location, "Owen's Sound," Georgian Bay. Real cowboys, ranches, horses, cattle and gun-running bandits, including the old sheriff in this film. The cast, actors from Hollywood, Alison [sic] Hayes, Jim Davis, John Hart (of The Last of the Mohicans fame), Tony Brown (The Boy and His Dog), Austin Willis and many other featured players. Saw some of the rushes on Saturday. Apparently the Director, Sam Newfield, is delighted with the photographic quality. The boss, Mr. S. Newfeld [sic], had a representative from 20th, Hollywood, visit the studio to view our efforts, he sent me congratulatory messages. The star, Alison Hayes, has received another contract from the company because of her good looks and performance, she also thanked me for my efforts on her behalf. So, you see, we are making pretty good headway over here.

It's a great country, food excellent, hospitality outstanding, and generous people who are willing to accept knowledge from persons who arrive here with experience and willing to teach them the up-to-date methods of our business, so enabling them to establish a sound foundation for producing feature films in this country which, although young, has terrific possibilities.[51]

John Bath's score is adequate and unobtrusive, with the sole exception of being a bit too "upbeat" immediately following the sad death of Tony's first dog. The film's lower budget—it had a negative cost of $123,000—becomes evident in a couple of places, the camera's shadow crossing Hayes as it dollies in for a close-up, and Prince's heavy panting almost drowning out the dialog in an early scene. Aside from those two minor quibbles, the film's technical aspects are otherwise adequate. *Harrisons Reports* gave the film an accurate assessment, calling it a "fair outdoor action melodrama," going on to say that "the simple story is a bit on the contrived side and is somewhat drawn out, despite the short running time. It is wholesome stuff, however, with enough viciousness on the part of a mean neighbor to draw sympathy to the hero, and as such should get by with undiscriminating family audiences."[52] The deaths of the two dogs, while bound to upset younger (and many older) viewers, are both handled offscreen.

Flaming Frontier was the brothers' second film for Regal, filming in and around Toronto in October 1957. Bruce Bennett, in the downhill slide of his career, co-stars with Jim Davis in a plot vaguely reminiscent of that of *The Wild Dakotas* a mere two years earlier. Bennett plays a half-breed Cavalry officer sent by President Lincoln to Fort Ridgeley, Minnesota to restore peace between the Sioux and the soldiers. Davis is the fort's unscrupulous, Indian-hating commander who, in cahoots with trader Cecil Lander and Ben Lennick, the territory's Indian agent, steals money and supplies intended for the Sioux. Bennett arrives at an uneasy truce with the Sioux's chief, Larry Solway, promising to set things right in exchange for chief's promise to keep his braves off the warpath. Davis and his cohorts violate the shaky truce, prompting the Sioux to attack.

Davis, Lander, and Lennick are all killed, with the result that the Sioux are now satisfied and peace returns. Bennett ends up marrying Paisley Maxwell, who had earlier left hubby Davis and fallen for Bennett's aging charms.

"A routine Cavalry-versus-Indians program melodrama," wrote *Harrisons Reports*, that "has enough robust action and excitement to get by with undiscriminating audiences.... Sam Newfield...strives mightily to incorporate as much vital entertainment values as attainable."[53] With a negative cost of $142,000 and worldwide rentals of $238,000, when distribution and promotional cost were factored in the film showed a loss of $25,000.

Flaming Frontier would prove to be the final production of Sig and Sam's long careers, and a rather unremarkable swan song at that.

Bruce Bennett takes a burning stick to the scar on his arm while a horrified Don Garrard looks on in **Flaming Frontier** (Regal Films/Twentieth Century Fox, 1958), Sig Neufeld executive producer, Sam Newfield producer and director.

Chapter 22:
The Twilight Years

One would have expected Sam to have continued in the industry as a director for television, since that's what so many of his contemporaries did, contemporaries that included William Beaudine and Jean Yarbrough. But he didn't. Son Joel explained:

The only time I really heard him discuss business was that he did not like television because the director lost all [say]. In other words, the actors became the prominent people. The actor could say 'This is how it's going to be, and if you don't like it, go away.' I hate what it did to them; he was a director, and he was no longer a director in TV. If it came down between one or the other, the director was gone. This is how it was, it was different, what was happening.[1]

Sam had turned his back on direction. Or, perhaps, direction had by now turned its back on Sam. Sig Jr. offered his assessment of Sam's years of success in the industry despite never having an agent, nor doing much (or needing to do much) of anything to promote his career.

He was so efficient at it, and got it all done quickly and didn't go over budget or schedule or things like that. That he was a terrific director? I honestly don't think so; in today's market he probably wouldn't be able to get a job, but in those days, he was fine for what he was doing. [Sam and the actors] got along well. He had a good sense of humor; he loved to joke around. It makes for a happy set, if the director's kind of leading everything and having fun and making people laugh, and keeping the thing going…and Sam did that. He had a good sense of humor. But in terms of being a great director, I don't think so.[2]

Sam's days as a director were over. It was no longer fun, and may not have been for some time. Joel thinks that it was during the silent era when his father derived the most enjoyment out of filmmaking, or at least that is his lasting impression. The 1920s were the years when every day was a learning experience, an immersion in the economical scheduling and production of films that would serve him so well over the years to come, and the years when he had the most fun doing so. The Silent Movie Theatre, which had opened in 1942, was located on Fairfax Avenue two blocks down from Canter's delicatessen, one of both Sig and Sam's favorite dining places. Every time Sam walked by the theatre on his way to or from Canter's, he would stop and take note of the film currently featured. He wouldn't go in, but would pause, lost in his nostalgic thoughts, wistfully ruminating on happier, more carefree days gone by.

"By the 1950s when I'm growing up," recalled Sam's grandnephew Tim Neufeld, "Sig doesn't socially see Sam, and he doesn't see his other brother [Morris], and doesn't see [his sister] Sadie, and the only 'family' I know growing up was my Uncle Bert and my grandparents. I have almost no recollection of Sam. I have vague recollection of Sam on a set of *The Last of the Mohicans*. I don't remember Sam ever coming over for any social occasions, same with Sadie."[3]

Without work to keep him busy, Sam doubled down on his gambling. His son Joel's military service had been deferred while he attended Pasadena's Art Center College of Design after graduating from high school. "I remember parking cars on Sunset Strip in those days when I was in college," recalled Joel, "and I always told people 'If you want to see actors, don't go to Hollywood Boulevard; go to Sunset Strip where all the agents are. Every person going in and out of a building is an actor."[4] Joel tells a story about celebrity, or being in close proximity to celebrity:

> I went back to New York with a friend from high school, when we graduated from high school, and I drove to New York. And we were in a bar, because you could drink at eighteen, and somehow somebody asked where we were from and we told them California, and people were buying us drinks, and we became stars. [I didn't realize the] interest in Hollywood...and they would mention actors I never heard of, who was their favorite.... It was very impressive, that we would become celebrities because we were from California.[5]

All good things come to an end, however, and Joel was eventually drafted into the Army for two years' service. His father's gambling resulted in one of Joel's more pleasant experiences. "He [Sam] loved Vegas," recalled Joel.

> He got to know pretty much everybody. The funniest story was when I was in the army and I took a couple of friends to Vegas, I was treated like a king because of my last name. These guys looked at me like "Who the hell are you?" [Sam] went to the Riviera almost all the time there, and he knew the pit bosses, and they would come and join us for breakfast. I went a couple of times with him when I got older. And he liked the horses.[6]

The addiction took its toll. "Sam did not take good care of himself at all, he just didn't," recalled his nephew, Sig Jr., thinking back to both his father's and uncle's later years.

> My dad took much better care of himself than Sam did. It's not that—he didn't drink or anything like that, but he just didn't take care of himself.... [His gambling] left him pretty much broke all the time; it cost him his family; his wife divorced him over it. It was a big problem. And my dad would sneak him a little bit of money here and there when he was flat out broke—my mother would kill my dad if she knew it.[7]

At one point in the late 1950s or 1960, Sam was hospitalized in the Motion Picture Hospital in Woodland Hills, and Joel visited him while in his uniform. Any thoughts he may have had about the reception he would receive were soon dashed. "I came down in uniform. I was complaining about [the uniform], and he got mad at me. He was very patriotic. He wanted to join the army.... He was very pro, very patriotic. And he got mad at me because I said something bad about the army."[8]

Sam's final six years were spent in relative obscurity. "I think he did some writing," recalled Joel when asked about this late period. "He did a lot of writing. He was left-handed, and he would write me a letter or something, and there was no way I could read it. It was the worst handwriting you would ever see. It all looked the same."

Sam lived at the Motion Picture Country House for the final few years. "He was at the actor's hospital at the end, out in the valley, which is where Jackie lived. The Motion Pictures House. And he had a ball out there. He ran into people he hadn't talked to in fifty years. And these were all these people who were dying, and it was a refuge for them all.... I would come down and visit him, and of course Jackie lived basically across the street from him. He wasn't there that long."

Sam had stomach problems for a number of years, so it may have been another example of the proverbial "boy who cried wolf." "Nobody took him very seriously, I don't think, and when they realized what it was, it was too late." It was, of course, cancer. Sam died on November 10, 1964; he was buried two days later at Mt. Sinai Memorial Park. Sam's ex-wife Violet outlived him by thirty years, dying in Los Angeles on December 23, 1994.

Sam's son Joel had a final say regarding the aftermath of his father's death. "When he died," recalled Joel, "Sam was qualified for a star on the [Hollywood] Walk of Fame. They contacted my sister [Jackie] about it; they wanted—in order to get the star you had to give them ten thousand dollars.' Joel paused in his story at this point, then concluded with his and Jackie's reaction to this request: "'Eh, I don't think so.'"[9]

Sig, on the other hand, had a much longer, and far more enjoyable, retirement, leaving the industry behind after those final two films for Regal up in Canada. "He wasn't one for hobbies," said his son Sig Jr. "[Sig and Ruth] travelled a bit, a lot more than they did when he was working. [He] basically lived out his life in leisure."[10] Sig and Ruth's son Stanley got the big break of his career in 1960 when he was hired to serve as assistant director of the popular television series *Naked City*. This necessitated relocating to New York, leaving their home at 4919 Mammoth Avenue behind. Sig and Ruth moved in as caretakers. Stanley's son Tim recalled that "there was a pool in the back

Retired Sig Neufeld and his wife Ruth circa 1968. *Courtesy of Tim Neufeld.*

yard—a small pool, and it's the San Fernando Valley—and my grandfather had never been swimming, never really had much free time. He wouldn't go in the pool until at least it was an hour after he ate because he was afraid of getting cramps, but he didn't know how to swim, he just wouldn't even put his feet in the water." Stanley sold the house a few years later, Sig and Ruth moving to an apartment two blocks away on Woodman Avenue.

Bert Sternbach was a constant companion throughout Sig's retirement, a friendship solidified over the past thirty-five years. "Bert Sternbach and my father became great friends for their whole lives once they met each other," recalled Sig Jr.,

and when [Sig] eventually retired [Bert] retired along when my dad did. But they always stayed close friends, and he was a confirmed bachelor—he never married—so we became sort of his family.
I always remember a trip in 1946, my mother got a new car right after the war—one of the first new cars to come out right after the war, because cars weren't made during the war—and we took a trip in the car, quite a long trip, and I got to drive because I was a sixteen-year-old teenager who wanted to do nothing but drive, so I drove them all and Bert came along with us and we did this big tour of the Pacific Northwest up into Canada and all around and back, and had a great time.[11]

Tim Neufeld, Sig's grandson, elaborated on Bert's relationship to the family:

Bert Sternbach about to embark on a flight back to Europe. *Courtesy of Tim Neufeld.*

> "[In the 1930s] they would take family vacations, and Bert would be part of the family vacation. So that's how close they were: they not only worked together—they *always* worked together—and when I had a car and was older and could take my grandpa out for lunch, which he used to like to do, Bert always came along because Bert lived literally in the apartment below my grandfather. There was a period of time when they bought a house—Sig and Ruth—in the valley, and [Bert] rented an apartment, like two doors away. When they were in Hollywood, [Bert] lived right next to them; he was always just there, he was just part of the family. I called him Uncle Bert—I only knew him as Uncle Bert—I never knew that he wasn't part of my family, and I grew up with him.... So Bert was part of the family, and very trusted in terms of running the productions.... [Bert] was Austrian and he spoke with an accent, and I remember in the fifties he flew back to Europe, and we all went to the airport to send him off to fly to Europe on one of the early jets, to go visit his family that was still there, who had miraculously survived the war....[12]

Bert Sternbach died on January 30, 1974. Sig had lost his brother by this time, and now he had lost his best friend.

As happens so often with people consumed by their work, little time and effort is spent on their children, and Sig was no exception. Now that he was retired, and his children grown adults, he spent a lot of time with his grandson Tim, who would frequently join Sig on excursions to some of his grandfather's favorite local restaurants. Sig loved the Hungarian fare served at Nickodell Restaurant on Melrose Avenue, just down the street from Paramount's main gate, but there were others. "He used to love to eat beef," recalled Tim, "and his favorite restaurant was Lawry's The Prime Rib in Los Angeles. As a kid we would go there a lot; he loved to go there because these were things in his youth he wasn't able to do."[13] And then there was baseball.

> [Sig] became a baseball nut. In those days the Dodgers were not on television, they were only on radio, with Vin Scully. He would religiously listen to those games with his little Sony transistor radio. My impression was during his working years all he did was work and spend time with his family; he had no hobbies. Baseball became sort of an obsession with him. I remember he would be listening to games all the time with Vin Scully. I went to a couple of games with him, and then my dad [Stanley] had worked for Gene Autry for a number of years, and Gene Autry bought the California Angels, which I think were called the Los Angeles Angels in the beginning. He called Gene Autry's office and got Autry's tickets to a game, and took my grandfather, and they were like the best seats in the house, and it was like one of the greatest days of his retirement. Even though he was a Dodgers fan, going to see the Angels, and sitting in the owner's seats.... I went with him to the Memorial Coliseum, which is where the Dodgers played initially, several times to games, and that brought him great joy to watch the game in person.[14]

Their excursions didn't always turn out as planned, such as the time Tim took his grandfather to the movies.

I took my grandfather to see *Blazing Saddles*, and of course he lived in the world of censorship, and I can tell you…he couldn't believe what he was seeing on the screen. Every five minutes he'd look over at me like he shouldn't be looking at the screen. And he kept saying "They would never allow this! They'd never allow this!" So it was a different world, the world of the Hays Office and censorship; they were very limited in what they could show on the screen.[15]

Health issues and the ravages of age were taking their unwelcome toll by this time.

He had cataract surgery, and he wore these very thick-frame glasses—he really couldn't see without them. The cataract surgery in those days was very primitive compared to what it is today. He used to blame it on all the time he spent in the editing room, squinting at black-and-white film. I'm sure the cataracts were independent of that, but that was his view, that it was all those years in the editing room that caused that.[16]

Sig and Ruth had celebrated their fiftieth wedding anniversary in 1970, and during these later years he would kid her, calling her "Toothless Ruthless." (Ruth had lost most of her teeth by this time, a casualty of the lack of proper dental care back in those earlier, far less affluent days.) He was devoted to Ruth, his responsibilities and day-to-day care increasing as she slowly slipped into the nether world of dementia. "He took care of her," said Tim. "He would cook her meals. He would go to the market every day. He would really care for her until the end."[17]

Sig Neufeld with his great granddaughter Pamela, grandson Tim's daughter, 1976. This was likely the last photo taken of Sig before his death three years later. *Courtesy of Tim Neufeld.*

The end came on April 9, 1977. Sig would carry on for another two years, a widower who had now lost all of those of his generation. Sister Sadie had died back in 1955. Brother Sam had died in 1964. Brother Maury had died in 1966. Friend Bert had died in 1974. And now Ruth.

With Ruth's passing, Sig Jr. moved his father back to Hollywood into a building that he owned on Laurel Canyon and Hollywood Boulevard. "And then he got pretty sick," recalled Tim. "He went to a nursing home in Santa Monica, which is near where my dad lived.... He was in a nursing home for a very short time.... He was admitted to St. John's Hospital, and Sig [Jr.] was on location, and Stan was on location; I was the only one here, and I saw him on the day he passed away."[18] The attending nurse noticed the ring that the Sterns had given him sixty years earlier, and told Tim that he should take it. "I didn't want to take it." The nurse persisted.

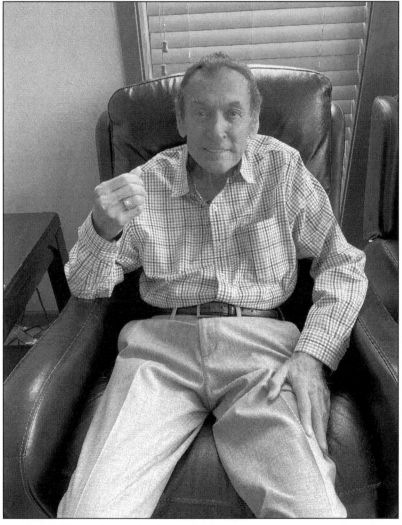

Sig Neufeld's son Sig Jr., displaying the ring that the Stern Brothers had given his father more than a century earlier; taken on May 26, 2022. Sig Jr. would pass on five months later. *Courtesy of Tim Neufeld.*

"But if you don't take it someone will steal it," and [she] took it off and he struggled. Even though he was almost in a coma, he struggled. He was fighting having that ring come off, because I think it was so important to him. And she handed me the ring, and I dropped it off with my dad's wife, and [Sig] passed away later on, later that day.[19]

Sig would follow Ruth on March 21, 1979.

Sig's two sons would carry on in his footsteps, perpetuating the Neufeld name in the industry for a number of years. Stanley would alternate between acting as a production manager and assistant director in both film and television. He served as production manager or executive in charge of production on television shows that included *Naked City*, *The Patty Duke Show*, and *Cagney and Lacey*, and films such as *Cotton Comes to Harlem*, *Death Wish*, and *Lipstick*. He would go on to supervise production at Orion Pictures on films that included *Amadeus*, *Platoon*, *Dances With Wolves*, and *Silence of the Lambs*, and later served as a bonding agent. Stanley retired in 2003 at age eighty when the bonding company closed its doors, enjoying another eleven years out of the "rat race" up until his death on December 26, 2014. He was ninety-one years old.

Sig's son Sig Jr. continued as an editor up until the 1970s, when he turned to direction. There's a gap in his credits from 1960 to 1967 which he's hard put to account for. "I was always working…I was probably back in editing…. We finished *The Mohicans* up in Canada. I went back home and couldn't get a job directing, so I went back to editing."[20] Once he became a director he stayed with it for over thirty years, helming TV shows that included *Lassie*, *Baretta*, *Kojak*, *The Incredible Hulk*, *T.J. Hooker*, *The New Mike Hammer*, *Scarecrow and Mrs. King*, and *Simon and Simon*. Sig Jr. retired from the industry in 2002, living a quiet life for the following two decades up until his death on October 28, 2022, at the age of ninety-one.

With Sig Jr.'s death, the Neufeld and Newfield connection to the motion picture and television industries finally came to an end.

Chapter 23:
The Neufeld-Newfield Legacy

So, what did the brothers have to show for their decades of sweat and labor in an unforgiving industry? Sig, for all his initiative, retired to a comfortable, upper middle-class life that lasted another two decades. Sam was less fortunate, a victim of his own uncontrollable proclivities, his gambling leading to the breakdown of his marriage and a few final years of fiscally challenged existence.

What they *did* have to show for it was the knowledge that they had collectively provided three decades' worth of entertainment to a huge segment of the nation's populace. Their target audience wasn't those with access to the thousands of theaters owned by the majors, rather those who depended on the smaller neighborhood theaters for their weekly fare, and those in the more remote parts of the country, the tens of thousands of theaters that peppered the South and the Midwest. Admittedly the brothers' films were modest by comparison to the films of the larger studios, but for many their films were the norm, the low budget fare that a huge segment of the filmgoing public had been weaned on and expected to see on a weekly basis, and usually enjoyed. These were the two-reel comedies that added some spice to the Universal program during the final years of the silent era, and the Westerns, mysteries, comedies, horror, and action-adventure outings that predominated for the following quarter century.

Along with the three decades' worth of entertainment they were responsible for, one must also consider the employment they provided. While the pay paled in comparison to that of the majors, there were hundreds of actors and technicians who never made it past the main gates of those larger studios, and were happy enough to find paying work with the independents. Aspiring actors attempting to make a name for themselves, along with veterans whose best days were behind them, all found a welcome from the independent producers, content to receive a paycheck, spartan though it may have been, rather than the unemployed alternative. As for the technicians, those who worked with Sig and Sam early on and had proven capabilities landed years- or decades-long jobs. Hans Weeren and Fred Myton are prominent examples of the former, while Jack Greenhalgh and Bert Sternbach notable beneficiaries of the latter. Good work was frequently rewarded with reasonably steady and dependable jobs.

Sig was also responsible for hiring some new acting talent for his films. Shirley Temple, only four-and-a-half-years-old and with a few shorts to her credit, had her first feature role in Sig's *Red-Haired Alibi* for Premier. Alan Ladd had his first credited appearance in Sig's *Hitler—Beast of Berlin*, and while director Sam didn't think the "too short, too small" actor would ever make it in an industry dominated by larger actors, time quickly proved him wrong. Sultry Julie London got her start at PRC as well, co-starring opposite Buster Crabbe in Sig and Sam's *Nabonga*. There were dozens of other fledgling actors who had early or first appearances in Sig's films, some who went on to modest careers and others who disappeared almost as quickly as they appeared, but none as notable as the three mentioned above. One cannot overlook Al St. John, however, whose career as a silent and early-sound comedian was well behind him when he found a new lease on his cinematic life in small parts in Westerns in the later 1930s, resulting in his long-term employment as "Fuzzy Q. Jones" by Sig at PRC, his popularity resurrected in a long string of Sam-directed Westerns from 1940 into 1946.

As for quality, it was all over the map. Hastily written screenplays coupled with spartan funding, overly familiar sets and settings, the performances of novice actors, and direction that was (for want of a better word) expeditious, the results could be routine, slapdash, and on very rare occasions almost unwatchable. That said, there were numerous exceptions found among the seemingly endless stream of cookie-cutter Westerns and other bland offerings, films that stood out as refreshingly different from the norm and, once in a while, superior to the films that came before and would likely follow. The films of PRC are frequently derided for their collective inferiority, but if one were to take a lengthy look at the subset of PRC's output that Sig and/or Sam were responsible for, one would come to realize that their output was several grades above so much of PRC's other offerings, both contracted from outside independent producers and manufactured in-house.

I'm partial, of course, but I feel that their film noir and mystery offerings were among their best. Have another viewing of *The Lady Confesses*, *Apology for Murder*, and *Money Madness* and you'll be pleasantly surprised at how engaging and well-acted these films are. Hugh Beaumont was the star of these (as well as the five "Michael Shayne" mysteries), an inarguable asset who delivers a believably understated performance and impresses with his relaxed ease and convincing ability to convey menace when the script called for it.

The endless stream of Westerns co-starring Buster Crabbe and Al "Fuzzy" St. John from 1941 into 1946, while eventually suffering somewhat due to the increasing overfamiliarity of their plots and the haste and budgetary limitations under which they were filmed, still always manage to provide an hour's worth of entertainment, sporadic action, and the seasoned, throwaway slapstick of St. John. The earlier Tim McCoy Westerns released by Puritan have a rugged, more bloodthirsty approach to them, far superior to McCoy's later series for Sam Katzman's Victory Pictures. *Bulldog Courage* and *Border Cabellero* are good examples of the Puritans, the latter relying on a device—McCoy's donning of a disguise—that works well in this particular film, but was driven into the ground in the later Victory series. *Outlaw Women* is another standout, and while it suffers from an unsatisfyingly "happy" ending, is otherwise refreshing in its offbeat approach to the usual Western fare, and in color—okay, Cinecolor—with atypically lavish sets to boot.

If action-adventure is your genre of choice, *Western Pacific Agent* delivers the goods, with refreshingly unusual location settings and a decidedly different villain for a change, the murderous psychopath played to the hilt by Mickey Knox, arguably the meatiest role of his long, fifty-plus year career. *Crashin' Thru Danger* benefits from the camaraderie of its three leads and their dangerous work as linemen, and the atypically bloodthirsty *Marked Men* is a standout for its grueling, desert-based sequences.

The horror-science fiction genre, while a far smaller part of the brothers' output, has some notable examples, the offbeat vampire chiller *Dead Men Walk*, and the underrated sci-fi, dinosaurs-on-the-loose *Lost Continent*. When it came to comedy, both brothers had had a firm grounding in the genre back with the Stern Brothers, but with the coming of sound were frequently let down by their comedically-challenged script writers. That said, Sam's silent shorts *Please Excuse Me* and *Buster's Spooks*, both of which have survived, are quite amusing and imaginative—not always the case with some of the Stern Brothers' later output—as well as Sig's later Tiffany Talking Chimp shorts, *The*

Blimp Mystery among the best of them. Once they switched over to feature production, comedies as such were fewer and farther between, although—and for better or worse—the brothers almost always shoehorned some questionable comic relief into their films, at the hands of former silent "stars" Syd Saylor, Jimmy Aubrey, and the like. St. John is the notable exception here, his character of "Fuzzy" always injecting some creative slapstick into the proceedings, and a welcome presence—to most viewers, at least—as sidekick to several of the Western leads, Buster Crabbe most prominent among them. The occasional full-blown comedy, such as *Hold That Woman!* and *The Kid Sister*, provides their share of well-earned laughs, and even the lesser *Danger! Women at Work* was a respectable offering, Patsy Kelly this one's saving grace. It was a rarity that either of the brothers dabbled in the musical genre, but when they did with films like *Harvest Melody* and *Swing Hostess*, the results were usually sufficiently entertaining, if only in their small, modest ways.

Viewers who enjoy this sort of lower budget fare benefit in a less obvious way, and that's due to the fact that most of these films never had their copyrights renewed, if they were ever even copyrighted at all. The result of this oversight is that almost all of these films are in the public domain, the preponderance of their sound output now available to view online for free at YouTube.com. Admittedly many of the films found there are sourced from 16mm prints previously used by television stations and in the hands of collectors, and somewhat battered and poorly duped as a result. Still, having *something* is better than *nothing*; try to track down the output of any of the major film companies and you'll quickly realize just how fortunate we are to have this plethora of public domain output at our electronic fingertips.

Recognition for the brothers' contributions to cinema has been fleeting at best, and history has, for the most part, chosen to ignore them. Which on one level is a shame, given that they provided so much entertainment, for so many people, over so many years. On the other hand, their films are comparatively minor offerings when judged against so much of the output of the majors, but this is an "apples or oranges" type of comparison. The brothers' output, along with that of the dozens of other little-remembered independent producers, represents a significant portion of the films released throughout cinema's lengthy history, and deserves to be remembered and respected for the entertainment it provided to a large swath of the filmgoing public.

B-film screenwriter C. Jack Lewis summed up the world of low budget filmmaking in a succinct fashion:

> During the era when I was around Hollywood, there seemed to be a sense of camaraderie among the actors, technicians, directors, and producers. They were all producing little pictures they knew would end up at the bottom of a double-feature bill, and they weren't competing with each other. They were competing only with themselves in attempting to turn out the best film possible, with the miniscule amounts of money available. Each film was a challenge and everyone involved willingly pitched in to get it made.[1]

This was Sig and Sam's world.

Afterword
By Tim Neufeld

When I was born in 1947, my grandfather, Sigmund Neufeld, and his brother, Sam Newfield, were still making "pictures" (as my grandfather frequently referred to them), and would continue to do so together for another eleven years. Unfortunately, I did not appreciate during their lives what they did and what they had done to escape dire poverty, and to have then made hundreds of motion pictures from the silent era to the age of television. My grandfather started in "the business" in 1911 in the cutting room at IMP, and worked continuously in the industry for forty-seven years. He brought Sam along as well in 1919, together with his other brother and brother-in-law.

About eighteen months ago, I had the great fortune to discover "Time is Money," Tom Reeder's amazing book about the Stern Brothers and their comedy companies, and to see the many references to my grandfather and to Sam, both of whom worked there up to the studio's end in 1929. My grandfather lived until 1979, and he and I became very close as the years went by. He had talked frequently about the Stern Brothers and his years working for them, from 1916 as a cutter and eventually as the manager of the studio when he was in his mid-twenties. He also frequently spoke of Baby Peggy and Brownie, the Wonder Dog, but I never thought to write it down or record him, or to ask the probing questions I should have. However, Tom's book filled in a lot of the details, and I then took the initiative to contact Tom and Gil Sherman, who was Julius Stern's grandson and writer of the book's Afterword. We had many productive discussions, which led to Tom's suggestion that a book about Sig and Sam and their many films would be a worthwhile undertaking. I was absolutely delighted and offered my services as an unpaid research assistant. Tom accepted, and the incredible journey of discovery began for me. This included travel to review documents, a trip to Hungary to try to take the story further back in time, finding photos I had never seen, meeting relatives I had either never met or had not seen for over fifty years, and countless other endeavors, all of which were so rewarding.

Some highlights included: meeting Sam's grandchildren and Sam's son Joel; hosting a family reunion and having them all share with me and my daughters, Pam and Kathy, recollections and photos for the book; spending significant time on interviews and research with my dear uncle, Sigmund Neufeld, Jr., who passed away during the journey; and traveling with my daughter Kathy to Madison, Wisconsin, to review and to hold in our hands the original PRC records for about 100 of Sig and Sam's films, including many signed by Sig and Sam.

With Tom's detailed research and writing, and the efforts of the Neufelds and the Newfields, the full story can now be told in this incredible book. It is a story about family, about overcoming poverty, about making hundreds of films on a budget, and of transitioning, surviving, and prospering from silent shorts to twenty-five years of features and, finally, to television, and it is about the films themselves, many of which Tom viewed. It is also a story about friendship: my grandfather and

Bert Sternbach were lifelong friends and colleagues for this entire journey, from Stern Brothers to "Last of the Mohicans," and I knew him only as Uncle Bert, who was always a part of all of our family gatherings.

I hope that you enjoy the book as much as we all enjoyed helping to make it happen. It was just over 100 years ago that the Stern Brothers gave my grandfather a diamond pinky ring, to thank him for his creativity as a cutter. He wore that ring until the day he passed away, my uncle wore it next, and it is now passed on to me and will be passed on for another 100 years to help us remember Sig and Sam.

Sig and Sam's journey was remarkable, and the Neufelds and the Newfields are so happy that it is now being shared with you.

Timothy Neufeld
Pasadena, California
December 2023

The Films of
Producer Sigmund Neufeld and Director Sam Newfield

These are the known and confirmed films of producer Sigmund Neufeld and his brother, director Sam Newfield.

They are listed in the order of release rather than broken out by Sigmund and Sam individually; films where only one of the two brothers were involved are intermingled, in release order, with their numerous joint efforts.

Because so many of their films were released on a state rights basis, release dates are in many cases approximates, and in some instances by month alone. These dates may not always jibe with those found in other sources, and in many cases an exact date is difficult, if not impossible, to determine.

This list is in all likelihood incomplete, as Sig was responsible for the production of films for which he never received credit, neither on screen nor in the trades. Similarly, Sam directed some lesser independent films without any sort of credit, and many others using an alias; "Sherman Scott" and "Peter Stewart" are the two aliases that are known, but it is possible that there were others that were used on an individual basis.

Which Is Which? (2-Reel Short): Released 10/13/1926. © Universal Pictures Corp. 04/26/1926. Stern Brothers Comedies/Universal Pictures. "The Excuse Maker" series. Director: Sam Newfield; Producer: Julius and Abe Stern; Story: William Anthony. Cast: Charles King.

Please Excuse Me (2-Reel Short): Released 11/10/1926. © Universal Pictures Corp. 06/26/1926. Stern Brothers Comedies/Universal Pictures. "The Excuse Maker" series. Director: Sam Newfield; Producer: Julius and Abe Stern; Story: William Anthony. Cast: Charles King, Constance Darling, Bud Jamison.

Jane's Engagement Party (2-Reel Short): Released 11/17/1926. © Universal Pictures Corp. 05/18/1926. Stern Brothers Comedies/Universal Pictures. "What Happened to Jane?" series. Director: Sam Newfield; Producer: Julius and Abe Stern; Story: Roy Evans. Cast: Wanda Wiley, Tony Hayes.

Jane's Predicament (2-Reel Short): Released 12/15/1926. © Universal Pictures Corp. 06/22/1926. Stern Brothers Comedies/Universal Pictures. "What Happened to Jane?" series. Director: Sam Newfield; Producer: Julius and Abe Stern; Story: Roy Evans. Cast: Wanda Wiley, Earl McCarthy.

What's Your Hurry? (2-Reel Short): Released 02/09/1927. © Universal Pictures Corp. 04/30/1926. Stern Brothers Comedies/Universal Pictures. "The Excuse Maker" series. Director: Sam Newfield; Producer: Julius and Abe Stern; Story: William Anthony. Cast: Charles King, Constance Darling.

Ask Dad (1-Reel Short): Released 02/27/1927. © Educational Film Exchanges, Inc. 02/16/1927. Cameo Comedies/Educational. Director: Sam Newfield; Producer: Jack White. Cast: Lewis Sargent, Audrey Ferris, Robert Burns, Henry Murdock.

Auntie's Ante (1-Reel Short): Released 05/08/1927. © Educational Film Exchanges, Inc. 05/02/1927. Cameo Comedies/Educational. Director: Sam Newfield; Producer: Jack White. Cast: Wallace Lupino, Madge Hunt, Robert Graves, Georgia O'Dell.

A Gym Dandy (1-Reel Short): Released 05/22/1927. © Educational Film Exchanges, Inc. 05/10/1927. Cameo Comedies/Educational. Director: Sam Newfield; Producer: Jack White. Cast: Phil Dunham, Estelle Bradley.

Jane's Sleuth (2-Reel Short): Released 06/22/1927. © Universal Pictures Corp. 03/31/1927. Stern Brothers Comedies/Universal Pictures. "What Happened to Jane?" series. Director: Sam Newfield; Producer: Julius and Abe Stern; Story: Roy Evans. Cast: Ethlyne Clair, Charles Dorety, Dorothy Wolbert.

My Mistake (2-Reel Short): Released 06/29/1927. © Universal Pictures Corp. 05/05/1927. Stern Brothers Comedies/Universal Pictures. "The Excuse Maker" series. Director: Sam Newfield; Producer: Julius and Abe Stern; Story: William Anthony. Cast: Charles King, Florence Allen, Lillian Worth, Baby Wally.

What an Excuse (2-Reel Short): Released 07/13/1927. © Universal Pictures Corp. 03/29/1927. Stern Brothers Comedies/Universal Pictures. "The Excuse Maker" series. Director: Sam Newfield; Producer: Julius and Abe Stern; Story: William Anthony. Cast: Charles King, Thelma Daniels, Max Asher, Bud Fine.

On Furlough (2-Reel Short): Released 07/27/1927. © Universal Pictures Corp. 06/09/1927. Stern Brothers Comedies/Universal Pictures. "Let George Do It" series. Director: Sam Newfield; Producer: Julius and Abe Stern. Cast: Sid Saylor, Jean Doree, Ethan Laidlaw.

Rushing Business (2-Reel Short): Released 08/31/1927. © Universal Pictures Corp. 06/09/1927. Stern Brothers Comedies/Universal Pictures. "Let George Do It" series. Director: Sam Newfield; Producer: Julius and Abe Stern. Cast: Sid Saylor, Joe Bonner.

Nize People (2-Reel Short): Released 10/10/1927. No copyright entry. Weiss Brothers-Artclass/National Distributors. "Izzy and Lizzy" series. Director: Sam Newfield; Producer: Billy West. Cast: Lucille Erwin, Bernie Glazer, Johnny Morris, Leo Sulky, Elfie Fay, Billy West, Jack Richardson.

The Disordered Orderly (2-Reel Short): Released 11/09/1927. © Universal Pictures Corp. 06/09/1927. Stern Brothers Comedies/Universal Pictures. "Let George Do It' series. Director: Sam Newfield; Producer: Julius and Abe Stern. Cast: Sid Saylor, Jean Doree.

On Deck (2-Reel Short): Released 11/30/1927. © Universal Pictures Corp. 06/09/1927. Stern Brothers Comedies/Universal Pictures. "Let George Do It' series. Director: Sam Newfield; Producer: Julius and Abe Stern. Cast: Sid Saylor, Jean Doree.

High Flyin' George (2-Reel Short): Released 01/25/1928. © Universal Pictures Corp. 09/10/1927. Stern Brothers Comedies/Universal Pictures. "Let George Do It' series. Director: Sam Newfield; Producer: Julius and Abe Stern. Cast: Sid Saylor, Jane Manners. (working title **Up in the Air**)

Man of Letters (2-Reel Short): Released 02/15/1928. © Universal Pictures Corp. 09/20/1927. Stern Brothers Comedies/Universal Pictures. "Let George Do It' series. Director: Sam Newfield; Producer: Julius and Abe Stern. Cast: Sid Saylor, Marie Wood, Dorothy Vernon, James T. Kelley.

George's False Alarm (2-Reel Short): Released 02/29/1928. © Universal Pictures Corp. 01/18/1928. Stern Brothers Comedies/Universal Pictures. "Let George Do It' series.

Director: Sam Newfield; Producer: Julius and Abe Stern. Cast: Sid Saylor, Marny Elwyn, Max Asher.

Watch, George! (2-Reel Short): Released 03/28/1928. © Universal Pictures Corp. 10/06/1927. Stern Brothers Comedies/Universal Pictures. "Let George Do It' series. Director: Sam Newfield; Producer: Julius and Abe Stern. Cast: Sid Saylor, Charlotte Dawn.

When George Hops (2-Reel Short): Released 04/25/1928. © Universal Pictures Corp. 10/19/1927. Stern Brothers Comedies/Universal Pictures. "Let George Do It' series. Director: Sam Newfield; Producer: Julius and Abe Stern. Cast: Sid Saylor, Ruby McCoy, Charlie Meakin, George Morrell, Allan Sears.

Sailor George (2-Reel Short): Released 05/09/1928. © Universal Pictures Corp. 02/03/1928. Stern Brothers Comedies/Universal Pictures. "Let George Do It' series. Director: Sam Newfield; Producer: Julius and Abe Stern. Cast: Sid Saylor.

George's School Daze (2-Reel Short): Released 05/30/1928. © Universal Pictures Corp. 11/23/1927. Stern Brothers Comedies/Universal Pictures. "Let George Do It' series. Director: Sam Newfield; Producer: Julius and Abe Stern. Cast: Sid Saylor.

When George Meets George (2-Reel Short): Released 06/20/1928. © Universal Pictures Corp. 12/20/1927. Stern Brothers Comedies/Universal Pictures. "Let George Do It' series. Director: Sam Newfield; Producer: Julius and Abe Stern. Cast: Sid Saylor, Thelma Daniels.

Buster Minds the Baby (2-Reel Short): Released 06/27/1928. © Universal Pictures Corp. 05/15/1928. Stern Brothers Comedies/Universal Pictures. "Buster Brown" series. Director: Sam Newfield; Producer: Julius and Abe Stern. Cast: Arthur Trimble, Lois Hardwick, Jerry the Dog, Merry Mae McKeen, Hannah "Oatmeal" Washington.

Big Game George (2-Reel Short): Released 07/18/1928. © Universal Pictures Corp. 12/16/1927. Stern Brothers Comedies/Universal Pictures. "Let George Do It' series. Director: Sam Newfield; Producer: Julius and Abe Stern. Cast: Sid Saylor.

Good Scout Buster (2-Reel Short): Released 07/25/1928. © Universal Pictures Corp. 05/15/1928. Stern Brothers Comedies/Universal Pictures. "Buster Brown" series. Director: Sam Newfield; Producer: Julius and Abe Stern. Cast: Arthur Trimble, Lois Hardwick.

Circus Daze (2-Reel Short): Released 08/1928. No copyright registered. Weiss Brothers/Artclass Pictures. Director: Sam Newfield/Charles Diltz. Cast: Poodles Hanneford, Betty Welsh, Edwin Argus, Franklin Bond.

Busting Buster (2-Reel Short): Released 08/15/1928. © Universal Pictures Corp. 05/15/1928. Stern Brothers Comedies/Universal Pictures. "Buster Brown" series. Director: Sam Newfield; Producer: Julius and Abe Stern. Cast: Arthur Trimble, Lois Hardwick, Jerry the Dog, Hannah "Oatmeal" Washington.

She's My Girl (2-Reel Short): Released 08/22/1928. © Universal Pictures Corp. 01/05/1928. Stern Brothers Comedies/Universal Pictures. "Let George Do It' series. Director: Sam Newfield; Producer: Julius and Abe Stern. Cast: Sid Saylor.

Half-Back Buster (2-Reel Short): Released 09/19/1928. © Universal Pictures Corp. 05/28/1928. Stern Brothers Comedies/Universal Pictures. "Buster Brown" series.

Director: Sam Newfield; Producer: Julius and Abe Stern. Cast: Arthur Trimble, Lois Hardwick, Jerry the Dog, Hannah "Oatmeal" Washington.

Buster Trims Up (2-Reel Short): Released 10/17/1928. © Universal Pictures Corp. 06/06/1928. Stern Brothers Comedies/Universal Pictures. "Buster Brown" series. Director: Sam Newfield; Producer: Julius and Abe Stern. Cast: Arthur Trimble, Lois Hardwick, Hannah "Oatmeal" Washington.

Teacher's Pest (2-Reel Short): Released 11/14/1928. © Universal Pictures Corp. 06/15/1928. Stern Brothers Comedies/Universal Pictures. "Buster Brown" series. Director: Sam Newfield; Producer: Julius and Abe Stern. Cast: Arthur Trimble, Lois Hardwick, Merry Mae McKeen, Jerry the Dog.

Watch the Birdie (2-Reel Short): Released 12/12/1928. © Universal Pictures Corp. 06/20/1928. Stern Brothers Comedies/Universal Pictures. "Buster Brown" series. Director: Sam Newfield; Producer: Julius and Abe Stern. Cast: Arthur Trimble, Lois Hardwick, Jerry the Dog.

Out at Home (2-Reel Short): Released 01/09/1929. © Universal Pictures Corp. 06/20/1928. Stern Brothers Comedies/Universal Pictures. "Buster Brown" series. Director: Sam Newfield; Producer: Julius and Abe Stern. Cast: Arthur Trimble, Lois Hardwick, Hannah "Oatmeal" Washington.

Hold Your Horses (2-Reel Short): Released 01/16/1929. © Universal Pictures Corp. 07/10/1928. Stern Brothers Comedies/Universal Pictures. "Mike and Ike" series. Director: Sam Newfield; Producer: Julius and Abe Stern. Cast: Joe Young, Ned La Salle, Dick Smith.

Have Patience (2-Reel Short): Released 02/06/1929. © Universal Pictures Corp. 07/05/1928. Stern Brothers Comedies/Universal Pictures. "Buster Brown" series. Director: Sam Newfield; Producer: Julius and Abe Stern. Cast: Arthur Trimble, Lois Hardwick.

Take Your Pick (2-Reel Short): Released 02/13/1929. © Universal Pictures Corp. 07/23/1928. Stern Brothers Comedies/Universal Pictures. "Mike and Ike" series. Director: Sam Newfield; Producer: Julius and Abe Stern. Cast: Joe Young, Ned La Salle.

The Newlyweds' Visit (2-Reel Short): Released 02/20/1929. © Universal Pictures Corp. 11/01/1928. Stern Brothers Comedies/Universal Pictures. "The Newlyweds and Their Baby" series. Director: Sam Newfield; Producer: Julius and Abe Stern. Cast: Jack Egan, Derelys Perdue, Lawrence McKeen.

She's a Pippin (2-Reel Short): Released 03/13/1929. © Universal Pictures Corp. 12/21/1928. Stern Brothers Comedies/Universal Pictures. "Mike and Ike" series. Director: Sam Newfield; Producer: Julius and Abe Stern. Cast: Joe Young, Ned La Salle, Emily Gerdes.

Tige's Girl Friend (2-Reel Short): Released 04/03/1929. © Universal Pictures Corp. 01/18/1929. Stern Brothers Comedies/Universal Pictures. "Buster Brown" series. Director: Sam Newfield; Producer: Julius and Abe Stern. Cast: Arthur Trimble, Lois Hardwick.

This Way Please (2-Reel Short): Released 04/10/1929. © Universal Pictures Corp. 01/08/1929. Stern Brothers Comedies/Universal Pictures. "Mike and Ike" series.

Director: Sam Newfield; Producer: Julius and Abe Stern. Cast: Joe Young, Ned La Salle.

Magic (2-Reel Short): Released 05/01/1929. © Universal Pictures Corp. 01/31/1929. Stern Brothers Comedies/Universal Pictures. "Buster Brown" series. Director: Sam Newfield; Producer: Julius and Abe Stern. Cast: Arthur Trimble, Lois Hardwick.

Delivering the Goods (2-Reel Short): Released 05/29/1929. © Universal Pictures Corp. 01/31/1929. Stern Brothers Comedies/Universal Pictures. "Buster Brown" series. Director: Sam Newfield; Producer: Julius and Abe Stern. Cast: Arthur Trimble, Lois Hardwick.

Chaperones (2-Reel Short): Released 06/05/1929. © Universal Pictures Corp. 01/15/1929. Stern Brothers Comedies/Universal Pictures. "Mike and Ike" series. Director: Sam Newfield; Producer: Julius and Abe Stern. Cast: Joe Young, Ned La Salle.

Buster's Spooks (2-Reel Short): Released 06/26/1929. © Universal Pictures Corp. 02/07/1929. Stern Brothers Comedies/Universal Pictures. "Buster Brown" series. Director: Sam Newfield; Producer: Julius and Abe Stern. Cast: Arthur Trimble, Lois Hardwick, Hannah "Oatmeal" Washington, Jerry the Dog, Albert Schaefer. (working title **Buster's Choice**)

Stop Barking (2-Reel Short): Released 08/21/1929. © Universal Pictures Corp. 02/07/1929. Stern Brothers Comedies/Universal Pictures. "Buster Brown" series. Director: Sam Newfield; Producer: Julius and Abe Stern. Cast: Arthur Trimble, Lois Hardwick.

Night Owls (2-Reel Short): Released 09/25/1929. © Universal Pictures Corp. 09/14/1929. Arthur Lake Comedies/Universal Pictures. Director: Sam Newfield; Screenplay: T. Page Wright, Bill Weber. Cast: Arthur Lake.

Too Many Women (2-Reel Short): Released 10/23/1929. © Universal Pictures Corp. 10/05/1929. Sid Saylor Comedies/Universal Pictures. Director: Sam Newfield; Screenplay: T. Page Wright, Bill Weber. Cast: Sid Saylor.

Doing His Stuff (2-Reel Short): Released 11/20/1929. © Universal Pictures Corp. 11/05/1929. Arthur Lake Comedies/Universal Pictures. Director: Sam Newfield, Harry Edwards. Cast: Arthur Lake.

Outdoor Sports (2-Reel Short): Released 01/01/1930. © Universal Pictures Corp. 06/03/1929. Sid Saylor Comedies/Universal Pictures. Director: Sam Newfield, Gus Meins; Story: T. Page Wright, Bill Weber. Cast: Sid Saylor

French Leave (2-Reel Short): Released 03/19/1930. © Universal Pictures Corp. 02/25/1930. Sid Saylor Comedies/Universal Pictures. Director: Sam Newfield; Screenplay: T. Page Wright, Bill Weber. Cast: Sid Saylor.

Fellow Students (2-Reel Short): Released 04/09/1930. © Universal Pictures Corp. 03/01/1930. Sid Saylor Comedies/Universal Pictures. Director: Sam Newfield; Screenplay: T. Page Wright. Cast: Sid Saylor.

Peek-A-Boo (2-Reel Short): Released 05/21/1930. © Universal Pictures Corp. 03/31/1930. Arthur Lake Comedies/Universal Pictures. Director: Sam Newfield; Screenplay: T. Page Wright, Bill Weber. Cast: Arthur Lake.

Sid's Long Count (2-Reel Short): Released 05/28/1930. © Universal Pictures Corp. 03/24/1930. Sid Saylor Comedies/Universal Pictures. Director: Sam Newfield; Screenplay: T. Page Wright, Bill Weber. Cast: Sid Saylor.

She's a He (2-Reels Short): Released 06/04/1930. © Universal Pictures Corp. 03/17/1930. Sunny Jim Comedies/Universal Pictures. Director: Sam Newfield. Cast: Sunny Jim McKeen.

Her Bashful Beau (2-Reel Short): Released 06/11/1930. © Universal Pictures Corp. 03/17/1930. Arthur Lake Comedies/Universal Pictures. Director: Sam Newfield; Screenplay: T. Page Wright, Bill Weber. Cast: Arthur Lake.

All Wet (2-Reel Short): Released 06/18/1930. © Universal Pictures Corp. 03/08/1930. Sid Saylor Comedies/Universal Pictures. Director: Sam Newfield. Cast: Sid Saylor.

The Beauty Parade (2-Reel Short): Released 07/02/1930. © Universal Pictures Corp. 03/31/1930. Sid Saylor Comedies/Universal Pictures. Director: Sam Newfield. Cast: Sid Saylor.

The Blimp Mystery (2-Reel Short): Released 07/28/1930. © Tiffany Productions, Inc. 07/17/1930. Tiffany Productions. Director: Sigmund Neufeld; Producer: Phil Goldstone; Story: Harry Fraser; Cinematography: Robert Cline; Dialogue: Jack Natteford; Settings: Ralph DeLacy. Cast: The Tiffany Talking Chimps (Chimps #1)

The Little Covered Wagon (2-Reel Short): Released 09/05/1930. © Tiffany Productions, Inc. 08/30/1930. Tiffany Productions. Director: Sigmund Neufeld; Producer: Phil Goldstone. Cast: The Tiffany Talking Chimps (Chimps #2)

The Little Big House (2-Reel Short): Released 10/15/1930. © Tiffany Productions, Inc. 10/16/1930. Tiffany Productions. Director: Sigmund Neufeld; Producer: Phil Goldstone. Cast: The Tiffany Talking Chimps (Chimps #3)

De Woild's Champeen (2-Reel Short): Released 11/26/1930. © Tiffany Productions, Inc. 11/28/1930. No copyright registered. Paul Hurst Comedies/Tiffany Productions. Director: Frank Strayer; Producer: Sigmund Neufeld; Story: Scott Darling. Cast: Paul Hurst, Nita Martan, Don Terry, Aggie Herring, Eddie Boland, Charlotte Merriam, Jack Kennedy. (Hurst #1)

The Little Divorcee (2-Reel Short): Released 12/01/1930. © Tiffany Productions, Inc. 12/05/1930. Tiffany Productions. Director: Sigmund Neufeld; Producer: Phil Goldstone. Cast: The Tiffany Talking Chimps (Chimps #4)

Ex-Bartender (2-Reel Short): Released 12/20/1930. © Tiffany Productions, Inc. 12/19/1930. Paul Hurst Comedies/Tiffany Productions. Director: Frank Strayer; Story: Scott Darling; Producer: Sigmund Neufeld. Cast: Paul Hurst, Robert Ellis, Frankyn Farnum, George Ovey. (Hurst #2)

The Tale of a Flea (2-Reel Short): Released 12/27/1930. No copyright registered. Paul Hurst Comedies/Tiffany Productions. Director: Frank Strayer; Producer: Sigmund Neufeld; Screenplay: W. Scott Darling. Cast: Paul Hurst. (Hurst #3)

Nine Nights in a Bar Room (2-Reel Short): Released 01/26/1931. © Tiffany Productions, Inc. 01/30/1931. Tiffany Productions. Director: Sigmund Neufeld; Producer: Phil Goldstone. Cast: The Tiffany Talking Chimps (Chimps #5) (working title probably **Sweet Patootie**)

Chasing Around (2-Reel Short): Released 03/23/1931. © Tiffany Productions, Inc. 05/24/1931. Tiffany Productions. Director: Sigmund Neufeld; Producer: Phil Goldstone. Cast: The Tiffany Talking Chimps (Chimps #6)

One Punch O'Toole (2-Reel Short): Released 03/23/1931. © Tiffany Productions, Inc. 03/20/1931. Paul Hurst Comedies/Tiffany Productions. Director: Sigmund Neufeld; Screenplay: Scott Darling, Sigmund Neufeld; Story: Scott Darling. Cast: Paul Hurst, Pert Kelton, Eddie Boland, Aggie Herring, Bud Jamison. (Hurst #4)

The Missing Link (2-Reel Short): Released 05/1931. No copyright registered. Paul Hurst Comedies/Tiffany Productions. Director: Frank R. Strayer; Producer: Sigmund Neufeld; Screenplay: Scott Darling. Cast: Paul Hurst. (Hurst #5)

Africa Squawks (2-Reel Short): Released 07/07/1931. © Tiffany Productions, Inc. 08/03/1931. Tiffany Productions. Director: Charles Lewis; Producer: Phil Goldstone. Cast: The Tiffany Talking Chimps (Chimps #7*)*

Apeing Hollywood (2-Reel Short): Released 08/16/1931. No copyright registered. Tiffany Productions. Director: Sigmund Neufeld; Producer: Phil Goldstone; Editor: Martin Cohn. Cast: The Tiffany Talking Chimps (Chimps #8)

Cinnamon (2-Reel Short): Released 10/04/1931. No copyright registered. Tiffany Productions. Director: Sigmund Neufeld; Producer: Phil Goldstone. Cast: The Tiffany Talking Chimps (Chimps #9)

Skimpy (2-Reel Short): Released 11/08/1931. No copyright registered. Tiffany Productions. Director: Sigmund Neufeld; Producer: Phil Goldstone. Cast: The Tiffany Talking Chimps (Chimps #10)

My Children (2-Reel Short): Released 12/28/1931. No copyright registered. Tiffany Productions. Director: Sigmund Neufeld; Producer: Phil Goldstone. Cast: The Tiffany Talking Chimps (Chimps #11) (working title **Gland Hotel**)

Discarded Lovers: Released 01/20/1932. No copyright registered. Premier Pictures/Tower Productions. Director: Fred Newmeyer; Producer: Sigmund Neufeld (uncredited); Screenplay: Edward T. Lowe; Story: Arthur Hoerl; Cinematography: William Hyer; Editor: Charles Hunt. Cast: Natalie Moorhead, Russell Hopton, J. Farrell MacDonald, Barbara Weeks, Jason Robards, Sharon Lynn, Fred Kelsey, Roy D'Arcy, Robert Frazer, Jack Trent, Allen Dailey.

Broadcasting (2-Reel Short): Released 01/31/1932. No copyright registered. Tiffany Productions. Director: Sigmund Neufeld; Producer: Phil Goldstone. Cast: The Tiffany Talking Chimps (Chimps #12) (working title **Ex-King**)

Shop Angel: Released 03/19/1932. No copyright registered. Premier Pictures/Tower Productions. Director: E. Mason Hopper; Producer: Morris R. Schlank; Supervisor: Sigmund Neufeld (uncredited); Screenplay: Edward T. Lowe; Story: Isola Forrester; Cinematography: Willaim Hyer. Cast: Marion Shilling, Holmes Herbert, Anthony Bushell, Walter Byron, Dorothy Christy.

Drifting Souls: Released 08/06/1932. No copyright registered. Premier Pictures/Tower Productions. Director: Louis King; Producer: Morris R. Schlank; Story: Barbara Hunter; Cinematography: William Hyer; Editor: Irving Birnbaum. Cast: Theodore Von Eltz, Lois Wilson, Raymond Hatton, Guinn Williams, Shirley Grey, Gene Gowing, Dorothy Vernon.

Exposure: Released 08/20/1932. No copyright registered. Premier Pictures/Tower Productions. Director, Screenplay: Norman Houston; Producer: Morris R. Schlank; Associate Producer: Sigmund Neufeld (as Sig Neufeld); Cinematography: Harry Forbes; Editor: Irving Birnbaum. Cast: Lila Lee, Walter Byron, Tully Marshall, Mary Doran, Bryant Washburn, Pat O'Malley, Lee Moran, Spec O'Donnell, Sidney Bracy, Nat Pendleton.

Red-Haired Alibi: Released 10/15/1932. No copyright registered. Premier Pictures/Tower Productions. Director: Christy Cabanne; Assistant Director: Sam Newfield; Producer: Sigmund Neufeld (as Sig Neufeld); Screenplay: Edward T. Lowe, Jr.; Story: Wilson Collison; Cinematography: Harry Forbes; Editor: Irving Birnbaum. Cast: Merna Kennedy, Theodore Von Eltz, Grant Withers, Purnell Pratt, Huntley Gordon, Fred Kelsey, Arthur Hoyt, Paul Porcasi, John Vosburgh, Shirley Temple.

Oh! My Operation (2-Reel Short): Released 12/28/1932. © Universal Pictures Corp. 12/05/1932. Universal Pictures. Director: James W. Horne; Story: Sam Newfield, J.A. Howe. Cast: Vincent Barnett, June Clyde, Walter Catlett, Dewey Robinson.

Daring Daughters: Released 03/25/1933. No copyright registered. Premier Attractions/Tower Productions. Director: Christy Cabanne; Assistant Director: Sam Newfield; Producer: Sigmund Neufeld; Screenplay: Sam Mintz; Cinematography: Harry Forbes; Editor: Irving Birnbaum. Cast: Marian Marsh, Kenneth Thompson, Joan Marsh, Bert Roach, Allen Vincent, Lita Chevret, Richard Tucker, Arthur Hoyt, Florence Roberts, Bryant Washburn Jr., Charlotte Merriam. (working title **Wise Girl/The Wise Girl**)

Reform Girl: Released 07/01/1933. No copyright registered. Premier Pictures/Tower Productions. Director: Sam Newfield (as Sam Neufeld); Producer: Sigmund Neufeld; Story: George W. Sayre; Cinematography: Harry Forbes; Editor: Lou Sackin. Cast: Skeets Gallagher, Noel Francis, Stanley Smith, Hale Hamilton, Dorothy Peterson, Ben Hendricks Jr., Robert Ellis, DeWitt Jennings.

The Important Witness: Released 07/15/1933. No copyright registered. Premier Pictures/Tower Productions. Director: Sam Newfield; Producer: Sigmund Neufeld; Screenplay: Douglas Doty; Story: Gordon Morris; Cinematography: Harry Forbes. Cast: Noel Francis, Dorothy Burgess, Donald Dillaway, Noel Madison, Robert Ellis, Charles Delaney, Harry Myers, Franklin Pangborn. (working title **Night Coach** [and **Public Stenographer**?])

Big Time or Bust: Released 11/10/1933. No copyright registered. Tower Productions. Director: Sam Newfield; Assistant Director: Leslie Simmonds; Producer: Sigmund Neufeld; Screenplay: George Wallace Sayre, from stage play "Excess Baggage"; Cinematography: Harry Forbes; Editor: Al Clark. Cast: Regis Toomey, Gloria Shea, Walter Byron, Edwin Maxwell, Charles Delaney, Paul Porcasi, Nat Carr. (working title **Headin' for Heaven**)

Wedding Belles (2-Reel Short): Released 1934. No copyright registered. Cavalcade Films Corp. Director: Sam Newfield; Cinematography: Otto Himm; Sound: Hans Weeren. Cast: Lloyd Hamilton, Eddie Gribbon, Arthur Housman, Gertrude Astor, Jack Del Rio.

Under Secret Orders: Released 01/01/1934. No copyright registered. Progressive Pictures. Director: Sam Newfield; Screenplay: Eustace L. Adams; Cinematography:

Jules Cronjager; Editor: Walter Thompson. Cast: Donald Dillaway, J. Farrell MacDonald, Nena Quartaro, Phyllis Barrington, Don Alvarado, Lafe McKee, Matthew Betz, Paul Ellis, Leon Holmes.

Marrying Widows: Released 05/18/1934. No copyright registered. Premiere Attractions/Tower Productions. Director: Sam Newfield; Producer: Sigmund Neufeld, Leslie Simmonds; Screenplay: Adele Buffington; Cinematography: Harry Forbes. Cast: Minna Gombell, Judith Allen, Johnny Mack Brown, Lucien Littlefield, Bert Roach, Sarah Padden, Arthur Hoyt, Virginia Sale, George Grandee, Otto Hoffman, Syd Saylor. (working title **Widows**)

Picnic Perils (2-Reel Short): Released 07/08/1934. © Universal Pictures Corp. 07/09/1934. Universal Pictures. Director: James W. Horne; Producer: Warren Doane; Story: W.P. Hackney, Sam Newfield. Cast: Sterling Holloway, Sylvia Picker.

Just We Two: (2-Reel Short): Released 08/08/1934. © Universal Pictures Corp. 07/27/1934. Universal Pictures. Director: James W. Horne; Story: W.P. Hackney, Sam Newfield. Cast: Grady Sutton, Sylvia Picker.

Beggar's Holiday: Released 08/17/1934. No copyright registered. Tower Productions. Director: Sam Newfield; Producer: Sigmund Neufeld; Screenplay: Adele Buffington; Cinematography: Harry Forbes. Cast: Hardie Albright, Sally O'Neil, J. Farrell MacDonald, Barbara Barondess, George Grandee, William Franklin.

The Fighting Trooper: Released 11/15/1934. © Ambassador Pictures, Inc. 11/20/1934. Ambassador Pictures. Director: Ray Taylor; Producer: Maurice Conn, Sigmund Neufeld (uncredited), Maurice Conn; Screenplay: Forrest Sheldon; Story: "Footprints" by James Oliver Curwood; Cinematography: Edgar Lyons; Editor: Ted Bellinger. Cast: Kermit Maynard, Charles Delaney, Barbara Worth, LeRoy Mason, Robert Frazer, George Regas, Walter Miller, Joseph W. Girard, Charles King, George Chesebro, Nelson McDowell, Lafe McKee, Arthur Ortego, Dauntless.

Northern Frontier: Released 02/01/1935. © Ambassador Pictures, Inc. 01/25/1935. Ambassador. Director: Sam Newfield; Producer: Sigmund Neufeld, Maurice Conn; Screenplay: Barry Barringer; Story: "Four Minutes Late" by James Oliver Curwood; Cinematography: Edgar Lyons; Sound Engineer: Hans Weeren. Cast: Kermit Maynard, Eleanor Hunt, LeRoy Mason, Walter Brennan, Ben Hendricks, Jr., Russell Hopton, J. Farrell MacDonald, Gertrude Astor, Lloyd Ingraham.

Wilderness Mail: Released 03/13/1935. © Ambassador Pictures, Inc. 05/10/1935. Ambassador. Director: Forrest Sheldon; Producer: Maurice Conn, Sigmund Neufeld (uncredited); Screenplay: Ben Cohen; Story: James Oliver Curwood; Cinematography: Arthur Reed; Sound Engineer: Corson Jewett; Editor: John English. Cast: Kermit Maynard, Fred Kohler, Paul Hurst, Doris Brook, Syd Saylor, Richard Curtis, Nelson McDowell, Kernan Cripps.

Red Blood of Courage: Released 04/20/1935. © Ambassador Pictures, Inc. 05/15/1935. Ambassador. Director: John English; Producer: Sigmund Neufeld, Maurice Conn; Screenplay: Barry Barringer; Story: James Oliver Curwood; Cinematography: Arthur Reed; Editor: Richard G. Gray. Cast: Kermit Maynard, Ann Sheridan, Reginald Barlow, Ben Hendricks Jr., George Regas, Nat Carr, Charles King.

Code of the Mounted: Released 06/08/1935. © Ambassador Pictures, Inc. 11/25/1935. Ambassador. Director: Sam Newfield; Producer: Sigmund Neufeld, Maurice Conn;

Screenplay: George Sayre; Story: James Oliver Curwood "Wheels of Fate"; Cinematography: Edgar Lyons; Editor: Jack English; Sound Engineer: Hans Weeren. Cast: Kermit Maynard, Robert Warwick, Jim Thorpe, Lillian Miles, Syd Saylor, Wheeler Oakman, Dick Curtis, Stanley Blystone, Roger Williams. (working title **Sandy of the Mounted**)

Branded a Coward: Released 08/01/1935. No copyright registered. Supreme Pictures. Director: Sam Newfield; Producer: A.W. Hackel; Screenplay: Earl Snell; Story: Richard Martinson; Cinematography: William Nobles; Editor: Earl Turner. Cast: Johnny Mack Brown, Billie Seward, Syd Saylor, Lloyd Ingraham, Lee Shumway, Roger Williams, Frank McCarroll, Yakima Canutt, Mickey Rentschler, Rex Downing. (working title **Brand of the Coward**)

Trails of the Wild: Released 08/07/1935. © Ambassador Pictures, Inc. 12/02/1935. Ambassador. Director: Sam Newfield; Producer: Sigmund Neufeld, Maurice Conn; Screenplay: Joseph O'Donnell; Story: James Oliver Curwood "Caryl of the Mountains"; Cinematography: Jack Greenhalgh; Editor: Jack English. Cast: Kermit Maynard, Monte Blue, Billie Seward, Theodore Von Eltz, Fuzzy Knight, Roger Williams, John Elliott, Wheeler Oakman, Robert Grazer, Charles Delaney.

You Can Be Had (2-Reel Short): Released 10/03/1935. © Universal Pictures Corp. 12/27/1935. Universal Pictures. Director: Sam Newfield; Producer: Bert Sternbach, Arthur Alexander. A Monkey comedy.

His Fighting Blood: Released 10/05/1935. © Ambassador Pictures, Inc. 11/25/1935. Ambassador. Director: John English; Producer: Sigmund Neufeld, Maurice Conn; Screenplay: Joseph O'Donnell; Story: James Oliver Curwood; Editor: Richard G. Gray; Sound Engineer: Hans Weeren. Cast: Kermit Maynard, Paul Fix, Polly Ann Young, Ben Hendricks Jr., Ted Adams, Joseph Girard, Frank La Rue, John McCarthy, Frank O'Connor, Charles King, Jack Cheatham, Edward Cecil, Ted Lorch.

Racing Luck: Released 10/31/1935. © Republic Pictures Corp. 10/14/1935. Winchester Pictures/Republic Pictures. Director: Sam Newfield; Producer: George A. Hirliman; Story, Screenplay: Jack O'Donnell, George Sayre; Cinematography: Edgar Lyons; Editor: Charles Hunt. Cast: William Boyd, George Ernest, Barbara Worth, Ernest Hilliard, Esther Muir, Onest Conley, Ben Hall, Henry Roquemore, Dick Curtis, Ted Caskey.

Timber War: Released 11/20/1935. © Ambassador Pictures, Inc. 04/06/1936. Ambassador. Director: Sam Newfield; Producer: Sigmund Neufeld, Maurice Conn; Screenplay: Barry Barringer; Story: "Hell's Gulch" by James Oliver Curwood; Cinematography: Jack Greenhalgh; Editor: Richard Wray; Sound Engineer: Hans Weeren. Cast: Kermit Maynard, Lucille Lund, Lloyd Ingraham, Wheeler Oakman, Roger Williams, Lawrence Gray, Robert Warwick.

Burning Gold: Released 12/16/1935. © Republic Pictures Corp. 01/28/1936 Winchester Productions/Republic Pictures. Director: Sam Newfield; Producer: George A. Hirliman; Screenplay: Earl Snell; Story: Stuart Anthony; Cinematography: Harry Forbes; Sound Engineer: Hans Weeren; Editor: Charles Hunt. Cast: William Boyd, Judith Allen, Lloyd Ingraham, Fern Emmett, Frank Mayo.

Bulldog Courage: Released 12/30/1935. © Puritan Pictures 01/14/1936. Excelsior Pictures/Puritan Pictures. Director: Sam Newfield; Producer: Sigmund Neufeld,

Leslie Simmonds; Screenplay: Joseph O'Donnell; Story: Frances Guihan, Joseph O'Donnell; Cinematography: Jack Greenhalgh; Editor: S. Roy Luby; Sound Engineer: Hans Weeren. Cast: Tim McCoy, Joan Woodbury, Paul Fix, Eddie Buzzard, John W. Cowell, William Karl Hackett, John Elliot, Eddie Cobb, Eddie Hearne, Jack Rockwell.

Thoroughbred: Released 1936. No copyright registered. Booth Dominion Productions/M-G-M. Director: Sam Newfield; Assistant Director: Jack Chisholm; Producer: J.R. Booth, Burt Kelly; Associate Producers: Arthur Gottlieb, Jack Goetz; Screenplay: Cyril B. DeLom, Keith Elda; Cinematography: Sam Levitt; Editor: Alex Myers; Sound Engineer: Harry Bellock. Cast: Toby Wing, Kenneth Duncan, Wheeler Oakman, Romeo Gaskins; Elliott Lorraine, Eric Clavering, Ruppert Lucas, Richard Townrow, William McIntyre, Edward Barrett, George Young. (working title **The King's Plate**)

Undercover Men: Released 1936. No copyright registered. Booth Dominion. Director: Sam Newfield; Assistant Director: John Chisholm; Producer: J.R. Booth; Screenplay: Murison Dunn; Cinematography: Sam Levitt; Editor: Alex Meyers; Sound Engineer: Harry Bellock. Cast: Charles Starrett, Adrienne Dore, Kenneth Duncan, Wheeler Oakman, Eric Clavering, Phil Brandon, Austin Moran, Gilmore Young, Grace Webster, Elliott Lorraine, Wilbur Freeman, Farnham Barter, Muriel Deane.

Stormy Trails: Released 1936. No copyright registered. Colony Pictures/State Rights. Director: Sam Newfield; Assistant Director: Eddie Mull; Producer: Arthur Alexander, Max Alexander; Screenplay: Phil Dunham; Story: E.B. Mann "Stampede"; Cinematography: Bob Cline; Editor: Charles Henkel. Cast: Rex Bell, Bob Hodges, Lois Wilde, Lane Chandler, Earl Dwire, Lloyd Ingraham, Karl Hacket, Earle Ross, Murdock McQuarrie, Jimmy Aubrey, Roger Williams.

Roarin' Guns: Released 01/27/1936. No copyright registered. Excelsior Pictures/Puritan Pictures. Director: Sam Newfield; Producer: Sigmund Neufeld, Leslie Simmonds; Screenplay, Story: Joseph O'Donnell; Cinematography: Jack Greenhalgh; Editor: S. Roy Luby; Sound Engineer: Hans Weeren. Cast: Tim McCoy, Rosalinda Price, Wheeler Oakman, Earl Hackett, John Elliott, Tommy Bupp, Jack Rockwell, Lou Meehan, Rex Lease.

Border Caballero: Released 03/01/1936. © Puritan Pictures 06/15/1936. Excelsior Pictures/Puritan Pictures. Director: Sam Newfield; Producer: Sigmund Neufeld, Leslie Simmonds; Screenplay: Joseph O'Donnell; Story: Norman S. Hall; Cinematography: Jack Greenhalgh; Editor: Holbrook N. Todd; Sound Engineer: Hans Weeren. Cast: Tim McCoy, Lois January, Ralph Byrd, Ted Adams, J. Frank Glendon, Earle Hodgins. (working title **Trail's End**)

Federal Agent: Released 04/10/1936. © Republic Pictures Corp. 04/19/1936. Winchester Pictures/Republic Pictures. Director: Sam Newfield; Screenplay: Robert Ellis; Story: Barry Barringer; Cinematography: Harry Forbes; Editor: Charles Hunt; Sound Engineer: Hans Weeren. Cast: Bill Boyd, Irene Ware, Don Alverado, Lenita Lane, George Cooper, Charles A. Browne.

Lightnin' Bill Carson: Released 04/15/1936. © Puritan Pictures 06/15/1936. Excelsior Pictures/Puritan Pictures. Director: Sam Newfield; Producer: Sigmund Neufeld, Leslie Simmonds; Screenplay: Joseph O'Donnell; Story: Arthur Durlam; Cinematography: Jack Greenhalgh; Editor: Jack English; Sound Engineer: Hans

Weeren. Cast: Tim McCoy, Lois January, Harry Worth, Rex Lease, Karl Hackett, John Merton.

Aces and Eights: Released 06/06/1936. No copyright registered. Excelsior Productions/Puritan Pictures. Director: Sam Newfield; Producer: Sigmund Neufeld, Leslie Simmonds; Screenplay: Arthur Durlam; Cinematography: Jack Greenhalgh; Editor: Jack English; Sound Engineer: Hans Weeren. Cast: Tim McCoy, Luana Walters, Rex Lease, Wheeler Oakman, Frank Glendon, Charles Stevens, Earle Hodgins, Jimmy Aubrey, Joseph Girard.

Go-Get-'Em, Haines: Released 06/15/1936. © Republic Pictures Corp. 06/29/1936. Winchester Pictures/Republic Pictures. Director: Sam Newfield; Producer: George A. Hirliman; Screenplay: George Sayre; Cinematography: Edgar Lyons; Editor: Charles Hunt. Cast: William Boyd, Sheila Terry, Eleanor Hunt, Lloyd Ingraham, LeRoy Mason, Jimmy Aubrey, Clarence Geldert, Lee Shumway, Louis Natheaux, Ernest Hilliard.

The Lion's Den: Released 07/06/1936. No copyright registered. Excelsior Pictures/Puritan Pictures. Director: Sam Newfield; Producer: Sigmund Neufeld, Leslie Simmonds; Screenplay: Jack Neville; Story: L.V. Jefferson; Cinematography: Jack Greenhalgh; Editor: Jack English; Sound Engineer: Hans Weeren. Cast: Tim McCoy, Joan Woodbury, Don Barclay, Frank Glendon, John Merton, Arthur Millett, Jack Rockwell, Dick Curtis.

Ghost Patrol: Released 08/03/1936. No copyright registered. Excelsior Pictures/Puritan Pictures. Director: Sam Newfield; Producer: Sigmund Neufeld, Leslie Simmonds; Story: Wyndham Gittens, Joseph O'Donnell; Assistant Director: William O'Connor; Editor: John English; Cinematography: Jack Greenhalgh; Sound Engineer: Hans Weeren. Cast: Tim McCoy, Claudia Dell, Walter Miller, Wheeler Oakman, Jim Burtis, Lloyd Ingraham, Dick Curtis, Jack Casey, Slim Whitaker, Artie Ortego, Art Dillard, Fargo Bussey.

The Traitor: Released 08/29/1936. No copyright registered. Excelsior Pictures/Puritan Pictures. Director: Sam Newfield; Producer: Sigmund Neufeld, Leslie Simmonds; Screenplay: John Neville, Joseph O'Donnell; Cinematography: Jack Greenhalgh; Editor: Jack English; Sound Engineer: Hans Weeren. Cast: Tim McCoy, Frances Grant, Karl Hackett, Jack Rockwell, Pedro Regas, Frank Melton, Dick Curtis, Dick Bottilier, Wally Wales, Ed Cobb, Wally West, Tina Menard, Soledad Jimenez, Frank Glendon.

Roarin' Lead: Released 12/09/1936. © Republic Pictures Corp. 12/09/1936. Republic Pictures. Director: Mack V. Wright, Sam Newfield; Producer: Nat Levine; Associate Producer: Sol C. Siegel; Screenplay: Oliver Drake, Jack Natteford; Cinematography: William Nobles; Editor: Murray Seldeen, William Thompson. Cast: "The Three Mesquiteers": Robert Livingston, Ray Corrigan, Max Terhune, Christine Maple, Hooper Atchley, Yakima Canutt, George Chesebro, Tommy Bupp, Mary Russell, Jane Keckley, Tamara Lynn Kauffman, Beverly Luff, Theodore Frye, Katherine Frye, Frank Austin, The Meglin Kiddies.

Bar-Z Bad Men: Released 01/20/1937. © Republic Pictures Corp. 01/20/1937. Republic Pictures. Director: Sam Newfield; Producer: A.W. Hackel; Screenplay: George H. Plympton; Story: James P. Olsen; Cinematography: Bert Longenecker;

Editor: Roy Claire. Cast: Johnny Mack Brown, Lois January, Tom London, Frank La Rue, Ernie Adams, Dick Curtis, Milt Morante, Jack Rockwell.

The Gambling Terror: Released 02/15/1937. © Republic Pictures Corp. 02/15/1937. Republic Pictures. Director: Sam Newfield; Producer: A.W. Hackel; Screenplay: George H. Plympton, Fred Myton; Cinematography: Bert Longenecker; Editor: Roy Claire. Cast: Johnny Mack Brown, Iris Meredith, Charles King, Dick Curtis, Ted Adams, Horace Murphy, Earl Dwire, Frank Ball, Bobby Nelson, Lloyd Ingraham, Emma Tansey, Budd Buster.

Lightnin' Crandall: Released 03/24/1937. © Republic Pictures Corp. 03/24/1937. Republic Pictures. Director: Sam Newfield; Producer: A.W. Hackel; Screenplay: Charles F. Royal; Story: E.B. Mann; Cinematography: Bert Longenecker; Editor: Roy Claire. Cast: Bob Steele, Lois January, Charles King, Earl Dwire, Ernie Adams, Frank La Rue, Horace Murphy, Lloyd Ingraham, Lew Meehan, Dave O'Brien. (working title **A Texan Rides**)

Trail of Vengeance: Released 03/29/1937. © Republic Pictures Corp. 03/29/1937. Republic Pictures. Director: Sam Newfield; Producer: A.W. Hackel; Screenplay: George H. Plympton, Fred Myton; Story: E.B. Mann; Cinematography: Bert Longenecker; Editor: S. Roy Luby, Tom Neff. Cast: Johnny Mack Brown, Iris Meredith, Warner Richmond, Karl Hackett, Earle Hodgins, Frank La Rue, Lew Meehan, Frank Ball, Dick Curtis.

Guns in the Dark: Released 04/14/1937. © Republic Pictures Corp. 04/14/1937. Republic Pictures. Director: Sam Newfield; Producer: A.W. Hackel; Screenplay: Charles F. Royal; Story: E.B. Mann; Cinematography: Bert Longenecker; Editor: Roy Claire. Cast: Johnny Mack Brown, Claire Rochelle, Syd Saylor, Ted Adams, Dick Curtis, Steve Clark, Jim Corey, Julian Madison, Roger Williams.

Melody of the Plains: Released 04/15/1937. No copyright registered. Spectrum Pictures. Director: Sam Newfield; Producer: Jed Buell; Associate Producer: George H. Callaghan; Screenplay: Bennett Cohen; Cinematography: Robert Kline; Editor: William Hess. Cast: Fred Scott, Al St. John, Louise Small, Billy Lenhart, David Sharpe, Slim Whittaker, Lew Meehan, Lafe McKee, Hal Price, Bud Jamison, Carl Matthews, White King the Horse. (working title **Song of the Prairie**)

Gun Lords of Stirrup Basin: Released 05/10/1937. © Republic Pictures Corp. 05/10/1937. Republic Pictures. Director: Sam Newfield; Producer: A.W. Hackel; Screenplay: George H. Plympton, Fred Myton; Story: Harry F. Olmstead; Cinematography: Bert Longenecker; Editor: Roy Claire. Cast: Bob Steele, Louise Stanley, Karl Hackett, Ernie Adams, Frank La Rue, Frank Ball, Steve Clark, Lew Meehan, Frank Ellis, Margaret Mann.

A Lawman Is Born: Released 06/21/1937. © Republic Pictures Corp. 06/21/1937. Republic Pictures. Director: Sam Newfield; Producer: A.W. Hackel; Screenplay: George H. Plympton; Story: Harry F. Olmstead; Cinematography: Bert Longenecker; Editor: Roy Claire. Cast: Johnny Mack Brown, Iris Meredith, Warner Richmond, Mary MacLaren, Dick Curtis, Earle Hodgins, Charles King, Frank La Rue, Al St. John, Steve Clark, Jack C. Smith.

Doomed at Sundown: Released 06/27/1937. © Republic Pictures Corp. 06/07/1937. Republic Pictures. Director: Sam Newfield; Producer: A.W. Hackel; Screenplay: George H. Plympton; Story: Fred Myton; Cinematography: Bert Longenecker; Editor:

Roy Claire. Cast: Bob Steele, Lorraine Hayes, Warner Richmond, Earle Dwire, Harold Daniels, David Sharpe, Horace Carpenter.

Boothill Brigade: Released 08/02/1937. © Republic Pictures Corp. 08/02/1937. Republic Pictures. Director: Sam Newfield; Producer: A.W. Hackel; Screenplay: George H. Plympton; Story: Harry F. Olmsted; Cinematography: Bert Longenecker; Editor: Roy Claire. Cast: Johnny Mack Brown, Claire Rochelle, Dick Curtis, Horace Murphy, Frank La Rue, Ed Cassidy, Bobby Nelson, Frank Ball, Steve Clark, Frank Ellis.

Arizona Gunfighter: Released 09/20/1937. © Republic Pictures Corp. 09/20/1937. Republic Pictures. Director: Sam Newfield; Producer: A.W. Hackel; Screenplay: George H. Plympton; Story: Harry F. Olmsted; Cinematography: Bob Kline; Editor: Roy Claire. Cast: Bob Steele, Jean Carmen, Ted Adams, Ernie Adams, Lew Meehan, Steve Clark, John Merton, Karl Hackett, A.C. Henderson, Frank Ball.

Moonlight on the Range: Released 10/06/1937. No copyright registered. Spectrum Pictures. Director: Sam Newfield; Producer: Jed Buell; Associate Producer: George H. Callaghan; Screenplay: Fred Myton; Story: Whitney Williams; Cinematography: Robert Cline; Sound Engineer: Hans Weeren. Cast: Fred Scott, Lois January, Al St. John, Dick Curtis, Frank La Rue, Jimmy Aubrey, Oscar Gahan, George Morrell, Carl Matthews, Wade Walker, Bill McCall, Shorty Miller, Jack Evans, Rudy Sooter.

Ridin' the Lone Trail: Released 11/01/1937. © Republic Pictures Corp. 11/01/1937. Republic Pictures. Director: Sam Newfield; Producer: A.W. Hackel; Screenplay: Charles F. Royal; Story: E.B. Mann; Cinematography: Robert Cline; Editor: S. Roy Luby. Cast: Bob Steele, Claire Rochelle, Charles King, Ernie Adams, Julian Rivero.

The Fighting Deputy: Released 12/05/1937. No copyright registered. Spectrum Pictures. Director: Sam Newfield; Producer: Jed Buell; Associate Producer: George H. Callaghan; Screenplay: William Lively; Story: Bennet Cohen; Editor: Arthur A. Brooks, William Hess; Production Management: Bert Sternbach; Sound Engineer: Hans Weeren. Cast: Fred Scott, Phoebe Logan, Al St. John, Marjorie Beebe, Charles King, Frank LaRue, Eddie Holden, Frank McKee, Jack Smith, Jack Evans, Sherry Tansey, White King the Wonder Horse.

Colorado Kid: Released 12/06/1937. © Republic Pictures Corp. 11/29/1937. Republic Pictures. Director: Sam Newfield; Producer: A.W. Hackel; Screenplay: Charles Francis Royal; Story: Harry F. Olmstead; Cinematography: Robert Cline; Editor: Roy Claire. Cast: Bob Steele, Marion Weldon, Karl Hackett, Ernie Adams, Ted Adams, Frank La Rue, Horace Murphy, Kenneth Duncan, Budd Buster, Frank Ball, John Merton.

Harlem on the Prairie: Released 12/09/1937. © Associated Features, Inc. 02/02/1938. Lincoln Pictures/Associated Features. Director: Sam Newfield; Producer: Jed Buell; Associate Producer: Sabin W. Carr; Supervisor: Maceo Sheffield; Screenplay: Fred Myton; Cinematography: William Hyer; Sound Engineer: Hans Weeren. Cast: Herbert Jeffries, F.E. Miller, Mantan Moreland, Spencer Williams, Connie Harries, Maceo B. Sheffield, George Randall, Nathan Curry, Lucius Brooks, Rudolph Hunter, Leon Buck, Ira Hardin, Edward Branden, James Davis.

Paroled - To Die: Released 01/10/1938. © Republic Pictures Corp. 12/30/1937. Republic Pictures. Director: Sam Newfield; Producer: A.W. Hackel; Screenplay: George H. Plympton; Story: Harry F. Olmsted; Cinematography: Robert Cline;

Editor: Roy Claire. Cast: Bob Steele, Kathleen Eliot, Karl Hackett, Horace Murphy, Steve Clark, Budd Buster, Sherry Tansey, Frank Ball, Jack Smith.

The Rangers' Round-Up: Released 02/15/1938. No copyright registered. Stan Laurel Production/Spectrum Pictures. Director: Sam Newfield; Producer: Jed Buell; Associate Producer: Bert Sternbach; Screenplay, Story: George Plympton; Cinematography: William Hyer; Editor: Robert Jahns; Sound Engineer: Hans Weeren. Cast: Fred Scott, Christine McIntyre, Karl Hackett, Al St. John, Syd Chatton.

Thunder in the Desert: Released 02/21/1938. © Republic Pictures Corp. 02/21/1938. Republic Pictures. Director: Sam Newfield; Producer: A.W. Hackel; Screenplay, Story: George H. Plympton; Cinematography: Robert Cline; Editor: Roy Claire. Cast: Bob Steele, Louise Stanley, Don Barclay, Ed Brady, Charles King, Horace Murphy, Steve Clark, Lew Meehan, Ernie Adams, Richard Cramer, Budd Buster.

Code of the Rangers: Released 03/09/1938. © Monogram Pictures Corp. 03/03/1938. Concord Productions/Monogram Pictures. Director: Sam Newfield; Producer: Maurice Conn; Screenplay, Story: Stanley Roberts; Cinematography: Jack Greenhalgh; Editor: Richard G. Wray; Sound Engineer: Hans Weeren. Cast: Tim McCoy, Rex Lease, Judith Ford, Wheeler Oakman, Edward Earle, Frank LaRue, Ed Piel, Sr., Kit Guard, Roger Williams, Jack Ingram, Hal Price, Budd Buster. (working title **Code of the Range**)

The Feud Maker: Released 04/04/1938. © Republic Pictures Corp. 04/04/1938. Republic Pictures. Director: Sam Newfield; Producer: A.W. Hackel; Screenplay: George H. Plympton; Story: Harry F. Olmsted; Cinematography: Robert Cline; Editor: Roy Claire. Cast: Bob Steele, Marion Weldon, Karl Hackett, Frank Ball, Budd Buster, Lew Meehan, Roger Williams, Forrest Taylor, Jack C. Smith, Steve Clark, Lloyd Ingraham.

Knight of the Plains: Released 05/07/1938. No copyright registered. A Stan Laurel Production/Spectrum Pictures. Director: Sam Newfield; Assistant Director: Charles Wayne; Producer: Jed Buell; Screenplay, Story: Fred Myton; Cinematography: Mack Stengler; Editor: Robert Jahns; Sound Engineer: Hans Weeren. Cast: Fred Scott, Al St. John, Marion Weldon, John Merton, Richard Cramer, Frank La Rue, Lafe McKee, Emma Tansey, Steve Clark, Jimmy Aubrey, Shery Tansey, Budd Buster. (working title **Paradise Valley**)

Gunsmoke Trail: Released 05/08/1938. © Monogram Pictures Corp. 05/10/1938. Concord Productions/Monogram Pictures. Director: Sam Newfield; Producer: Maurice Conn; Screenplay: Fred Myton; Story: Robert Emmett; Cinematography: Jack Greenhalgh; Editor: Martin G. Cohn. Cast: Jack Randall, Louise Stanley, Al St. John, Henry Roquemore, Ted Adams, John Merton, Harry Strang, Jack Ingram, Kit Guard, Hal Price, Al Bridges.

Songs and Bullets: Released 05/15/1938. No copyright registered. A Stan Laurel Production/Spectrum Pictures. Director: Sam Newfield; Producer: Jed Buell; Associate Producer: Bert Sternbach; Screenplay: George Plympton, Joseph O'Donnell; Story: George Plympton; Cinematography: Mack Stengler; Editor: Robert Jahns; Sound Engineer: Hans Weeren. Cast: Fred Scott, Al St. John, Alice Ardell, Charles King, Karl Hackett, Frank La Rue, Richard Cramer, Budd Buster, Jimmie Aubrey, Lew Porter, Sherry Tansey.

Phantom Ranger: Released 05/27/1938. © Monogram Pictures Corp. 05/23/1938. Concord Productions/Monogram Pictures. Director: Sam Newfield; Producer: Maurice Conn; Screenplay: Joseph O'Donnell; Story: Joseph O'Donnell, Stanley Roberts; Cinematography: Jack Greenhalgh; Editor: Richard G. Wray. Cast: Tim McCoy, Suzanne Kaaren, Karl Hackett, John St. Polis, John Merton, Edward Earle, Robert Frazer, Harry Strang, Charles King, Dick Cramer, Tom London, Bruce Warren, Jimmy Aubrey, Donald Dean. (working title **Ridin' Gent**)

Desert Patrol: Released 06/06/1938. © Republic Pictures Corp. 06/06/1938. Republic Pictures. Director: Sam Newfield; Producer: A.W. Hackel; Screenplay: Fred Myton; Cinematography: Robert Cline; Editor: Roy Claire. Cast: Bob Steele, Marion Weldon, Rex Lease, Ted Adams, Forrest Taylor, Budd Buster, Steve Clark, Jack Ingram, Julian Madison.

Durango Valley Raiders: Released 08/22/1938. © Republic Pictures Corp. 08/22/1938. Republic Pictures. Director: Sam Newfield; Producer: A.W. Hackel; Screenplay: George H. Plympton; Story: Harry F. Olmsted; Cinematography: Robert Cline; Editor: Roy Claire. Cast: Bob Steele, Louise Stanley, Karl Hackett, Ted Adams, Forrest Taylor, Steve Clark, Horace Murphy, Jack Ingram.

Crashin' Thru Danger: Released 09/15/1938. No copyright registered. Excelsior Pictures. Director: Sam Newfield; Producer: Sigmund Neufeld, Leslie Simmonds; Screenplay: Norman Houston; Cinematography: James Brown; Editor: Jack English; Sound Engineer: Hans Weeren. Cast: Ray Walker, Sally Blane, Guinn Williams, James Bush, Guy Usher, Robert Homans, Syd Saylor, Dick Curtis, Margaret O'Connell, Alexander Schoenberg. (aka **Crashing Through Danger**, **Crashing Thru Danger**, and **Crashin' Through Danger**; working title **Hell Breaks Loose**)

Lightning Carson Rides Again: Released 10/10/1938. No copyright registered. Victory Pictures/State Rights. Director: Sam Newfield; Assistant Director: Charles Henry; Producer: Sam Katzman; Screenplay, Story: E.R. O'Dasi; Cinematography: Marcel Picard; Editor: Holbrook N. Todd; Sound: Hans Weeren; Production Manager: Ed W. Rote; Settings: Fred Preble. Cast: Tim McCoy, Joan Barclay, Ted Adams, Bob Terry, Forrest Taylor, Ben Corbett, Slim Whitaker, Frank Wayne, Jane Keckly, Karl Hackett, Reed Howes, Frank La Rue, James Flaven.

Frontier Scout: Released 10/21/1938. © Fine Arts Pictures. 10/21/1938. Fine Arts Pictures/Grand National Pictures. Director: Sam Newfield; Producer: Franklin Warner; Associate Producer: Maurice Conn; Screenplay: Frances Guihan; Cinematography: Jack Greenhalgh; Editor: Richard G. Wray; Sound Engineer: Hans Weeren. Cast: George Houston, Al St. John, Beth Marion, Alden Chase, Dave O'Brien, Jack Smith, Budd Buster, Walter Byron, Dorothy Fay, Jack Ingram, Minerva Urecal, Kenneth Duncan, Slim Whitaker, Kit Guard, Carl Mathews, Joseph W. Girard, Mantan Moreland. (working titles **The Westerner** and **Wild Bill Hickok**)

Six Gun Trail: Released 11/25/1938. No copyright registered. Victory Pictures/State Rights. Director: Sam Newfield; Assistant Director: Charles Henry; Producer: Sam Katzman; Screenplay, Story: E.R. O'Dasi; Cinematography: Marcel Picard; Editor: Holbrook N. Todd; Sound: Hans Weeren; Production Manager: Ed W. Rote; Settings: Harry Reif. Cast: Colonel Tim McCoy, Nora Lane, Ben Corbett, Alden Chase, Ted Adams, Don Gallaher, Bob Terry, Karl Hackett, Frank Wayne, Hal Carey.

The Terror of Tiny Town: Released 12/01/1938. © Principal Productions, Inc. 07/19/1938. Principal Productions/Columbia Pictures. Director: Sam Newfield; Assistant Director: Gordon S. Griffith; Producer: Jed Buell; Associate Producer: Abe Meyer, Bert Sternbach; Screenplay: Fred Myton; Cinematography: Mack Stengler; Editor: Martin G. Cohn, Richard G. Wray. Cast: Billy Curtis, Yvonne Moray, Little Billy, Bill Platt, Joan Bambury, Joseph Herbst, Charles Becker, Nita Krebs, George Ministeri, Karl Casitzky, Johnnie Fern.

Trigger Pals: Released 01/13/1939. © Cinemart Productions, Inc. 01/13/1939. Cinemart Productions/Grand National Pictures. Director: Sam Newfield; Assistant Director: Bert Sternbach; Producer: Philip N. Krasne; Associate Producer: Robert Hampton Ford; Screenplay: George Plympton, Ted Richmond; Cinematography: Jack Greenhalgh; Editor: Roy Luby; Sound Engineer: Hans Weeren. Cast: Art Jarrett, Lee Powell, Al St. John, Dorothy Faye, Ted Adams, Nina Guilbert, Stanley Blystone, Ernie Adams, Earl Douglas, Frank La Rue, Ethan Allen.

Code of the Cactus: Released 02/25/1939. No copyright registered. Victory Pictures/State Rights. Director: Sam Newfield; Assistant Director: Bert Sternbach; Producer: Sam Katzman; Screenplay, Story: Edward Halperin; Cinematography: Marcel Picard; Editor: Holbrook N. Todd; Sound Engineer: Hans Weeren; Production Manager: Ed W. Rote; Settings: Fred Preble. Cast: Tim McCoy, Ben Corbett, Dorothy Short, Ted Adams, Alden Chase, Dave O'Brien, Forrest Taylor, Bob Terry, Slim Whitaker, Frank Wayne.

Texas Wildcats: Released 04/10/1939. No copyright registered. Victory Pictures/State Rights. Director: Sam Newfield; Assistant Director: Bert Sternbach; Producer: Sam Katzman; Screenplay, Story: George H. Plympton; Cinematography: Marcel Picard; Editor: Holbrook N. Todd; Sound Recording: Glen Glenn; Production Manager: Ed W. Rote; Settings: Fred Preble. Cast: Tim McCoy, Joan Barclay, Ben Corbett, Forrest Taylor, Ted Adams, Avando Reynaldo, Bob Terry, Dave O'Brien, Frank Ellis, Reed Howes, Slim Whittaker.

Outlaw's Paradise: Released 04/19/1939. No copyright registered. Victory Pictures/State Rights. Director: Sam Newfield; Assistant Director: Bert Sternbach; Producer: Sam Katzman; Screenplay, Story: Basil Dickey; Cinematography: Marcel Picard; Editor: Holbrook N. Todd; Sound Recording: Glen Glenn; Production Manager: Ed W. Rote; Settings: Fred Preble. Cast: Tim McCoy, Joan Barclay, Benny Corbett, Ted Adams, Forrest Taylor, Bob Terry, Don Gallaher, Dave O'Brien, Jack Mulhall.

Six-Gun Rhythm: Released 05/13/1939. © Arcadia Pictures Corp. 05/13/1939. Arcadia Pictures/Grand National Pictures. Director: Sam Newfield; Producer: Sam Newfield (uncredited); Associate Producer: Norman Haskall; Screenplay: Fred Myton; Story: Ted Richmond; Cinematography: Art Reed; Editor: Robert Crandall; Sound Engineer: Hans Weeren. Cast: Tex Fletcher, Joan Barclay, Ralph Peters, Reed Howes, Bud McTaggert, Ted Adams, Walter Shumway, Kit Guard, Carl Mathews, Art Davis, Bob Fraser, Jack McHugh, Sherry Tansey. (working title **Rhythm Rides the Range**)

Straight Shooter: Released 08/12/1939. No copyright registered. Victory Pictures/State Rights. Director: Sam Newfield; Assistant Director: Bert Sternbach; Producer: Sam Katzman; Screenplay: Basil Dickey, Joseph O'Donnell; Cinematography: Art Reed; Editor: Holbrook N. Todd; Sound Recording: Hans

Weeren; Production Manager: Ed W. Rote; Settings: Fred Preble. Cast: Tim McCoy, Julie Sheldon, Ben Corbett, Ted Adams, Reed Howes, Forrest Taylor, Budd Buster, Carl Mathews.

The Fighting Renegade: Released 09/01/1939. No copyright registered. Victory Pictures/State Rights. Director: Sam Newfield; Assistant Director: Bert Sternbach; Producer: Sam Katzman; Screenplay, Story: William Lively; Cinematography: Art Reed; Editor: Holbrook N. Todd; Sound Recording: Hans Weeren; Production Manager: Ed W. Rote. Cast: Tim McCoy, Joyce Bryant, Ben Corbett, Ted Adams, Budd Buster, Dave O'Brien, Forrest Taylor, Reed Howes, John Elliot.

Torture Ship: Released 10/22/1939. No copyright registered. Producers Pictures Corp./Producers Distributing Corp. Director: Victor Halperin; Producer: Sigmund Neufeld (uncredited); Screenplay: Milton Raison; Story: "A Thousand Deaths" by Jack London; Cinematography: Jack Greenhalgh; Editor: Holbrook N. Todd; Sound Engineer: Hans Weeren. Cast: Lyle Talbot, Irving Pichel, Julie Bishop, Sheila Bromley, Anthony Averill, Russell Hopton, Julian Madison, Eddie Holden, Wheeler Oakman, Stanley Blystone, Leander de Cordova, Dmitri Alexis, Skelton Knaggs. (working title **The Island of Fear**)

Hitler—Beast of Berlin: Released 10/29/1939. No copyright registered. Producers Pictures Corp./Producers Distributing Corp. Director: Sam Newfield (as Sherman Scott); Producer: Ben N. Judell; Associate Producer: Sigmund Neufeld; Screenplay: Shepard Traube, from his story "Goose Step"; Cinematography: Jack Greenhalgh; Editors: Robert Crandall, Holbrook N. Todd (uncredited); Sound Engineer: Hans Weeren. Cast: Roland Drew, Steffi Duna, Greta Granstedt, Alan Ladd, Lucien Prival, Vernon Dent, John Ellis, George Rosener, Bodil Rosing, Hans Von Twardowski, Joel Newfield, Jacqueline Newfield. (released as censor-imposed **Beasts of Berlin** in several states, and elsewhere under the MPPDA-imposed **Goose Step**)

Flaming Lead: Released 11/1939. No copyright registered. Colony Pictures/State Rights. Director: Sam Newfield; Producer: Max Alexander, Arthur Alexander; Screenplay: Joseph O'Donnell, Cinematography: Art Reed; Editor: Holbrook N. Todd. Cast: Ken Maynard, Eleanore Stewart, Dave O'Brien, Walter Long, Tom London, Reed Howes, Ralph Peters, Carleton Young, Kenneth Duncan, Bob Terry, Joyce Rogers.

Trigger Fingers: Released 11/01/1939. No copyright registered. Victory Pictures/State Rights. Director: Sam Newfield; Assistant Director: Bert Sternbach; Producer: Sam Katzman; Screenplay, Story: Basil Dickey; Cinematography: Bill Hyer; Editor: Holbrook N. Todd; Production Manager: E.W. Rote; Settings: Fred Preble; Sound Recording: Hans Weeren. Cast: Tim McCoy, Ben Corbett, Jill Martin, Joyce Bryant, Carleton Young, John Elliott, Bud McTaggart, Ralph Peters, Forrest Taylor, Kenne Duncan.

Fighting Mad: Released 11/05/1939. No copyright registered. Criterion Pictures/Monogram Pictures. Director: Sam Newfield; Assistant Director: Herman E. Webber; Producer: Philip N. Krasne; Screenplay: George Rosener, John Rathmell; Cinematography: Jack Greenhalgh; Editor: Roy Luby; Sound Engineer: Hans Weeren. Cast: James Newill, Sally Blane, Benny Rubin, Dave O'Brien, Milburn Stone, Walter Long, Warner Richmond, Ted Adams, Chief Thunder Cloud, Ole Olson, Horace Murphy.

Buried Alive: Released 11/06/1939. No copyright registered. Producers Pictures Corp./Producers Distributing Corp. Director: Victor Halperin; Producer: Ben Judell, Sigmund Neufeld (uncredited); Screenplay: George Bricker; Story: William A. Ullman, Jr.; Cinematography: Jack Greenhalgh; Editor: Holbrook N. Todd; Sound Engineer: Hans Weeren. Cast: Beverly Roberts, Robert Wilcox, George Pembroke, Ted Osborn, Paul McVey, Alden Chase, Don Rowan, Peter Lynn, Norman Budd, Bob McKenzie, Wheeler Oakman, Ben Alexander, Boyd Irwin, Edward Earle, Dave O'Brien.

The Invisible Killer: Released 11/14/1939. No copyright registered. Producers Pictures Corp./Producers Distributing Corp. Director: Sam Newfield (as Sherman Scott); Producer: Ben Judell; Associate Producer: Sigmund Neufeld; Screenplay: Joseph O'Donnell; Story: Carter Wayne's novel "Murder for Millions"; Cinematography: Jack Greenhalgh; Editor: Holbrook N. Todd; Sound Engineer: Hans Weeren. Cast: Grace Bradley, Roland Drew, Jeanne Kelly, David Oliver, William Newell, Boyd Irwin, Clen Wilenchick, Frank Coletti, Sydney Grayler, Alex Callam, Harry Worth, Ernie Adams. (working title **Wanted for Murder**)

Mercy Plane: Released 12/04/1939. No copyright registered. Producers Pictures Corp./Producers Distributing Corp. Director: Richard Harlan; Producer: Ben N. Judell; Associate Producer: Sigmund Neufeld; Screenplay: William Lively; Cinematography: Jack Greenhalgh; Editor: Holbrook N. Todd. Cast: James Dunn, Frances Gifford, Matty Fain, William Pawley, Harry Harvey, Forbes Murray, Edwin Miller, Duke York.

Death Rides the Range: Released 01/13/1940. No copyright registered. Colony Pictures/State Rights. Director: Sam Newfield; Producer: Max Alexander, Arthur Alexander; Screenplay: Bill Lively; Cinematography: Art Reed; Editor: Holbrook N. Todd. Cast: Ken Maynard, Fay McKenzie, Ralph Peters, Julian Rivero, Charles King, John Elliott, William Castello, Sven Hugo Borg, Michael Vallon, Julian Madison, Kenneth Rhodes, Tarzan.

The Sagebrush Family Trails West: Released 01/14/1940. No copyright registered. Producers Pictures Corp./Producers Distributing Corp. Director: Sam Newfield (as Peter Stewart); Producer: Sigmund Neufeld; Screenplay: William Lively; Cinematography: Jack Greenhalgh. Cast: Bobby Clark, Earle Hodgins, Nina Guilbert, Joyce Bryant, Minerva Urecal, Archie Hall, Kenneth Duncan, Forrest Taylor, Carl Mathews, Wally West.

Texas Renegades: Released 01/21/1940. No copyright registered. Producers Pictures Corp./Producers Distributing Corp. Director: Sam Newfield (as Peter Stewart); Associate Producer: Sigmund Neufeld; Screenplay: Joseph O'Donnell; Story: Robert Emmett; Cinematography: Jack Greenhalgh; Editor: Holbrook N. Todd; Sound Engineer: Hans Weeren. Cast: Tim McCoy, Nora Lane, Kenneth Duncan, Lee Prather, Harry Harvey, Earl Gunn, Hal Price, Bud McClure, Joe McGuinn, Raphael Bennett, Buel Bryant, Arnold Clack.

Secrets of a Model: Released 05/04/1940. © Continental Pictures Corp. 12/06/1939. Continental Pictures/State Rights. Director: Sam Newfield; Producer: J.D. Kendis; Screenplay: Sherman Lowe, Arthur St. Claire; Cinematography: Jack Greenhalgh; Editor: George Merrick; Sound Engineer: Hans Weeren; Production Manager: Melville P. De Lay. Cast: Sharon Lee, Harold Daniels, Phyllis Barry, Bobby Watson, Grace Lenard, Julien Madison, Eddie Borden.

I Take This Oath: Released 05/20/1940. © Producers Releasing Corp. 05/14/1940. Sigmund Neufeld Productions/Producers Releasing Corp. Director: Sam Newfield (as Sherman Scott); Assistant Director: Melville De Lay; Producer: Sigmund Neufeld; Screenplay: George Bricker; Story: William A. Ullman, Jr.; Cinematography: Jack Greenhalgh; Editor: Holbrook N. Todd; Sound Engineer: Hans Weeren. Cast: Gordon Jones, Joyce Compton, Craig Reynolds, J. Farrell MacDonald, Veda Ann Borg, Mary Gordon, Robert Homans, Guy Usher, Brooks Benedict, Edward Peil, Sr. (working title **Sons of the Finest**; rereleased as **Police Rookie**)

Frontier Crusader: Released 06/17/1940. © Producers Releasing Corp. 05/22/1940. Sigmund Neufeld Productions/Producers Releasing Corp. Director: Sam Newfield (as Peter Stewart); Assistant Director: Douglas Bridges; Producer: Sigmund Neufeld; Screenplay: William Lively; Story: Arthur Durham; Cinematography: Jack Greenhalgh; Editor: Holbrook N. Todd; Production Manager: Bert Sternbach; Sound Engineer: Hans Weeren. Cast: Tim McCoy, Dorothy Short, Lou Fulton, Karl Hackett, Ted Adams, John Merton, Forrest Taylor, Hal Price, Frank La Rue, Kenne Duncan.

Hold That Woman!: Released 06/28/1940. © Producers Releasing Corp. 06/22/1940. Sigmund Neufeld Productions/Producers Releasing Corp. Director: Sam Newfield (as Sherman Scott); Assistant Director: Melville De Lay Producer: Sigmund Neufeld; Screenplay: George Bricker; Story: Raymond L. Schrock, William Pierce; Cinematography: Jack Greenhalgh; Editor: Holbrook N. Todd; Production Manager: Bert Sternbach; Sound Engineer: Hans Weeren. Cast: James Dunn, Frances Gifford, George Douglas, Rita La Roy, Martin Spellman, Eddie Fetherston, Guy Usher, Paul Bryar, Ed Miller, John Dilson, Dave O'Brien, Anna Lisa, William Hall, Marie Rice, Frank Meredith, Art Miles. (working title **Skip Tracer**)

Billy the Kid Outlawed: Released 07/20/1940. © Producers Releasing Corp. 07/12/1940. Sigmund Neufeld Productions/Producers Releasing Corp. Director: Sam Newfield (as Peter Stewart); Assistant Director: Melville De Lay; Producer: Sigmund Neufeld; Screenplay: Oliver Drake; Cinematography: Jack Greenhalgh; Editor: Holbrook N. Todd; Production Manager: Bert Sternbach; Sound Engineer: Hans Weeren. Cast: Bob Steele, Louise Curry, Al St. John, Carleton Young, John Merton, Joe McGuinn, Ted Adams, Walter McGrail, Kenne Duncan, Reed Howes, George Chesebro, Budd Buster.

Gun Code: Released 07/29/1940. © Producers Releasing Corp. 07/25/1940. Sigmund Neufeld Productions/Producers Releasing Corp. Director: Sam Newfield (as Peter Stewart); Assistant Director: Melville De Lay; Producer: Sigmund Neufeld; Screenplay: Joseph O'Donnell; Cinematography: Jack Greenhalgh; Editor: Holbrook N. Todd; Production Manager: Bert Sternbach; Sound Engineer: Hans Weeren. Cast: Tim McCoy, Inna Gest, Lew Fulton, Alder Chase, Carleton Young, Ted Adams, Robert Winkler, Dave O'Brien, George Chesebro, Jack Richardson, John Elliott. (working title **Border Crossing**)

Marked Men: Released 08/28/1940. © Producers Releasing Corp. 08/28/1940. Sigmund Neufeld Productions/Producers Releasing Corp. Director: Sam Newfield (as Sherman Scott); Assistant Director: Melville De Lay; Producer: Sigmund Neufeld; Screenplay: George Bricker; Story: Harold Greene; Cinematography: Jack Greenhalgh; Editor: Holbrook N. Todd; Production Manager: Bert Sternbach; Sound Engineer: Hans Weeren. Cast: Warren Hull, Isabel Jewell, John Dilson, Paul Bryar,

Charles Williams, Al St. John, Budd L. Buster, Art Miles, Eddie Fetherston, Ted Erwin, Lyle Clement, Gray Shadow. (aka **Desert Escape**)

Arizona Gang Busters: Released 09/16/1940. © Producers Releasing Corp. 09/11/1940. Sigmund Neufeld Productions/Producers Releasing Corp. Director: Sam Newfield (as Peter Stewart); Assistant Director: Melville De Lay; Producer: Sigmund Neufeld; Screenplay: William Lively; Cinematography: Jack Greenhalgh; Editor: Holbrook N. Todd; Production manager: Bert Sternbach; Sound Engineer: Hans Weeren. Cast: Tim McCoy, Pauline Haddon, Lew Fulton, Forrest Taylor, Julian Rivero, Arno Frey, Paul Ellis, Kenneth Duncan, Jack Rutherford, Elizabeth La Mal, Otto Reichow, Lita Cortez.

Am I Guilty?: Released 09/27/1940. No copyright registered. Supreme Pictures. Director: Sam Newfield (as Samuel Neufeld); Producer: A.W. Hackel; Screenplay: Sherman Lowe; Cinematography: Robert Cline; Editor: S. Roy Luby. Cast: Ralph Cooper, Sybyl Lewis, Lawrence Criner, Sam McDaniel, Marcella Moreland, Arthur T. Ray, Reginald Fenderson, Matthew Jones, "Pigmeat" Markham, Jesse Brooks, Napoleon Simpson. (working title **Free Clinic**)

Billy the Kid in Texas: Released 09/30/1940. © Producers Releasing Corp. 09/30/1940. Sigmund Neufeld Productions/Producers Releasing Corp. Director: Sam Newfield (as Peter Stewart); Assistant Director: Melville De Lay; Producer: Sigmund Neufeld; Screenplay: Joseph O'Donnell; Cinematography: Jack Greenhalgh; Editor: Holbrook N. Todd; Production Manager: Bert Sternbach; Sound Engineer: Hans Weeren. Cast: Bob Steele, Terry Walker, Al St. John, Carleton Young, Charles King, John Merton, Frank La Rue, Charles Whittaker.

Riders of Black Mountain: Released 11/11/1940. © Producers Releasing Corp. 11/02/1940. Sigmund Neufeld Productions/Producers Releasing Corp. Director: Sam Newfield (as Peter Stewart); Assistant Director: Melville De Lay; Producer: Sigmund Neufeld; Screenplay: Joseph O'Donnell; Cinematography: Jack Greenhalgh; Editor: Holbrook N. Todd; Production Manager: Bert Sternbach; Sound Engineer: Hans Weeren. Cast: Tim McCoy, Pauline Hadden, Rex Lease, Ralph Peters, Julian Rivero, Edward Peil, Sr., Frank La Rue, Ted Adams, Jack Rutherford, Alden Chase, George Chesebro, Dirk Thane.

The Devil Bat: Released 12/13/1940. © Producers Releasing Corp. 12/17/1940. Sigmund Neufeld Productions/Producers Releasing Corp. Director: Jean Yarbrough; Producers: Jack Gallagher, Sigmund Neufeld (uncredited); Associate Producer: Guy V. Thayer, Jr.; Screenplay: John Thomas Neville; Story: George Bricker; Cinematography: Arthur Martinelli; Editor: Holbrook N. Todd; Production Manager: Melville De Lay. Cast: Bela Lugosi, Suzanne Kaaren, Dave O'Brien, Guy Usher, Yolande Mallott, Donald Kerr, Edward Mortimer, Gene O'Donnell, Alan Baldwin, John Ellis, Arthur Q. Bryan, Hal Price, John Davidson, Billy Griffith, Wally Rairdon.

Billy the Kid's Gun Justice: Released 12/27/1940. © Producers Releasing Corp. 12/25/1940. Sigmund Neufeld Productions/Producers Releasing Corp. Director: Sam Newfield (as Peter Stewart); Producer: Sigmund Neufeld; Screenplay: Tom Gibson; Cinematography: Jack Greenhalgh; Editor: Holbrook N. Todd; Production Manager: Bert Sternbach; Sound Engineer: Hans Weeren. Cast: Bob Steele, Al St. John, Louise Currie, Carleton Young, Charles King, Rex Lease, Ken Duncan, Forrest Taylor, Ted Adams, Al Ferguson, Karl Hackett, Ed Peil, Sr., Julian Rivero, Blanca Visher.

The Lone Rider Rides On: Released 01/10/1941. © Producers Releasing Corp. 01/08/1941. Sigmund Neufeld Productions/Producers Releasing Corp. Director: Sam Newfield; Assistant Director: Melville De Lay; Producer: Sigmund Neufeld; Screenplay: Joseph O'Donnell; Cinematography: Jack Greenhalgh; Editor: Holbrook N. Todd; Production Manager: Bert Sternbach; Sound Engineer: Hans Weeren. Cast: George Houston, Hillary Brooke, Al St. John, Karl Hackett, Lee Powell, Forrest Taylor, Frank Hagney, Jay Wilsey, Frank Ellis, Curley Dresden.

Billy the Kid's Range War: Released 01/24/1941. © Producers Releasing Corp. 01/16/1941. Sigmund Neufeld Productions/Producers Releasing Corp. Director: Sam Newfield (as Peter Stewart); Assistant Director: Melville De Lay; Producer: Sigmund Neufeld; Screenplay: William Lively; Cinematography: Jack Greenhalgh; Editor: Holbrook N. Todd; Production Manager: Bert Sternbach; Sound Engineer: Hans Weeren. Cast: Bob Steele, Al St. John, Joan Barclay, Carleton Young, Rex Lease, Milton Kibbee, Karl Hackett, Ted Adams, Julian Rivero, Alden Chase, Howard Masters, Buddy Roosevelt, Ralph Peters.

The Lone Rider Crosses the Rio: Released 02/28/1941. © Producers Releasing Corp. 02/24/1941. Sigmund Neufeld Productions/Producers Releasing Corp. Director: Sam Newfield; Assistant Director: Melville De Lay; Producer: Sigmund Neufeld; Screenplay: William Lively; Cinematography: Jack Greenhalgh; Editor: Holbrook N. Todd; Production Manager: Bert Sternbach; Sound Engineer: Hans Weeren. Cast: George Houston, Al St. John, Roquell Verria, Charles King, Julian Rivero, Alden Chase, Thornton Edwards, Howard Masters, Jay Wilsey, Frank Ellis, Frank Hagney, Phillipi Turich. (working title **The Lone Rider Across the Rio**)

Outlaws of the Rio Grande: Released 03/07/1941. © Producers Releasing Corp. 03/05/1941. Sigmund Neufeld Productions/Producers Releasing Corp. Director: Sam Newfield (as Peter Stewart); Assistant Director: Melville De Lay; Producer: Sigmund Neufeld; Cinematography: Jack Greenhalgh; Editor: Holbrook N. Todd; Production Manager: Bert Sternbach; Sound Engineer: Hans Weeren. Cast: Tim McCoy, Virginia Carpenter, Charles King, Ken Duncan, Ralph Peters, Karl Hackett, Rex Lease, Phillip Turich, Frank Ellis, Thornton Edwards, Joe Dominguez.

Billy the Kid's Fighting Pals: Released 04/18/1941. © Producers Releasing Corp. 04/09/1941. Sigmund Neufeld Productions/Producers Releasing Corp. Director: Sam Newfield (as Sherman Scott); Assistant Director: Melville De Lay; Producer: Sigmund Neufeld; Screenplay: George Plympton; Cinematography: Jack Greenhalgh; Editor: Holbrook N. Todd; Production Manager: Bert Sternbach; Sound Engineer: Hans Weeren. Cast: Bob Steele, Al St. John, Phyllis Adair, Carleton Young, Charles King, Curley Dresden, Edward Peil, Sr., Hal Price, George Chesebro, Forrest Taylor, Budd Buster, Julian Rivero.

The Lone Rider in Ghost Town: Released 05/16/1941. © Producers Releasing Corp. 05/10/1941. Sigmund Neufeld Productions /Producers Releasing Corp. Director: Sam Newfield; Assistant Director: Melville De Lay; Producer: Sigmund Neufeld; Screenplay: Joe O'Donnell; Cinematography: Jack Greenhalgh; Editor: Holbrook N. Todd; Production Manager: Bert Sternbach; Sound Engineer: Hans Weeren. Cast: George Houston, Al St. John, Alaine Brandes, Budd Buster, Frank Hagney, Alden Chase, Reed Howes, Charles King, George Chesebro, Edward Peil, Sr. (working title **The Lone Rider Gallops to Glory**; aka **Ghost Mine**)

Billy the Kid in Santa Fe: Released 07/11/1941. © Producers Releasing Corp. 07/03/1941. Sigmund Neufeld Productions/Producers Releasing Corp. Director: Sam Newfield (as Sherman Scott); Assistant Director: Melville De Lay; Producer: Sigmund Neufeld; Screenplay: Joseph O'Donnell; Cinematography: Jack Greenhalgh; Editor: Holbrook N. Todd; Production Manager: Bert Sternbach; Sound Engineer: Hans Weeren. Cast: Bob Steele, Al St. John, Rex Lease, Marin Sais, Dennis Moore, Karl Hackett, Steve Clark, Hal Price, Charles King, Frank Ellis, Dave O'Brien, Ken Duncan.

Texas Marshal: Released 07/14/1941. © Producers Releasing Corp. 05/26/1941. Sigmund Neufeld Productions /Producers Releasing Corporation. Director: Sam Newfield (as Peter Stewart); Assistant Director: Melville De Lay; Producer: Sigmund Neufeld; Screenplay: William Lively; Cinematography: Jack Greenhalgh; Editor: Holbrook N. Todd; Production Manager: Bert Sternbach; Sound Engineer: Hans Weeren. Cast: Tim McCoy, Art Davis, Kay Leslie, Karl Hackett, Edward Peil, Sr., Charles King, Dave O'Brien, Budd Buster, John Elliott, Wilson Edwards, Byron Vance.

The Lone Rider in Frontier Fury: Released 08/08/1941. © Producers Releasing Corp. 08/02/1941. Sigmund Neufeld Productions/Producers Releasing Corp. Director: Sam Newfield; Assistant Director: Melville De Lay; Producer: Sigmund Neufeld; Screenplay: Fred Myton; Cinematography: Jack Greenhalgh; Editor: Holbrook N. Todd; Production Manager: Bert Sternbach; Sound Engineer: Hans Weeren. Cast: George Houston, Al St. John, Hillary Brooke, Karl Hackett, Ted Adams, Archie Hall, Budd Buster, Virginia Card, Ed Peil, Sr., John Elliott, Tom London, Frank Ellis.

The Lone Rider Ambushed: Released 08/29/1941. © Producers Releasing Corp. 08/21/1941. Sigmund Neufeld Productions/Producers Releasing Corp. Director: Sam Newfield; Producer: Sigmund Neufeld; Screenplay: Oliver Drake; Cinematography: Jack Greenhalgh; Editor: Holbrook N. Todd; Sound Engineer: Hans Weeren. Cast: George Houston, Al St. John, Maxine Leslie, Frank Hagney, Jack Ingram, Hal Price, Ted Adams, George Chesebro, Ralph Peters, Steve Clark.

Mr. Celebrity: Released 10/10/1941. © Producers Releasing Corp. 10/08/1941. Producers Releasing Corp. Director: William Beaudine; Executive Producer: George R. Batchellor; Producer: Martin Mooney; Screenplay: Martin Mooney; Original Story: Martin Mooney and Charles Samuels; Cinematography: Arthur Martinelli; Editor: Robert Crandall; Production Manager: Dick L'Estrange; Sound Engineer: Ben Winkler. Cast: Buzzy Henry, James Seay, Doris Day, William Halligan, Gavin Gordon, Laura Treadwell, John Ince, Johnny Berkes, Larry Grey, Clara Kimball Young, Francis X. Bushman, Jim Jeffries. (Sigmund Neufeld handled the actual production duties, sans credit.)

Billy the Kid Wanted: Released 10/24/1941. © Producers Releasing Corp. Sigmund Neufeld Productions/Producers Releasing Corp. 10/04/1941. Director: Sam Newfield (as Sherman Scott); Assistant Director: Melville De Lay; Producer: Sigmund Neufeld; Screenplay: Fred Myton; Cinematography: Jack Greenhalgh; Editor: Holbrook N. Todd; Production Manager: Bert Sternbach; Sound Engineer: Hans Weeren. Cast: Buster Crabbe, Al St. John, Dave O'Brien, Glenn Strange, Charles King, Slim Whitaker, Howard Masters, Choti Sherwood, Joel Newfield, Budd Buster, Frank Ellis.

The Lone Rider Fights Back: Released 11/07/1941. © Producers Releasing Corp. 10/16/1941. Sigmund Neufeld Productions/Producers Releasing Corp. Director: Sam Newfield; Assistant Director: Melville De Lay; Producer: Sigmund Neufeld; Screenplay: Joseph O'Donnell; Cinematography: Jack Greenhalgh; Editor: Holbrook N. Todd; Production Manager: Bert Sternbach; Sound Engineer: Hans Weeren. Cast: George Houston, Al St. John, Dorothy Short, Dennis Moore, Frank Hagney, Charles King, Frank Ellis.

Billy the Kid's Round-Up: Released 12/12/1941. © Producers Releasing Corp. 11/14/1941. Sigmund Neufeld Productions/Producers Releasing Corp. Director: Sam Newfield (as Sherman Scott); Assistant Director: Melville De Lay; Producer: Sigmund Neufeld; Screenplay: Fred Myton; Cinematography: Jack Greenhalgh; Editor: Holbrook N. Todd; Production Manager: Bert Sternbach; Sound Engineer: Hans Weeren. Cast: Buster Crabbe, Al St. John, Carleton Young, Joan Barclay, Glenn Strange, Charles King, Slim Whitaker, John Webster.

Texas Manhunt: Released 01/02/1942. © Producers Releasing Corp. 12/08/1941. Sigmund Neufeld Productions/Producers Releasing Corp. Director: Sam Newfield (as Peter Stewart); Assistant Director: Melville De Lay; Producer: Sigmund Neufeld; Screenplay: William Lively; Cinematography: Jack Greenhalgh; Editor: Holbrook N. Todd; Production Manager: Bert Sternbach. Cast: Lee Powell, Art Davis, Bill Boyd, Julie Duncan, Frank Hagney, Karl Hackett, Dennis Moore, Frank Ellis, Arno Frey, Eddie Phillips.

The Lone Rider and the Bandit: Released 01/16/1942. © Producers Releasing Corp. 01/14/1942. Sigmund Neufeld Productions/Producers Releasing Corp. Director: Sam Newfield; Assistant Director: Melville De Lay; Producer: Sigmund Neufeld; Screenplay: Steve Braxton; Cinematography: Jack Greenhalgh; Editor: Holbrook N. Todd; Production Manager: Bert Sternbach. Cast: George Houston, Al St. John, Dennis Moore, Vicki Lester, Glenn Strange, Jack Ingram, Milt Kibbee, Karl Sepulveda, Eddie Dean, Slim Whitaker, Slim Andrews.

Raiders of the West: Released 02/13/1942. © Producers Releasing Corp. 01/15/1942. Sigmund Neufeld Productions/Producers Releasing Corp. Director: Sam Newfield (as Peter Stewart); Assistant Director: Melville De Lay; Producer: Sigmund Neufeld; Screenplay: Oliver Drake; Cinematography: Jack Greenhalgh; Editor: Holbrook N. Todd; Production Manager: Bert Sternbach; Sound Engineer: Hans Weeren. Cast: Bill Boyd, Art Davis, Lee Powell, Virginia Carroll, Charles King, Glenn Strange, Rex Lease, Slim Whitaker, Milton Kibbee, Lynton Brent.

Billy the Kid Trapped: Released 02/20/1942. © Producers Releasing Corp. 01/30/1942. Sigmund Neufeld Productions/Producers Releasing Corp. Director: Sam Newfield (as Sherman Scott); Assistant Director: Melville De Lay; Producer: Sigmund Neufeld; Screenplay: Joseph O'Donnell; Cinematography: Jack Greenhalgh; Editor: Holbrook N. Todd; Production Manager: Bert Sternbach; Sound Engineer: Hans Weeren. Cast: Buster Crabbe, Al St. John, Bud McTaggart, Ann Jeffreys, Glenn Strange, Walter McGrail, Ted Adams, Jack Ingram, Milt Kibbee, Eddie Phillips, Budd Buster.

The Lone Rider in Cheyenne: Released 03/20/1942. © Producers Releasing Corp. 02/10/1942. Sigmund Neufeld Productions/Producers Releasing Corp. Director: Sam Newfield; Associate Director: Melville De Lay; Producer: Sigmund Neufeld;

Screenplay: Oliver Drake, Elizabeth Beecher; Cinematography: Jack Greenhalgh; Editor: Holbrook N. Todd; Production Manager: Bert Sternbach. Cast: George Houston, Al St. John, Dennis Moore, Ella Neal, Roy Barcroft, Lynton Brent, Kenne Duncan, Milton Kibbee, J. Merrill Holmes, Karl Hackett, Jack Ingram, George Chesebro.

Rolling Down the Great Divide: Released 04/24/1942. © Producers Releasing Corp. 04/08/1942. Sigmund Neufeld Productions/Producers Releasing Corp. Director: Sam Newfield (as Peter Stewart); Assistant Director: Melville De Lay; Producer: Sigmund Neufeld; Screenplay: George Milton; Cinematography: Jack Greenhalgh; Editor: Holbrook N. Todd; Production Manager: Bert Sternbach; Sound Engineer: Hans Weeren. Cast: Bill Boyd, Art Davis, Lee Powell, Wanda McKay, Glenn Strange, Karl Hackett, Jack M. Holmes, Ted Adams, Jack Ingram, John Elliott.

The Mad Monster: Released 05/15/1942. © Producers Releasing Corp. Sigmund Neufeld Productions/Producers Releasing Corp. 05/07/1942. Director: Sam Newfield; Assistant Director: Melville De Lay; Producer: Sigmund Neufeld; Screenplay: Fred Myton; Cinematography: Jack Greenhalgh; Editor: Holbrook N. Todd; Production Manager: Bert Sternbach; Sound Engineer: Hans Weeren. Cast: Johnny Downs, George Zucco, Anne Nagel, Glenn Strange, Sarah Padden, Gordon Demain, Mae Busch, Reginald Barlow, Robert Strange, Henry Hall, Edward Cassidy, Eddie Holden, John Elliott, Charles Whitaker, Gil Patric.

Men of San Quentin: Released 05/22/1942. © Producers Releasing Corp. 05/12/1942. Producers Releasing Corp. Director: William Beaudine; Producers: Martin Mooney and Max M. King; Executive Producer: George R. Batchellor; Screenplay: Ernest Booth; Original Story: Martin Mooney; Cinematography: Clark Ramsay; Editor: Dan Milner; Production Manager: Dick L'Estrange; Sound Engineer: Ben Winkler. Cast: J. Anthony Hughes, Eleanor Stewart, Dick Curtis, Charles Middleton, Jeffrey Sayre, George Breakston, Michael Mark, John Ince, Joe Whitehead, Skins Miller, Jack Seay, Jack Cheatham, Drew Demarest. (Sigmund Neufeld handled the actual production duties, sans credit.)

Billy the Kid's Smoking Guns: Released 05/29/1942. © Producers Releasing Corp. 05/21/1942. Sigmund Neufeld Productions/Producers Releasing Corp. Director: Sam Newfield (as Sherman Scott); Assistant Director: Melville De Lay; Producer: Sigmund Neufeld; Screenplay: George Milton; Cinematography: Jack Greenhalgh; Editor: Holbrook N. Todd; Production Manager: Bert Sternbach; Sound Engineer: Hans Weeren. Cast: Buster Crabbe, Al St. John, Dave O'Brien, John Merton, Milton Kibbee, Ted Adams, Karl Hackett, Frank Ellis, Slim Whitaker, Budd Buster, Joel Newfield, Joan Barclay.

Texas Justice: Released 06/12/1942. © Producers Releasing Corp. 06/01/1942. Sigmund Neufeld Productions/Producers Releasing Corp. Director: Sam Newfield; Associate Producer: Melville De Lay; Producer: Sigmund Neufeld; Screenplay: Steve Braxton; Cinematography: Jack Greenhalgh; Editor: Holbrook N. Todd; Production Manager: Bert Sternbach; Sound Engineer: Hans Weeren. Cast: George Houston, Al St. John, Wanda McKay, Claire Rochelle, Dennis Moore, Archie Hall, Slim Whitaker, Edward Peil, Sr., Karl Hackett, Julian Rivero. (aka **The Lone Rider in Texas Justice**)

Tumbleweed Trail: Released 07/10/1942. © Producers Releasing Corp. 06/19/1942. Sigmund Neufeld Productions/Producers Releasing Corp. Director: Sam Newfield (as

Peter Stewart); Assistant Director: Melville De Lay; Producer: Sigmund Neufeld; Screenplay: Fred Myton; Cinematography: Jack Greenhalgh; Editor: Holbrook N. Todd; Production Manager: Bert Sternbach; Sound Engineer: Hans Weeren. Cast: Bill Boyd, Art Davis, Lee Powell, Marjorie Manners, Jack Rockwell, Charles King, Karl Hackett, George Chesebro, Frank Hagney.

Jungle Siren: Released 08/14/1942. © Producers Releasing Corp. 08/07/1942. Sigmund Neufeld Productions/Producers Releasing Corp. Director: Sam Newfield; Assistant Director: Melville De Lay; Producer: Sigmund Neufeld; Screenplay: George W. Sayre, Sam Robins; Story: George W. Sayre, Milton Raison; Cinematography: Jack Greenhalgh; Editor: Holbrook N. Todd; Production Manager: Bert Sternbach; Sound Engineer: Hans Weeren. Cast: Ann Corio, Buster Crabbe, Paul Bryar, Evelyn Wahl, Arno Frey, Milt Kibbee, Jess Brooks, Manart Kippen, James Adamson, Greco the Chimpanzee.

Law and Order: Released 08/21/1942. © Producers Releasing Corp. 02/05/1943. Sigmund Neufeld Productions/Producers Releasing Corp. Director: Sam Newfield (as Sherman Scott); Assistant Director: Melville De Lay; Producer: Sigmund Neufeld; Screenplay: Sam Robins; Cinematography: Jack Greenhalgh; Editor: Holbrook N. Todd; Production Manager: Bert Sternbach; Sound Engineer: Hans Weeren. Cast: Buster Crabbe, Al St. John, Dave "Tex" O'Brien, Sarah Padden, Wanda McKay, Charles King, Hal Price, John Merton, Ken Duncan, Ted Adams.

Prairie Pals: Released 09/04/1942. © Producers Releasing Corp. 02/19/1943. Sigmund Neufeld Productions/Producers Releasing Corp. Director: Sam Newfield (as Peter Stewart); Assistant Director: Melville De Lay; Producer: Sigmund Neufeld; Screenplay: Patricia Harper; Cinematography: Jack Greenhalgh; Editor: Holbrook N. Todd; Production Manager: Bert Sternbach; Sound Engineer: Hans Weeren. Cast: Bill Boyd, Art Davis, Lee Powell, Esther Estrella, Charles King, John Merton, Jack M. Holmes, Kermit Maynard, I. Stanford Jolley. (aka **Frontier Marshall in Prairie Pals**)

Border Roundup: Released 09/18/1942. © Producers Releasing Corp. 02/10/1943. Sigmund Neufeld Productions/Producers Releasing Corp. Director: Sam Newfield; Assistant Director: Melville De Lay; Producer: Sigmund Neufeld; Screenplay: Stephen Worth; Cinematography: Jack Greenhalgh; Editor: Holbrook N. Todd; Production Manager: Bert Sternbach; Sound Engineer: Hans Weeren. Cast: George Houston, Al St. John, Dennis Moore, Patricia Knox, Charles King, I. Stanford Jolley, Edward Peil, Sr., Jimmy Aubrey, John Elliott. (aka **Lone Rider in Border Roundup**)

Sheriff of Sage Valley: Released 10/02/1942. © Producers Releasing Corp. 02/01/1943. Sigmund Neufeld Productions/Producers Releasing Corp. Director: Sam Newfield (as Sherman Scott); Assistant Director: Melville De Lay; Producer: Sigmund Neufeld; Screenplay: George W. Sayre, Milton Raison; Cinematography: Jack Greenhalgh; Editor: Holbrook N. Todd; Production Manager: Bert Sternbach; Sound Engineer: Hans Weeren. Cast: Buster Crabbe, Al St. John, Dave "Tex" O'Brien, Maxine Leslie, Charles King, John Merton, Kermit Maynard, Hal Price.

Along the Sundown Trail: Released 10/19/1942. © Producers Releasing Corp. 02/01/1943. Sigmund Neufeld Productions/Producers Releasing Corp. Director: Sam Newfield (as Peter Stewart); Assistant Director: Melville De Lay; Producer: Sigmund Neufeld; Screenplay: Arthur St. Claire; Cinematography: Jack Greenhalgh; Editor: Holbrook N. Todd; Production Manager: Bert Sternbach; Sound Engineer: Hans Weeren. Cast: Art Davis, Bill Boyd, Lee Powell, Julie Duncan, Charles King, Karl

Hackett, Howard Masters, John Merton, Jack Ingram, Kermit Maynard. (aka **Frontier Marshall Along the Sundown Trail**)

Outlaws of Boulder Pass: Released 10/28/1942. © Producers Releasing Corp. 02/05/1943. Sigmund Neufeld Productions/Producers Releasing Corp. Director: Sam Newfield; Assistant Director: Melville De Lay; Producer: Sigmund Neufeld; Screenplay: Steve Braxton; Cinematography: Jack Greenhalgh; Editor: Holbrook N. Todd; Production Manager: Bert Sternbach; Sound Engineer: Hans Weeren. Cast: George Houston, Al St. John, Dennis Moore, Marjorie Manners, I. Stanford Jolley, Karl Hackett, Charles King, Ted Adams, Ken Duncan, Frank Ellis. (aka **Lone Rider in Outlaws of Boulder Pass**)

The Mysterious Rider: Released 11/20/1942. © P.R.C. Pictures, Inc. 11/20/1943. Sigmund Neufeld Productions/Producers Releasing Corp. Director: Sam Newfield (as Sherman Scott); Assistant Director: Melville De Lay; Producer: Sigmund Neufeld; Screenplay: Steve Braxton; Cinematography: Jack Greenhalgh; Editor: Holbrook N. Todd; Production Manager: Bert Sternbach; Sound Engineer: Hans Weeren. Cast: Buster Crabbe, Al St. John, Caroline Burke, John Merton, Edwin Brien, Jack Ingram, Slim Whitaker, Kermit Maynard, Ted Adams. (aka **Billy the Kid in The Mysterious Rider**; reissued in cutdown version in 1947 as **Panhandle Trail**)

Overland Stagecoach: Released 12/11/1942. © Producers Releasing Corp. 02/08/1943. Sigmund Neufeld Productions/Producers Releasing Corp. Director: Sam Newfield; Assistant Director: Melville De Lay; Producer: Sigmund Neufeld; Screenplay: Steve Braxton; Cinematography: Jack Greenhalgh; Editor: Holbrook N. Todd; Production Manager: Bert Sternbach; Sound Engineer: Hans Weeren. Cast: Bob Livingston, Al St. John, Dennis Moore, Julie Duncan, Glenn Strange, Charles King, Ted Adams, Julian Rivero, Budd Buster, Art Mix. (aka **Lone Rider in Overland Stagecoach**)

The Kid Rides Again: Released 01/27/1943. © Producers Releasing Corp. 01/16/1943. Sigmund Neufeld Productions/Producers Releasing Corp. Director: Sam Newfield (as Sherman Scott); Assistant Director: Melville De Lay; Producer: Sigmund Neufeld; Screenplay: Fred Myton; Cinematography: Jack Greenhalgh; Editor: Holbrook N. Todd; Production Manager: Bert Sternbach; Sound Engineer: Hans Weeren. Cast: Buster Crabbe, Al St. John, Iris Meredith, Glenn Strange, Charles King, I. Stanford Jolley, Ed Peil, Sr., Ted Adams, Slim Whitaker. (aka **Billy the Kid in The Kid Rides Again**)

Dead Men Walk: Released 02/10/1943. © Producers Releasing Corp. 01/26/1943. Sigmund Neufeld Productions/Producers Releasing Corp. Director: Sam Newfield; Assistant Director: Melville De Lay; Producer: Sigmund Neufeld; Screenplay: Fred Myton; Cinematography: Jack Greenhalgh; Editor: Holbrook N. Todd; Production Manager: Bert Sternbach; Sound Engineer: Hans Weeren. Cast: George Zucco, Mary Carlisle, Nedrick Young, Dwight Frye, Fern Emmett, Robert Strange, Hal Price, Sam Flint.

Wild Horse Rustlers: Released 02/12/1943. © Producers Releasing Corp. 02/10/1943. Sigmund Neufeld Productions/Producers Releasing Corp. Director: Sam Newfield; Assistant Director: Melville De Lay; Producer: Sigmund Neufeld; Screenplay: Steve Braxton; Cinematography: Robert Cline; Editor: Holbrook N. Todd; Production Manager: Bert Sternbach; Sound Engineer: Hans Weeren. Cast: Bob Livingston, Al

St. John, Linda Johnson, Lane Chandler, Stanley Price, Frank Ellis, Karl Hackett. (working title **Western Saboteurs**; aka **Lone Rider in Wild Horse Rustlers**)

Queen of Broadway: Released 03/08/1943. © Producers Releasing Corp. 01/26/1943. S&N Productions/Producers Releasing Corp. Director: Sam Newfield; Assistant Director: Melville De Lay; Executive Producer: Sigmund Neufeld; Producer: Bert Sternbach, Sam Newfield (uncredited); Screenplay: Rusty McCullough, George Wallace Sayre; Story: George Wallace Sayre; Cinematography: Jack Greenhalgh; Editor: Holbrook N. Todd; Sound Engineer: Hans Weeren. Cast: Rochelle Hudson, Buster Crabbe, Paul Bryar, Emmett Lynn, Donald Mayo, Isabel La Mal, Blanche Rose, Henry Hall, John Dilson, Mil Kibbee, Vince Barnett, Jack Mulhall, Snowflake.

Fugitive of the Plains: Released 03/12/1943. © Producers Releasing Corp. 03/02/1943. Sigmund Neufeld Productions/Producers Releasing Corp. Director: Sam Newfield; Assistant Director: Melville De Lay; Producer: Sigmund Neufeld; Screenplay: George W. Sayre; Cinematography: Jack Greenhalgh; Editor: Holbrook N. Todd; Production Manager: Bert Sternbach; Sound Engineer: Hans Weeren. Cast: Buster Crabbe, Al St. John, Maxine Leslie, Jack Ingram, Kermit Maynard, Karl Hackett, Hal Price, George Chesebro, Frank Ellis, John Morton. (reissued in cutdown version in 1947 as **Raiders of Red Rock**)

My Son, the Hero: Released 04/05/1943. © Producers Releasing Corp. 03/23/1943. Atlantis Pictures/Producers Releasing Corp. Director: Edgar G. Ulmer; Assistant Director: Melville De Lay; Producer: Peter R. Van Duinen; Screenplay, Story: Doris Mallot, Edgar G. Ulmer; Additional Dialog: Sam Newfield; Cinematography: Robert Cline, Jack Greenhalgh; Editor: Charles Henkel, Jr.; Sound Engineer: Hans Weeren. Cast: Patsy Kelly, Roscoe Karns, Joan Blair, Carol Hughes, Maxie Rosenbloom, Luis Alberni, Joseph Allen Jr., Lois Collier, Jennie Le Gon, Nick Stewart, Hal Price, Al St. John, Elvira Gurcy, Isabel La Mel, Maxine Leslie.

Death Rides the Plains: Released 05/07/1943. © Producers Releasing Corp. 05/15/1943. Sigmund Neufeld Productions/Producers Releasing Corp. Director: Sam Newfield; Assistant Director: Melville De Lay; Producer: Sigmund Neufeld; Screenplay: Joseph O'Donnell; Story: Patricia Harper; Cinematography: Robert Cline; Editor: Holbrook N. Todd; Production Manager: Bert Sternbach; Sound Engineer: Hans Weeren. Cast: Bob Livingston, Al St. John, Nica Doret, Ray Bennett, I. Stanford Jolley, George Chesebro, John Elliott, Kermit Maynard, Silm Whitaker, Karl Hackett. (aka **Lone Rider in Death Rides the Plains**)

Western Cyclone: Released 05/14/1943. © Producers Releasing Corp. 05/10/1943. Sigmund Neufeld Productions/Producers Releasing Corp. Director: Sam Newfield; Assistant Director: Melville De Lay; Producer: Sigmund Neufeld; Screenplay: Patricia Harper; Cinematography: Robert Cline; Editor: Holbrook N. Todd; Production Manager: Bert Sternbach; Sound Engineer: Hans Weeren. Cast: Buster Crabbe, Al St. John, Marjorie Manners, Karl Hackett, Milton Kibbee, Glenn Strange, Charles King, Hal Price, Kermit Maynard, Bud Osborne. (aka **Billy the Kid in Western Cyclone**; reissued in cutdown version in 1947 as **Frontier Fighters**)

The Black Raven: Released 05/31/1943. © Producers Releasing Corp. 04/19/1943. Sigmund Neufeld Productions/Producers Releasing Corp. Director: Sam Newfield; Assistant Director: Melville De Lay; Producer: Sigmund Neufeld; Screenplay: Fred Myton; Cinematography: Robert Cline; Editor: Holbrook N. Todd; Production Manager: Bert Sternbach; Sound Engineer: Hans Weeren. Cast: George Zucco,

Wanda McKay, Noel Madison, Byron Foulger, Robert Middlemass, Charles Middleton, Robert Randall, Glenn Strange, I. Stanford Jolley.

Wolves of the Range: Released 06/21/1943. © Producers Releasing Corp. 06/18/1943. Sigmund Neufeld Productions/Producers Releasing Corp. Director: Sam Newfield; Assistant Director: Melville De Lay; Producer: Sigmund Neufeld; Screenplay: Joseph O'Donnell; Cinematography: Robert Cline; Editor: Holbrook N. Todd; Production Manager: Bert Sternbach; Sound Engineer: Hans Weeren. Cast: Bob Livingston, Al St. John, Frances Gladwin, I. Stanford Jolley, Karl Hackett, Ed Cassidy, Jack Ingram, Ken Duncan, Budd Buster, Bob Hill. (aka **Lone Rider in Wolves of the Range**)

The Renegade: Released 07/01/1943. © P.R.C. Pictures, Inc. 07/01/1943. Sigmund Neufeld Productions/Producers Releasing Corp. Director: Sam Newfield; Assistant Director: Melville De Lay; Producer: Sigmund Neufeld; Screenplay: Joe O'Donnell; Story: George Milton; Cinematography: Robert Cline; Editor: Holbrook N. Todd; Production Manager: Bert Sternbach; Sound Engineer: Hans Weeren. Cast: Buster Crabbe, Al St. John, Lois Ranson, Karl Hackett, Ray Bennett, Frank Hagney, Jack Rockwell, Tom London, George Chesebro. (aka **Billy the Kid in The Renegade**; reissued in cutdown version in 1947 as **Code of the Plains**)

Cattle Stampede: Released 08/16/1943. © Producers Releasing Corp. 08/21/1943. Sigmund Neufeld Productions/Producers Releasing Corp. Director: Sam Newfield; Assistant Director: Melville De Lay; Producer: Sigmund Neufeld; Screenplay: Joseph O'Donnell; Cinematography: Robert Cline; Editor: Holbrook N. Todd; Production Manager: Bert Sternbach; Sound Engineer: Corson Jowett. Cast: Buster Crabbe, Al St. John, Frances Gladwin, Charles King, Ed Cassidy, Hansel Werner, Ray Bennett, Frank Ellie, Steve Clark, Roy Brent, John Elliott, Budd Buster. (aka **Billy the Kid in Cattle Stampede**)

Danger! Women at Work: Released 08/23/1943. © P.R.C. Pictures, Inc. 08/23/1943. Jack Schwarz Productions/Producers Releasing Corp. Director: Sam Newfield; Assistant Director: Melville De Lay; Producer: Jack Schwarz; Associate Producer: Harry D. Edwards; Screenplay: Martin Mooney; Story: Gertrude Walker, Edgar G. Ulmer; Cinematography: Ira Morgan; Editor: Robert O. Crandall; Production Manager: Bert Sternbach; Sound Engineer: Corson Jowett. Cast: Patsy Kelly, Mary Brian, Isabel Jewell, Wanda McKay, Betty Compson, Cobina Wright, Sr.

Law of the Saddle: Released 08/28/1943. © Producers Releasing Corp. 09/18/1943. Sigmund Neufeld Productions/Producers Releasing Corp. Director: Melville De Lay; Assistant Director: Al Schnee; Producer: Sigmund Neufeld; Screenplay: Fred Myton; Cinematography: Robert Cline; Editor: Holbrook N. Todd; Production Manager: Bert Sternbach; Sound Engineer: Corson Jowett. Cast: Bob Livingston, Al St. John, Betty Miles, Lane Chandler, John Elliott, Reed Howes, Curley Dresden, Al Ferguson, Frank Ellis. (aka **Lone Rider and Law of the Saddle**)

Blazing Frontier: Released 09/01/1943. © Producers Releasing Corp. 08/21/1943. Sigmund Neufeld Productions/Producers Releasing Corp. Director: Sam Newfield; Assistant: Melville De Lay; Producer: Sigmund Neufeld; Screenplay: Patricia Harper; Cinematography: Robert Cline; Editor: Holbrook N. Todd; Production Manager: Bert Sternbach; Sound Engineer: Hans Weeren. Cast: Buster Crabbe, Al St. John, Marjorie Manners, Milton Kibbee, I. Stanford Jolley, Frank Hagney, Kermit Maynard, George Chesebro, Frank Ellis.

Tiger Fangs: Released 09/10/1943. © P.R.C. Pictures, Inc. 10/09/1943. Jack Schwarz Productions/Producers Releasing Corp. Director: Sam Newfield; Assistant Director: Lou Perlof; Producer: Jack Schwarz; Associate Producer: Fred McConnell; Screenplay: Arthur St. Claire; Cinematography: Ira Morgan; Editor: George M. Merrick; Production Manager: George M. Merrick; Sound Engineer: Ben Winkler. Cast: Frank Buck, June Duprez, Duncan Renaldo, Howard Banks, J. Farrell MacDonald.

Raiders of Red Gap: Released 09/30/1943. © P.R.C. Pictures, Inc. 10/10/1943. Sigmund Neufeld Productions/Producers Releasing Corp. Director: Sam Newfield; Assistant Director: Alex Finlayson; Producer: Sigmund Neufeld; Screenplay: Joseph O'Donnell; Cinematography: Robert Cline; Editor: Holbrook N. Todd; Production Manager: Bert Sternbach; Sound Engineer: Lyle Willey. Cast: Bob Livingston, Al St. John, Myrna Dell, Ed Cassidy, Charles King, Kermit Maynard, Roy Brent, Frank Ellis, George Chesebro. (aka **Lone Rider in Raiders of Red Gap**)

Devil Riders: Released 11/05/1943. © P.R.C. Pictures, Inc. 11/06/1943. Sigmund Neufeld Productions/Producers Releasing Corp. Director: Sam Newfield; Assistant Director: Melville De Lay; Producer: Sigmund Neufeld; Screenplay: Joseph O'Donnell; Cinematography: Robert Cline; Editor: Bob Crandall; Production Manager: Bert Sternbach; Sound Engineer: Lyle Willey. Cast: Buster Crabbe, Al St. John, Patti McCarthy; Charles King, John Merton, Kermit Maynard, Frank LaRue, Jack Ingram, George Chesebro, Ed Cassidy.

Harvest Melody: Released 11/22/1943. © P.R.C. Pictures, Inc. 11/22/1943. Producers Releasing Corp. Director: Sam Newfield; Assistant Director: Melville De Lay; Producer: Walter Colmes; Screenplay: Allan Gale; Story: Martin Mooney, Ande Lamb; Cinematography: James Brown; Editor: Holbrook N. Todd; Production Manager: Bert Sternbach; Sound Engineer: Corson Jowett. Cast: Rosemary Lane, Johnny Downs, Charlotte Wynters, Sheldon Leonard, Luis Alberni, Claire Rochelle, Syd Saylor, Marjorie Manners, Henry Hall, Billy Nelson, Frances Gladwin, Marin Sais, Herbert Hayes.

The Drifter: Released 12/20/1943. © P.R.C. Pictures, Inc. 12/01/1943. Sigmund Neufeld Productions/Producers Releasing Corp. Director: Sam Newfield; Assistant Director: Melville De Lay; Producer: Sigmund Neufeld; Screenplay: Patricia Harper; Cinematography: Robert Cline; Editor: Holbrook N. Todd; Production Manager: Bert Sternbach; Sound Engineer: Lyle Willey. Cast: Buster Crabbe, Al St. John, Carol Parker, Jack Ingram, Kermit Maynard, Roy Brent, George Chesebro, Ray Bennett, Jimmy Aubrey, Slim Whitaker.

Nabonga: Released 01/25/1944. © P.R.C. Pictures, Inc. 01/30/1944. Sigmund Neufeld Productions/Producers Releasing Corp. Director: Sam Newfield; Assistant Director: Melville De Lay; Producer: Sigmund Neufeld; Screenplay: Fred Myton; Cinematography: Robert Cline; Editor: Holbrook N. Todd; Production Manager: Bert Sternbach; Sound Engineer: Corson Jowett. Cast: Buster Crabbe, Barton MacLane, Fifi D'Orsay, Julie London, Bryant Washburn, Herbert Rawlinson, Prince Modupe, Jackie Newfield, Nbongo the Gorilla. (working titles **Drums of the Jungle**, **Jungle Fury**, and **Jungle Terror**; aka **Nabonga Gorilla**)

Frontier Outlaws: Released 03/04/1944. © P.R.C. Pictures, Inc. 04/04/1944. Sigmund Neufeld Productions/Producers Releasing Corp. Director: Sam Newfield; Assistant Director: Melville De Lay; Producer: Sigmund Neufeld; Screenplay: Joseph

O'Donnell; Cinematography: Robert Cline; Editor: Holbrook N. Todd; Production Manager: Bert Sternbach; Sound Engineer: Art Smith. Cast: Buster Crabbe, Al St. John, Frances Gladwin, Marin Sais, Charles King, Jack Ingram, Kermit Maynard, Edward Cassidy, Emmett Lynn, Budd Buster, Falcon the Horse.

Thundering Gun Slingers: Released 03/25/1944. © P.R.C. Pictures, Inc. 03/15/1944. Sigmund Neufeld Productions/Producers Releasing Corp. Director: Sam Newfield; Assistant Director: Melville De Lay; Producer: Sigmund Neufeld; Screenplay: Fred Myton; Cinematography: Robert Cline; Editor: Holbrook N. Todd; Production Manager: Bert Sternbach; Sound Engineer: Glen Glenn. Cast: Buster Crabbe, Al St. John, Frances Gladwin, Karl Hackett, Charles King, Jack Ingram, Kermit Maynard, Budd Buster, George Chesebro, Falcon the Horse.

The Monster Maker: Released 04/15/1944. © P.R.C. Pictures, Inc. 04/15/1944. Sigmund Neufeld Productions/Producers Releasing Corp. Director: Sam Newfield; Assistant Director: Melville De Lay; Producer: Sigmund Neufeld; Screenplay: Pierre Gendron, Martin Mooney; Story: Lawrence Williams; Cinematography: Robert Cline (uncredited); Editor: Holbrook N. Todd; Production Manager: Bert Sternbach; Sound Engineer: Ferol Redd. Cast: J. Carrol Naish, Ralph Morgan, Tala Birell, Wanda McKay, Terry Frost, Glenn Strange, Alexander Pollard, Sam Flint, Ace. (working title **The Devil's Apprentice**)

Valley of Vengeance: Released 05/05/1944. © P.R.C. Pictures, Inc. 05/15/1944. Sigmund Neufeld Productions/Producers Releasing Corp. Director: Sam Newfield; Assistant Director: Melville De Lay; Producer: Sigmund Neufeld; Screenplay: Joseph O'Donnell; Cinematography: Jack Greenhalgh; Editor: Holbrook N. Todd; Production Manager: Bert Sternbach; Sound Engineer: Glen Glenn. Cast: Buster Crabbe, Al St. John, Evelyn Finley, Donald Mayo, David Polonsky, Glenn Strange, Charles King, John Merton, Lynton Brent, Jack Ingram, Bud Osborne, Nora Bush, Steve Clark, Falcon the Horse.

The Contender: Released 05/10/1944. © P.R.C. Pictures, Inc. 05/10/1944. S&N Productions/Producers Releasing Corp. Director: Sam Newfield; Assistant Director: Melville De Lay; Producer: Bert Sternbach; Executive Producer: Sigmund Neufeld (uncredited); Screenplay: George Sayre, Jay Doten, Raymond Schrock; Story: George Sayre, Jay Doten; Cinematography: Robert Cline; Editor: Holbrook N. Todd; Sound Engineer: Ferol Redd. Cast: Buster Crabbe, Arline Judge, Julie Gibson, Donald Mayo, Roland Drew, Milton Kibbee, Glenn Strange, Sam Flint, Duke York, George Turner. (working titles **Ringside** and **My Boy**)

Fuzzy Settles Down: Released 07/25/1944. © P.R.C. Pictures, Inc. 07/12/1944. Sigmund Neufeld Productions/Producers Releasing Corp. Director: Sam Newfield; Assistant Director: Melville De Lay; Producer: Sigmund Neufeld; Screenplay, Story: Louise Rousseau; Cinematography: Jack Greenhalgh; Editor: Holbrook N. Todd; Production Manager: Bert Sternbach; Sound Engineer: Glen Glenn. Cast: Buster Crabbe, Al St. John, Patti McCarty, Charles King, John Merton, Frank McCarroll, Hal Price, John Elliott, Ed Cassidy, Robert Hill, Falcon the Horse.

Rustlers' Hideout: Released 09/02/1944. © P.R.C. Pictures, Inc. 09/02/1944. Sigmund Neufeld Productions/Producers Releasing Corp. Director: Sam Newfield; Assistant Director: Melville De Lay; Producer: Sigmund Neufeld; Screenplay, Story: Joseph O'Donnell; Cinematography: Jack Greenhalgh; Editor: Holbrook N. Todd; Production Manager: Bert Sternbach; Sound Engineer: Glen Glenn. Cast: Buster

Crabbe, Al St. John, Patti McCarty, Charles King, John Merton, Terry Frost, Hal Price, Lane Chandler, Al Ferguson, Frank McCarroll, Ed Cassidy, Falcon the Horse. (working title **Phantom of Wild Valley**)

Swing Hostess: Released 09/08/1944. © P.R.C. Pictures, Inc. 09/08/1944. Sigmund Neufeld Productions/Producers Releasing Corp. Director: Sam Newfield; Producer: Sigmund Neufeld; Screenplay: Louise Rousseau, Gail Davenport; Story: Louise Rousseau "Records for Romance"; Cinematography: Jack Greenhalgh; Editor: Holbrook N. Todd; Production Manager: Bert Sternbach; Sound Engineer: Max Hutchinson. Cast: Martha Tilton, Iris Adrian, Charles Collins, Cliff Nazarro, Harry Holman, Emmett Lynn, Betty Brodel, Claire Rochelle, Paul Porcasi, Terry Frost, Phil Van Zandt, Earle Bruce.

Wild Horse Phantom: Released 10/28/1944. © P.R.C. Pictures, Inc. 10/28/1944. Sigmund Neufeld Productions/Producers Releasing Corp. Director: Sam Newfield; Assistant Director: Harold E. Knox; Producer: Sigmund Neufeld; Screenplay, Story: George Milton; Cinematography: Jack Greenhalgh; Editor: Holbrook N. Todd; Production Manager: Bert Sternbach; Sound Engineer: Arthur Smith. Cast: Buster Crabbe, Al St. John, Elaine Morey, Kermit Maynard, Budd Buster, Hal Price, Robert Meredith, Frank Ellis, Frank McCarroll, Bob Cason, John Elliott, Falcon the Horse.

I Accuse My Parents: Released 11/04/1944. © P.R.C. Pictures, Inc. 12/15/1944. Alexander-Stern Productions/Producers Releasing Corp. Director: Sam Newfield; Assistant Director: Melville De Lay; Producer: Max Alexander; Screenplay: Harry Fraser, Marjorie Dudley; Story: Arthur Caesar; Cinematography: Robert Cline; Editor: Charles Henkel, Jr.; Sound Engineer: Arthur B. Smith. Cast: Mary Beth Hughes, Robert Lowell, John Miljan, Vivienne Osborne, George Meeker, Edward Earle, George Lloyd, Patricia Knox, Florence Johnson, Richard Bartell.

Oath of Vengeance: Released 12/09/1944. © P.R.C. Pictures, Inc. 12/09/1944. Sigmund Neufeld Productions/Producers Releasing Corp. Director: Sam Newfield; Assistant Director: Harold E. Knox; Producer: Sigmund Neufeld; Screenplay: Fred Myton; Cinematography: Robert Cline; Editor: Holbrook N. Todd; Production Manager: Bert Sternbach; Sound Engineer: Arthur Smith. Cast: Buster Crabbe, Al St. John, Mady Laurence, Jack Ingram, Charles King, Marin Sais, Karl Hackett, Kermit Maynard, Hal Price, Frank Ellis, Falcon the Horse.

His Brother's Ghost: Released 02/03/1945. © P.R.C. Pictures, Inc. 03/03/1945. Sigmund Neufeld Productions/Producers Releasing Corp. Director: Sam Newfield; Assistant Director: Harold E. Knox; Producer: Sigmund Neufeld; Screenplay, Story: George Milton; Cinematography: Jack Greenhalgh; Editor: Holbrook N. Todd; Production Manager: Bert Sternbach; Sound Engineer: Arthur Smith. Cast: Buster Crabbe, Al St. John, Charles King, Karl Hackett, Archie Hall, Roy Brent, Bud Osborne, Bob Cason, Frank McCarroll, George Morrell.

The Kid Sister: Released 02/06/1945. © P.R.C. Pictures, Inc. 02/06/1945. Sigmund Neufeld Productions/Producers Releasing Corp. Director: Sam Newfield; Assistant Director: Melville De Lay; Producer: Sigmund Neufeld; Screenplay, Story: Fred Myton; Cinematography: James Brown; Editor: Holbrook N. Todd; Production Manager: Bert Sternbach; Sound Engineer: Max Hutchinson. Cast: Roger Pryor, Judy Clark, Frank Jenks, Constance Worth, Tommy Dugan, Richard Byron, Minerva Urecal, Ruth Robinson, Peggy Wynne.

Shadows of Death: Released 04/19/1945. © P.R.C. Pictures, Inc. 04/19/1945. Sigmund Neufeld Productions/Producers Releasing Corp. Director: Sam Newfield; Assistant Director: Melville De Lay; Producer: Sigmund Neufeld; Screenplay, Story: Fred Myton; Cinematography: Jack Greenhalgh; Editor: Holbrook N. Todd; Production Manager: Bert Sternbach; Sound Engineer: Glen Glenn. Cast: Buster Crabbe, Al St. John, Dona Dax, Charles King, Karl Hackett, Edward Hall, Frank Ellis, Bob Cason.

The Lady Confesses: Released 05/16/1945. © P.R.C. Pictures, Inc. 05/16/1945. Alexander-Stern Productions/Producers Releasing Corp. Director: Sam Newfield; Assistant Director: Harold E. Knox; Producer: Alfred Stern; Screenplay: Helen Martin; Story: Irwin R. Franklyn; Cinematography: Jack Greenhalgh; Editor: Holbrook N. Todd; Sound Engineer: Arthur B. Smith. Cast: Mary Beth Hughes, Hugh Beaumont, Edmund MacDonald, Claudia Drake, Emmett Vogan, Barbara Slater, Edward Howard, Dewey Robinson, Carol Andrews. (working title **Undercover Girl**)

Gangster's Den: Released 06/14/1945. © P.R.C. Pictures, Inc. 07/14/1945. Sigmund Neufeld Productions/Producers Releasing Corp. Director: Sam Newfield; Assistant Director: Melville De Lay; Producer: Sigmund Neufeld; Screenplay, Story: George Plympton; Cinematography: Jack Greenhalgh; Editor: Holbrook N. Todd; Production Manager: Bert Sternbach; Sound Engineer: Charles Althouse, Glen Glenn. Cast: Buster Crabbe, Al St. John, Sydney Logan, Charles King, Emmett Lynn, Kermit Maynard, Edward Cassidy, Stan Jolley, George Chesebro, Karl Hackett, Michael Owen.

Stagecoach Outlaws: Released 08/17/1945. © P.R.C. Pictures, Inc. 08/17/1945. Sigmund Neufeld Productions/Producers Releasing Corp. Director: Sam Newfield; Assistant Director: William A. O'Connor; Producer: Sigmund Neufeld; Screenplay, Story: Fred Myton; Cinematography: Jack Greenhalgh; Editor: Holbrook N. Todd; Production Manager: Bert Sternbach; Sound Engineer: Glen Glenn. Cast: Buster Crabbe, Al St. John, Frances Gladwin, Ed Cassidy, Stanford Jolley, Kermit Maynard, Bob Cason, Robert Kortman, Steve Clark.

Apology for Murder: Released 09/27/1945. © P.R.C. Pictures, Inc. 09/27/1945. Sigmund Neufeld Productions/Producers Releasing Corp. Director: Sam Newfield; Producer: Sigmund Neufeld; Screenplay, Story: Fred Myton; Cinematography: Jack Greenhalgh; Editor: Holbrook N. Todd; Production Manager: Bert Sternbach; Sound Engineer: Ben Winkler. Cast: Ann Savage, Hugh Beaumont, Russell Hicks, Charles D. Brown, Pierre Watkin, Sarah Padden, Norman Willis, Eva Novak, Budd Buster, George Sherwood, Wheaton Chambers. (working titles **Single Indemnity** and **Highway to Hell**)

Border Badmen: Released 10/10/1945. © P.R.C. Pictures, Inc. 10/10/1945. Sigmund Neufeld Productions/Producers Releasing Corp. Director: Sam Newfield; Assistant Director: William O'Connor. Producer: Sigmund Neufeld; Screenplay, Story: George Milton; Cinematography: Jack Greenhalgh; Editor: Holbrook N. Todd; Production Manager: Bert Sternbach; Sound Engineer: Lyle Willey. Cast: Buster Crabbe, Al St. John, Lorraine Miller, Charles King, Raphael Bennett, Archie Hall, Budd Buster, Marlyn Gladstone, Marin Sais.

Fighting Bill Carson: Released 10/31/1945. © P.R.C. Pictures, Inc. 10/31/1945. Sigmund Neufeld Productions/Producers Releasing Corp. Director: Sam Newfield; Assistant Director: William O'Connor; Producer: Sigmund Neufeld; Screenplay,

Story: Louise Rousseau; Cinematography: Jack Greenhalgh; Editor: Holbrook N. Todd; Production Manager: Bert Sternbach; Sound Engineer: Lyle Willey. Cast: Buster Crabbe, Al St. John, Kay Hughes, Stanford Jolley, Kermit Maynard, Bob Cason, John L. Buster, Bud Osborne.

White Pongo: Released 11/02/1945. © P.R.C. Pictures, Inc. 08/10/1945. Sigmund Neufeld Productions/Producers Releasing Corp. Director: Sam Newfield; Producer: Sigmund Neufeld; Screenplay, Story: Raymond L. Schrock; Cinematography: Jack Greenhalgh; Editor: Holbrook N. Todd; Production Manager: Bert Sternbach; Sound Engineer: John Carter. Cast: Richard Fraser, Maris Wrixon, Lionel Royce, Al Eben, Gordon Richards, Michael Dyne, George Lloyd, Larry Steers, Milton Kibbee, Egon Brecher, Joel Fluellen. (working titles **Congo Pongo** and **White Gorilla**)

Prairie Rustlers: Released 11/07/1945. © P.R.C. Pictures, Inc. 11/20/1945. Sigmund Neufeld Productions/Producers Releasing Corp. Director: Sam Newfield; Assistant Director: William O'Connor; Producer: Sigmund Neufeld; Screenplay, Story: Fred Myton; Cinematography: Jack Greenhalgh; Editor: Holbrook N. Todd; Production Manager: Bert Sternbach; Sound Engineer: Lyle Willey. Cast: Buster Crabbe, Al St. John, Evelyn Finley, Karl Hackett, Stanford Jolley, Bud Osborne, Kermit Maynard.

Lightning Raiders: Released 01/07/1946. © P.R.C. Pictures, Inc. 12/10/1945. Sigmund Neufeld Productions/Producers Releasing Corp. Director: Sam Newfield; Assistant Director: Stanley Neufeld; Producer: Sigmund Neufeld; Screenplay, Story: Elmer Clifton; Cinematography: Jack Greenhalgh; Editor: Holbrook N. Todd; Production Manager: Bert Sternbach; Sound Engineer: Lyle Willey. Cast: Buster Crabbe, Al St. John, Mady Laurence, Henry Hall, Steve Darrell, Stanford Jolley, Karl Hackett, Roy Brent, Marin Sais, Al Ferguson.

Mantan Messes Up: Released 02/10/1946. No copyright registered. Lucky Star Productions/Toddy Pictures. Director: Sam Newfield (John Reese on some promotional posters); Producer: Ted Toddy. Cast: Mantan Moreland, Monty Hawley, Jo Rhetta, Daryce Bradley, Lola Carrington, Raymond Harris, Lena Horne, Eddie Green, Buck and Bubbles, Nina Mae McKinney, Red Caps, The Four Tones, Bo Jinkins.

The Flying Serpent: Released 02/20/1946. © P.R.C. Pictures, Inc. 02/01/1946. Sigmund Neufeld Productions/Producers Releasing Corp. Director: Sam Newfield (as Sherman Scott); Producer: Sigmund Neufeld; Screenplay, Story: John T. Neville; Cinematography: Jack Greenhalgh; Editor: Holbrook N. Todd; Production Manager: Bert Sternbach; Sound Engineer: Frank McWhorter; Script Clerk: Violet Newfield. Cast: George Zucco, Ralph Lewis, Hope Kramer, Eddie Acuff, Wheaton Chambers, James Metcalfe, Henry Hall, Milton Kibbee, Budd Buster, Terry Frost. (working title **The Feathered Serpent**)

House-Rent Party: Released 03/10/1946. No copyright registered. Toddy Pictures. Director: Sam Newfield; Producer: Ted Toddy; Screenplay: Sam Newfield, Ted Toddy; Cinematography: Jack Etra; Editor: Elmer J. McGovern; Production Manager: Sandra Hickman; Sound Engineer: Nelson Minnerly. Cast: Pigmeat Markham, John "Rastus" Murray, Alfred Cortez, David Bethea, Claude Demetri, Rudolph Toombs, Bill Dillard, Lance Taylor, Lou Swarz, Hannah Sylvester, Kay Freeman, Willie Drake, Oozie Mallon's Jitterbugs, Macbeth's Calypso Band.

Gentlemen with Guns: Released 03/27/1946. © Pathe Industries, Inc. 06/22/1946. Sigmund Neufeld Productions/Producers Releasing Corp. Director: Sam Newfield; Producer: Sigmund Neufeld; Screenplay, Story: Fred Myton; Cinematography: Jack Greenhalgh; Editor: Holbrook N. Todd; Production manager: Bert Sternbach; Sound Engineer: Lyle Willey. Cast: Buster Crabbe, Al St. John, Patricia Knox, Steve Darrell, George Chesebro, Karl Hackett, Budd Buster, Frank Ellis.

Fight That Ghost: Released 04/10/1946. No copyright registered. Toddy Pictures. Director: Sam Newfield; Producer: Ted Toddy; Screenplay: Sam Newfield, Ted Toddy; Cinematography: Jack Etra; Editor: Elmer J. McGovern; Production Manager: Sandra Hickman; Sound Engineer: Nelson Minnerly. Cast: Pigmeat Markham, John Rastus Murray, Alberta Pryne, Percy Verwayne, David Bethea, Claire Leyba, Bill Dillard, George Wiltshire, Wen Talbert, Clarice Graham, Ray Allen, Rudolph Toombs, Milton Woods, Sidney Easton.

Murder Is My Business: Released 04/10/1946. © Pathe Industries, Inc. 06/18/1946. Sigmund Neufeld Productions/Producers Releasing Corp. Director: Sam Newfield; Assistant Director: Stanley Neufeld; Producer: Sigmund Neufeld; Screenplay: Fred Myton; Story: Brett Halliday; Cinematography: Jack Greenhalgh; Editor: Holbrook N. Todd; Sound Engineer: Earl Sitar. Cast: Hugh Beaumont, Cheryl Walker, Lyle Talbot, George Meeker, Pierre Watkin, Richard Keene, David Reed, Carol Andrews, Julia McMillan, Helen Heigh, Ralph Dunn, Parker Garvie, Virginia Christine, Donald Kerr.

Pigmeat Markham's Laugh Hepcats: Released 06/1946. No copyright registered. Toddy Pictures. Director: Sam Newfield. Cast: Pigmeat Markham, Monte Hawley, Lillian Randolph, Laurence Criner, Johnny Taylor, Vernon McCalla, Millie Monroe. (aka **Pigmeat's Laugh Hepcats**)

Ghost of Hidden Valley: Released 06/03/1946. © Pathe Industries, Inc. 06/03/1946. Sigmund Neufeld Productions/Producers Releasing Corp. Director: Sam Newfield; Assistant Director: Stanley Neufeld; Producer: Sigmund Neufeld; Screenplay, Story: Ellen Coyle; Cinematography: Art Reed; Editor: Holbrook N. Todd; Production Manager: Bert Sternbach; Sound Engineer: Glen Glenn. Cast: Buster Crabbe, Al St. John, Jean Carlin, John Meredith, Charles King, Jimmy Aubrey, Karl Hackett, John L. Cason, Silver Harr, Zon Murray.

Larceny in Her Heart: Released 07/10/1946. © Pathe Industries, Inc. 06/18/1946. Sigmund Neufeld Productions/Producers Releasing Corp. Director: Sam Newfield; Assistant Director: Stanley Neufeld; Producer: Sigmund Neufeld; Screenplay: Raymond L. Schrock; Story: Brett Halliday; Cinematography: Jack Greenhalgh; Editor: Holbrook N. Todd; Production Manager: Bert Sternbach; Sound Engineer: Earl Sitar. Cast: Hugh Beaumont, Cheryl Walker, Ralph Dunn, Paul Bryar, Charles Wilson, Douglas Fowley, Gordon Richards, Charles Quigley, Marie Harmon, Lee Bennett, Julia McMillan, Milton Kibbee. (working titles **Crime on My Hands** and **Crime in the Night**)

Prairie Badmen: Released 07/17/1946. © Pathe Industries, Inc. 07/09/1946. Sigmund Neufeld Productions/Producers Releasing Corp. Director: Sam Newfield; Assistant Director: Stanley Neufeld; Producer: Sigmund Neufeld; Screenplay, Story: Fred Myton; Cinematography: Robert Cline; Editor: Holbrook N. Todd; Production Manager: Bert Sternbach; Sound Engineer: Glen Glenn. Cast: Buster Crabbe, Al St.

John, Patricia Knox, Charles King, Ed Cassidy, Kermit Maynard, John L. Cason, Steve Clark, Frank Ellis, John L. Buster. (working title **Dangerous Men**)

Queen of Burlesque: Released 07/24/1946. © Pathe Industries, Inc. 07/04/1946. Alexander-Stern Productions/Producers Releasing Corp. Director: Sam Newfield; Assistant Director: Louis Germonprez; Producer: Arthur Alexander, Alfred Stern; Screenplay: David A Lang; Cinematography: Vincent J. Farrar; Editor: Jack Ogilvie; Production Manager: Norman Cook; Sound Engineer: John Carter. Cast: Evelyn Ankers, Carleton Young, Craig Reynolds, Rose La Rose, Emory Parnell, Murray Leonard, Nolan Leary, Gordon Clark, Alice Fleming, Jacqueline Dalya, Red Marshall, David Frisco, Charles King.

Terrors on Horseback: Released 08/14/1946. © Pathe Industries, Inc. 08/14/1946. Sigmund Neufeld Productions/Producers Releasing Corp. Director: Sam Newfield; Assistant Director: Stanley Neufeld; Producer: Sigmund Neufeld; Screenplay, Story: George Milton; Cinematography: Jack Greenhalgh; Editor: Holbrook N. Todd; Production Manager: Bert Sternbach; Sound Engineer: Lyle Willey. Cast: Buster Crabbe, Al St. John, Patti McCarty, Stanford Jolley, Kermit Maynard, Henry Hall, Karl Hackett, Marin Sais, Budd Buster, Steve Darrell, Steve Clark.

Overland Riders: Released 08/21/1946. © Pathe Industries, Inc. 08/21/1946. Sigmund Neufeld Productions/Producers Releasing Corp. Director: Sam Newfield; Assistant Director: Stanley Neufeld; Producer: Sigmund Neufeld; Screenplay, Story: Ellen Coyle; Cinematography: Jack Greenhalgh; Editor: Holbrook N. Todd; Production Manager: Bert Sternbach; Sound Engineer: Earl Sitar. Cast: Buster Crabbe, Al St. John, Patti McCarty, Slim Whitaker, Bud Osborne, Jack O'Shea, Frank Ellis, Al Ferguson, John L. Cason, George Chesebro, Lane Bradford.

Blonde for a Day: Released 08/29/1946. © Pathe Industries, Inc. 07/06/1946. Sigmund Neufeld Productions/Producers Releasing Corp. Director: Sam Newfield; Assistant Director: Stanley Neufeld; Producer: Sigmund Neufeld; Screenplay: Fred Myton; Story: Brett Halliday; Cinematographer: Jack Greenhalgh; Editor: Holbrook N. Todd; Production Manager: Bert Sternbach; Sound Engineer: Franklin Hansen. Cast: Hugh Beaumont, Kathryn Adams, Cy Kendall, Marjorie Hoshelle, Richard Fraser, Paul Bryar, Mauritz Hugo, Charles Wilson, Sonia Sorel, Frank Ferguson, Claire Rochelle. (working title **Blondes on the Loose**)

Outlaws of the Plains: Released 09/22/1946. © Pathe Industries, Inc. 09/22/1946. Sigmund Neufeld Productions/Producers Releasing Corp. Director: Sam Newfield; Assistant Director: Stanley Neufeld; Producer: Sigmund Neufeld; Screenplay: A. Fredric Evans; Story: Elmer Clifton; Cinematography: Jack Greenhalgh; Editor: Holbrook N. Todd; Production Manager: Bert Sternbach; Sound Engineer: Elden Ruberg. Cast: Buster Crabbe, Al St. John, Patti McCarty, Charles King, Jr., Karl Hackett, Jack O'Shea, Bud Osborne, Budd Buster, Roy Brent, Slim Whitaker.

Gas House Kids: Released 10/28/1946. © P.R.C. Pictures, Inc. 10/07/1946. Sigmund Neufeld Productions/Producers Releasing Corp. Director: Sam Newfield; Assistant Director: Stanley Neufeld; Producer: Sigmund Neufeld; Screenplay: Elsie and George Bricker, Raymond L. Schrock; Story: Elsie and George Bricker; Cinematography: Jack Greenhalgh; Editor: Holbrook N. Todd; Production Manager: Bert Sternbach; Sound Engineer: John Carter. Cast: Robert Lowery, Billy Halop, Teala Loring, Carl Switzer, David Reed, Rex Downing, Rocco Lanzo, Hope Landin, Ralph Dunn, Paul Bryar,

Nannette Vallon, Charles Wilson. (working titles **East Side, West Side** and **East Side Rascals**)

Lady Chaser: Released 11/25/1946. © Pathe Industries, Inc. 11/25/1946. Sigmund Neufeld Productions/Producers Releasing Corp. Director: Sam Newfeld; Assistant Director: Stanley Neufeld; Producer: Sigmund Neufeld; Screenplay: Fred Myton; Story: G.T. Fleming-Roberts; Cinematography: Jack Greenhalgh; Editor: Holbrook N. Todd; Production Manager: Bert Sternbach; Sound Engineer: Charles Kenworthy. Cast: Robert Lowery, Ann Savage, Inez Cooper, Frank Ferguson, William Haade, Ralph Dunn, Paul Bryar, Charles Williams, Garry Owen, Marie Martino. (working title **Lady Killer**)

Three on a Ticket: Released 04/05/1947. © Pathe Industries, Inc. 03/03/1947. Sigmund Neufeld Productions/Producers Releasing Corp. Director: Sam Newfeld; Assistant Director: Stanley Neufeld; Producer: Sigmund Neufeld; Screenplay: Fred Myton; Story: Brett Halliday; Cinematography: Jack Greenhalgh; Editor: Holbrook N. Todd; Production Manager: Bert Sternbach; Sound Engineer: John Carter. Cast: Hugh Beaumont, Cheryl Walker, Paul Bryar, Ralph Dunn, Louise Currie, Gavin Gordon, Charles Quigley, Douglas Fowley, Noel Cravat, Charles King, Brooks Benedict. (working title **The Corpse Came Calling**)

Jungle Flight: Released 08/22/1947. © Paramount Pictures Inc. 08/22/1947. Paramount Pictures. Director: Sam Newfeld (as Peter Stewart); Producer: William H. Pine, William C. Thomas; Screenplay: Whitman Chambers; Story: David Lang; Cinematography: Jack Greenhalgh, Fred Jackman, Jr.; Editor: Hal Gordon. Cast: Robert Lowery, Ann Savage, Barton MacLane, Douglas Fowley, Douglas Blackley, Curt Bois, Duncan Renaldo.

The Sea Hound: Released 09/04/1947. © Columbia Pictures Corp. 09/04/1947-12/11/1947. Esskay Productions/Columbia Pictures (15-part serial). Director: Sam Newfeld (five days' work only, uncredited; replaced by Mack V. Wright and Walter B. Eason); Producer: Sam Katzman; Screenplay: George H. Plympton, Lewis Clay, Arthur Hoerl; Cinematography: Ira H. Morgan; Editor: Earl Turner; Production Manager: David Katzman Cast: Buster Crabbe, Jimmy Lloyd, Pamela Blake, Ralph Hodges, Robert Barron, Hugh Prosser, Rick Vallin, Jack Ingram, Spencer Chan, Milton Kibbee, Al Baffert, Stan Blystone, Robert Duncan, Pierce Lyden, Rusty Westcoat.

Adventure Island: Released 10/10/1947. © Paramount Pictures Inc. 10/10/1947. Paramount Pictures. Cinecolor. Director: Sam Newfeld (as Peter Stewart); Producer: William H. Pine, William C. Thomas; Screenplay: Maxwell Shane; Story: Robert Louis Stevenson, Lloyd Osborne "Ebb-Tide"; Cinematography: Jack Greenhalgh; Editor: Howard Smith; Sound Engineer: John Myers. Cast: Rory Calhoun, Rhonda Fleming, Paul Kelly, John Abbott, Alan Napier.

Money Madness: Released 04/15/1948. © Film Classics Inc. 04/01/1948. Sigmund Neufeld Productions/Film Classics. Director: Sam Newfeld (as Peter Stewart); Assistant Director: Stanley Neufeld; Producer: Sigmund Neufeld; Screenplay: Al Martin; Cinematography: Jack Greenhalgh; Editor: Holbrook N. Todd; Production Manager: Bert Sternbach; Sound Engineer: Ben Winkler. Cast: Hugh Beaumont, Frances Rafferty, Harlan Warde, Cecil Weston, Ida Moore, Danny Morton, Joel Friedkin, Lane Chandler. (working title **The Easy Way**)

The Counterfeiters: Released 05/28/1948. © Twentieth Century-Fox Film Corp. 05/11/1948. Reliance Pictures/Twentieth Century Fox. Director: Sam Newfield (as Peter Stewart); Assistant Director: Stanley Neufeld; Executive Producer: Bert M. Stearn, Harry Hendel; Producer: Maurice Conn; Screenplay: Fred Myton, Barbara Worth; Story: Maurice H. Conn; Cinematography: James S. Brown, Jr.; Editor: Martin G. Cohn; Sound Engineer: John R. Carter. Cast: John Sutton, Doris Merrick, Hugh Beaumont, Lon Chaney, Jr., George O'Hanlon, Douglas Blackley, Herbert Rawlinson, Pierre Watkins, Don Harvey, Fred Coby, Joyce Lansing, Gerard Gilbert. (aka **Triple Cross**)

Lady at Midnight: Released 08/15/1948. © Pathe Industries, Inc 08/11/1948. John Sutherland Productions/Eagle-Lion Films. Director: Sam Newfield (as Sherman Scott); Assistant Director: Stanley Neufeld; Producer: John Sutherland; Screenplay, Story: Richard B. Sale; Cinematography: Jack Greenhalgh; Editor: Martin Cohn; Production Manager: Bert Sternbach; Sound Engineer: Ben Winkler. Cast: Richard Denning, Frances Rafferty, Lora Lee Michel, Ralph Dunn, Nana Bryant, Jackie Searle, Harlan Warde, Claudia Drake, Ben Welden.

Miraculous Journey: Released 09/01/1948. © Sigmund Neufeld Pictures, Inc. 09/20/1948. Sigmund Neufeld Pictures/Film Classics. Cinecolor. Director: Sam Newfield (as Peter Stewart); Assistant Director: Stanley Neufeld; Producer: Sigmund Neufeld; Screenplay, Story: Fred Myton; Cinematography: Jack Greenhalgh; Editor: Holbrook N. Todd; Production Manager: Bert Sternbach; Sound Engineer: Ben Winkler. Cast: Rory Calhoun, Audrey Long, Virginia Grey, George Cleveland, June Storey, Thurston Hall, Jim Bannon, Carole Donne, Tom Lane, Flame the Dog, Jim the Crow, Charlie the Chimp. (working title **Jungle Blindness**)

Unknown Island: Released 11/24/1948. © Albert Jay Cohen Productions, Inc. 12/01/1948. Albert Jay Cohen Productions/Film Classics. Cinecolor. Director: Jack Bernhard; Assistant Director: Clarence Eurist; Sigmund Neufeld Presents (unconfirmed; Promotional Stills Only); Producer: Albert J. Cohen; Screenplay: Robert T. Shannon, Jack Harvey; Story: Robert T. Shannon; Cinematography: Fred Jackman, Jr.; Editor: Harry Gerstad; Production Manager: Rudolph E. Abel; Sound: Max Hutchinson. Cast: Virginia Grey, Philip Reed, Richard Denning, Barton MacLane, Richard Wessel, Daniel White, Philip Nazir. (working title **The Unbelievable**; this credit for Neufeld is probably erroneous)

The Strange Mrs. Crane: Released 01/01/1949. © Pathe Industries, Inc. 12/18/1948. John Sutherland Productions/Eagle-Lion Films. Director: Sam Newfield (as Sherman Scott); Assistant Director: Stanley Neufeld; Producer: John Sutherland; Screenplay: Al Martin; Story: Frank Burt, Robert Libott; Cinematography: Jack Greenhalgh; Editor: Martin Cohn; Production Manager: Bert Sternbach; Sound Engineer: Ben Winkler. Cast: Marjorie Lord, Robert Shayne, Pierre Watkin, James Seay, Ruthe Brady, Claire Whitney, Mary Gordon, Chester Clute, Dorothy Granger, Charles Williams.

State Department: File 649: Released 02/15/1949. © Film Classics, Inc. 01/17/1949. Sigmund Neufeld Pictures/Film Classics. Cinecolor. Director: Sam Newfield (as Peter Stewart); Assistant Director: Stanley Neufeld; Producer: Sigmund Neufeld; Screenplay, Story: Milton Raison; Cinematography: Jack Greenhalgh; Editor: Holbrook N. Todd; Production Manager: Bert Sternbach; Sound Engineer: Ben Winkler. Cast: Virginia Bruce, William Lundigan, Jonathan Hale, Frank Ferguson,

Richard Loo, Philip Ahn, Raymond Bond, Milton Kibbee, Victor Sen Yung, Lora Lee Michel, John Holland, Harlan Warde, Carole Donne, Barbara Woodell, Robert Stephenson, Lee Bennett, H.T. Tsiang, Joseph Crehan, Ray Bennett, Nana Bryant. (working title **File 649: State Department**)

Wild Weed: Released 07/15/1949. No copyright registered. Hallmark Productions. Director: Sam Newfield (as Sherman Scott); Assistant Director: Stanley Neufeld (uncredited); Producer: Richard Kay; Executive Producers: Jack Jossey, Kroger Babb; Screenplay: Richard H. Landau; Story: Arthur Hoerl; Cinematography: Jack Greenhalgh; Editor: Richard Currier, Seth Larsen; Sound: William Randall. Cast: Alan Baxter, Lyle Talbot, Lila Leeds, Michael Whelan, Mary Ellen Popel, Doug Blackley, David Holt, Don Harvey, David Gorcey, Jack Elam, Dick Cogan. (aka **She Shoulda Said No!** and **The Devil's Weed**)

Radar Secret Service: Released 01/28/1950. © Lippert Productions, Inc. 01/10/1950. Lippert Pictures. Director: Sam Newfield; Executive Producer: Robert L. Lippert; Producer: Barney Sarecky; Screenplay: Beryl Sachs; Cinematography: Ernest Miller; Editor: Carl Pierson; Sound Engineer: Earl Snyder. Cast: John Howard, Adele Jergens, Tom Neal, Myrna Dell, Sid Melton, Ralph Byrd, Robert Kent, Pierre Watkins, Tristram Coffin, Riley Hill, Robert Carson, Kenne Duncan. (working title **Radar Patrol**)

Western Pacific Agent: Released 03/17/1950. © Lippert Productions, Inc. 03/10/1950. Lippert Pictures. Director: Sam Newfield; Producer: Sigmund Neufeld; Associate Producer: Irving Kay; Screenplay: Fred Myton; Story: Milton Raison; Cinematography: Ernest Miller; Editor: Carl Pierson; Production Manager: Bert Sternbach; Sound: Glen Glenn. Cast: Kent Taylor, Sheila Ryan, Mickey Knox, Morris Carnovsky, Robert Lowery, Sid Melton, Frank Richards, Dick Elliott, Ted Jacques, Anthony Jochim, Lee Phelps, Carla Martin, Margia Dean, Gloria Gray, Vera Marshe, Jack Geddes.

Motor Patrol: Released 06/29/1950. © Lippert Productions, Inc. 06/15/1950. Lippert Pictures. Director: Sam Newfield; Producer: Barney Sarecky; Associate Producer: Murray Lerner; Screenplay: Maurice Tombragel, Orville Hampton; Story: Maurice Tombragel; Cinematography: Ernest Miller; Editor: Stanley Frazen; Production Manager: Bert Sternbach; Sound Engineer: Glen Glenn. Cast: Don Castle, Jane Nigh, Bill Henry, Gwen O'Connor, Reed Hadley, Onslow Stevens, Dick Travis, Charles Victor, Sid Melton, Frank Jenks, Frank Jacquet, Lt. Lou Fuller, Charles Wagenheim, Margia Dean, Joe Greene, Carla Martin, Don Avelier, Irene Martin.

Hi-Jacked: Released 07/15/1950. © Lippert Productions, Inc. 07/10/1950. Lippert Pictures. Director: Sam Newfield; Executive Producer: Murray Lerner; Producer: Sigmund Neufeld; Screenplay: Fred Myton, Orville Hampton; Story: Ray Schrock, Fred Myton; Cinematography: Phil Tannura; Editor: Edward Mann; Production Manager: Bert Sternbach. Cast: Jim Davis, Marsha Jones, Sid Melton, David Bruce, Paul Cavanagh, Ralph Sanford, Iris Adrian, George Eldredge.

Three Desperate Men: Released 01/12/1951. © Mayflower Productions, Inc. 01/15/1951. Mayflower Productions/Lippert Pictures. Director: Sam Newfield; Assistant Director: Jack Berne; Executive Producer: Murray Lerner; Producer: Sigmund Neufeld; Screenplay, Story: Orville Hampton; Cinematographer: Jack Greenhalgh; Editor: Carl Pierson; Production Manager: Bert Sternbach; Sound Engineer: Max Hutchinson. Cast: Preston Foster, Jim Davis, Virginia Gray, Monte

Blue, Ross Latimer, Sid Melton, John Brown, Rory Mallinson, William Haade, Margaret Seddon, House Peters, Jr., Anthony Jochim, Joel Newfield. (working titles **Three Outlaws** and **The Daltons' Last Raid**)

Fingerprints Don't Lie: Released 02/23/1951. © Spartan Productions, Inc. 04/10/1951. Spartan Productions/Lippert Pictures. Director: Sam Newfield; Assistant Director: Stanley Neufeld; Producer: Sigmund Neufeld; Screenplay: Orville Hampton; Story: Rupert Hughes; Cinematography: Jack Greenhalgh; Editor: Harry Reynolds; Production Manager: Bert Sternbach; Sound Engineer: Glen Glenn. Cast: Richard Travis, Sheila Ryan, Sid Melton, Tom Neal, Margia Dean, Lyle Talbot, Michael Whalen, Richard Emory, Rory Mallinson, George Eldridge, Dee Tatum.

Mask of the Dragon: Released 03/17/1951. © Spartan Productions, Inc. 04/10/1951. Spartan Productions/Lippert Pictures. Director: Sam Newfield; Assistant Director: Stanley Neufeld; Producer: Sigmund Neufeld; Screenplay: Orville Hampton; Cinematography: Jack Greenhalgh; Editor: Carl Pierson; Production Manager: Bert Sternbach; Sound Engineer: Glen Glenn. Cast: Richard Travis, Sheila Ryan, Sid Melton, Michael Whalen, Lyle Talbot, Richard Emory, Mr. Moto, Dee Tatum, Jack Reitzen, Karl Davis, John Grant, Eddie Lee, Ray Singer, Carla Martin, Curt Barrett's Trailsmen.

Skipalong Rosenbloom: Released 04/20/1951. © Wally Kline Enterprises 02/14/1951. Wally Kline Enterprises/Eagle-Lion Classics. Director: Sam Newfield; Producer: Wally Kline; Screenplay: Dean Reisner, Eddie Forman; Story: Eddie Forman; Cinematography: Ernest Miller; Editor: Victor Lewis, J.R. Whitrredge. Cast: Maxie Rosenbloom, Max Baer, Hillary Brook, Raymond Hatton, Jackie Coogan, Jacqueline Fontaine, Fuzzy Knight, Ray Walker, Sam Lee, Al Shaw, Joe Greene, Dewey Robinson. (aka **The Square Shooter**)

Lost Continent: Released 08/17/1951. © Tom Productions, Inc. 08/15/1951. Tom Productions/Lippert Pictures. Director: Sam Newfield; Assistant Director: Stanley Neufeld; Executive Producer: Robert L. Lippert; Producer: Sigmund Neufeld; Associate Producer: Jack Leewood; Screenplay: Richard H. Landau, Orville Hampton (uncredited); Story: Carroll Young; Cinematography: Jack Greenhalgh; Editor: Phil Cahn; Production Manager: Bert Sternbach. Cast: Cesar Romero, Hillary Brooke, Chick Chandler, Sid Melton, John Hoyt, Hugh Beaumont, Whit Bissell, Acquanetta, Murray Alper.

Leave It to the Marines: Released 09/28/1951. © Tom Productions, Inc. 08/15/1951. Tom Productions/Lippert Pictures. Director: Sam Newfield (as Samuel Newfield); Producer: Sigmund Neufeld; Screenplay: Orville Hampton; Cinematography: Jack Greenhalgh; Editor: Carl Pierson; Production Design: Bert Sternbach; Sound: Glen Glenn. Cast: Sid Melton, Mara Lynn, Gregg Martel, Ida Moore, Sam Flint, Doug Evans, Margia Dean, Richard Monohan, William Haade, Jack George, Paul Bryar, Ezelle Poule, Will Orleans, Richard Farmer, Jimmy Cross.

Sky High: Released 10/12/1951. © Tom Productions, Inc. 08/08/1951. Tom Productions/Lippert Pictures. Director: Sam Newfield (as Samuel Newfield); Producer: Sigmund Neufeld; Screenplay: Orville Hampton; Cinematography: Jack Greenhalgh; Editor: Carl Pierson; Production Manager: Bert Sternbach; Sound: Glen Glenn. Cast: Sid Melton, Mara Lynn, Sam Flint, Doug Evans, Fritz Feld, Mark Krah, Margia Dean, Paul Bryar, Thayer Roberts, Don Frost, John Pelletti, Ernie Veneri,

John Phillips, Will Orleans, Peter Damon. (working titles **Up and At 'Em** and **Off We Go**)

Outlaw Women: Released 05/02/1952. © Howco Productions 12/18/1951. Howco Productions/Lippert Pictures. Presented by J. Frances White, Joy N. Houck; Director: Sam Newfield, Ron Ormond; Assistant Director: Clark Paylow, William Nolte; Producer: Ron Ormond; Associate Producer: June Carr; Screenplay: Orville Hampton; Cinematography: Ellis W. Carter, Harry C. Neumann; Editor: Hugh Winn; Sound: Glen Glenn. Cast: Marie Windsor, Richard Rober, Carla Balenda, Jackie Coogan, Allan Nixon, Jacqueline Fontaine, Billy House, Richard Avonde, Lyle Talbot, Maria Hart, Leonard Penn, Tom Tyler, Lou Lubin, Cliff Taylor, The Four Dandies, Connie Cezon, John Martin, Mary Hill, Sandy Sanders, Diane Fortier, Paul Gustine, Angela Stevens, Ted Cooper, Hazel Neilson, Clark Stevens, Riley Hill.

Scotland Yard Inspector: Released 10/31/1952. © Exclusive Films, Ltd. 11/05/1952. (British) Intercontinental Pictures/Exclusive Films/Lippert Pictures. Director: Sam Newfield; Assistant Director: Basil Keyes; Producer: Anthony Hinds; Screenplay: Orville Hampton, adapted from a popular B.B.C. serial by Lester Powell; Cinematography: Walter Harvey; Editor: James Needs; Production Manager: John Pinky Green; Sound: Bill Salter. Cast: Cesar Romero, Lois Maxwell, Bernadette O'Farrell, Lloyd Lamble, Geoffrey Keen, Campbell Singer, Alistair Hunter, Mary Mackenzie, Frank Birch, Wensley Pithey. (British title **Lady in the Fog**)

The Gambler and the Lady: Released 12/26/1952. © Exclusive Films Ltd. 12/16/1952. Exclusive Films Ltd/Lippert Pictures. Director: Sam Newfield, Patrick Jenkins; Assistant Director: Ted Holliday; Producer: Anthony Hinds; Cinematography: Walter Harvey; Editor: Maurice Rootes; Production Manager: Pinky Green; Sound Engineer: Bill Salter. Cast: Dane Clark, Kathleen Byron, Naomi Chance, Meredith Edwards, Anthony Forwood, Eric Pohlmann, Julian Somers, Anthony Ireland. (British title **In the Money**)

Sins of Jezebel: Released 10/23/1953. © Jezebel Productions, Inc. 12/05/1953. Jezebel Productions/Lippert Pictures. Director: Reginald LeBorg; Assistant Director: Clark Paylow; Executive Producer: Robert L. Lippert, Jr.; Producer: Sigmund Neufeld; Screenplay: Richard Landau; Cinematography: Gilbert Warrenton; Editor: Carl Pierson; Production Supervisor: Stanley Neufeld; Sound Engineer: Earl Snyder. Cast: Paulette Goddard, George Nader, Eduard Franz, John Hoyt, Ludwig Donath, John Shelton, Margia Dean, Joe Besser.

Thunder Over Sangoland: Released 04/08/1955. © Arrow Productions, Inc. 06/13/1955. Arrow Productions/Lippert Pictures. Director: Sam Newfield; Producer: Rudolph C. Flothow; Screenplay: Sherman L. Lowe; Editor: Dwight Caldwell. Cast: Jon Hall, Ray Montgomery, Marjorie Lord, House Peters, Jr., Myron Healy.

Last of the Desperados: Released 12/01/1955. © Associated Film Releasing Corp. 02/10/1956. Sigmund Neufeld Productions/Associated Film Releasing Corp. Director: Sam Newfield; Producer: Sigmund Neufeld; Screenplay: Orville Hampton; Cinematography: Eddie Linden; Editor: Holbrook N. Todd; Production Manager: Bert Sternbach; Sound: Ben Winkler. Cast: James Craig, Jim Davis, Barton MacLane, Margia Dean, Dona Martel, Myrna Dell, Bob Steele, Stanley Clements. (working title **The Story of Pat Garrett**)

The Wild Dakotas: Released 02/1956. © Associated Film Releasing Corp. 04/06/1956. Sigmund Neufeld Productions/Associated Film Releasing Corp. Director: Sam Newfield; Assistant Director: Herbert Glazer; Producer: Sigmund Neufeld; Screenplay: Thomas W. Blackburn; Cinematography: Kenneth Peach; Editor: Holbrook N. Todd; Production Manager: Bert Sternbach; Sound Recording: Jack Lilly. Cast: Bill Williams, Coleen Gray, Jim Davis, John Litel, Dick Jones, John Miljan, Lisa Montell, Stan Jolley, Wally Brown, Iron Eyes Cody, Bill Dix.

The Three Outlaws: Released 08/22/1956. © Associated Film Releasing Corp. 07/02/1956. Sigmund Neufeld Productions/Associated Film Releasing Corp. Director: Sam Newfield; Producer: Sigmund Neufeld; Screenplay: Orville Hampton; Editor: Dwight Caldwell; Production Manager: Bert Sternbach; Sound Recording: Jack Lilly. Cast: Neville Brand, Alan Hale, Bruce Bennett, Jose Gonzalez Gonzalez, Jeanne Carmen, Rudolfo Hoyos, Robert Christopher, Robert Tafur, Lillian Molieri, Vincent Padula.

Frontier Gambler: Released 09/05/1956. © Associated Film Releasing Corp. 07/02/1956. Sigmund Neufeld Productions/Associated Film Releasing Corp. Director: Sam Newfield; Assistant Director: Harold Knox; Producer: Sigmund Neufeld; Screenplay: Orville Hampton; Script Supervisor: Violet McComas; Cinematography: Eddie Linden; Editor: Dwight Caldwell; Production Manager: Bert Sternbach; Sound Recording: Ben Winkler. Cast: John Bromfield, Coleen Gray, Kent Taylor, Jim Davis, Margia Dean, Veda Ann Borg, Stanley Andrews, Nadene Ashdown, Tracey Roberts, Roy Engel, John Merton, Frank Sully. (working title **Frontier Queen**)

Wolf Dog: Released 07/1958. © Twentieth Century-Fox Film Corp. 04/17/1958. Regal Films (Canada)/Twentieth Century Fox. Regalscope. Director: Sam Newfield; Assistant Director: Bert Marotta; Executive Producer: Sigmund Neufeld (uncredited); Producer: Sam Newfield; Screenplay: Louis Stevens; Cinematography: Frederick Ford; Editor: Douglas Robertson; Production Manager: Bert Sternbach. Cast: Jim Davis, Allison Hayes, Tony Brown, Austin Willis, Don Garrard, Juan Root, B. Braithwaite, Lloyd Chester, Syd Brown, Daryl Masters, Les Rubie, Ed Holmes, John Nevette, John Paris, Jay MacDonald, Prince the Dog. (working title **A Boy and His Dog**)

Flaming Frontier: Released 08/1958. © Twentieth Century-Fox Film Corp. 06/26/1958. Regal Films (Canada)/Twentieth Century Fox. Regalscope. Director: Sam Newfield; Assistant Director: Bert Marotta; Executive Producer: Sigmund Neufeld (uncredited); Producer: Sam Newfield; Screenplay: Louis Stevens; Cinematography: Frederick Ford; Editor: Douglas Robertson; Production Manager: Bert Sternbach; Sound: Ben Brightwell. Cast: Bruce Bennett, Jim Davis, Paisley Maxwell, Cecil Linder, Ben Lennick, Peter Humphreys, Larry Solway, Bill Walsh, Larry Mann.

TV SERIES:

Ramar of the Jungle (1953-54). Director: Sam Newfield (14 episodes) and others; Executive Producers: Rudolph C. Flothow, Leon Fromkess; Star: Jon Hall

Captain Gallant of the Foreign Legion (1955). Director: Sam Newfield (4 episodes) and others; Producer: Gilbert Ralston; Cast: Buster Crabbe, Cullen "Cuffy" Crabbe, Fuzzy Knight

Hawkeye and the Last of the Mohicans (1957). Director: Sam Newfield (36 episodes) and others; Producers: Leon Fromkess, Sigmund Neufeld; Cast: John Hart, Lon Chaney Jr.

The Adventures of Tugboat Annie (1957). Director: Sam Newfield (2 episodes) and others; Producer: Anthony Veiller, Leon Fromkess, Sigmund Neufeld; Cast: Minerva Urecal, Walter Sande

Endnotes

Chapter 1: We Gotta Get Out of This Place
[1] Likely in the town of Oradea, now a part of Rumania
[2] "Dictionary of Occupational Titles Part 1: Definitions of Titles" Washington, DC: United States Government Printing Office, June 1939, page 398
[3] Tim Neufeld interview, June 20, 2022
[4] *Twelfth Census of the United States*, data enumerated on June 5, 1900
[5] Tim Neufeld interview, June 20, 2022
[6] Ibid.
[7] 1905 *New York State Census*
[8] According to Tim Neufeld, "Jackie, Sam's daughter, specifically told me that the clothing was the photographer's clothing, inside a photo studio." Jacqueline "Jackie" Newfield was Sam Newfield's daughter. (Tim Neufeld interview, July 29, 2022)
[9] *Thirteenth Census of the United States*, data enumerated on April 21, 1910
[10] Interview with Sigmund Neufeld, Jr. and Tim Neufeld, June 20, 2022
[11] Ibid.
[12] Ibid.
[13] Jack Cohn, "Fourteenth Street," *Film Daily*, February 28, 1926, p.57
[14] Julius Stern, "Reminiscences of a Studio Manager, Part 1," *Moving Picture World*, June 5, 1915, p.1592
[15] Cohn, "Fourteenth Street," *Op. Cit.*
[16] "The Imp Moves," *Moving Picture World*, September 3, 1910, p.523
[17] "Julius Stern," *The Implet*, January 27, 1912, p.2
[18] Drinkwater, John, *The Life and Adventures of Carl Laemmle* (London: William Heinemann Ltd, 1931), p.126
[19] Ibid., p.95
[20] Neal Gabler, *An Empire of Their Own* (New York: Anchor Books/Doubleday, 1988), p.59
[21] Cohn, *Op. Cit.*
[22] "A Saturday Success and Sensation, the IMP 'Split'!", *The Implet*, January 27, 1912, p.8
[23] Carl Laemmle, "Splitting the Splits!", *The Implet*, April 27, 1912, p.8
[24] In fairness to Laemmle and IMP, it should also be noted that they were early introducers of the occasional two-reel subject at this same time, with offerings such as *Shamus O'Brien* and *Lady Audley's Secret* (both early-mid 1912)
[25] "The IMP Film Company's California Plant," *The Implet*, February 24, 1912, p.2
[26] "Photographs of the IMP Players," *The Implet*, January 27, 1912, p.8
[27] 1915 *New York State Census*
[28] 1916 *New York City Directory*
[29] "Universal Eastern Forces Thinning," *Moving Picture World*, June 24, 1916, p.2244
[30] "Greater Number of Eastern 'U' Players Now in the West," *Motion Picture News*, June 24, 1916, p.3921
[31] Tim Neufeld interview, June 20, 2022
[32] Sigmund Neufeld Draft Registration card, dated June 5, 1917

Chapter 2: There Comes a Time in Every Young Man's Life
[1] "Julius Stern," *Moving Picture World*, November 4, 1916, p.633
[2] Samuel Neufeld [sic] Draft Registration card, dated September 12, 1918
[3] Tim Neufeld interview, June 20, 2022
[4] Joel Newfield interview, October 18. 2022. Marguerite Sheffler, daughter of actor Jackie Morgan who worked at Century 1921-22, relayed this interesting anecdote in an email dated November 4, 2022: "My dad remembered shooting a movie and everyone ate roast beef sandwiches for lunch. For some reason, my dad didn't have a sandwich and he was the only one who didn't get sick." Sam and Sig's mother's sandwiches, perhaps?
[5] Sig Neufeld Jr. interview, June 27, 2022
[6] Sigmund Neufeld-Ruth Auld marriage license, dated March 9, 1920
[7] *Fourteenth Census of the United States*, data enumerated on January 23, 1920
[8] Sig Neufeld Jr. interview, June 24, 2022

9 "Most Serious Man in Film Company is Laugh Censor," paper unknown, December 7, 1921, page unknown
10 "Stern Bros. Appoint Production Manager," *Motion Picture News*, December 2, 1922, p.2812; "Chas. Wallach Takes Up Duties in Signal Corps," *Motion Picture News*, October 27, 1917, p.2886
11 Gilbert Sherman interview, June 24, 2022
12 Lee Royal, *The Romance of Motion Picture Production* (Los Angeles: Royal Publishing Company, 1920), p.30
13 "Where to Find People You Know," *Camera!*, November 11, 1922, p.6
14 "Alterations in Century Staff," *Motion Picture News*, November 25, 1922, p.2674
15 "Julius Stern Adds Herman Raymaker to Century's Staff," *Exhibitors Trade Review*, November 25, 1922, p.1633
16 "Edwards to Direct Bud Messinger for Century," *Motion Picture News*, December 2, 1922, p.2811
17 "Short Stuff," *Film Daily*, February 4, 1923, p.10
18 "Engage 'Pinto' for Devising Comedy," *Los Angeles Evening Express*, January 10, 1923, p.20
19 "Made Head of Century Script Building Department," *Exhibitors Trade Review*, February 2, 1924, p.29
20 "Stern Brothers to Meet," *Moving Picture World*, September 29, 1923, p.403
21 "Sterns Improving Studios," *Camera!*, December 30, 1922, p.13
22 "Large Program is Planned for Century Films," *Los Angeles Times*, January 18, 1925, p.73; "Big Outlay for Century," *Exhibitors Trade Review*, March 21, 1925, p.50
23 "Production Manager Breaks Arm," *Exhibitors Trade Review*, April 25, 1925, p.22
24 Stanley Neufeld Birth Certificate, dated May 1, 1923
25 Correspondence with Tim Neufeld, June 21, 2022
26 Telegram from Sigmund Neufeld to Julius and Abe Stern in Paris, France, dated August 16, 1926
27 The *1926 Film Daily Year Book* would identify Alexander as Century's Casting Director and Purchasing Agent, p.701
28 "Stern Brothers Start Work in New Studio," *Universal Weekly*, October 2, 1926, p.23
29 "Stern Bros. Resume Work In New Western Studios," *Moving Picture World*, October 2, 1926, p.292
30 Thomas Reeder, *Time is Money! The Century, Rainbow, and Stern Brothers Comedies of Julius and Abe Stern* (BearManor Media, 2021)
31 Tim Neufeld interview, July 29, 2022
32 Neal Gabler, *Walt Disney: The Triumph of the American Imagination* (New York: Alfred A. Knopf, 2006), p.90
33 According to both son Sig Neufeld Jr. and grandson Tim Neufeld, Sigmund and Sam would playfully argue over which spelling was correct, although it's likely that Neufeld is the correct spelling. Various documents over the years would incorrectly yield other spellings as well, such as Neufeldt and Neufield. On both his 1918 and 1942 Draft Registration cards, Sam signed his name as "Samuel Neufeld", so it's evident that his argument for the Newfield surname was baseless. Sam's son Joel chimed in: "I'm still not sure where they came from. They were saying when they came to America neither one of them spelled their name correctly. Sam took it the English way—'Newfield'—and 'Neu' was the other with Sig. The correct spelling from what I understand was German—'Neufelt.' And they went from Germany to Hungary and then to the United States. Now those are the stories I heard, but I have no idea how true they are." (Joel Newfield interview, October 18, 2022)
34 "Marion-Davis Team," *Film Daily*, December 5, 1926, p.20
35 "Three Stern Brothers Companies Start Work On New Comedies," *Universal Weekly*, August 27, 1927, p.23
36 "In and Out of Town," *Motion Picture News*, January 14, 1928, p.131
37 "Five Stern Brothers Units in Work Soon," *Film Daily*, January 23, 1928, p.7; "Julius Stern Goes to Coast to Launch Comedy Product for Coming Season," *Universal Weekly*, January 28, 1928, p.40
38 "Sam Newfield Leaves for Coast," *Film Daily*, January 15, 1928, p.2
39 "Thrill Comedies the Latest Public Demand Says Sig. Newfield, Stern Studio Manager," *Universal Weekly*, February 4, 1928, p.26. While this piece was attributed to Sigmund, it's very possible that it was written by one of the Sterns' publicists
40 Ibid.
41 "Inside Stuff: Picture," *Variety*, September 5, 1928, p.24

[42] Telegram from Carl Laemmle, Hot Springs Ark, to Stern Pictures Corporation., 6048 Sunset Blvd, Hollywood Calif., dated February 16, 1929
[43] "On the Dotted Line," *Los Angeles Evening Post-Record*, April 6, 1929, p.12
[44] "Universal Two-Reel Comedies That Will Click Big Laughs," *Universal Weekly*, July 13, 1929, pp.28-29; "Sid Saylor Starts New Comedy Series," *Universal Weekly*, April 13, 1929, p.32
[45] "A Little from Lots," *Film Daily*, April 11, 1929, p.7
[46] Half-page ad congratulating Carl Laemmle for his twenty years in the business, *Motion Picture News*, November 30, 1929, p.63

Chapter 3: A Different Breed of Comedian
[1] "Honor Roll," *Film Daily*, November 9, 1918, p.2838
[2] "Plans Series of Westerns," *Film Daily*, October 20, 1920, p.3
[3] "Looks Like a Busy Season at the Hollywood Studios," *Exhibitors Herald*, January 24, 1925, p.32
[4] "John M. Stahl Joins Tiffany; Fine Arts Studio Purchased," *Exhibitors Herald*, November 5, 1927, p.31
[5] "Sig Neufeld Heads Novelty Shorts of Tiffany's Program," *Exhibitors Herald*, May 24, 1930, p.47
[6] "Paul Hurst to Star for Tiffany," *Exhibitors Daily Review and Motion Pictures Daily*, July 16, 1930, p.2
[7] "'Classics in Slang' Series of Six to Be Made as Talkies," *Hollywood Filmograph*, July 26, 1930, p.10
[8] "Pictures," *Variety*, August 20, 1930, p.33
[9] "Pert Kelton Signed," *Exhibitors Daily Review and Motion Pictures Today*, March 27, 1930, p.2
[10] Dan Thomas, "Movie Chat," *Times Herald* (Olean, New York), July 21, 1930, p.9
[11] "Meet Mrs. Lewis!", *Exhibitors Daily Review and Motion Pictures Today*, September 18, 1930, p.12
[12] "Music, Comedy and Travel in Tiffany's 62 Short Features," *Exhibitors Herald-World*, August 30, 1930, p.47
[13] "Tiffany Rumored in Field to Buy," *Inside Facts of Stage and Screen*, February 15, 1930, p.9
[14] "Tiffany Will Expand Coast Studio Property," *Film Daily*, July 1, 1930, pp.2, 8
[15] "One Punch O'Toole," *Film Daily*, March 29, 1931, p.11
[16] "Tiffany Studio Maintains Busy Working Schedule," *Film Daily*, December 29, 1930, p.6
[17] "Paul Hurst's Damage," *Variety*, April 22, 1931, p.5
[18] Wheeler W. Dixon and Audrey Brown Fraser, *I Went That-A-Way: The Memoirs of a Western Film Director, Harry L. Fraser* (Metuchen, New Jersey: The Scarecrow Press, Inc., 1990), pp.110-111
[19] "Chimps Learn to Act at New School," *Calgary Herald*, June 13, 1931, p.24
[20] "Complete Fourth Chimp Comedy," *Film Daily*, September 24, 1930, p.6
[21] J.L.K., "Tiffany Previews Newest Shorts," *Exhibitors Daily Review and Motion Pictures Today*, September 25, 1930, p.2
[22] "The Little Covered Wagon," *Motion Picture News*, August 30, 1930, p.56
[23] Ibid.
[24] "The Little Divorcee," *Exhibitors Herald-World*, December 1, 1930, p.30
[25] "The Little Divorcee," *Motion Picture News*, December 6, 1930, p.121
[26] "Nine Nights in a Bar Room," *Exhibitors Daily Review and Motion Pictures Today*, December 26, 1930, p.4
[27] "Clever Chimpanzees Newest Movie Stars," *Calgary Herald*, October 28, 1930, p.5
[28] "Chasing Around," *Motion Picture*, July 1931, p.80
[29] "Tiffany," *Exhibitors Herald-World*, December 6, 1930, p.6
[30] Ralph Wilk, "Hollywood Flashes," *Film Daily*, June 3, 1931, p.6; "Tiffany Chimps Will Burlesque 'Cimarron'," *Calgary Herald*, June 10, 1931, p.5
[31] Sig Neufeld Jr. interview, June 27, 2022
[32] *Hollywood Filmograph* July 5, 1930, p.24
[33] "Who's Who in Hollywood," *1937 Film Daily Presents the Product Guide and Directors Annual*, p.240
[34] "Phil Goldstone Resigns as Tiffany Studio Head," *Film Daily*, April 25, 1930, p.1
[35] "Phil Goldstone to Stay with Tiffany," *Exhibitors Daily Review and Motion Pictures Today*, May 2, 1930, p.6; "Goldstone On Leave of Absence from Tiffany," *Motion Picture News*, May 3, 1930, p.25
[36] "No Split—Goldstone," *Variety*, July 9, 1930, p.4
[37] James P. Cunningham, "Industry Statistics: Number 82," *Film Daily*, November 1, 1929, p.3
[38] "34 Features Tentatively Set by Tiffany," *Film Daily*, December 30, 1930, pp.1-2
[39] "Educational Rules Tiffany Sales Force," *Motion Picture Herald*, April 25, 1931, pp.12, 51

[40] "Off the Record," *Motion Picture Daily*, July 20, 1931, p.2
[41] "Charney, Goldstone in Lab. Field," *Motion Picture Herald*, December 19, 1931, p.22
[42] "Africa Squawks," *Film Daily*, August 2, 1931, p.11
[43] "Neufeld in Split with Tiffany-Educational on Chimp Shorts," *Motion Picture Herald*, October 10, 1931, p.37
[44] "Broadcasting," *Film Daily*, January 17, 1932, p.10
[45] "Bud Barsky-Sig Neufeld of Famous Comedies Productions, Ltd.," *1931 Film Daily Year Book*, p.134
[46] Tim Neufeld interview, June 27, 2022

Chapter 4: What Poison Does to the Body (1932-1934)
[1] "Voice of the Industry," *Motion Picture Herald*, December 5, 1931, p.78
[2] "Cut Budgets for Shorts," *Motion Picture Herald*, November 21, 1931, p.32
[3] "Independents' Economy Wins Bank Recognition." *Film Daily*, January 21, 1932, p.1,12. Gluckman would also be referred to as "Sam Gluckman" in a subsequent article in *Variety*: "New Indie Firm," May 24, 1932, p.4
[4] Ibid.
[5] "New Independent Firm Planning 18 Features," *Film Daily*, November 1, 1931, p.1
[6] "Tower Productions, Inc. Plans Eight Releases," *Film Daily*, January 5, 1932, p.2
[7] "Discarded Lovers," *Film Daily*, January 3, 1932, p.8
[8] "Shop Angel," *Film Daily*, March 6, 1932, p.11
[9] "The Shop Angel," *Hollywood Filmograph*, February 20, 1932, p.6
[10] "Morris R. Schlank and Sid [sic] Neufeld Produce Their Second [sic] Feature," *Hollywood Filmograph*, May 21, 1932, p.9
[11] "Third Tower Film Starts," *Film Daily*, May 18, 1932, p.5
[12] "Drifting Souls," *Film Daily*, August 9, 1932, p.9
[13] "'Drifting Souls' with Lois Wilson," *Harrison's Reports*, August 13, 1932, p.130
[14] "Obituaries: Morris Schlank," *Variety*, July 5, 1932, p.47
[15] "Neufeld Heads Premier," *Variety*, July 12, 1932, p.6
[16] "Tower's Fourth in Work," *Film Daily*, July 15, 1932, p.2
[17] "26 Productions Slated By Goldstone's New Unit," *Film Daily*, May 15, 1932, p.5
[18] "New Indie Firm," *Variety*, May 24, 1932, p.4
[19] "Neufeld, Director, Father of Baby Girl," *Los Angeles Evening Citizen News*, February 28, 1933, p.1
[20] "In Dad's Footsteps," *Hollywood Filmograph*, August 13, 1932, p.9
[21] "Christy Cabanne to Direct," *Hollywood Filmograph*, September 3, 1932, p.11
[22] "Premier's Mintz Orig.," *Variety*, October 11, 1932, p.27
[23] Also referred to as *The Wise Girl* or *Wise Girl*, depending on the source
[24] "Filmograph's Bulletin Board," *Hollywood Filmograph*, November 5, 1932, p.16
[25] "Republic Studios," *Hollywood Filmograph*, November 5, 1932, p.5
[26] "Tiffany Rumored in Field to Buy," *Inside Facts of Stage and Screen*, February 15, 1930, p.9
[27] "Daring Daughters," *Film Daily*, April 25, 1933, p.3
[28] "Christy Cabanne," *Hollywood Filmograph*, November 5, 1932, p.2
[29] "Daring Daughters," *Motion Picture Herald*, April 15, 1933, p.30
[30] "Independents Seek Means to Keep Going," *Hollywood Reporter*, March 11, 1933, p.3
[31] "Efforts Made to Avert Shutdown," *Van Nuys News*, March 13, 1933, p.19
[32] "Studios Dark as Troubles Ironed Out," *San Antonio Light*, March 15, 1933, p.15
[33] When asked by his grandson Tim about the effects of the Great Depression on his livelihood, Sig would chuckle and respond (paraphrased) "For those of us in the picture business, there was no Depression; we were always busy." Sig's son Sig Jr. elaborated: "The film industry did great during the Depression because people had nothing to do but go to the movies…it was a nickel to go to the movies." (Tim Neufeld and Sigmund Neufeld Jr. interview, June 27, 2022)
[34] "Film Employes [sic] Row with Studio Over Pay Slash," *Berkeley Daily Gazette*, April 13, 1933, p.3
[35] "Walkout Closes 11 Film Studios," *Bakersfield Californian*, July 25, 1933, p.8
[36] "Sig Neufeld Places 'Reform Girl' In Work," *Hollywood Reporter*, January 28, 1933, p.3
[37] "11 Coast Studios Bid for Indie's Prods.," *Variety*, February 7, 1933, p.7
[38] "Neufeld, Director, Father of Baby Girl," *Op. Cit.*

[39] "Reform Girl," various letters to Dave Brill and R.J. Fannon, Capitol Film Exchange dated July 22, 1933 and August 7, 1933; undated internal document; file A1418-77, Box 220, 25402, Motion Picture Division, New York State Archives, Albany, New York

[40] "Reform Girl," *AFI Catalog*, https://catalog.afi.com/Film/5228-REFORM-GIRL?sid=ca25caec-9b4e-42c0-a30c-1caf3c1d5d27&sr=9.788989&cp=1&pos=0

[41] "Reform Girl," *Variety*, December 12, 1933, p.29

[42] "Tower Finishes Seventh," *Film Daily*, February 2, 1933, p.5

[43] "Buys 'Public Stenographer'" *Variety*, March 7, 1933, p.21; "'Night Coach' Bought By Neufeld for Premier," *Film Daily*, March 4, 1933, p.2

[44] "'Night Coach' Starts," *Variety*, May 16, 1933, p.23

[45] 'The Important Witness," *Film Daily*, September 6, 1933, p.11

[46] Chic., "The Important Witness," *Variety*, July 15, 1933, pp.20, 56

[47] "The Important Witness," *Film Daily*, September 6, 1933, p.11

[48] Chic., "The Important Witness," *Op. Cit.*

[49] "Drafting of Film Code Was Long and Arduous Task," *Film Daily*, December 1, 1933, p.5

[50] "29 Producers Join in Plea for Retention of Twin Bills," *Film Daily*, October 4, 1933, p.8

[51] "Big Time or Bust," *Harrisons Reports*, December 16, 1933, pp.198-199

[52] According to producer Sam Sherman, his parents met during a 1935 screening of this film in New York. Sherman's father encouraged his son's growing interest in film, which eventually led to a decades-long immersion in the film industry as the producer and distributor of low budget films. I'd like to think that Newfield's low budget *Big Time or Bust* was in some subconscious way the inspiration for Sherman's love of seat-of-the-pants filmmaking. Which, of course, is a rather absurd notion. Sam Sherman. *When Frankenstein Met Dracula* (Murania Press, 2019), p.19

[53] "Neufeld Joins Roach," *Motion Picture Daily*, November 23, 1933, p.8

[54] "Dad Says," *Hollywood Filmograph*, November 11, 1933, p.4

[55] "New Studio Named," *Hollywood Filmograph*, November 11, 1933, p.11

[56] Phil M Daly, "Along the Rialto, "*Film Daily*, August 18, 1934, p.3

[57] "Premiere [sic] to Sennett," *Hollywood Reporter*, February 2, 1934, p.6

[58] "Tower Completes Series," *Film Daily*, March 23, 1934, p.14

[59] "Marrying Widows," *Motion Picture Daily*, April 6, 1934, p.8

[60] "Marrying Widows," *Film Daily*, May 18, 1934, p.10

[61] "Gets Foreign Rights," *Film Daily*, September 14, 1933, p.2

[62] "Double Bill Factor," *Motion Picture Herald*, May 19, 1934, pp.25-26

[63] E.W. Hammons, "Hammons Hits Twin Bills," *Motion Picture Daily*, December 8, 1934, pp.1, 16

Chapter 5: The Conning of Sigmund (1934-1935)

[1] "Units for Mascot," *Philadelphia Exhibitor*, May 1, 1934, p.26

[2] "Mascot Set on 12 for '34-'35 List," *Motion Picture Daily*, May 22, 1934, p.5

[3] "Mascot Announces 12 Titles," *Motion Picture Herald*, May 26, 1934, p.24

[4] "Who's Who in Hollywood," *Film Daily*, February 26, 1937, p.11

[5] Ralph Wilk, "A Little from Lots," *Film Daily*, July 7, 1934, p.3

[6] "Kermit Maynard to Make Series for Conn. Firm," *Film Daily*, July 23, 1934, pp.1-2

[7] Louella O. Parsons, *Dayton Herald* (Ohio), July 20. 1934, p.32

[8] "Herbert Aller Joins Ambassador," *Film Daily*, August 2, 1934, p.2

[9] "Closes Deals on Maynard Films," *Film Daily*, August 25, 1934, p.2

[10] Buck Rainey, *Heroes of the Range* (Waynesville, North Carolina: The World of Yesterday, 1987), p.73

[11] "Riding Crown of Kermit Maynard to Go Undefended," *Los Angeles Times*, August 27, 1934, p.5

[12] "Northern Frontier," *Film Daily*, February 8, 1935, p.7

[13] Boyd Magers, "An Interview With...Beth Marion," Boyd Magers' *Western Clippings* web site. http://www.westernclippings.com/interview/bethmarion_interview.shtml

[14] "Incorporations: California," *Variety*, November 13, 1934, p.23; "Ambassador Pictures, Inc.," *1935 Film Daily Year Book*, p.562

[15] "The Fighting Trooper," *Motion Picture Daily*, November 1, 1934, p.8

[16] John Brooker, *The Happiest Trails* (CP Entertainment Books, 2017), pp.209-211

[17] "The Red Blood of Courage," *Film Daily*, April 20, 1935, p.6

[18] "Wilderness Mail," *Film Daily*, March 9, 1935, p.3

[19] "Wilderness Mail," *Motion Picture Daily*, July 5, 1935, p.12
[20] Brooker, p.209
[21] Mark Thomas McGee, *Talk's Cheap, Action's Expensive: The Films of Robert L. Lippert* (Albany, Georgia: BearManor Media, 2014), p.2
[22] "Northern Frontier," *Motion Picture Daily*, February 8, 1935, p.7
[23] "Northern Frontier," *Film Daily*, February 8, 1935, p.7
[24] "Conn to Start Kyne Series," *Film Daily*, May 4, 1935, p.2
[25] In the opinion of Republic cowboy star Monte Hale, "The kids didn't like you singing or hugging the girl too much. They just wanted you to pet your horse, ride him and chase outlaws." ("Monte Hale," *Films of the Golden Age*, Summer 2023 #113, p.31)
[26] "State Rights: Code of the Mounted," *Philadelphia Exhibitor*, July 15, 1935, p.54
[27] "Research Council Begins Task of Improving Studio Standards," *Motion Picture Herald*, August 20, 1932, p.10
[28] "Plan Television Broadcast of 'Journey's End'," *Los Angeles Evening Express*, April 4, 1930, p.29
[29] "Television at Home," *Los Angeles Times*, April 5, 1930, p.22
[30] "Electrical," *Motion Picture Insider*, June 1935, p.57
[31] "Trails of the Wild," *Film Daily*, November 29, 1935, p.13
[32] "Trails of the Wild," *Variety*, December 4, 1935, p.15
[33] "What the Picture Did for Me," *Motion Picture Herald*, February 1, 1936, p.55 (P.G. Held, New Strand Theatre, Griswold, Iowa)
[34] "Curwood's Story Action Thriller," *The Dothan Eagle* (Dothan, Alabama), December 14, 1935, p.9
[35] Mike Fitzgerald, "An Interview With...Lucille Lund," Boyd Magers' *Western Clippings* web site. http://www.westernclippings.com/interview/lucillelund_interview.shtml

Chapter 6: The Real McCoy (1935-1937)

[1] *Los Angeles Times*, March 13, 1935, p.13; "Simmonds and Neufeld Form Producing Firm," *Film Daily*, March 14, 1935, p.1
[2] "It's Excelsior Pics Now," *Variety*, April 3, 1935, p.6
[3] Ralph Wilk, "A Little from Lots," *Film Daily*, April 6, 1935, p.4
[4] "Seals Issue On 104 Films in 2 Months," *Film Daily*, February 3, 1936, pp.1, 12
[5] Ralph Wilk, "A Little from Hollywood Lots," *Film Daily*, March 19, 1935, p.6
[6] "New Indie Firm Formed," *Film Daily*, January 7, 1935, p.1
[7] "Tim McCoy Westerns On State Right Market," *Film Daily*, February 12, 1935, p.1
[8] Tim McCoy with Ronald McCoy, *Tim McCoy Remembers the West* (University of Nebraska Press, 1988), pp.243-244
[9] Michael R. Pitts, *Poverty Row Studios, 1929-1940* (Jefferson, North Carolina: McFarland & Company, Inc., 1997), p.291
[10] "Simmonds, Neufeld Set On Tim McCoy Westerns," *Film Daily*, September 25, 1935, p.2
[11] Ralph Wilk, "A Little from Lots," *Film Daily*, March 30, 1936, p.6
[12] "Bulldog Courage," *Motion Picture Daily*, February 17, 1936, p.10
[13] "The Lion's Den," *Film Daily*, August 25, 1936, p.4
[14] "The Lion's Den," *Motion Picture Daily*, August 25, 1936, p.5
[15] Bral., "The Lion's Den," *Variety*, September 2, 1936, p.2
[16] "Tim McCoy at Ideal Friday and Saturday," *Corsicana Daily Sun* (Corsicana, TX), February 19, 1937, p.10
[17] One of the frequently used, money-saving devices among B western directors and their editors was to take a shot of horsemen riding in one direction, use it, then flip the negative and reuse it so that it looked like different footage.
[18] "Crashin' Thru Danger," *Film Daily*, November 11, 1938, p.4

Chapter 7: Sam, Sans Sig (Part 1: 1932-1936)

[1] "New Montmartre Continues to Command Attention of Amusement World," *Hollywood Filmograph*, September 16, 1933, p.5
[2] "You Can Be Had," *Motion Picture Daily*, January 31, 1936, p.6
[3] "You Can Be Had," *Motion Picture Herald*, February 8, 1936, p.62
[4] "What the Picture Did for Me," *Motion Picture Herald*, April 25, 1936, p.84

[5] Possibly later in 1934; there was a brief announcement in the press in August of Hamilton's attempt at a comeback in shorts. See Wood Soames, "Curtain Calls," *Oakland Tribune*, August 24, 1934, p.25
[6] Although Producer Ben Judell would resurrect Progressive in 1938 for an additional three releases
[7] "Under Secret Orders," *Film Daily*, December 6, 1933, p.7
[8] "Under Secret Orders," *Variety*, December 12, 1933, pp.19, 29
[9] "Who's Who in Hollywood," *Film Daily*, March 7, 1938, p.13
[10] Wear., "Branded a Coward," *Variety*, October 23, 1935, p.31
[11] "Distribution," *Philadelphia Exhibitor*, November 15, 1935, p.13
[12] "Theatres at Sulphur," *Sulphur Times-Democrat* (Sulphur, Oklahoma), April 9, 1936, p.4
[13] "Nine Production Companies Organize," *Motion Picture Herald*, May 26, 1934, p.24
[14] "Saal Reported Lining Up Indie Exchange Group," *Film Daily*, July 12, 1934, p.2; "Yates Wants Indie Exchanges Merged," *Motion Picture Daily*, August 6, 1934, pp.1-2
[15] "Select Prods. to Start One in West, One in East," *Film Daily*, October 12, 1934, p.2
[16] George Hirliman, "Cut Operating Costs," *1933 Film Daily Year Book*, p.117
[17] "Yates and Hirliman Signing Up Talent," *Motion Picture Daily*, November 20, 1933, p.1
[18] "Liberty, Mascot Join Republic," *Motion Picture Herald*, June 15, 1935, p.59
[19] "Dickering on Wm. Saal As Republic Sales Head," *Film Daily*, January 28, 1936, pp.1, 3
[20] "Select Finishes One, Starts Another," *Film Daily*, March 9, 1935, p.2
[21] "Racing Luck," *Film Daily*, November 19, 1935, p.8
[22] "Racing Luck," *Motion Picture Herald*, October 31, 1935, p.68
[23] "Burning Gold," *Film Daily*, December 16, 1935, p.8
[24] "Burning Gold," *Variety*, December 16, 1935, p.15
[25] "Federal Agent," *Motion Picture Herald*, April 11, 1936, p.85
[26] "Movie Menage to Board Ship," *News-Pilot* (San Pedro, CA), January 19, 1935, p.5
[27] "Passengers Go Movie," *Oakland Tribune*, February 12, 1935, p.20
[28] "Go-Get-'Em, Haines," *Film Daily*, June 15, 1936, p.13
[29] "Eight Films in Color," *Motion Picture Herald*, September 7, 1935, p.37
[30] "Canada's Richest Heir Seeks License to Rewed Phila. Girl," *Morning Post* (Camden, NJ), January 22, 1938, p.6
[31] "Foreign Market," *1932 Motion Picture Almanac*, p.1932
[32] "'Lab' Men to Make M-G-M Quota Films," *Motion Picture Daily*, August 9, 1935, pp.1, 3; "New Firm to Make 12 Films in Canada," *Film Daily*, January 19, 1934, p.1
[33] "Lining Up Equipment for Toronto Film Studio," *Film Daily*, March 22, 1934, pp.1, 9
[34] "Production Venture Started in Ottawa," *Motion Picture Daily*, May 20, 1935, pp.1-2
[35] "Three Ottawa Girls Have Chance to Become Motion Picture Stars," *Ottawa Journal*, June 12, 1935, p.14
[36] "Metro Coin, All Rights to Booth For 6 Quota Pix," *Variety*, August 7, 1935, p.7
[37] "'Lab' Men to Make M-G-M Quota Films," *Op. Cit.*
[38] "Purely Personal," *Motion Picture Daily*, August 8, 1935, p.2
[39] "Booth Starts First Feature in Canada," *Variety*, August 21, 1935, p.13
[40] "First 'Quota' Film in Work," *Motion Picture Herald*, October 12, 1935, p.51
[41] "Thoroughbred," *Philadelphia Exhibitor*, May 1, 1936, p.31
[42] "Two Booth Companies, So Booth Dominion Changes," *Motion Picture Herald*, March 14, 1936, p.75
[43] "Heart Attack Is Fatal to Col. J.R. Booth, Jr.," *Film Daily*, October 13, 1941, p.5
[44] "National Film Takes Over Century Studios for Sound," *Variety*, April 3, 1929, p.7
[45] "Trem Carr Filming First All-Dialogue Feature Production," *The Film Mercury*, June 14, 1929, p.1
[46] "The Alexander Brothers Offer Stage Space," *Hollywood Filmograph*, June 3, 1933, p.5
[47] "Alexander to Produce," *Hollywood Reporter*, March 13, 1934, p.1; "Alexander-'U' Deal," *Hollywood Reporter*, March 20, 1934, p.6
[48] "Cineglow Building." *Hollywood Reporter*, March 20, 1934, p.2
[49] "'Thunder Over Texas' Beacon Production," *Hollywood Filmograph*, September 8, 1934, p.3
[50] "Normandy Pictures Corporation," *1936 Film Daily Year Book*, p.252
[51] "Production Personnel: Colony Pictures, Inc.," *1937 Film Daily Product Guide and Directors Annual*, p.424
[52] "Stormy Trails," *Film Daily*, December 23, 1936, p.10

[53] "Stormy Trails," *Variety*, December 23, 1936, p.62
[54] "News of Dailies," *Variety*, April 14, 1937, p.79
[55] Produced and completed under this title, but released as *International Crime*
[56] "Alperson Planning 26 Feature Films," *Motion Picture Daily*, March 30, 1938, pp.1, 8
[57] "GN Future Hinges on Trustee Loyd Wright's Trip to Gotham," *Boxoffice*, August 6, 1938, p.40
[58] "Gene Austin to Make Four," *Film Daily*, July 28, 1938, p.7; "Sings While He Rides," *Variety*, August 3, 1938, p.6; "Standard in Deal for Westerns by Alexander," *Boxoffice*, October 1, 1938, p.79
[59] "Production Personnel: Colony Pictures, Inc.," *1938 Film Daily Year Book*, p.71
[60] "Colony Plans 12 Films," *Motion Picture Daily*, April 5, 1939, p.4
[61] "Get Out the Hay Bags," *Variety*, March 29, 1939, p.39; "Lewis' Hollywood Arrival Presages New Studio," *Boxoffice*, April 1, 1939, p.31
[62] "Flaming Lead," *Showmen's Trade Review*, July 1, 1939, p.9
[63] "SAG-Agent Deal," *Variety*, February 8, 1939, p.52
[64] "Henkel Charges Plot in SMPFE Suspension," *Film Daily*, November 10, 1939, p.11
[65] "Act on Laemmle Claim," Variety, *December* 20, 1939, p.6
[66] Mike Fitzgerald, "An Interview with…Fay McKenzie," Boyd Magers' *Western Clippings* web site. http://www.westernclippings.com/interview/faymckenzie_interview.shtml

Chapter 8: Sam, Sans Sig (Part 2: 1936-1940)
[1] Tim Neufeld interview, June 27, 2022
[2] "Neufield [sic] Berthed at Col," *Variety*, August 19, 1936, page unknown
[3] Sigmund Neufeld Jr. interview, July 15, 2022
[4] "Jed Buell Now Head of Sennett Publicity," *Inside Facts of Stage and Screen*, January 25, 1930, p.3
[5] "Plans Feature Comedies," *Motion Picture Daily*, July 3, 1934, p.11
[6] "Studios Rush Work on 44 Feature Films," *Motion Picture Herald*, May 25, 1935, p.44
[7] "Callaghan, Buell Top De Luxe Film Outfit," *Variety*, July 1, 1936, p.6
[8] "DeLuxe Pictures," *Motion Picture Herald*, July 4, 1936, p.43
[9] Cedric Belfrage, "Talkies While You Wait," *Motion Picture*, August 1930, p.31
[10] "Romance Rides the Range," *Motion Picture Herald*, September 26, 1936, p.43
[11] Boyd Magers, "The Westerns of…Fred Scott," Boyd Magers' *Western Clippings* web site. http://www.westernclippings.com/westernsof/fredscott_westernsof.shtml
[12] "Melody of the Plains," *Hollywood Reporter*, March 29, 1937, p.3
[13] "Melody of the Plains," *Film Daily*, April 2, 1937, p.9
[14] Magers, "The Westerns of…Fred Scott," *Op. Cit.*
[15] "Moonlight on the Range," *Boxoffice* July 31, 1937, p.17
[16] "Moonlight on the Range," *Philadelphia Exhibitor*, August 1, 1937, p.43
[17] "All-Negro Musical Western," *Film Daily*, October 12, 1937, p.5
[18] Buell served as president, Sternbach as vice president, and Carr as secretary-treasurer
[19] "Dusky Mustangers," *Variety*, October 13, 1937, p.4; "Buell Firm Re-Named," *Film Daily*, October 21, 1937, p.20
[20] Neufeld family lore has it that Sig was somehow involved in the production of this film, but this has not been confirmed. Tim Neufeld recalled "visiting the Autry Museum with my Dad [Stanley] when it first opened and… seeing Herb Jeffries' poster with Sam's name on it there, and my Dad saying that it was my grandfather's film …" Correspondence with Tim Neufeld, October 5, 2023
[21] "The Bronze Buckaroo Rides Off Into the Sunset," *npr music*, Terry Gross host, May 27, 2014. www.npr.org/transcripts/316339183
[22] "Sheffield Supervises New Race Picture Featuring Westerns," *California Eagle* (Los Angeles), October 21, 1937, p.8; Ralph Wilk, "A Little from Lots," *Film Daily*, October 22, 1937, p.7
[23] "Something New," *Motion Picture Herald*, October 23, 1937, p.29
[24] "Harlem on the Prairie," *Film Daily*, February 5, 1938, p.4
[25] "Harlem on the Prairie," *Motion Picture Daily*, November 24, 1937, p.5
[26] "'Harlem' for the Rialto," *Film Daily*, January 26, 1938, p.4
[27] "Western Agreement is Canceled by SAG," *Boxoffice*, June 30, 1945, p.41
[28] Randy Skretvedt, *Laurel and Hardy: The Magic Behind the Movies* (Beverly Hills, CA: Moonstone Press, 1987), p.332

[29] "Stan Laurel On His Own," *Film Daily*, March 4, 1937, p.6
[30] "Stan Laurel Forms New Producing Firm, *Motion Picture Daily*, November 15, 1937, p.10
[31] "Porter Tuning Gallopers," *Variety*, November 10, 1937, p.43
[32] "Newfield Megging Westerns," *Film Daily*, November 22, 1937, p.9
[33] "Boots and Saddles Aide," *Variety*, December 15, 1937, p.7
[34] "The Rangers Roundup," *Motion Picture Herald*, February 5, 1938, p.48
[35] "Rangers Roundup," *Film Daily*, February 9, 1938, p.7
[36] "Knight of the Plains," *Motion Picture Daily*, April 28, 1938, p.6
[37] Misspelled in the credit as "Shery Tansey"
[38] "Songs and Bullets," *Film Daily*, May 20, 1938, p.8
[39] "Buell Blows Laurel, Back to Prod. On Own," *Variety*, April 13, 1938, p.6
[40] Skretvedt, p.333
[41] "Sennett Talks Releasing Deal for Laurel Comedies," *Film Daily*, September 13, 1938, p.2. The little people who would have played Laurel's parents were culled from the cast of *The Terror of Tiny Town*, widely advertised as "Jed Buell's Midgets." This took place shortly after Sol Lesser failed to exercise his option to finance another film starring "Buell's Midgets"
[42] "A New Independent Enters Film Scene," *Boxoffice*, November 26, 1938, p.36
[43] "Singer Midgets to Appear in 'Terror of Tiny Town'," *Film Daily*, April 15, 1938, p.3
[44] Neufeld family lore has it that Sig was somehow involved in the production of this film as well: Sig's grandson Tim Neufeld recalls overhearing a porch-based discussion circa 1958 between his father Stanley, Sig's son, and another filmmaker about the possibility of filming a sequel to *The Terror of Tiny Town*, a film which Tim had heard referred to as one of "Grandpa's pictures" on several occasions. This, needless to say, never came to fruition, and a solid connection between Sig and the original film has not yet been confirmed.
[45] Ralph Wilk, "A Little from Lots," *Film Daily*, April 27, 1938, p.23
[46] "Lingual Trouble," *Variety*, May 25, 1938, p.6
[47] Anna Kerchy and Andrea Zittlau, editors, *Exploring the Cultural History of Continental European Freak Shows and 'Enfreakment'* (Newcastle upon Tyne, England: Cambridge Scholars Publishing, 2012), p.200
[48] "Midgets Star in Cow Opera," *Detroit Free Press*, May 30, 1938, p.5
[49] "All-Midget Feature Called Greatest Novelty in Years," *Altoona Tribune* (Altoona, PA), December 15, 1938, p.8
[50] Some sources give 1877 as a birth date for Platt
[51] Some sources give 1887 as a birth date for Becker
[52] "All-Midget Feature Called Greatest Novelty in Years," *Op. Cit.*
[53] "Midgets in Pix Travesties," *Film Daily*, June 13, 1938, p.3
[54] "Pee-Wees' to Make Series of Pictures," *Variety*, July 20, 1938, p.17
[55] "All-Midget Feature Called Greatest Novelty in Years," *Op. Cit.*
[56] "Hyman Goes East," *Boxoffice*, July 16, 1938, p.34
[57] When the L. Wolfe Gilbert Music Publishing Co. published five songs from the film prior to the film's release, this song was titled "Wedding of Jack and Jill." It's listed as "Mister Jack and Missus Jill" in the released film's credits. See Ralph Wilk, "A Little from Lots," *Film Daily*, July 26, 1938, p.4
[58] "The Terror of Tiny Town," *Hollywood Spectator*, July 23, 1938, p.8
[59] "What the Picture Did for Me," *Motion Picture Herald*, April 8, 1939, p.71 (Sam Kimball, Cornish Theatre, Cornish, Maine)
[60] "A Cycle?," *Variety*, April 27, 1938, p.5
[61] "Little Billy to Open Midget Nitery in H'wood, Lower Case All the Way," *Variety*, September 21, 1938, p.43
[62] "Inside Stuff: Pictures," *Variety*, September 28, 1938, p.23
[63] "Theatres – Exchanges," *Variety*, November 23, 1938, p.21
[64] "Independent Ranks Glow With Promise for New Season," *Boxoffice*, September 17, 1938, p.87
[65] "Mayer is Defendant in $500,000 Slander Suit," *Boxoffice*, November 12, 1938, p.8
[66] Letter from Lee L. Goldberg to Leon Fromkess, dated October 8, 1940
[67] Joel Newfield interview, October 18, 2022
[68] "Roarin' Lead," *Film Daily*, April 24, 1937, p.7
[69] "What the Picture Did for Me," Motion Picture Herald, December 11, 1937, p.70 (Sammie Jackson, Jackson Theatre, Flomaton, Alabama)

[70] "Hackel's Shoot-'Em-Ups," *Variety*, June 6, 1936, p.37
[71] "Trail of Vengeance," *Variety*, June 23, 1937, p.33
[72] "A Lawman is Born," *Film Daily*, June 28, 1937, p.18
[73] "A Lawman is Born," *Motion Picture Daily*, July 2, 1937, p.9
[74] "Boothill Brigade," *Variety*, September 29, 1937, p.15
[75] "Juvenile Signs to Make Seven; Starting Soon," *Exhibitors Herald*, June 11, 1927, p.42
[76] Bobby J. Copeland, *Charlie King: We Called Him "Blackie"* (Madison, North Carolina: Empire Publishing, Inc., 2003), p.38
[77] "Gun Lords of Stirrup Basin," *Motion Picture Daily*, May 21, 1937, p.7
[78] "Gun Lords of Stirrup Basin," *Boxoffice*, June 5, 1937, p.31
[79] And just who was this film's editor? Advance materials and reviews cite S. Roy Luby as the editor, but the film's opening credits name Roy Claire. This is the case on some of the other Republic Westerns as well.
[80] "Republic Lineup Totals 54, Including 24 Westerns," *Boxoffice*, June 5, 1937, p.11
[81] Ralph Wilk, "A Little from Lots," *Film Daily*, July 30, 1937, p.9
[82] "Arizona Gunfighter," *Variety*, September 29, 1937, p.15
[83] "The Arizona Gunfighter," *Motion Picture Daily*, September 23, 1937, p.4
[84] "Ridin' the Lone Trail," *Motion Picture Daily*, October 29, 1937, p.16
[85] "'Colorado Kid' Fair Bob Steele Western," *Film Bulletin*, January 1, 1938, p.8
[86] "Colorado Kid," *Film Daily*, December 11, 1937, p.4
[87] "Paroled—To Die," *Film Daily*, January 11, 1938, p.10
[88] "Paroled to Die," *Motion Picture Daily*, January 10, 1938, p.6
[89] "Thunder in the Desert," *Variety*, May 18, 1938, p.12
[90] "Feud Maker," *Variety*, July 20, 1938, p.13
[91] "Desert Patrol," *Film Daily*, June 3, 1938, p.6
[92] "What the Picture Did for Me," *Motion Picture Herald*, April 8, 1939, p.72 (E.M. Freiburger, Paramount Theatre, Dewey, OK)
[93] "What the Picture Did for Me," *Motion Picture Herald*, June 3, 1939, p.58 (C. Fismer, Lyric Theatre, Hamilton, OH)
[94] "Steele, Western Star, Dropped by Hackel," *Motion Picture Daily*, June 24, 1938, p.2
[95] "Conn's Concord to Make 8 Westerns for Monogram," *Film Daily*, November 13, 1937, pp.1, 3
[96] "Code of the Rangers," *Film Daily*, April 13, 1938, p.6
[97] "Code of the Rangers," *Variety*, April 13, 1938, p.15
[98] "What the Picture Did for Me," *Motion Picture Herald*, April 23, 1938, p.63 (Harry M. Palmer, Temple Court Theatre, Washington, IN)
[99] "What the Picture Did for Me," *Motion Picture Herald*, October 22, 1938, p.54 (Cecil Ward, Stone Theatre, Bassetts, VA)
[100] Mike Fitzgerald, "An Interview With...Suzanne Kaaren," Boyd Magers' *Western Clippings* web site. http://www.westernclippings.com/interview/suzannekaaren_interview.shtml
[101] "Phantom Ranger," *Film Daily*, June 20, 1938, p.6
[102] "Phantom Ranger," *Variety*, June 22, 1938, p.12
[103] David J. Hanna, "Hollywood," *Film Bulletin*, July 3, 1937, p.11
[104] "Gunsmoke Trail," *Variety*, June 22, 1938, p.14
[105] "Frontier Scout," *Film Daily*, September 16, 1938, p.7
[106] "Frontier Scout," *Boxoffice*, September 17, 1938, p.37
[107] "Fine Arts Signs George Houston," *Motion Picture Herald*, August 6, 1938, p.52
[108] "Independents Denote Action As Plans Form, Cameras Roll," *Boxoffice*, November 12, 1938, p.8; "Start Jarrett Western," *Film Daily*, November 11, 1938, p.4
[109] "Weekend Highlights Within the Industry," *The Exhibitor*, January 11, 1939, p.9
[110] Hanna, "Notes About Films and Film People," *Independent Exhibitors Film Bulletin*, December 3, 1938, p.13
[111] "Trigger Pals," *Boxoffice*, January 21, 1939, p.27
[112] "Trigger Pals," *Variety*, January 11, 1939, p.13
[113] "What the Picture Did for Me," *Motion Picture Herald*, November 25, 1939, p.51 (F.W. Lineham, Rialto Theatre, New Britain, CT)
[114] "Tex Fletcher Signed for Series by Grand National," *Boxoffice*, November 26, 1938, p.20
[115] "Six-Gun Rhythm," *Variety*, June 21, 1939, p.26

[116] "Activity Pervades Grand National," *Boxoffice*, January 14, 1939, p.38
[117] "Six-Gun Rhythm," *Op. Cit.*
[118] "'Unit Basis' Plan GN Likelihood," *Boxoffice*, February 18, 1939, p.47
[119] "4 GN Films Set for Release," *Boxoffice*, May 6, 1939, p.54
[120] "Shooting on Screen and in Auditorium," *Boxoffice*, November 11, 1939, p.88
[121] "Film Lots Suffer Cuts in Staff," *Oakland Tribune*, April 18, 1938, p.7
[122] "Confidence of Independents Augurs Well for Big Season," *Boxoffice*, September 10, 1938, p.28
[123] "Independent Unit Revived on Coast," *Motion Picture Daily*, October 13, 1938, p.1
[124] "Confidence of Independents Augurs Well for Big Season," *Op. Cit.*
[125] "Sam Katzman to Produce 8 Westerns with Tim McCoy," *Film Daily*, September 6, 1938, p.2
[126] Tom Weaver, "Katz-Mania," *Films of the Golden Age*, Winter 2007/08, Number 51, p.70
[127] "Chatter," *Variety*, May 1, 1935, p.54; "Coming and Going," *Film Daily*, May 24, 1935, p.2
[128] "Katzman's Indie Series," *Variety*, June 16, 1935, p.37
[129] "Victory Making Eight Peter Kyne Features," *Film Daily*, May 27, 1935, p.6
[130] "A Boom Looms on Independent Lots," *Boxoffice*, July 30, 1938, p.32. *Boxoffice* placed filming at International Studios; see "Independent Stride Firm; Cameras Turn on Several," *Boxoffice*, September 3, 1938, p.35
[131] "Official Probe Asked in Movie Studio Fire," *Ventura County Star Free Press* (CA), January 7, 1938, p.3
[132] McCoy and McCoy, p.250
[133] Thomas Baird, "Time and the Cowboys," *World Film News*, August 1938, p.167 (reprint of "Theatre: Last Roundup" that appeared in the May 16, 1938 issue of *Time*)
[134] "In Receivership Problem to Court," *Corpus Christi Caller Times*, May 8, 1938, p.13
[135] McCoy and McCoy, p.251. Buck Rainey puts McCoy's outlay at $100,00, and says that gave McCoy 51% of the stock; see Rainey, *Heroes of the Range*, p.104
[136] "Weiss' Coast Line-Up," *Variety*, June 20, 1928, p.16
[137] "Sternbach Enters New Field," *Motion Picture World*, April 11, 1925, p.565
[138] "Incorporations," *Variety*, October 24, 1933, p.31
[139] "The Drunkard," *Oakland Tribune*, June 16, 1935, p.37
[140] Pitts, p.438
[141] Bernstein had been one of the original five stockholders in L-Ko back when it was first incorporated in July 22, 1914, along with Henry Lehrman, Sam Behrendt, Alfred P. Hamberg, and Abe Stern.
[142] "Independent Producers Association Revives to Negotiate with Studio Unions on Scales," *Boxoffice*, October 15, 1938, p.68
[143] "What the Picture Did for Me," *Motion Picture Herald*, November 25, 1938, p.77 (Harry M. Palmer, Temple Court Theatre, Washington, IN)
[144] "Victory Takes Space," *Variety*, December 28, 1938, p.20
[145] "Code of the Cactus," *The Exhibitor*, May 17, 1939, p.313
[146] "Code of the Cactus," *Motion Picture Herald*, January 14, 1939, p.37
[147] "Victory's 20 to Include 12 Specials, 8 Westerns," *Film Daily*, January 18, 1939, p.8
[148] "Faralla is Preparing Third with Guizar," *Boxoffice*, March 11, 1939, p.49
[149] Read Kendall, "Around and About in Hollywood," *Los Angeles Times*, December 5, 1938, p.26
[150] "Katzman Starting Third McCoy," *Film Daily*, November 28, 1938, p.8
[151] "Outlaws Paradise," *Boxoffice*, April 22, 1939, p.26
[152] "Outlaw's Paradise," *Variety*, April 26, 1939, p.12
[153] Anthony Thomas, "Tim McCoy," *Films in Review*, April 1968, Vol XIX, No. 4, pp.221-222
[154] "Straight Shooter," *Variety*, May 15, 1940, p.18
[155] With the exception of the rousing song, "Men of the Prairie," that accompanies the opening credits. Atypical for the series, this one has lyrics as well.
[156] "Fighting Renegade," *Variety*, September 6, 1939, p.19
[157] "20 Victory Giddy-Ups," *Variety*, January 11, 1939, p.7
[158] David James Hanna, "Why is Independent Production Dying?," *Film Bulletin*, January 11, 1939, p.11
[159] Ibid.

Chapter 9: Ben Judell Shoots for the Big Time (Sig, Sam, and PPC/PDC, 1939-1940)

[1] "Brevities of the Business," *Motography*, October 26, 1912, p.340
[2] "Judell Goes to Chicago," *Motion Picture News*, September 11, 1915, p.59
[3] "B.N. Judell Forms His Own Exchange," *Exhibitors Herald*, February 16, 1918, p.37
[4] "Judell Sets 4 Exchanges to Handle Progressive Pix," *Film Daily*, November 29, 1937, p.2
[5] "Judell's New Company," *Motion Picture Herald*, April 23, 1938, p.12. *Rebellious Daughters* was announced under the working title *Wayward Daughters*, and *Slander House* as *Scandal House*.
[6] "Judell Company to Make and Sell 36," *Motion Picture Herald*, June 3, 1939, p.53
[7] "Independent Filming Spurred by Judell," *Boxoffice*, June 10, 1939, p.34. Judell's hiring of Sig to supervise the six production units suggests that Sig may have held a similar position elsewhere during the nearly three-year period he was absent from mention in the trades, performing a similar function at Columbia or some other, larger studio
[8] "Film Comeback by Senior Laemmle," *Boxoffice*, July 8, 1939, p.28
[9] "Ben Judell's First Five on Schedule Announced," *Boxoffice*, July 15, 1939, p.31
[10] "Film Production is Spurred by Judell," *Boxoffice*, September 16, 1939, p.68
[11] "Judell Building," *Motion Picture Herald*, August 26, 1939, p.49
[12] The film's opening credit attribution aside, George Sayre and Harvey Huntley were named as the writers in "Indie Producers Set Their 1940 Program," *Motion Picture Herald*, August 5, 1939, pp.13-14
[13] "Judell Shift; Other Indes [*sic*] Are Active," *Boxoffice*, August 12, 1939, p.50
[14] "Torture Ship," *Motion Picture Herald*, September 16, 1939, p.63
[15] Herb., "Torture Ship," *Variety*, November 29, 1939, p.14
[16] "Torture Ship," *The Exhibitor*, November 1, 1939, p.409
[17] "Torture Ship," *Film Daily*, November 22, 1939, p.6
[18] A word of warning: Depending on the film lengths provided in contemporary reviews, all the copies of *Torture Ship* that can be found at YouTube.com are missing at least nine minutes of the film's opening scenes, and possibly as much as fourteen minutes. These prints open abruptly with the escaped killers already on board Pichel's ship, well aware of their potential fate, and plotting their revenge and escape.
[19] Margaret Talbot, *The Entertainer: Movies, Magic and My Father's Twentieth Century* (New York: Riverhead Books, 2012), p.359
[20] "Buried Alive," *Film Daily*, November 6, 1939, p.8
[21] "Buried Alive," *The Exhibitor*, December 13, 1939, p.432
[22] "Mercy Plane," *The Exhibitor*, March 6, 1940, p.483
[23] "Mercy Plane," *The Exhibitor*, February 28, 1940, p.18
[24] Ralph Wilk, "A Little from Lots," *Film Daily*, June 22, 1930, p.4; Ralph Wilk, "Hollywood Flashes," *Film Daily*, June 10, 1931, p.7
[25] A similar move took place at Universal in the 1940s, when producer Ben Pivar's name had become ubiquitous in the credits of that company's B-level productions. Encouraged to come up with a pseudonym for occasional use, he cobbled together the name "Neil P. Varnick," "Neil" chosen from his son's first name, and the "P. Varnick" portion a slight reworking of his family's original surname, "Pivarnick." Another example of hiding behind multiple aliases were those employed by director-screenwriter Harry Fraser. Fraser would usually direct using variations of his own name, but when it came to screenwriting and assistant directing would employ multiple alternatives, Munro Talbot, Wayne Carter, Edward Weston, Weston Edwards, Harry O. Jones, and Harry C. Christ among others.
[26] "Production Notes," *The Exhibitor*, September 27, 1939, p.19
[27] Sigmund Neufeld, Jr. interview, July 15, 2022
[28] "The Invisible Killer," *Film Daily*, February 9, 1940, p.6
[29] "The Invisible Killer," *The Exhibitor*, January 24, 1940, p.455
[30] "Work Will Start on Movie Soon," *Arizona Republic* (Phoenix), October 27, 1939, p.31
[31] "Producers Pictures Lines Up Series of Westerns," *Daily News* (Los Angeles), November 2, 1939, p.20
[32] "Judell's Arizona Studio to Open in a Gay Way," *Boxoffice*, October 21, 1939, p.30; "Change PDC Production Schedule at Prescott," *Boxoffice*, December 9, 1939, p.86
[33] "Movie Completed at Granite Dells," *Arizona Independent Republic* (Phoenix), December 17, 1939, p.2
[34] "Ben Judell," *Motion Picture Daily*, December 5, 1939, p.7
[35] "Exhibs Jump at Gratis Booking," *Showmen's Trade Review*, September 9, 1939, p.4

[36] "Producers Distributing Corporation," *Boxoffice*, August 26, 1939, insert
[37] "Production," *The Exhibitor*, November 29, 1939, p.31
[38] "Ben Judell," *Motion Picture Daily*, December 5, 1939, p.7
[39] "The Sagebrush Family Trails West," *The Exhibitor*, February 28, 1940, p.18
[40] "Sagebrush Family Trails West," *The Movies...and the People Who Make Them*, 1940 Volume II Number 39, p.126
[41] "New Company Formed By PPC Creditors," *Boxoffice*, March 23, 1940, p.34
[42] "Filming of Western Starts at Prescott," *Arizona Independent Republic*, December 19, 1939, p.46
[43] Letter from Shepard Traube to Joseph I. Breen, Motion Picture Producers and Distributors of America, dated May 15, 1939. Margaret Herrick Library Digital Collections, Margaret Herrick Library, Academy of Motion Picture Arts and Sciences
[44] Letter from Joseph I. Breen to B.F. Zeidman, dated May 17, 1939. Margaret Herrick Library Digital Collections, Margaret Herrick Library, Academy of Motion Picture Arts and Sciences
[45] "Indie Producers Set Their 1940 Programs," *Motion Picture Herald*, October 5, 1939, pp.13-14; Jimmie Fidler, "Jimmie Fidler in Hollywood," *Santa Ana Register* (CA), September 12, 1939, p.11
[46] "Hitler...Beast of Berlin" ad, *Showmen's Trade Review*, September 9, 1939, p.13
[47] Fidler, *Op. Cit.*
[48] Fidler, *Op. Cit.*
[49] "'Beast of Berlin' Put Into Production Mill," *Boxoffice*, September 23, 1939, p.42
[50] "Anti-Nazis Get Full Picture of Crisis," *Boxoffice*, September 23, 1939, p.42
[51] Paul Harrison, "Harrison in Hollywood," *Edwardsville Intelligencer* (Illinois), November 2, 1939, p.3
[52] Letter from Joseph I. Breen to Producers Pictures Corporation, dated September 19, 1939. Margaret Herrick Library Digital Collections, Margaret Herrick Library, Academy of Motion Picture Arts and Sciences
[53] Breen would refer to Julius as "Ben Judell Sr." in his correspondences
[54] Joseph I. Breen letter to Francis S. Harmon, head of the eastern Production Code Administration office, dated October 23, 1939. Margaret Herrick Library Digital Collections, Margaret Herrick Library, Academy of Motion Picture Arts and Sciences
[55] "Concentrates of the News," *Los Angeles Times*, September 20, 1939, p.15
[56] Arnie Bernstein, *Swastika Nation* (New York: St. Martin's Press, 2013), p.217
[57] "Production Notes," *The Exhibitor*, September 27, 1939, p.19
[58] "'Beast of Berlin' Put Into Production Mill," *Op. Cit.*
[59] Joel Newfield interview, October 18, 2022
[60] Bernstein, p.218
[61] Joseph I. Breen letter to Ben Judell, dated November 3, 1939. Margaret Herrick Library Digital Collections, Margaret Herrick Library, Academy of Motion Picture Arts and Sciences
[62] "Title 'Goose Step' Brings Hays Okay," *Boxoffice*, December 9, 1939, p.67
[63] "'Beasts of Berlin' Gets Okay as Censors Reverse," *Film Daily*, November 13, 1939, pp.1, 6
[64] "Beasts of Berlin," *Motion Picture Herald*, October 29, 1939, p.42
[65] "Seal for 'Berlin' Waits on National Title Change," *Film Daily*, November 16, 1939, pp.1, 7
[66] "Three Censor Boards Approve 'Hitler'," *Boxoffice*, November 18, 1939, p.13
[67] Ben R. Crisler, "Beasts of Berlin," *New York Times*, November 20, 1939, p.15
[68] "Beasts of Berlin," *Variety*, November 22, 1939, p.16
[69] "Goose Step," *Motion Picture Review*, February 1940, p.4
[70] "Movie Making is Halted," *Arizona Independent Republic*, January 1, 1940, p.32
[71] "Rathner to Head Revamped PDC, PPC; Pathe Active," *Film Daily*, February 26, 1940, pp.1, 4
[72] Sig's wife Ruth was vice president, and brother Sam secretary; Bert Sternbach was both production manager and casting director. Incorporated on March 27, 1940, the company would remain on the books until early 1960
[73] "New Company Formed By PPC Creditors," *Boxoffice*, March 23, 1940, p.34
[74] "Producers Releasing Corp. Incorporates in New York," *Film Daily*, April 3, 1940, p.2
[75] "Pathe is Financing Neufeld for PRC," *Boxoffice*, April 27, 1940, p.35
[76] "Producers Releasing Corp. Plans Thirty-eight," *Motion Picture Herald*, May 11, 1940, p.40
[77] "Judell Successors Plan Two Features a Month," *Boxoffice*, April 6, 1940, p.38
[78] "Neufeld Boosts Program," *Motion Picture Daily*, April 25, 1940, p.7; "Neufeld Productions Ups '40-41 Film Total to 36," *Boxoffice*, May 4, 1940, p.36
[79] "Pathe is Financing Neufeld for PRC," *Op. Cit.*

Chapter 10: Like a Phoenix from the Ashes (Sig, Sam, and PRC, Part 1, 1939-1941)

[1] Joel Newfield interview, October 18, 2022
[2] "Fighting Mad," *The Exhibitor*, November 15, 1939, p.415
[3] Or at least it was thought to be so at the time. While it was widely believed that Iron Eyes Cody was a Native American, time would prove that he was actually of Italian parentage.
[4] "Secrets of a Model," *Film Daily*, April 18, 1940, p.4
[5] "What the Picture Did for Me," *Motion Picture Herald*, July 20, 1940, p.42 (A.C. Myrick, State Theatre, Lake Park, Iowa)
[6] "Hackel Back at Rep.," *Variety*, November 4, 1942, p.8
[7] "A.W. Hackel Recovers," *Film Daily*, March 22, 1939, p.2
[8] "Major Film Company Signs Ralph Cooper," *Indianapolis Recorder*, June 1, 1940, p.11
[9] Distributor Henry Sonnenshine "was the first person to place an all-colored film into big time theatres in New York. He crashed RKO and Loews with Ralph Cooper's film, 'Dark Manhattan' which broke records and attracted a larger gross than 'The Good Earth' and 'Dead End' playing at opposition houses." See "Sonnenshine of Staff of Supreme Pics," *California Eagle* (Los Angeles), May 16, 1940, p.10
[10] Earl J. Morris, "Supreme Pix Co.'s A.W. Hackel Making Four with Cooper," *Pittsburgh Courier*, May 11, 1940, p.21
[11] "John Jenkins Distributor for Supreme Pictures Corp.," *Boxoffice*, August 10, 1940, p.57
[12] "Apollo, N.Y.: Am I Guilty?," *Variety*, October 2, 1940, p.56
[13] "Am I Guilty?," *Variety*, October 2, 1940, p.25
[14] "Hackel's 2-Pic Mono Deal," *Variety*, May 14, 1941, p.4
[15] "PRC Announces Lineup," *The Exhibitor*, May 8, 1940, p.16
[16] "Highlights of Production Happenings: Producers Releasing Corp.," *The Exhibitor*, July 10, 1940, p.14a
[17] "Pathe Pictures, Ltd., to Handle PRC Lineup," *Film Daily*, June 7, 1940, p.4; "Pathe British Deal," *Boxoffice*, June 15, 1940, p.27
[18] These and all subsequent budgetary figures are culled from the United Artists collection of the Wisconsin Center for Film and Theater Research at the University of Wisconsin-Madison, and supplemented by input from Karl Thiede. All figures quoted are rounded to the nearest dollar
[19] "I Take This Oath," *The Exhibitor*, May 29, 1940, p.536
[20] "I Take This Oath," *The Movies…and the People Who Make Them*, September 28, 1940, p.128
[21] "Hold That Woman," *Film Daily*, July 12, 1940, p.6
[22] Chudnow earned a mere $50 for his contributions to *I Take This Oath*—his first collaboration for Sig—which included the main title's "The Lady Takes a Chance" along with eleven other compositions. Contract between Sigmund Neufeld Productions and David Chudnow of Screen Music, Inc., dated May 1, 1940; Wisconsin Center for Film and Theater Research (WCFTR), United Artists collection, University of Wisconsin-Madison
[23] Tim Neufeld interview, July 22, 2022
[24] "The Karma of Becoming American," Denshō, https://densho.org/catalyst/the-karma-of-becoming-american/
[25] "Producers Sets New Program for Season," *Motion Picture Daily*, August 2, 1940, p.8; "New Independent Distributor Lists 38 for 1940-1941," *Motion Picture Herald*, August 3, 1940, p.20
[26] "Wandering Around Hollywood," *Showmen's Trade Review*, January 11, 1941, p.19
[27] "O. Henry Briggs Named PRC Head," *Film Daily*, September 26, 1940, p.2; "Briggs Succeeds Rathner As President of PRC," *Boxoffice*, December 28, 1940, p.17
[28] "Rathner Schedules Seven for Early P-R-C Release, *Boxoffice*, November 9, 1940, p.16
[29] "Briggs Visiting Exchanges En Route to West Coast," *Film Daily*, January 28, 1941, p.2
[30] Joseph I. Breen letter to Sigmund Neufeld, dated June 24, 1940. Margaret Herrick Library Digital Collections, Margaret Herrick Library, Academy of Motion Picture Arts and Sciences
[31] *Gun Code* Pennsylvania censor notes dated August 30, 1940. Margaret Herrick Library Digital Collections, Margaret Herrick Library, Academy of Motion Picture Arts and Sciences
[32] "Arizona Gang Busters," *The Exhibitor*, September 25, 1940, p.14
[33] "What the Picture Did for Me," *Motion Picture Herald*, November 22, 1941, pp.73-74 (E.L. Ornstein, Rialto Theatre, Marengo, Indiana)
[34] "Riders of Black Mountain," *Motion Picture Daily*, October 29, 1940, p.3
[35] "Outlaws of the Rio Grande," *Motion Picture Daily*, February 24, 1941, p.5
[36] Anthony Thomas, p.2234

[37] Earlier undated *Tempe News* article quoted in Jay Mark, "Lousy Movie's Best Scenes are Those of 1940 Tempe," *Arizona Republic* (Phoenix), March 28, 2008, p.6

[38] Letter from Adolph Schimel to Leon Fromkess, dated July 8, 1940. WCFTR, UA collection, University of Wisconsin-Madison

[39] "What the Picture Did for Me," *Motion Picture Herald*, February 8, 1941, p.48 (C. Frank Deane, Abbott Theatre, Huntington, West Virginia)

[40] Mike Fitzgerald, "An Interview With…Louise Currie," Boyd Magers' *Western Clippings* web site. http://www.westernclippings.com/interview/louisecurrie_interview.shtml

[41] In his autobiographical *White Horse, Black Hat: A Quarter Century on Hollywood's Poverty Row* (The Scarecrow Press, 2002, p.50), screenwriter C. Jack Lewis claims that Fuzzy Knight was originally set to be Crabbe's sidekick in the series, but backed out at the last minute and headed over to Universal. "In the original script, Fuzzy Knight was going to appear as himself, Fuzzy. With Al St. John in place, the director saw no need to change the name and Al played a character called Fuzzy in this and subsequent Westerns. Slowly, he adopted a character called Fuzzy Q. Jones and became known to fans around the world as Fuzzy, not Al St. John." The accuracy of this is questionable, especially since St. John was using the character name Fuzzy in the earlier, late 1930s Fred Scott series. Unless, of course, he was confusing the Crabbe series with the Fred Scott series.

[42] Mario DeMarco, *Battlin' Bob Steele*, as quoted in Bobby J. Copeland's *Charlie King: We Called Him "Blackie"*, p.12

[43] "Billy the Kid in Texas," *The Exhibitor*, October 23, 1940, p.14

[44] "Billy the Kid in Texas," *Variety*, November 20, 1940, p.18

[45] "Billy the Kid's Range War," *Variety*, March 12, 1941, p.16

[46] "Billy the Kid's Range War," *Motion Picture Herald*, December 13, 1941, p.46 (E.L. Ornstein, Rialto Theatre, Marengo, Indiana)

[47] "Bob Steele's the Real McCoy," *Morning Herald* (Hagerstown, MD), September 19, 1941, p.5

[48] Brought in with a negative cost of $11,634. Screenwriter George Plympton received $200 for his efforts. WCFTR, United Artists collection, University of Wisconsin-Madison

[49] Negative cost $12,816. Screenwriter Joseph O'Donnell only received $150 for this one. WCFTR, United Artists collection, University of Wisconsin-Madison

[50] "What the Picture Did for Me," *Motion Picture Herald*, November 30, 1940, p.50

[51] Undated copy of 1940-41 contract between Sigmund Neufeld Productions and Producers Releasing Corporation of America. WCFTR, University of Wisconsin-Madison, United Artists Series 2G, Box 26, Folder 401b

[52] Document summarizing agreement between Producers Releasing Corporation of America and Sigmund Neufeld Productions, Inc. dated April 18, 1941. WCFTR, UA Series 2G, Box 26, Folder 401a

[53] *The Devil Bat*'s final negative cost was $21,371

[54] Don Leifert, "Producers Releasing Corp., Part 2," *Filmfax*, August 1989, No. 16, p.71

[55] "Clowns, Circuses, Cactus, Cirees," *Boxoffice*, December 14, 1940, p.40

[56] Letter from assistant secretary George Fleitman, Producers Releasing Corp., to Sigmund Neufeld Productions, dated some time in 1947. WCFTR, UA Series 2G, Box 26, Folder 404

[57] The overages on Sigmund Neufeld Productions for the 1940-41 season amounted to $3,943 for four films: *I Take This Oath*, *Hold That Woman!*, *Marked Men*, and *The Lone Rider Crosses the Rio*. When deductions of $2,436 were made for advances and credits in excess of the other films' contract prices, the balance due to Sig was $1,507. Leon Fromkess letter and "Statement of Account" to Sigmund Neufeld, dated (month illegible) 15, 1941. WCFTR, UA collection, University of Wisconsin-Madison

[58] Sigmund Neufeld letter to Harry Rathner, dated October 13, 1940. WCFTR, UA Series 2G, Box 26, Folder 401b

[59] "PRC Assigns Neufeld," *Boxoffice*, October 26, 1940, p.30-A

[60] *The Lone Rider Crosses the Rio* exceeded its spartan budget by nearly $2,000, coming in with a negative cost of $13,706

[61] "The Lone Rider Rides On," *Boxoffice*, March 1, 1941, p.34

[62] "Hollywood," *Showmen's Trade Review*, April 5, 1941, p.36

[63] Lange and Porter were paid $305 for their compositions, which included "Under the Prairie Skies," "Sweet Susannah," and "Spring Valley." WCFTR, UA collection, University of Wisconsin-Madison

[64] Signed contract between George Houston and Eddy Graneman, PRC Director of Advertising and Publicity, dated October 11, 1940. WCFTR, UA collection, University of Wisconsin-Madison
[65] "The Lone Rider in Ghost Town," *Film Daily*, May 9, 1941, p.7
[66] "The Lone Rider Ambushed," *Film Daily*, October 31, 1941, p.10
[67] "The Lone Rider Fights Back," *Film Daily*, December 24, 1941, p.8

Chapter 11: Growing Up in Hollywood – Part 1
[1] Sigmund Neufeld Jr. interview, July 22, 2022
[2] Joel Newfield interview, May 11, 2023
[3] Joel Newfield interviews, October 18, 2022, and May 11, 2023
[4] Sigmund Neufeld Jr. interview, June 24, 2022
[5] Sigmund Neufeld Jr. interview, July 15, 2022
[6] Stanley Neufeld, Directors Guild of America interview by Kevin Koster. https://www.dga.org/Craft/VisualHistory/Interviews/Stanley-Neufeld.aspx
[7] Ibid.
[8] Sigmund Neufeld Jr. interview, July 15, 2022
[9] Sigmund Neufeld Jr. interviews, July 15 and 22, 2022
[10] Sigmund Neufeld Jr. interview, August 10, 2022
[11] Sigmund Neufeld Jr. interview, July 15, 2022
[12] Joel Newfield interview, October 18, 2022
[13] Sigmund Neufeld Jr. interview, July 15, 2022
[14] Joel Newfield interview, October 18, 2022
[15] Sigmund Neufeld Jr. interview, June 27, 2022
[16] Tim Neufeld interview, June 27, 2022
[17] Ibid.
[18] Ibid.
[19] Kathy Neufeld interview, June 27, 2022
[20] Sigmund Neufeld Jr. interview, June 27, 2022
[21] Tim Neufeld interview, June 27, 2022
[22] Sigmund Neufeld Jr. interview, August 10, 2022

Chapter 12: Buster Joins Fuzzy (Sig, Sam, and PRC, Part 2, 1941-1942)
[1] "Consolidated Advances $1,000,000 to P.R.C.," *Motion Picture Herald*, March 1, 1941, p.23
[2] "P.R.C. Additional Funds From Consolidated," *Motion Picture Herald*, June 28, 1941, p.60; "Mortgage of Chattels, Pledge and Assignment" between Consolidated Film Industries, Inc. and Producers Releasing Corporation, dated June 18, 1941. WCFTR, UA collection, University of Wisconsin-Madison
[3] "PRC to Convene in Chi. Mar. 22-24," *Showmen's Trade Review*, March 15, 1941, p.4
[4] Contract between Producers Releasing Corporation of America and Sigmund Neufeld Productions, Inc. dated August 1, 1941. WCFTR, UA Series 2G, Box 26, Folder 402
[5] "PRC Into the Ring With 42 Next Year," *Boxoffice*, March 29, 1941, p.19
[6] "PRC to Make 42 Pictures," *Showmen's Trade Review*, March 29, 1941, p.8
[7] Document summarizing agreement between Producers Releasing Corporation of America and Sigmund Neufeld Productions, Inc. dated August 1, 1941. WCFTR, UA Series 2G, Box 26, Folder 403
[8] Production Contract between Producers Releasing Corporation of America and Sigmund Neufeld Productions, Inc. dated April 30, 1942. WCFTR, UA Series 2G, Box 26, Folder 402
[9] "The Hollywood Scene," *Motion Picture Herald*, May 24, 1941, p.38
[10] "Neufeld Gets Stories, *Motion Picture Daily*, May 26, 1941, p.6; "Stepped Up Production for Decree Sales Still the Planning Keynote," *Motion Picture Herald*, May 31, 1941, p.25
[11] Ralph Wilk, "Hollywood Speaking," *Film Daily*, June 27, 1941, p.8
[12] "Studios Buy 16 Stories for Production During Week," *Motion Picture Daily*, June 5, 1941, p.6
[13] "Signal Tower," *The Newhall Signal* (Newhall, CA), August 29, 1941, page unknown
[14] "'Buster' Crabbe Says July 4th at Clear Lake Happiest He's Had Since He Was a Kid," *Globe-Gazette* (Mason City, Iowa), July 5, 1941, p.2
[15] Frank Leyendecker, "'Billy, the Kid, Wanted' Good Starter for Buster Crabbe Westerns," *Film Bulletin*, October 24, 1941, p.6
[16] John Tibbetts, "Buster Crabbe," *American Classic Screen*, July/August 1977, p.10

17 Ibid., p.9
18 Joel Newfield interview, October 18, 2022
19 "Billy the Kid Wanted," *Film Daily*, November 28, 1941, p.6
20 Patricia Harper, "The Minimum Basic Flat Deal," *The Screen Writer*, April 1946, p.19
21 "Correspondence," *The Screen Writer*, Volume 1 - July 1945-May 1946, p.48
22 Boyd Magers, "Characters and Heavies: Glenn Strange," Boyd Magers' *Western Clippings* web site. http://www.westernclippings.com/heavies/glennstrange_charactersheavies.shtml
23 "Billy the Kid Trapped," *Motion Picture Herald*, February 20, 1942, p.612
24 "Billy the Kid's Smoking Guns," *Motion Picture Herald*, August 22, 1942, p.854
25 Sigmund Neufeld Jr. interview, July 15, 2022
26 Neil Summers, "Action Actors by Neil Summers: Dave O'Brien," Boyd Magers' *Western Clippings* web site. http://www.westernclippings.com/stuntmen/daveobrien_stuntmen.shtml
27 "Law and Order," *Film Daily*, October 15, 1942, p.6
28 "Sheriff of Sage Valley," *Variety*, December 9, 1942, p.16
29 "PRC to Show First Year Profit, Directors Told," *Film Daily*, July 9, 1941, p.4
30 "PRC Sales Ahead 100%—Greenblatt," *Motion Picture Herald*, November 8, 1941, p.40
31 "Appoint Greenblatt P.R.C. Sales Chief," *Motion Picture Herald*, April 19, 1941, p.25
32 "Lee Powell Killed in Action," *Film Daily*, September 1, 1944, p.2
33 "Deal With Meyer Stern Gives PRC 100% Coverage," *Film Daily*, March 26, 1941, p.2
34 Not to be confused with yet *another* Boyd, William "Stage" Boyd (1889-1935), long dead by this time
35 "PRC Signs Radio Star," *Motion Picture Herald*, September 20, 1941, p.66
36 "Final Screening of Program at Grand," *Newark Advocate* (Newark, Ohio), February 14, 1942, p.7
37 Contract between Sigmund Neufeld Productions, Inc. and William Boyd, dated July 25, 1941. WCFTR, UA Series 2G, Box 26, Folder 401b
38 "Texas Manhunt," *The Exhibitor*, December 24, 1941, p.913
39 Copeland, pp.35-36
40 Ibid., p.36
41 "Prairie Pals," *The Exhibitor*, October 7, 1942, p.1124
42 Brought in with a negative cost of $13,267
43 Sam had evidently caught on to just how boring it was for viewers to watch Houston's singing in these films, so he repeatedly cut away to inserts of Fuzzy who would be rolling a cigarette, fumbling with a canteen, chewing tobacco, or some other bit of business simply to relieve the visual tedium
44 "No Equine Injuries in Neufeld Pictures," *Panama City News-Herald* (Panama City, FL), September 14, 1941, p.4
45 "Well Balanced Program at the Riviera," *The News Tribune* (Tacoma, Washington), January 13, 1944, p.10
46 "Rowland Lee to Engineer Return of Frankenstein," *Los Angeles Times*, November 15, 1938, p.A14
47 "British Banning 'Horror' Pix for the Duration," *Film Daily*, September 16, 1942, p.5
48 "Creepy Pix Cleaning Up," *Variety*, March 31, 1943, pp.7, 46
49 La Guardia, who had it in for the burlesque shows since the beginning of his administration, finally took action when some rogue strippers began to work so-called "flashing" into their acts. This involved the quick repositioning of the wearer's G-string, affording a quick glimpse of the nether regions to the more attentive members of the audience. Needless to say, a crowd pleaser. (Leslie Zemeckis, *Behind the Burly Q*, New York: Skyhorse Publishing, 2013, p.204)
50 "PRC All-Out for Corio; 7-Day Shooting Sked Now," *Variety*, February 25, 1942, p.6
51 Ibid.
52 "PRC May Change Name to Pathe," *Motion Picture Herald*, August 1, 1942, p.15
53 PRC-supplied promotional piece, as printed in "Lovely Ann Corio Is Sensational On Screen," *Morning Herald* (Uniontown, PA), August 31, 1942, p.2
54 "PRC Sets Product Deal with Two Warner Zones," *Film Daily*, October 16, 1942, p.2
55 Leon Fromkess letter to O. Henry Briggs, dated July 2, 1942. WCFTR, UA collection, University of Wisconsin-Madison
56 Leon Fromkess letter to PRC comptroller Joseph Lamm, dated March 19, 1943. WCFTR, UA collection, University of Wisconsin-Madison
57 "PRC Sells 7-Picture Unit," *Showmen's Trade Review*, October 31, 1942, p.23
58 "PRC's Package Plan Calls for 2 Features Under One Catchy Title," *Showmen's Trade Review*, September 12, 1942, p.23

59 "'Jungle Siren' Silly Melodrama Has Selling Angles," *Film Bulletin*, August 14, 1942, p.22

60 While Max King was credited as co-producer of Beaudine's *Men of San Quentin* (05/22/1942) along with Martin Mooney, Sig was the actual behind-the-scenes producer, continuing to receive 20 % of the overages for this film for years to come. Sig had a similar arrangement for producer Mooney's earlier *Mr. Celebrity* (10/10/1941), also directed by Beaudine, for which he received 12 ½ % of the overages. Letter from assistant secretary George Fleitman, Producers Releasing Corp., to Sigmund Neufeld Productions, dated some time in 1947. WCFTR, UA Series 2G, Box 26, Folder 404

Chapter 13: The War Takes a Bite (Sig, Sam, and PRC, Part 3, 1942-1943)

1 "Cut Pix Costs to Bone," *Variety*, November 4, 1942, pp.3, 20

2 "Producers Agree on 10-24% Reduction in Raw Stock," *Motion Picture Herald*, August 8, 1942, p.12

3 "SWG's Negotiation Request Heeded," *Boxoffice*, April 12, 1940, p.22

4 Sigmund Neufeld Jr. interview, July 22, 2022

5 "Independent Producers Set Property Stockpile," *Motion Picture Daily*, October 28, 1942, pp.1, 7

6 James Francis Crow, "Film War Saving Drive Picks Up Speed as All Industry Rallied," *Los Angeles Evening Citizen-News*, April 23, 1942, p.6

7 "Pathe Paid $750,000 for PRC Control; Prod., Distrib Setup Continue," *Variety*, January 14, 1942, p.7 put the acquisition at 85% of PRC's stock, but the subsequent purchase of a remaining 32% of the stock accurately placed to initial acquisition at 68%.

8 "Neufeld Leases Studio," *The Exhibitor*, January 28, 1942, p.7; "Pathe Now Owns 100 Per Cent of PRC Stock," *Motion Picture Herald*, February 28, 1942, p.46

9 "PRC May Change Name to Pathe," p.15

10 "PRC Convenes On Coast May 4," *Motion Picture Herald*, March 28, 1942, p.70; "PRC Holds Meeting," *The Exhibitor*, April 1, 1942, p.7

11 "Batcheller Quits PRC," *Variety*, April 29, 1942, p.5; "Fromkess Heads PRC Production," *Film Daily*, April 28, 1942, pp.1, 7

12 "Producers Releasing Corp.," *Film Daily*, May 7, 1942, p.8

13 "PRC to Have 18 Westerns and 24 Features," *Motion Picture Herald*, May 9, 1942, p.21

14 "PRC is Moving to Talisman Studios," *Motion Picture Herald*, September 12, 1942, p.60

15 "Production Periscope," *The Exhibitor*, May 26, 1943, p.11

16 Peter Bogdanovich, *Who the Devil Made It* (New York: Alfred A. Knopf, Inc., 1997), p.124

17 "Who's Who in Hollywood," *Film Daily*, October 5, 1942, p.4

18 "PRC Announces Titles of 24 Features; 18 Westerns Comprising 1942-43 Schedule," *Showmen's Trade Review*, July 18, 1942, p.6

19 "Fugitive of the Plains," *The Exhibitor*, April 7, 1943, p.1240

20 "What the Picture Did for Me," *Motion Picture Herald*, May 22, 1943, p.49 (M.L. London, Gem Theatre, East Boston, Massachusetts)

21 "What the Picture Did for Me," *Motion Picture Herald*, June 5, 1943, p.49 (Charles A. Brooks, Ritz Theatre, Marshfield, Maryland)

22 "Western Cyclone," *Variety*, June 16, 1943, p.16

23 John Tibbetts, "Buster Crabbe," *American Classic Screen*, July/August 1977, pg.9

24 "'Buster' Crabbe Says July 4th at Clear Lake Happiest He's Had Since He Was a Kid," p.2

25 Florence "Flobelle" Moore St. John, interviewed by Sam Gill in Sterling, Kansas, October 3, 1965

26 John Tibbetts, p.10

27 Buster Crabbe letter to Tim Neufeld, September 6, 1973

28 "'Buster' Crabbe Says July 4th at Clear Lake Happiest He's Had Since He Was a Kid," *Op. Cit.*

29 "Hollywood," *Showmen's Trade Review*, April 24, 1943, p.37

30 "Sound Truck Bottleneck Nips Indie Producers; Majors Well Supplied," *Variety*, July 1, 1942, p.27

31 Boyd Magers, "The Westerns of…Bob Livingston," Boyd Magers' *Western Clippings* web site. http://www.westernclippings.com/westernsof/boblivingston_westernsof.shtml

32 Ibid.

33 "Hollywood," *Showmen's Trade Review*, June 19, 1943, p.48

34 "Wolves of the Range," *The Exhibitor*, July 14, 1943, p.1302

35 "Wolves of the Range," *Variety*, June 14, 1944, p.10

36 "Studio Size-Ups," *Film Bulletin*, October 18, 1943, p.16

37 Herb A. Lightman, "Out of This World!," *American Cinematographer*, September 1951, p.377

³⁸ W.G.C. Bosco, "Aces of the Camera: Jack Greenhalgh, A.S.C.," *American Cinematographer*, January 1945, pp.7, 18
³⁹ Ibid., p.18
⁴⁰ "Aces of the Camera: Vincent J. Farrar," *American Cinematographer*, August 1946, p.294
⁴¹ "Queen of Broadway," *Film Daily*, November 24, 1942, p.6
⁴² Stanley had gone to work for his father immediately after finishing high school. He can be spotted in the cast and crew photos for *Tumbleweed Trail* and manning the clap board for *The Mad Monster* and *Texas Justice*, all three films in production at different times in early 1942
⁴³ "To the Colors!," *Film Daily*, October 20, 1942, p.20
⁴⁴ Stanley Neufeld, Directors Guild of America interview by Kevin Koster. https://www.dga.org/Craft/VisualHistory/Interviews/Stanley-Neufeld.aspx
⁴⁵ Joel Newfield interview, October 18, 1942
⁴⁶ Hugh Dixon, "Hollywood," *Pittsburgh Post-Gazette*, June 29, 1944, p.24
⁴⁷ Sigmund Neufeld Jr. interview, August 10, 2022
⁴⁸ "PRC Buys 'Package' Radio Show," *Motion Picture Herald*, April 10, 1943, p.15
⁴⁹ "Producers Releasing," *Film Bulletin*, May 17, 1943, p.18
⁵⁰ "Danger! Women at Work," *Motion Picture Herald*, July 17, 1943, p.1426
⁵¹ "'Danger! Women at Work' with Patsy Kelly and Mary Brian," *Harrisons Reports*, July 24, 1943, p.118
⁵² "Danger! Women at Work (PRC)," *Photoplay*, October 1943, p.119
⁵³ "What the Picture Did for Me," *Motion Picture Herald*, September 18, 1943, p.58 (Army Theatre No. 2, Ft. Bragg, North Carolina)
⁵⁴ "Creepy Pix Cleaning Up," *Op. Cit.*
⁵⁵ Ibid.
⁵⁶ Ed Raiden, "Wandering Around Hollywood," *Showmen's Trade Review*, October 3, 1942, p.41
⁵⁷ Leifert, "Producers Releasing Corp., Part 2," *Filmfax*, p.72
⁵⁸ "Dead Men Walk," *The Exhibitor*, January 6, 1943, p.18
⁵⁹ "Dead Men Walk," *Harrisons Reports*, January 9, 1943, p.6
⁶⁰ "Dead Men Walk," *Showmen's Trade Review*, January 16, 1943, p.34
⁶¹ "Dead Men Walk," *Motion Picture Daily*, February 16, 1943, p.6
⁶² "Dead Men Walk," *Variety*, April 7, 1943, p.8
⁶³ "'The Black Raven' Below-Par Horror Film," *Film Bulletin*, July 26, 1943, p.20
⁶⁴ "Creepy Pix Cleaning Up," *Op. Cit.*
⁶⁵ "The Black Raven," *Motion Picture Daily*, March 16, 1943, p.6
⁶⁶ "The Black Raven," *Motion Picture Herald*, March 20, 1943, p.1215
⁶⁷ "Summary Production Cost" sheets for *The Black Raven*, dated March 1, 1943; David Chudnow's contract assigning all rights to his compositions for *The Black Raven*, dated February 26, 1943. WCFTR, UA collection, University of Wisconsin-Madison
⁶⁸ "Hollywood," *Showmen's Trade Review*, January 23, 1943, p.28
⁶⁹ Letter from Ben Schwalb to R. George Fleitman, dated September 12, 1944. WCFTR, UA collection, University of Wisconsin-Madison
⁷⁰ "Hollywood," *Showmen's Trade Review*, April 17, 1943, p.37
⁷¹ "Production Notes from the Studios," *Showmen's Trade Review*, February 13, 1943, p.22

Chapter 14: Slaves of Formula (Sig, Sam, and PRC, Part 4, 1943-1944)
¹ "Producers Releasing," *Op. Cit.*
² Not all eight of these "Bill" Westerns would be released during the 1943-44 season, nor would a consistent eight be released in any subsequent season, with one exception. That said, twenty-four Crabbe Westerns would be released over the next three seasons with a final lone entry spilling into the 1946-47 season, accounting for the eight entries filmed in any given season, 1943-44 through 1945-46.
³ "PRC Plans 40 Films for New Season," *Motion Picture Herald*, June 19, 1943, p.44. "40 Films" and "16 Westerns" were incorrectly stated in this article, but corrected to "42" and "18" shortly thereafter.
⁴ "PRC Announces Titles of 24 Features; 18 Westerns Comprising 1942-43 Schedule," *Showmen's Trade Review*, July 18, 1942, p.6
⁵ "PRC Expanding and Altering Its Setup," *Showmen's Trade Review*, May 29, 1943, p.30
⁶ "Producers Releasing," *Film Bulletin*, July 12, 1943, p.10

[7] "Production Notes from the Studios," *Showmen's Trade Review*, September 18, 1943, p.34
[8] "Designate Officers of PRC Productions," *Motion Picture Daily*, September 8, 1943, p.10
[9] "PRC Acquires Fine Art Studio for $305,000," *Film Daily*, September 22, 1943, p.7
[10] "PRC Productions Formed," *Showmen's Trade Review*, September 18, 1943, p.36
[11] *State of California Department of Public Health Certificate of Death* for Hans Hugo Herman Weeren, dated August 6, 1943
[12] Production Contract between Producers Releasing Corporation of America and Sigmund Neufeld Productions, Inc. dated July 15, 1943. WCFTR, UA Series 2G, Box 26, Folder 404
[13] Documents summarizing agreement between Producers Releasing Corporation of America and Sigmund Neufeld Productions, Inc. dated August 10 and August 13, 1943. WCFTR, UA Series 2G, Box 26, Folders 404 and 405
[14] "PRC Gross on Westerns Up 47 Per Cent," *Motion Picture Herald*, February 20, 1943, p.24
[15] "Blazing Frontier," *Motion Picture Daily*, April 10, 1943, p.4
[16] John Todd, "In Hollywood," *The Times* (Munster, Indiana), November 10, 1943, p.28
[17] "The Devil Riders," *Motion Picture Herald*, February 12, 1944, p.1754
[18] "Frontier Outlaws," *The Exhibitor*, April 5, 1944, p.1483
[19] "Frontier Outlaws," *Motion Picture Daily*, May 25, 1944, p.7
[20] "Frontier Outlaws," *Showmen's Trade Review*, June 10, 1944, p.18
[21] "Frontier Outlaws," *Motion Picture Herald*, August 5, 1944, p.2030
[22] "The Drifter," *Film Daily*, June 14, 1943, p.6
[23] Copeland, pp.40-41
[24] "Valley of Vengeance," *Showmen's Trade Review*, July 15, 1944, p.15
[25] "Valley of Vengeance," *Motion Picture Daily*, August 8, 1944, p.12
[26] "Valley of Vengeance," *Film Daily*, August 28, 1944, p.13
[27] PRC accounting department head David P. Wiener letter to Leon Fromkess, dated May 4, 1944. WCFTR, UA collection, University of Wisconsin-Madison
[28] "Fuzzy Settles Down," *Independent Film Journal*, December 9, 1944, p.32
[29] "Fuzzy Settles Down," *Motion Picture Herald*, December 2, 1944, p.2202
[30] Contract between PRC Pictures, Inc. and Sigmund Neufeld Productions, Inc. dated March 10, 1944. WCFTR, UA Series 2G, Box 26, Folder 405
[31] "Coast Flashes," *Motion Picture Daily*, September 30, 1943, p.2; "Academy Gets Members," *The Exhibitor*, October 6, 1943, p.14
[32] S&N's officers were Sternbach as president, Violet Newfield as vice-president, and Sam as secretary-treasurer
[33] Frederick C. Othman, "Hollywood Film Shop," *Chico Record* (Chico, CA), July 1, 1943, p.2
[34] "PRC Prepares 25 Films for Early Production," *Motion Picture Herald*, April 24, 1943, p.29
[35] "'Tiger Fangs' Frank Buck Feature Has Serial-Like Plot," *Film Bulletin*, December 10, 1943, p.22
[36] "Tiger Fangs," *Film Daily*, September 27, 1943, p.4
[37] "Tiger Fangs," *Harrisons Reports*, September 18, 1943, p.150
[38] "Who's Who in Hollywood," *Film Daily*, June 26, 1944, p.6
[39] A handwritten contract, dated August 6, 1943, and "Signed for Radio Rogues By Jimmy Hollywood," took "all responsibility for any and all impersonations done by us," absolving Sigmund Neufeld Productions "from any and all suits or legal difficulties that might arise from use of same." WCFTR, UA collection, University of Wisconsin-Madison
[40] "Harvest Melody," *Film Daily*, October 6, 1943, p.9
[41] "Harvest Melody," *Motion Picture Daily*, October 6, 1943, p.7
[42] "Harvest Melody," *Motion Picture Herald*, October 9, 1943, p.1574
[43] "Harvest Melody," *Showmen's Trade Review*, October 9, 1943, p.11
[44] "What the Picture Did for Me," *Motion Picture Herald*, March 11, 1944, p.62 (W.C. Pullin, Linden Theatre, Columbus, Ohio)
[45] "What the Picture Did for Me," *Motion Picture Herald*, December 16, 1943, p.43 (Ralph Raspa, State Theatre, Rivesville, West Virginia)
[46] "What the Picture Did for Me," *Motion Picture Herald*, May 20, 1944, p.40 (Robert Floeter, Burton Theatre, Flint, Michigan)
[47] "What the Picture Did for Me," *Motion Picture Herald*, May 6, 1944, p.48 (Harriet Pilliod, La France Theatre, Swanton, Ohio)
[48] "What the Picture Did for Me," *Motion Picture Herald*, December 9, 1943, p.40 (W.J. Fleischer, New Franklin Theatre, Franklin, Minnesota)

[49] Letter from Leon Fromkess to O. Henry Briggs, dated June 26, 1943. WCFTR, UA collection, University of Wisconsin-Madison
[50] Letter from Leon Fromkess to Walter Colmes Productions, dated July 15, 1943. WCFTR, UA collection, University of Wisconsin-Madison
[51] It's possible (but as yet confirmed or dismissed) that Sigmund Neufeld Productions may have had a similar, behind-the-scenes arrangement with other producers' films. *The Lady Confesses*, an Alexander-Stern Production produced by Alfred Stern, is a possibility, given the commonality of some of its crew members
[52] Letter from attorney Herbert T. Silverberg to Sigmund Neufeld Productions, Inc. dated October 12, 1943. WCFTR, UA collection, University of Wisconsin-Madison
[53] Letter from Leon Kaplan to Herbert T. Silverberg, dated November 10, 1947. WCFTR, UA collection, University of Wisconsin-Madison
[54] "Walter Colmes to Produce Six Pictures for Republic," *Film Daily*, November 3, 1943, p.2
[55] "The Contender," *Motion Picture Daily*, May 9, 1944, p.7
[56] Leon Fromkess letter to PRC general sales manager Leo J. McCarthy, dated December 14, 1943. WCFTR, UA collection, University of Wisconsin-Madison
[57] Leon Fromkess letter to Bert Sternbach, dated January 27, 1944. WCFTR, UA collection, University of Wisconsin-Madison
[58] Eugene S. Goodwin of Kaplan & Livingston letter to George Fleitman, dated September 5, 1944. WCFTR, UA collection, University of Wisconsin-Madison
[59] "Nabonga," *Motion Picture Herald*, March 4, 1944, p.1783
[60] "Jungle Thriller 'Nabonga,' Will Be on Iowa Bill," *The Courier* (Waterloo, Iowa), May 28, 1944, p.20
[61] "At the Princess," *Boone News Republican* (Boone, Iowa), July 28, 1944, p.3
[62] "Nabonga," *The Exhibitor*, January 26, 1944, p.1447
[63] "Nabonga," *Motion Picture Daily*, February 24, 1944, p.11
[64] "Hollywood," *Showmen's Trade Review*, March 20, 1943, p.42
[65] Sigmund Neufeld letter to PRC Pictures, Inc. dated December 16, 1943; Leon Fromkess telegram to PRC comptroller Joe Lamm dated December 24, 1943; Arthur Johnson telegram to Joseph Lamm dated December 27, 1943. WCFTR, UA collection, University of Wisconsin-Madison
[66] "Production Notes from the Studios," *Showmen's Trade Review*, August 26, 1944, p.36
[67] Tom Weaver, *Poverty Row Horrors!* (Jefferson, North Carolina: McFarland & Company, Inc., 1993), p.150
[68] "The Monster Maker," *Film Daily*, March 10, 1944, p.6

Chapter 15: The Entrance of Noir (Sig, Sam, and PRC, Part 5, 1944-1945)
[1] "PRC Pictures Plans National Distribution," *Motion Picture Herald*, February 5, 1944, p.51
[2] "Briggs Quits PRC's Posts," *Film Daily*, January 31, 1944, pp.1, 3
[3] "Fromkess Elected PRC President," *Motion Picture Herald*, July 22, 1944, p.34
[4] "PRC to Release 40 Films Next Year: Fromkess," *Motion Picture Herald*, February 26, 1944, p.42
[5] "Hollywood," *Showmen's Trade Review*, June 10, 1944, p.38
[6] Sigmund Neufeld "Production Contract" with PRC Pictures, Inc., dated May 23, 1944. WCFTR, UA collection, University of Wisconsin-Madison
[7] "PRC to Release 40-45 For Next Season," *Motion Picture Herald*, July 1, 1944, p.16
[8] "PRC Announces 40 in 1944-45 Season," *The Exhibitor*, July 5, 1944, p.14
[9] John Tibbetts, "Buster Crabbe," *American Classic Screen*, July/August 1977, p.10
[10] "Production Contract" between PRC Pictures Inc. and Sigmund Neufeld Productions, dated May 23, 1944. WCFTR, UA collection, University of Wisconsin-Madison
[11] "Shadows of Death," *Motion Picture Daily*, January 25, 1945, p.7
[12] "Gangsters Den," *Motion Picture Daily*, March 8, 1945, p.9
[13] "What the Picture Did for Me," *Motion Picture Herald*, November 10, 1946, p.36 (Nick Raspa, State Theatre, Rivesville, West Virginia)
[14] "Stagecoach Outlaws," *Motion Picture Herald*, July 14, 1945, p.2542
[15] "Shadows of Death," *Motion Picture Herald*, January 20, 1945, p.2278
[16] "Stagecoach Outlaws," *Showmen's Trade Review*, July 27, 1945, p.30B
[17] "Rustlers Hideout," *Motion Picture Daily*, November 6, 1944, p.8
[18] Buster Crabbe letter to Tim Neufeld, dated September 6, 1973
[19] "Wild Horse Phantom," *The Exhibitor*, November 1, 1944, p.1608
[20] "Oath of Vengeance," *The Exhibitor*, November 15, 1944, p.1616

[21] "His Brother's Ghost," *The Exhibitor*, January 24, 1945, p.1654
[22] "Stagecoach Outlaws," *Variety*, October 3, 1945, p.20
[23] "'Buster' Crabbe Says July 4th at Clear Lake Happiest He's Had Since He Was a Kid," *Globe-Gazette* (Mason City, Iowa), July 5, 1941, p.2
[24] Joel Newfield interview, May 11, 2023
[25] Sigmund Neufeld Jr. interview, July 22, 2022
[26] Joel Newfield interviews, October 18, 2022 and May 11, 2023
[27] Sigmund Neufeld Jr. interview, July 22, 2022
[28] Sigmund Neufeld Jr. interview, August 10, 2022
[29] Sigmund Neufeld Jr. interview, June 27, 2022
[30] Sigmund Neufeld Jr. interview, July 22, 2022
[31] Ibid.
[32] Sigmund Neufeld Jr. interview, August 10, 2022
[33] "Sigmund Neufeld Productions" ad, *Boxoffice Barometer*, November 11, 1944, p.113
[34] "Neufeld is Producing Several for PRC," *Motion Picture Herald*, November 11, 1944, p.32
[35] "Sigmund Neufeld Productions" ad, *1945 Film Daily Year Book*, p.450
[36] "Hollywood," *Showmen's Trade Review*, May 1, 1943, p.35
[37] "PRC Has Large Backlog," *Showmen's Trade Review*, June 26, 1943, p.43
[38] "Production Notes from the Studios," *Showmen's Trade Review*, May 27, 1944, p.37
[39] "Swing Hostess," *The Exhibitor*, September 20, 1944, p.1587
[40] "'Swing Hostess' with Martha Tilton and Iris Adrian," *Harrisons Reports*, October 7, 1944, p.163
[41] "Swing Hostess," *Motion Picture Herald*, October 28, 1944, p.2157
[42] "Swing Hostess (PRC)," *Photoplay*, February 1945, p.115
[43] PRC upped the season's standard contract of $60,000 per to $70,000 for this one film
[44] Jay Livingston and Ray Evans wrote the song "Stop the Hubbub, Bub" for Judy Clark to sing in this film, but it was either cut or never filmed in the first place. "Production Notes from the Studios," *Showmen's Trade Review*, November 4, 1944, p.74
[45] "The Kid Sister," *Variety*, March 21, 1945, p.10
[46] "The Kid Sister," *Showmen's Trade Review*, June 23, 1945, p.20
[47] "Kid Sister," *Film Daily*, March 20, 1945, p.8
[48] "The Kid Sister," *Motion Picture Herald*, February 10, 1945, p.2309
[49] "The Kid Sister," *Motion Picture Daily*, February 2, 1945, p.3
[50] "'The Kid Sister' with Judy Clark and Roger Pryor," *Harrisons Reports*, February 10, 1945, p.23
[51] "I Accuse My Parents," *Motion Picture Daily*, October 25, 1944, p.11
[52] "The Lady Confesses," *Film Daily*, March 30, 1945, p.12
[53] "'The Lady Confesses'…Well-Made Budgeteer," *Box Office Digest*, March 31, 1945, p.9
[54] Edba., "The Lady Confesses," *Variety*, June 27, 1945, p.16
[55] "The Lady Confesses," *Showmen's Trade Review*, March 31, 1945, p.8
[56] "The Lady Confesses," *Motion Picture Herald*, March 31, 1945, pp.2381-2382

Chapter 16: Growing Up in Hollywood – Part 2
[1] Joel Newfield interview, October 18, 2022
[2] Ibid.
[3] Sigmund Neufeld Jr. interview, July 22, 2022
[4] Joel Newfield interview, October 18, 2022
[5] Joel Newfield interview, May 11, 2023
[6] Joel Newfield interview, October 18, 2022
[7] Ibid.
[8] Tim Neufeld interview, June 27, 2022
[9] Stanley Neufeld interview, Directors Guild of America, conducted by Kevin Koster, April 30, 2013. https://www.dga.org/Craft/VisualHistory/Interviews/Stanley-Neufeld.aspx
[10] Ibid.

Chapter 17: A Formula That Was Working (Sig, Sam, and PRC, Part 6, 1945-1947)
[1] These two films were shot using the DuPont monopack process, but Ansco monopack was being considered for future productions if available ("Studio Size-Ups," *Film Bulletin*, July 23, 1945, p.38)

[2] "50 in 1945-46; Eight in Color," *Motion Picture Herald*, July 7, 1945, p.40; "PRC to Produce 50 Pictures in 1945-1946," *The Exhibitor*, July 11, 1945, p.8

[3] Sigmund Neufeld Productions' "Production Contract" with PRC Productions, Inc., dated October 2, 1945.

[4] "Studio Size-Ups," *Film Bulletin*, August 10, 1945, p.26

[5] Sigmund Neufeld Jr. interview, August 10, 2022

[6] "Studio Size-Ups," *Film Bulletin*, August 10, 1945, *Op. Cit.*

[7] "Insider's Outlook," *Motion Picture Daily*, September 6, 1945, p.2

[8] "Reeves Espy in Charge at PRC Studio as Leon Fromkess Resigns Post as President," *Showmen's Trade Review*, September 1, 1945, p.10

[9] "Kenneth Young President of PRC Pictures, Inc.," *Motion Picture Herald*, September 8, 1945, p.18; "Young New Studio Head for PRC; Stolz Promoted," *Motion Picture Herald*, September 15, 1945, p.48

[10] "Studio Size-Ups," *Film Bulletin*, September 17, 1945, p.24

[11] "Independent Film Production Reaches New Peaks in Hollywood," *Variety*, January 9, 1946, p.77

[12] "Studio Size-Ups," *Film Bulletin*, April 15, 1946, p.14

[13] Bogdanovich, p.595

[14] *Not* based on Neil Miller's short story of the same title that appeared in the March 1928 issue of *Clues Detective* magazine

[15] "Apology for Murder," *Motion Picture Herald*, September 9, 1945, p.57

[16] "Apology for Murder," *Motion Picture Daily*, September 14, 1945, p.4

[17] "Apology for Murder," *Variety*, September 27, 1945, p.20

[18] This $2,250 figure is crossed out on the Production Budget sheet, and $4,500 handwritten next to it. This was to cover the additional $2,250 of negative cost for the film's eight-day shoot. WCFTR, UA collection, University of Wisconsin-Madison

[19] Letter from PRC Assistant Sales manager Lloyd Lind to Russell Holman, Paramount Pictures, dated December 20, 1945. WCFTR, UA Series 2G, Box 26, Folder 407

[20] $45,000, upped in September to $47,250; the final negative cost $45,854

[21] Some sources state sixty-seven- and sixty-eight-minute running times

[22] "Schirmer Photoplay Series," *Moving Picture World*, February 12, 1916, p.1041

[23] "Up-to-the-Minute Entertainment from Transcription Headquarters," *Broadcasting*, September 15, 1936, p.35; "Behind the Microphone," *Broadcasting*, August 1, 1939, p.39

[24] "Obituaries: Leo Erdody," *Variety*, April 13, 1949, p.71

[25] Thirty-one inserts and 195 ½ feet of footage in total, according to a summary in the film's file, for which they paid $250. WCFTR, UA collection, University of Wisconsin-Madison

[26] It's likely that Wrixon was misremembering Corrigan as Cameron, although I suppose it's possible that Cameron was coaxed into that second blonde gorilla costume.

[27] Leifert, "Producers Releasing Corp., Part 2," *Filmfax*, p.74

[28] "Quetzalcóatl," Encyclopedia Britannica, https://www.britannica.com/topic/Quetzalcoatl

[29] *The Flying Serpent*'s working title was *The Feathered Serpent*

[30] "Production Budget" records for *The Flying Serpent*, dated December 11, 1945

[31] "Studio Size-Ups," *Film Bulletin*, June 11, 1945, p.26

[32] Budgets ranged from $22,000 for the earlier entries, and $22,500 for the later ones

[33] John Tibbetts, "Buster Crabbe," *American Classic Screen*, July/August 1977, p.10. Production records for three of these final films reflect five- and six-day shooting schedules

[34] "Hollywood," *Motion Picture Daily*, August 16, 1946, p.10

[35] "Production Budget" records for *Ghost of Hidden Valley*, dated May 8, 1946

[36] Bogdanovich, p.125

[37] "Unions Peril Us, Film Man Says," *Los Angeles Times*, June 19, 1947, pp.1-2

[38] "'Buster' Crabbe Says July 4th at Clear Lake Happiest He's Had Since He Was a Kid," *Globe-Gazette* (Mason City, Iowa), July 5, 1941, p.2

[39] Ultimately ranging from a low of $3,909.67 for *Panhandle Trail* to a high of $5,022.16 for *Gun Trouble*. WCFTR, UA Series 2G, Box 26, Folder 404

[40] "PRC Reissues Six Westerns Under New Titles," *Motion Picture Herald*, May 10, 1947, p.50

[41] Letter from Emil K. Ellis to C. Warren Sharpe, Pathe Industries, Inc. dated January 3, 1949. WCFTR, UA Series 2G, Box 26, Folder 404

[42] Letter from James M. King, Jr. at Eagle-Lion Films, Inc. to Emil K. Ellis, dated February 7, 1949. WCFTR, UA Series 2G, Box 26, Folder 404

[43] Letter from Emil K. Ellis to James King, Jr., Eagle-Lion Films, Inc., dated February 9, 1949. WCFTR, UA Series 2G, Box 26, Folder 404
[44] Eagle-Lion Studios, Inc. Inter-Office Communication from Fletcher J. Williams to A. E. Bollengier, dated February 22, 1949. WCFTR, UA Series 2G, Box 26, Folder 404
[45] Letter from A. E. Bollengier to Emil K. Ellis, dated March 25, 1949. WCFTR, UA Series 2G, Box 26, Folder 404
[46] "More Features Added to PRC 45-46 Schedule," *Motion Picture Daily*, July 2, 1945, p.6; "Studio Size-Ups," *Film Bulletin*, November 12, 1945, p.14
[47] Sheila Graham, "Notes in Brief About New Films and Stars," *Dayton Daily News*, November 18, 1945, p.61
[48] "Hollywood Film Shop," *Butte Montana Register*, March 7, 1946, p.4
[49] "Production Budget" records for *Murder is My Business*, dated January 25, 1946. WCFTR, UA collection, University of Wisconsin-Madison
[50] Joseph I. Breen letter to Sigmund Neufeld, dated November 14, 1945. Margaret Herrick Library Digital Collections, Margaret Herrick Library, Academy of Motion Picture Arts and Sciences
[51] "'Murder is My Business' with Hugh Beaumont and Cheryl Walker,' *Harrisons Reports*, March 9, 1946, p.38
[52] "Murder is My Business," *Film Bulletin*, March 18, 1946, p.8
[53] Aaron Sutcliffe, "80th Anniversary of Joe Louis' Knockout Over Jack Roper," *Boxing Insider* web site. https://www.boxinginsider.com/columns/80th-anniversary-of-joe-louis-knockout-over-jack-roper/
[54] Joel Newfield interview, May 11, 2023
[55] Myton's flat fee was $1,500 for this film
[56] Final negative cost $54,820, $2,310 under budget
[57] "'Blonde for a Day' with Hugh Beaumont and Kathryn Adams," *Harrisons Reports*, August 3, 1946, pp.122-123
[58] "Blonde for a Day," *Motion Picture Herald*, August 10, 1946, pp.3137-3138. An arguable opinion, of course; regardless, Sig paid himself $2,625 for this film, his brother Sam $2,000 for directing, and son Stanley $752 for assisting
[59] "Blonde for a Day," *Motion Picture Daily*, August 1, 1946, p.5
[60] "Rank, Pathe in Distrib Deal," *Film Bulletin*, December 24, 1945, p.32
[61] "Thomas PRC President; Lind Vice-President," *Showmen's Trade Review*, December 29, 1945, p.9
[62] "Eagle-Lion at PRC," *Showmen's Trade Review*, June 1, 1946, p.32
[63] "Eagle-Lion's Plans," *Showmen's Trade Review*, June 15, 1946, p.48
[64] "No Change of Pace at PRC," *Showmen's Trade Review*, June 8, 1946, p.60
[65] "Seidelman's PRC Post Refutes E-L Merger Talk," *Variety*, June 5, 1946, p.7
[66] "Studio Size-Ups," *Film Bulletin*, June 24, 1946, p.18
[67] "Studio Size-Ups," *Film Bulletin*, July 8, 1946, p.18
[68] "Studio Personalities," *Boxoffice*, March 10, 1945, p.68
[69] Ivan Spear, "Hollywood Report," *Boxoffice*, May 19, 1945, p.30
[70] "May Lineup Totals 33, More if Strike Ends," *Boxoffice*, April 28, 1945, pp.67-68
[71] "Production Notes from the Studios," *Showmen's Trade Review*, November 24, 1945, p.46
[72] "Inside Stuff—Pictures," *Variety*, April 10, 1946, p.30
[73] "Queen of Burlesque," *Showmen's Trade Review*, July 6, 1946, p.26
[74] "Queen of Burlesque," *Motion Picture Daily*, July 3, 1946, p.12
[75] "Queen of Burlesque," *Box Office Digest*, June 22, 1946, p.8
[76] "Queen of Burlesque," *Motion Picture Herald*, July 6, 1946, p.3078
[77] Erskine Johnson, "Impulses and Hips Difficult to Control, Rose La Rose Finds," *Huron Daily Huronite and Plainsman*, April 21, 1946, p.13.
[78] Crabbe and Sig would be back in the news in early 1951, when Crabbe filed for damages in the amount of $500,000 against Sig Neufeld Productions, charging breach of a 1943 contract. Neither the details of this suit nor its outcome are known. ("In the News," *Los Angeles Evening Citizen News*, February 5, 1951, p.14)
[79] "Curved Finger Gets Glenn Ride," *Valley Times* (North Hollywood), July 3, 1946, p.5; "Eagle-Lion Progressing," *Showmen's Trade Review*, July 6, 1946, p.52
[80] "Television Gets Films," *Motion Picture Daily*, July 15, 1940, p.1
[81] "Alexanders Prep Lardner Vidpix," *Variety*, March 5, 1952, p.29
[82] "PRC Ends Singing Western," *Showmen's Trade Review*, July 27, 1946, p.34

[83] "Neufeld's Film for PRC," *Showmen's Trade Review*, August 3, 1946, p.48
[84] Several others made out extremely well on this shoot: Stanley Neufeld received $940 for assisting Sam, and Bert Sternbach received $1,750 for keeping an eye on the budget. Oddly enough, Jack Greenhalgh received a mere $604 for his work here, consistent with his salaries for previous films for Sig, but somewhat surprising given his long relationship with Sig, the outstanding work he did on this film, and its nine-day duration
[85] "PRC Very Much Alive," *Showmen's Trade Review*, August 24, 1946, p.38
[86] "Majestic," *Shamokin News-Dispatch*, January 9, 1947, p.9
[87] "PRC to Expand—Thomas," *Film Bulletin*, September 16, 1946, p.30
[88] "Drop Low Budget Pix from PRC's Program," *Film Daily*, November 26, 1946, pp.1, 6
[89] Sigmund Neufeld Jr. interview, July 22, 2022
[90] Letter from Sigmund Neufeld, "noted and agreed to" by Leon Fromkess, to PRC Pictures, Inc., dated May 16, 1946; Letter from Arthur B. Johns, PRC Productions, Inc., to C. Warren Sharpe, Pathe Industries, Inc., dated May 16, 1946. WCFTR, UA collection, University of Wisconsin-Madison
[91] Internal PRC Productions document from Arthur B. Johnson to George Fleitman, dated February 15, 1947. WCFTR, UA collection, University of Wisconsin-Madison
[92] Telegram from Harry Thomas to George Fleitman, PRC Pictures, Inc., dated May 13, 1947; Telegram from George Fleitman to Harry Thomas, dated May 14, 1947. WCFTR, UA collection, University of Wisconsin-Madison
[93] Internal PRC Productions document from Arthur B. Johnson to George Fleitman, PRC Pictures, Inc., dated June 2, 1947. WCFTR, UA collection, University of Wisconsin-Madison
[94] "Miscellaneous Independents," *Film Bulletin*, July 8, 1946, p.18

Chapter 18: Set Adrift (Sam, Sans Sig, 1946-1949)
[1] "Toddy to Make Colored Features in the East," *Film Daily*, November 23, 1945, p.6; "Newfield Directing Negro Feature," *Showmen's Trade Review*, November 24, 1945, p.47
[2] "Astor to Start Second Negro Musical on Monday," *Film Daily*, November 28, 1945, p.3
[3] Million Dollar Pictures had been formed in the mid-1930s "by black actor, dancer, and longtime Apollo Theatre emcee Ralph Cooper, black stage actor George Randol, and Hollywood producers Harry and Leo Popkin" (Mel Watkins, *On the Real Side* (New York: Simon & Schuster, 1994), p.354)
[4] "Toddy Pictures Company Collection," Special Collections of the Margaret Herrick Library, Academy of Motion Picture Arts and Sciences
[5] David F. Friedman, *A Youth in Babylon* (Buffalo, New York: Prometheus Books, 1990), p.58
[6] "Toddy Pictures Weighs Expanded Production," *Film Daily*, February 4, 1946, p.6
[7] "Toddy Signs Markham for Four," *Motion Picture Herald*, March 2, 1946, p.21
[8] Watkins, p.351
[9] Friedman, p.58
[10] Watkins, p.357
[11] "Flashes," *Box Office Digest*, May 11, 1946, p.18
[12] "Legion of Decency Reviews Twelve New Productions," *Motion Picture Herald*, May 3, 1947, p.30
[13] "Jungle Flight," *Film Bulletin*, March 3, 1947, p.36
[14] "Jungle Flight," *Harrisons Reports*, March 1, 1947, p.36
[15] "Jungle Flight," *Motion Picture Daily*, February 24, 1947, p.7
[16] "Jungle Flight," *Variety*, April 21, 1947, p.10
[17] "Briefs from the Lots," *Variety*, September 25, 1946, p.7
[18] "Pine and Thomas to Test Prerelease Bookings," *Boxoffice*, August 9, 1947, p.24
[19] "Ad Budget is Quadruple for Pine-Thomas Film," *Boxoffice*, September 27, 1947, p.47
[20] "Bobby-Soxers Heeded," *Showmen's Trade Review*, April 19, 1947, p.38
[21] "Transcriptions to Exploit P-T's 'Adventure Island'," *Showmen's Trade Review*, August 2, 1947, p.11
[22] "Showmen Ahoy!," *Motion Picture Herald*, September 6, 1947, p.51
[23] Red Kann, "Who Says It Must Be Millions or Nothing?" *Motion Picture Herald*, January 24, 1948, p.24
[24] "Cinecolor," Wikipedia.org. https://en.wikipedia.org/wiki/Cinecolor
[25] "Adventure Island," *Motion Picture Herald*, August 16, 1947, p.1832
[26] "Exhibitor Has His Say," *Boxoffice*, May 18, 1948, p.2 (D.W. Trisko, Ritz Theatre, Jerome, Arizona)

[27] "Studios Have a Record backlog of 207 Films," *Motion Picture Herald*, February 8, 1947, p.12
[28] "Schooners to Be Used," *Valley Times* (North Hollywood), April 14, 1947, p.1112
[29] It's interesting to note that the *Seaward*'s owner, Charles A. Williams, sued Paramount and William Pine in Los Angeles federal court for $8,700 *a month after* Sam's accident, for damage done to the schooner during the filming of *Adventure Island*. Presumably the damage had been dealt with before the schooner was rented to Katzman for filming. ("Par, Pine Sued for $8,700 Damage to Boat," *Variety*, June 11, 1947, p.21)
[30] "Film Director Hurt on Ship," *Los Angeles Times*, May 17, 1947, p.9; "Newfield Seriously Hurt," *Showmen's Trade Review*, May 31, 1947, p.43
[31] "Who's Who in Hollywood," *Film Daily*, July 21, 1948, p.12; "Studio Size-Ups," *Film Bulletin*, March 15, 1948, p.17
[32] "Financial and Trade Notes," *Television Digest*, October 7, 1950, p.4
[33] "Skipalong Rosenbloom," *Motion Picture Daily*, April 20, 1951, p.6
[34] "'Skipalong Rosenbloom' with Maxie Rosenbloom and Max Baer," *Harrisons Reports*, April 20, 1951, p.82
[35] "Distrib Syndicate Buys 'Skipalong' Pic," *Variety*, February 14, 1951, pp.3, 16
[36] "Actor Bob Mitchum Caught at Film Colony Dope Party," *Long Beach Press-Telegram* (Long Beach, California), September 1, 1948, p.1
[37] Shawn Wilkinson, "Dancing with Insanity: The Lila Leeds Story—In Her Own Words! (Part 3)," *Filmfax*, December/February 2017-18, No. 150, p.68
[38] *Op. Cit.*
[39] "Big Chi News is Return of Vaude; With 'Judge,' Wow $35,000; 'Champ' Giant 32G, 'Wild Weed' Tame 12G," *Variety*, July 20, 1949, p.11
[40] "Reefer Pic's Chi Preem," *Variety*, July 13, 1949, p.18
[41] Friedman, pp.51-52
[42] "National Legion of Decency," *The Exhibitor*, May 16, 1950, p.18
[43] "Ohio Sup. Ct. Upholds Ban on 'Wild Weed'," *Variety*, June 14, 1950, p.31
[44] "UK Ban on 'Devil's Weed'," *Motion Picture Daily*, December 20, 1951, p.3
[45] Vale, V. and Juno, Andrea, Editors, *RE/SEARCH: Incredibly Strange Films* (San Francisco, CA: RE/SEARCH Publications, 1986). "Interview with Dave Friedman" conducted by Jim Morton, p.105

Chapter 19: The Baby of the Industry (Film Classics, 1948-1949)
[1] "New Distrib. Co. Formed," *Film Bulletin*, May 3, 1943, p.23
[2] "Film Classics Opens Drive for Major Company Status," *Boxoffice*, September 27, 1947, p.13
[3] "Cinecolor Takes Film Classics," *Motion Picture Herald*, October 18, 1947, p.20
[4] "Studio Roundup," *Showmen's Trade Review*, January 24, 1948, p.31
[5] "Along the Rialto," *Film Daily*, March 9, 1948, p.4
[6] "Sigmund Neufeld Pictures to Release Through FC," *Boxoffice*, April 3, 1948, p.55
[7] "'Miraculous Journey' Neufeld First for FC," *Film Daily*, April 8, 1948, p.8
[8] "Neufeld Buys Novel," *Valley Times* (North Hollywood), February 16, 1948, p.15
[9] "Briefs from the Lots," *Variety*, February 25, 1948, p.7
[10] Louella Parsons, *Philadelphia Inquirer*, June 6, 1950, p.29; Louella Parsons, *The Tribune* (Scranton, PA), June 8, 1950, p.25
[11] "Four rental lots are offering financial assistance to indie producers in the form of secondary and completion money, including deferred payment of rental costs. These offers are contingent on the past records of the producers and on the quality of the stories they have in mind." Nassour Studios was one of the four. ("Remember When It Was Tough to Rent Space?" *Variety*, February 25, 1948, p.7)
[12] "Nassour Space to Neufeld," *Boxoffice*, September 4, 1948, p.43; "Lundigan, Bruce Headline 'File 649'," *Los Angeles Times*, September 7, 1948, p.29
[13] "Host John E. Peurifoy," *Boxoffice*, October 2, 1948, p.55
[14] "State Department—File 649," *Motion Picture Daily*, February 11, 1949, p.4
[15] "State Department—File 649," *Variety*, February 16, 1949, p.13
[16] "State Department—File 649," *Showmen's Trade Review*, February 12, 1949, p.34
[17] "Bernhard and Kranze Cited for 'File 649'," *Motion Picture Daily*, February 24, 1949, p.2
[18] "EL-FC Merges, to Tackle Majors With 'Quality' Pics," *Film Bulletin*, June 5, 1950, p.9

[19] "ELC Aims: More Product, Lower Costs, Higher Fees," *Film Bulletin*, February 12, 1951, p.11
[20] "History Lesson...UA Style," *Motion Picture Exhibitor*, April 17, 1959, p.9
[21] Sigmund Neufeld letter to PRC treasurer A.E. Bollengier, dated April 1, 1949. WCFTR, UA collection, University of Wisconsin-Madison
[22] Eagle-Lion Films treasurer D.J. Melamed letter and "Recap of Remittance" to Sigmund Neufeld Productions, dated September 27, 1949. WCFTR, University of Wisconsin-Madison, United Artists Series 2G, Box 26, Folder 405

Chapter 20: When Hero Catch Crook, Time for Picture to End (Lippert, 1950-1953)
[1] "Organization of Screen Guild is Moving Ahead," *Motion Picture Herald*, February 16, 1946, p.32
[2] "Lippert Renames Screen Guild Prod.," *Motion Picture Daily*, June 2, 1949, p.2
[3] McGee, p.18
[4] "Lippert Heads New Financing Company," *Motion Picture Daily*, June 27, 1949, p.2
[5] "'Exhibitor Lethargy' Flayed By Lippert," *Motion Picture Daily*, February 11, 1949, pp.1, 4
[6] "TV is Endangering Theatre Business, Lippert Maintains," *Motion Picture Daily*, February 3, 1950, pp.1, 3
[7] "Lippert Lists 33 for '50," *Motion Picture Daily*, September 13, 1949, pp.1, 3
[8] "Two-a-Month Set from Lippert," *Motion Picture Daily*, September 28, 1949, p.2
[9] "Lippert Releases Go to Three a Month," *Motion Picture Daily*, October 5, 1949, p.2
[10] "Hollywood Newsreel," *Showmen's Trade Review*, December 10, 1949, p.30
[11] "Train Surprise Movie Setting," *Berkeley Daily Gazette*, December 16, 1949, p.13
[12] "Western Pacific Agent," *Motion Picture Daily*, March 23, 1950, p.5
[13] Patrick McGilligan and Paul Buhle, *Tender Comrades* (New York: St. Martin's Griffin, 1997), pp.353-354
[14] "Nassour Company to Make Action Pictures," *Motion Picture Daily*, May 23, 1945, p.2
[15] "Independents: Lippert Productions," *Film Bulletin*, May 8, 1950, p.19
[16] "Motor Patrol," *Motion Picture Daily*, May 10, 1950, p.6
[17] "'Motor Patrol' with Don Castle, Jane Nigh and Reed Hadley," *Harrisons Reports*, May 13, 1950, p.76
[18] "Motor Patrol," *Variety*, May 10, 1950, p.16
[19] "Motor Patrol," *The Exhibitor*, May 24, 1950, p.2854
[20] Paul Woodbine, "The Write Approach: An Interview with Screenwriter Orville H. Hampton," *Filmfax*, April/May 1998, No. 66, pp.61-63
[21] "Hi-Jacked," *Motion Picture Daily*, June 23, 1950, p.4
[22] Ibid.
[23] "Hi-Jacked," *Variety*, July 19, 1950, p.2887
[24] Frederick Rappaport, "Prolific Pragmatist," *Filmfax*, August/September 1993, No.40, p.39
[25] Lightman, p.377
[26] Edward M. Gray was president; Rudolph Monter and Sig were vice-presidents; William Cane treasurer; and Victor Mindlin secretary. Offices were located at 9118 Sunset Boulevard. ("Mutual TV Productions Capitalized at $1,000,000," *Variety*, August 9, 1950, p.31; "Film Report," *Broadcasting-Telecasting*, September 4, 1950, p.55)
[27] Walter Ames, "Biscailuz Opens Sheriff's Records for Video Audience; Olivier, Leigh Duo Tonight," *Los Angeles Times*, November 6, 1950, p.26; "Tele Chatter," *Variety*, November 15, 1950, p.40
[28] "MTP Named Defendant in Non-Payment Suit," *Broadcasting-Telecasting*, June 6, 1954, p.36; "SAG Files Suit to Collect Residual TV Film Payments," *Broadcasting-Telecasting*, October 15, 1956, p.68
[29] "Gary Cooper, Lippert Set Moderate-Budget Indie," *Variety*, October 18, 1950, p.4; "Studio Size-Ups," *Film Bulletin*, November 6, 1950. P.25
[30] McGee, pp.42-43
[31] *The Dalton Gang's Last Raid* according to some sources
[32] "Lippert Will Start Three in September," *Motion Picture Daily*, August 22, 1950, p.3
[33] Actor Kim Spaulding's alternate credit on a few films
[34] "Briefs from the Lots," *Variety*, October 11, 1950, p.20
[35] "Lippert Forms New Production Company," *Motion Picture Daily*, December 19, 1950, p.8
[36] "Briefs from the Lots," *Variety* June 28, 1950, p.22
[37] "Science Moving Too Fast for Fiction Film," *San Mateo Times*, May 3, 1951, p.15

[38] "Start of 'Lost Continent' Advanced from June to Feb.," *Film Bulletin*, January 29, 1951, p.31
[39] Lightman, p.351
[40] While *American Cinematographer* stated that the jungle sets were constructed at the Goldwyn Studios as well, William Fogg claims that they were at the Nassour Studios, assembled in 1948 and previously used for Lippert's *Jungle Goddess* (1948) and Nassour's *Africa Screams* (1949). (William Fogg, "Rediscovering Robert Lippert's Lost Continent," *Filmfax*, January/March 2005, No. 105, p.110)
[41] Lightman, *Op. Cit.*
[42] Woodbine, pp.63-64
[43] Pat Jankiewicz, "The Wit and Wisdom of Whit Bissell," *Filmfax*, September 1990 No.22, p.77
[44] Rappaport, p.39
[45] "Exhibitors Forum," *Film Bulletin*, December 31, 1951, p.27
[46] Sid Melton interviewed by Tom Weaver, *The Astounding B Monster* web site, http://www.bmonster.com/profile38.html
[47] "'Tell It to the Marines' with Sid Melton and Mary [sic] Lynn," *Harrisons Reports*, June 14, 1952, p.95
[48] The "HOW" in Howco represented the initials of the partners' last names, Houck, Ormond, and White
[49] McGee, p.163
[50] "News of the Territory," *The Exhibitor*, February 20, 1952, p.NT-3; "Film Report," *Broadcasting*, March 10, 1952, p.78
[51] "Lippert Eyes % Deals, Retains Levin to Check," *Film Bulletin*, March 10, 1952, p.15
[52] Mike Fitzgerald, "Interview with…Marie Windsor," Boyd Magers' *Western Clippings* web site. http://www.westernclippings.com/interview/mariewindsor_interview.shtml
[53] Will Hammer was William Hinds' adopted stage name, originating with his two-man act "Hammer and Smith"
[54] Marcus Hearn and Alan Barnes, *The Hammer Story: The Authorised History of Hammer Films* (London: Titan Publishing Group Ltd., 2007), pp.10-11
[55] McGee, p.41
[56] "Lippert in Joint UK Production Deal," *Motion Picture Daily*, September 5, 1951, p.16
[57] "U.K. Union Strife Halts Lippert Film," *Motion Picture Daily*, November 7, 1951, p.8
[58] "The Hollywood Scene," *Motion Picture Herald*, April 19, 1952, p.35
[59] "Exclusive Speed," *Kinematograph Weekly*, April 3, 1952, p.22
[60] Ibid.
[61] "'Bigger' Movies Urgent—Lippert," *The Independent Film Journal*, October 3, 1953, p.11
[62] Ibid. According to Lippert biographer McGee, a second, 1-1.85 ratio version was filmed as well for distribution to the smaller theatres unequipped to handle the wider format
[63] "Lippert Sets Meetings On 'Sins of Jezebel'," *Motion Picture Herald*, September 19, 1953, p.16
[64] "Random Shots," *Broadcasting-Telecasting*, October 5, 1953, p.32
[65] "As the hypnotic heroine, Miss Goddard fans her eyelashes, swings a bare midriff with pendulum precision and weighs crises of religion and state as though a wad of gum were parked behind the royal tiara." ("The Screen in Review," *New York Times*, January 9, 1954, p.12)
[66] "'Jezebel' in Color at St. Francis," *San Francisco Examiner*, November 14, 1953, p.11

Chapter 21: Too Many Fuzzys (AFRD, Regal Films, and Television, 1953-1958)
[1] Joel Newfield interview, October 18, 2022
[2] Ibid.
[3] Ibid.
[4] Karl Whitezel, "Buster Crabbe is Captain Gallant of the Foreign Legion," *Filmfax*, June/July 2001, No. 85, pp.60-62. Screenwriter C. Jack Lewis has a different take on it in his *White Horse, Black Hat*, p.51: "Al St. John, according to all reports, was well into the sauce. His inclusion was nixed by the money men. But the other Fuzzy, named Knight, had not had a drink in nearly two years. He was signed…"
[5] "Captain Gallant of the Foreign Legion," *Variety*, February 16, 1955, p.31.
[6] Tim Neufeld interview, July 29, 2022
[7] "Baumgarten Planning Action Picture Slate," *Independent Film Journal*, September 3, 1955, p.17
[8] "Baumgarten Rolling Low-Budget Yipees," *Variety*, October 26, 1955, p.7
[9] "Ex-Banker Baumgarten Ups Budgets for Ten Associated Features," *Variety*, January 11, 1956, p.4

[10] Rappaport, p.39
[11] "Last of the Desperados," *Variety*, January 25, 1956, p.6
[12] "The Wild Dakotas," *Motion Picture Exhibitor*, July 25, 1956, p.4189
[13] "Diverted 'Dakotas'," *Variety*, December 14, 1955, p.13; "On the Wire," *Independent Film Journal*, February 18, 1956, p.16
[14] Ted Okuda, "Beauty Meets the Beast of Piedras Blancas: Jeanne Carmem," *Filmfax*, July/August 1995, No. 51, p.54
[15] "The Three Outlaws," *Motion Picture Daily*, September 11, 1956, p.6
[16] Ibid.
[17] "The Three Outlaws," *Motion Picture Exhibitor*, August 22, 1956, p.4205
[18] "Frontier Gambler," *Motion Picture Exhibitor*, September 5, 1956, p.4214
[19] "31 Inde Dist. Deals Lined Up By MacMillen," *Film Bulletin*, March 12, 1951, p.11
[20] "Film Report," *Broadcasting-Telecasting*, March 31, 1952, p.156
[21] "Film Maker: Leon Fromkess," *Broadcasting-Telecasting*, September 13, 1954, p.101
[22] "Small to Produce TV Series in Canada," *Motion Picture Daily*, July 6, 1956, p.2; "Gives Canada Major Vidpix Stake; 3-Way Production Set at $1,500,000," *Variety*, July 11, 1956, pp.35, 40
[23] "'Mohicans' Goes on Location In Canada with 1,300-Job Bonanza," *Variety*, October 17, 1956, pp.39, 44
[24] "The International Scene: Canada-Canadian Comment," *Motion Picture Exhibitor*, August 8, 1956, p.10
[25] Sigmund Neufeld Jr. interview, July 15, 2022
[26] Tom Weaver, *Eye On Science Fiction* (Jefferson, North Carolina: McFarland & Company, Inc., 2003), p.148
[27] Sigmund Neufeld Jr. interview, July 15, 2022
[28] Weaver, *Eye On Science Fiction*, p.146
[29] Joel Newfield interview, October 18, 2022
[30] Gillian Pritchard, "The Last of the Mohicans Pioneer Television Effort," *The Expositor* (Branford, Ontario), October 25, 1956, p.31
[31] Tim Neufeld interview, July 15, 2022
[32] Weaver, *Eye On Science Fiction*, pp.147-148
[33] Sigmund Neufeld Jr. interviews, July 15 and 22, 2022
[34] Sigmund Neufeld Jr. interview, June 27, 2022
[35] Ibid.
[36] Joel Newfield interview, May 11, 2023
[37] Tim Neufeld interview, July 15, 2022
[38] Sigmund Neufeld Jr. interview, July 22, 2022
[39] Joel Newfield interview, October 18, 2022
[40] "Hawkeye and the Last of the Mohicans," *Variety*, January 23, 1957, p.31
[41] Weaver, *Eye On Science Fiction*, p.149
[42] "'Tugboat Annie' Rolls in Canada," *Variety*, July 31, 1957, p.91
[43] "Normandie Sets Second Outdoor TV Series," *Motion Picture Daily*, March 22, 1957, p.4
[44] "Network Notes," *Montreal Star* (Montreal, Quebec), December 19, 1957, p.24
[45] "Regal Films Formed By E.J. Baumgarten," *Motion Picture Daily*, June 21, 1956, p.2
[46] "Welcome to Regal," *Motion Picture Exhibitor*, November 7, 1956, p.4
[47] "20th Plots Replenished Library," *Variety*, November 7, 1956, p.4
[48] "Lippert Theatres' New HQ," *Variety*, October 10, 1956, p.24
[49] "Two Regal Productions in Canada for 20th-Fox Aid Industry There," *Motion Picture Daily*, August 20, 1957, p.2; "The International Scene," *Motion Picture Exhibitor*, September 4, 1957, p.10
[50] "Victoria," *Shamokin News-Dispatch* (Shamokin, Pennsylvania), September 3, 1958, p.9; "At the Theaters," *Springfield News-Sun* (Springfield, Ohio), March 31, 1959, p.8
[51] Fred Tonge, "Tell Us When You Get a Job," *Film & TV Technician*, October 1957, pp.135, 142
[52] "'Wolf Dog' with Jim Davis, Allison Hayes and Tony Brown," *Harrisons Reports*, July 26, 1958, p.119
[53] "Flaming Frontier," *Motion Picture Daily*, August 12, 1958, p.6

Chapter 22: The Twilight Years
[1] Joel Newfield interview, October 18, 2022
[2] Sigmund Neufeld Jr. interview, August 10, 2022

[3] Tim Neufeld interview, July 29, 2022
[4] Joel Newfield interview, October 18, 2022
[5] Ibid.
[6] Ibid. Joel later emphasized the treatment they received: "Free everything: Free show. Free dinner. Free room. Everything, because of him." Joel Newfield interview, May 11, 2023
[7] Sigmund Neufeld Jr. interview, August 10, 2022
[8] Joel Newfield interview, October 18, 2022
[9] Ibid.
[10] Sigmund Neufeld Jr. interview, July 15, 2022
[11] Sigmund Neufeld, Jr. interview, June 27, 2022
[12] Tim Neufeld interview, June 27, 2022
[13] Tim Neufeld interview, June 20, 2022
[14] Tim Neufeld interview, July 15, 2022
[15] Tim Neufeld interview, July 22, 2022
[16] Tim Neufeld interview, July 15, 2022
[17] Ibid.
[18] Tim Neufeld interview, July 29, 2022
[19] Ibid.
[20] Sigmund Neufeld Jr. interview, July 22, 2022

Chapter 23: The Neufeld-Newfield Legacy
[1] Lewis, *White Horse, Black Hat*, p.229

Bibliography

Books/Periodicals:

Bogdanovich, Peter. *Who the Devil Made It*. New York: Alfred A. Knopf, Inc., 1997

Brooker, John. *The Happiest Trails*. CP Entertainment Books, 2017

Copeland, Bobby J. *Charlie King: We Called Him "Blackie"*. Madison, North Carolina: Empire Publishing, Inc., 2003

Dixon, Wheeler. *Producers Releasing Corporation: A Comprehensive Filmography and History*. Jefferson, North Carolina: McFarland & Company, Inc., 1986

Dixon, Wheeler W., and Fraser, Audrey Brown. *I Went That-A-Way: The Memoirs of a Western Film Director, Harry L. Fraser*. Metuchen, New Jersey: The Scarecrow Press, Inc., 1990

Doyle, Billy H. *The Ultimate Directory of the Silent Screen Performers*. Metuchen, New Jersey: The Scarecrow Press, Inc., 1995

Fenin, George N., and Everson, William K. *The Western: From Silents to the Seventies*. New York Penguin Books, 1973

Friedman, David F., with De Nevi, Don. *A Youth in Babylon*. Buffalo, New York: Prometheus Books, 1990

Gabler, Neal. *Walt Disney: The Triumph of the American Imagination*. New York: Alfred A. Knopf, 2006

Hearn, Marcus, and Barnes, Alan. *The Hammer Story: The Authorised History of Hammer Films*. London: Titan Publishing Group Ltd., 2007

Isenberg, Noah. *Edgar G. Ulmer: A Filmmaker at the Margins*. Los Angeles: University of California Press, 2014

Koszarski, Richard. *"Keep 'Em in the East"*. New York: Columbia University Press, 2021

Lewis, C. Jack. *White Horse, Black Hat: A Quarter Century on Hollywood's Poverty Row*. Lanham, Maryland: The Scarecrow Press, Inc., 2002

Massa, Steve. *Lame Brains and Lunatics: The Good, The Bad, and The Forgotten of Silent Comedy*. Albany, Georgia: BearManor Media, 2013

McCoy, Tim, with McCoy, Ronald. *Tim McCoy Remembers the West*. University of Nebraska Press, 1988

McDuffie, Jerome; Piggrem, Gary; Woodworth, Steven E. *United States History*. Piscataway, New Jersey: Research & Education association, 2004

McGee, Mark Thomas. *Talk's Cheap, Action's Expensive: The Films of Robert L. Lippert*. Albany, Georgia: BearManor Media, 2014

McGilligan, Patrick, and Buhle, Paul. *Tender Comrades*. New York: St. Martin's Griffin, 1997

Miller, Don. *B Movies*. New York: Ballantine Books, 1988

_____. *Hollywood Corral*. New York: Popular Library Publishers, 1976

Okuda, Ted. *Grand National, Producers Releasing Corporation, and Screen Guild/Lippert*. Jefferson, North Carolina: McFarland & Company, Inc., 1989

Papp, Susan M. *Hungarian Americans and Their Communities of Cleveland*. Cleveland Ethnic Heritage Studies, Cleveland State University, 1990

Pitts, Michael R. *Poverty Row Studios, 1929-1940*. Jefferson, North Carolina: McFarland & Company, Inc., 1979

Rainey, Buck. *Heroes of the Range*. Waynesville, North Carolina: The World of Yesterday, 1987

Reeder, Thomas. *Stop Yellin': Ben Pivar and the Horror, Mystery, and Action-Adventure Films of His Universal B-Unit*. Albany, Georgia: BearManor Media, 2011

_____. *Time is Money! The Century, Rainbow, and Stern Brothers Comedies of Julius and Abe Stern*. Orlando, Florida: BearManor Media, 2021

Sante, Luc. *Low Life*. New York: Vintage Books, 1991

Skretvedt, Randy. *Laurel and Hardy: The Magic Behind the Movies*. Beverly Hills, California: Moonstone Press, 1987

Stein, Michael; Okuda, Ted; Wilson, James J.J., editors. *Filmfax: The Magazine of Unusual Film & Television*. Evanston, Illinois, 1989-2018, No.s 16, 22, 40, 51, 66, 81, 150

Steinbrunner, Chris, and Penzler, Otto. *Encyclopedia of Mystery and Detection*. New York: McGraw-Hill Book Company, 1976

Talbot, Margaret. *The Entertainer: Movies, Magic and My Father's Twentieth Century*. New York: Riverhead Books, 2012

Tibbets, John C., and Welsh, James M., editors. *American Classic Screen* magazine. Topeka, Kansas: The Traditions Press, 1977, Volume 1 Number 6

Weaver, Tom. *Eye On Science Fiction*. Jefferson, North Carolina: McFarland & Company, Inc., 2003

_____. *Poverty Row Horrors!* Jefferson, North Carolina: McFarland & Company, Inc., 1993

Zemeckis, Leslie. *Behind the Burly Q: The Story of Burlesque in America*. New York, New York: Skyhorse Publishing, Inc., 2013

Web Sites:

AFI Catalog of Feature Films (aficatalog.afi.com)

Ancestry (ancestry.com)

British Newspaper Archive, The (britishnewspaperarchive.co.uk)

Chronicling America: Historic American Newspapers (chroniclingamerica.loc.gov)

Classic Horror Film Board, The (tapatalk.com/groups/monsterkidclassichorrorforum)

FamilySearch (familysearch.com)

Internet Archive (archive.org)

Koster, Kevin. *Visual History with Stanley Neufeld.* Directors Guild of America, Visual History Program, 2013. Craft / Visual History (dga.org/craft/visualhistory/interviews/stanley-neufeld.aspx)

Lantern Search Platform. Wisconsin Center for Film and Theater Research, University of Wisconsin-Madison (lantern.mediahist.org)

Magers, Boyd. *Western Clippings* (westernclippings.com)

Media History Digital Library (mediahistoryproject.org)

Motion Pictures, 1912-1939: Catalog of Copyright Entries (gutenberg.org/ebooks/51836)

Motion Pictures, 1940-1949: Catalog of Copyright Entries (gutenberg.org/ebooks/58237)

Motion Pictures, 1950-1959: Catalog of Copyright Entries (gutenberg.org/ebooks/59656)

Newspapers by Ancestry (newspapers.com)

NewspaperArchive by Storied (newspaperarchive.com)

Raleigh Studios (raleighstudios.com)

Index

A Boy and His Dog 397, 399

A Garden By the Sea (song) 301

A Gym Dandy 22, 416

A Lady of Chance 124

A Lawman Is Born 125, 128, 427

A Little Song (song) 152, 301

A Man and His Soul 301

A Star is Born 58

A Texan Rides 427

A Thousand Deaths (story) 162, 432

A Thousand Summers 170

A Woman of Affairs 124

A Yank in Libya 231-232

Abbott and Costello 263

Abbott, Bud 263

Abbott, John 331, **332**, 452

Abel, Rudolph E. 453

Academy of Motion Picture Arts and Sciences 52, 69, 262

Ace, the Wonder Dog 273

Aces and Eights **79**, 80, 426

Acquanetta 368, **370**

Action Pictures 353

Adams, Ernie 126, **131-132**, 135

Adams, Kathryn **314**

Adams, Stella 23

Adams, Ted 77, 126, 128, **134**, 135, 137, 142, 149, 153, 155-158, 177, 187-188, **189**, 192, **193**, 201, 215, **216**, 221

Adrian, Iris 284

Adventure Island 329, **330**, 331, **332**, 345

Adventures of Billy the Kid (series) 182, 186, 192

Adventures of Bob and Bill, The 130

Adventures of Sherlock Holmes, The 227

Adventures of Tarzan, The 10

Adventures of Tugboat Annie, The (TV series) **396**, 397

Advertising Advisory Council 173

AFRC (see Associated Film Releasing Corp.) **384**, 389

Africa Screams 263

Africa Squawks 41, 421

After the Thin Man 227

Alberni, Luis 266

Albert Jay Cohen Productions 347, **348**

Alberti, Signor 107

Albright, Hardie 59

Alexander, Arthur **86**, 98-99, **100-101**, 102, **104**, 148, 232, 234, 240, 255, **288**, **317**, 319

Alexander, Frieda 98

Alexander, Max 15, 21, **27**, 44, 98-99, **100-101**, 102, **104**, 228, 232, 244, 255, 262, 287, 319

Alexander, Richard 103

Alexander-Stern Productions, Inc. 112, 232, 255, 262, 282, 289, 295-296, 324

Alice (series) 21-22

All Wet 240

Allen Judith 59-60

Allen, Irving 309

Aller, Herbert 61

Alliance Film Corporation 218

Along Came a Woman 61

Along the Sundown Trail 222, 441

Alperson, Edward L. 101

Alpert, Manny 399

Alt, Al 16

Am I Guilty? 180, **181**, 435

Ambassador Pictures 61, **62-63**, **65**, **67-68**, 69, **70**, 71, **72**, 73, 77, 85, 97, 138, 147, 166, 200, 245

And the Angels Sing (song) 282

Andrews, Carol 311
Andrews, Jack 383
Andrews, Stanley 388
Angel Street (play) 176
Angelus Productions 60
Ankers, Evelyn **317**, 318
Annakin, Ken 197
Ansara, Michael 395
Anthony, William 20
Anything Once (story) 61
Apeing Hollywood **37-38**, 42, 421
Apology for Murder xiv, 297-298, **299-300**, 301, 309, 410, 448
Arbuckle, Roscoe "Fatty" 115, 259
Arcadia Pictures 85, **143**
Ardell, Alice 116
Argyle, John 262
Arizona Gang Busters 188, 435
Arizona Gunfighter **134**, 428
Arlen, Richard 343
Arliss, George 343
Armstrong, Billy 9
Arrow Productions, Inc. **382**, 391
Arson Squad 232
Artclass Pictures **23**, 147, **148**
Asch, Nathan 99
Asher, Harry 176, **186**, **209**
Asher, Max 15
Ask Dad 22, 415
Associated Features, Inc. 110, 112
Associated Film Releasing Corp. (AFRC) **384-390**, 397
Associated Features 110, 112
Associated Producers 295
Associated Screen Studios 95
Association of Cine and Allied Technicians 376

Astor, Gertrude **87**
Atchley, Hooper 123
Aubrey, James "Jimmy" 77, 80, 94, 116, 149, 306, 411
Audio Pictures, Ltd. 391
Auld, Alice 12
Auld, Ruth Emma (see Neufeld, Ruth)
Auntie's Ante 22, 415
Austin, Gene 101
Autry, Gene 134, 138-139, 405
Avonde, Richard 374
B.F. Zeidman Productions, Ltd. 171
B.N. Judell, Inc. 161
Babb, Kroger 341-342
Baby Peggy Montogomery **15**, 16, 413
Bachman, John C. 197
Bad Penny 90
Baer, Max 144, **338**
Baker, Bob 236
Balcon, Michael 343
Baldwin, Alan 196
Balenda, Carla 375
Ball, Frank 132, 135-136
Ballentino, Umberto Alexander (see also Jeffries, Herb) 110
Bambury, Joan 119
Banner Productions 333
Bannon, Jim 346-347
Barclay, David 217
Barclay, Don 80-81, 136
Barclay, Joan **143**, 144, 151, 154, **155**, 156, 215
Baretta (TV series) 408
Barlow, Reginald 66
Barnes, Alan 375
Barnett Brothers Circus 218
Baron of Arizona, The 359
Barringer, Barry 73

Barry, Phyllis 19

Barsky Chimp Comedies **40**, 41

Barsky, Bud 41

Bartell, Eddie 266

Barter, Farnham 97

Barthelmess, Richard 165

Barton, Charles 263

Bar-Z Bad Men 125, **126**, 131, 426

Batcheller, George R., Jr. 187, **205**, 235, 237

Batcheller, George R., Sr. 187

Bath, John 399

Baum, Louis 61

Baumgarten, E.J. 384-385, 390, 397

Baxter, Alan 339-340

Beacon Productions 99

Beasts of Berlin (see also *Hitler – Beast of Berlin*) 173-174

Beatty, Clyde 263

Beaudine, William 196-197, 231, 322, 325, 401

Beaumont, Hugh 289, **290**, 298, **299-300**, 309, **310**, 311, **312-315**, 322, 334, 343, **344**, 345, **368-369**, 410

Beauty Parade, The 420

Becker, Charles 117, 119

Beckwith, Madeline 31

Beebe, Marjorie 109

Beggar's Holiday 59, 423

Bell Automatic Cinema Machines 162

Bell, Rex 99, **100**

Bellamy, Madge 125

Bellinger, Ted 64

Bellock, Harry 97

Benedict, Brooks 322

Benjamin, Robert S. 176

Bennett, Bruce 388-389, 399, **400**

Bennett, Constance 343

Bennett, Spencer Gordon 232

Bergman, Henry 9

Berlin Revolts 236

Berne, Joseph 266

Bernhard, Jack 348

Bernhard, Joseph 349, 351

Bernstein, Elmer 371

Bernstein, Isadore 150-151

Besser, Joe 380

Betz, Matthew 71

Beyond the Pecos 306

Big Bluff, The 60

Big Game George 25, 417

Big Time or Bust **57**, 58, 422

Big U 46

Billy Carson (series) xiv, 261, 276, 282, 297, 304

Billy the Kid (1930) 125

Billy the Kid in Cattle Stampede (see also *Cattle Stampede*) 443

Billy the Kid in Santa Fe 194, 437

Billy the Kid in Texas 192, 435

Billy the Kid in The Kid Rides Again (see also *The Kid Rides Again*) 441

Billy the Kid in The Mysterious Rider (see also *Mysterious Rider, The*) 441

Billy the Kid in The Renegade (see *Renegade, The*) 443

Billy the Kid in Western Cyclone (see *Western Cyclone*) 443

Billy the Kid Outlawed 192, 434

Billy the Kid (series) viii, ix, xiv, 162, 182, 186, 192, 194, 211, 218, 237, 239, 240, 255-257, 261, 308

Billy the Kid Trapped 215, 438

Billy the Kid Wanted 211, **213**, 438

Billy the Kid's Fighting Pals **194**, 436

Billy the Kid's Gun Justice **193**, 436

Billy the Kid's Range War 194, 436

Billy the Kid's Round-Up viii, 214, **216**, 438

Billy the Kid's Smoking Guns 215, **216**, **282**, 439

Biograph 48, 90, 196

Biophone Sound Recording 98

Birch, Frank 377

Birell, Tala 272-273, **274**

Biscailuz, Los Angeles County Sheriff Eugene 359

Bisceglia, Geremino (see also *Fletcher, Tex*) 143

Bissell, Whit 368, **369**, 370

Black Cat, The 244

Black Raven, The 227, 244, 249, 252, **253**, 254-255, 443

Black Rider Westerns (series) 354

Blackley, Douglas 328, 334, 349

Blackmer, Sydney 197

Blane, Sally 73, 83-84, 177-178

Blazing Frontier 256-257, **258-259**, 260, 444

Blazing Saddles 406

Blazing Stewardesses 244

Blimp Mystery, The 34, **35**, 37, 42, 411, 420

Blonde for a Day 309, **314-315**, 316, 322, 450

Blondes on the Loose 314, 451

Blood Feast 325

Blue Ribbon Comedies 116

Blue, Monte 71

Bluebeard 244

Blumenfeld Theatres 353

Blumenfield, Joe 324, 353

Blummer, Jon 333

Blystone, Jack 9

Bobby Clark Day 168

Bois, Curt 328

Boland, Eddie 32

Bombs Over Burma 231, 252

Bonner, Joe 15

Bonney, William 257

Bonwick, George 235

Booth Canadian Films, Ltd. 98

Booth Dominion Productions, Ltd. 85, 95, **96**, 98, 391

Booth, J.R. (John Rudolphus) 95

Booth, J.R. (John Rudolphus), Jr. 95, **98**

Boothill Brigade 125, **129**, 130, 428

Border Badmen 304, 448

Border Caballero 77, 78, 114, 125, 147, 151, 425

Border Crossing (see also *Gun Code*) 188, 434

Border Roundup 223, 440

Borg, Sven Hugo 103

Boss of Boom Town 306

Bowery Boys, The (series) **319**, 320

Bowery Champs 147

Boyd, Bill "Cowboy Rambler" 218, **219-221**, 222

Boyd, William "Bill" 90-91, **92-94**

Boyd, William "Stage" 91

Boyhood Days 15

Bradbury, Robert Adrian (see *Steele, Bob*) 130

Bradbury, Robert N. 88, 130

Bradford, William 385

Bradley, Doryce 327

Bradley, Grace 166-167

Brady, Ed 136

Brady, Ruthe 337

Brand of the Coward (see *Branded a Coward*) 88, 424

Brand, Neville 387, 389

Branded a Coward 88, **89**, 90, 124-125, 424

Brandon, Phil 97, **98**

Brash, Henry 295

Brecher, Egon 302

Breen, Joseph I. 171-173, 188

Brenda Starr, Reporter 333

Brian, Mary 248

Bricker, Elsie 320

Bricker, George 164, 196, 320

Bride of Frankenstein 51

Briggs, O.H(enry). 186, **209-210**, 231, **233**, 235, **236**, 255, **256**, 275

Brigham Young – Utah Miracle Man 162

Bright Shaw, The 165

Bring 'Em Back Alive (book) 262

British Board of Film Censors 342

British Lion 375

Broadcasting 41, **42**

Broadway Big Shot 196

Brock, Lou 231

Brodel, Betty 284

Brodine, Norbert 245

Bromfield, John 390

Bronze Buckaroo, The 112

Brook, Doris 66

Brooke, Hillary 199, 201-202, 338, 368

Brooker, John xii, 65, 67

Brooks, A(rthur).A. 325

Brooks, Jess Lee 230

Brower, Otto 61-63

Brown, Charles D. 298, 300

Brown, Harry Joe 245

Brown, James S., Jr. 84, 267

Brown, Johnny Mack 59-60, 88, **89**, 90, 124-125, **126-129**, 130, 139

Brown, Tony 397, **398**, 399

Brownie the Wonder Dog **14**, 15, 413

Bruce, Earle 285

Bruce, Virginia 349, **350-351**

Bryan Foy Studios 52, 146

Bryant Joyce 157-159, 168-169

Bryar, Paul 185, 190, **191**, 230, 246, 312, 314-315, 320, 322, 372

Buchanan, Jack 262

Buck Rogers 211

Buck, Frank 262, **263**, 264

Buell, Jed 59, **106**, 107, **108**, **110-111**, 112, **113**, 115, **116**, 117, **118, 120**, 121-122, 137, 149, 185, 187, 196, 209, 213, 325

Buffalo Bill 146

Bulldog Courage 74, **75**, 76, 410, 425

Bupp, Tommy 76-77, 123

Buried Alive **164**, 433

Burning Gold 90, 92, 424

Burr, C.C. 117

Burtis, Jim 81

Bush, James 83-84

Bushell, Anthony 46

Bushman, Francis X. 48

Buster Brown (series) 16, 19, 23, 26-27

Buster Crabbe Show, The (TV series) 382

Buster, Budd L. 158, 200-202, **304-305**

Buster's Spooks 26, 410

Busy Lizzie 23

But Not for Love (play) 170

Butterbeans and Susie 181

Byrd, Ralph 77, 124, 196, **354**, 355

Byron, Allan 248

Byron, Kathleen 377

Byron, Richard 286

Byron, Walter 46, **47**, 58

C. Schirmer, Inc. 301

Cabanne, Christy 48-49, **50**, 51

Caesar, Arthur 287

Cagney and Lacey (TV series) 408

Cagney, James 100, 356

Cailliet, Lucien 350

Caldwell, Dwight 381

Calhoun, Rory 329, 331-332, **346-347**

Caliente Kid (story) 211

California Zephyr 355

Call of the Jungle 231

Callaghan, George H. 107
Callam, Alex 166
Calling Dr. Death 251
Cameo Comedies 22
Cameron, Rod 302, 306
Campbell, William 31
Canadian Broadcasting Company (CBC) 391, **392**, 395, **396**
Candy and Coco 101
Cane, William 359
Canutt, Yakima 89, 123
Capital Film Exchange 44
Capital Pictures 107
Captain Gallant of the Foreign Legion (TV series) 382, **383**
Captain Silver's Log of the Sea Hound (comic strip) 333
Captured in Chinatown 148
Card, Virginia 201
Carey, Hal 152
Carlin, Jean 306
Carlisle, Mary 211, **212**, 251-252
Carmen, Jean 134
Carmen, Jeanne **388**, 389
Carnival Show 105
Carnovsky, Morris **356**
Carr, Nat 58
Carr, Sabin W. 110, 112
Carr, Trem 62, 90, 99, 262
Carradine, John 244
Carreras, Enrique 375
Carreras, James 375
Carreras, Michael 375-377
Carroll, Leo G. 176
Carroll, Madeleine 343
Carter, Douglas 345
Cason, John L. 306

Cassidy, Ed 129-130, 242
Castello, William 103
Castle, Don **357**, 358
Castle, Peggie 384
Cats and the Fiddle 181
Cattle Stampede 237, 443
Caught Cheating 30
Cavalcade Films Corp 85, **87**
CBC (see Canadian Broadcasting Company)
CBS (see Columbia Broadcasting System)
Cedars of Lebanon Hospital 52, 256, 334
Celentano, Ralph 38
Century Comedies xiii, 8, 10-11, 13, 15-16, **17**, 18, **19-20**, 21-22, 28, 31, 147, 166, 207
Chadwick Studios 235-236, 256
Chadwick, I.E. 262, 307
Chambers, Dudley 363-365
Chambers, Wheaton 302
Champion 341
Chance, Naomi 377
Chandler, Chick 368, **369**
Chaney, Lon, Jr. 228, 334, **335**, 391, **392**, 393-394, 396
Chaplin Studios 11-12
Chaplin, Charles 12
Chapman, Jules K. 343
Chase, Alden 149, 151, 164, 200
Chasing Around 37, 421
Chatton, Syd 113-114, 266
Chesebro, George 123, **305**
Chester Comedies 31
Chicago Musical College 114
Child Bride 179
China Clipper 228
Chisholm, John "Jack" 97
Christine, Virginia 311
Christopher, Robert 387

Chudnow, David 185, 196, 226, 254, 267

Cimarron 39

Cinecolor Corporation 343, 349

Cinecolor Finance Corporation 343, 345

Cinecolor Process 329, 331-332, 343, 347, 350-351, 373-374, 410

Cineglow Sound System 99

Cinema Sound, Inc. 70

Cinemart Productions 85, 142

Cinemascope 378, 397, 399

Cinematograph Films Act of 1927 95, 375

Cinephone 51

Cinnamon **39**, 421

Circus Capers 23

Circus Daze **23**, 417

Cisco Kid Productions, Inc. 112

Citizen Kane 273

Clack, Bobby 168

Clair, Ethlyne 20

Clark, Bobby 162, **168**, 169

Clark, Dane 377, **378**

Clark, Judy 285, **286**

Clark, Steve 135-136

Classics in Slang (series) 30, 32

Clavering, Eric 97, **98**

Clay, Lewis 333

Cleveland, George 346

Clifton, Elmer 228, 231-232, 262, 317

Cline, Robert 100, 244, 249, 254, 276

Clute, Chester **337**

Clyde, Andy 107

Coast Picture Productions 176

Cobb, Edmund "Eddie" 75

Code of the Cactus 147, 149, **153**, 159, 431

Code of the Mounted 67, **68**, 424

Code of the Plains 308, 443

Code of the Range 429

Code of the Rangers 138, 429

Cody, Iron Eyes 178

Coffin, Tristram 355

Cohen, Albert Jay 347, **348**

Cohn, Jack 4, **6**, 14, 105

Cohn, Martin G. 61, 337

Coleman, Bennie **366**

Coletti, Frank 166

College Sweetheart 107

Collier, John, Commissioner of Indian Affairs 146

Collins, Charles **284**

Collins, G. Pat 359

Collins, Lew 306

Colmes, Walter 262, 264, **265**, 266-267

Colony Pictures Corp. 85, 98-99, **100-101**, 102-103, **104**, 244-245

Colorado Kid 134-135, 428

Columbia Pictures xi, 4, 48, 52, 74, 85, 105, **106**, 114, **118**, 119, **120**, 125, 145, 160, 213, 234, 237, 256, 266-267, 272, 294, 325, **333**, 381

Colvig, Vance DeBar 15

Compson, Betty 249

Compton, Joyce 183

Concord Productions 85, **138**, **140**, 147

Congo Pongo 298, 448

Conn Studios 146

Conn, Maurice H. 61, **62-63**, 64, **65**, **67-68**, 70, 72, 73, 91, **138**, **140**, 141, 334 , **335**

Consolidated Film Exchange 61, 90, 325

Consolidated Film Industries 90, 209, 235

Consolidated Pictures, Inc. 148

Consolidated Studios 357

Consumers Park 4

Consumers Park Brewing Company 4

Contender, The 254, 262, **268-269**, 270, 313, 445

Continental Pictures 180

Convict Battalion (story) 254

Coogan, Jackie 374-375

Cook, Grant L. 41

Cooper, Gary **360**

Cooper, Inez 321-322

Cooper, Jack 15

Cooper, James Fenimore 393

Cooper, Ralph 180, **181**, 182

Coquette 125

Corbett, Ben 151-152, **153**, 154, 156, **157**, 158-159

Corby, Francis 19-20, 24, 26, **27**

Corio, Ann 228, **229-230**, 231-232, 272

Corpse Came Calling, The (see also *Three On a Ticket*) 322, 451

Corrigan, Ray "Crash" 122-123, **124**, 241, 270, **271**, 272-273, **274**, 302, 347

Corriganville 241, 279, 304

Cortez, Ricardo 244

Cotton Club Tramp Band 105

Cotton Comes to Harlem 408

Counterfeiters, The 334, **335**, 452

Cowboy Afoot (story) 211

Cowboy G-Men (TV series) 359

Cowboy Rambler Band 219

Cowboys Never Walk (story) 211

Cowell, John W. 75-76

Coyle, Ellen 306

Coyle, John T. 197, 209, 231

Crabbe, Buster viii, xiv, 115, 211-212, **213**, 215, **216-217**, 218, 223, 228, **230**, **237-239**, 240, 243, 245, **246-247**, 257, 258-259, 260-262, **268-269**, 270-272, 275-277, **278-279**, 282, 291, **292**, 297, **304-305**, 306, **307-308**, 309, 316, 318, **333**, 334, 382, **383**, 409-411

Crabbe, Cullen "Cuffy" 382, **383**

Craig, James **384**, 385-386

Cramer, Richard "Dick" 114-115

Crashin' Through Danger 73, 83, **84**, 410, 430

Crashin' Thru Danger (see *Crashin' Through Danger*) 430

Crashing Through Danger (see *Crashin' Through Danger*) 430

Crashing Thru Danger (see *Crashin' Through Danger*) 430

Crawford, Joan 124-125

Crespinel, William Thomas 331

Crevenne, Marcel 383

Crime in the Night (see also *Larceny in Her Heart*) 312, 450

Crime on My Hands 450

Criner, Laurence 180

Crisler, Ben R. 174

Criterion Pictures 41, 85, **177**

Crosby, Bing 292

Crowley, William X. 325

Cummings, Constance 343

Cummins, Sam 341

Cunard, Grace 10

Currie, Louise 192-193, 322

Currier, Richard 340

Curry, Louise (see Currie, Louise)

Curse, The 105

Curti, Georgio 295

Curtis, Billy 117, **118**, 119-120

Curtis, Dick (see Curtis, Richard)

Curtis, Richard 69, 82, 125, **126-127**, 128-130

Curwood, James Oliver 61-63, 71

Cutler, Lester 197, 231, 262

D'Arcy, Roy 44

D'Orsay, Fifi 270-272

Da Pello, Rosina 318

Dahl, Arlene 376

Dailey, Allen 44

Dalton's Last Raid, The 360

Daly, Phil M. 59

Dalya, Jacqueline **317**, 318

Damaged Good 41

Danger! Women at Work **248**, 249, 262, 411, 443

Dangerous Men 316, 450

Daniels, Harold **179**

Daring Daughters **50**, 51, 422

Dark Manhattan 180

Darling, Constance 19

Darling, Scott 30, 32

Darmour, Larry 41, 51, 90

Darrell, Steve **305-306**

Dauntless 64

Davenport, Gail 282

David and Bathsheba 378

Davis, Art **219-221**, 222

Davis, Audry 219

Davis, Benny 266

Davis, Elmer 233

Davis, George 23

Davis, Jim **358**, 359, **361**, 362, **384-385**, 386, 397, 400

Davis, Karl "Killer" 364

Davis, Rufe 124

Davis, Virginia 22

De Fee, Lois 118

De Luxe Pictures 107

Dead End (play) 320

Dead End Kids and Little Tough Guys, The (series) 320

Dead Men Walk xiv, 227, 244, 249, **250-251**, 255, 301, 410, 442

Dead On Course 376

Dean, Eddie 221

Dean, James 287

Dean, Margia 363, **364**, 372, 385, 389

Death on the Wing (story) 73

Death Rides the Plains 241, 442

Death Rides the Range 103, **104**, 433

Death Wish 408

Decent (story) 99

Decker, Sam 122

Delaney, Charles 64, 71

De Lay, Melville P. 185, 241, **243**, 254, 294, 311

Delinquent Daughters 161, 272

Delinquent Parents 161

Dell, Claudia 82

Dell, Myrna 355

DeMarco, Mario 193

DeMille, Cecil B. 378

Denning, Richard 335-336

Denny, Reginald 60

Dent, Vernon 173

Derr, E.B. 187, 197, 209

Desert Escape (see also *Marked Men*) 435

Desert Patrol 134, **137**, 430

Desperate Cargo 196

Destination Moon 365

Detour 244, 300

Devil Bat, The **195**, 225, 302, 435

Devil Riders 257, 259-260, 444

Devil's Apprentice, The 272, 445

Devil's Weed, The 339, **340**, 453

Devine, Andy 292

DeWoild's Champeen **32**, 420

Dickey, Basil 156, 158

Dietrich, Marlene 119

Dillaway, Donald 55, 88

Dilson, John 191

Diltz, Charles **23**

Discarded Lovers 44, **45**, 421

Disney, Roy 51

Disney, Walt 21-22, 51, 335, 366

Dix, Richard 39, 343

Dixie Film Exchange 325
Dixie Jamboree 272
Dixie National 325
Dodd, Jimmy 124
Dogville Comedies 31
Doing His Stuff 28, 419
Dollar Bills, The 328
Dominion Motion Pictures, Ltd. 98
Donath, Ludwig 379
Donne, Carole 346
Dooley, Jed 20
Doomed at Sundown 130, **133**, 134, 428
Dore, Adrienne 97, **98**
Dorety, Charles 23, 26
Doten, Jay 268
Doty, Douglas 54
Double Indemnity 258
Double Spots 107
Douglas, George 186
Down By the Old Alamo (song) 201
Down on the Sunset Trail (song) 119
Downing, Rex 320
Downs, Johnny **225**, 226, 228, 264-267
Doyle, Sir Arthur Conan 367
Dracula 225, 252
Dragnet (radio series) 359
Drake, Claudia 289, 336
Drake, Oliver 123, 232, 262
Dreifuss, Arthur 231, 262
Dresden, Curley **216**
Dresser, Davis 309
Drew, Roland 166-167, 173-174, 268, **269**
Drifter, The 257, 260, **261**, 444
Drifting Souls **46**, 421
Drums of the Jungle 270, 445
Drunkard, The 148

Drunkard; or, The Fallen Saved, The (play) 148
Dudley, Marjorie 287
Duke is Tops, The 180
Duke of the Navy 197
Dumas, Alexander 122
Duna, Steffi 173-174
Duncan, Bud 87
Duncan, Ken (aka Kenneth, Kenne) 95-97, **98**, 170, 188, 190, 355
Dunham, Phil 9, 99
Dunlap, Paul 359, 370, 385, 389
Dunlap, Scott R. 139, 262
Dunn, James **165**, **184**, 185
Dunn, Murison 97
Dunn, Ralph 311, 314, 321-322, **336**
Dunne, Irene 39
Duprez, June 264
Durango Valley Raiders 134, 137, 430
Durlam, Arthur 74
Dwire, Earl 100, 126-127, 131, 133
Dyne, Michael 302
E & R Jungle Films 31
Eagle Lion Classics **338**, 339, 351
Eagle's Brood, The 91
Eagle-Lion Films xi, 257, 267, 308-309, 315-317, 320, 322, 324, 328, 335, **336-337**, 352
Earle, Jack 15-16
Eason, Walter B. 333, 334
East Side Kids (series) 147, 319-320
East Side Rascals 320, 451
East Side, West Side 320, 451
Easy Way, The 343, 452
Ebb Tide 329
Ebb-Tide, The (story) 329
Eben, Al 302
Edison, Thomas 4

Educational Pictures /Film Exchange 22, 40-41, 49, 52, 60, 87, 101

Edwards, Harry 15

Edwards, Meredith 378

Ehrlich, Emilie 381

Eldredge, George 363

Eldredge, Roy 180-181

Eliot, Kathleen 135

Elliot, John 71, 76, 103, 201

Ellis, Emil K. 308-309

Ellis, Frank **305-306**

Ellis, John 196

Emergency Landing 196

Emmett, Fern 252

Emmett, Robert 67, 162, 295

Emory, Richard 363, **364**

Enchanted Forest, The **295**

Engle, Billy 16, **17**

English, John "Jack" **63**, **65**, 66, 68-69, 74, 79, 81, 84, 116

Enright, Ray 228

Erdody and His Famous Orchestra 301

Erdody, Leo Wald 196, 298, 301, 304, 345

Ernest, George 91

Erwin, Ted **191**

Esper, Dwain 179

Espy, Reeves 296

Esskay Productions **333**

Eureka Productions 341

Evans, Doug 45, 371

Ex-Bartender 32, 420

Excelsior Pictures 73-74, 76, **84**, 125, 149, 159, 166, 245

Excess Baggage (stage play) 56

Exclusive Films Limited 375, **376**, **378**, 380

Excuse Maker, The (series) 19-20

Exhibitors Screen Service, Inc. 90

Ex-King 41, 421

Exposure 47, 49, 422

Ex-Racketeer 254

F.B.O. (see Film Box Office)

Fain, Matty **165**

Fairbanks, Douglas 48

Fairbanks, William 29

Falcon the Horse 259

Famous Comedies Productions, Ltd. 40, 41

Fare Enough 16

Farmer, Frances 329

Farrar, Vincent J. 245, 317

Fatima (novel) 345

Faye, Dorothy 142

Federal Agent 90-92, **93**, 425

Federation of the Motion Picture Industry 56

Feld, Fritz 372

Ferguson, Frank 315, 321-322, 350

Fetherston, Eddie **191**

Feud Maker 134, 136, 429

Fidler, Jimmie 172

Fier, Jack 61

Fifth Musketeer, The 197

Fight That Ghost 325, 327, 449

Fighting Bill Carson 304, 448

Fighting Deputy, The 107, 109, **110**, 114, 158, 428

Fighting Mad **177**, 178, 432

Fighting Renegade, The 145, 147, 157, 432

Fighting Trooper, The 63-64, 66, 423

File 649: State Department 331, **348-351**, 357, 453

Film Box Office (F.B.O.) 130-131, 213

Film Classics xiv, 213, 257, 343, **344-349**, 350, 394

Film Laboratories of Canada, Ltd.

Fine Arts Pictures 95

Fine Arts Studio 85, **141**

Fingerprints Don't Lie 363, **364**, 454

Finney, Edward 262

First National 30, 45, 87, 125, 213, 245

Fischer, Margarita 7

Fisher, Ross 245

Fitzgerald, Mike 103, 139

Fix, Paul 66, 76

Flame the Dog 346

Flaming Disc, The 13

Flaming Frontier 397, 399, **400**, 457

Flaming Lead 101, 103, 432

Flash Goordon 211

Flash Gordon Conquers the Universe 211

Flash Gordon's Trip to Mars 211

Fleming, Rhonda 329, **330**, 331, **332**

Fleming-Roberts, G.T. 321

Fletcher, Tex **143**, 144, 219

Flint, Sam 183, 372

Flothow, Rudolph C. **382**

Fluellen, Joel 302

Flying Serpent, The 196, 257, 282, 298, 301-302, **303**, 317, 449

Fog Island 227

Fontaine, Jacqueline 375

Fontaine, Lili 395

Footprints 61, 63

Foran, Dick 139

Forbes Randolph Kentucky Jubilee Singers 31

Forbes, Harry **27**, 48-50, 58-59, 99

Ford, Francis 10

Ford, Frederick 398

Ford, Wallace 343

Foreman, Carl 360

Forman, Eddie 338

Forwood, Anthony 378

Foster, Preston **361**, 362-363

Foulger, Byron 253

Four Keltons, The 30

Four Tones, The 111

Fowley, Douglas 312, 322, 328

Fox Fims 7, 29-30, 38, 48, 49-50, 52, 61, 87, 106, 115, 125, 145, 166, 242, 245

Fox Monkeys, The 31

Fox, Wallace 262, 306

Foy, Bryan 52, 145-146, 316

Francis Ford Studio **20**, 21

Francis, Noel 52, **53**, **55**

Frankel, David 20

Frankenstein 81, 225

Franklin Productions 339

Franz, Eduard 379-380

Fraser, Harry 32-33, 101, 107, 231, 262, 272, 287, 325

Fraser, Richard 272, 302, 315

Frazer, Robert 44, 64, 71

Freaks 118

Fred Waring and His Pennsylvanians 266

Free Clinic 435

Freeman, Wilbur 97

Freidberg, Sidney 176

French Leave 28, 419

Frenke, Dr. Eugene 121

Frey, Arno 220, 230, 263-264

Friedman, David F. 325-326, 341-342

Frijoles (song) 111

Fromkess, Leon 122, 182, **186**, 209, 231, **233**, 235, 236, 237, 254-255, **256**, 262, 267, 269-270, 272, **275**, 295-296, 298, 304, 281, **382**, 390-391, **392**, 397

Frontier Crusader 182, 187, 434

Frontier Fighters 308, 443

Frontier Frameup (story) 211

Frontier Gambler 384, 389-390, 456

Frontier Marshal Along the Sundown Trail (see also *Along the Sundown Trail*) 441

Frontier Marshal in Prairie Pals (see also *Prairie Pals*) 440

Frontier Marshal (series) xiv, 186-187, 218-219

Frontier Outlaws 257, 260, 445

Frontier Scout **141**, 197, 430

Frost, Terry 272-273, 303

Frye, Dwight 251-252

Frye, Katherine 123

Fugitive of the Plains 237, **238**, 308, 442

Fuller, Sam 353

Fulton, Lou **187**

Fury (TV series) 391

Fuzzy Settles Down 243, 257, 261, 446

Gabler, Neal 22

Gale, Allan 267

Gallagher, Jack **195**

Gallagher, Skeets 52, **53**

Gambler and the Lady, The 377, **378**, 455

Gambling Terror, The 125-126, **127**, 167, 427

Gambling with Souls 178

Gang War 180

Gangs, Inc. 177

Gangster's Den 276-277, **294**, 447

Gangsters on the Loose 180

Garbo, Greta 124

Garfield, John 356

Garner, Don 395

Garrard, Don 398, **400**

Garvie, Parker 311

Gas House Kids 301, 318, **319**, 320, 322, 451

Gas House Kids Go to Hollywood 320

Gas House Kids Go West 320

Gaskins, Romeo 96

Gaumont British 218, 343

Geldert, Clarence 93

Gell, William J. 182, 210

Gendron, Pierre 272

General Foreign Sales Corp. 60

Gentlemen with Guns 304, **305-306**, 317, 449

George's False Alarm 416

George's School Daze 417

German American Bund 166, 173, 175

Gest, Inna **187**

Ghost Mine 437

Ghost of Hidden Valley 304, 306, 449

Ghost Patrol 81, **82**, 426

Ghost Town Gold 122

Gibson, Hoot 100

Gibson, Julie 268-269

Gibson, Tom 107

Gifford, Frances **165**, **184**, 185

Gill, George 176, **186**, **209-210**

Ginsberg, Henry 58

Girard, Joseph W. 78, 80

Girl and the Gorilla, The **270**

Girls for Rent 244

Gittens, Wyndham 74

Gladwin, Frances **242**, 243

Gland Hotel 41, 421

Glass Key, The 177

Glendon, J. Frank 77, 80-82

Glenn, Glen 147, 240, 256

Gluckman, Herman 44, 48

Glucksman, Joe 43-44

God's Country 353

Goddard, Paulette **379**, 380

Goetz, Jack 95

Go-Get-'Em Haines 90-93, **94**

Gold Medal Films 44

Goldberg, Lee 122, **186**

Goldberg, Rube 23

Golden Gate Productions 324, 353

Golden Turkey Awards, The (book) 119

Goldstone, Phil 29, **30**, 33-34, 36, 39-41, 48, 51, 56, 98, 145

Goldwyn Studios 48, 257, 366-367

Goldwyn, Samuel 320, 391

Gombell, Minna 59-60

Gonzalez Gonzalez, Jose 387-388

Good Scout Buster 417

Goodman, Benny 282-283

Goose Step (movie; see *Hitler – Beast of Berlin*) 172-173, 175, 432

Goose Step (short story) 170-171

Gorcey, Leo 320

Gordon, Eddie 16

Gordon, Gavin 322

Gordon, Huntley 49

Gordon, Mary **183-184**

Gordon, Milton 391

Gornel, David 381

Gottlieb, Arthur 95, 391-392

Gottlieb, Harold 316

Graham, Sheila 309

Grand Hotel 41

Grand National 85, 94, 99-101, 130, 141-143, 144, 178, 197, 245, 256

Grand National Studios 162, 173

Grandin, Francis J. 7

Granstedt, Greta 173

Grant, Frances 82

Gray, Coleen 386, **390**

Gray, Edward M. 359

Gray Shadow 191

Gray, Virginia **362**

Grayler, Sydney 166

Great Radium Mystery, The 13

Great Western Productions, Inc. 10, 112

Greco the Chimpanzee 229

Green Pastures, The 111

Green, George 359

Greenblatt, Arthur 218, 236, 255

Greene, Clarence 295

Greenhalgh, Jack 66, 71, 74, 76-77, 80-82, 138, 164, 166-167, 173, 182, 185, 192, **219**, **224-225**, **233**, **236**, 244-245, **246**, 249, 251, 276, **278**, **280**, **282**, 289, **294**, **297**, 298, 304, 306, 311, **315**, 320, 328, 335, 337, **341-342**, 345, **346**, 347, 350-351, 359, 360, **366**, 367-368, 385, 409

Gregory, Ena 15

Grey, Harry 124

Grey, Virginia 346-347, 363

Gribbon, Eddie 87

Griffith, D.W. 48

Grippo, Jan 320

Grofe, Ferde 301

Gross, Dave 74

Guihan, Frances 141

Guilbert, Nina 168-169

Guilty Parents 178

Gun Code **187**, 188, 434

Gun Lords of Stirrup Basin 130, **132**, 133-134, 427

Gundelfinger, Alan M. 331

Guns in the Dark 125, **128**, 427

Gunsmoke (TV series) 212, 215

Gunsmoke Trail 138-139, **140**, 429

Haade, William 321, **361**, 363

Hackel, A.W. **88-89**, 122, 124-125, **126-129**, 130-131, **132-134**, **136-137**, 138, 145-146, 180, **181**, 182, 213, 262

Hackett, Karl **75**, 76-78, 80, 82, 99, 113-115, 132, 135, **136**, 137, 139, 149, 187, 201-202, **220**

Hackney, W.P. 85

Hagenbeck-Wallace Circus 146

Hager, Clyde 105

Hagney, Frank 200, 220, 257, 259, 369

Hal Roach Studios 52, 58, 117, 339

Hale, Alan **387**, 389

Hale, Jonathan 388

Half-Back Buster 417

Half-Buck 121

Half-Buck Goes West 121

Half-Buck Hits the Trail 121

Half-Buck Rides Again 121

Hall Room Boys (series) 15

Hall, Henry 302

Hall, Huntz 320

Hall, Jon 381, **382**

Hall, Thurston 346

Hall, William 185

Halliday, Brett 309, 311-312, 322

Hallmark Productions **341-342**

Halop, Billy 320

Halperin Productions 41

Halperin, Edward 153

Halperin, Victor 162, **163-164**, 166, 232

Ham and Bud 87

Hamilton, Lloyd **87**

Hammer Film Productions 375, 380

Hammer, Will 375

Hammon, H.W. 40, 60, 101

Hampton, Orville 357-358, 363, 367, 371, 377, 385, 387

Handcuffed 99

HANL (see Hollywood Anti-Nazi League) 172

Hanna, David James 159-160

Hanneford, Poodles **23**, **148**

Hardwick, Lois 26

Hardy, Oliver 112

Harlan, Richard **165**, 166

Harlem on the Prairie 110, **111**, 112, 122, 185, 428

Harlem Rides the Range 112

Harley-Merry Studiom4

Harper, Patricia 213-214, 258, 276

Harris Disc Recording 50

Harrison, Paul 172

Harry Sherman Productions, Inc. 112

Harryhausen, Ray 369

Hart, John 391, **392**, 393-394, 396, 399

Hart, Maria 375

Harvest Melody xiv, 243, 262, 264, **265**, 266-267, 411, 444

Harvey, Don 334, **335**, 339

Harvey, Harry 165, 170

Harvey, Walter 377

Harwin, Dixon R. 231, 262

Hatton, Raymond 124, 190, 338

Have Patience 418

Hawkeye and the Last of the Mohicans (see *Last of the Mohicans, The*) 457

Hawkeye's Homecoming (TV show episode) 395

Hayes, Allison 397-399

Hayes, Lorraine 133-134

Hays Office 171, 173, 180, 261, 406

Headin' for Heaven 56, 422

Hearn, Marcus 375

Heigh, Helen 311

Hell Breaks Loose (see *Crashin' Thru Danger*) 73, 430

Hell's Devils 177

Hendricks, Ben Jr. 66, 69

Henkel, Charles V. 99, 102-103

Henry Lehrman Comedies 87

Henry, Bill 359

Henry, Charles 147

Henry, Gale 10

Hepburn, Katherine 156, 264

Her Bashful Beau 420

Herbert, Holmes 46

Here's to Happiness (play) 265

Herman, Al 15-16, 232, 262

Herzog, Karl 255, **256**, 345

Hicks, Russell 298-300

High and Mighty (story) 211

High Flyin' George 24, **25**, 416

High School Confidential! 274

Highway to Hell 298, 448

Hi-Jacked **358**, 359, 385, 454

Hill, Riley 355

Hill, Robert F. 13, 107, 148, 243

Hilliard, Ernest 91, 93

Hillyer, Lambert 306

Hinds, Anthony 375. **376**

Hirlicolor 94

Hirliman, George A. 90, **92**, 94, 145

His Adopted Daughter 282

His Brother's Ghost 276, 278, 447

His Fighting Blood 66, 69, 424

Hitchcock, Alfred 45, 329, 343

Hite, Les 110

Hitler – Beast of Berlin 162, 166, **171**, 172-174, **175**, 176-177, 185, 217, 245, 409, 432

Hodgins, Earle 77, **79**, 80, 113-114, 129, 169

Hoerl, Arthur 44, 333

Hoffman, Dr. Samuel J. 340

Hoffman, Maurice H. 29, 90

Hold On 16

Hold That Woman! xiv, 182, **184**, 185, 191, 411, 434

Hold Your Horses 26, 418

Holden, Eddie 109

Holiday, Billie 181

Hollingsworth, Violet Evelyn 48

Hollywood Anti-Nazi League (HANL) 172

Hollywood Films 44

Hollywood Studios 41

Holman, Harry 284

Holt, David 339

Homans, Robert 83-84, 182, **183**

Homolka, Oscar 329

Hop Harrigan (comic strip) 333

Hop Harrigan America's Ace of the Airways 333

Hopalong Cassidy 91-92, 219

Hopper, E. Mason 45-46

Hopper, Hedda 265

Hopton, Russell 44

Horne, James W. 85

Hoshelle, Marjorie 315

Hot Curves 30

Hot Off the Press 147

Houck, Joy N. 373

House Across the Street, The 342

House-Rent Party 325, **326**, 327, 449

Housman, Arthur 87, 94

Houston, George 115, **141**, 162, 186-187, **197-202**, 211, **223**, 224, 241

Houston, Norman **47**, 48

Howard, John 355

Howco Productions 373, **374**

Howe, Jay "Kitty" 9, 16, **17**

Howell, Alice 9-10

Howes, Reed 102, 143-144, 149, 151, 154, 158

Howling Hollywood 23

Hoxie, Al 43

Hoxie, Jack 48

Hoyt, John 368, **369**, 379

Hudson, Rochelle 245, **246-247**

Hughes, Mary Beth 287, 289, **290**

Hugo, Mauritz 315

Hull, Warren 190, **191**

Hunt, Eleanor 68, 93-94

Hurst, Paul 30-31, **32**
Huston, Walter 343
Hutchinson, Craig 9
Huth, Harold 232
Hyer, William "Bill" 44-46
Hygienic Productions 341
Hyman, Louis 119
I Accuse My Parents 282, **287-288**, 446
I Can't Escape 99
I Shot Jesse James 274, 353
I Take This Oath 182, **183-184**, 187, 434
Ideal Studios 325
IMP xiv, 3, **4**, 5, **6**, 7-8
IMP Split 6
Implet, The 6-7
Important Witness, The 54, 55, 422
IMPPA (see Independent Motion Picture Producers Association) 51, 145, 234, 307
In the Money 377, 456
Incredible Hilk, The (TV series) 408
Independent Moving Pictures Company 3, **4**
Independent Motion Picture Producers Association (IMPPA) 51, 145, 262, 307
Ingraham, Lloyd 81, 93, 100, 126
Inner Sanctum Mysteries 250
Inside Information 148
Inside the Law 231
Institute of Musical Arts 197
International Alliance of Theatrical Stage Employees (IATSE) 51
International Amphitheatre, Chicago 146
International Film Classics 343
International Studios 52, 56, 117, 151
Invasion U.S.A. 274
Invisible Killer, The 166, **167**, 173, 433
Invisible Man Returns, The 225
Invisible Woman, The 225

Iron Eyes Cody 178
Island of Fear, The (see also *Torture Ship*) 162, 432
Israel, Sam 316
Iverson Ranch 206, **236**, 304
Izzie and Lizzie (series)
James, Judge William P. 101
Jamison, Bud 19, 32
Jane Eyre 273
Jane's Engagement Party 19, 415
Jane's Predicament 415
Jane's Sleuth 416
January, Lois 77-78, 125, 131
Jarrett, Art **142**, 143
Jed Buell Productions 113
Jeffries, Herbert 110, **111**, 112
Jenkins, Patrick 377
Jenks, Frank 285
Jergens, Adele 355
Jeritza 107
Jerry the Dog 26-27
Jewell, Edward 350
Jewell, Isabel 190-191, 248
Jezebel Productions **379**
Jive Junction 255, 262
John Sutherland Productions 335, 336-337
Johnson, Arthur 255, **256**, 324
Johnson, W. Ray 262
Jo-Jo from Mexico (song) 114
Jolley, I. Stanford **222**, 242, 253, 257
Jones, Buck 150
Jones, Gordon 182-183, **184**
Jones, Governor R. T. 168
Jones, James 23, 85
Jones, John J. 353
Jones, Marsha 359

Journey's End 70

Jowett, Corson 256

Joy Theatres 373

Judell, Ben N. 160-162, **165**, 166-173, 176

Judell, Clara 161

Judell, Harvey 161

Judell, Julius 172

Judge Steps Out, The 341

Judge, Arline 248, 268, **269**

Julliard School 197

Jungle Blindness 345, 452

Jungle Flight 328, **329**, 332, 451

Jungle Fury 270, 445

Jungle Night 345

Jungle Siren 225, 228, **229-230**, 231, **232**, 440

Jungle Terror 270, 445

Just We Two 85, 423

Kaaren, Suzanne 139

Kahn, Richard C. 112

Kane, Joseph 122

Kann, Red 296

Karas, Anton 264

Karloff, Boris 244, 343

Katzman, Hortense 145

Katzman, Sam 54, 88, **145**, 146-147, **149-150**, **152-155**, 156, **157**, 158, **159**, 160, 169-170, 185, 234, 256, 262, 320, **333**, 334, 410

Kay, Richard 339, **341**

KBS Productions 90, 95

Kearns, Carroll D. 307

Keen, Geoffrey 376

Keene, Richard 311-312

Keene, Tom 138-139

Keeping Up with the Joneses (series) 23, 26

Kelly, Albert H. 197

Kelly, Burt 95, **96**

Kelly, Patsy **248**, 249, 411

Kelly, Paul 331

Kelsey, Fred 44, 49

Kelton, Pert 31-32

Kendall, Cy 314

Kendis, J.D. **178**, 179-180

Kennedy, Joseph P. 130

Kennedy, Merna 49

Kent, Robert 328, 334, **335**, 339, 355

Kent, Willis 88

Kerr, Donald 196

Keystone Comedies 7, 115

Kibbee, Milton 215, 230, 257, **259**, 268, **269**, 282, 350

Kid Rides Again, The 237, 441

Kid Sister, The xiv, 282, 285, **286**, 287, 411, 447

King Brothers 197

King Kong 370

King, Charles 19-20, 23, **24**, 64, 66, 69, 103, 109, 114-115, **116**, 126, 128, 131-132, 135-136, **189**, 190, 192-193, 200, **202**, 212, 214, 218, 221-222, 259-261, **279**, **294**, 306, 322, 337, 375

King, Henry 378

King, Louis **46**

King's Plate, The 95, **96**

Kingsley, Stanley 320

Kirkland, David 9

Klein, New York Rep. Arthur 351

Kline, Richard 145

Kline, Robert (see Cline, Robert)

Kline, Wally **338**, 339

Knight of the Plains 113-114, 429

Knight, Fuzzy 71, **338**, 382

Knox, Mickey 355, **356**, 357, 410

Kohler, Fred 66-67

Kojak (TV series) 408

Korda Brothers 375

Korngold, Erich Wolfgang 274

Kornmann, Mary 107

Koster, Henry 378

Kozinsky, Frank 197

Kozinsky, Maurice 197

Krah, Mark 372

Kramer, Hope 303

Kranze, B.G. 351

Krasne, Philip N. **142**, **177**

Kraushaar, Raoul 340

Krebs, Nita 119-120

KTTV Television Studios 365, 373, **379**

Kuhn, Fritz 173

Kulick, Bert 176, **186**, 209

Kyne, Peter B. 146

La Guardia, Fiorello 228

La Rose, Rose 318

La Roy, Rita 185

La Rue, Frank 192, 259

La Salle, Ned 26

Ladd, Alan 173-174, 177, 409

Lady at Midnight 335, **336**

Lady Chaser 318, **321**, 322

Lady Confesses, The xiv, 282, 289, **290**, 309, 410, 447

Lady in the Fog (see also *Scotland Yard Inspector*) **376**, 455

Lady Killer (see also *Lady Chaser*) 321, 451

Lady's in Distress (song) 178

Laemmle Film Service 4

Laemmle, Carl xiv, 3-4, **5**, 6, 27-28, 106, 244

Lafflets (series) 21

Lake, Arthur 28

Lamb, Ande 266

Lamble, Lloyd 376

Lamont, Charles **14**, 19

Landau, Richard H. 366-367, 379-380

Landers, Lew 232

Lane, Lola 54

Lane, Nora **152**, 170

Lane, Rosemary 264, **265**, 266-267

Lang, David A. 317

Lang, Fritz 227

Langdon, Harry 107, 196

Lange, Johnny 152, 199

Lanzo, Rocco 320

Larceny in Her Heart 301, 309, **312-313**, 316, 322, 450

LaRocque, Rod 100

LaRue, Al "Lash" 115, 305-306

Lasky, Art 268

Lassie (TV series) 103, 391, 408

Last Alarm, The 197

Last of the Desperados **384-385**, 456

Last of the Mohicans, The 391, **392**, 393, 395-397, 399, 401, 408, 414, 457

Last Smile, The 18

Latimer, Ross **361**, 362

Laugh-O-Grams (series) 21

Laurel and Hardy 43, 109

Laurel, Stan 112, **113**, 114-115, **116**, 117

Law and Order 218, 440

Law of the .45s 122

Law of the Saddle 241, **243**, 444

Le Saint, E.J. 7

Leal, John 122

Lease, Rex 78-80, **137**, 138, 148

Leave It to the Marines 358, 371, **373**, 455

LeBorg, Reginald 354, 379-380

Lee, Lila 47

Lee, Sharon (see also Walker, Cheryl) **179**, 311

Leeds, Lila 339-340, **341-342**

Lehrman, Henry xiii, 7, 9-10, 28, 87

Leifert, Don 252

Lenard, Grace 180

Lennick, Ben 399-400

Leonard, Robert Z. 29

Leonard, Sheldon 264-266

LeRoy, Mervyn 378

Leslie, Maxine **201**, 218, **238**

Lesser, Sol 118-119, 121, 211

Let George Do It (series) 19-20, 23-24, **25**

Levine, Nat 51, **61**, 90, 122, **124**

Levitt, Gene 383

Levitt, Sam 95

Levy, Eady 375

Lewis, Charles 31, 36

Lewis, Jerry 70

Lewis, Joe 313

Lewis, Joseph H. 232, 262

Lewis, Ralph 303

Lewis, Sybyl 180

Liberty Pictures 90

Lightnin' Bill Carson 78, 84, 125, 150, 425

Lightnin' Crandall 130-131, 427

Lightning Carson Rides Again 145, **150**, 154, 157, 430

Lightning Raiders 294, **304**, 448

Lincoln Pictures, Inc. 85, 110, **111**

Lincoln, Elmo 10

Lind, Lloyd 297

Linden, Eddie 385

Linden, Eric 100

Lion's Den, The **80**, 81, 426

Lippert Productions 213, 257, 291, 328, 336, 353, **354**, 355, **356-358**, 359, **361-362**, 363, **364-366**, **368-370**, 371, **372-374**, **376**, **378-379**, 381, 384, 394

Lippert, Robert L. xiv, 353-354, 359, **360**, 363, 365-368, 371, 375-376, 378, 380, 384, 397

Lipstick 408

Lisa, Anna 185

Listen to the Mockingbird (song) 124

Little Annie Rooney 191

Little Big House, The 36, 37, 420

Little Billy (Rhodes) **106**, 119, 121

Little Covered Wagon, The 34, **35**, 36-37, 420

Little Divorcee, The 36-37, 420

Littlefield, Lucien **59**, 60

Lively, William "Bill" 103, 158, 162, 165, 169

Livingston, Monte 345

Livingston, Robert "Bob" 115, 122-123, **124**, 139, 223-224, **241-243**, 244, 253

L-Ko Komedy Kompany xiii, xiv, 7, **8-10**, 28, 147

Lloyd, Betty 62

Lockwood, Margaret 343

Loder, John 343

Logan, Phoebe 109

London Films 375

London, Jack 162, **163**, 164

London, Julie 270-272, 409

London, Tom 101-102, 125-126

Lone Ranger Rides Again, The 242

Lone Ranger, The 142

Lone Rider Ambushed, The 201-202, 437

Lone Rider and Law of the Saddle (see *Law of the Saddle*) 444

Lone Rider and the Bandit, The 223-224, 438

Lone Rider Crosses the Rio, The **198**, 436

Lone Rider Fights Back, The **202**, 438

Lone Rider Gallops to Glory, The 199, 437

Lone Rider in Border Roundup (see *Border Roundup*) 440

Lone Rider in Cheyenne, The **223**, 439

Lone Rider in Death Rides the Plains (see *Death Rides the Plains*) 442

Lone Rider in Frontier Fury, The 201, 437

Lone Rider in Ghost Town, The **199-200**, 20, 437

Lone Rider in Outlaws of Boulder Pass (see *Outlaws of Boulder Pass*) 441

Lone Rider in Overland Stagecoach (see *Overland Stagecoach*) 441

Lone Rider in Raiders of Red Gap (see *Raiders of Red Gap*) 444

Lone Rider in Texas Justice, The (see *Texas Justice*) 440

Lone Rider in Wild Horse Rustlers (see *Wild Horse Rustlers*) 442

Lone Rider in Wolves of the Range (see *Wolves of the Range*) 443

Lone Rider Rides On, The **197**, 198, 218, 436

Lone Rider (series) 141, 186, 197, 211, 223, 237, 241, 257

Long, Audrey **346-347**

Long, Harry 23

Long, Walter 101

Longenecker, Bert T. 125, 129-130, 133-134

Loo, Richard 349

Lord, Marjorie **337**

Loring, Teala 320

Lorraine, Elliott 96-97

Lorraine, Louise **14**

Lost Continent 358, **366**, 367, **368-370**, 371, 385, 410, 455

Lost World, The (novel) 367

Lourie, Eugene 340

Lowell, Robert 287, **288**

Lowery, Robert 320, **321**, 322, 328, **329**, 355-356

Luby, S. Roy 74

Lugosi, Bela **195**, 196, 244, 375

Lund, Lucille 72

Lundigan, William 349, **350-351**

Lydon, Jimmy 306

Lynn, Emmett 284

Lynn, Mara 371, **372-373**

Lynn, Sharon 44

Lyons and Moran 15

Lyons, Eddie 7

Lyons, Edgar 64, 68-69, 91, 93-94

M 227

M & A Productions 7 232

M Squad (TV series) 391

MacDonald, Edmund 289

MacDonald, J. Farrell 44, 59, 263-264

MacDonald, William Colt 122

MacFadden, Hamilton 232

Mack Sennett Pictures Corporation 117

Mack Sennett Studios 59, 106

Mack, Hughie 10

MacLane, Barton 270-272, 328, **329**, 386

MacMurray, Fred 298

Mad Ghoul, The 227

Mad Monster, The 215, **225-227**, 228, **280**, **292**, 439

Madison, Julian 103, 128, 179

Madison, Noel 54, 253

Magers, Boyd xi, 107-108, 215, 241

Magic 419

Magnificent Obsession 86

Majestic Pictures Corp. 48, 56, 90, 122

Mallinson, Rory 362

Mallot, Doris 244

Mallott, Yolande 196

Man from Guntown, The 74

Man from Headquarters, The 61

Man of Letters 416

Mancunian Studios 376

Maniac 179

Mann, E.B. 99

Mann, Hank 43, 46

Manners, Jane 24, **25**

Manners, Marjorie 265-266

Mantan Messes Up 122, 325, **327**, 448

Maple, Christine 123

March of Time (series) 173

Marie Antoinette 227

Marion, Beth 62, 141

Marion, Edna 16, 23

Marked Men xiv, 190, **191**, 192, 195-196, 410, 435

Markham, Dewey "Pigmeat" 180, 182, 325, **326**, 327

Marrying Widows **59**, 125, 423

Marsh, Joan 51

Marsh, Marian 51

Marshall, Herbert 343

Marshall, Tully 30, **47**

Martel, Gregg 373

Martin, Al 337, 343

Martin, Jill 158

Martin, Marian 318

Martin, Mr. Joe 31, 34

Martin, Mrs. Joe 31, 34

Martino, Marie **321**

Marvin, Lee 397

Mascot Pictures Corporation 59, 61-63, 90, 122, 125

Mask of Dijon, The 232

Mask of the Dragon 363-364, **365**, 454

Mason, John 181

Mason, LeRoy 64

Masters, Howard **213**

Mathews, Carl 113-114

Maxwell, Edwin 58

Maxwell, Lois 376

Maxwell, Paisley 400

May, Betty 15

May, Herbert 167

Mayer, Louis B. 30

Maynard, "Tex" 61

Maynard, Ken 62, **101**, 102-103, **104**

Maynard, Kermit 61-62, **63**, 64, **65**, 66, **67-68**, 69, **70**, 71, **72**, 73, 97, 149, 218, 222, **237**, 240, **279**, **308**, 319

Mayo, Donald 245-246, **247**, 268-269

MCA (see Music Corporation of America) 391

McCall, William "Bill" **148**

McCann, Irving G. 307

McCarroll, Frank **89**

McCarthy, Leo J. 231, 269, 275, 295

McCarthy, Patti 259-260

McClure, Doug 291

McComas, Robert 381

McComas, Violet 389

McCoy, Tim 74, **75-76**, 77, **78-80**, 81, **82-83**, 84, 114, 125, **138**, 139, 145-147, **149-150**, 151, **152-155**, 156, **157**, 158, **159**, 162, 169, **170**, 176, 182, 186, **187**, 188, **189**, 190, 209, 211, 218, 333, 410

McCulley, Johnston 211

McElwaine, Don 296

McGee, Mark Thomas 355, 360

McGilligan, Patrick 356

McGuinn, Joe 192

McIntyre, Christine 113

McKay, Wanda 218, 221, 249, 253, 272-273

McKean, Donald C. 262

McKee, Lafe 109, 115

McKeen, Lawrence 20, 28

McKeen, Sunny Jim 28

McKenzie, Robert "Bob" 77, 103

McKenzie, Eva 103

McKenzie, Fay 103-104

McManus, George 20

McMillan, Julia 311

McMillon, Don 399

McPhail, Addie 23

McTaggart, Bud 211, 215

Medved Brothers 119

Meehan, George 54

Meehan, Lew 132, **133-134**, 135

Meeker, George 287, 311

Meins, Gus 19-20, 24, 26, 28

Melody Lingers On, The 198

Melody of the Plains 107, **108**

Melton, Frank 82

Melton, Sid 291, 336, 355-356, **357**, 358, 363, **364**, 368, **369**, 371, **372-373**

Melzac, Vincent 391

Mercury Laboratories 145

Mercy Plane **165**, 166, 185, 433

Meredith, Iris 126-129

Meredith, John 306

Merkel, Una 248

Mermaid Comedies 22

Merrick, Doris 334

Merrick, George M. 228, 232

Merton, John 77-78, 80, 114-115, 139, 188, 192, 215, 218, 222, **237**, 259

Messick, Dale 333

Messinger, Buddy 15

Metcalfe, James 302

Metro 48, 301

Metro-Goldwyn-Mayer (see also M-G-M) 29-30

Metropolitan Pictures, Inc. 110

Metropolitan Studios 52, 99

M-G-M 29-31, 36, 41, 45, 52, 74, 85, 95, 105, 112, 118, 124-125, 139, 144, 234, 258, 335, 378

Michael Shayne (series) xiv, 295, 309, **310**, 313, 318, 322, 335, 410

Michel, Lora Lee 335, **336**

Mickey Mouse 24

Middlemass, Robert 253

Middleton, Charles 253

Midnight Follies 23

Mike and Ike (series) 23, **24**, 26

Miles, Art **191**

Miles, Lillian 68

Miljan, John 287, **288**

Milland, Ray 329

Miller Brothers 101 Ranch Wild West Show 74

Miller, Ernest 354

Miller, F.E. 110-111

Miller, Walter 64, 81

Millet, Arthur 80-81

Million Dollar Haul 148

Million Dollar Productions 180, 325

Milton, George 277

Mindlin, Victor 359

Minsky's Burlesque 228

Minstrel Man 262, 285, 301

Minto Skating Club 95

Mintz, Charles 22

Mintz, Sam 50

Miracle Kid, The 197

Miraculous Journey 301, **345-347**

Misbehaving Husbands 96

Missing Link, The 32, 421

Mister Jack and Missus Jill (song) 119

Mistress Caroline 34

Mitchum, Robert 339, 342

Modupe, Prince 270

Mojave Kid, The 130

Molieri, Lillian 388

Mom and Dad 341

Money Madness 301, 343, **344**, 345, 410, 452

Monogram Pictures/Studios 29, 48, 84-85, 90, 99, 130-131, 136, **138**, 139, **140**, 147, 160, **177**, 178, 182, 186, 190, 197, 211, 218, 228, 231, 234, 237, 240, 331, 333

Monogram Ranch 211

Monster Maker, The 270, 272, **273-274**, 286, 445

Montana Moon 125

Monter, Rudolph 255, 359

Montgomery, Baby Peggy **15**, 16

Mooney, Martin 197, 231, 234, 248, 254, 266, 272, 295

Moonlight on the Range 107-108, 428

Moore, Dennis "Smoky" 223

Moore, Vin 9

Moorhead, Natalie **45**

Moran, Austin 97

Moran, Lee 15, 47

Morante, Milburn "Milt" 126, 148-149

Moray, Yvonne 117, **118**, 119-120

Moreland, Mantan 110-111, 122, 180, 325, **327**

Moreland, Marcella 180

Morey and Sutherland Studios 318

Morgan, Ira H. 263

Morgan, Ralph 272, **273**

Morris, Chester 54

Morris, Dave 10

Morris, Earl J. 180

Morris, Gordon 54

Mortimer, Edward 196

Morton, Danny 344

Motion Picture Distributing and Sales Company, The 5

Motion Picture Financial Corp. 353

Motion Picture Patents Company 4

Motion Picture Producers and Distributors of America (MPPDA) 171

Motor Patrol **357**, 358, 454

Mountan, D.J. 145

MPPDA (see Motion Picture Producers and Distributors of America) 172-173

Mr. Smith Goes Ghost 325

Muir, Esther 91

Mummy's Ghost, The 227, 394

Mummy's Hand, The 225, 227

Mummy's Tomb, The 227

Murder Is My Beat 274

Murder Is My Business 309, **310**, 311, 317, 449

Murietta Hot Springs 47

Murphy, Denny 399

Murphy, Horace 129, 135

Murray, Charlie 30

Murray, John "Rastus" **326**, 327

Murray, Mae 29

Murray, Zon 306

Music Box Revue 24

Music Corporation of America (MCA) 391

Musical Fantasies 31

Mutual Burlesque Circuit 228

Mutual Film Corporation 48, 161

Mutual Television Productions 359

My Boy 446

My Children 41, 421

My Dream Rose (song) 301

My Mistake 416

My Son, the Hero **244, 262, 442**

Mycroft, Walter C. 231, 262

Myers, Alex 97

Myers, Zion 15, 31

Mysterious Rider, The **237**, 308, 441

Mystery of the Mary Celeste, The 375

Myton, Fred 110, 114-115, 117, 119, 127, 133, 201, 212-213, **214**, 225, 253-254, 276-277, 285-286, 298, 311-312, 314, 321-322, 334, 346, 409

Nabonga 217, 270, 271, 272, 409, 445

Nabonga Gorilla 217, 445

Nader, George 380

Nagel, Anne 225-226, 228

Naish, J. Carrol 272-273

Naked City (TV series) 403, 408

Napier, Alan 331-332

Napoleon and Sally 31, 34

Nassour Studios 334, 349. 353, 357-358

Nassour, Edward 357

Nat Ross Productions 74

National Concert and Artists Corporation 248

National Film Recording Company/Studios 98

National Legion of Decency 328, 342

National Recovery Act (NRA) 56

National Screen and Consolidated Film 61

National Screen Service Corp. 379

Natteford, Jack 32, 34, 123

Naughty Stewardesses, The 244

Navy Relief Society 29

Nazarro, Cliff 107, **284**

NBC (National Broadcasting System) 319, 357, 382

Neal, Tom 197, 355, 363

Nebenzal, Seymour 231, 262

Negro News Review (series) 325

Nelson, Billy 265-266

Nelson, Bobby 126-127, 129

Nelson, Eva 9

Neufeld, Josephine 1-2, **3**, 7, 11-13, 18, **204**

Neufeld, Marie **293-295**, 343, **345**,

Neufeld, Morris "Maury" 2, **3**, 7, 11, 13, 18, 204, 207-208, 401, 407

Neufeld, Ruth 11, **12**, 13, **18**, 28, 62, **73**, **203**, 204, 206, 207, **217**, 243, **293**, 294, **295**, 360, **383**, **403**, 404-408

Neufeld, Sadie 2, **3**, 7, 11, 13, 18, **207**, 401, 407

Neufeld, Samuel (see Newfield, Samuel "Sam")

Neufeld, Sigmund "Sig"

    Early Days 2, **3**, 4-8

    Universal **3**, 4-8

    Stern Brothers: L-Ko, Century, Stern Brothers Comedies 9, **10-11**, 12-13, **14**, 15-16, **18**, 20-21, 24-26, **27**, 28

    Tiffany 29-31, **32**, **35-37**, **39**, 41, **42**

    Tower Productions/Premier Attractions **43**, 44-45, **46-47**, 48, **49-50**, 51-52, **53**, 54, **55**, 56, **57**, 58, **59**, 60

    Ambassador Pictures 61-62, **63**, 64, **65**, 66, **67-70**, 72

    Puritan/Excelsior Pictures **73**, 74, **75-76**, **78-80**, **82-84**

    1937-39, Whereabouts Unknown 105

    Producers Distributing Corp./Producers Pictures Corp. 161-162, **163-165**, 166, **167**, 169, **170-171**, 172-174, 176

    Producers Releasing Corp. (PRC) 182, **183-184**, 185, **186-187**, **189**, 190, **191**, 192, **193-194**, 195-196, **197-202**, **209-210**, 211-212, **213**, 214-215, **216-217**, **219-225**, 227-228, **229-230**, 231, **232-233**, 234, **235-239**, 240, **241-243**, 244-245, **247**, 248-249, **250-251**, **253**, 254-255, **256**, 257, **258-259**, 260, **261**, 262, 267, 270, **271**, 272, **273-276**, 277, 278-280, 281, **282-285**, 286, 290, **295**, 296 **297**, 298, **301**, **303-308**, 309, **310**, 311, **312-314**, 316, 318, **319**, 320, **321**, 322, **323**, 324

    Film Classics 343 **344-351**

    Lippert Productions 354-355, **356**, 357, **358**, 359-360, **361**, 363, **364-366**, 367, **368**, 371, **372-373**, **379**, 380

    Associated Film Releasing Corp. (AFRC) 383, **384-387**, **389-390**

    Regal Films/Twentieth Century-Fox **398**, **400**

    Television 359, 391, **392**, 393-394, 397

    Retirement 401, **403**, 404-405, **406-407**, 408

    Miscellaneous xi, xiii-xv, 91, 110, 125, 145, 147-150, 159, 328, 335, 411, 413-414

Neufeld, Sigmund, Jr. xi, xiii, 2-4, 12-13, 28, 43, 73, 105, 166, **203**, 204, 206, **207**, 208, **217**, 248, 280-281, 291, 296, 360, 390-395, 397, 401-404, **407**, 408, 413

Neufeld, Simon 1-2

Neufeld, Stanley **18**, 41-42, **73**, 203, **205**, 207, **224-225**, **246**, 247, **292-293**, **295**, 306, 311, 335, **341**, 343, 345, **348**, 381, **382**, **387**, 388, 390-391, **393**, 394, **396**, 397, 403-405, 408

Neufeld, Timothy Lee xi-xii, 2, 8, 21, 41, 105, 185, 207, 277, 293, 343, 383, 393, 401, 403-405, 413-414

Neumann, Kurt 365

Neville, John "Jack" Thomas 74, 196-197, 302, 304

New Grand National 101

New Mike Hammer, The (TV series) 408

Newell, William 166

Newfield, Billy 213

Newfield, Jacqueline "Jackie" xi, **52**, 173, **175**, 203, **207**, 217, **271**, 272, **291**, 292, 336, 381, 402-403

Newfield, Joel Clark xi-xiii, 11, 88, 119, 122, 173, **175**, 177, 203, 206, **207**, 212, **213**, **216**, 217, 247, 279-280, **291**, 292, 313, **362**, 363, 381, 393, 395, 401-403, 413

Newfield, Samuel "Sam"

    Early Days 2, **3**, 7

    Stern Brothers: Century, Stern Brothers Comedies 11, 13, 16, **17**, 18-20, 22, **23-25**, 26, **27**, 28

    Director-for-hire 1930s 105-10

    Universal 11, 13, 16, **17**, 18-20, 22, **23-25**, 26, **27**, 28-29, 31, 39, 85, **86**

    Tower Productions/Premier Attractions 48, **50**, **52-55**, **57**, 58, **59**, 60

    Ambassador Pictures, 65-67, **68**, 69, **70**, 71, **72**

    Puritan/Excelsior Pictures 73-74, **75-76**, 77, **78-80**, 81, **82-84**

    Cavalcade Film Productions 87

    Progressive Pictures 88

    Supreme Pictures 88, **89**, 90, 180, **181**, 182

    Winchester Productions 90-91, **92-94**

    Booth Dominion Productions 95, **96**, 97-98

    Colony Pictures 98-100, **101**, 102-103, **104**

    Spectrum Pictures 105, 106, 107, **108**, 109, **110**

    Associated Features **110-111**

    Stan Laurel Productions **113**, 114-115, **116**, 117

    Principal/Columbia: *The Terror of Tiny Town* 117, **118**, 119, 121, 122

    Republic Pictures 122-123, **124**, 125, **126-129**, 130-131, **132-134**, 135, **136-138**

Concord Pictures/Monogram **138**, 139, **140**

Grand National: Fine Arts, Cinemart, Arcadia **141-143**, 144

Victory Pictures 144-147, **149-150**, 151, **152-155**, **157**, 158, **159**

Producers Distributing Corp. (PDC)/Producers Pictures Corp. (PPC) 161-162, 166, **167**, 169, **170-171**, 173-174, **175**, 176-177

Criterion Pictures **177-178**

J.D. Kendis 177-**179**, 180

Producers Releasing Corp. (PRC) 182, **183-184**, 185, **187**, 188, **189**, 190, **191**, **193-194**, 196, **197-202**, 212, **213**, 215, **216**, 217-218, **219-225**, 227-228, **229-230**, 231, 234, **235**, **237-239**, 240, **241-243**, 244-245, **246-248**, 249, **250-251**, 252, **253**, 254-257, **258-259**, 260, 261, 262, **263**, 264, **265**, 266-267, **268-269**, 270, **271**, 272, **273-274**, 276-277, **278-280**, 281, **282-286**, 287, **288**, 289, **290**, 295, **297**, 298, **301**, **303-308**, 310, 311, **312-314**, 316, **317**, 318, **319**, 320, **321**, 322, **323**

Toddy Pictures 325, **326-327**

Pine-Thomas Productions 328, **329-330**, **332**

Banner Pictures **333**, 334

Reliance Pictures 334, **335**

Eagle-Lion/John Sutherland Productions 335-338

Eagle Lion Classics **338**, 339

Franklin Productions 339, **340-342**

Film Classics 343, **344-351**, 352

Lippert Productions **354**, 355, **356-358**, 359, **361**, 363, **364-365**, 367, **368-370**, 371, **372-374**, **376**, 377, **378**, 380

Exclusive Films Ltd. **376**, 377, **378**

Associated Film Releasing Corp. (AFRC) **384-390**

Regal Films/Twentieth Century-Fox **398**, 399, **400**

Television **354**, **381-383**, 391, **392**, 393-395

Retirement 401-403, 407

Miscellaneous xi-xv, xvi, 409-411, 413-414

Newfield, Violet 48, **52**, 206-207, **224**, 291, **381**, **386**, **388-389**, 403

Newill, James "Jim" 178

Newlyweds and Their Baby, The (series) 19-20, 23, 28

Newlyweds' Visit, The 418

Newmeyer, Fred 44, **45**. 107, 232

Nigh, Jane 357-358

Nigh, William 197, 262

Night Coach 54, 422

Night Coach (story) 54

Night Owls 28, 419

Nine Nights in a Bar Room 36-37, 420

Nixon, Allan 374-375

No More Frontier 170

Nolan, Lloyd 309

Nolte, William 325

Normandie Productions Ltd. 391, **392**, **396**, 397

Northern Frontier 67-69, 423

Northwest Trail 353

Nosseck, Max 197

Novak, Eva 10

Novelty Pictures Company 148

NRA (see National Recovery Act) 56

Nu-Atlas Musicals 105

Numa Pictures Corporation 10

O'Brien, Dave "Tex" 101-102, 141, 149, **153**, 154, 156, 158, 178, 185, 196, 211-212, **213**, 215, **216-217**, 232, 255

O'Brien, George 89

O'Brien, Willis 369-370

O'Connor, Gwen 357

O'Dasi, E.R. 150-151

O'Connell, Ann 186

O'Donnell, Gene 196

O'Donnell, Joseph "Jack" 74, 91, 114-115, 123, 167, 193, 200, 202, 215, 260, 276

O'Donnell, Spec 47, 337

O'Farrell, Bernadette 376

O'Hanlon, George 334

O'Neil, Sally 59

O'Shea, Oscar 394

Oakman, Wheeler 68, 71, 76-77, 80-82, 95-97, **98**, 138, 164

Oath of Vengeance 276, 278, 279, 446

Off His Trolley 16, **17**

Off We Go 371, 455

Office of War Information 233

Oh Nursie! 16

Oh! My Operation 85, 422

Old Cactus Joe (song) 199

Olenick, Jerry 161

On Deck 416

On Furlough 416

One Big Mistake 325

One Frightened Night 61

One Million B.C. 369

One Punch O'Toole 31, 421

One Way Trail (story) 211

Only a Song (song) 301

Ormond, Ron 354, 373, **374**

Orth, Louise 9

Osborn, Ted 164

Osborne, Vivienne 287, **288**

Othman, Frederick C. 263

Our Dancing Daughters 124

Out at Home 418

Outcault, Richard F. 16

Outdoor Sports 28, 419

Outlaw Deputy, The 74

Outlaw Women 373, **374**, 410, 459

Outlaws of Boulder Pass 223, 441

Outlaws of the Plains 277, 304-305, 318, 451

Outlaws of the Rio Grande **189**, 190, 436

Outlaw's Paradise 145, 154, **155**, 156, 431

Overland Riders 304, 450

Overland Stagecoach 223-224, 241, 301, 441

Overland with Kit Carson 168

Pacemakers 237, 255

Pacific Producing Company 10

Package Plan 231

Padden, Sarah **59**, 218, 298

Pal, George 365

Panama Pacific 93

Panhandle Trail 308, 441

Panther's Claw, The 197

Paper Bullets 177

Papillon 197

Paradise Island 30

Paradise Valley 429

Paradise Valley (song) 114

Paramount Pictures viii, 29, 38, 41, 45, 52, 59, 66, 95, 115, 125, 144, 177, 213, 228, 234, 236, 298-299, 328, **329-330**, **332**, 405

Paroled - To Die 134-135, **136**, 429

Parsons, Lindsley 262

Parsons, Louella O. 51, 347

Pathé Laboratories/Pathe Pictures Ltd. 52, 107, 130, 176-177, 182, 186-187, 195, 210, 213, 235, 245, 255, 296-297, 299, 308, 315-317, 322, 351

Patty Duke Show, The (TV series) 408

Pawley, William **165**

Payson, Blanche 15

Peach, Kenneth 385, 387

Pecos Troublemakers 145

Peek-A-Boo 419

Peerce, Jan 105

Peerless 29

Pembroke, Georgen 164

Pembroke, Scott 19-20

Pendleton Round-Up 62

Pendleton, Nat 47

Penn, Leonard 374

Pete Smith Comedies 217

Pete the Pup 20, 26

Peters, Ralph 102-103, 144

Peurifoy, John E. 349

Peyser, Seymour 176

Phantom Guns 145

Phantom of Wild Valley 446

Phantom Ranger **138**, 139, 430

Phil Goldstone Productions 29-30

Philippi, Louis 122

Picard, Marcel (see Le Picard, Marcel)

Pichel, Irving 162, 164

Pickford, Mary 125, 196

Picnic Perils 85, 423

Piel, Edward Jr. **199**

Pierce, Warren H. 233

Pierson, Carl 354

Pigmeat Markham's Laugh Hepcats (aka *Pigmeat's Laugh Hepcats*) 325, 449

Pine Ridge Farms 391

Pine, William H. xv, 328, 331

Pine-Thomas Productions 236, 328, **329-330**, 331, **332**, 345

Pinto 15

Pithey, Wensley 377

Placeritas Ranch 211

Plan Nine from Outer Space 251

Platt, Bill 117, 119-120

Play Girl, The 125

Please Excuse Me 19, 410, 415

Plympton, George H. 114-115, 123, 125, 127, 130, 133, 277, 333

Pohlmann, Eric 377, **378**

Police Rookie 434

Pollard, Harry 7

Popel, Mary Ellen 339

Popkin, Harry 325

Porcasi, Paul 285

Porter, Lew 111-115, 119, 152, 185, 199, 345

Powdersmoke Range 122

Powell, Lee **142**, 211, 218, **219-222**

Powers, Patrick 51

Poynter, Nelson 233

Prairie Badmen 304, **308**, 316, 450

Prairie Pals 222, 440

Prairie Rustlers 294, 304, 448

Prather, Lee 120

Pratt, Purnell 49

PRC Productions, Inc. 235, 255-256, 324, 345

Preble, Fred 147, 162, 174, 185

Premier Attractions **43**, 45-50, 52, 56, 59-60, 409

Premier Pictures 73

Price, Hal 135

Price, Byron 233

Price, Rosalinda 76-77

Price, Vincent 176

Prince Modupe 270

Prince the Dog 397, **398**, 399

Principal Productions 85, **106**, **118**, 119, 149

Prison Girl 231

Prison Train 171

Prisoner of Japan 231

Problem Child, The 117

Producers Distributing Corp. (PDC) 161, **163-165**, **167-168**, **170-171**, **175**, 176-177

Producers Pictures Corp. (PPC) 161, **163-168**, 169, **170-171**, 172-173, **175**, 176-177, 182, 185

Producers Releasing Corp. (PRC) xi, xiii-xv, 69, 122, 141, 147, 157, 176-177, 182, **183-184**, 185, **186-187**, 188, **189**, 190, **191**, 192, **193-195**, 196, **197-202**, **209-210**, 213, 215, **216**, 217-218, **219-227**, 228, **229-230**, 231, **232**, 234, **235-239**, 240, **241-243**, 244-245, **246-248**, 249, **250-251**, 252, **253**, 254-255, **256**, 257, **258-259**, 260, **261**, 262, **263**, 264, **265**, 266-267, **268-269**, 270, **271**, 272, **273-276**, 277, **278-280**, 281, **282-286**, 287, **288**, 289, **290**, 292, **294-295**, 296, **297**, 298, **299-301**, **303-308**, 309, **310**, **312-315**, 316, **317**, 318, **319**, 320, **321**, 322, **323**, 324, 328, 331, 335, 343, 345, 381, 390-391, 393-394, 409-410, 413

Producers Specials 255

Production Code 171-172, 365

Progressive Pictures Corporation 85, 88, 161

Progressive Studios 153-154

Pryor, Roger 285-286

Psycho 45

Public Stenographer 54, 422

Puppy Love (series) 28

Puritan Pictures 74, **75-76**, **78-80**, **82-83**, 84-85, 147, 150, 159, 166, 245, 410

Queen of Broadway 245, **246-247**, 255, 270, 292, 301, 442

Queen of Burlesque 297, **317**, 318, 450

Queenie the Horse 15

Quo Vadis 378

Quota Quickies 375

Racing Luck 90-91, **92**, 424

Radar Patrol 354, 453

Radar Secret Service **354**, 355, 357-358, 453

Rafferty, Frances 335-336, 343-345

Raiders of Red Gap 241, 244, 444

Raiders of Red Rock 308, 442

Raiders of the West 221, 438

Rainbow Comedies 10, **17**

Rainbow Pictures 107

Raine, Norman Reilly 397

Rains, Claude 343

Raison, Milton 162, 230, 245-246, 350

Ramar of the Jungle (TV series) 354, 381, **382**, 391, 457

Randall, Jack 132, 138-139, **140**

Randall, Lorraine 133-134

Randall, Rebel 200

Randall, Robert 253

Range Busters, Inc. 112

Rangers' Round-Up, The **113**, 114, 429

Rank, J. Arthur 315

Ranson, Lois **239**

Rappaport, Frederick 359

Rathmell, John 178

Rathner, Harry 161, 173, 176, **186**, 198

Ravina Rink 95

Rawlinson, Herbert 270, 334

Ray, Bernard B. 231

Ray, Nicholas 287

Rayart Productions 62, 99

Raymaker, Herman 15

Rebel Without a Cause 287

Rebellious Daughters 161

Records for Romance (story) 282

Red Blood of Courage **63**, **65**, 66, 69, 423

Red Skelton Hour, The (TV series) 217

Red-Haired Alibi 48-49, 409, 422

Reed, Art 102, 153

Reed, Carol 343

Reed, David 311, 320

Reefer Madness 217

Reform Girl 52, **53**, 422

Regal Films xiv, 397, **398**, 399, **400**, 404

Regal Productions, Inc. 94

RegalScope 397-398

Regas, George 66, 82

Regas, Pedro 264

Reif, Elias 350

Reif, Harry 147

Reisner, Dean 338

Reitzen, Jack 364

Reliance Pictures 334, **335**

Renaldo, Duncan 124, 263-264

Renegade, The 237, **239**, 308, 443

Renfrew of the Royal Mounted 178

Reno 106

Republic Pictures Corporation 65, 85, 90-91, **92-94**, 122-123, **124**, 125, **126-129**, **132-134**, **136-137**, 138-139, 167, 180, 187, 194, 224, 228, 234-235, 242, 244, 266-267

Republic Studios 50, 52

Return of the Terror 145

Revier, Harry 179

Revolt of the Zombies 153

Revue Productions 391

Reynolds, Craig 183, **317**, 318

Rhodes, Billy "Little Billy" 106, 119-121

Rhodes, Kenneth 103

Rhythm Rides the Range 143, 431

Richards, Gordon 302, **312**, 313

Richmond, Warner 127-129, **133**, 176

Richmond, Ted H. 187, 197, 209, 231

Ride 'Em, Cowboy, Ride 'Em (song) 201

Riders of Black Mountain **189**, 190, 435

Riders of the Dawn 139

Riders of the Santa Fe 306

Ridin' Gent 430

Ridin' the Lone Trail 134-135, 428

Rin Tin Tin (dog) 397

Ringling Bros. and Barnum & Baily Circus 74, 146

Ringside 446

Ripley, Arthur 232, 235, 262

Ripley-Monter 255

Ritchie, Billie 9

Ritter, Tex 232

Rivero, Julian 103, 135

Riverside Studios 376

RKO 29, 52, 105, 107, 122, 139, 144, 185, 234, 341

Roach, Bert 10, 59

Roach, Hal 18, 43, 52, 58-59, 112, 116-117, 339, 369

Road Show Pictures 101

Roaming Cowboy, The 107

Roarin' Guns **76**, 426

Roarin' Lead 122, **124**, 426

Robards, Jason 44

Robe, The 378

Rober, Richard 374-375

Robert L. Lippert Productions 353

Roberts, Beverly 164

Robertson-Cole 48

Robinson, Clarence 180

Robinson, Dewey 289

Robinson, Edward G. 292

Robinson, Ruth 285-286

Robson, William N. 383

Rochelle, Claire 128, **129**, 135, 264

Rocketship X-M 347, 358

Rockwell, Jack 82, 125

Rogell, Al 245

Rogers, Gene 9

Rogers, Roy 138

Rolling Down the Great Divide **221**, 313, 439

Rolling Stone (series) 31

Romance of Roaring Valley (story) 211

Romance Rides the Range 107

Romero, Cesar 368, **369-370**, **376**, 377

Roosevelt, Franklin D. 56, 171, 302

Root, Juan 398

Rose, Billy 211

Rosen, Phil 197

Rosenblatt, Sol A. 56

Rosenbloom, Maxie 206, **338**

Rosener, George 178

Rote, Ed W. 147

Rothacker, Colonel Watterson 233

Rothschild, Harry S. 391

Rough Rider (series) 190

Rouse, Russell 295

Rousseau, Louise 261, 282

Rowland, William 262

Royal Canadian Mounted Police 97, 397

Rubel, Beno 21

Rubin, Benny **177**, 178

Runyon, Damon 246

Rushing Business 416

Rustlers' Hideout 276-277, 446

Ruttstein, Louis 176

Ryan, Sheila 356, 363, **364-365**

S&N Productions 245, 255, 262, 270, 292

Saal, William 90-91

Sachs, Beryl 354

Sackheim, Jerry 99

SAG (see Screen Actors Guild)

Saga of Smoky Farm (story) 211

Sagebrush Family (series) 162, 182

Sagebrush Family Across the Rio Grande, The 169

Sagebrush Family at the Rodeo, The 169

Sagebrush Family Fights Rustlers, The 169

Sagebrush Family Meets the Outlaws, The 169

Sagebrush Family on a Dude Ranch, The 169

Sagebrush Family Rides On, The 169

Sagebrush Family Stakes a Claim, The 169

Sagebrush Family Trails West, The 166-167, **168**, 169, 182, 433

Sailor George 417

Sailor, Beware! 170

Sais, Marin 266

Saland, Nat 145

Sale, Richard B. 336

Salkow, Sidney 395

Sally 30

Salome (opera) 107

Sam Katzman Productions 333

Samson and Delilah 378

Samuel Goldwyn Productions 391

Samuels, Jackson 399

Sande, Walter 397

Sandy of the Mounted 68, 424

Sanford, Ralph 359

Sanforth, Clifford 325

Sarecky, Barney 354, **354**, **357**, 358

Sarecky, Lou 61

Sarong Girl 231

Sarong Review 231

Saturday Evening Post (magazine) 397

Sauber, Harry 295-296

Savage, Ann 298, **299-300**, 321, 328

Saville, Victor 343

Sax, Sam 295

Saylor, Syd (aka Sid) 20, 24, **25**, 26, 28, 39, 64, 84, 89, 122, 124, 128, 232, 266, 411

Sayre, George W. 52, 56, 91, 94, 162, 230, 245-246, 268, 276

Scarecrow and Mrs. King (TV series) 408

Schaefer, Albert 26

Schaffner, Franklin J. 197

Schenck, Aubrey 316

Schlank, Mel 48

Schlank, Morris R. **43**, 46-48

School Romance 15

Schrock, Raymond L. 268, 312, 314, 320

Schroeder, Doris 359

Schüfftan, Eugen 392

Schwab, Pierre 383

Schwalb, Ben 296

Schwarz, Jack 231, **248**, 255, 262, **263**, 272, 295, 324

Schwarzwald, Milton 105

Scotland Yard Inspector 334, **376**, 377, 455

Scott, Alice **293**

Scott, Fred 107, **108**, 109, **110**, 112-115, **116**, 117, 122-123, 139, 158

Scott, Lester 51

Scott, Marie 247

Scott, Sherman 85, 166, **167**, **171**, 173, 182, **183-184**, 191, 194, 198, 212, **213**, **216**, 218, **237**, 257, 303, 328, 335, **336-337**, **341**, 415

Scott, Zachery 376

Screen Actors Guild (SAG) 112, 145, 397

Screen Guild Productions 331, 353

Screencraft 54, 145

Script Building Department 15, 147

Scully, Vin 405

Sea Hound, The **333**, 334, 451

Searle, Jackie 336

Seay, James **337**

Seconds 252

Secrets of a Co-Ed 231-232

Secrets of a Model **178-179**, 180, 311, 434

Secrets of a Model School 180

Secrets of a Sorority Girl 232

Seddon, Margaret 363

Seiderman, Maurice 273

Sekely, Steve 232, 262

Selby, Gertrude 9

Select Pictures 90

Selig, William N. 61

Selznick, David O. 329, 346

Sen Yung, Victor 349

Sennett, Mack 7, 18, 52, 59, 87, 106, 115, 117, 121, 277

Senorita Chula (song) 301

Seward, Billie 71, 88

Shadow Murder Case, The 101

Shadow, The (series) 100

Shadows of Death 276-277, 447

Shane, Maxwell 332

Sharpe, David 134

Shayne, Robert 337

She Shoulda Said "No"! 342, 453

She's a He 28, 420

She's a Pippin 418

She's My Girl 417

Shea, Gloria **57**, 58

Shearer, Norma 124

Sheffield, Maceo B. 110-111

Shefter, Bert 363

Sheldon, Forrest 63, 65-66, **67**

Sheldon, Julie 156, **157**

Shelton, John 380

Sheridan, Ann 66

Sheridan, James 115

Sheriff of Sage Valley 218, 440

Sherman, Gilbert xii, 14, 413

Sherwood, Choti **213**

Sherwood, George 300

Shilling, Marion 45

Shop Angel 45, 421

Short, Dorothy **153**, 188, 202

Showmen's Pictures 145

Shuffle Along (revue) 111

Shumway, Lee 93

Sid's Long Count 420

Sigmund Neufeld Pictures, Inc. **345-350**

Sigmund Neufeld Productions, Inc. 112, 176, 185, 195-196, 198, 210, 213, 234, 245, 255, 262, 267, 271, 275, 294, 296, **297**, 298, 304, 307, 324, 343, **344**, 352, 384-385

Simmonds, Joe 43-44, 48, 54, 56, 59, 73-74

Simmonds, Leslie 54, 73, **75-76**, **78-80**, **82-84**

Simon and Simon (TV series) 408

Sin of Nora Moran, The 41

Singer Midgets, The 117

Singer, Campbell 377

Singer, Leo 117, 121

Singer, Walberga 117

Singing Buckaroo, The 107

Singing Six Guns 145

Single Indemnity 298, 448

Sins of Jezebel 378, **379**, 380, 384, 456

Six-Gun Rhythm **143**, 144, 219, 431

Six-Gun Trail 152, 156, 159, 430

Six-Shootin' Sheriff 101

Skimpy 41, 421

Skip Tracer 434

Skipalong Rosenbloom 338, 365, 454

Skippy 41

Skirball, Jack H. 143

Skouras, Spyros 375, 397

Sky High 358, 371, **372**, 373, 455

Slander House 161

Slater, Barbara 289

Slaughter Trail 359

Slaves in Bondage 178

Sloan, James 262

Small, Edward 198, 334, 391

Smith, Dick (see Smith, Richard)

Smith, Ernie **366**

Smith, Noel 9, 15

Smith, Paul Gerard 317

Smith, Richard "Dick" 9

Smith, Roland 180

SMPFE (see Society of Motion Picture Film Editors, The) 102-103

Snooky the Humanzee 31, 34

Snyder, Earl 354

Soanes, Wood 144

Social Service Pictures of Hollywood 180

Society of Motion Picture Film Editors, The (SMPFE) 102, 234

Solomon, Louis 74

Solway, Larry 399

Song of Old Wyoming 295

Song of the Prairie 107, 427

Songs and Bullets 113, 115, **116**, 123, 429

Songs and Saddles 101

Sono Art-World Wide 29, 106, 131

Sons of the Finest 182, 434

Sophisticrats, The 170

Sorel, Sonia 315

Sound Technicians Local 695 234

Sparrows 196

Spartan Productions 363, **364-365**

Spectrum Pictures 85, 107, **108**, **110**, 112, **113**, **116**, 139, 149, 244

Spellbound 329

Spitfires 237, 255

Square Shooter, The 454

St. Claire, Arthur 264

St. John, Al "Fuzzy" xiv, 107, 109, **113**, 114-115, **116**, 123, **129**, 139, 141, **142**, 156, 182, **191**, 192, 193-194, **198-202**, 211-212, **213**, 215, **216**, 218, 222, **223-224**, **233**, **237**, **239**, 240, **241**, 242-243, 257-258, **259**, 260, **261**, 275-277, **278-279**, **294**, **304-308**, 382, 409-411

St. John, Flobelle 240

St. Polis, John 139

Stage & Screen Productions, Inc. 148

Stagecoach Outlaws 276-278, 447

Stahl, John M. 30

Stampede (story) 99

Stan Laurel Corporation 112, 117

Stan Laurel Productions 85, **113**, **116**, 117, 185

Stander, Lionel 266

Stanley, Louise 132, 136-137, 139

Stanwyck, Barbara 298

Star System 10

Starrett, Charles 95, 97, **98**

State Department: File 649 331, **348-351**, 357, 453

State Rights 29, 43, 74, 77, 85, 88, 99, 101, 107, 113, 138, 148, 160-161, 180, 415

Steele Saddle 194

Steele, Bob xiv, 88, 115, 124, 130-131, **132-133**, 134-135, **136**, 137-138, 145, 169, 176, 182, 186-187, 192, **193**, 194, 211, 215, 232, 261, 386

Steiner, Max 274

Stengler, Mack 119

Stephenson, David 316

Stephenson, Robert 350

Sterling Film Exchange 29

Sterling, Merta 10

Stern Brothers 13, 19, 21, **24**, 29, 47, 54, 58, 69, 207, 240, **407**, 410, 413-414

Stern Brothers Comedies xiii-xiv, 8, 18-19, 28, 49, 85

Stern Productions 112

Stern, Abe xiii, 7, **8**, 18, 98-99, 232

Stern, Alfred 99, 101, 232, 255, 289, **290**, 317

Stern, Frieda 98

Stern, Herman 101

Stern, Joseph 99

Stern, Julius xii-xiii, 3-4, **5**, 7, **8**, 9-10, 14, **15-16**, 18, 24, 27, 98-99, 232, 413

Sternbach, Bert Nathan **14**, 15-16, **23**, **27**, 85, **86**, 107, 110, 113, 117, 147, **148**, 149, 158, 162, 166-167, 185, **219**, **224-225**, **229**, **233**, 234, 245, **246**, 247-248, 254-255, 262, **268-269**, **271**, 276, 278, 280, **282**, 292, **294**, 296, **297**, 298, 306, 335, 343, 345, 360, 385, 391, **404**, 405, 409, 414

Stevenson, Robert (director) 343

Stevenson, Robert Louis 329

Stewart, Eleanore 101-102

Stewart, Peter 85, 162, 166, **170**, **187**, **189**, 190, **193**, 194, 198, 218, **219-222**, **235**, 257, 328, 332, 334, **335**, 343, **344-345**

Stoloff, Ben 316

Stone, Milburn 177

Stop Barking 26-27, 419

Storey, June 346-347

Stormy Trails 99, **100**, 102, 425

Story of Pat Garrett, The 384, 456

Straight Shooters 156, **157**, 432

Stranahan, F. Stewart 146

Strange Mrs. Crane, The 335, **337**, 453

Strange, Glenn 212, 214-215, 221, **225**, 226, **227**, 228, **253**, 268-269, 273, **280**

Strayer, Frank R. 31-32, **33**

Strickfaden, Kenneth 81

Sultan's Daughter, The 231

Sunny Jim (series) 28

Sunshine Comedies 7, 87

SuperScope 235 387

Supreme Pictures Corporation 85, 88, **89**, 90, 124-125, 138, 145, 180, **181**, 244

Sutherland Studio 318, 320-321, 328, 335, 343, 354

Sutherland, John 322, 335, **336-337**

Sutton, Grady 107

Sutton, John 334, **335**

Swain, Mack 10

Swamp Woman 228, 231-232

Sweet Patootie 37, 420

Sweetheart of Sigma Chi, The 211

Swellhead, The 30

Swing Hostess xiv, 275, 282, **283-285**, 411, 446

Switzer, Carl 320

Sydney, George 30

Sylos, F. Paul 366

Syndicate Pictures 29, 131

T.J. Hooker (TV series) 408

Take Your Pick 418

Talbot, Lyle 162, 164, 311, 339, 364, 374

Tale of a Flea, The 32, 420

Tales of Billy the Kid (series) 162

Talisman Studios 59, 73, 90, 107, 145, 171, 187, 236

Tallman, William 384

Talmadge, Richard 30

Tansey, Emma 115, 126

Tansey, Robert (Emmett) (aka Robert Emmett) 67, 162, 295

Tansey, Sherry 115

Tartakoff, Meyer 325

Tarzan the horse 325

Tarzan's Revenge 122

Tarzan the Fearless 211

Tarzan, the Police Dog (series) 148

Tatum, Dee 363-365

Taylor, Forrest 137, 149, 153-154, 157-158

Taylor, Kent 355-356

Taylor, Ray 63-65, 122, 306

Teacher's Pest 418

Tec-Art Studios 31, 39, 50-51

Technicolor/Technicolor Corporation 30-31, 331, 335

Teitelbaum, Emmanuel "Mannie" 7, **207**, **224-225**, **246**, **278**

Teitelbaum, Eugenia 13

Television Programs of America (TPA) 391, **392**, **396**

Temple, Shirley 49, 409

Terhune, Max 122-123, **124**

Terror of Tiny Town, The **106**, 117, **118**, 119, **120**, 121-122, 137, 431

Terrors on Horseback 304, **307**, 450

Terry, Bob 99, 149, **150**, 151, 154, 156

Terry, Sheila 93-94

Texas Justice 223, **224**, 440

Texas Manhunt **219**, **220**, 438

Texas Marshal 190, 437

Texas Marshal (series) xiv, 211, 218

Texas Renegades 162, 166, 169, **170**, 182, 433

Texas Wildcats 145, 153, **154**, 431

These Are Our Children (TV series) 359

They Had to See Paris 272

They Raid By Night 231

Third Man, The 364

Thirty for Tonight 282

This Gun for Hire 177

This Way Please 418

Thomas, Dan 31

Thomas, Harry H. 297

Thomas, Senator John William Elmer 172

Thomas, William C. 328, **329-330**

Thompson, Fred 245

Thoroughbred **96**, 425

Three DeLovelies, The 105

Three Desperate Men 359-360, **361-362**, 454

Three Mesquiteers, The 122-123, **124**

Three Mesquiteers, The (series) 122, 134, 138-139, 224, 241-242

Three Musketeers (novel) 122

Three on a Ticket 314, 318, 322, **323**, 328, 451

Three Outlaws, The 360, 384, **387-388**, 456

Three Stooges, The 114, 124

Thunder in the Desert 134, 136, 429

Thunder Over Sangoland 381, 456

Thundering Gun Slingers 257, 260, 445

Thurn-Taxis, Alexis 262

Tierney, William 334

Tiffany Productions 29-30, **32**, 34, 39-41, 44, 46, 48, 69-70, 90, 131, 166

Tiffany Studios 31, 40-41, 44, 87

Tiffany Talking Chimps 35-36, **38-39**, **42**, 86

Tiffany Talking Chimps (series) 31, 41, 85, 244, 410

Tiffany-Stahl 30

Tige's Girl Friend 418

Tiger Fangs 262, 263, 444

Tilton, Martha 282, **283**, 284-285

Tim McCoy's Real Wild West and Rough Riders of the World 146

Timber War 67, 71, **72**, 424

Todd, Holbrook 74, 147, 166, 185, 188, 234, 254, 267, 276, 289, 298, 303, 306, **323**, 345, 385, 394-395

Todd, Mabel 248

Toddy Pictures 325, **326-327**

Toddy, Ted 325-326

Tom Productions 366, **368-370**, **372-373**

Tombragel, Maurice 357

Tomorrow We Live 244

Tondeleyo and Lopez 181

Too Many Winners 322, 335

Too Many Women 419

Toombs, Rudolph 327

Toomey, Regis **57**, 58

Torture Ship 162, **163**, 164-165, 432

Touch of Evil 273

Tower Productions 43, 44, **45-47**, 48, **50**, **53**, **55**, 56, **57**, **59**, 60, 85, 125

TPA (see Television Programs of America)

Trader Horn 41

Trail of Vengeance 125, 127, 427

Trail's End 425

Trail's End (song) 178

Trails of the Wild 67, **70**, 71, 200, 424

Traitor, The 82, **83**, 84, 426

Traube, Shepard 170-172, 176

Travis, Richard 363, **364-365**

Trent, Jack 44

Trigger Fingers 158, **159**, 432

Trigger Pals **142**, 149, 218, 431

Trigger Smith 168

Trigger Trail 306

Trimble, Arthur 16, 19, 26-27

Triple Cross 334, 452

Trocadero 267

Trust, The 4

Tumbleweed Trail 222, **235**, 236, 440

Turner, Doreen 19, 26

Twentieth Century Fox 309, 334, **335**, 343, 375, 378, 397, **398**, **400**

Twenty Thousand Leagues Under the Sea 366

Two Thousand Maniacs 325

Two-Gun Lady 384

Two-Gun Man from Harlem 112

Tyler, Tom 124, 146, 211

Ullman, Elwood 54

Ulmer, Edgar G. 236, 244, 248, 255, 262, 274, 298, 300-301, 306, 316

Unbelievable, The 453

Under Secret Orders 88, 423

Undercover Girl 447

Undercover Men 95, 97, **98**, 425

United Artists xi, 52, 125, 160, 234, 335, 341, 351

United Players, Inc. 21

Universal (Pictures Corporation) 21, 24, 28-30, 44, 48-49, 52, 74, 85, **86**, 105, 166, 192, 211, 225-228, 234, 236, 242, 244, 250, 252, 266, 306, 325, 343, 294, 409

Universal Animated Weekly 14

Universal City 8, 28, 46

Universal Film Manufacturing Company 3, 5-8, 15-16, 29, 31, 161, 213, 281

Universal Weekly 24

Unknown Island 347, **348**, 452

Up and At 'Em 371, 455

Up in the Air 24, 416

Urecal, Minerva 386, **396**, 397

Usher, Guy 185, 196

Vacation Days 333

Vagabond Dreams Come True (song) 111

Vallee, Rudy 41

Valley of Vengeance 257, 261, 445

Vallon, Michael 103

Vampire Bat, The 41

Van Duinen, Peter R. 244, 248, 262

Van Gogh, Vincent 193

Van Zandt, Phil 284, **285**

Vaughn, James 316

Veidt, Conrad 343

Victor, Charles 357

Victory Caravan 234

Victory Pictures 85, 144-147, **149-150**, **152-155**, **157**, **159**, 160, 169-170, 185, 256, 333, 410

Victory Specials 237, 255

Vidor, King 125

Vigal, Johnny 181

Vitagraph 130

Vogan, Emmett 289, **290**

Voice of Hollywood, The (series) 31

Von Eltz, Theodore 49

Von Stroheim, Erich 232

Von Twardowski, Hans 174

Voss, Frank "Fatty" 9

V-Specials 237, 255

Wages of Sin, The 318

Wahl, Evelyn 230

Walker, Cheryl **179**, **310**, 311-312, 314, 322

Walker, Gertrude 248

Walker, Ray 83, **84**

Walker, Terry 192

Wallach, Charles 14

Wally Kline Enterprises **338**

Walsh, Raoul 343

Walters, Luana 80

Wanted for Murder 162, 166, 433

Ward, Warwick 262

Warde, Harlan 336, 344-345

Warner Bros. 302

Warrenton, Gilbert 379

Washington, Hannah "Oatmeal" 26

Watch George! 417

Watch the Birdie 418

Water Follies of 1941 211

Waterfront 232

Watkins, Mel 327

Watkin, Pierre 298, 300, 311, 334, 337, 355

Watson, Bobby 180

Wayne, Carter 162

Wayne, Frank 149, 151

Wayne, John 124

Weaver, Tom 146, 274, 371, 393, 396

Wedding Belles **87**, 422

Weeks, George 262

Weeren, Hans 44, **69**, 70, 74, 87, 107, 110, 113-114, 147, 166, 185, **224-225**, 234, 240, **246**, 254, 256, 409

Weiss Brothers/Artclass Pictures **23**, 147, **148**

Weiss Productions 148

Weiss, Louis 148, 272

Weldon, Marion 114-115, 135-137

Welles, Orson 273

Welsh, Betty **23**

West, Mae 85, 285, 385

Westen, Al 325

Western Agreement, The 112

Western Cyclone 237, 239, 308, 443

Western Film Exchange 161

Western Pacific Agent 355, **356**, 357-358, 410, 453

Western Pacific Railroad 355

Western Saboteurs 442

Western Star Production Company 29

Westerner, The 430

Weston, Cecil 343, 345

WH Films 375

Whale, James 70

Whalen, Michael 339, 363-364

What an Excuse 416

What Happened to Jane? (series) 19-20

What's Your Hurry? 415

Whelp of the Fox (story) 211

When George Hops 417

When George Meets George 417

Which Is Which? 19, 415

Whirlwind Horsemen 101

Whistler, The (radio series) 337

Whitaker, Slim 149

White Gorilla 272, 282, 448

White Pongo 272, 282, 298, **301**, 302-303, 448

White Zombie 41, 153, 162

White, J. Frances 373

White, Jack 22

Widows 59, 423

Wilcox, Robert **164**, 165

Wild Bill Hickok 80, 141, 430

Wild Dakotas, The 384, **386**, 387, 399, 456

Wild Horse Phantom 276, **278**, 446

Wild Horse Round-Up 62

Wild Horse Rustlers **241**, 442

Wild Weed 339, **340-342**, 352, 453

Wilde, Lois 100

Wilder, Billy 298

Wilderness Mail **67**, 423

Wildfire, the Story of a Horse 353

Wiley, Wanda 16, 18-20

Willey, Lyle 256

Williams, Bill 386

Williams, Charles 322

Williams, Guinn 73, 83, **84**

Williams, Roger **89**

Williams, Sidney 234

Williams, Spencer Jr. 110-111

Willis, Austin 398-399

Willis, Norman 300

Wilson, Lois 46

Winchester Pictures 85, 90-91, **92-94**

Windsor, Marie 374-375

Wing, Toby 95, **96**, 97

Winkler, Ben 256

Winkler, George 22

Winkler, Margaret 22

Winkler, Robert 187-188

Winters, Charlotte 265

Winters, Johnny **106**

Winters, Ted 399

Wisbar, Frank 232

Wise Girl 50, 422

Wise, James 219

With Daniel Boone Thru the Wilderness 130

With Davy Crockett at the Fall of the Alamo 130

With Sitting Bull at the Spirit Lake Massacre 130

Withers, Grant 49

Witney, William 65

Witwer, H.C. 30

Wolf Dog 397, **398**, 456

Wolf Man, The 225

Wolf, Sam 51

Wolves of the Range 241, **242**, 443

Wood, Ed 251

Wood, Harley 158

Woodbine, Paul 367

Woodbury, Joan 76, 80-81

World Gone Mad, The 41

World Symphony Orchestra 301

World Wide 29, 40, 131

Worth, Barbara 64, 91, **92**, 334

Worth, Constance 285-286

Worth, Harry 78

Wright, Cobina, Sr. 248-249

Wright, Mack V. 122, **124**, **333**, 334

Wrixon, Maris 302

Yanks Are Coming, The 229

Yarbrough, Jean **195**, 196, 383, 401

Yates, Herbert J. 90, 209, 235

You Can Be Had 85, **86**, 148, 424

Young, Carleton 158, 192, 211, 214-215, **216**, 318

Young, Joe 26, **148**

Young, John S. 296

Young, Kenneth M. 296

Young, Nedrick **250**, 251-252

Young, Raymond E. 296

Young, Robert 343

Young, Robert R. 296, 315-316, 322-323

Young, Roland 343

Your Heart Belongs to Her (song) 389

Yung, Victor Sen 349

Zeidman, Bennie 171

Ziegfeld Follies 24

Ziehm, Arthur 60

Zucco, George 225, **226**, 227-228, 249, **250-251**, 252, **253**, 302-304

Other Books By Thomas Reeder

Time Is Money!
The Century, Rainbow, and Stern Brothers Comedies
of Julius and Abe Stern

Mr. Suicide
Henry "Pathe" Lehrman and the Birth of Silent Comedy

Stop Yellin'
Ben Pivar and the Horror, Mystery, and Action-Adventure Films
of His Universal B-Unit

Poetic Justice

Other Books From SPLIT REEL

Pokes & Jabbs:
The Before, During and After of the Vim Films Corporation
by Rob Stone

The Pokes & Jabbs Picture Book
Compiled by Rob Stone

Story By Grover Jones
Compiled and Filmography by Rob Stone

Victor Moore & His Klever Komedies
Compiled by Steve Massa & Rob Stone

The Klever Komedies Picture Book
by Rob Stone & Steve Massa

Laurel or Hardy:
The Solo Films of Stan Laurel and Oliver "Babe" Hardy
by Rob Stone

SPLIT REEL LLC
P.O. Box 946 · Culpeper, VA 22701
info@split-reel.com · www.split-reel.com
(540) 521-9826

Split Reel LLC publishes books and other media related to the performing arts. We specialize in silent film with a focus on providing detailed, deeply researched works that highlight lesser-known aspects of the entertainment industry.